BOLLINGEN SERIES LIX · 3

PAUL FRIEDLÄNDER

PLATO

3

THE DIALOGUES
Second and Third Periods

TRANSLATED FROM THE GERMAN
BY HANS MEYERHOFF

BOLLINGEN SERIES LIX

PRINCETON UNIVERSITY PRESS

THIS IS THE THIRD OF THREE VOLUMES
CONSTITUTING THE FIFTY-NINTH PUBLICATION
IN A SERIES SPONSORED BY
BOLLINGEN FOUNDATION

Originally published in German as
Platon, III: *Die Platonischen Schriften, Zweite und
Dritte Periode* (2nd edition) by W. de Gruyter &
Co., Berlin, 1960.

For this translation, the notes have been considerably corrected and supplemented; the text has been revised to a lesser extent.—P. F.

LIBRARY OF CONGRESS CATALOGUE CARD NO. 57–11126
MANUFACTURED IN THE UNITED STATES OF AMERICA
DESIGNED BY ANDOR BRAUN

Prefatory Note

I was fortunate to have Hans Meyerhoff as my translator. His mastery of both the German and the English language, his literary talent, and his thorough philosophical background combine in his translation. We were, moreover, able during several years to discuss many problems that came up, a collaboration that enriched both of us and also added to our friendship. This was abruptly ended by the accident in which Hans Meyerhoff was killed, thus shattering the rich promise of the future. For this last volume it meant that we were unable to discuss his translation. Certain others, including myself, helped to shape the final text. The notes, not his work but that of several collaborators, have been checked by me.

I am most grateful to Mrs. Ruth Spiegel for the patient and understanding work she put into the final shaping of the text and notes of *Plato* 2 and 3. Special thanks are due to her also for the detailed and well-thought-out indexes to these two volumes. It is a pleasure to thank also Mrs. Jean Kyle Booher who, besides performing the major task of preparing *Plato* 1 for the press and indexing it, continued to serve as an adviser for the other two volumes. My thanks are due to Mr. William McGuire and Mr. Wolfgang Sauerlander, of the Bollingen Series staff, for their steady concern and their willingness to give advice when needed.

There should not be missing in this last volume of my Plato work the expression of my gratitude to Bollingen Foundation, which generously helped me for many years when I had little or no help from Germany.

Last not least, I should thank Charlotte Friedländer, my wife, for her great share in the work and for her constant aid.

It is for a special reason that I owe thanks to R. G. Hoerber. His review of my second volume (in *Classical Philology*, LXII: 1, January, 1967) drew my attention to an oversight in my interpretation of the *Laches*. I have made comment on this in Chapter XXIII, note 36.

P. F.

Los Angeles, California
April, 1968

PUBLISHER'S NOTE

The first volume of this work, *Plato: An Introduction* (1958), contains seventeen chapters, each an independent study of an aspect of Plato's thought, his creative work, and his relation to modern thinkers, and a chapter on Plato as jurist by Huntington Cairns. A new edition is in preparation, with revisions and additional annotation.

The second volume, *Plato: The Dialogues, First Period* (1964), contains Chapters I–XIX, which interpret the works of Plato's early creative period, the "ascent."

The third volume, *Plato: The Dialogues, Second and Third Periods*, contains Chapters XX–XXXI. These take up the central and late dialogues, the works of Plato's major creative periods. At the end of this final volume, there is an Afterword, "On the Order of the Dialogues."

Table of Contents

SECOND PERIOD

THE CENTRAL DIALOGUES

TWENTY

Symposium

SOMEDAY when the history of Platonism is written, one of its most important chapters will have to deal with the influence of the *Symposium* on later ages.[1] In this respect, only the *Timaeus* and the *Republic* compare with the *Symposium*.

In this dialogue as in no other, Socrates is shown as a man at once sociable and lonely, and highest praise is bestowed on him. Thus, Socrates could not be the narrator here as in the *Lysis* or the *Protagoras*, nor could the dialogue do without a narrator as the *Gorgias* or the *Phaedrus*.[2] As in the *Phaedo*, there had to be a brief introductory conversation between someone who was present on the occasion and someone else or others who want to hear the report. In both dialogues, this introductory or frame conversation leads up to the question, "What, then, were the speeches made on this occasion?"—only to lead beyond speeches into the world of dramatic action and into the realm of silence and the ineffable.

It is more difficult to deal with the question of why Plato, in the *Symposium*, put the actual events so far back in time before the date of the report. The feast described occurred in the year 416, for Plato took the first victory of the brilliant young poet Agathon—an occasion undoubtedly long remembered—as an opportunity to stage the speeches on the subject of love. Why, then, does he let so many years elapse between the events and the report? The device is so important that Plato supplies an elaborate account of the history of the tradition and even gives an erroneous impression, soon repudiated, that the feast had taken place only recently (172BC). To be sure, the significance of the event and the speeches is enhanced if it is true that they have been remembered so long that even now people are most anxious to hear about them. Moreover, this manner of presentation enables Plato to depict the feast as a historical event (the narrator has asked Socrates himself for confirmation), and at the same time to eliminate unessential features. Aristodemos who was a witness could not remember everything and Apollodoros who is transmitting the report by Aristodemos has in turn forgotten some things, so that what is presented is only what is "most memorable" (178A, 180C). Here is a symbolic demonstration of the Platonic process of re-creating actual events in a dialogue.[3] Yet even this is not explanation enough.

There is another dialogue, the *Parmenides*, in which we find a conversation that took place a long time ago, with a detailed report as to how it was transmitted. Socrates as a young man meets with Parmenides who is very old. Thus, the difficulties concerning the "doctrine of *Ideas*" did not come to light yesterday, but have been thought about for a long time. Similarly, here in the *Symposium*, we are told that Socrates many years ago made a speech on the subject of *Eros*, the knowledge of which he had received "a long time ago"—as he repeats twice (201DE)—from Diotima. He was a young man when he learned about the way of *Eros*, the way leading toward the highest beauty and true being. It is after a long time has passed that, at the banquet, he speaks of this experience again. And the effect of this occasion lasts in turn until the day when it is revived in the account of Apollodoros. The lasting presence of the occasion is confirmed in the prelude, and beyond this, timeless being is immersed in the stream of time because it is in and for man. Even more: splendor and gaiety intermingle with deep seriousness as we recall that, at the very time Apollodoros is reporting about the banquet, the catastrophe of Alkibiades and the defeat of Athens have already occurred and the death of Socrates is probably to be expected within a year.[4]

It is the same Apollodoros who is mentioned in the *Apology* (34A) when Socrates lists the names of friends who are present at the trial and are supporting him. There the name of Apollodoros is put beside Plato's and is the last in a long list so that he

is likely to be remembered. Yet even if in reading the *Symposium*
we should not remember this detail, we cannot forget that the
same Apollodoros is seen and heard in passionate outbreaks of
grief both at the beginning and at the very end of the *Phaedo*
(59AB, 117D). "You know the man and his nature," as it is said
there (59B 1). The *Symposium* and the *Phaedo* belong to the
same period. Which of them is earlier cannot be decided. But in a
deeper sense, the two are "contemporary," for it is inconceivable
that when Plato chose Apollodoros as narrator in the *Symposium*
he did not think of the historical event, i.e., the presence of
Apollodoros, his deeply felt presence, at the death of Socrates.
Plato could have selected some other member of the Socratic
circle to report on Agathon's feast. In choosing Apollodoros he
intended, if not solely then at least primarily, to make the reader
conscious of death in the midst of the banquet and the speeches
about love, even as the two themes were consciously connected
in his own mind. As the voice of Eros is heard in the dialogue on
death so a reminder of death is sounded, softly but noticeably,
in the prelude to the speeches on love and is later heard in the
speeches themselves.

Even the frame conversation presents a number of people. FRAME
There is Aristodemos, the only person who was present at 172A–174A
Agathon's feast; to him we ultimately owe the report. There is
Apollodoros, who reports what he has heard. Both represent
the type of disciple, passionately devoted but unproductive and
slightly ridiculous, who may always be found in the circle
gathered around a great man. Aristodemos goes barefoot, like
his master, whose "most devoted admirer among the men of
those days" he is said to be. For unknown reasons, Apollodoros
bears the epithet "mild" or "soft" (μαλακός), in grotesque contrast to his character here in the *Symposium*.[5] He considers
everybody "miserable" (κακοδαίμονες), with the exception of
Socrates. This is indeed true in a deeper sense—i.e., when
Socrates is taken as the measure. In the outer circle these two
are closest to Socrates. Then there is a certain Phoenix, who
serves as the bridge in the tradition between Aristodemos and
Apollodoros, and a certain Glaukon, who is most anxious to
hear about the famous conversation and "only recently" sought

out Apollodoros to ask him about it. The name Glaukon cannot but make us think of Plato's brother who, at the beginning of the *Republic* and of the *Parmenides*, appears—unmistakably—as the son of Ariston and the brother of Adeimantos. The scene at the beginning of the *Republic* is reminiscent of the *Symposium* in its very words.[6] This is Plato's way of suggesting his own participation in the events described without ever appearing in his own person in any dialogue (as Aristotle and Cicero, for example, do).

Then, representing a vague tradition, there is a "Somebody" who had heard Phoenix' report but could not say anything definite about it. And finally, the furthest removed, there are those to whom Apollodoros is speaking. They remain nameless. He refers to them as rich men (173c) and, as he is contrasting their talk with the "speeches on philosophy," a contrast of two principles of life comes into view in eloquent sentences, as it does, for example, at the beginning of the *Republic*. Their clash is symbolized in the clash of words (οἴομαι—οὐκ οἴομαι, 173D). Still, we must not overlook the fact that the desire for money is interpreted later as a kind of love, or love in its most primitive form (205D), and that those here abused by Apollodoros are also the occasion (because they are curious) for giving this report about Agathon's feast. Yet only Aristodemos enters into the inner circle of the conversation, and he merely as a silent listener. In that circle are men of a higher rank who, in turn, are outranked by the incomparably greater stature of Socrates.

Another point is to be noted in connection with this frame conversation. At its opening we hear about the "get-together of Agathon, Socrates, and Alkibiades." We are supposed to keep this in mind, wondering why Alkibiades is not among the guests, and wait expectantly until he—always acting differently from others—breaks in upon the banquet. We may also look back to the *Protagoras* where Alkibiades, although mentioned in the very first words of the dialogue, does not join the conversation until much later (336B). What is still a relatively external device in the *Protagoras* becomes a main formative principle in the *Symposium*.

The narrative leading into the actual conversation does not start with Agathon's banquet, but describes—again in similarity to the *Protagoras*—Socrates on his way to the banquet. In Xenophon's *Symposium*, Socrates is one of the guests from the very beginning. Plato makes him a latecomer to the feast. Since he will have the last word among the speakers, his presence is singled out from the start.

PRELIMINARY
CONVERSATION
174A–176A

In the introductory report Socrates is first shown as a social person, and so he will be shown in the greater part of the dialogue. Then, in conscious contrast, Plato describes him as the thinker lost in inner reflection. The playful conversation with Aristodemos, who as reporter must be present from the beginning, culminates in the word "beautiful." Aristodemos asks Socrates why he has dressed up so beautifully. "So that I would go in beauty to the house of a man of beauty," Socrates replies. This note of playfulness is resumed later, for when Alkibiades arrives, he charges jealously that Socrates has contrived to find a place at the table next to the fairest (213c). Is this not more than mere play? Love—as Diotima says at the height of the dialogue—is "procreation in beauty." Thus, the most important theme is sounded at the very beginning in the manner of a social pleasantry, somewhat as in the *Hippias Major*, the dialogue about beauty that begins with the words "Hippias the beautiful."

But does not the correlation "go in beauty . . . to the man of beauty" have another special meaning? Does it not suggest the question, raised in the *Lysis*, whether friendship is a relationship between the like or the unlike? This would refer here to a very ironic kind of likeness. That we are not mistaken in these surmises is soon shown in the first exchange between Socrates and Agathon (175c *et seq.*), the brief skirmish, full of irony, over "wisdom." Even now (174A *et seq.*) this impression is reinforced by the playful exchange with Aristodemos. The play is on the proverb that the good go unbidden to the feast of the inferior. Homer turned it around to say that the worse go to the feast of the better. Now we turn it once again to say that the good go to the feast of the good. And Aristodemos, who feels inferior, is embarrassed to go to the banquet of a "wise" man.

All these are variations on the theme of like to like and unlike to unlike, a theme to be sounded again in the *Symposium* in the speeches of Eryximachos and Agathon. Its intrinsic relationship to the problem of friendship is known to us from the *Lysis*. When this interlude ends on the Homeric note of the "two going together" (σύν τε δύ᾽ ἐρχομένω), we must remember that Aristotle cites this very phrase when he begins his discourse on the nature of friendship (*Nicomachean Ethics* VIII 2 1155ᵃ 15), and that the remainder of the *Symposium* itself deals with various forms of this friendly "duality"—now Socrates and Aristodemos, next Socrates and Agathon, and finally Socrates and Alkibiades. Here is the first stage in which the same basic relationship is depicted.

Next Socrates in his loneliness is shown, especially the effect that his being lost in deep thought outside has upon the festive gathering inside and the mounting tension generated by this. The lonely man—so Socrates will appear again in the encomium of Alkibiades (220CD). It is no accident that he is revealed in this dialogue as a lonely man. Xenophon wants to show that the great man is capable also of fun and playfulness (ἐν ταῖς παιδιαῖς). But Plato always has the whole Socrates before his eyes, so that the more he reveals Socrates' sociability, the more he must show the lonely streak in the same character. Yet, the meaning of this episode transcends biography. The "polarity of loneliness and communication" is, according to Jaspers, a characteristic aspect of human existence.[7] It is this polarity that manifests itself in Socrates more strikingly than in anybody else.

175D–176A   After Socrates has finally come inside, we witness a brief exchange between him and the host. This takes place within the frame of Socrates' changing his position: first he sits down, and then he reclines.[8] There is talk about where the newcomer should take his seat, but this talk soon shifts to a mock debate on wisdom and how it can be communicated from one person to another. The playful analogy proposed by Socrates, that wisdom does not flow from the fuller into the emptier man as water runs from the fuller into the emptier vessel, suggests a basic principle of Socratic education. Agathon, full of knowledge, and Socrates as the ignorant man are poised in ironic counterpoint.

A brief conversational interlude introduces the various INTERLUDE 176A–178A speakers at the banquet and then leads to the topic of their speeches: love. Agathon and Socrates we have met, but now when the actual drinking together is about to begin with all the customary ritual, Pausanias is the first to speak. In the *Protagoras* (315DE), this same Pausanias listens to Prodikos' sounding off his wisdom, and beside him sits a strikingly handsome young man. "I seem to have heard," Socrates observes casually, "that his name is Agathon, and I should not be surprised if he were Pausanias' favorite." This incident goes back about fifteen years before the dramatic date of the *Symposium*, but it is the same Pausanias who here in the house of Agathon speaks first after the host. In other words, their friendship has lasted.

Aristophanes need not be introduced to anybody. It is taken for granted without a word that the famous writer of comedies should be a guest in the home of a writer of tragedies who has just earned his first spurs, and we look forward to the end of the dialogue (223CD) when only these two poets are left to keep up with Socrates and he "compels them to acknowledge . . ." In addition to Aristodemos, whose role is confined to that of reporter, two other guests are mentioned: Eryximachos, the physician, and Phaidros. We should remember them from the *Protagoras* (315c) where they sat at the feet of "Professor" Hippias as he discoursed on matters of natural science. Thus, it is fitting that Eryximachos here indulges in a few generalities on excessive drinking, and is obviously Phaidros' friend. For Phaidros "is accustomed to follow the advice of Eryximachos, especially in medical matters," and Eryximachos has "often heard Phaidros say . . ." And this brings us to the topic of the speeches.

No poet (so Phaidros claims) has ever composed an encomium in honor of the great god Eros, and no orator has ever discoursed in praise of love; hence, this should be done tonight. How strange! Both in the *Antigone* and in the *Hippolytus*, the chorus addresses a passionate song to Eros, and much earlier the poet Alkaios had praised love as the "mightiest of the gods."

As Aristophanes complains later in the dialogue (189c) that there are no temples of the great god, so Euripides had voiced a similar complaint in the song of his chorus: we do not honor love in ritual and cult. Thus, what is declared here, setting the stage for the contest of speeches to follow, already had been said in reproach by others. That the reproach is not altogether justified is shown by the choric songs, by the ancient sanctuary of Eros in Thespiai (where the statue of Eros by Praxiteles was to be dedicated, probably within Plato's lifetime), and finally, by the famous altar created just at the entrance to the Academy.[9] Plato knew the choric songs and the altar better than we do. The altar inscription from the age of the Peisistratides addressed to the "cunning, ingenious Eros" is echoed in Diotima's words (203D 6). Thus, a great deal of social talk is mixed into what we have heard so far. Then when we hear Phaidros complaining that "until now nobody has dared to sing an appropriate hymn in praise of love," how can we think of anybody but Plato and the daring task he has set himself?

In the context of the speeches we must, above all, pay attention to Socrates. Plato assigns him the last place at the table. "It will be more difficult for us whose place is last, but we shall be contented if those who precede us have spoken well" (177E). We know, then, that he will be listening, and we must judge by his standards. Only Socrates might possibly be justified in pronouncing a negative judgment on everything that is said by the talented and intelligent men who precede him. At the same time, being on his side we cannot admire uncritically everything that is said.[10]

Let us look ahead in the dialogue to some of the brief *interludes* during which the dimensions of social existence, as it were, will emerge in the midst of the long and timeless speeches.

INTERLUDE 185c–185E Aristophanes, who is due to speak in third place, is prevented from doing so by an attack of hiccups. A brief conversation on the subject ensues between him and the physician, who then speaks in place of the patient. We have pointed out earlier[11] how significantly this playful interlude is subordinated to the ultimate goal of the dialogue. Similar playful meaning continues in the

INTERLUDE 189A–189c interlude that occurs between the speeches of the same two men.

A new vista opens in the break introduced after the speech INTERLUDE 193D–194E of Aristophanes. Here the ground is laid for the speech of Agathon—indeed not only for his speech, but for Socrates' speech as well. In this interlude, Socrates breaks his silence by confessing that he is deeply worried about what will be left for him to say after all the others have spoken. Again, we are directed toward the final goal. And as Socrates draws Agathon into conversation about the relationship of the "many" to the "wise," and as Agathon does not know how to go on and Phaidros, guardian of the rules for the contest, warns him not to let himself be seduced by the dialogical power of Socrates, we sense how this power is gradually mobilized against the type of "long speeches" that ultimately are not appropriate to a search for truth. We may ask again—as we did previously (175c *et seq.*)—who in this circle belongs to the many and who to the wise.

PHAIDROS. We have met him in the *Protagoras* among the I 1 178A–180B audience of Hippias. We know him from the *Phaedrus* as a follower of Lysias. His speech here will praise love first for its origin among the most ancient race of gods, and then for its benefits to mankind. This is a rhetorical schema, and the speech undoubtedly reflects contemporary thought even though Phaidros calls upon the testimony of the ancient poets and wise men.[12] It is not only that he imputes to the heroic age a type of male Eros alien to it. Also he recasts, in his critical fancy, the mythical figures of the great Aeschylus so that they fit better into his own system. The reforming appeal, "one should . . . ," "one ought to . . ." (178E 3), which leads him to envisage in his imagination a whole army of lovers, is also a youthful trait. But what does this speech mean in the whole movement of thought of which it is a part?

Eros as a "great god," a world-creating power, akin to the primordial powers: this view will not be essentially changed by the subsequent speakers except for Agathon, who will oppose to this cosmogonic Eros the youthful Eros no less powerful and perfect than the other. Both traditional mythical images of Eros are necessary so that, by contrast, Diotima's vision may surprisingly reveal that "Eros is not a god, but a great demon."

As the creative power in the universe, this love celebrated by Phaidros encompasses the widest sphere. At the same time, its effects on human existence are most far-reaching. Love alone—not kinship or wealth—is the guide toward the good life. It is the motive behind a sense of shame at what is ugly and behind the striving for what is beautiful (ἐπὶ τοῖς καλοῖς φιλοτιμίαν). Without it neither state nor individual can produce great and beautiful works. This necessary link between love and beauty, alluded to repeatedly here, points directly forward to Diotima's speech. And Alkibiades will confess later on that he feels ashamed of his life in the presence of Socrates—and in his presence only. The essential effect of Eros on man's life (in the Greek and Platonic sense, on man's life in the state) is brought out immediately. Its effect is virtue, *arete*. This is the dominant theme also of Diotima's doctrine, but it is only through her that the familiar word *arete* is given new content and direction. In the speech of Phaidros there prevails, almost throughout, the pre-Socratic connection between virtue and male courage that as a definition was overcome in the *Laches*.

Mythical illustrations from the heroic past conclude the speech, both clarifying and enhancing what has been said. They celebrate the sacrificial death of one lover for another, and here a distinction is made that sounds strange to us. When the beloved sacrifices himself for the sake of the lover, this is more highly honored by the gods than the reverse. One might interpret this by suggesting that sacrifice can be taken for granted in the case of the lover who is carried away by his passion, but not so in the case of the object of the passion. Yet, the view is justified here on different grounds. The lover is more divine than the beloved, because he is inspired by the god (θειότερον γὰρ ἐραστής παιδικῶν· ἔνθεος γάρ ἐστι, 180B).[13] The argument sounds like hairsplitting as it is advanced by Phaidros, and it seems grotesque if we think of Eryximachos—until we remember that Socrates is present as a silent listener. Socrates is the great lover. It is rare that the disciples bear him the affection (ἀγαπᾶν) that is fitting. When they do so, however, the gods do them a favor. Thus, the concluding part of this speech aims at Socrates, god-inspired, although the speaker himself neither intends nor recognizes this. In other words, Socrates is the magnet giving direction and meaning to the generalities.

Once we have grasped this we may ask whether the reader should not think of Socrates earlier (179A 6) when Phaidros, envisaging an army of lovers in his imagination,[14] says, "They will not desert each other." Later when Alkibiades in his praise of Socrates talks about their comradely loyalty in combat, the same phrase about "not deserting each other" occurs twice (220E 1, 221A 5). And must we not also think of Socrates at the beginning of the mythical part of Phaidros' speech when it is said that only lovers resolve to die for others? Then follow illustrations from mythology. Orpheus, who did not dare to die "for the sake of love," is sent back from Hades without having reached his goal. A shadow (φάσμα) is shown to him, but the woman herself (αὐτήν) is not returned. Alcestis, on the contrary, who died "out of love," and Achilles, who did more than die for another (ὑπεραποθανεῖν) inasmuch as he followed Patroklos in death (ἐπαποθανεῖν), are honored by the gods for their sacrifice.

The significance of these mythical cases is seen still more clearly in Socrates' own speech where Diotima celebrates, in a literal echo, the same heroes and their sacrifice (208D). The Herakleitean tension between love and death is coming to the fore. Do we read too much in if we place Socrates among these heroes? Surely not, since, in the *Apology* (28CD), it is he who celebrates Achilles as his heroic model. And was it not Socrates who "dared" and "reached the goal"? Did he not see the "things themselves" instead of their "shadows"? Did he not die "for the sake of love"—"for the others"?[15]

PAUSANIAS. In the *Protagoras*, he is among the audience listening to Prodikos. His speech here, even more than that of Phaidros, shows training in rhetoric, all the more so because the speech is based on the contrast (rhetorically accentuated) between two kinds of love.[16] This duality itself is not strange in the context of the mythical tradition. Hesiod (*Erga* 77 *et seq.*), for example, affirmed that there was not *one* goddess "Strife"

I 2
180c–185c

(Eris) but two, a good one and an evil. It is hard to imagine that Plato did not have this dual Eris in mind when he had his Pausanias construct the dual Eros. Noble and common love, noble and common lovers, are contrasted with each other. In this contrast, the power of the god is, if possible, enhanced still further and his relationship to virtue accentuated. Love is "common" when the lovers love the body more than the soul, when they choose the young and the ignorant as objects of their love, and when they leave each other as soon as the bodily bloom passes (ἅμα τῷ τοῦ σώματος ἄνθει λήγοντι, 183E). Thus, the "kind of love is disposed of that is pleasure-driven and merely pleasure-seeking."[17]

Noble love impels toward the mature. In following it we move toward a noble inner disposition (ἤθους χρηστοῦ ἐραστής, 183E) and a love (we must imagine Pausanias looking across the table at Agathon) that "is lifelong, for it becomes one with the everlasting."[18] If the speaker is carried away by reforming zeal to proclaim this as a law (χρῆν δὲ καὶ νόμον εἶναι), we are entitled to look back to the flirtation at the beginning of the *Protagoras*, as well as to the contrast between Socrates and the lovers of Alkibiades as shown in the *Alcibiades Major*. For there the many are those who here serve Eros Pandemos. They pass as the bloom of youth passes (τοῦ σώματος . . . ἐπειδὴ λήγει ἀνθοῦν, *Alcibiades* 131c) because they "did not love Alkibiades at all, but only his body," whereas only then does Socrates approach the young man for an education moved by love.[19]

Throughout the entire speech of Pausanias, there runs as a common theme—through the distinction between two kinds of love, through the analysis of erotic customs in different states, and through his reforming proposals (χρῆν, 181D; δεῖ, 184c) —something hardly discussed, practically taken for granted. It is the connection, almost the union, between the love of youth and philosophy or, where the speaker goes most fully into his subject, philosophy and gymnastics (182c).[20] Philosophy, in turn, is linked with virtue (184D) so that the theme struck in the speech of Phaidros is continued in a fuller prelude to the Socratic theme.[21] It need not be mentioned that for Socrates the word "philosophy" has an entirely different meaning. Nevertheless, this is a preparatory stage and, toward the end of the speech by Pausanias, we read about the noble bond between the lover who can contribute to "prudence and every kind of virtue" (εἰς φρόνησιν τε καὶ ἄλλην ἀρετήν) and the youth who "gives himself" in order to acquire "education and other wisdom."

It is often said that Plato made Pausanias as a true sophist praise the refined love of the physical organism. This may be correct, but it is not the whole story. Diotima, too, will say that love begins with love for a beautiful body. Thus, we must realize that while the speech of Pausanias leads into the vicinity of the Socratic sphere, it still is far removed from the center. Agathon will say later (194E) that every speaker had made the mistake that instead of praising the god, he had praised the benefits conferred by the god upon mankind. Since Socrates accepts Agathon's principle (199C, 201D), we must also approach our criticism from this perspective.

Pausanias, indeed, has inquired into the nature of love neither deeply enough nor with Socratic precision, and has been too empirical in his emphasis on the effects of love. He did distinguish between a noble love and an ugly love, to be sure, but only Diotima will show that this contrast presupposes a higher power set above these two opposing forces—just as in the *Gorgias* (495C *et seq.*), and even in the *Philebus* (12C *et seq.*), the distinction between a noble and a common pleasure is resolved by a *tertium quid* that emerges between or beyond both. Pausanias is far removed from such reflections. How could it be otherwise? The fact that there is ambiguity in his speech reveals a fundamental uncertainty on his part. Nevertheless, a great many things he says will appear as stages on the way to Socrates when we look back later from Socrates' speech to that of Pausanias.

ERYXIMACHOS. We have met him in the *Protagoras* as a student of natural science. Appropriate to this background are both the form and content of his speech, which displays the same formal rigor we find in some of the Hippokratic writings.[22]

I 3
185E–188E

Here, however, is not this rigor exaggerated as the different sections sharply separated from each other invariably culminate in a conceptual schema? Technical pride and a critical attitude are to be esteemed, but does not pride here turn into vanity and criticism into an excessively critical hairsplitting, especially in the critique of Herakleitos to whose "harmony of opposites" the doctrine of the speaker is indebted in many respects? According to Eryximachos' view of cosmic principles, it is possible to classify the art of medicine with the art of cookery. Even this might do if he did not go on to say that the goal of both arts is "to enjoy pleasure without sickness" (187E). Nor may we disregard the accompanying music—the noisy attack of hiccups from Aristophanes and, at the end, his resounding sneeze after he has tickled his nose as prescribed. Yet, despite the ironic aspects of the *mise en scène*, we must not overlook the content of the speech and its necessary place in the construction of the whole dialogue.

Plato has the scientist and physician speak in order to extend into the realm of nature, the universe, and the dimension of transcendence the same tendencies that Pausanias had pursued earlier in the human and social sphere. Thus, Eryximachos begins with a critique of the previous speaker. Pausanias did not pursue the right principle to its conclusion, he says, and with the words, love is "great and wonderful," he also refers to the praise of the cosmogonic Eros at the beginning of Phaidros' speech. Cosmic love as the counterpart of human love—in this respect, as in others, the *Lysis* is predecessor to the *Symposium*. In the *Lysis* (215E), we read that just as in life opposites must be friends, so are the most opposite among the elements most akin to each other. The *Symposium* puts passionate love in place of friendship. Still, as in the *Lysis*, so here primary forces or beings oppose each other, now in a more complex relationship (*Symposium* 186D, 188A). They may be hostile to each other, as they are in principle. The good Eros then creates harmony among them whereas the evil Eros makes them strive for union in destructive excess. A dual Eros who rules in the universe: this view very much resembles that of Empedokles, another scientist and physician, according to whom the two opposing primordial powers of love and strife produce the combinations and separations of bodies in the universe. If we think of the historic development of the human mind as surveyed by Socrates in the *Phaedo* (95E *et seq.*), the theory of Eryximachos, like that of his predecessor, Empedokles, belongs to an early age before the turn toward the *logoi*.

The principle of the dual Eros is pursued through the various stages. The art of medicine, besides which gymnastics and agriculture are merely mentioned, deals with the world of the human body. Music and astronomy deal with the harmonies and disharmonies in the sphere of sounds and that of heavenly bodies. As astronomy is the means for reaching the cosmic level, so the art of divination (suggesting the religious sphere) leads upward to the level of the divine. This is the kind of ascent Plato always employs. It is worked out to perfection in the structure of education in the *Republic* and in the world-structure of the *Timaeus*. The speech of Eryximachos anticipates both constructions down to the very words that are used.[23] Rhythm and harmony are envisaged as the principles of order in the soul and in the universe, and the art of music as the loving desire for this educational work in the soul. When this ascent sketched here reaches the level described as the "communion between gods and men" (ἡ περὶ θεούς τε καὶ ἀνθρώπους κοινωνία) or as the level of "all sacrifices and the province of divination" (θυσίαι πᾶσαι καὶ οἷς ἡ μαντικὴ ἐπιστατεῖ), we have again moved in the direction of Diotima.[24] According to her, the realm of the demonic, to which Eros belongs, is pervaded by the "art of divination and the priestly art concerned with sacrifices, mysteries, and incantations" and "with the exchanges and replies between gods and men" (ἡ ὁμιλία καὶ ἡ διάλεκτος θεοῖς πρὸς ἀνθρώπους, 203A). The dogmatic scientist ends where Diotima begins.

As the direction toward virtue first laid out by Phaidros is continued in the speech of Pausanias, so the view of the world of gods and men first taken by Phaidros (178A) has been enlarged now by Eryximachos into a view encompassing all the realms of being, from the human body upward to the divine. But the concept of a double Eros breaks up the unity envisaged by the first speaker and, necessary as this break-up was in order to penetrate deeper, it calls for a new unity. For anybody who has learned anything from Plato must know that the distinction between a good Eros and a bad Eros will not do—that a god can never be bad. In fact, we may take a superficial contradiction at the beginning of Pausanias' speech (first specifying that one must honor every god and then qualifying that one must praise only the good Eros[25]) as a suggestion that, although we may encounter a greater abundance of phenomena here than in the speech of Phaidros, this solution still will not do. That the divine sphere must remain untouched by anything defective is the insight to be reaffirmed in the end. And for the same reason, Eros must be put into the in-between realm of the demonic. Thus, this dissonance is resolved only very late. For the time being, we hear an entirely new melody.

I 4
189c–193D

ARISTOPHANES. He is seated in third place at the table, and his speech should have come, therefore, in the middle of the five speeches preceding Socrates'. In giving Aristophanes an attack of hiccups so that he becomes the fourth speaker instead of the third, Plato invites us to think, for a moment, about the speech of Aristophanes if it had come at the time originally set for it.[26]

It is apparent, to begin with the human or social content, that the four other speakers form two pairs of friends, Phaidros and Eryximachos, Pausanias and Agathon. Even as Aristophanes is alone among the guests in this human situation, so his speech is the furthest removed from the speeches of the others. The four speeches again form two pairs, although in a sense different from the pairs of men who deliver them. The speeches of Phaidros and Agathon belong together by contrast, since Phaidros celebrates the oldest of the gods and Agathon, the youngest. The other two speeches are linked because the theme of the double Eros introduced by Pausanias is confirmed by Eryximachos. Aristophanes is the sharpest critic—Mankind has not yet grasped the power of love—and he is the most radical in pointing toward what might almost be called an "existential anthropology." Human existence is fragmentary and in danger of becoming more so. From this premise there follows the powerful and virtually ethical demand: the true nature of love consists in overcoming this fragmentary state through striving for wholeness. And at the same time, Aristophanes' speech employs the most powerful aesthetic and mythological images.

Myth is invoked here in pointed contrast to the kind of sociology and natural science revealed by the previous two speakers, against whom Aristophanes directs himself.[27] Mythology was alluded to by them only in recalling the ancient genealogies of Eros. In the speech of Socrates, myth will find its limited place; here it fills the whole world. What was missing before is to be shown now by means of a concrete, poetic description. We are to "perceive" the "power" of love (189c). We sense the mythmaker in the formal principle of telling a story that is loosely continuous and repetitive,[28] a form handled here, however, by a poet who can create an abundant stream of fantasy and words, along with a delightful and grotesque play of images. That is the Aristophanes in Plato.

At its beginning and end the speech of Aristophanes grows into cosmic dimensions. Mankind in its original state is akin to the heavenly bodies, both in shape and in movement, and it is our hope that love will restore this original state in us. This cosmic level, to which Eryximachos had also risen, is glimpsed again in Diotima's significant words that, through love, "the universe is fastened in and with itself." This theme will be completely unfolded only in the *Phaedrus* and in the *Timaeus*. In the *Symposium*, we lose sight of it after the speech of the man of science, for Aristophanes—and later Agathon and Diotima—deal primarily with love in the world of man.

Aristophanes ranks the ways of love among human beings according to the value—i.e., according to the degree of masculinity that enters into the relationship. The highest place is given to the love of one male for another, especially the love of men who are valiant and concerned with the affairs of the state. In this relationship, it is said, we find the depth of feeling at the first encounter, the yearning never to let go of the other, and the sure presentiment that such a desire must aim at something deeper than the satisfaction of a physical drive. That Aristophanes should interpret all these riddles from the perspective of a *single* point beyond experience constitutes the greatness of this construction. The interpretation itself, that love is the desire of the incomplete for completion, of the half for the whole (191A, 192E), is a playful turn, at once betraying the speaker's own emotion and moving his listeners. Aristotle[29] is not altogether wrong in his prosaic and mocking critique of this image derived from the "speeches on love." Given such a desire for melting together, either both partners must perish, namely, in the act of melting together, or else one of the partners must perish because he fails in this endeavor. Only Socrates, and Diotima speaking through him, will put knowledge in place of the vague presentiment that love is rooted in the beyond. Only Socrates will follow Diotima's ladder of love upward to the good, and teach, with direct reference (205D *et seq.*) to the speech of Aristophanes, that the "whole" is nothing if it is not understood as the perfect or the good.

15   AGATHON. He criticizes all his predecessors[30] on the ground
194E–197E   that they talked not about Eros but only about his works, and announces that he for one will talk first about the god and later about the works. This criticism is not quite fair, for Phaidros had made the same distinction earlier. Nevertheless, it is true that Phaidros said relatively little about the nature of love and that the praise of love in the other speeches turned increasingly upon its works, near or far. We thus return to the topic of the nature of love, and since Socrates later explicitly adopts the order proposed by Agathon (201D), it is clear that we are turning in the direction where the discussion will culminate. What is right and essentially new, however, can be said only then. Thus, love is shown here for the last time in a traditional image at once opposed as well as complementary to that developed in the speech by Phaidros (195AB). In that speech, Eros was the primeval, creative power; here he is the youthful, playful god of love. These are the two traditional mythical images, and from them both, but especially from the latter, the novel view developed by Socrates will distinguish itself surprisingly. Agathon rounds out the circle begun by Phaidros.

The *Lysis* successively takes up these four propositions, that
(*1*) love is between the unlike, (*2*) love is between the like,
(*3*) in love, that which is neither good nor bad but rather in
between strives upward toward perfection, and (*4*) love is the
desire of the incomplete for completion. All four views—as we
showed previously[31]—are taken over into the *Symposium*. The
third view, the most profound, will be expressed by Diotima
in the form of a myth that surpasses the three myths incorporated by Plato into the pre-Socratic prelude of the *Symposium*.
The fourth view was represented in the tale told by Aristophanes. But the "complementary" (οἰκεῖον), as Socrates later
(205E) will say reproachfully, is in itself indifferent toward
value. Hence, it must be raised to the level of the good if it is to
be the goal of true love. The doctrine of opposites appeared in
the scientific world-view of Eryximachos. There the opposites
came to rest in a state of balance so that no energy was left, as it
were, to be used for striving toward something higher than
themselves. The doctrine of equals is reserved for Agathon, who
uses it to construct his image of the youthful Eros. Here there is
no tension at all. Little should we wonder that the image retains
a playful appearance without any heroic trait.

While Agathon only implicitly opposes the view of Eryximachos—so that the new knowledge of Socrates and Diotima
may rise above this contrast—he openly takes a stand against
Phaidros. The creation of the world could not have been subject
to the rule of love but must rather have been the work of blind
necessity (ἀνάγκη), if we are to believe the stories about the
origin of the gods and their battles (εἰ ἐκεῖνοι ἀληθῆ ἔλεγον,
195c). (This qualification, viewed in light of the critique of
mythology in the *Euthyphro* and in the *Republic*, would lead to
a destruction or a transformation of the ancient myths.) Necessity refers—if we look ahead toward the *Timaeus*—to what is
totally devoid of meaning and form. Thus, Agathon is right in
exposing a false theology, except that his own view of love is
not serious enough to take the place of the other. The two opposing views, then, cancel rather than complement each other.

As far as language and style are concerned, Agathon's speech
is the most seductive of all. Even though the portrait here of

Agathon is an ironic parody of this disciple of Gorgias, Plato has given him a magical power of words with full enjoyment that cannot be for the sake of satire alone. His listeners, surely not insignificant men, are delighted.[32] And even as Agathon goes furthest in the demand that Socrates later will acknowledge and no matter how differently develop (the demand, that is, that we must deal with the nature of the god), so also are there individual traits in Agathon's speech that seem to anticipate the image of love in the speech of Socrates. For Agathon proceeds in his praise of the god by calling him "perfect" (εὐδαιμονέστατον), first, by virtue of being the most beautiful, and second, by virtue of being the best. He is the most beautiful because "love and ungrace (ἀσχημοσύνη) are always enemies" and love "does not dwell amidst the ugly" (196AB). He is the best because the virtues, all four of them, go with love (196B–D). The gods themselves, including Zeus, the ruler, have learned their essential skills from love. In these words, "the works of the gods were set in order only when love, obviously love of beauty, came among them," we hear for a moment something about the true aim of love. And in his first words, Socrates will describe this relation between love and beauty as indispensable, in explicit reference to the words of Agathon (197B, 201A).

Despite these suggestions, however, and precisely because Agathon has set himself the goal of dealing with the nature of love, we feel his conceptual failure all the more strongly. To see this failure we need only compare his speech to that of Aristophanes. Did Plato intend to show that, on this level, all conceptual power and all myth-creating power as well—indeed, all power as such—had spent itself? Was this why he placed at the end this most playful image, a construction in which the youthful Eros is said to be, among many other things, the master of poetry (196E)? Is Plato mobilizing all the splendor of words and the dance of rhythms in order to show that this refinement of means, this softening of the ethical substance, and this vanishing of the conceptual content represent an extreme, and that a radical turn is called for to break out of this circle? How little experience of life Agathon has if he can say that the present age —it is, among other things, the age of the Peloponnesian War!

—is ruled by love and is a period of peace and friendship. At any rate, the sober questions soon to be posed by Socrates will be in sharpest contrast to the speech of Agathon. This speech is so organized, however, that Socrates can use the same model when he is outlining his surprisingly new image of love in contrast to this conventional view.

Let us remember, in conclusion, who the historical Agathon was. He was a representative of the *dolce stil nuovo* in which musical and rhetorical forms become ends in themselves, destroying the serious spirit of tragedy. Would not Plato have succumbed to this style had he remained a writer of tragedies? Thus, did he not depict in Agathon a danger threatening himself that Socrates helped him overcome? And do we not catch a glimpse, between Agathon's speech and the ensuing questions by Socrates, of an aspect of the educational work that Plato himself experienced and is now transmitting to others?

The noisy cheers greeting Agathon's hymn are put into words by Socrates, whose delight at the "magic" of speeches by others we know from the *Protagoras* (328D), the *Apology* (17A), and the *Menexenus* (235A). As soon as the ironic acclaim has reached its height, however, the same ironic tone turns toward criticism. Twice (199AB) Socrates drops the word "truth" under the disguise of irony, and suddenly the magic of what we have heard so far is dispelled, whether it was superficial or deep, full of content or full of sound. What was serious and what was not will now be tested anew by the inquiring mind of Socrates directed toward the world of being. 198A–199c

SOCRATES. With Socrates the dialogical power breaks through, even as it could barely be held back in the interlude just concluded. As Socrates sets out to accomplish his dual task—to show the lack of foundations in the previous speeches and to lay the foundations for his own—dialogue is his only mode of expression. The rules of the banquet will compel him also to deliver a speech later on, but this speech, in turn, is soon broken up into dialogue. II
199c–212c

Three points are made in the conversation with Agathon. First, there is no such thing as "love as such," but only "love 199c–201c for somebody or something." Love is "intentional." This piece of knowledge (a piece of phenomenology and a truly Socratic-Platonic insight into reality) corresponds to the view expressed elsewhere (*Sophist* 262E 5) that there is no such thing as "speech as such," but only "speech about something" (λόγος τινός). It may be found in similar form in the *Lysis* (218D) when we hear that friendship is "for the sake of something." And even as in the *Lysis* we ascended from this to the "highest love" (πρῶτον φίλον) and to a first glimpse of the Forms, so here this sober proposition is the basis for everything else that follows in the *Symposium* up to the vision of "beauty itself."

The second point is that love is desire (ἐπιθυμία) of something we lack or are in want of (οὗ ἐνδεής ἐστι, 200E). This, too, we encountered in the *Lysis*, where it is said that love (φιλία) is a desire for something of which we are in want (οὗ ἂν ἐνδεὴς ᾖ, 221D). There we moved next to the proposition that love is directed toward what is fitting or complementary (οἰκεῖον). Here in the *Symposium* the goal is greater, for, as his third point, Socrates takes over from Agathon's speech the incontrovertible proposition that love is love of beauty. This is linked now with the first two points, and we see that beauty is the "something" to which love is intrinsically related, and that beauty is what love desires eternally and therefore must be "in want of."

"Beautiful" and "good," however, are usually (or practically) but two names for the same thing. Thus, dialectically we have established the basic points: there is love and there is beauty or the good, with love by its very nature both lacking and desiring beauty or the good. Agathon admits he has not understood any of what he was talking about. Indeed, these first simple assertions have made all the previous foundations insecure. Yet, it is also the case that what was said previously is given its true meaning in these new formulations, especially the contingent connection between love and beauty in Agathon's speech.

201D–203A   Now Socrates begins his own speech, which immediately turns into a conversation he had with Diotima when he was young.[33] Diotima even taught him, so he says, the things he has just clarified in the preliminary conversation with Agathon. This shows that these principles developed in advance are essential to the argument. What follows is based upon them. The realm "in between" is singled out—"between" beautiful and ugly, good and evil, wise and foolish. This is the realm to which Eros belongs since he does not possess but rather desires. In mythical language, Eros is called a "great demon" in contrast to the god to whom perfection (εὐδαιμονία) is assigned. Love is reduced in status but only for the purpose that something higher may come into view toward which it necessarily strives and through which it is endowed with singular dignity among all other "intermediates."[34] The good was not conceived radically enough as long as love was called beautiful, good, and a god.

This conceptual clarification of the nature of love is rendered concrete now in the language of myth. The "in-between" status of love is confirmed with its parents representing opposites, the mother Poverty and the father Plenty. The necessary relationship to the beautiful is shown in that the act of procreation takes place at the feast of Aphrodite, the beautiful. In this Eros, the lover of the beautiful, we now perceive more and more traits that make him at the same time a lover of wisdom, i.e., a philosopher, and closely connected, we perceive also traits of Socrates (much as in Agathon's Eros there were traits of Agathon).[35] Diotima herself says that she has painted Eros in the colors of the lover whereas Agathon borrowed his colors from the beloved. We are to realize the full meaning of this only when we see Socrates himself in the lover. The masculine features of this love, tense, warlike, hunterlike, are in explicit contrast to the softness sounded in the words and rhythms of Agathon. Again, we see the contrast that Plato had in mind when he chose Agathon as the predecessor in the *Symposium* to Socrates.

203A–204C

Having clarified the nature of love and its object, we inquire into its effects on man. Love desires that it possess the beautiful and good. Thus, ultimately, it desires "happiness," εὐδαιμονία.

204C–207A

(This takes us back, we might note, to the end of Aristophanes' speech.) Love is conceived here in a general sense, so that what is called "love" in a specific sense must be distinguished from the general concept. Yet, the same law applies to the narrower, human sphere. Love is directed toward the "other half," is a "striving toward the whole," only if this whole is at the same time "good." And this thought completes rather than destroys the principal theme of the speech of Aristophanes.

Love aims at possessing the good, at possessing it forever, i.e., for eternity, and at procreation in beauty, by means of which it is possible for human beings to partake of eternity or immortality. The necessary connection between love, divinity, and procreative desire for the beautiful, as well as the incompatibility of the beautiful with the ugly and the unshapely (ἀνάρμοστον): these themes take over what was true in the speech of Agathon, that love is always at war with the unshapely or ungraceful (ἀσχημοσύνη), and that love does not dwell with the ugly (196AB, 197B). These truths now rest, however, on the knowledge made secure by Socrates in his preliminary conversation with Agathon. They are linked, furthermore, with the new theme of immortality or the overcoming of death.

207A–209E What has been said up to this point is the general foundation. "These things she taught me at various times when she spoke of love," Socrates says (207A). On these foundations there now rise, as a second level and then a third, the higher insights and the highest mystery. On the second level ("once she asked me . . ."), we extend our view first to include the world of animals. This is the "natural" kind of attitude, expressed earlier by Eryximachos, which serves here to enlarge the base of operations, as it were. Preservation and immortality—these are the goals of the species and of the life of the individual, from physical and mental life upward to the highest spiritual activities.[36] Viewed in this perspective, the sacrifice of life for the sake of love and the mythical examples that Phaidros cited acquire a new meaning. The tension between love and death is felt again. But the heroic death is raised here to the dimension of the immortal. Immortal is the memory of the heroes, immortal is their virtue, and their loving longing aims at the immortal.

Viewed in this perspective, finally, education acquires a new meaning; it is procreation in the soul. Agathon earlier had playfully attributed all "four virtues" to love. Phaidros and Pausanias had spoken more seriously about the intrinsic relationship between love and virtue, and they had necessarily touched on the sphere of the state. Now this theme is resumed— by Socrates-Diotima. Love as a creative drive in the soul is a drive for eternity aiming at the education of the beloved, education for the community, for the state.[37] "The greatest and fairest wisdom by far is that which is concerned with the ordering of states and family, and is called temperance and justice" (209A). The poems of Homer and Hesiod, the laws of Lykurgos and Solon and even of non-Greeks: these are monuments to eternity. (And do we go against Plato's intention if we remember that he is a thinker and poet himself, that he is about to found his own state, and that he will write the *Laws*?)

At last and on the highest level, Diotima shows the ascent from the first stage of love upward to the vision of beauty itself. That is the fulfillment of the mystery for the sake of which everything else preceded (210A).[38] It had been missing in the speech of Socrates and all the more so in the speeches of the others. If we read their speeches from the perspective of this highest level, we are able to separate out in them what is authentic and unauthentic, right and wrong. And what remains acquires new meaning—the community of lovers referred to by Phaidros and Pausanias, the ascent through all realms upward to the divine described by Eryximachos, the "wholeness" that according to the myth of Aristophanes existed in the beginning and is to be regained in the end, the union of beauty and love celebrated by Agathon. Thus, the worth of all the previous speeches may be measured by the degree to which they approximate the goal set here by Socrates-Diotima. It is not that they lead in stages toward this goal, but rather that they approach it in a different sense. For collectively they rise above the common or chaotic world that intrudes into the prelude as the sphere of money-making, and, into the banquet as such, as

209E–212C

wild drunkenness. Yet they remain far below the world of Socrates and Diotima and acquire their meaning and worth only in this perspective.

III
212C–222B

ALKIBIADES. When, as in the aporetic dialogues, Socrates asked one of his "What is . . .?" questions, or when, as in the *Gorgias*, he brought the Forms or *Ideas* into our field of vision, the context was his educational work, or his struggle with adversaries, or his development of a conceptual movement. Yet the *Symposium* shows Socrates for once not as the educator or the fighter, but almost as the mouthpiece through whom some higher being is announcing its wisdom. For this reason it is indispensable that after the path to the Forms has been shown, i.e., after clarification in words, there should follow a human-active movement revealing the nature of the goal. The pronouncements of the priestess could not be the end of the work. There had to be a concluding part in which the ascent to the heights would be depicted in the reality of actual life. The *Symposium* reaches its climax in the episode involving Alkibiades. In the *Symposium*, as in the *Republic*—different as the two works may be in every other respect—the Forms are "in the middle."

212C–215A

The sounds of flutes heard in the house stopped when the speeches began (176E). Now they are heard again outside. With the drunken Alkibiades, life in its wildness breaks in upon the formal company. Drunkenness, on the one hand, belongs to the realm of chaos. (Later, for example, the chaotic interruption of a band of revelers—223B—will ruin the order of the banquet.) Everybody must sense the tension generated even by mere mention of the name Alkibiades. And here we meet the man who, coming now to celebrate Socrates, will detach himself from every Socratic bond and become the ruin of Athens.[39] On the other hand, drunkenness dissolves all social barriers: *in vino veritas* (214E). Only the madness of drunkenness, somehow akin to the madness of the lover, of the poet, or of the philosopher, could speak as Alkibiades will—without restraint and without shame.

Plato has Alkibiades first take a seat and then recline on the couch, and between these two movements there occurs a decisive turn not unlike that at the beginning when Socrates joined the company. The turn here is away from Agathon, to whom Alkibiades first pays polite tribute as "the most beautiful and the most intelligent," towards Socrates who deserves this praise in quite a different sense. Much is concealed behind the playful banter. Alkibiades complains that Socrates had managed by devious means to have his place next to the most handsome. This applies not only, as intended, to Agathon, but also to Alkibiades himself, for in making room for him (213AB) Socrates also manages to have Alkibiades next to himself at the table. The newcomer reproaches Socrates for always lying in wait and appearing suddenly at the most unexpected places. Behind this bantering play of Alkibiades, we sense the seriousness of the situation for the young men who would unexpectedly find themselves confronted by the critical eye of Socrates. The beginning of the *Alcibiades Major* is the most moving illustration of such an encounter. The first words Alkibiades addresses to Socrates in the *Symposium* (213C) remind us in a literal sense of the passionate outburst with which he interrupts his long silence in the *Alcibiades* (104D).

We are supposed to see this connection and measure the distance that separates the present encounter from the earlier one, going back half a lifetime. In the playful charge made here by Socrates (*Symposium* 213D) that Alkibiades is annoying him with jealousy and that his madness and love (φιλεραστία) have become unbearable, we sense the passion Socrates generates in another person, here an egocentric individual. Alkibiades himself expresses the general experience by saying towards the end that Socrates deceives his young followers: he appears as if he were the lover and they the beloved, yet he is always more the beloved than the lover (222B). In the *Alcibiades Major*, this experience is transformed into the dramatic movement of the dialogue from the beginning to the end. Behind Alkibiades' daring joke that Socrates would lay hands on him if he were to love anybody else in the presence of Socrates, we sense the deeper meaning that Socrates is indeed the only one who deserves to be praised. And even as in the prophecies of Diotima love began to acquire the traits of the master himself, so Socrates now becomes the object of the last encomium in praise of Eros.

215A–222B   At the center of the speech of Alkibiades, we find the strange simile of the statues of Seilenos which, on being opened, reveal the most precious images of gods. Here the basic attitude of the younger man is total surrender, that of the master clear knowledge and perfect discipline with regard to every kind of temptation and impulse, temperance (σωφροσύνη), courage (ἀνδρεία, καρτερία), and prudence (φρόνησις) in the sharing of a night with the beautiful youth as in the dangers of battle. This core is surrounded, however, by an exterior shell of "strangeness" (ἀτοπία) and "irony." It is the shell one must penetrate—and yet can do so only for moments. It is in the core that mysterious attraction and painful repulsion intersect each other and shake the beholder. This is the area pictorially represented in the comparison with Marsyas and again with the statues of Seilenos. It is an analogy pursued on a large scale at the beginning of Alkibiades' speech and then once more referred to at the end (to let us see the surroundings more concretely, as it were) in the context of the "deception" by which Socrates confuses his young followers (222AB).

Yet all these things we should rather read in Plato's own words since a restatement cannot but weaken them. Here, however, the relationship between Diotima's prophecies and the encomium of Alkibiades ought to be considered.[40] We can understand what the master has done to Alkibiades only when we keep in mind that Socrates has climbed the ladder upward to the vision of the Forms and that he embodies this ascent in his own existence. Alkibiades may be surprised at Socrates' disdaining his beauty. We know, however, that Socrates has long since passed beyond the lowest stage, where love is "of a single beautiful body." He not only has entered upon the third stage, where one "gives birth to discourse that improves the young" (210c); he has reached the highest stage, where one beholds the eternal Form of beauty and the prototype of the virtues. For it is only at this highest stage that the "reality of virtue itself is brought forth, and not its copies" (212A).

We must infuse Diotima's revelation into the experiences

of Alkibiades in order to see these experiences in their full
scope. And we must see Socrates at once in his human contact
with others and as the philosopher ascending to the realm of
Form (*Eidos*) if we are to do justice to the full range of this
portrait.

Another aspect not to be missed is that through Alkibiades
Plato is speaking here for himself (215CD). Beautiful Olympos
himself had learned his divinely moving melodies from Marsyas,
the ugly satyr, and all later players of flute, good or bad, derive
from this teaching. Exactly the same kind of moving power in-
heres in the simple speech of the new Marsyas-Socrates: "When
we hear you speak or even when we hear your words through
somebody else, we are shaken and under a spell," says Alkibiades. Thus, Plato points to his own place and task as a follower of the master. And from this very perspective, among
others, we may consider whether it really makes sense that
Plato in his later works would retain the person of Socrates
only from habit. Did not the music of this new Marsyas still
sound within him in his old age?

What Alkibiades had called up in a profound interpenetration   222c–223d
of seriousness and levity is heard as an echo in the social game
involving Socrates, Agathon, and Alkibiades. It culminates in
the scene where Agathon changes his place and lies down on
the couch to the right of Socrates. As Socrates first had his place
beside Agathon and then managed, by a ruse, to have Alkibiades
lie down between himself and Agathon, so now at the end
Socrates has his place between the two men of "beauty." In
this position, drawing beauty unto himself, we see Socrates just
before confusion takes over with the drunken, noisy revelers.
Even the narrator, Aristodemos, succumbs to the confusion of
drunkenness and sleep. Yet Socrates remains untouched by the
disturbance, at the end alone, but before that in the company of
the two poets, Aristophanes and Agathon. "He is drinking
clockwise from a large goblet" with them, thus even formally
confirming the victory of order over disorder. He is "discours-
ing" with them, and then, victorious to the end, he "compels
them to acknowledge" that the poet of tragedy who truly
masters his art (τέχνη) must be a poet of comedy also.

This view goes against the firm Greek tradition to which Plato himself subscribes, or seems to, in the *Republic* (III 395A). The question is so important to him that he keeps it in mind over decades, from the *Ion* (534C) to the *Laws* (VII 816DE).[41] In the *Ion*, it is said that the distinction between tragic and comic art consists in the fact that each poet creates by divine dispensation (θείᾳ μοίρᾳ), but he who works with art and knowledge (τέχνη καὶ ἐπιστήμη) would combine both within himself.[42] Thus, Aristophanes and Agathon—so we must read Socrates—do not create from knowledge. Socrates, on the other hand, combines art and knowledge. How so? In his existence he is the satirist, the ironic man, the man of knowledge, the fighting man, and the man of death. And does not Plato's own work, with Socrates at its center, cancel both "tragedy" and "comedy" even as it claims to supersede all earlier poetry? Tragedy and comedy are not to be understood here in the sense that the *Symposium* as a comedy (it sometimes is so called) or a satyr-play is to be contrasted with the tragedy of the *Phaedo*. In the *Phaedo*, as we hear at the very beginning of the dialogue itself, there is an "unusual mixture of pleasure and pain," the participants laugh as well as cry, and death is conquered by immortality. In the *Symposium*, we sense sorrow behind the splendor of the banquet. The poet Conrad Ferdinand Meyer urges us to hear the "drowsy flutes of death" at the end of the feast. But we have seen that the thought of death is present right from the beginning in the figure of Apollodoros who is reporting and whose passionate outbursts we remember from the *Phaedo*. Phaidros' speech celebrates the sacrifices of the heroes, and the tension between love and death is felt in the words of Diotima. Much as the *Symposium* and the *Phaedo* are works of contrast and complement, both contain what Socrates calls the "whole tragicomedy of life" (*Philebus* 50B).[43]

In the end, Socrates is alone, the only one to conquer drunkenness and sleep, as in the *Phaedo* he is the only wise one to remain unshaken by the tears of the women and friends. Now he goes to the Lyceum, i.e., to his day's work, compared with which this night was a magnificent exception. After the speeches on the nature of love, he goes to the active confirmation of love. And only in the evening does he go home to rest.

The *Symposium* stands out among all the dialogues of Plato. Xenophon felt challenged to compete with the *Symposium* and the *Apology* (which is remarkable in quite a different manner), and indeed wrote two works of his own using precisely the same titles. He was successful at least in the sense that a long row of "Symposia" and "Symposiaka" followed his and Plato's models. Plutarch's nine books of *Symposiaka*, the fifteen books of Athenaeus' *Deipnosophistes*, and the six books of *Saturnalia* of Macrobius all are attempts to give collections of literary excerpts an entertaining form. Nowadays, however, in spite of its Platonic origin, nobody cares about this literary form of late antiquity. As a form it served simply as a preserving frame, and only the ancient fragments preserved by it are of importance to us now.

The effect of Plato's *Symposium* on later history is dramatically apparent in the pages of the "Commentarium" appended by Marsiglio Ficino to his translation of the dialogue. There he reports how Lorenzo de' Medici, going back to ancient custom, founds a new symposium as a regular institution. As its president (*"architriclinus"*), he appoints Francesco Bandini. Bandini sets the seventh day of November (the date of Plato's birth and death) as the day for the celebration. He chooses nine members, Ficino himself the ninth, and calls them to a meeting in Careggi (*"in agro Caregio"*). When all have gathered, he recites to them the speeches from Plato's *Symposium*—in Ficino's translation, to be sure—and asks each of them to interpret one of the seven speeches. Lots are cast, and Giovanni Cavalcanti is chosen to interpret the first speech, the speech of Phaidros. Even if Ficino's account is "edited" here and there, the task was set and executed: the first modern Academy was founded.

In the English-speaking world, "symposium" long ago became a word in ordinary language. In this process, it lost the high meaning it had in Plato's time, and by the eighteenth century may have fallen so low as to mean "table talk" and "hodgepodge." Shelley's English translation of the *Symposium* helped to restore meaning to the title word, and at the beginning of the twentieth century, G. L. Dickinson—with Plato's help—raised the word to its ancient nobility in his dialogue, *A Modern Symposium*. This work of Dickinson's deals with contemporary politics, and the participants are modern Englishmen. At the end of the dialogue, we are told what the title implies: "Greece stands eternally at the threshold of the new life. Forget her, and you sink back, if not to the brutes, to the insect."

About 1870, the German painter Anselm Feuerbach, then living in Italy, painted two fine pictures. These were two versions of the same great imaginative subject, Plato's *Symposium*. No other work of Plato's could offer such an abundance of figures in action. Agathon stands in the center, turning to the left where Alkibiades and his retinue are shown as they break in upon the gathering. The other guests at the banquet are seated or are lying down behind Agathon, filling the right side of the picture. And among them, Socrates stands out by his mien and his profile.

TWENTY-ONE

Phaedo

THE *Apology* veils behind a speech in court what Plato intended to reveal: the existence of the philosopher confronted with the ultimate decision. In the *Gorgias*, the court of Athens is contrasted with the court beyond, thus raising the Form of true justice above the sphere of the temporal on earth. The *Meno* refers knowledge to the realm of eternal being and—with the help of the Orphic doctrine of the transmigration of souls—proves the immortality of the soul by showing that it partakes of the truth of being. All these aspects come together, at the height of Plato's creativeness, in the *Phaedo*.

In this dialogue, therefore, more than in any other, it is impossible to separate "what happened" from "what was said" (58c 7), to distinguish between events and philosophical content, as in frame and picture.[1] Truth of being and reality of life, *Idea* and existence, are related to each other necessarily and intrinsically. If Socrates had obeyed the message of the official in charge of administering the poison and had remained silent on the last day of his life, he would have had little to say to posterity. No disciple would have carried his teachings into the world as Phaidon does here, and Plato would not have presented, over a period of fifty years, through Socrates (or in the presence of Socrates), the crucially important things he himself meant to communicate or struggle against. But what can a philosopher who is completely concerned with the subject matter, yet at the same time always is expressing his own being, say before his death, and what can he talk about then except philosophy, death, and immortality? Given the magnitude of the task as well as the human limitations, the arguments do not completely reach their goal (107AB). This is so even when we are dealing with courage and temperance. So, for a conversation about death and immortality more than at any time, we need the presence of a man who will conduct it bravely and meet his end fearlessly and nobly.

FRAME
CONVERSATION
57A–59C
    The first words emphasize that Phaidon was present "himself," that he is reporting as an eyewitness. We sense the tension stretching from this affirmation to the brief remark, seemingly quite matter of fact: "Plato, I believe, was sick" (59B). In his written work, Plato's own name occurs only here and twice in the *Apology*, there (*Apology* 34A, 38B) merely as part of the official record of the court proceedings, as it were. Here in the *Phaedo* the indefinite "I believe" is significant. Phaidon speaks from a distance. He has only a vague relationship to Plato. Without the qualification, "I believe," Plato would not have mentioned his own name here. To do so must have been important enough, however, partly to justify before posterity why he was absent, and partly—for him still more importantly —to justify the freedom of inventing the conversations according to his own design while giving an exact record of the situation itself.

    It is no accident that the dialogue dealing with death is named after Phaidon, the beautiful and the young. Love and death are joined in a Herakleitean tension. Let us think ahead to the critical moment later when we do not know whether the argument will live or die, whether it will find or miss the meaning of life and death. At this moment, Socrates puts his hand on the beautiful hair of Phaidon, who is sitting at his feet. This touch of the one nearest to him—"your mortal body, this narrow sanctuary"—seems to put new life into the philosophical argument that had threatened to collapse.

    The same love that was near the dying man carries the message of his death into the wide world of the living, for Phaidon will tell in Phlius the story of the last hours of Socrates. By transferring the frame conversation to a place outside Athens, Plato is able to record a number of things that, being well known, could hardly have been told among Athenians. At the same time, the significance of the great event is shown as its effects extend beyond Athens to the world at large in widening circles. Phlius is a stage between Athens and the world at large—to begin with, a stage between Athens and Elis, Phaidon's home. (He will later transmit the Socratic tradition from his school at Elis.) Again, it is no accident that Echekrates, who first receives the message, is a Pythagorean and that Phlius was known as the seat of a Pythagorean community.[2] The contemporary reader must have thought of this community when he heard about the circle gathered around Echekrates, although it is worth noting that Plato portrays this group hardly at all. Echekrates represents a stage between common sense and the level of Socrates-Plato. This is the same stage that is represented in the dialogue itself by Simmias and Kebes, and on it the Pythagorean doctrine of the soul and mathematics are seen as propaedeutic to knowledge in Plato's sense. It is quite appropriate that the two men who are trained in philosophy should put up the stronger opposition in the conversation itself, for in doing so they also help Socrates fulfill his philosophical mission.

The reference to the trial as already known in Phlius (58A) makes us look back to the *Apology*. There, at an earlier stage of his work, Plato presents us with the portrait of the philosopher and his existence confronted by the ultimate decision. The *Apology* culminated in this conviction: death is "good" to him who is a "good" man. It justified this conviction—bypassing the seriousness of the question, as it were—by arguing that, after death, we may expect a state of dreamless sleep or the continuation of a philosophical life, the only life worth living. Thus, death would be not the end of life, but perhaps even an improvement of it. This was said for the benefit of the public, the large audience in court.

The *Phaedo* transforms this view into a new context. What, in the *Apology*, was concealed behind the simple word "good" is revealed here as the realm of Forms, or *Ideas*. The prospect of continuing the life of the philosopher in Hades—the prospect, that is, of continuing the search for the good—and the insight that no evil can come to the good man from outside, are now made secure in the knowledge that the soul by its very nature belongs to the world of eternal Forms, of true being, of the good, of transcendence. Anybody who looks, in the "proofs of immortality" offered in the *Phaedo*, for dogmatic demonstration in support of childlike hopes must be assuming that in the *Apology* a different Socrates, the "historical" Socrates, is heard, in contrast to the "Platonic" Socrates of the *Phaedo*. Against this view we shall at least try to show how little these readers in search of dogmatic answers are following Plato's own clues. Above all we must not allow an interpretation of this later dialogue to amount to a leveling down or a freezing of Plato's thought.

The reference to the trial, then, connects the *Phaedo* with the *Apology*, the work to which it corresponds at an earlier stage. At the same time, a theme is sounded that will run through the entire *Phaedo*. The friends gather in the room of the courthouse, which is situated near the prison (59D). This, to be sure, is part of the historical report, but we may wonder if it would have been worth mentioning if Plato had not intended to call up the memory of the trial explicitly—"in the courthouse where the trial took place." Later when Socrates begins to speak he looks upon his audience, in a serious and significant play, as his judges before whom he must defend himself more successfully (he hopes) than before his other judges (63B and E, 69DE). This contrast is kept up to the end. When, in the closing myth, the judges of the dead pronounce sentence upon those guilty of murder and, in turn, upon him who "has purified himself by means of true philosophy" (*Phaedo* 113E–114C), we need hardly think back to the *Apology*—where there is an appeal to the true judges in Hades in contradistinction to the alleged judges in life (*Apology* 41A)—in order to realize what contrast Plato has always had in mind.

Only outside Athens could one report in such detail about the circumstances that postponed the execution of Socrates. Did Plato merely wish to record what actually happened, in the manner of a historian? If so, why go back into the prehistory of the custom, into the legend of how Theseus "saved" and "was saved" and how Apollo was the "savior"? When we enter the prison itself, we learn that Socrates has composed a hymn to

Apollo. The hymn to the god, on the one hand, and the practice
of a philosophical life, on the other, illuminate in ironic reflection the Socratic response to the call received in a dream: "Practice the arts of the Muses!" Is not the philosophical life represented as a hymn to Apollo, the savior, to whose service the
Socrates of the *Apology* dedicated his educational work?[3] And
even if the story about dream and hymn were to be interpreted as
a mere record of some actual happening, such an interpretation
fails in connection with a later episode that is entirely filled with
an Apollonian spirit. In this episode, related between the second
and third levels of the dialogue (84E *et seq.*), Socrates serves
Apollo as a fellow servant with the singing swans. Even as they
are said to sing more and more beautifully as they are about to
join the god whose servants they are, so Socrates believes himself endowed with no less prophetic powers derived from the
same master to whom he is dedicated (ἱερὸς τοῦ αὐτοῦ θεοῦ).
There, at the outset, Apollo is invoked—Apollo, the saving,
prophetic, and musical god who guarantees sublime order and
lawfulness—so that his presence may be felt to the end.

Pindar had written unforgettably about music as the symbol
of order in man and society and about Apollo as the patron in
both spheres.[4] We may also recall how often Apollo and the
singing swans figure in the mythical biographies about Plato.[5]
There Plato is said to descend from Apollo himself. Plato's
parents are shown sacrificing on Hymettos to Pan, to the
nymphs, and to Apollo, while bees are busy pouring honey into
the infant's mouth. In the night before Plato becomes Socrates'
disciple, Socrates has a dream in which a featherless infant swan
takes refuge on his knees and then flies away singing and in full
plumage. The dying Plato dreams of himself as a singing swan
who flies from tree to tree; no hunter can shoot him down. The
Pythagorean Simmias interprets this dream as follows: Everybody would try to grasp Plato's thoughts, but each one would
make the interpretation fit his own thinking. (Do we not do so to
this day?)

We enter the prison at the moment when Socrates—after re-
ceiving the message of what is going to happen to him today,
and after sending off the lamenting Xanthippe—is sitting up

INTRODUCTORY
CONVERSATION
59C–63E

on his bed (60B 1). After a while he lets his legs down towards the ground (61c 10). Then the philosophical conversation commences. Between one posture and the other, there is a preliminary conversation not unlike that which takes place in the *Symposium* between the moments of Socrates' sitting down and his lying down. Here in the *Phaedo*, we see how Socrates rubs his leg and we hear how he begins to talk, calmly as from a distance, about the inseparability of pleasure and pain. The scene is in striking contrast to what just preceded, especially the noisy lamentations. Yet it is no accident that Phaidon, in the frame conversation, had described the "mixture of pleasure and pain" as the state in which he and all others found themselves on this day (59A). Each time the mixture is called "strange" (ἄτοπον, 59A 5, 60B 4). We sense the similarity, and also the difference. Socrates speaks in a contemplative mood about what "men call pleasure" as if it did not concern him, whereas the others are deep in their state of passion. No less is it an accident that these affects later figure prominently as something to be avoided by the philosopher (64D), a nailing of the soul to the body (83D). Socrates is no Stoic, but we learn right away how little these matters touch him.

The poetry to which the conversation now turns in connection with Aesop's fables is similarly of peripheral yet at the same time deeply ironic significance. Socrates tells about the dream-figure's calling to him, "Practice the arts of the Muses!" And now, on the one hand, an ironic tension is set up between his saying that he is no storyteller or inventor of myths (μυθολογικός)—he who had just sketched a fable as Aesop might have invented it—and the mythical aspects of the dialogue itself. These mythical aspects are soon to be heard (61E 2) with increasing significance until they culminate in the great myth in which this very Socrates, a stranger to myths, conceals his ultimate thoughts. On the other hand, Socrates plays ironically with the ordinary kind of poetry (τὴν δημώδη μουσικήν, 61A), which he is practicing in prison, and with the true musical work of his life. The level to which Socrates seemingly has descended in the making of his poems is represented by the literary work of Euenos who knows a little of everything, and is treated, with

noticeable scorn, as a money-making sophist in the *Apology*
(20B) and as a technician of oratory in the *Phaedrus* (267A).
Socrates does not wish to enter into competition with this kind
of poetry (60D), but as a "philosopher" he calls upon Euenos—
in vain, as Simmias remarks—to follow him as soon as possible. But by this Socrates does not mean that he should pass into
the other life by violent means, however, for that would not be
lawful (οὐ θέμιτον).

   With these words, Socrates lowers his feet to the ground.
This new posture marks the beginning of the actual conversation
in which we must learn "to examine carefully the journey into
the beyond as well as talk about it in mythical images" (διασκο-
πεῖν τε καὶ μυθολογεῖν). Thus, one method alone is not enough.
The reader is supposed to ask, "Why not?" and then learn in
what follows how to distinguish between the two approaches.
How profound is the advice to Euenos! Death as something
good—that sounds paradoxical. Death as something good that
we must not bring about—that sounds even more enigmatic.
These paradoxes are made clear only in a preliminary way. The
first is clarified by referring to the hope that we shall meet good
men in the other life also, and the conviction that we shall be
with the gods who are good. The second paradox is clarified
with reference to the Orphic doctrine by which "we men are
here on a sort of guard post from which we must not run
away."[6]

   The second paradox, among other things, transposes the
basic problem of the *Crito* into the symbolism of the *Phaedo*.
The first paradox, among other things, reminds us of the end
of the *Apology* (40c *et seq.*). The hope expressed there is raised
here into the dimension of transcendence, since the false an-
tagonism of life and death postulated by common sense is overcome by the fact that the gods who are good rule over both
realms. This means, furthermore, that human existence finds
its completion in death, as inescapable as it is mysterious. And
for this same reason, human existence lacks completion if an
arbitrary end is put to life.[7] Thus, from death we are directed
back to life that faces towards death. Moreover, in calling upon
the ancient myths Socrates issues another demand to the living:

In the beyond, the good are much better off than the wicked. This mythical form carries the moral imperative that runs through the whole dialogue, reappearing repeatedly, always present beneath the surface. Nor is it an accident that, at this point, the faithful Kriton is permitted to interrupt with the message from the official who will administer the poison. Socrates should refrain as much as possible from talking, he says. For once Socrates does not obey; his life's work is in question. It is now, in fact, that the dialectical discussion gets under way. Through it the power of conviction will be given to what has been merely alluded to so far.

I
63E–69E   The topic of this first discussion is not just a "proof of immortality" in general. Its point of departure is, rather, the strange readiness for death on the part of Socrates. This attitude does not seem to make sense to his friends, and it must insult the gods who are good masters. This insistent objection from his Pythagorean associates gives Socrates the opportunity to point out that readiness for death is the natural attitude of the philosophic life. For true philosophy means to learn how to die. This is the imperative whose influence has been felt through the ages.[8] The many, to be sure, misunderstand the orientation toward death, or the attitude of being worthy of death. They turn it, as the fate of Socrates shows, into its paradoxical opposite. What is death, according to the general view? It is the separation of the soul from the body. What is a philosophic life? It is indifference to the pleasures of the body or needs of the body in general, and "a turning toward the soul" (64D–65A). As far as the specific task imposed upon the philosopher—the development of reason or intelligence—is concerned, the physical senses are a hindrance. Even the keenest senses, sight and hearing, do not yield the truth of being. Especially when confronted with the highest task, which is knowledge of justice, beauty, and goodness itself, or in short, knowledge of being, the philosopher must turn pure thought-itself to pure being-itself. Even the linguistic correspondence points to the relationship between knowledge and its object, to the fact that the soul is akin to the *Eidos* and perhaps *Eidos* akin to soul (65C, 66A, 66E). The desires of the body are responsible for wars and civil

strife (thus the political theme is sounded); they interfere with philosophy and disturb our thinking even when we do advance to philosophizing. Therefore, life—the union of body and soul —is the enemy of philosophy. Only in death, "if at all," can we attain true knowledge.

Death, i.e., the liberation of the soul from the body, turns out to be the fulfillment of the philosophic life, and the fear of death, within this existential context, to be "most unreasonable." This argument on behalf of the consistently reasonable attitude that characterizes a philosophic life is expanded in several respects. In every other kind of life, the brave are "courageous from fear" and the temperate are "temperate from intemperance." Hence, such generally acknowledged virtues as courage and temperance are meaningful only in the context of a philosophic life oriented toward death, because only in such a life is reason (φρόνησις) the "true coin." Other lives, as the *Protagoras* (356c *et seq.*) had scornfully shown, do not have such a secure standard and can only calculate quantities of pleasure and pain. In the beginning of the discussion here in the *Phaedo* (62B), the "mystery doctrine" that we are "in this life as on a guard post" had been touched. Later on (67CD), Orphic images are invoked to describe the separation of the soul from the body, as for example "purification" and "release from the chains of the body." These mystery strains mount toward the end of the passage (69c). In the mystery doctrines, Socrates finds "hints" (αἰνίττεσθαι) pointing toward the reality he has in mind. Purgation (καθαρμός) corresponds to temperance, justice, courage, and reason. The uninitiated, who in Hades "shall lie in the mud," and the initiated and purified, who "shall dwell with the gods"—these correspond in the mysterious language of mysticism to the unphilosophical lives and the philosophical lives. Plato employs this language here, at the beginning, in the middle, and at the end, as if he wished to make sure that just when he had firmly established the rule of reason (φρόνησις) in life and death, the "enigmatic character of existence" would not be neglected.

The "speech of defense" is finished (69E). What is its essential meaning? It is not concerned with proving the "immortality of the soul" as the later conversations are—whether in fact or in appearance. Here, on the contrary, life and death of the philosopher are interpreted as a consistently meaningful whole, or as "the desire to become pure spirit" (Schleiermacher). But all the elements that will recur in the later "proofs of immortality" are present: the rule of reason, the direction toward the world of Forms, the fulfillment of a philosophic life in death, and the symbolic language of the mysteries as pointing toward the existence of the philosopher. For the first time we have entered into the circle that will be drawn, on an expanding and concentric scale, in the remainder of the dialogue.[9]

II
69E–84B

We pass into the area of the second circle with an objection raised by Kebes—and let us not forget how much there is of Kebes in all of us! He agrees with what has been said, but also calls attention to what is questionable from the average man's point of view. Suppose the soul after its separation from the body goes nowhere, but dissolves like breath or smoke? Thus, while in the previous conversation we had a simple and clear account of the life of the philosopher, we are confronted now with a popular and materialistic concept of the soul. This calls for discussion, but words like "mythical speech" (διαμυθο-λογῶμεν), "likely" (εἰκός), and "opinion" (δόξα) indicate the level of discussion into which Plato now draws his Socrates.

II 1
69E–72E

Socrates again begins by referring to the profound premonitions contained in the mystery doctrines. More specifically, he cites the doctrine of the rebirth of the soul, for if this could be proved, it would suffice to dispose of the objection. Presently the view is expanded so that it goes beyond the fate of mankind. The universe itself is represented as being in continuous movement between opposites. This aspect of nature is dominant in the theories of Herakleitos and Empedokles, and finds a close approximation later on in Melissos, particularly in his formulation (*Vorsokr.* 30 [20] B 8, par. 3) that "the living dies and becoming originates from the non-living." Thus, as the terminology indicates, Socrates adopts the view of natural philosophy according to which we may infer, from the perennial transformation of life and death, death and life, or from the cyclical movement of becoming, "that the souls must exist somewhere and be reborn thence." This sublime view of life in the language of natural philosophy takes its stand beside the mysteries. Man is given a place in the order of the universe; the "balance of the great scale" applies to him as well.

This expansion, magnificent as it is, has two defects that are to be noticed by the attentive reader. For a large number of the opposites cited, we can say there is a more or less, i.e., a state "between" the opposites: larger and smaller, stronger and weaker, better and worse, and so forth. Yet the first two pairs of opposites (we lose sight of them, as it were, in the cumulative massing of evidence) were of an entirely different kind: beautiful and ugly, just and unjust (70E 2–3). Kebes does not notice the difference between what is absolute and what is relative. Otherwise, he would not reply affirmatively to the question of whether "everything" comes into being from its opposite, but would add: You have just shown us some being that does not "come to be" (71A 9–11). That we are not reading into the text what Plato did not intend to be there may be seen clearly toward the end of the dialogue (103A 4) when "one of the company" refers back to this discussion about opposites and Socrates, "with a quick turning of the head"—a physiognomic characteristic recorded earlier by Aristophanes (*Clouds* 362)—embarks upon clarifying the distinction between the world of being and the world of becoming.

The other defect is as follows. A price has been paid for expanding the view into the world-order of natural philosophy. The separate nature of the soul has been sacrificed. Life and death are envisaged as purely natural phenomena like sleeping and waking. It is not a matter of my death and yours or your life and mine. The soul, too, is a natural phenomenon. What is lacking in this view is the "soul" conceived as the (rational) self whose preservation is a matter of concern to man caring about his fate. Existence is lacking, one would say today. Thus, of the two points raised by Kebes as deserving to be proved— "that the soul exists when man has died and that it possesses some power, i.e., reason or intelligence" (70B)—only the first has come into its own. It is no accident that Kebes, after Socrates has apparently finished, adds a second argument opening with the words, "There is also . . ."[10]

The second argument is the theory of recollection. To learn means to "re-call" what we once knew in a previous life. Kebes has "often" heard Socrates expound this view, and now Simmias wants to be reminded of the proofs for it. How strange. Must not every reader be aware that it was Pythagoras, the master of Kebes and Simmias, who appealed to this doctrine of pre-existence? Empedokles had pointed specifically to the man of superior wisdom who could remember ten or twenty previous lives.[11] In the *Meno* (81BC), Socrates introduced the discussion of this subject by citing a solemn passage in Pindar referring to the souls sent back into this life by the queen of Hades. Nothing like that is in the *Phaedo*. Here we are not dealing with mystic-ecstatic experiences, however much the term "recollection" alludes to them. Instead, we are dealing with the "innate ideas" that much later will figure prominently in the epistemological theories of Descartes, Leibniz, and Kant.[12]

Socrates first "recalls" the doctrine with the help of arguments familiar from the *Meno*. Then the phenomenon of recollection, which, in the *Meno* (81CD), was only touched upon by referring to the "kinship of the whole of nature with each other," is approached on a broad scale. There is recollection due to contiguity and to similarity.[13] In the case of similarity, however, an additional factor must be mentioned, namely, that one thing is less than the other or does not quite equal the other. And so the concept of equality comes into view. As again and again in Plato, equal things are contrasted with the equal-itself. The things that we call equal or that appear to be equal are still unequal. They are both similar to the Form of equality and, at the same time, different from it.[14] The way of gaining a knowledge of the equal-itself from this Herakleitean tension between the equal and the unequal fits into the previous analysis of the phenomenon of recollection. We perceive that the objects of experience are not equal, but that there is in them a "tendency" or a "striving" (βούλεται, ὀρέγεται) to become equal. In perceiving them "we remember" the equal-itself which we must have "known before" (προειδέναι). This insight is then extended beyond the equal to the good, the beautiful, the just, and the pious—in short, to everything "upon which we imprint the seal being-itself" (τὸ «ὃ ἔστι»). These things, too, we must have known before we came into this life. All of this is an expansion upon the *Meno*. But here in the *Phaedo*, at the end of the demonstration (76D *et seq.*), the meaning of it is stated emphatically. The pre-existence of the soul depends upon the being of the eternal essences. Just as (ὥσπερ) they have real being, so (οὕτως) did the soul exist previously. Their existence and the pre-existence of the soul condition each other. Just as (ὁμοίως) there is essential being, so there is the pre-existence of the soul. This analogy is affirmed three times.

In the *Meno*, the half-mythical doctrine of recollection served to establish the possibility of knowledge and, ultimately, the knowledge of Forms. Conversely, here the knowledge of Forms is used as the basis for guaranteeing the immortality of the soul. But now it turns out that, according to the present version, we can infer only the pre-existence of the soul, not its survival. This is hardly the sort of conclusion that matters most to us who are human like Simmias and Kebes. Reminded of this defect, Socrates combines the doctrine of recollection with the earlier view according to which life generates from death, thus supplementing pre-existence by life after death. The proof seems to be complete, yet Plato suggests immediately that he does not think so, for he proposes "further discussion of the matter" (77D).[15] And, indeed, the power of conviction that each demonstration lacks on its own cannot be brought about by joining two complementary parts of the demonstrations—very unlike parts, besides. What remains most significant is the intrinsic relationship between soul and *Eidos*. Yet myths of the beyond and theories of natural philosophy might rather cloud the purity of this view, granted that mythical premonitions are significant and that the cyclical movement ascribed to the universe was an important insight. Neither mythology nor natural philosophy, nor knowledge of the Forms—even though all three be combined—can satisfy the childlike wish to see one's life prolonged beyond death and to have a proof for such survival.

The "child in us" demands magic charms in order to be calm about the soul's fate after life. Man's fear lest the soul upon leaving the body be dispersed by the wind has not been assuaged. We are still dealing with the popular view of the soul as breath, a material substance but made of finer stuff. Socrates takes up the view, albeit in irony and playfulness. In this third section, the context continues to be theories of nature and, as we shall see, Plato tries to gain from this source all that he can.

The fear that the soul might be dispersed arises from within the concepts of natural philosophy. Empedokles, Anaxagoras, and the Atomists had used the concepts of combination and separation. As far as bodies or atoms are concerned, Leukippos and Demokritos might have said as well that what is composite may be broken up into its component parts, but that what is not composite is indestructible. It takes Plato, however, to contrast the visible, composite nature of physical objects with the kind of being, invisible (at least to human eyes, 79B), incomposite, and non-physical, that is to be attributed to the eternal Forms. These two types of being are then co-ordinated to the body and the soul of man, whereupon it turns out that the soul is "more similar" to the invisible.

The same result is gained still more strikingly by reflecting on the functions of the soul. There are the senses which grasp the physical objects. There also is the soul which reaches toward "being itself." For in contrast to the confusion and unrest in the sensory world, the world that the soul dwells in is pure, eternal, everlasting, and unchanging. And since the soul is akin to this being (περὶ ἐκεῖνο), its wanderings are at an end and it remains always itself. This state of being is called intelligence or reason (φρόνησις). The essential nature of the philosopher had been described in similar words during the first stage of the dialogue.[16] Can there be a stronger proof for the immortality, or rather the eternity, of the soul?

Yet, as was said, we are still dealing with natural philosophy or, more precisely, with the popular conception of the soul as breath, a finer stuff in the body. Thus, the discussion descends again to this level. The soul "has a far and away greater resemblance (ὅλῳ καὶ παντὶ ὁμοιότερον) to everlasting, unchanging being than to its opposite" (79E). Again, since the soul rules over the body, it is "like" (ἔοικεν) the divine and the ruling principle. Hence, it is "altogether indestructible, or nearly so" (80B). In sum, the soul is "most like" (ὁμοιότατον) the divine, the immortal, the intelligible; it is of a single Form and indestructible, whereas the body is most like the opposite. Thus, the clear view we had previously gained is muddied again because of the comparison between soul and body. Instead of radical separation and contrast, we are adopting a misleading comparative method that only the "child in us" would call a "proof of immortality." Plato pursues it emphatically, furthermore, as if he meant to suggest that here where we are trying to prove too much, we are ultimately not proving anything. (But this is no external critique, as so many in the literature are. We are merely following the critical suggestions that Plato himself has liberally distributed.[17]) Moreover, we learn that this failure to clearly grasp the essence happens not only in thought, but again and again in life as well. To become pure soul or pure spirit is a task never completely realized in the life of man. Yet, it is a demand that the philosopher, his eyes upon death, makes of himself and of others. Soon we shall hear this more explicitly.

In the *Meno*, too, the soul's vision of the Forms, or *Ideas*, was connected with both eschatology and a moral injunction. This is no accidental or capricious link, for if thinking does not pass the test of action, it is incomplete in the life of man. Or, according to the *Republic* (540A), those who have reached the highest knowledge of eternal being must be compelled to apply to actual life what they have seen and learned. The eschatological view puts man, both as a thinker and as an agent, before the court of eternity, with the concrete power and the solemnity of ancient tradition by which myth surpasses conceptual thought. Thus, the threefold link connecting knowledge of Forms, mythical eschatology, and moral demand is deeply grounded throughout the *Phaedo* as a whole. It has been seen on the first level, and now again on the second as the two other parts join the chain of "proofs" in the center of which is the knowledge of Forms. The eschatology rests on the distinction between body and soul that dominated—and muddied—the proof to the end. The pure soul of the philosopher, which (as was said on the first level, 81A 1 ∼ 67E 5) has practiced dying, departs into the realm it resembles, the invisible, divine, immortal, and intelligible. It is released from the body and from its wanderings. The soul that is uncleansed and weighted down by the body is dragged back into the visible world and, depending upon its character, is reincarnated in various physical shapes.

These visions of the beyond, interspersed with repeated occurrences of the word "probable," are connected—by means of a "therefore" (τοιγάρτοι)—to the moral theme. This theme had intruded quietly, yet clear, into the very beginning of the conversation (63D) and then again halfway through the second stage (72E 1–2). Now, with solemn emphasis, Socrates calls for release and purification. The goal of the mysteries becomes the goal of philosophy. Philosophy is pure knowledge and a turning away from the affects, pleasure and pain, desire and fear, that obscure the clarity of knowledge and rivet the soul to the body.[18] Vision of the truly divine—a vision achieved through strenuous and continuous work of thought—is now the goal, not any longer of the mystic, but of the philosopher. His death is the passing of the soul into the realm akin to itself. Thus, at the end, there is once more this essential core of the proof (here seen without its all too earthly shell) for the indestructibility of the soul. From this perspective, the ironic thinker looks down upon the fear . . . (He addresses his two partners directly and repeats in his last words, so that the distance may be all the more noticeable, the very words that Kebes used [70A] in launching the discussion on this second stage.[19]) The ironic thinker looks down, then, upon the childlike fear that the soul, on its release from life, may be scattered by the wind.

III
84c–115A
Long silence. The first words that break it indicate that the partners have been critical of what was said before. Their keeping silent, therefore, has significance the reader should heed.

At the same time, the silence also marks a sharp break— We are approaching the highest level. Before we do so, the nature of the problem is brought up once more. To know the truth about it in this life is impossible or at least very difficult. Yet, to infer from this fact that one should prematurely desist from further inquiry would be cowardly. If we cannot attain perfect knowledge, we must be satisfied with the humanly best argument—unless there is somebody, as Simmias mysteriously says, who could make the journey of life on the raft of a divine *logos*. So a decision is made beforehand with regard to the certainty about what can at best be said on the subject under discussion. A decision also is made about the necessity of inquiring continuously. The secret of the Socratic life once again is wrapped in enigmatic allusions.

The discussion itself proceeds from two objections. The objection raised by Simmias goes far beyond the early, materialistic conception of the soul as smoke or breath. Suppose, it is said now, that body and soul are related like a musical instrument and its harmony. This analogy would satisfy the condition that the soul is invisible, incorporeal, and something beautiful and divine, yet it would not guarantee its existence after death. The objection raised by Kebes (86E *et seq.*) is as follows. So far we have proved only the pre-existence of the soul, its life after death, and its superiority over the body. But we have not proved eternal life, for, according to the previous arguments, it is not impossible that the soul might use up many bodies and in the end still perish.

III 1a
85E–88B

Plato seems to advance at least the first of these two objections because it must have been highly attractive to him. The predicates invisible, incorporeal, beautiful, divine, call the Forms to mind. Moreover, how important the Pythagorean concept of harmony was or became for Plato, and especially for his view of the soul, may be seen just from one aspect of his work—that in the *Timaeus* the world-soul is constructed mathematically according to harmonic proportions.[20] Yet, as soon as the analogy is transferred back to the relationship between an instrument and its harmony, there is the danger that it makes the soul into a function, however noble, of the body. Even in this case, we might ask—must ask, in Plato's spirit—whether the harmonic proportion really is nothing else but a function of the instrument or, conversely, whether the instrument perhaps translates the eternal harmony into concrete sounds. The objection raised by Kebes again envisages the soul, in accordance with the general views of natural philosophy, as a kind of extremely fine substance. Both objections show that the soul has not been recognized as something radically different from the body, and that we fail to recognize the pure, distinct essence of the soul as soon as we introduce physical notions into the discussion.

INTERLUDE
88c–91c

Here is a critical place in the dialogue. Discomfort and doubts arise among those present on the occasion. Uneasiness spreads even into the frame conversation itself, where Echekrates—he, too, is a Pythagorean, we must remember—finds himself at home with the view that the soul is a harmony but nevertheless confesses doubts about what has been said so far. At this threatening moment, Socrates displays most nobly his understanding kindness, his "courage," and his ability "to come to the rescue of the *logos*." He senses the prevailing mood, a dangerous mood, and fights against it by interpreting it as "misology" (comparable to "misanthropy") and by exposing its cause. It is due not to the *logos* itself but to our defective treatment of the *logos*. Nowhere is the dignity of thought shown more movingly than when Socrates strokes young Phaidon's hair and admonishes him not to cut it, following the custom, for the sake of Socrates—for Socrates, as we read between the lines, does not die—but to cut it if the argument should die and we cannot bring it back to life. Then, with a new appeal to manliness (ἀνδριστέον) and concern for the truth, Socrates proceeds to refute the objections.

III 1b
91c–95e

The doctrine of recollection remains the foundation. Dubious as the participants may have been about everything else, all of them agreed on this point. But the doctrine of recollection and the harmony view of the soul are not compatible with each other.[21] Harmony does not exist prior to the instrument. Hence, according to a principle whose full significance will be worked out later, a view that "rests on a certain probability without proof" must be rejected in favor of a view that rests "on sound foundations." The harmony view, however, may be easily refuted on other grounds as well. It is incompatible with the fact that the soul rules over the body opposing the passions, whereas the harmony of an instrument is a function of its physical construction. Again, the harmony view is incompatible with the fact that the soul itself may be in a state of harmony or disharmony. The view rejected here is dangerous because it does not seem to allow for norms in ethics. The soul is not simply a harmony. Rather, to achieve a state of harmony is a moral demand imposed upon the soul. In the *Republic* (443DE), it is justice that integrates the three "forms" (or parts) of the soul into a harmony like the harmony of sounds produced on three strings attuned to each other. Thus, in rejecting the tempting thesis put up by Simmias, Socrates affirms that the soul is something far "more divine."

Here we should pause and ask whether we might not often differ from Simmias. Is a harmony really "later" than the instrument? Or rather does it not determine what the instrument must be like in order to produce, here and now, more or less perfectly, a harmony that exists "before" and "after"? Does harmony really follow upon the elements of which it is composed or rather does it not guide them? Does not harmony mean what it says, namely, the attunement of sounds into a higher unity? Is it really true that one soul cannot be more "soul" than another? Is not the soul of Socrates incomparably more "soul" than that of any of us? Is it really the case that no harmony can be more harmonious than another? Are there not simpler and richer melodies, more or less perfect melodies—and souls?

Even so, and even if we do not agree with what Simmias is assenting to, or denying, and try instead to learn from our own dissent, it is clear that the identification of soul with a harmony is a metaphor. In the *Poetics* and the *Rhetoric*, Aristotle deals with the nature and kinds of metaphors extensively and searchingly. In the areas of his concern, he distinguishes metaphors that are sublime from those that are useful and those that are ridiculous. In the *Ethics* and the *Metaphysics*, the term "metaphorical" is an expression of criticism.[22] "On the basis of certain robability, but without proof"—this is Socrates' judgment with regard to the impressive view identifying the soul with a harmony.

The objection raised by Kebes is still more important for the further course of the conversation. It is explicitly restated by Socrates, but, strangely enough, is not actually refuted. Instead, Socrates subordinates it to a more general problem, "the inquiry into the causes within the field of becoming and perishing." These words refer to the conceptual language of natural philosophy—from Anaximander and Parmenides on.[23] The purpose of introducing the Kebes argument, as we witness here, is to overcome this type of natural philosophy by the philosophy of Forms, or more correctly (since Plato never thought of discarding natural philosophy), to subordinate it to the philosophy of Forms.

III 2
95E–102A

Socrates pauses for a considerable time before he begins to speak. We sense the opening of an entirely new movement, and soon we are on so different a level that the objection raised by Kebes has completely disappeared from sight.

The path surveyed by Socrates, and told about as if it were the path of his own philosophical development, consists of three stages. The first stage represents the passionate search for a solution of problems in the context of natural philosophy or science. Physical principles are used to explain nature. Mind or spirit, including knowledge itself, appears as the result of physical causes. From the very beginning of this account, the diversity of opinions invites misgivings. In the end there is total confusion, for simple biological or mathematical phenomena, like growth, or addition, or the relation of greater than, cannot be accounted for on this level. The second stage introduces the concept of "mind" by Anaxagoras as a way out of the confusion. This seems to provide an explanation of nature by which every phenomenon is interpreted according to the principle of the good, or perfect order of the whole. To his disappointment, however, Socrates realizes that this "mind" is not to be understood as an agent spiritualizing nature through the principle of perfection, but that it invariably is discarded in favor of a materialistic theory of causation. The most significant

and topical illustration for the failure of the Anaxagorean concept of mind is this: it provides no explanation of why Socrates
chooses to stay in prison awaiting his death when he might just
as well have escaped. The basic theme of the *Crito* is alluded to,
and what looked like a chapter in the history of philosophy
turns out to be connected with the very core of Socratic existence.

The third stage represents a radical change in direction. From
the things we turn to the *logoi*, to the thoughts, concepts, definitions, and whatever else is included in the meaning of this Greek
word—"pure reason," one might be tempted to say. This
change seems to be an act of renunciation, and yet Socrates does
not wish to forever renounce the possibility of acquiring a
knowledge of nature (99c) even as Plato did not. Nature or
cosmos is the foundation in the concluding myth here in the
Phaedo and then again in the *Republic*. The *Timaeus* will complete what Anaxagoras set out to do and failed. And even here
in the *Phaedo* (99a *et seq*.), Socrates outlines with complete
clarity the twofold system of causes, teleological and material,
that prevails in the world-view of the *Timaeus*. And in the *Laws*,
finally, the starry heavens and the soul are joined to lead us upward to a view of the divine.[24]

Here in the *Phaedo*, Socrates states that the turn to the *logoi*
is a second-best method (δεύτερος πλοῦς), only to retract the
statement then for all practical purposes (99e 6 *et seq*.). This is
an ironic play that still troubles interpreters of Plato, as it is
supposed to. It should serve as a warning to the logicians as
well as the non-logicians among us.[25]

The new "logical" method is then described in general terms.
On each occasion Socrates takes the "most powerful" proposition as a hypothesis (ὑποθέμενος) and posits as true whatever
agrees with this. He had used the same method previously in
his criticism of Simmias (92c). The purely formal statement is
given content now as Socrates goes back to the "well-worn"
theme of *Ideas* and specifies the beautiful-, the good-, and the
great-in-and-by-itself as the objects of the hypothesis.[26] The
relationship of particulars to the *Ideas*, or Forms, cannot be
determined unambiguously in conceptual language; it is ren-

dered by such metaphors as presence, communion, or something like it.[27] The problem of how a thing becomes greater or smaller, how one becomes two, may be solved now whereas it remained in a state of confusion on the second level of the dialogue (70D *et seq.*) and even on the present level (at 96D *et seq.*) when we were engaged in cutting things up and putting them together. Finally, we return once more to the formal mode, and direct our attention to a series of progressively higher hypotheses until we reach the ultimate that would be "satisfactory" (ἱκανόν). The systematic nature of this ordering is insisted upon in contrast to eristic caprice (101E). Similarly, even as late as the *Philebus* (17A), the crucial difference between the dialectical method and the eristic method is said to be that the dialectical, but not the eristic, demarcates precisely the orderly stages between the one and the many.

As the path to that goal is shown, the partners are asked to give their lively assent, and this assent spreads out into the frame conversation just as previously the mood of depression and skepticism had spread. We must read these two digressions, in which Echekrates stops being a listener and becomes a speaker himself, in strict correspondence with each other (88c *et seq.* ∼ 102A). Earlier, when the conceptual analysis was conducted in the context of natural science, there was room for misology. Now we have reached a method that guarantees true knowledge. Certainly, this survey of systems does not correspond to the development of the historical Socrates—and hardly to that of the historical Plato. Socrates did not begin with natural science, and he did not end with the Platonic method. And for Plato, the philosophy of nature was not a beginning but a final, peripheral expansion, however much he may have known earlier about Anaxagoras and Herakleitos. What is described here in the *Phaedo* is rather the development taken by Greek philosophy from Thales to Plato, again not as a historical account (to which Plato is essentially indifferent), but as the way philosophy discovers itself.[28] And now we can see the full meaning of this interlude for the dialogue as a whole. At the same time as the path of purification in philosophical thought becomes visible, the conversation about the soul rises beyond the level on which concepts derived from natural science predominate, and reaches the level of the pure philosophy of Forms.

The final proof rests on the foundation of this method. It is III 3 102A–107B not only the Form itself that excludes its opposite, or "does not admit its opposite." Also such phenomena that always contain their appropriate Form,[29] as fire the Form of heat, snow the Form of cold, or the number three the Form of the uneven— these, too, either perish at the advance of their opposites or withdraw. What follows from this with respect to our problem is that the nature of the soul consists in the life it gives to the body in which it dwells. Hence, the soul cannot admit its opposite, death. That which does not admit *thanatos* is *a-thanatos* or death-less, and thus is indestructible like a god or like the Form of life, to which the soul is assimilated here. Hence, it is not destroyed by death, but withdraws. Our souls are indeed "in Hades."

How should we understand this? We look back once more to the passage where the groundwork is laid for this proof. Opposites exclude each other, not only in themselves but "in us" as well. At this point (103A), a Somebody in the audience interrupts—the only time in the whole dialogue—calling attention to a contradiction with what had been said earlier (70D), namely, that opposites are generated from each other. While praising the courage of the person, who remains nameless, Socrates points to the basic difference between what was said then and now. The interruption is necessary in order to show concretely the difference between the two levels, then. And it has to be an indefinite Somebody who speaks, not Simmias or Kebes, since both of them have followed Socrates to the new level.

The difference consists in the fact that previously the context was the world of things or objects (πράγματα), and now it is prototypes; then it was bodies, now it is *logoi*. It follows that, in this new context, that which contains the Form cannot be thought of as a bodily thing, but must be conceived as something akin to the Form itself. "Soul," therefore, is not a living thing that, in conjunction with the body, forms the natural being called man. Just as the pure Form of life resists death, so does the *Form*like and lifelike soul. The "kinship" or "similarity" of the soul with the Form (*Eidos*) is so intensified here that the soul in its very existence seems to be included in the realm of Form. That is the meaning of the final statement (clothed in mildly mythological language) about the "souls in Hades"—if we follow Plato's own interpretation proposed in the *Cratylus* (403A). Hades is the in-visible, that which cannot be grasped by the physical senses.

When we look back once more to the lower level where the discussion was conducted in the context of natural philosophy, we may better appreciate the degree of sublimation achieved in this later concept of the soul. It is doubtful that our own interpretation can do justice to the heights of the conception. To be sure, traditional criticism, both modern and ancient, rarely has done so—ancient criticism beginning for us with Straton, the Peripatetic—because, among other things, it has accepted the objection by the Somebody but overlooked Socrates' refutation of the objection.[30] Moreover, do we not invariably find in ourselves something of the Kebes who selfishly insists on a firm guarantee that his little self never perish? For Plato, however, "purification"—the word of the mysteries—is the cornerstone of the whole work.[31] Purification is the task imposed upon the life of the philosopher. Death is a type of purification. And the proofs for the immortality of the soul are progressively purified.

Is it surprising, or is it inherent in the nature of human thought, that this purification does not progress to pure perfection? Plato, as we see, has the participants express criticism of this last proof. Simmias has doubts owing to the magnitude of the subject and the weakness of man. Socrates, too, insists that the original assumptions always be examined anew. If this be done, he is convinced, they will follow the *logos*—with the immediately added qualification, "as far as it is humanly possible." Yet this qualification, in turn, is canceled by an affirmation of certainty: If this has become clear to you (he obviously is pointing to the realm of Forms), you will be at an end of your search. The dialectics of doubt and certainty is as genuinely Socratic-Platonic as is the fact that it promises to come to rest in some firm foundation.

As in the *Meno* and in the lower stages of the *Phaedo*, so now
on the third and highest level, two elements—moral demand
and a view of the beyond—are added or built into the conceptual
conversation about the immortality of the soul. Just as "knowledge, will, and faith" belong together as the three components
of the Christian world,[32] so do *"logos, ethos,* and myth" belong together in Plato's. In the *Meno* (86B), Socrates based
his defense of the eternity of the soul upon the conviction that
the truth of being was in it. He added to this the demand that
the uncertainty necessarily accompanying a conceptual analysis
of such a topic must be compensated for by the energetic pursuit
of inquiry "which makes us 'manly.' " He is resolved to fight
for this pursuit in word and deed. "Deed" stands as the last
word in this long section of the *Meno*.

Similarly, here in the *Phaedo*, the conceptual analysis ending
on the dialectical tension between doubt and certainty is now
continued with the exhortation that the soul requires care, all
the more care, since it is a matter of caring not only for this life
but for eternity. And then, at the end of the whole discussion
(114D *et seq.*), there occurs another warning not to indulge in
the pleasures of the body but to practice the pleasures of learning, to adorn the soul not with adornment of the body but with
its own adornment. In between is the great myth of the beyond.
Wherever the lines of life are extended beyond all possible experience, Plato in the solemn language of ancient tradition employs a myth that complements these lines and reflects back on
life itself. Previously anticipated at the earlier stages of the
Phaedo, the myth finally becomes autonomous on the largest
possible scale.

As far as the content of this myth is concerned, we may refer
to what we have said before.[33] Here we simply shall try to suggest once more how the proofs and the myths of the *Phaedo* are
to be read. The "child in us" would like to transform death into
a counterfeit life. Only suffering may induce in some people a
longing for the end. The philosopher, being "ignorant," cannot
convert either hope into certainty. Yet he does not succumb to
despairing doubt. Instead, he adopts the courageous attitude
of the inquiring mind and tries to distill—out of popular con-

ceptions, eschatological visions of the devout, scientific speculations of ancient natural philosophers, and, ultimately, out of his own knowledge of the Forms—some clear idea not so much about the nature of death as about the nature of life. He does not have time, as it is said in the *Phaedrus*, to think about whether Boreas really abducted Oreithyia from this rock or some other one. Still less does he have time, now, at the threshold of death, to think about whether there is such a thing as a judgment of the dead and reincarnation in the literal sense. What he perceives is that the call to virtue (*arete*), to community, and to a perfect life, received from entirely different sources, coincides with the doctrine of the sacred myth and thereby is reinforced. The conception that the soul separated from the body is purified and enters into purgatory remains a dogma.[34] But it is precisely this liberation and purification that the philosopher seeks. Thus, viewed from the perspective of life, this convergence of different lines is an affirmation of the philosophical vocation. Viewed from the perspective of death, it is the realization of how unphilosophical the fear of death is (for it is an attempt to evade the fulfillment of life). The philosopher does not disturb the faith according to which the soul passing through death's gate enters into a world of splendor and magnificent sights. He rather takes these images as symbols for his own ascent to the realm of light and true Forms. And since like can be known only by like—i.e., being, the eternal, and Form can be known only by what is akin to them—these visions of the beyond once more reinforce in the philosopher the resolution to live in the image of eternity.

There is no other dialogue, as we have said earlier, in which the theoretical results of the conversation are more deeply rooted in the existential context. *The last day of Socrates*: this reality is present from the beginning and is kept alive, by a word or a moving gesture, throughout the whole dialogue as it mounts to its final climax.

CONCLUDING PART
115B–118

There is little to be said about the report of Socrates' death, for is there anyone to whom Socrates' death does not speak in its own words? The insights gained during the philosophical conversation are carried over into the last words and gestures, into Socrates' message to his friends "to care for themselves"

(115B), into his appeal to them when they burst into tears—
"Be calm and strong!" (117E), and into the orders he gives for
his funeral in a wonderful mixture of jest and seriousness (115C
et seq.). They cannot bury Socrates. Only his body can be
buried, and this they should do "according to custom," not in
the spirit of Cynics, that is, but in a genuinely Socratic spirit.
The entire sequence, Socrates' wishing to offer a libation of the
redeeming potion to the gods, the renouncing of this wish, the
prayer, the covering of his body, and the order to sacrifice a
cock to Asklepios—this last scene is of such symbolic meaning
and transparent depth that it can only lose by interpretation.

Thus, let there be but a few words about some details. The
man who administers the poison appears twice in the dialogue.
At the beginning (63D), he warns Socrates to speak as little as
possible lest the poison have to be administered "twice and
three times."[35] Socrates for once does not obey, since to give up
this conversation would be to deny his very being. If necessary,
the man should prepare a cup "even twice and three times." In
the *Gorgias* (498E), in the *Philebus* (60A), and in the *Laws*
(956E), Plato uses the proverb: "Even twice and three times the
good (or the right)!" It is hardly imaginable that he would not
have had in mind this "proverb," as he calls it in the *Philebus*,
since he has Socrates repeat the same words for emphasis. This is
connected with the brief scene toward the end when Socrates
asks the same man administering the poison whether it is permissible to offer a libation to the gods. To offer poison to the
gods? That would be a sacrilege but for the fact that the poison
here is something good, a healing power. And this, in turn, is
in harmony with the last prayer to the gods for a happy journey
and with the last order—the sacrifice to the god of healing.

The report speaks simple truth, thereby acquiring the significance of symbol.

The *Phädon* of Moses Mendelssohn (1767) and Lamartine's
La mort de Socrate (1823) are copied, with modifications, after
Plato's *Phaedo*. Both of the later works derive the description
of events and at least part of the philosophical conversation from
Plato's dialogue. Mendelssohn even begins and concludes his

own work with an exact translation from the original, and moves away from it only where he thinks it is necessary "to adjust the philosophical proofs to the taste of our time." In Lamartine's poem, in which "metaphysics and poetry are sisters, or rather one," the Greek original in its content, conversation, and form is Christianized, a transformation to which no other work of Plato's could lend itself as well as the *Phaedo*.

TWENTY-TWO

Republic

Integration of the Dialogue "Thrasymachus": The Hostile Power

WE MIGHT COMPARE the *Republic* to a city built in stages according to a magnificent and uniform plan— a city that has incorporated, as a suburb, a settlement dating back to earlier times. This comparison rests on an assumption few would question today: that Book I of the *Republic* was originally a dialogue of Plato's early period, at least planned as such and probably written down. Customarily it is referred to under the name of the *Thrasymachus*. We have discussed it as one of the "aporetic dialogues in search of a definition."[1] Those who argue that this hypothesis cannot be proved must make two assumptions which are far harder to accept: first, that while Plato, during the period of the aporetic dialogues, inquired into all the other virtues, he would have omitted "justice," and second, that at the height of his career as a writer, Plato would or even could have composed the beginning of the *Republic* in the structure and linguistic form characteristic of him at a much earlier literary stage.

We should also note that the opening scene in the *Republic* is very similar to that in the *Symposium*. Both scenes are set in a harbor town, in the Piraeus and in the Phaleron. In both scenes, someone is walking toward Athens (πρὸς τὸ ἄστυ, *Republic* 327B 1, 327C 4; εἰς ἄστυ, *Symposium* 172A 2). In both, there is somebody calling from behind and afar (πόρρωθεν, ὄπισθεν, *Republic* 327B 2 and 4; *Symposium* 172A 3), asking the other to stop (περιμεῖναι, *Republic* 327B 3. οὐ περιμενεῖς; *Symposium* 172A 5). Yet, the contrast is all the more striking. Whereas Agathon's victory is celebrated in his own home in Athens, the great conversation about the state takes place near the harbor Piraeus and in the house of the rich half-citizen Polemarchos. We may venture to say that even as Plato could not have chosen the house of a half-citizen as the setting for the speeches on love, so he would not have chosen such a setting for his work on the ideal state—if this scene had not already been fixed in the *Thrasymachus*. It was indeed a suitable setting for the struggle with the sophistic immoralist who had come to Athens on a visit from the Bosporos. Then Plato retained the setting when he decided to use this struggle as the introduction to the great work. He also retained the time. The conversation still begins in the evening, even though this means, considering the length of the discussion as a whole, that it would have to extend throughout the night and far into the next day.[2] The *Laws* begins in the early morning, a much more natural arrangement, as Plato himself must have thought. In the writing of the *Republic*, however, such questions of space and time were negligible as compared with the central fact that the construction of the true state would make no sense without the struggle that precedes and accompanies it.

The dialogue *Thrasymachus* is full of violent struggle. Beginning with the second book of the *Republic*, this dramatic movement yields to a quiet discussion, the appropriate mood for the construction of the state. It is most characteristic that, at the beginning of Book II, the hostile power that is to be overthrown is represented in new form by Glaukon and Adeimantos, Plato's brothers. They differ from Thrasymachos; they are not real opposition. They only restate his case (358B 7) and bring together all the currently prevailing arguments on justice and injustice (358C, 362E). It is all the more important that genuine struggle has preceded, for injustice must be fought and overcome dialectically before the new realm of justice rooted in the *logos* can be founded.

Yet it would be inadequate to interpret this situation merely in terms of before and after, for Thrasymachos does not leave the conversation. Even later on he is mentioned as being present. As is said toward the end of Book IX (590c), the best man— and we know the best man is he in whom the divine is the ruling principle—should rule over the lesser like master over slave, not, as Thrasymachos thought, in order to harm the slave but in order to do him good. And if it seems that the conflict has practically died down here, we are taught differently elsewhere. When it is announced by Socrates that not the young but the old should practice philosophy, this principle (so it is said in Book VI 498c) will find opposition among the audience, and Thrasymachos will be the first to express it. In the *Gorgias* (484c), Kallikles—the man of power, developed out of the Thrasymachos of the earlier dialogue—defended the thesis that only the young should engage in philosophy whereas the mature man should resolutely enter into what is generally called "political life." Thus, it is no accident that Thrasymachos' opposition is explicitly mentioned in this passage of the *Republic*. For, let us add, Socrates' principle contradicts the attitude of all those who know politics or the political life only as the usual struggle for power.

Later, at the beginning of Book VIII (545A), it is said that we shall consider first the defective types of government so that we can measure pure justice and injustice by the degrees of happiness and unhappiness they bring to mankind. Only then will we know whether we should choose justice or, following Thrasymachos, injustice. Thus, it is merely an urbane irony for Socrates to add that he and Thrasymachos have now become friends and had not been enemies even before (498cD). On the contrary, the hostility of the power represented by Thrasymachos, and fought and conquered by Socrates, is secretly present all along. For it is not the case that Plato, in his period of maturity, considered the passionate struggle of his earlier years as finished. The struggle serves to secure the foundation for the construction to follow. From an aesthetic point of view, this is shown by the use of the *Thrasymachus* as the opening book for the *Republic*—or, in Plato's own words (357A), as the prelude to the *logos*—and by the personal presence of the powerful adversary throughout the entire work. Above all, it is the fact that this preliminary struggle not only precedes the constructive parts to follow, but remains in constant tension with them—it is this fact, more than any other, that makes the *Republic* a genuine dialogue and not a treatise arbitrarily forced into dialogue form.[3]

In our previous discussion of the *Thrasymachus*,[4] we singled out a section that Plato must have inserted when he placed the originally independent dialogue as the prelude to the *Republic*. This revision must be examined now with regard to its meaning for the work as a whole.

Unshaken by Socrates' arguments, Thrasymachos in a long speech (343B–344E) unfolds the nature of tyranny, celebrating it as the expression of the highest power and the greatest happiness. Then before Socrates proceeds to counterattack (348C *et seq.*), there occurs the section Plato here inserted. Surprisingly, it refers us (ἔτι γὰρ τὰ ἔμπροσθεν ἐπισκεψώμεθα, 345B 9) to a struggle that already lies behind us—namely, the critique of the view that "justice is the advantage of the stronger."

In this critique, Socrates had shown (341D) that each art aims by its very nature at perfection (τελέαν εἶναι) and that perfection consists in fulfilling its proper function (αὐτὴ αὑτῇ τὸ συμφέρον σκέψεται, 342B 1). As this is in medicine, and in racing horses, so it is in the art of ruling, which therefore can never aim at the benefit of the rulers. Now, in the inserted section, we learn again that each art yields only the benefit peculiar to itself (ὠφελίαν ἰδίαν, 346A 6). And as this is in medicine, and in navigation, so it is in the art of ruling, which therefore can never aim at the benefit of the rulers.

To the question, "Why go over the same ground again in similar words and examples?" the answer is, "Evidently because of the puzzling paradox that follows." For the paradox is that no true ruler governs willingly (345E). He must be induced to rule by rewards or punishment. This is stated so provocatively that Glaukon, who has not yet entered into the conversation, asks for an explanation. Socrates then shows that the ordinary rewards, money and honor, are not truly desirable. In fact, the expressions "love of money" (φιλάργυρον) and "love of honor" (φιλότιμον) actually have a pejorative meaning.

Moreover, the punishment referred to just before consists in being governed by the worse. Thus, "if a city of good men were to come into being" (πόλις ἀνδρῶν ἀγαθῶν εἰ γένοιτο, 347D 2), nobody would compete for power. This line, however, is dropped. Instead, the struggle is launched against the firm position of Thrasymachos by going back to the beginning (ἐξ ἀρχῆς, 348B 8).

Who are the rulers who must be compelled to govern against their will? What reward is worth more than money and honor? We can answer these questions only if we look forward to the later books of the *Republic*. There we learn: The rulers are the philosopher-kings. The reward is a life dedicated to the pursuit of knowledge. Philosophy rises above the desire for honor and riches. What must such a state be like, we may ask, in which such rulers reap such a reward and the corresponding punishment? This is suggested here from afar by the conditional, "if a city of good men were to come into being." Yet, however distant, it is only in this passage in all of Book I that the ideal state emerges, like a mirage, in contrast to tyranny. Then immediately it disappears again. By inserting this transitional piece, Plato intended to call up this vision—though only for a moment and more as puzzle and question mark. Still, in doing so, he gave in this early work, the *Thrasymachus* (a dialogue on one plane, so to speak), a hint of the dimension in depth in which the *Republic* moves from the second book on.

The Speeches of Glaukon and Adeimantos—Restatement of the Hostile Power

In order to turn definitely from the problem of justice to a discussion of the just state, Plato has Glaukon, described as highly energetic (ἀνδρειότατος ὤν), express a protest that Thrasymachos abandoned his position too soon.[5] Glaukon then sets out to restate the argument so as to make it clear, by contrast, what power justice and injustice have "in and for themselves in the soul" of the possessor, irrespective of external consequences. Adeimantos' speech follows his brother's. The hostile power that Socrates must overthrow (καταπαλαῖσαι, 362D 8) gathers in these two great speeches of Plato's brothers. They

I B
358B–367E
BOOK II

reveal the terrible disintegration of human norms that Socrates alone can heal—and reveal it all the more the less the two
brothers express their own views.

First we recall the content of these speeches, then inquire
into their sources in Plato's earlier thought, and, last, observe
how they in large part determine the structure of the *Republic*
as a whole.

358B–362c   THE SPEECH OF GLAUKON. This speech consists of three parts.
BOOK II   The first part proceeds from the thesis that "by nature" to do
wrong is good and to suffer wrong is evil, or, more pointedly,
that (by nature) the best thing is to go unpunished for doing
wrong and the worst thing is to suffer wrong without having
the power to avenge oneself. It is then shown, in a genealogy
of morals (γένεσις καὶ οὐσία τῆς δικαιοσύνης), how this original
state of affairs was ruined because, from weakness, human beings reached a mutual agreement (νόμους τίθεσθαι καὶ συνθήκας)
which they called (ὀνομάσαι) "justice": Every man refrains from
doing wrong on the condition that everybody else does so, too.
Any man who has the power, however, to break this convention
would be foolish if he did not do so.

The second part of Glaukon's speech proves and interprets
this view by reference to Gyges and his ring. A just man acts
out of weakness. Nobody is willingly just (οὐδεὶς ἑκὼν δίκαιος)
but only as a result of coercion. This statement is diametrically
opposed to the Socratic-Platonic view that it is impossible to do
wrong willingly. Put differently: the Socratic-Platonic paradox
is in contradiction to common sense. For everybody is said to
be convinced that it is more advantageous to practice injustice
than justice; hence, everybody believes that injustice is "good."

The third part of Glaukon's speech submits the two opposing
ways of life to judgment (κρίσις)—the life of the just man and
the life of the unjust man. The unjust life is envisaged as dressed
up with a reputation of justice, with the power of persuasion
and violent action. The just life is devoid of all this; i.e., although it is just, it is stripped even of the reputation of justice.
The fate of the just man is then depicted as, in helplessness, the
suffering of the worst imaginable misery. But the unjust man,

reaping the fruits of his power, is admired among men and even among gods—according to the pernicious conception encountered in the *Euthyphro*. Thus, a simple calculus of happiness shows how much the life of the unjust is to be preferred to the life of the just.

Glaukon's speech has antecedents in Plato's work. Kallikles spoke a similar language in the *Gorgias* (482c *et seq.*), and his speech, in turn, was prefigured by that of Thrasymachos in the early dialogue which is now Book I of the *Republic* (343B *et seq.*).[6] All three speeches oppose the customary, but hypocritical, value attributed to just and unjust, derive this value from fear and weakness, and, in the end, link injustice with happiness and justice with unhappiness. Starting with the *Gorgias*, this situation is described by distinguishing between "convention" (*nomos*) and "nature" (*physis*), and the significance of the calculus of happiness is heightened by a reminder of the fate of Socrates. In addition to the warnings of Kallikles, we hear in the *Republic* echoes of Polos' threats (the same threats of torture and painful death). On the whole, Glaukon's speech— representing not his own views but those most commonly held —is weaker in tone than that of Kallikles, yet stronger in structure and in its elaboration upon the two ways of life that confront each other "as if they were two statues" (361D). One theme of the Kallikles speech had to be dropped: his opposition to philosophy as the goal of life and his insistence that it must be confined to the education of the young. Since the *Republic* will be concerned with education on a systematic scale, this struggle had to be shifted to a later part (Book VI 487c *et seq.*) and is eliminated, therefore, from Glaukon's speech, which deals mainly with principles.

It is characteristic that, at the end of the respective works in which these speeches occur, there is a reference again to each of them. For in the end the view these speeches present is overcome. This struggle dominates each work, creating a field of tension of expanding scope. In the dialogue *Thrasymachus*, this tension extends through the second part of the conversation with Thrasymachos. At the end, it is considered proven that the just are "happy" and the unjust "miserable" (354A; cf. 344B).

In the *Gorgias*, the same tension extends through the whole conversation with Kallikles until his threats—"You will be dizzy and gape openmouthed; you will have your ears boxed with impunity; when you are dragged into court, you will be put to death"—are repeated by Socrates himself and are overcome by the conviction: Yes, any man may kill me, but his action will be unjust and hence evil (521B). Again, the threats are rejected in the myth, where Socrates pays Kallikles back. "Before the judge in the underworld, you will gape openmouthed and you will be dizzy and anybody who so chooses may box your ears" (527A).

In the *Republic*, finally, the same tension extends over a much larger area. It determines the general structure of the work, in fact, from the beginning of the second book to the end of the tenth. Glaukon's speech culminates in the comparison of the two ways of life and in the question, Which is the happier? This question is decided at the end of Book IX after the varieties of "defective constitutions" have been examined and, concurrently, the descending stages of the good, or of happiness, in life. Later still, in Book X (612B), the ring of Gyges reappears when it has been shown that the soul of the just man would do right with or without the ring. It turns out that the fate Glaukon had predicted for the just man—that he would suffer disgrace, misery, and torture (361E)—applies instead to the soul of the unjust (613DE).[7] Then, as in the *Gorgias*, the final answer to the original question is given in the words of a myth.

It is obvious that these progressive stages are not just an expansion but rather an enrichment of the internal structure, adding new dimensions. The concluding part of the *Thrasymachus* is based upon the contrast, and upon this contrast only, of justice and injustice, happiness and power. The same contrast appears in the *Gorgias*, but it is used there as a basis for comparing two ways of life, philosopher versus political orator. These two ways still confront each other in the same political domain, the actual state. As far as the *Gorgias* goes, the just man, the philosopher, has not attained his own domain, the ideal state founded on justice. This move is achieved in the *Republic*. Returning to the original contrast as presented in the *Thrasy-*

machus (and incorporating the dialogue itself), the *Republic* transforms the contrast into the basic conflict between two political systems: the ideal state (Books II–VII) as against the defective constitutions (Books VIII and IX). The gain made in the *Gorgias* is nowise lost in the *Republic*. And as for the two ways of life contrasted in the *Gorgias*, the philosophical life is transformed in the *Republic* into the educational system of the ideal state, and the life of the rhetorician and politician is incorporated into the series of defective constitutions, until finally, at the extreme end of this series, the power—or anti-power—represented by Kallikles is present again as the soul of the tyrant "that is least able to do as it wishes."[8]

THE SPEECH OF ADEIMANTOS. Glaukon described—from the perspective of immoralism, not from his own conviction—the happy fate of the unjust and the unhappy fate of the just. He did so in terms of the consequences ensuing from each way of life. As we have mentioned, this view is repudiated at the end of Book IX by demonstrating that the just is happy and the unjust unhappy. But it would not be enough for Plato to refute injustice only by an analysis of its consequences. To overcome the hostile power it must be shown that justice is intrinsically good and injustice intrinsically evil. The speech of Adeimantos serves to prepare the ground for this demonstration. In demanding this proof, i.e., in inquiring into the intrinsic nature of justice and injustice, the speech must proceed in a context that makes it possible to set off pure justice and pure injustice. This leads to another aspect of the speech, that it brings together the arguments characteristic of a half-baked, disguised type of "injustice" which is very popular, and very dangerous, precisely because it does not dare take the radical view expounded in Glaukon's speech.

Popular praise of "justice," so Adeimantos begins his speech, is based not on its nature but on the rewards it brings, fame and benefits among men, favor among the gods both on earth and beyond this life. Another way (ἄλλο εἶδος, 363E 5) of looking at justice is still worse. It is called "fair" but said to be difficult to acquire, whereas injustice—although called "disgraceful"

362E–367E
BOOK II

(αἰσχρόν)—is said to be pleasant and easy to win. "Fair" and "disgraceful," to be sure, are judgments by convention (νόμος); in truth, injustice is more advantageous than justice. Even the gods often bestow happiness upon the unjust and misfortune upon the just in accordance with their general nature, which is changeable and subject to external influence. The effect of these views upon the young is that they decide that what counts is the appearance of virtue, not the reality. One must surround himself with the illusion or shadow image of virtue (σκιαγραφία ἀρετῆς), which although not easy is not impossible, especially if good use is made of the art of rhetoric. But one must not believe that the gods are looking behind the façade. For (so we hear in an obvious reference to Gorgias' treatise *On Nature or Not-Being* and to Protagoras' treatise *On the Gods*) either the gods do not exist at all or they do not care about human affairs or they may be persuaded to change their minds. If we observe the rites of the mysteries, moreover, the gods will protect us against punishment in the next world. The effect of these arguments is to shake the dignity of justice in its inner being. If we disregard the case of the exceptional person endowed with rare genius or clear knowledge (θείᾳ φύσει ἢ ἐπιστήμην λαβών) in moral matters, it is a fact that the general mass of people subscribe to the view that a man is just (moral) only because he lacks the strength for unjust (immoral) action.

So much for the diagnosis of the moral crisis. This disintegration of norms or confusion in the structure of society has its cause, shall we say, or rather its most manifest and terrifying counterpart, in man's conception of the gods. Man himself is such a nonentity that he simply declares the gods to be nonexistent, or he projects his own instability upon the gods. This results in the view that there is no necessary or firm connection between what the gods dispense and man's goodness or evil, or the view that the gods can be persuaded to change their minds, or that punishment in the beyond can be avoided, by means of prayer and ritual.

The chief responsibility for spreading these false doctrines and for contributing to the moral confusion in general falls, however, upon the poets. This theme runs through the entire speech of Adeimantos. Hesiod tells us "how smooth is the way to evil-doing" (364D), and according to Simonides, "appearances master even the truth" (365c). Beginning with the ancient heroes —and through whom do they speak but the poets?—right and wrong always have been praised or censured for the effect they have, never for their intrinsic nature (366E). And even more important is the fact that the dangerous theology derives not only its spread but its support from the poets. Homer, Musaios, and Orpheus are responsible for the false belief that by performing appropriate rites man can escape punishment for the wrong he has done, or that sacrifice and prayer will persuade the gods to change their minds. Thus, the theme of the *Euthyphro* finds its completion in the *Republic*, for Socrates' opposition to this pseudo-theology is part of the indictment drawn up against him (*Euthyphro* 6A). The struggle against traditional mythology that runs through the *Republic* is Plato's counterattack, deeply grounded in the fate of Socrates.

Plato's brothers, then, are spokesmen for the existing crisis without having lost their own faith in "justice." It is they who urgently appeal to Socrates for a new justification, inasmuch as the older doctrines have not been able to make secure the conviction—otherwise there would not be a crisis now—that doing wrong is the greatest evil and doing right is the greatest good. The appeal aims specifically at the intrinsic nature of the concepts, and away from their practical consequences. What do the concepts of right and wrong, of justice and injustice, mean in and by themselves? How can it be proved that injustice is evil and justice good by the effect that each has on the soul itself? Only Socrates can answer these questions (as Adeimantos insistently concludes), because he has given his entire life to them. With words like these, which Plato has his brothers speak in strong emphasis, Plato shows how the problem of justice and its solution—i.e., the *Republic* as a whole—is founded upon the Socratic existence.

If, as we did before in the case of Glaukon's speech, we now ask how far Adeimantos' speech determines the structure of the whole work, we must start out from the basic question as to the intrinsic nature of justice. This question is answered in Book IV where, in two comprehensive inquiries, the system of the virtues is developed, first with respect to the state (427D–434B), then with regard to the individual soul (434D–444E). In both systems "justice" comes last. It is the final object of the whole search. Ultimately, it turns out to be the strict order that holds the corresponding systems together in the true sense. Thus, the quest for the intrinsic nature of justice reaches its goal. And it is no accident that, as this dual inquiry in Book IV gets under way, there is a clear reference to the last words in the speech of Adeimantos (II 367E 4). We must inquire into the nature of justice and injustice, and discover which of the two a man must have in order to reach his perfection, "irrespective of whether his condition is known or not to all gods and men" (ἐάν τε λανθάνῃ ἐάν τε μὴ πάντας θεούς τε καὶ ἀνθρώπους, IV 427D 6).

Book IV points not only forward but also backward in the structural design of the *Republic*. It points backward in that the parallelism between state and individual soul is introduced in Book II, immediately following the speech of Adeimantos, with the recognition that justice must be found in both (368DE). There follows, from Book II into Book IV, the construction of the city—the "soul" writ large. When this construction has progressed as far as necessary, the search for justice can go forward: the system of the virtues is developed. The speech of Adeimantos points forward, too, in that it is concerned with the nature not only of justice, but also of its opposite, injustice. The inquiry into injustice is undertaken as soon as the question of justice has been settled. A further reference to the words of Adeimantos, "irrespective of whether it is known or not" (ἐάν τε λανθάνῃ ἐάν τε μή, IV 445A 2), shows that the important thing is to distinguish between appearance and reality. The inquiry into injustice is broken off, however, at the end of the fourth book when it has hardly begun, and is resumed only at the beginning of the eighth book. Books VIII and IX contain the discussion of the disintegrating souls and the corresponding types of government, down to the most unjust. At the end of Book IX, the discussion concentrates again upon the "inner city," and rises, in Book X, to a vision of the immortal soul. But justice is the guiding theme throughout, and at the end

(X 612B), we find another reference to Adeimantos' request
(II 367D) that we must discover what justice is in itself irrespective of "reward and judgment." If Adeimantos suggested that
man might be able to hide from the gods (365c), this possibility
is revealed as an illusion now that, at the end, we have completed
the ascent into the sphere of true being and the good, i.e., the
sphere of the divine. For we have learned that the gods must
necessarily love the good man and hate the evil one (612E).

These comments so far deal with only one aspect of the structural significance of Adeimantos' speech. There is another
aspect, whose power is not felt uniformly throughout the entire
work, but is sensed in individual episodes. The speech of
Adeimantos held the poets, and their dangerous theology,
responsible for the moral crisis, as we have seen. It is Plato's
struggle against this theology and thus—*seemingly*—against
poetry itself that emerges as a constant concern in recurring
episodes throughout the *Republic*.

The struggle emerges even in Book II. We have hardly
been introduced to the class of guardians when the question
arises—it cannot be posed too soon—how to educate them
(376c). Education begins with myths or fables. The beginning
is all-important everywhere. The young soul is easily molded.
Its nourishment must be regulated from its earliest period.
Fairy tales are not quite cut to the measure of the *Republic*, as it
were. But "myth," after all, also refers to legends of the gods
and heroes, and "in this larger context we shall see the smaller."

377A–379A
BOOK II

Here the conversation turns, for the first time—the direction
was foreshadowed in the speech of Adeimantos—to the struggle
with Homer and Hesiod, the poets who created "false and
deceiving myths" and did now know how to "deceive truly."
(This, in short, would have been their proper task.) A false
myth is the story about the struggle of Kronos against his
father Uranos, or of Zeus against Kronos. Such stories set the
worst possible example for young minds. The theme of the
Euthyphro, already alluded to in the speech of Adeimantos,
comes through here more clearly and then is sensed again when
Socrates proclaims that in the city to be founded, all stories and
representations of gods fighting against gods will be forbidden.[9]

What, then, are the true stories to be put in the place of the false ones? Socrates declines to deal with this question "at present" (379A 1), perhaps pointing forward to the concluding myth of the *Republic* or even to the *Timaeus* and the *Critias*.

379A–383C
BOOK II

For the present, we learn only about the basic principles by which poets must proceed if they are to produce true myths. They are the basic principles of theology (τύποι περὶ θεολογίας, 379A 5). God is good, is the first principle; the gods do not change, is the second. These principles rule out any myth in which the gods cause evil, and any myth that deals with the changing nature of the gods or with deceptions on their part. The systematic significance of these principles will appear later. Here it suffices to see how the speech of Adeimantos closely connects the moral crisis with poetry and theology, and how, along with the educational work, as its precondition and point of departure, a struggle is launched against the great poetic tradition—with the intention of replacing its basic conceptions by a purer view of the deity.

386A–392C
BOOK III

The struggle against the poets continues. The next question is, What moral attitudes are to be inculcated as desirable in the new city? In each case—whether it is courage (386A), seriousness (οὐ φιλογέλωτας, 388E), moderation (389D), or the lack of greed (390D)—in each case the fight goes against Homer, who is said to be cultivating just the opposite: fear because he gives a false picture of the next world, and every form of excess because of the way he misrepresents the heroes.

392C–397E
BOOK III

There is still more to come. Continuing with the matter of musical education, Socrates deals—in a separate chapter, one might say—with the problem of poetic expression (περὶ λέξεως). Beginning with Homer, he distinguishes between poetic narration (διήγησις) and imitative (dramatic) representation (μίμησις), and the mixture of the two. He raises the question of whether the guardians should be permitted to use the mimetic type—i.e., above all, but not exclusively, dramatic poetry—and decides that an affirmative answer to this question would violate the basic principle established for the founding of the city. Such transformation into an alien genre is forbidden so long as every man is permitted to do only one thing and not many things, and

so long as education is concerned with producing a good man
(ἀνὴρ ἀγαθός, 395D 6). Consequently, harmonies and rhythms
must also be free of sharp variations (μεταβολαί, 397B 6). For
"with us man is not twofold or manifold, since every man does
one thing" (397E).

It surely is no accident that, throughout this long section
dealing with education (from 376D to 398C), Adeimantos is the
partner in the conversation, for the task of fighting against the
poets first emerged as part of his speech. This struggle continues
throughout the *Republic*, not as an integral part of the basic
structure of the work, as we have said, but rather in intermittent
episodes.

A brief digression, explicitly labeled as such (ἐξέβημεν, 568D 4),
occurs at the end of Book VIII. A verse from Euripides—
"tyrants are wise by keeping company with the wise"—gives
another opportunity to say explicitly that we cannot admit
the poets of tragedy into our state because they sing the praises
of tyranny. But they will enjoy high honors in other states—the
higher the honor the further such states are removed from the
ideal state, with the highest honor under a tyranny and in a
democracy. In addition to reflecting Plato's own experience in
Athens and Syracuse, this thought contains a general observation. Just as a definite type of man corresponds to a certain type
of government, so does a definite type of poet correspond. And
the distance separating true poetry from current tragedy is a
measure also of the distance separating the true state from tyranny. We may surmise what kind of dramatic poetry—at once
tragedy and comedy—Plato associates with the true state.

How important this subject of poetry was for Plato may be
seen from the long interlude at the beginning of the tenth book,
where, shortly before the concluding myth, the theme recurs of
how the new state must be the enemy of mimetic poetry. We
have tried elsewhere to show that Plato is speaking in this
passage of himself, although in disguise.[10] Now we must show
how this passage in Book X differs essentially from the discussion in Book II to which it is related. The general situation has
changed: first, because the ascent to the world of Forms occurs
between the two discussions; second, because in this ascent an

568A–568D
BOOK VIII

595A–608B
BOOK X

ordered system of the stages of knowledge has been discovered; and third, because the growth of the perfect state has been witnessed, along with its counterpart, the orderly constitution of man's soul. As a result, statements that, in Book II, were still preliminary and empirical now have a systematic foundation.

If we consider the ordered system—Forms, objects in the world of appearance, and mimetic representation of these objects—then we see that the "poet of tragedy who is an imitator occupies third place from the king and the truth" (597E).[11] If we consider the stages of knowledge, we know that the artist who is an imitator does not, as the maker of a thing, have "right opinion" about the value of the work he is imitating, let alone the clear knowledge of him who uses it; at best he has an illusory image (εἰκασία, 511E). If we consider the true structure of state and soul, we know that the more "poetically" the poet works, the more he must strengthen the passionate element in these structures at the price of reason and that, in doing so, he must disturb the balance and order in these structures—yet our sole task is to achieve such balance and order. Thus, at the end of the whole work, formal judgment is pronounced upon Homer. The reader, who has suspected, ever since Adeimantos' speech in Book II, what is to be "Homer's" share in the moral catastrophe, realizes how "unjust" the new state must be toward the ancient epic, precisely because this state is destined to restore eternal justice.

Tragic poetry was included in the *Gorgias* (502B) among the arts of flattery, along with playing on the flute and lyre and with dithyrambic poetry. For tragic poetry proved to be a kind of rhetoric and therefore suffered the same condemnation; it serves "pleasure" and thus is an enemy of philosophy. As all the forces and struggles present in the *Gorgias* return in the *Republic*, so does the struggle against tragedy. And like everything else, this struggle also is transferred to a different dimension. Tragedy, together with its ancestor, Homer, is included now among the defective kinds of government; hence, it must be kept out of the ideal state. What was momentarily caught sight of in the *Gorgias* reappears constantly throughout the *Republic*, like wellsprings that have their source in the speech of Adeimantos at the beginning of the second book.

The Origin of the Human Community

The smallest human community originates from need—i.e., from the fact that human beings are not self-sufficient. The most primitive type of social organization restricted to what is most necessary (ἀναγκαιοτάτη πόλις) consists of four or five men complementing each other in their work. It is gradually enlarged by adding other indispensable and complementary functions. This original city remains a simple product, however, so simple that the delightfully playful description of its daily life and festivals evokes a protest on Glaukon's part. There is developed now out of this "healthy society," as Socrates calls it, or out of this "community of pigs," as Glaukon protests, a second society described as "luxurious" (τρυφῶσα) or "in a state of fever" (φλεγμαίνουσα). The list of new professions that are added is characteristic: musicians, poets, rhapsodes, handicrafters, wet nurses, barbers, cooks—in short, representatives of all those arts called, in the *Gorgias*, "arts of flattery" and equated with the pleasure principle. Even the physicians are here (II 373D) in worse company than in the *Gorgias*. They are needed much more in a society of fevered complexion than in a healthy state, where, in fact, there had been no mention of them at all. The territory becomes too small for the rising population; hence, the next step is to reach out for the territory of one's neighbor. (Again, the *Gorgias* had shown the close connection between pleasure and *pleonexia*.) And so there is war, and a new class emerges in society—the class of soldiers or "guardians." The next question asks what their "nature" must be so that they are "good" guardians, and soon the combination of "manliness" and "gentleness" (πρᾳότης) is singled out as necessary.

At this point (376C), where the discussion turns to the education of the guardians, and Adeimantos again takes the place of Glaukon as partner in the long conversation to follow, there

II 1
368E–376C
BOOK II

is a natural break. We may ask here what this inquiry into the origins of human society means in the context of the work as a whole.

"When we look at the state as coming into existence, coming into existence not in the literal sense, but in the higher sense of discourse and thought (γιγνομένην λόγῳ), we shall also be able to see how justice and injustice originate in and are co-ordinated with it" (369A). In other words, we are able to grasp its nature by considering its growth "from its very beginnings and origins." A necessary and meaningful process of growth takes place before our eyes. The word "nature" and the verbal expressions referring to original growth (κατὰ φύσιν, φύεσθαι) are repeated constantly throughout this initial description (370A et seq.).[12] Added to these are other expressions, also repeated constantly, referring to need (χρεία, δεῖσθαι, προσδεῖσθαι, ἐνδεής) and necessity (δεῖ). For inherent in the "nature," or essence, of a thing are demands which must be satisfied so that the thing may realize its own nature. What, then, does this process of growth mean in the structure of the work as a whole, granted that Plato does not inquire into the origins of human society in the manner of our contemporary studies in sociology or prehistory?[13] We may suggest this: Plato's city, ultimately, grows out of these origins. Hence, it is a product of organic growth, not a machine. And just as true origins continue to determine later stages of development, so these origins must also reach up into the perfect state.

Now we are supposed to discover justice in this process. Thus, as soon as the "healthy society" has come into existence, the question again is (371E 12): Where do we find justice in it? The answer does not sound very promising, for it says that justice is to be found in the mutual need (ἐν χρείᾳ) that the complementary elements have for each other. This is almost less than we learned in the Thrasymachus, where it was said that justice is concerned with the areas of business, community, and need (συμβόλαια, κοινωνία, χρεία, I 333A et seq.). Indeed, we have not yet come to a point where more can be said. For justice in the strict sense exists only in the context of the Forms, or Ideas.

Why does Plato formulate the question here, then, and suggest an answer, however tentative? The principle of justice, as will be shown later, consists in "doing one's own," i.e., in the self-discipline exercised by each class of society and by each function of the soul in restricting itself to its own proper task. The same principle of doing one's own is anticipated here in a preliminary form. The workmen will produce more and better things when each of them performs the one task that is appropriate to his own nature (370c). Thus, "doing one's own" is a principle essentially rooted in every "natural" human community before it is raised by Plato to the level of the ideal state.

This principle is badly misunderstood, however, if it is interpreted as selfishness or proud independence. A person may "do his own" either for his own benefit or for the benefit of the community, as Socrates points out at the beginning in order to distinguish these alternatives (369E 2 – 370A 4). The word "common" and its derivatives are used repeatedly (369E 5, 370D 6, 371B 5, 371E 2). "Sharing" (371B 4) is another expression for the same principle, and "not for himself" (370c 9) is its negative counterpart. "Doing one's own," therefore, is a constructive social principle—and is so understood on the higher levels—only when it aims at the benefit of the community. Thus, after the simile of the cave and its interpretation are behind us, and when the philosopher has found his proper task in the ideal state, we read again: "They will share with each other" (VII 519E 4); they must "care for each other" (520A 8); it is forbidden that "everyone take the course that pleases him" (520A 3). We well may ponder to what extent this highest level of the *Republic* is anticipated in the origins of Plato's construction of the state.

What Socrates presents here belongs to a general tradition of speculation about the origins of human culture.[14] In Greece, this tradition begins with Hesiod's myths about the different ages of mankind and about the role of Prometheus, and is continued in the poetic works that make Orpheus the founder of human culture. In the *Prometheus* of Aeschylus, and in the great chorus of Sophocles' *Antigone*, this theme of the earliest beginnings of mankind is transformed into a series of tragic events. What was ancient myth in epic poetry and in tragedy becomes a part of rational prehistory with Anaxagoras and Archelaos. Demokritos continues along these lines, as Protagoras perhaps did earlier—although we do not know how little or how much we should attribute to him in the tale told by Plato's Protagoras. This myth on the origins of mankind must contain traditional material, but we do not know how extensively. Besides, Plato has made it his own property. How closely this mythical account is related to the origins of society as described here in the *Republic* may be seen from the fact that both list the same five professions, almost in the same order, as constituents of the original city.

Let us consider next the manner in which Socrates presents this primitive history of mankind in the *Republic* and how his partners respond to the invention. "Perhaps so," Adeimantos replies (370A 5) when the construction of the small community based on the division of labor principle is presented. We hear the same "perhaps" when Socrates declares that the original community, now somewhat enlarged, is "complete" (371E 9). When Socrates himself picks up this second "perhaps" (372A 3), we may recall that he began the whole construction by a prefacing "perhaps" (368E 7). Thus, Glaukon's explosive protest does not occur all of a sudden, as might appear to be the case if we paid no attention to the repeated "perhaps."

Looking back from this construction of the primitive state, we saw that its predecessor was to be found in the myth told by Protagoras. Looking forward, we realize that the ideal state grows out of this original community as envisaged by Socrates. The ideal state retains the separation of functions, conceived now on a large scale, and it raises the principle of justice, already implicit in the primitive state, to the level of the ruling virtue. At this height Socrates will refer to the mode of being to be attributed to this ideal state in a phrase, as strikingly simple as it is untranslatable, that combines *mythos* and *logos:* ἣν μυθολογοῦμεν λόγῳ (501E 4).

Mythos and *logos*, or play and seriousness, interpenetrate even on the lowest level, and the repeated "perhaps" is a symbol for this conjunction. With what has been said so far, we have practically answered the question raised so often as to how the "healthy community" that Glaukon calls a "community of pigs" is to be understood. It is unthinkable that Plato, at any time, regarded this primitive community as an ideal state of nature in the sense of a *Utopia* or a *Contrat social*. Nor is there any indication whatever that, in this portrait, he is ridiculing the concept of a utopian state formulated by some other thinker or poet, or that he is incorporating some other formulation into his own work. Such speculations obscure the basic insight that what is developed here in organic growth is the prototype of the just state as it "perhaps" existed at one time. When Glaukon crudely refers to it as a community of pigs, he is judging the healthy community from the perspective of the subservience to desires which will transform it into a feverish state.

Why, finally, does Plato present this sequence of two stages of development? This, too, must have been a matter of principle, not a matter of history or polemics. The healthy community contains the prototype of the principle of justice, but it is without *logos* and, hence, without virtue (*arete*) in the sense of perfect being. So it is only "natural" that the primitive impulse of physical life, "desire"—which, ultimately, is the source of injustice—gradually prevails in this community that is insecure in its foundations. This is the same process which, viewed from the level of the true state, will lead to the defective types of government. Thus, this contrast is inherent also in "nature." Yet, as even the worst one among the defective types is still sustained, as it were, by the faint reflection cast by the pure type, so here, in the present context, the "sick" community is not totally devoid of healthy substance. War originates from evil, but even then it is a question whether its effects are always evil (373E). More important, the principle of the healthy state is employed presently in connection with the selection of the guardians. The farmer or cobbler does not serve as a soldier, as he does in most historical societies. On the contrary, the class of soldiers is separated off lest one man do many things.

The guardians are endowed with those polar qualities, courageous spirit and a desire for learning, which, though contrary, must for this very reason be combined. In this, however, the analogy with the watchdog (375E) shows how far we still are engaged in a preliminary approach. In the luxurious or sick community we encounter the forces that must be subdued so that Plato's realm may be founded. Yet, impulse and desire (ἐπιθυμία) aiming at pleasure, as well as energy or high-spiritedness (θυμοειδές), are also "by nature." Hence, they cannot and should not be eradicated, but must be assigned their proper place so that the whole will be perfect.

Thus, in the ideal state, both the "healthy society" and the "luxurious" one are raised to a new level (with the luxurious deprived of its excesses, or "purified," 399E 5).

The Education of the Guardians

II 2a–2c
376C–412B
BOOKS II–III
MUSIC, GYMNASTICS, AND JUSTICE. The need for guardians has hardly been stated when the question arises, how to educate them. This not only indicates how much Plato's state is an educational project, but also emphasizes that the construction of this state from its very beginnings (368DE) is designed to show "in large letters" the possibilities to be realized in each individual soul. In each of us (so we may hope, at least) there is a disposition toward "courage," i.e., some quality which, from the perspective of the state as a whole, corresponds to the class of the guardians. Yet, even this subject, the education of the guardians, is not autonomous. It is integrated presently into the over-all structure of the work—the search for justice or its opposite. In the end, it is said that the two arts, gymnastics and music, in which this education of the guardians consists, are not meant or not merely meant to improve body and soul, as the customary view has it (376E). Both arts serve the soul, i.e., the essential nature of man. More specifically, both arts are designed to reconcile the two contrary qualities decisive in the selection of the guardians (375E)—courageous spirit (τὸ θυμοειδές) and intellectual striving (τὸ φιλόσοφον).

What does all this have to do with justice? It goes to the heart of the matter if we consider that justice in the state—or "rightness," as we might call it more appropriately—consists in each class's doing its own. This practice rests, however, on the harmonic relationship of the forces at work in the educational process. And this connection is clearly seen at the begin-

ning of Book VIII, in that the process of disintegration is attributed to the decline in the value of these powers, music and
gymnastics (especially the decline in the value of music as compared with gymnastics, so that the young generation grows
more a-musical—546D, 548C). Here is confirmation of the
thesis that the correspondence between gymnastics and music,
on the one side, and justice, on the other, as set up at the opening of the educational section, is due not to some formal principle of organizing the material conveniently, but to a meaningful connection in depth.

THE WORDS. We begin with "musical" education, or more
specifically, with the concrete subject of "words," i.e., stories
taken in a broad sense. These are of two kinds, true stories
"that say of things how they are," and false or deceptive stories.
Both types belong to education. First, we take up the deceiving
stories, the myths. The implication is that we shall deal later
with the true stories. This expectation is not fulfilled, however,
and not because Plato changed his plan of organization,[15] but
because "truth" is to be found only on the level where reason
encounters the world of true being. In other words, this is one
of the numerous passages at this middle stage of the *Republic*
that point forward to the highest stage in Books V–VII.

Although it is not said explicitly, there is an ingredient of
truth in the deceptive myths also.[16] With respect to the basic
ways of teaching about the gods (τύποι περὶ θεολογίας),[17] two
principles are set up by which the traditional myths of creation
must be purged. The first principle is that God is good. Hence,
he cannot be the cause of evil, and all the stories that depict
Zeus or any other god in the role of doing evil must be banished.
The second principle is that change and deception are incompatible with the nature of a god. Hence, all stories about the
metamorphoses of gods must be repudiated, as well as those in
which a god presents a deceptive appearance as if he were
changing into a different shape.

In this critique of myths and in the form of myth itself, we
perceive hints that will become true knowledge only in the
central part of the *Republic*.[18] The Form of the Good—the simile

II 2a
376D–392C
BOOKS II–III

of the cave identifies it with the image of the sun—rises above the world of gods with their different names, whereas evil, or falsehood, is attributed to what is represented by the cave (or, in the *Timaeus*, by the "receptacle"). The assertion that the gods are unchangeable will be rendered, on the level of dialectics, as the view that pure being is eternal. Pure knowledge will be revealed as the opposite of falsehood. And being and knowledge will be strictly related to each other, the one as "divine" as the other. Thus, the light of truth and reality radiating from this highest level is visible even on the lower level.

After this discussion of the principles that must be observed in the stories of "gods, demons, heroes, and the world beyond" (392A), there remains the question of how the poets should speak about men. As soon as this question is posed, however, it is deferred as premature. For in order to deal with it, we would first have to refute definitively the praise of injustice as stated by Thrasymachos and repeated here in similar words (III 392B; cf. I 343C). But to refute this would mean to have already discovered the "nature of justice" (οἷόν ἐστι δικαιοσύνη, 392C 2)—as we will do not until Book IV. It would also mean discovering that justice, "by its intrinsic nature, is of advantage to its possessor"—as will be guaranteed by the scale of happiness at the end of Book IX. Both of these later parts are here anticipated. The work as a whole, then, will conclude with the great myth that deals with "gods, demons, heroes, and the world beyond," and yet, at the same time and in a deeper sense, deals with human beings, showing—no longer by general rules but by example—"how one should speak of them."

392c–398B
BOOK III

Here continues the struggle against imitative poetry, discussed earlier (pp. 75ff.) in connection with Adeimantos' speech. This speech seemed to deviate from the search for justice in raising the question about the poetic forms appropriate to the ideal state. One hint particularly deserves to be noticed. "Perhaps," Socrates says (394D 7–9), "this question is much more far-reaching. I do not know yet, but wherever the wind of the argument blows, there we shall follow." Nothing more is heard of this indefinite promise. Yet in reading about the different kinds of poetry (394AB), we cannot but notice that Plato's own form of the dialogue, although never "simple narration," falls to a great extent into the category of "imitative" poetry. This is true of the pure dialogues, like the *Euthyphro*, the *Gorgias*, and the *Phaedrus*. And often in Plato's works narration is combined with dramatic representation, as in narrated dialogues like the *Symposium*, the *Phaedo*, and the *Republic*. Subsequently Socrates will assert that tragedy and comedy, though apparently very similar, are nevertheless so different that the same poet is incapable of producing both. But should we not recall the final scene of the *Symposium* where Socrates "compels" Aristophanes and Agathon "to admit" that both types of poetry must be combined in the same poet? And let us question further. When, in contrast to this view, human nature is "split up" (*Republic* III 395B) into smaller and smaller pieces, does Plato really intend that we should say, with Adeimantos, "most true," i.e., accept this splitting up of human nature, instead of thinking of Plato's own work that is in sharpest possible contrast to such a process? In short, we cannot but realize, here in the *Republic* as well as at the end of the *Symposium*, that Plato is speaking for himself. He is at least suggesting what place in the ideal state is to be assigned to his own literary work—to his dialogues, where narration and mimesis, as well as tragedy and comedy, are combined and superseded by philosophy.

HARMONY AND RHYTHM. After the "words"—i.e., the subjects and kinds of poetry—there follows, in a separate section, a discussion of harmonies and rhythms, already touched on earlier in the dialogue (397BC). As far as details are concerned, Socrates twice appeals to the work of Damon, the musical theorist —from whom we could learn more about the subject.[19] If Damon's *Areopagiticus* were less of a fragment to us—the title of the work characterizes it as a solemn speech delivered before the highest court of Athens—we would know more about Plato's indebtedness to it, or how much he omitted from it as inessential for his purpose, and how far he went beyond his predecessor.

Certain harmonies and rhythms are eliminated as inappropri-

II 2b
398c–403c
BOOK III

ate for the true state; only a few are retained as appropriate. The selection is designed to develop and reconcile the warlike, manly, and active dispositions with the peaceful, gentle, and moderate dispositions—an interaction of polar qualities that for Plato are essential aspects of human nature, and have already been designated as decisive criteria in the selection of the guardians. The discussion then turns to the general characteristics of rhythm and harmony. Here the affinity is shown that exists between right rhythm, right harmony, right speech (λέξις), beautiful form and shape (εὐσχημοσύνη), the beauty of character (εὐήθεια). This is the dimension in depth, as it were, of the musical qualities, reaching into the inner life of man. Their dimension in breadth is visible in the products of the arts and crafts, in the body and in all living things. Since man is always surrounded by these products, formed or deformed, and is touched by them in the depths of his being, music even in its seemingly sensuous elements provides the most effective nourishment for the young soul. Rhythm and harmony—so viewed in breadth and depth—prepare the soul so that "when reason comes," a man will recognize her (because of his education) and welcome her as kin (402A).

When reason comes . . . This does not happen here on this level of education in constructing the state. Thus, the phrase points forward to the highest level of the *Republic* (Books V–VII), to the path by way of mathematics to the Forms, the realm of order, and the Form of the Good. But why is it that just the sensuous elements of music are preparation for this goal? We cannot here go into all the ramified connections ascribed to rhythm and harmony in Plato's writings, from his earliest period on. It must suffice to point out that, according to the *Laws* (664E *et seq.*), rhythm is the term for order in movement, harmony for order in voices; that, according to the *Timaeus* (90D), the soul's task consists in re-creating in itself the orderly movement of the universe, its harmony and cycles (ἁρμονίας τε καὶ περιφοράς); that, according to the *Gorgias* (507E *et seq.*), "proportion is a mighty power among men and gods" holding together "heaven and earth by community, friendship, order, discipline, and justice." If we add that the word *logos* refers not only to "reason" but also to relations among num-

bers, and that this second meaning is always present, it becomes still more evident why rhythm and harmony are to prepare the ground for rational discourse. Both are orderly systems, on different levels of sublimation. Musical education
produces "harmony and balance, not knowledge." This Socrates will say later (VII 522A), looking back to the earlier
discussion, only to embark soon after on the theory of numbers
that prepares the way to the realm of reason, the way from
the world of becoming to the world of being.

As the perfect musical education is related to knowledge,
so are the respective objects related. "The musical education is
not complete until we can recognize the Forms, or qualities
(εἴδη), of discipline, courage, liberality, and greatness of mind
(ἐλευθεριότης, μεγαλοπρέπεια), and other Forms akin to them, as
well as their opposites, moving about[20] in their various embodiments, or manifestations (ἐνόντα ἐν οἷς ἔνεστιν)—until we
recognize the Forms themselves and their copies."[21] This is the
way musical education is envisaged, in every respect a preparation for pure knowledge, a necessary prerequisite without which
we could not set out on the dialectical path toward knowledge.
"Forms" (εἴδη) are the objects of both disciplines. The difference is that in pure knowledge the mind grasps the nature of
true being without the help of perception, whereas in music
only objects are perceived. Here (i.e., in the real world) they
move about in various embodiments, and in addition to the
embodiments or qualities of discipline (sophrosyne) and courage,
the embodiments of their opposites also move about. In the
realm of knowledge, however, the charioteer-mind beholds the
Forms, and only them, as they are in themselves, enthroned
upon a holy seat (Phaedrus 247D, 254B). Without an education
in music, then, there can be no education in philosophy. A man
who in his formative years has not learned rhythm and harmony, and has not experienced discipline and what is akin to
it or opposite to it in its various embodiments, cannot ascend
on the path toward the pure Forms of self-discipline and the
good.

Eros. In the *Symposium* and the *Phaedrus* (250c *et seq.*), we
are shown the way upward from physical beauty to eternal

402D–403C

beauty, and how for us the physical kind is a necessary precondition to the eternal. As in these dialogues love is the guide in the ascent, so here in the *Republic* love is present in its preliminary stage, and here, as well as in the two other dialogues, love—for a moment—bears the features of Socrates. The man educated in music loves another who combines beauty of body and soul, and if there is a defect in the other, it can be only on the side of physical appearance (as in Socrates and in Theaitetos). This love masters the powerful impulse which, without moderation and discipline, may become a veritable madness. So the discussion yields a moral principle (403A 7–8): "To love rightly is to love with moderation and a sense for music someone who is disciplined and beautiful." In the new state to be founded, this principle is expressed in the law that a lover should treat his beloved as a father does his son—a lesson experienced by Alkibiades in the night he spent with Socrates (*Symposium* 219CD). The section on music here in the *Republic* culminates in a portrayal of love that is circumscribed by moral demands and legal rules but is ultimately determined by the fact that (as in the *Symposium*) "beauty is the object of love." For (*Republic* 403C) "the realm of music finds its fulfillment in the love of the beautiful."[22]

"When reason comes . . ." This was said (402A) in anticipation. Should we not ask, then, what happens to this musical *Eros* on the higher level of the *Republic?* As the present discussion concludes on the note of "love," so love emerges briefly in the course of the conversation in Book V as soon as the word *philo-sopher* makes its appearance (474C *et seq.*). There we will pass from those who love only beautiful voices, colors, and figures to those few and rare who are capable of beholding "beauty itself," those who "love to see the truth, the real being" (τῆς ἀληθείας φιλοθεάμονες, 475E). A man who truly desires to know—as is said somewhat later, in the fight against those who despise philosophy (VI 490B)—does not dwell in the world of many things and appearances, but ascends toward the world of true being and seeks to grasp it by means of the power in his soul akin to it. Then his labors (ὠδῖνες), which— as in the *Symposium* (206E) and in the *Phaedrus* (251E 5)—are

necessarily a part of love, come to an end. Thus, at the height
of the *Republic*, the philosophical *Eros* supersedes the musical
Eros. The description of the stages of love Plato reserved for
the *Symposium*.

GYMNASTICS—PHYSICIAN AND JUDGE. There follows a brief discussion of gymnastics, or physical education. Here it would be
even more inappropriate than in the case of music to lose ourselves in technical details. The important thing for Plato was
to counter the erroneous view that gymnastics has its own
raison d'être. Hence, to begin with (403D), we find a critique of
the view—it threatens to take over in our own time again—
that the training of the body accomplishes the same end as the
"training" of the soul. The fact is just the reverse. The founder
of the city, therefore, must educate the mind (διάνοια) so that
it can set rules concerning the details of education, physical
education or gymnastics included. At the end of the discussion,
the customary view that gymnastics serves the body and music
serves the soul (376E) is overcome by a higher synthesis
(411E). Both gymnastics and music serve the soul in ensuring
the right harmony between its opposites—the power of courage
and the power of knowledge—and the guardians need both.
For this reason, the intimate connection of the two arts is described first in terms of complementary functions (404E):
gymnastics produces physical health, music spiritual health.
Later it is described in terms of the right mixture: an excess
of gymnastics makes man too tough, an excess of music too
soft (410D). Only the right proportion of the two arts produces
the right harmony in the soul. Thus, within this section we
witness another ascent from one level to another—if slight,
still clearly an ascent in the true Platonic spirit.

But must not one be puzzled to discover that, between these
two levels describing gymnastics, the intervening discussion is
about physicians and judges? The matters discussed include
what they should be like and, even more, what they should
not be like, and how those who fall into this second category
must as far as possible be excluded from the ideal state. We
leave it to the physicians and judges of today to read the memo-

II 2c
403C–412B
BOOK III

rable details thoughtfully. Here we inquire instead into the meaning of the digression. To clarify it, we may go back to the system of the arts as set forth in the *Gorgias*.[23]

There we found that as legislation was related to the function of the judge, so gymnastics was related to medicine. Body and soul, precaution and restoration—these were the dual principles employed in the system of the *Gorgias*. The system is now revised in a way characteristic of the stage we are at in the *Republic*. Everything is the same except that we find *music* in the place of legislation. This is understandable as soon as we realize that, in the *Republic*, almost the whole subject of legislation is replaced by education, and that the modes of music and the laws of the state are co-ordinated in a striking manner according to the views of Damon, theoretician of both music and politics (424c). "The modes of music are never altered without simultaneously unsettling the foundations of the state." Parallel to the system of the genuine arts, in the *Gorgias*, we found the arts of flattery, or pseudo-arts. Of these, sumptuous cookery—the "Syracusan table" and "Sicilian delicacies" (404D)—is merely alluded to here in the *Republic*. Much more is heard of rhetoric, the worst of this class. As in the *Gorgias*, rhetoric is said here (*Republic* 405BC) to protect men from "justice" (or punishment). In the *Gorgias*, rhetoric was described as the caricature of the law courts; here it is said to be "still worse than the courts of law," which obviously do not enjoy a high reputation either. Yet now we have come to a point where the two dialogues, despite a similar structure, differ from each other.

In the *Gorgias*, the intention was to devalue rhetoric within the context of the state as it exists. Here in the *Republic*, the intention is to work out a difference in value, within the system of genuine arts, in the context of the founding of a new state. To be sure, with his sense of reality Plato knows that even the best state cannot dispense with physicians and judges. Still, their work is needed all the more, the worse the state is. Better than medicine is gymnastics, and better than the law is—music, in the profound sense that entitles Plato to assign musical education a place here corresponding to legislation in the system of the *Gorgias*. (It is likely that Damon had already inferred this important correlation from the twofold meaning of the word *nomos*—law and tonal structure—and had drawn from it his own conclusions with regard to music and politics.) Thus, the meaning of this apparent digression on physician and judge in the midst of the section on education has become clear. For medicine and law are now restricted in their respective value in order to secure the highest rank for education.

Conclusion of the Preliminary Construction of the City

In this part, at the end of which Socrates will proclaim, with ironic emphasis, that the state (not "is founded . . ." but) "may be founded for you, son of Ariston" (427c 6),[24] various lines of thought cross each other. The institutions are perfected further. By means of repeated tests the "rulers" and, below them, the "auxiliaries" are selected from the class of "guardians" (412B *et seq.*). A "camp ground" is chosen for the guardians. They must live in the simplest quarters (415D *et seq.*), and they must not own any personal property (416D *et seq.*). Yet, as a matter of fact, Plato regulates very little, and makes it clear throughout that even these few institutions are not ends in themselves. They serve the sole purpose of assigning to each class its appropriate task so as to ensure the ordered unity of the state as a whole. Specific regulations with regard to appearance, dress, the market, and the law courts are explicitly omitted (425B *et seq.*)—probably because of discussions current at the time. But any approach that focuses on these external aspects fails, as usual, to catch the real meaning, which may be formulated as follows. Education has priority over the institutions that by an inner necessity grow out of it. The guardhouse must be located, of course, where the guardians can best subdue the enemy within and repel the enemy without (415DE); i.e., it must be so located physically that the guardians can fulfill their proper function. Yet what matters more is that it be located in a spiritual realm—"in music" (424D).[25]

For an understanding of the work as a whole, we must carefully note the numerous indications that we only seem to have reached the goal and actually are still on a preliminary level.

Glaukon, to be sure, thinks the education is now complete. Most readers feel as he does, and so do all those who believe that Plato ever envisaged this construction of the city as a thing complete in itself. Socrates, however, points forward (414B, 416B) to Books VII and VIII, i.e., to the highest level of education and the true center and summit of the whole work. Even the discussion of special institutions—arrangements for the possession of wives, for marriage, and for the procreation of children—is postponed (423E). This introduces a peculiar tension which is used in Book V to propel the conversation to its highest level, and there we shall actually hear about the rulers, their education and their function. Looking back (VI 502E *et seq.*) to the present discussion, Socrates will comment ironically that reason had stepped aside and concealed herself out of fear that she might stir up these very matters that are now put forward. Thus, Plato later confirms what is implicit in this earlier section, that he has indeed postponed the discussion, and that the reader should feel this postponement as an element of tension revealing that there is an ascent—an ascent to the mystery.[26]

At the end of this chapter, we shall discuss the mythical line of the work, the dimension that comes into view now as soon as the blueprint of the new city appears to be finished. Socrates invents the educational myth of the earthborn and the different metals of which they are composed. Let us concentrate here on the meaning of this fairy tale. Birth from the earth shows the unity provided by having the same mother. The different metals signify the multiplicity. Upon both Plato bases the founding of his state. The individual institutions and regulations are derived from this starting point. The guardians—and only they—are allowed to own no private property, or practically none (416D *et seq.*). The happiness of the individual is determined by his share in the happiness of the whole community, not vice versa (420BC). Riches and poverty must be equally excluded from the city lest it fall apart into two separate social factions (421D *et seq.*). The city must not be too large or too small; not too large because a large size may threaten the unity within, not too small because a small size increases the danger that every man may do all sorts of things instead of "doing his own," and also, it seems, because in a state that is too small, the available resources are too scarce (423BC). If the descendants of the guardians do not meet the requirements laid down for this class, they will be relegated to the class of manual laborers. Conversely, if there is somebody in the general population who is endowed with the qualities of a guardian, he will move up into the class of guardians (415BC, 423CD).

"A unity out of parts of different nature" (ἐξ εἴδει διαφερόντων) —this is Aristotle's definition of the state (*Politics* II 1261ᵃ 15 *et seq.*). "Equality in which opposites are contained and complement each other" (τὸ ἴσον ἀντιπεπονθός)—this is for him the principle preserving the state. These are excellent formulations characterizing the nature of Plato's state. Precisely because this nature consists in a delicate balance of forces, the true state is constantly threatened by decay (φθορά). Disintegration had already entered into the beginnings of the state when the pleasure principle, the natural principle of life, made its appearance (see p. 83, above). Now the fairy tale concludes with the prophecy that the state will perish when men of iron or bronze become its guardians. Original endowment and education—the first before the second—are, if rightly used, the preconditions for building the right state. Hence, both also contribute, in their interaction, to the disintegration of the state. And, indeed, how does decay set in, according to Book VIII (545D *et seq.*)? With a defect in education, i.e., in arithmetic. The failure to compute the difficult number that determines marriages leads to a corruption of man's physical nature. In line with this development, the balance between musical and gymnastic education is upset in the case of those guardians who no longer are completely suited to their task. Thus, all the specific institutions of the ideal state are designed to make it secure against the forces of decay that are a constant and immediate threat owing to selfishness, private property, the desire for individual happiness, and change in the musical style.[27]

These counterforces are powerful enough to be given brief and dramatic expression. As Glaukon had protested earlier against the original, healthy state by calling it a community of pigs, so now—as the founding of the new state is tentatively completed (419A)—Adeimantos interrupts by objecting that Socrates has given the guardians duties to perform but no happiness, no enjoyment (μηδὲν ἀπολαύουσι). This objection is so important that it is taken up again in Book V (465E *et seq.*). There the power that creates the state opposes the individual's claim for happiness, "the senseless, childish phantasm of happiness," as being destructive of the whole because the guardian seeks no longer to be a guardian, but to be happy. Only the happiness (eudaemonia) of the entirety, or the community as a whole, is recognized as a legitimate standard (421A, 466B). Thus, the answer to the objection will be found in the proof of happiness, demanded by Glaukon at the beginning of Book II and to be given only near the end of the work (IX 580B *et seq.*).

The constant threat of decay—Plato postponed the actual analysis of this phenomenon until Books VIII and IX—is anticipated here in the brief reference to what is characteristic of a defective state. Opposed to the city which we are founding, and for which we are legislating only basic principles, there stands—*Athens*. There, as everybody must realize though it is not mentioned by name, is Athens, with its business of legislating for everything, a practice comparable to that of the patient who tries all sorts of cures and medicines instead of changing his way of life (425E *et seq.*). The true nature of the new city is seen all the more clearly by contrast.

A final detail is still missing in this preliminary survey: religious worship and services for the dead. To legislate about these matters, however, is not for men. It is for Apollo, the Delphic "oracle," to select among the various traditional rites and cults (427BC). Looking ahead to the highest level, we note the contrast that no mention whatever is made there of religious worship by the living. Only posthumous honors due the philosophers are briefly mentioned (540BC). For the class of guardians, religion is tradition purified. For the class of philosophers, religion is the vision of the highest perfection itself, a perfection of which even Helios, the brightest and most illuminating of all the gods, is but a reflection. Since we must always think of the individual soul, writ small, as the counterpart to the large structure of the state, and since the quality of guardianship is not extinguished in the soul of the philosopher but is surpassed through philosophy, it follows that traditional religion is not extinguished in the soul of the philosopher either but is absorbed in the highest knowledge of the One-Good and in the feeling of reverence accompanying this knowledge.

The Search for Justice

Constantly felt as tension in the background—see pp. 84f.—the search for justice is resumed immediately after the preliminary completion of the new city and then is continued to the last part of Book IV. This shows the necessary connection between the two concepts, state and justice, a reciprocal relationship since the ideal state is a state founded on justice and since justice can be realized only in the community. The present section of the dialogue is organized according to two structural elements —the parallelism between state and individual, and the contrast between justice and injustice. For this reason, we hear first about the virtues in the state (427D–434E), and then about the virtues in the individual soul (434E–435C, 441C–444C). Before this second topic can be discussed, however, it is necessary to deal with the inner structure of the individual soul (435C–441C). At the end of the section, the discussion comes to the matter of the vices, especially injustice, but the over-all structure of the work (p. 117, below) requires that this topic, scarcely mentioned, be dropped—to be resumed only in the eighth book.

Justice, as if it were self-understood, is defined within the context of the whole system of the virtues. Plato's mind was such that he should not be suspected of intending to set up, for some reason, a system of "the four cardinal virtues"—a system which might then be taken out of context and recorded as a paragraph of "Plato's ethics."[28] How little dogma there is in this discussion of justice may be seen from the fact that Plato used the formula "doing one's own" as a definition of *sophrosyne* in the *Charmides* (161B), and now in the *Republic* (433A) uses it as a definition of justice. In the *Symposium* (209A), justice and moderation almost fuse into a unity on which the order of the community is based. Piety, which is so important a virtue in

II 2e
427D–445E
BOOK IV

the older moral literature, and even in the *Apology* was for
Plato the central virtue seen in Socrates, is not included at all
in the *Republic*—or, as we suggested (pp. 96f.), is included only
indirectly. This shows how Plato attuned the "system" of the
virtues to the system of the state and the individual soul.[29]
Otherwise, he might have come back to the five virtues of the
Protagoras. Whether there are four virtues or five did not matter as much as that they formed a system.

But why a system? The answer requires a further question,
for why did the early dialogues inquiring into a single virtue
have to end inconclusively? Does not this aporetic outcome mean
that the inquiry into courage or moderation cannot be conducted
by isolating these virtues from each other, for the reason that
the essence of each can be discovered only in relation to the
others? Only a system, then, can guarantee that each single
virtue is right in itself. Courage and moderation, for example,
are then coupled with each other in a state of tension which
keeps courage from degenerating into violence and moderation
from degenerating into shy modesty. Only a *sy-stem* can hold
together the integrated structure of state and soul.

That the problem of unifying the virtues in one virtue concerned Plato from the beginning may be seen through a comparison of the *Protagoras* with the aporetic dialogues in search
of a definition. In the *Protagoras*, this unity is achieved violently and prematurely, as it were. In an aporetic dialogue, the
outcome of the conversation shows that, by isolating the virtues
from each other, the analysis must necessarily end inconclusively. Plato can show how both of these approaches must
miss the truth because he has his goal clearly in mind, as we
see in the *Gorgias*. For as Kallikles tears courage apart from
self-discipline, affirming courage and despising self-discipline
(and thus showing that he does not understand courage either),
Socrates counters with the image of the cosmos of the soul in
which self-discipline combines not only with justice and piety,
but with courage as well, into an indissoluble unity of perfection. Here, then, we find a system of four virtues—not quite the
same as in the *Republic*—as an expression of order against the
forces of destruction. This theme is also taken over into the

new dimension of the *Republic* after the forces of injustice are overcome and the new community of the city is established. We may add that a system of knowledge, justice, and discipline is suggested also in the *Alcibiades Major,* where it is put more as a question than an answer and is comprehensible only from the perspective of the *Republic.* The *Alcibiades,* however, focuses explicitly on the structure of the state, more so than the *Gorgias* which is concerned primarily with the structure of the individual soul.[30]

Even though the twofold system of virtues that is presented here in the *Republic* comes at the end of a long development and represents a major step linking the two structures, state and soul, it must be made clear that we are still dealing with preliminary matters. Between the two systems comes the section "on the soul" and its three "forms" (εἴδη). It is here (435D) that we find the statement, alluded to before, that we cannot get anywhere by the methods (μέθοδοι) employed so far, and that another and longer way must be taken to reach our goal. The present discussion, however, is said to be adequate for what we have discovered so far—for the system of virtues in the state. This system, then, is just as preliminary as the doctrine of the soul that follows and the system of virtues in the individual co-ordinated with the system of virtues in the state.

The other and longer way is, no doubt, the ascent of the cognizant soul to the realm of Forms. In fact, Plato himself later (504B) refers explicitly to this passage here in the fourth book. Almost at the end of the work, before *dike* sits in judgment over the immortal soul, we are shown the purity, unity, and eternity of the soul. We look down on its previous state when it was "deformed by association with the body and with other evils" (611c). On this level of knowledge, "we shall be able to distinguish more clearly justice and injustice and all the matters that we have discussed." From this perspective, the system of virtues and of the soul—and of the state as well, must we not add?—as we find them in Book IV recede to the level of preliminary or tentative findings.

How could it be otherwise, when "reason" is not yet present on this level of education? Indeed, we should take a look first at what Socrates, in outlining the four virtues, means by "wisdom" or "knowledge" (428B *et seq.*, 442C). In the over-all structure of the city, it means "good counsel" (as in *Alcibiades Major* 125E), i.e., the practical wisdom that is needed in order to deal properly with the internal and external affairs of the city. Similarly, in the structure of the soul, this "knowledge" corresponds to the kind of wisdom required to keep each separate element as an integral part of the whole. Knowledge of the Forms or *Ideas* lies far in the distance and high above the level of the present discussion. Thus, the concluding remark made by Socrates (429A 5-6), "We have found one of the four, I know not how," must be understood in its ironic ambiguity so that we know how to take Glaukon's reply that he is "satisfied" with these findings.

The second virtue is manliness or courage (429A *et seq.*, 442BC). In many respects, the discussion here is reminiscent of the *Laches*, as when, for example (corresponding to *Laches* 191DE), the four types of affects against which manliness must prevail are grouped in a system both psychological and ethical. Manliness is still confined, however, to the class of soldiers although there is a reference (430C 3) to its "civic" nature, beyond the strictly military sphere. It is constantly emphasized (429C 1 and 7, 430B 3) that we are still in the field of "opinion"—even though it is "right opinion" that the law conveys by means of this education in music and gymnastics. The analogy with a perfect process for dyeing material so that the color cannot be washed out afterwards shows that we are still on a preliminary and practical level, as is confirmed by the concluding remark that "later we shall learn more about this subject."

The third virtue is moderation or self-discipline (430D *et seq.*, 442CD). It is described as a kind of concord or harmony. This musical metaphor occurs at both the beginning and the end of the discussion, pointing to the fact that concord among the different classes and forces in state and soul is a basic requirement. Then the expression "self-mastery" (τὸ κρεῖττω ἑαυτοῦ) is called on to clarify the meaning of *sophrosyne* or self-discipline. The sophistic argument—undoubtedly derived from contemporary discussions—that in order to be master of himself, a man must also be his own servant, is barely mentioned yet yields to a true insight. The very expression shows that there is a better element and a worse element in the soul and that the better should rule over the worse, or the worse should submit to the better by mutual agreement. Both parts should be of the same opinion—again, "opinion" as a preliminary stage of knowledge—as to which should be in control and which should obey.

There remains justice (432B *et seq.*, 442D *et seq.*) as the fourth virtue and as the centrifugal force which, counterpoised to the centripetal force of self-discipline, sustains the whole edifice. For, "as we have heard from others and as we have often said ourselves,"[31] justice consists in "everybody's doing his own." It is, then, the principle we have followed from the very beginning in founding the state. But is it not rather silly (βλακικόν τι πάθος) simply to come back, after all these labors, to what we established in the beginning? This is not quite the case, since we were "required" (δεῖν, 433A 2) to establish what "by nature" is present in every good society, i.e., in a city state constructed "according to nature." And we do not come back to it in the primitive, natural sense of the cobbler's sticking to his last and the farmer's sticking to the soil. We deal with it, instead, in a mature form, as it were, or transformed on a higher level where each class in society and each element of the soul restricts itself to performing the task appropriate to its nature. Yet, again, we must realize that we have reached only a resting place on the way upward. We have not yet entered on the world of pure knowledge and eternal Forms. This world opens up later, and the Form of justice will then be mentioned again explicitly (517E). The concluding myth, finally, will convey to us the highest order in the vision of a cosmic harmony superseding and regulating all other types of order. The world-spindle, the lots drawn for life, and the court of eternal justice— these are manifestations of justice far above the level we have reached in Book IV here.[32]

What demands Plato makes on us! He shows the system of the virtues before we have reached the level of pure knowledge, and compels us to ask what the system will be like after knowledge has disclosed the realm of Forms. He places the structure of the soul before us so that it is seen from the outside, so to speak, as if it were an object,[33] and then leads us to another and higher stage where the soul has gained true knowledge of itself, of its eternity, its unity, and its power to behold true being. The system of the virtues and the threefold soul cannot be separated from the construction of the three-class state. This state, therefore, also is raised to a new level by the dimension of philosophy that emerges in its midst. Viewed in this perspective, the "doctrines" about the soul, the virtues, and the state lose their doctrinal and static character. They are stages on the way to the *Idea* of the Good, and when we have climbed high enough, they remain behind—the systems of the soul, the virtues, and the state. The state, too, loses its temporal, earthly character; it becomes a myth (VI 501E). Yet it is not reduced to a "mere myth," but is raised to the higher mode of existence where fable is infused with the *Ideas*.

The Three Waves

III 1
449A–473E
BOOK V Three waves break in upon us, each one more powerful than the other. With this pictorial metaphor, Plato raises the conversation to its highest level. This level is reached—and on it everything that has been said before will suddenly be transformed—when we come to the core of the whole *Republic*, the incredible paradox that philosophers be kings, and that the ideal state will not be realized unless they are (473CD). From then on, this new knowledge will stand at the center and direct our view to the realm of true being.

To this realm, then, we are carried by the wave that threatened to drown us. Precisely because this wave is so overwhelming, Plato does not introduce it by itself, but as the third and last wave long kept in the background. Two paradoxes precede it. These paradoxes are not of the same overwhelming power, however, but of such a kind that they might have been dealt with on the level we are now leaving. For there we had already heard (423E) about the community of wives and children, a matter which was then postponed. This question now becomes the second wave. And even as it holds back the third wave, so the second is intentionally held back by the first, i.e., by the question of whether women should receive the same education as men in music and gymnastics.

These are paradoxical proposals, and Plato plays with them —*pour épater le bourgeois*—by having the women exercise naked with the men in the gymnasium and by elaborating on the institution of communal marriage, with many amusing and even grotesque details.[34] Yet, he is deeply serious behind the jest. For here, as everywhere in the *Republic*, it is not the institution that matters to him, but the principle represented by it. In principle, as many as possible should be able to share in the education provided by the state. In principle, the forces that tear the state apart are the greatest evil and those that bind it together are the greatest good, and the strongest bond is forged by a communion of pleasure and pain (462AB). The more striking the paradox, the clearer the principle. Besides, may we not say that at least in this aspect of education, our own society has moved much closer to adopting Plato's paradox?

The third and most radical paradox is concealed, as it were, behind these preliminary paradoxes. All the excitement is concentrated on them in order to deceive the reader as to what is yet to come. This is the meaning of the interlude at the beginning of Book V, the most dramatic interlude in the dialogue since Glaukon and Adeimantos, at the beginning of Book II, replaced Thrasymachos. These excited murmurs among the listeners, this interference of Polemarchos and even of Thrasymachos himself, this curiosity to learn about such dubious matters as the community of wives and the procreation of children —all these maneuvers (what fitting irony!) are designed to bring the conversation face to face with true being.[35]

But let us consider more carefully the peculiar way in which the approach to the goal is veiled, how the third and crucial question—the third wave—is smuggled in, as it were. The first wave raises two questions: first, whether the education in music and gymnastics is of benefit to the women guardians, and second, whether it is possible. In the case of the second wave, Socrates puts aside the question of whether it is possible —thus we are held in suspense—and turns instead to a discussion of how the community of wives and children should be organized and why this institution is beneficial (458B). Later he will examine the question of whether it is possible, and his partner intimates that, without this promise, he would have raised the question himself. Yet, against all expectations, the course of the conversation shifts again. There follows a digression on military service for both men and women (466E *et seq.*). Still another digression follows, dealing with the rules of war to be observed among the Greeks (469B *et seq.*). This digression has a deep inner connection with the main theme, for it is designed to show that the Greeks are "friends by nature." Hence, they cannot engage in "war" (πόλεμος) with each other, but only in "strife" or "factionalism" (στάσις). Thus, the Greek nation seems to be subsumed under the same principle of "friendship" that binds the ideal state together, the nation, ultimately, envisaged as the city writ large.

Nonetheless, serious and important as these matters are and as much as Plato speaks here not as an "unworldly idealist" but as a political realist addressing—in vain—a message to all the Greek states, his warning at this point is primarily to postpone and veil the ultimate goal he is pursuing. Socrates, so his partner objects (471C), would like to go on digressing in order to evade the question that remains to be answered, the question whether these things are possible. What things? Originally, the community of wives (466D)—but suddenly we find that the question is of a much larger order. For we are asking now "whether it is possible that this state we have been founding can come into existence and, if so, how" (471C). After such detours, delays, and ruses, we finally see before us the third and biggest wave (472A, 473C).

From the various subsidiary themes interwoven into this section, only one is selected for comment here. The false view (453E *et seq.*) that men and women must perform different tasks because their natures are different rests on making false "divisions" (διαίρεσις) in the concepts, or rather in the essences or "Forms" (εἴδη). It is argued that if we divide the class of human beings into male and female and assign to each sex a certain task, it follows that the other sex cannot be admitted to this task. This method disregards the aim of the division. We might just as well divide mankind into those who are bald and those who are long-haired and then conclude that if the bald are cobblers, the long-haired must not be permitted to practice the same craft. That is an eristic, not dialectic, method of division. The dialectic method does not operate by arbitrarily selecting a coupled pair of concepts and by co-ordinating them with another pair selected just as arbitrarily. On the contrary, it must pay close attention to the concepts of difference and identity and to the aim intended by the division.

The method of division (and synopsis) belongs to the relations among Forms. Thus, it was present in Plato's mind, at least as a future objective, as soon as he began to develop his own philosophy.[36] It is not without a hidden purpose that here as he is about to embark upon the world of Forms, Plato inserts, "by the way," a critique of the eristic method of division and gives us at least a hint about the true method.[37] Later, when the philosopher is mentioned and we enter upon a new level, the highest level of the dialogue, one of the first moves is a set of divisions (διαιρῶ, 476A 9) distinguishing between "philosophy," on one side, and the "love of sounds and sights and of the arts," on the other, between "beauty itself," on one side, and its embodiment in images single and dimmed, on the other, between waking and dreaming, between knowledge and opinion.

The Central Thesis of the "Republic" and Its Victorious Confirmation

In the *Seventh Letter* (326AB), Plato says that the paradoxical conviction that only the union of government and philosophy could save a state from perishing was already with him when he made his trip to Sicily at the age of forty. This, then, is the seed out of which grew the founding of the ideal state. We have shown how Plato emphasized this paradox by employing all sorts of detours and ruses to hold it back. Once it is out in the open, it must be defended against the powers of *doxa*, common opinion, as one might say, that finds a *para-dox* (473E 4, 490A 5) both incomprehensible and irritating.

The hostile resistance is expressed in two attacks, the first

III 2
473E–502C
BOOKS V–VI

launched by Glaukon (473E), and the second by Adeimantos
(487B). The meaning of the paradox is clarified in overcoming
this resistance. And after the paradox has emerged victorious,
the philosopher can set out to gain the highest goal (502c–
541B).

The first thrust is made by "many people of considerable
standing." They take off their coats, pick up the nearest weapon
at hand, and go after Socrates. In short, they enforce "people's
justice."[38] They are not described by name or even by profession or type. They represent the indefinite threat of the collec-
tive. Nor do they attack any specific point in the general thesis.
They have no counterarguments. They simply strike out.

Socrates meets the attack by inquiring into the nature of the
philosopher. Every reader knows that, behind this inquiry,
there is the reality of the strange life of the philosopher as
represented by Socrates more than by anybody else. And behind the attack by the indefinite many, there looms from afar
his indictment, defense, and death. Here Socrates concentrates
on the meaning of the word "philosopher" and what, strictly
speaking, it says about the kind of life a philosopher leads. He
loves knowledge. He loves—this takes us back to the *Eros*
theme of the dialogue (pp. 89ff., above). It is in the nature of
love that it loves its object completely. Hence, the philosopher
loves wisdom completely, and in this pursuit, he desires to behold
the truth (τῆς ἀληθείας φιλοθεάμων, 475E) and "to approach and
apprehend beauty itself" (476B).

What this means is explained by an ontological schema. The
three epistemological stages—*knowledge, ignorance*, and, in between, *opinion*—correspond strictly to three ontological stages
of *being, not-being*, and, in between, the world of *becoming*.
"Becoming" is characterized here, in a Parmenidean sense, as
"both being and not-being," even as other features of this discussion are Parmenidean. This ontological analysis is tentative,
and later it will be superseded by a more complete analysis
(VI 504E *et seq.*). It suffices, however, to make the point at
stake here, that the philosopher is oriented toward the realm
of true being.

In this way, the paradoxical life of the philosopher is revealed in its real meaning. He is, indeed, "para-doxan," i.e., besides and beyond opinion. In so far as "love" (which is part of the philosopher's name) aims at true being, all other loves can be shown—by means of the method of division—to be oriented toward inferior modes of being, as, for example, the love of honor (φιλότιμος), or the love of the arts (φιλότεχνος), or the love of spectacles (φιλοθεάμων) in the ordinary sense of the term, quite different from the philosopher's being enamored of the "spectacle" of truth (475E 4). These other loves aim at things that "tumble about in the region between true being and not-being" (479D). They are concerned not with *philo-sophy*, love of wisdom, but with *philo-doxy*, love of appearance and opinion. The ontological schema has clarified the situation to such an extent—as is shown all the more effectively without being put into words—that all the people who threatened to attack Socrates are now classified as lovers of opinion, below the lovers of wisdom.

Still, the paradoxical thesis that philosophers be kings has not been clarified. This is now done on the ontological basis just considered. Knowledge of the realm of truth and being is the foundation also for the social world, whose function is to legislate on what is beautiful, just, and good, and to preserve existing laws. For only this kind of knowledge "opens one's eyes." If, in addition, knowledge combines with experience and with the different virtues, then the proof for the thesis is complete. From the ontological perspective, it is evident, indeed, that the nature of the philosopher "must" include all virtues, i.e., all original forces,[39] for kinship with and membership in the realm of being is incompatible with any kind of want or original defect. Inner balance (ἔμμετρος φύσις) is the appropriate state of the philosophical character since it must not have an excess of any of the original dispositions. This philosophical character is made perfect by education, and by the process of reaching the maturity of age. Education points to the crucial discussion to follow; the maturity of age shows that natural disposition remains a factor throughout. Those, then, who are endowed with the right disposition, who receive the right education and mature accordingly, should be the rulers of the state.

484A–487A
BOOK VI

Thus, we have come to see the central thesis of the *Republic*—
in the context of "reason." But at this very point, Adeimantos
expresses the opposite view, countering "reason" (*logos*) by
average experience. This is the view that a man becomes useless for the social or political world if he gives his whole life
to philosophy instead of restricting philosophy to his youth.
We know this complaint from the speech of Kallikles in the
Gorgias (484c). And we have seen (p. 69, above) how Plato
in reformulating this speech in the second book of the *Republic*
postponed the refutation of this one complaint until he had
reached the present stage in the sixth book. Here he is able,
by means of this refutation, to expand upon the nature of the
philosophical state and simultaneously to prepare the ground
for the education of the philosopher.

The complaint serves to clarify the nature of the state. The
state, so Adeimantos says in the name of the many, does not
know what to do with the philosopher. At best the philosopher
is "useless"—and for a while the word "useless" moves to
the center.[40] What the many say is true, Socrates replies, to
the surprise of his colloquist and to our surprise as well, except
that they talk like a mutinous crew who consider the true expert
in the art of navigation as "useless" or a "stargazer and babbler." These same epithets of derision were, in Plato's youth,
bandied about on the stage and in the market place, and were
applied to men of enlightenment, natural scientists, and orators.
The wording (488e) also echoes clearly the attack upon Socrates himself in the *Clouds* of Aristophanes. What is true, then,
in this view of the many? The philosopher is indeed useless in
the present state. Yet this situation condemns not (as the
majority believe) the philosopher, but the present state. Philosophical existence—so we infer—requires the true state which
comes into being because the philosopher guides it toward the
world of true being and in which he therefore would no longer
be useless.

The customary charge leveled against philosophers makes
still another point. Philosophers not only are said to be useless,
but many of them are said to be "quite vicious" (παμπόνηροι,
487D 2, 489D 3). This charge reveals something about the

philosophical nature itself. We must go back to the basic disposition of the philosopher, that he is filled with love for true
being. The consequences of this passion are that he strives toward true being, to mate with it and to beget intelligence and
truth in order to live in knowledge and in truth and thus to be
released from his pain. To achieve this end he must cultivate
the "choir" of virtues in which are combined such opposite
excellences as justice and discipline, on the one hand, courage
and pride, on the other, and also quick intelligence and memory.
Yet, along with all these noble qualities—so we see again even
as we have seen from the beginning (p. 83, above)—there
goes the danger of possible "corruption." The stronger the
plant, the more dangerous is a nourishment not suitable for it,
is the analogy. Thus, men of mediocre nature are not exposed
to the danger. In short, what is justified in the charge that the
many bring against the philosopher only points to the steep
ascent mastered in the philosophical existence, and to the need
for (492A), and the responsibility entailed by, an education in
philosophy. (Of this truth present-day enemies of Plato's
philosophy—Arnold Toynbee in the forefront—do not seem to
have an inkling, for they are ignorant that they are following
the lead of the many.[41])

Before we reach the highest level where the education of the
philosopher-king is the subject of discussion, the urgency of
the whole problem must be underlined more explicitly. We
have not yet explored all the possible ways in which the "corruption of the philosophic nature" may be envisaged. For Plato
two names are indissolubly linked with this possibility—
Socrates, whom even Plato's *Apology* could not acquit, as far as
the many are concerned, of the senseless charge that he was
corrupting the youth, and Alkibiades, the foremost example of
a man who, though endowed with the nature of a philosopher
and ruler, was corrupted in life. The indictment of Socrates may
be heard in the very words of this passage (492A), just as
previously the attack upon him was heard in the *Clouds* of
Aristophanes. Thus, we may realize all the more clearly how
threatened the life of a philosopher is. Every reader must have
been reminded of Socrates in the words about the punishment

in store for the recalcitrant educators—"loss of civic rights, confiscation of property, and death" (492D). The individual is helpless against the tyrannical power of the mass.[42] Plato's despair about the possibility of having a true educator in the present conditions of society goes so far that he thinks a person can be "saved" by divine grace only (492E et seq.). Thus, when charges similar to those against Socrates are brought against other "teachers of wisdom" (sophists), we must remember that they indeed belong to the mass and have educated their pupils in the opinions of the many. In other words, the indictment of Socrates boomerangs against his accusers, i.e., against the many, who are unphilosophical in their nature (494A). It strikes the professional educators, who are part of the mass, and exempts precisely Socrates whose educational work appears as the saving act of a god.

Next, as far as Alkibiades is concerned, it has always been recognized that this passage (494B et seq.) suggests his likeness. Yet it has not been recognized that here the main features of the dialogue *Alcibiades Major* are integrated as well. From the general theme of a highly talented and high-minded nature, applicable to Dion and to Plato himself, the description here in the *Republic* singles out—more and more distinctly—the very features that Socrates, at the beginning of the earlier dialogue, points out in Alkibiades. He belongs to a great city. He is rich and wellborn, tall and handsome.[43] These gifts inspire him with the unbounded hope to rule not only over Greeks but also over barbarians, and so he is filled with empty imaginings.[44] "Somebody" comes to address him and tell him the truth: that he is devoid of reason and in need of it, and that he cannot acquire it without giving himself completely to this pursuit. First, he finds it difficult to listen to this counsel because he is surrounded by evil influences; but then, since he is of good disposition and feels akin to what he is told, he begins to pay attention, and his mind is turned toward philosophy. The "somebody" in the *Alcibiades Major* is Socrates. And the unique movement of this small but incomparable work is delineated here, on the large scale of the *Republic*, in its most condensed form. At the end of the *Alcibiades* (132A, 135E) are the words of concern that Alkibiades "may be corrupted by the people of Athens." And this corruption of the most highly gifted individual is shown here in the *Republic* as the danger against which the founding of the new city must protect us.

Inferior people occupy the place vacated by those who are philosophically gifted, but threatened. Thus, as Plato says in words with autobiographical overtones,[45] the success of a philosophical life is a rare accident (495c *et seq.*). Dion rightly is identified as the man of noble and well-bred nature who was saved by exile (496B).[46] Theages is mentioned as a member of the Socratic circle who was kept out of politics by his sickly body—and Socrates briefly refers, in ironic understatement, to his own demonic voice that has kept him out of politics. We cannot miss being reminded of the dialogue *Theages*, which shows the demonic power that must secretly co-operate with the educational work. For this power is not to be forgotten in the rational program of education that follows here. Complete success—something Plato did not claim for himself or even for Socrates—could be attained only if a man of philosophical disposition and education were to find a "suitable society," i.e., the "best state." And so we are brought back to the *Republic*. Something, however, is still missing in this state; it is, in fact, the main thing, without which the state must perish (497D 9). The *logos*, philosophy, philosophical education—these do not have a secure place as yet in the state. Ever since we were directed toward this goal, in the section on the musical pre-education (402A), we have been held in suspense about the solution, postponed now for so long.

Yet, we still have not reached the point where, with a new upbeat, the construction of the philosophical education will begin (502c). We still are moving—sharply focusing upon this point—along previous lines. We have come this far because Adeimantos cited the view of the many, according to whom philosophy, although appropriate for the education of the young, would make unsuited for political life those who gave it too much time. Now we are in a position to counter with the opposite, and stipulate that a philosophical education only appropriate to their age should be given to boys, that, with advancing years, philosophical pursuits should be intensified, and that in a man's old age, philosophy should be his chief occupation (497E *et seq.*). This is another hint at the project to follow. At the same time, it is a reply to the many, who through Adeimantos had protested against spending too much time on philosophy.

This protest was only one part, however, of the great movement launched by Socrates in the paradox of the philosopherking. Against the many—among whom we now meet (498D *et seq.*) the wordy and eristic orators in courtrooms and lecture halls—we have ever more successfully defended the need for a philosophical education. Now, near the end of this section, the central paradox from which we set out is repeated emphatically (499BC, 501E). We have learned that philosophy is an advance toward the world of order and eternal being, in which there is no injustice and no wrong. The vision of perfection stirs in him who is akin to it the impulse to copy it. Thus, the true philosopher seized by the "compulsion" to create something in the sphere of the worldly state will exercise his art, like a great painter of the order of Polygnotos, looking upward to the divine prototype.[47] The resistance of the opponents is thus overcome. The proof that this enterprise, however difficult, is possible has been carried through successfully. Only the path of education itself still must be shown exactly. And, almost at the end, there is the strange reference to the compulsion that must be laid upon the philosopher (500D 4), indicating that there remains the task of determining how the philosopher is to take up his work in the ideal state.

In sketching the development of this section, we have passed by the following detail. At the very place where the philosophical education was shown to be necessary, extending in various degrees through the different periods of life, there was a hint pointing beyond the limits of human life on earth. The pure (or almost pure) philosophical life of the old man is such that his life beyond would correspond to it (498C). And, says Socrates, the energy we have invested in convincing our opponents either will be crowned by success here and now or will be profited from in a future life when we are born again (498D).

Twice, suddenly, strangely, and only for a moment, then, the concluding myth of the whole work is sounded in anticipation, and the moral imperative inherent in the myth of the soul becomes audible even here.

The Education of the Philosophers and Their Integration into the State

We have come to the highest and most difficult task: the education of those destined to become "saviors of the state." Everything is to be taken up once more almost from the beginning (ἐξ ἀρχῆς, 502ε 2). Once more the difficulties of the previous discussion are emphasized. The intentional shrinking from what is to come (503AB, 504B) points to the steep and rare life of the philosopher. Why so rare? This is explained now more clearly than before. Since the highest and most manifold demands are made upon the philosopher, his nature must be universally gifted. It must unite those diametrically opposed dispositions, aggressive energy of the spirit and firm restraint (ἀνδρεία and σωφροσύνη). In the *Statesman*, this is still said to be the task of the philosopher-ruler: to reconcile these two basic dispositions in the state. From this we gather how rare an accident it must be for these dispositions to be combined in a single person. And as rare as such individuals are, so difficult is the path marked for them in attaining the "highest objects of study" (μέγιστα μαθήματα, 503ε). This path is the "other, longer way around" (504B) that came into sight from afar (435D) when there was still hope, as Socrates put it in ironic concealment, of avoiding it. It is from this perspective that the previous analysis of justice and the other virtues, along with the doctrine of the tripartite soul, is reduced to the level of a preliminary, tentative discussion. It was not "appropriate," as the partner thought. The goal, and hence the right "measure," was lacking. The highest object must be something greater, and ethics and psychology must be worked out now beyond their preliminary versions.

The highest object of knowledge, then, is very difficult. And yet—suddenly—it appears to be quite easy, for it is "the Form of the Good." "You have often heard," Socrates says, that this is the highest object of knowledge, for whenever we seriously discussed some serious subject, we were talking, ultimately, about what is good or perfect. All men desire the good. Some think it is pleasure; others think it is thought (φρόνησις).

These are the two basic positions that oppose each other. Considering that the same two positions will later oppose each other as points of departure in the *Philebus*, it is very clear that Plato is concerned with more than a topical confrontation of contemporary views. The important question is not whether Aristippos is to be identified as the author of the "hedonistic" view, or Antisthenes, the Megarians, or Socrates himself as author of the "intellectualistic" view. The important thing is rather that pleasure is the natural desire of the physical organism as knowledge is the natural desire of the mind. Here Plato wants to show that the mind is conscious of its own nature only if it is conscious of its desire for knowledge of the good, not just for knowledge as such. (This theme was first touched on in the *Charmides* and the *Euthydemus*.) Even the body is capable, however, of distinguishing between good and bad pleasures. (Plato used this distinction in the *Gorgias*, we may recall, in order to refute a radical hedonism.[48]) Thus, the two views—pleasure and knowledge—though each necessarily one-sided and seemingly opposed to the other, point to a common goal beyond themselves, the good. Yet it remains unclear what this good actually is.

This much is clear, however, amidst all the conjecturing or divining (μαντεύεσθαι, 505E 1, 506A 6 and 8): Even though men may strive for appearances in ordinary life, a person desiring the good is not satisfied with appearances but aims at being. Hence, the essential task of the guardians is to know the good. The good: it is sighted beyond the just and the beautiful (506A), and a glimpse of it reduces the system of the virtues developed in Book IV to a tentative status. The suspense mounts as the reader expects to be brought face to face with the good itself. Yet what we do reach here in the *Republic* is deeply significant in our understanding of Plato.[49] The average mind expects that the more intelligent person can answer every question put to him. So Glaukon keeps urging Socrates to reveal his own views (δόγματα) about the good (506A *et seq.*). But Plato uses Socratic ignorance (506c) to resist this pressure. What Socrates has just sighted in the distance, he veils again because he must do so; for though he "will omit" (παραλείπειν) a great deal, he "will not leave anything out intentionally" (ἑκὼν οὐκ ἀπολείψω, 509c).

We shall not trace once more the movement by which the good in its paradoxical state of "being beyond being" is sighted —and yet remains invisible. Only these general remarks may be added. Throughout the whole work we can follow the mounting tension, quite clearly at least from the passage in Book IV (435D) where we are promised a "longer and harder way." This is a tension directed toward the central core of the work. But there is hesitation and evasion in moving toward this goal. Just as it seems to be within reach, evasion again asserts itself as a counterforce. It is not accidental that the structure of the *Republic* is determined by this movement and countermovement, for this dual aspect is in the nature of the good. On the one hand, the good is the goal that inescapably determines the direction for every real movement; yet, on the other hand, language must come to a stop because the good is beyond being and, hence, beyond words.

Once we have sighted the good—and simultaneously have lost it from sight—we must reformulate the structure of being and knowledge adopted earlier (476c *et seq.*) when the philosopher was first introduced. Then it sufficed to adopt a Parmenidean schema: knowledge and ignorance, on the one side, being and not-being, on the other, and in between these poles, opinion, corresponding to the objects in the world of becoming. Now we have moved to a higher level. Nothing, to be sure, is said about ignorance and not-being. Although these radically negative concepts conceal a serious problem (to be dealt with in the *Theaetetus* and the *Sophist*), they do not apply to actual life. Even deep in the cave, as we soon shall hear, there is a faint reflection of the fire against the wall so that the shadows are set off. In life there is only being and knowledge, however shadowy and confused. What is new here is that the simple contrast of knowledge and opinion, world of being and world of becoming, is reformulated in the harmonious system of four modes of knowledge corresponding to four modes of being. This fourfold path joined together by geometric proportion carries us upward to the Form of the Good.

This new ontology as it is worked out at the end of Book VI provides the basis for what follows in Book VII. The simile of the cave leads from darkness to the vision of the sun—and back again into the cave (514A–517A). Its interpretation leads from the world of visible appearances to the world of the Intelligible culminating in the "*Idea* of the Good, the essence of perfection" —and back again to the world of becoming (517A–518B). The program of education proceeds, both epistemologically and ontologically, beyond gymnastics and music to the realm of rational discourse and, passing through the mathematical sciences, leads to dialectics and on the "dialectical path" upward to the vision of the good—and back again to practical life within the state (518B–535A). Three times, then, we are shown the path upward to the highest goal. Each time the path bends back to return to life in the human community, impressing upon us the moral obligation to take part in this life.

To close the circle by bending back to the beginning—this is also the meaning of the remainder of Book VII. At the beginning of Book VI, we learned, on the basis of the earlier (Parmenidean) doctrine of being and knowledge, what qualities the rulers must have in order to be selected as philosopher-kings (485A *et seq.*). Now these same qualities are cited, sometimes in the same words, sometimes differently. Yet, after the new ontology has been worked out at the end of Book VI, and after the path leading to the good has been cleared, we realize that these specifications have somehow acquired a new content. Thus, the objects of knowledge to which the soul must conform (484B 1, 535A *et seq.*) are recognized now as those sciences of order that lead upward to the realm of true being. As before (485CD, 535DE), the candidate must be a lover of truth to whom falsehood and deception are alien (ἀψευδής). But it is only now that we recognize the gradually purified Forms of being and knowledge, only now that we learn that the *Idea* or Form of the Good is the source of "truth and reason" (ἀλήθειαν καὶ νοῦν, 517c).

The bending back by which the circle is closed goes still farther, reaching back to the preliminary education outlined in the second and third books.[50] There we anticipated the *logos*, to which, ultimately, all types of gymnastics and music are directed (ἐλθόντος δὲ τοῦ λόγου, III 402A 3). Now, after completing the work of the *logos*, we can look back upon these propaedeutic disciplines as a kind of playful grasp of the objects of knowledge (as, indeed, mathematical elements cannot be overlooked in gymnastics and music). Thus, the beginning and all but final stages of the educational process are clearly related to each other. Yet, the most perfect integration of the educational system occurs, at the end of Book VII, in the specific periods of life set aside for the education of the philosopher-king. Here the ultimate concern is not with the numbers of years, i.e., whether the education in gymnastics should last two years or three (537B), or whether the training in dialectics should last four years, or five, or six (539DE). What matters is something more important: that the whole life cycle, consisting of education and action, theory and practice, must be uniformly integrated so that even the highest and rarest experiences have their proper place, and so that even the most lonely man is compelled to return to active service on behalf of the community.

Corruption

The *Thrasymachus* depicts the basic tension between just and unjust. The *Gorgias* transforms this theme into a struggle between philosophy and rhetoric during which the tension gradually rises to a new pitch. Step by step, "injustice" represented by rhetoric loses ground—and with each step, philosophy representing the sphere of "justice" gains ground. In the *Republic*, this basic tension is expressed in the contrast between the ideal state in the first place (Books II to VII) and then the defective types of government. The opposing forces, now represented as types of government, have thus changed their place. This change was possible because Plato used the *Thrasymachus* as a prelude to the *Republic*, so that the struggle against injustice has been fought out in advance, as it were, before the founding of the new city begins. The change was necessary because the nature of the defective states can be understood only from the perspective of the ideal state. A gradual ascent from the defective states to the ideal state cannot be envisaged. There is no step that would lead from even the best type of real state to the ideal, for the ideal state is a being completely of its own kind.

In a solemn spirit but with an admixture of playfulness as well, Plato constructed the perfect state out of basic facts of human life, thereby showing that the city he was founding, even though it be a wishful image, nevertheless corresponded to the natural laws of life. In a parallel fashion, he now envisages under the image of corruption the relationship of the empirical states to the perfect state. He reduces the empirical varieties to four basic types of governments and men, and he presents their respective distance from the ideal state and from the philosopher-king as a process of degeneration that leads in stages from the Form of justice to the most extreme forms of injustice. For what we find here is "not a comparison of different historical types of government but an analysis of constructive and destructive forces in the community."[51]

As the growth of the ideal state is anticipated in the myth of the creation of mankind told by Protagoras in the dialogue named after him (322A *et seq.*), so now Hesiod's myth of the five ages of man serves as the prototype for the process of corruption—even though it is also based on experience, including our own. Plato had cited the myth much earlier when he described how the different metals were mixed into human nature (415A). Now he comes back to it, mentioning Hesiod by name (546E). He begins this discourse on disintegration by solemnly invoking the Muses, "like Homer" (545D)—or rather like Hesiod—and presently, in the same solemn tone, constructs the nuptial number (which still troubles mathematicians today). Hesiod was both a poet and a thinker; Plato combines myth with mathematics in a still higher unity.

At each of the four stages of disintegration, as far as both the

government and the individual are concerned, Plato first describes the process of transformation (μεταβολή) into the new
type, and then describes the characteristics of this type. Thus,
each stage is in four parts. It is all the more noticeable that this
scheme, strictly observed at three stages, is expanded at the
last stage, that of tyranny, in order to raise the question about
the happiness enjoyed in this type of government and by this
type of man (556D et seq., 571A, 576B et seq.). This leads to the
examination that occupies the central part of Book IX (576B–
588A): the account of the happiness in store for the philosopher
and for the tyrant. Everything that precedes aims at this final
reckoning. When at last it comes, Plato shows the importance
of the theme by having Glaukon again take the place of his
brother as partner in the conversation. By this move we are
reminded that it was Glaukon who demanded this account of
happiness—at the end (361D) of his great speech in Book II.

Thus, the stages of corruption down to the level of tyranny
and the tyrant are clearly derived from a simple basic model
that was originally conceived in Plato's own mind and is integrated here, by way of the different stages, with Hesiod's myth
of the five ages of man. At the end of the *Thrasymachus*, there is
an account of the happiness of the unjust man. In the *Gorgias*,
first through Polos, then through Kallikles, the problem is expanded by inquiring into the happiness of the political orator,
the representative of the principle of injustice and, as it were,
a tyrant without an empire. The contrast of principles is translated, in the *Gorgias*, into a contrast of ways of life, and, in the
Republic, into the contrast of types of government. Instead of
the original simple contrast, however, there is a series of stages
in the *Republic*. Yet these are presented in such a way that the
sharp polarity comes through again in the end.

The unhappiness of the tyrant is shown here in three ways.
The first demonstration (576c–580c) is derived from the description of the type itself. The soul of the tyrant, like the
tyrannical state, is consumed by passions and, hence, is unfree.
In other words, despite all license, this type of state or
individual can do "least as he likes" (ἥκιστα ποιήσει ἃ ἂν
βουληθῇ, 577E), and the complete tyrant is in fact the complete

slave. So we hear in the very same words one of the main themes of the conversation with Polos in the *Gorgias* (οὐδὲν γὰρ ποιεῖν ὧν βούλονται, 466E). There the contrast between caprice (ἃ δοκεῖ) and a genuine act of will was made even more explicit. Here in the *Republic*, we find instead a richer abundance of observation, dominated, moreover, by the parallelism between state and individual so that the portrayal of the specific traits is intensified.

While the first demonstration of unhappiness is based directly on the portrayal itself, the other two proofs will involve a discussion of the concept of pleasure. This provides another link with the *Gorgias*, even as it is not accidental that, here in the *Republic*, the image of the sieve or leaky vessel is reinvoked as a symbol of the soul destroyed by pleasure or desire.[52] Yet this echo only serves to remind us that there is a profound difference between the two treatments of this topic. Instead of a radical struggle against pleasure—and even in the course of this, the difference between "better" and "worse" pleasures became significant—we find now, in the *Republic*, a graded system of pleasures. These pleasures are no longer simply fought but, as is increasingly characteristic of Plato in his later years, are ordered and integrated systematically.

The second demonstration (580D–583B) proceeds from the three "forms" (εἴδη, classes or parts) of the city and the soul. To each "form" there corresponds a desire appropriate to it— for money and acquisition, for victory and honor, for knowledge and wisdom, respectively. We are familiar with this grading from the *Phaedo* (68c, 82c). It also served as a guide to an understanding of the defective types of states, i.e., to explain the fall from the ideal state into timocracy and then into oligarchy. Now we are to learn, however, not only that a specific type of ruler and a specific kind of human nature correspond to each desire, but also—and this is new—that a specific kind of pleasure so corresponds. In other words, the desire of the philosopher is not, as in the *Phaedo* and the *Gorgias*, opposed to pleasure as such. For there is a kind of pleasure that belongs specifically to the desire of the philosopher. Only he can decide why philosophical pleasure is to be preferred to the others, for only he knows them all and only he has the proper tool for making this decision—the power of reason.

The third demonstration (583B–588A) is the most basic and profound. Anticipating results of the *Philebus*, it applies, surprisingly enough, the concept of truth to the nature of pleasure. In the *Gorgias*, pleasure, as something completely transitory, still seemed to be radically opposed to truth and the good. Now, however, genuine pleasure is looked upon as something positive. It is contrasted to apparent pleasure, which, strictly speaking, is only a kind of sublimated pain. The apparent pleasure rises—on an imaginary scale—from the bottom to a median point, or point of indifference; the genuine pleasure rises from the median point upward; and the error of the customary interpretation consists in mistaking a conditional superiority for an unconditional one.

A second consideration is still more important. Every desire has its source in a state of depletion; hence, it aims at completion; and the state of being refilled produces pleasure. But that which is filled and that which relieves a want differ in degrees of being and truth (οὐσία καὶ ἀλήθεια). Of these the soul has more than the body, knowledge more than eating and drinking. The pleasure co-ordinated with the act of refilling (or completion) also has different degrees of truth or reality. No longer, as in the *Gorgias* and the *Phaedo*, are truth and goodness opposites of pleasure. Even the pleasures of the body have their place and justification. The point is not to deny the claim of desire, but to subordinate it to reason. Thus the philosopher, too, knows all types of pleasure. But even as his soul is an ordered city in which there is no enemy within and no factionalism, or civil war (στάσις), so is there a hierarchy of pleasures in his soul ordered according to the degree of "truth" each contains.

Thus, the corruption of governments and of the human types associated with them corresponds to a decline also in true pleasure. At the end, when the distance separating the happiness of the philosopher from that of the tyrant is expressed in the playfully serious proportion of $729:1$ ($= 3^6:1$), we once more are made conscious of the ordered scale of political and human types that provides the general frame for the radical contrast between philosopher and tyrant.

The Last Ascent

Plato could not conclude the dialogue on this lowest level of corruption even if the final balance sheet of happiness had not been a reminder of the highest goal. Here, where he finally answers the question raised in Glaukon's speech at the beginning of Book II and thus closes the outer circle, the symmetry of the work alone demanded that Book I, the old dialogue *Thrasymachus* used anew and integrated, also be counterbalanced by—let us say, for the time being, *by something*.

The *Republic* grew out of the *Gorgias*. The *Gorgias* culminated in a myth of the beyond. If the myth was an organic component of the earlier work, it could not be absent from the later and greater work. The something, therefore, had to contain a mythical element.

What we have derived here from the aesthetic structure and the organic growth of the *Republic* may be understood on a higher level as being determined by a philosophical necessity. From Glaukon's speech in Book II on, the happiness of the just as against that of the unjust has been an open question. Even though the meaning of the word "happiness" (εὐδαιμονία) contains different and contradictory elements—perfect being, and pleasure—the desire for happiness is legitimate, for it is a natural impulse of life itself. But the kind of balance sheet of happiness drawn up here in the *Republic* toward the end of Book IX, on the model of pleasures, is incomplete and inadequate. And we need not say this merely in general terms, since we derive the same conclusion from an important passage in the *Laws* (V 732D *et seq.*).

There we find a comparison of different ways of life according to the degrees of pleasure and pain they contain. The general result is that, as compared with the contrary ways of life, a life of virtue not only is more advantageous in every other respect, but also is superior in "pleasure" and "joy" (κρατεῖ τῷ χαίρειν πλείω, 733A; ἡδίω εἶναι, 734D). This comes as the last "preamble" (προοίμιον) before the civil code itself is expounded. Its place in the work shows the importance of this comparison. And this importance may be explained by saying that man's life is involved, to the highest degree, in pleasure, pain, and desire (732E). Also, *as legislators*, we are dealing with men, not with gods. This is Plato's "natural" way of thinking, even—and especially—in his old age.

The preceding preambles in the *Laws* deal, on the other hand, with the gods, and with "what, after the gods, is the most divine thing in man—the soul" (726A). How we are to preserve and cultivate this divine thing, how it is corrupted by partaking of evil, what is the natural order of soul and body and possessions, and what follows from this order as far as education and legislation are concerned—all these matters are impressed upon us in solemn words. This is the "divine" aspect of things, to be followed by the balance of pleasures and pains in the "human" dimension. The two aspects complement each other necessarily. The human balance alone would be a vulgar hedonism; the divine level alone would be too high for human beings. This is how Plato always felt, as early as the *Protagoras*.[53] We realize why the *Republic* could not end with the account of human happiness. Here, too, this "human" perspective divorced from the "divine" would be only half the story and, hence, false. In the *Republic*, Plato had to place this account of higher happiness in that sphere where the soul comes face to face with true being.

Let us add a final point. Plato developed the *Republic* out of the thematic structure of the dialogue *Thrasymachus*. At the beginning of this early work we hear (through the old Kephalos) a reference, in a popular and noncommittal sense, to life after death, its rewards and punishments. Since this theme was mentioned before the discussion moved into the sphere of Socratic examination, it could not have any further consequences in the *Thrasymachus*. But as this theme grew in the development of Plato's work, he must have felt compelled, in the *Republic*, as soon as he used the earlier dialogue as its prelude, to complement at the end the tentative reference at the beginning by a genuine Platonic myth of the beyond.[54]

Previously we have been guided by the organic affinities between the *Gorgias* and the *Republic*. Now it must be said that, despite their affinities, the two works also differ significantly in structure. The *Gorgias* ascends in a uniform movement toward the level where Socratic power asserts itself ever more effectively and where the myth of life after death emerges as the natural culmination of the whole work. The structure of the *Republic* is quite different. Its highest peak is necessarily in the middle, in the founding of the ideal state itself. Then follows the descent through the defective constitutions. Although this part ultimately concludes with the balance sheet of happiness by which the highest Form again comes into view, a myth of the beyond could not organically follow immediately after the descent. A longer way was needed to reach this goal.

As point of departure, we may take knowledge of the nature of order (κόσμος, τάξις), which is what Socrates establishes through those renewed attacks in his struggle with Kallikles in the *Gorgias* (503D *et seq.*). What is ordered is good. What is disordered is bad, everywhere—in the object produced by the craftsman or artist, in the body, and in the soul. The order of the soul, however, is tantamount to the reign of law (*nomos*) and virtue (*arete*). This, in turn, provides a clue to the meaning of punishment, chastisement, discipline, and restrictions (κολάζειν). Punishment restores the order that was violated, and therefore punishment is better than what the many desire—licentiousness, lack of discipline (ἀκολασία), and escape from punishment (505A *et seq.*, 507D). Later in the *Gorgias'* critique of the great statesmen, the metaphor appears comparing man to a domestic animal that is tame when his trainers take him in hand but then grows wilder than he was to begin with, because of bad care, i.e., lack of discipline. He bites, kicks, and butts with his horns. The task of the true statesman and educator is to make man "tamer"—or, dropping the metaphor, "more just" (516A *et seq.*).

In the *Republic* (588B *et seq.*) we find, right after the balance of happiness, the construction of the soul as a fantastic compound of a man, a lion surrounded by snakes, and a many-headed beast having all over itself tame and wild animal heads which it can produce and change by itself.[55] The whole, in turn, is contained inside a single man representing the living body. This picture reflects the states of the human soul. There is the state of order when these elements so joined together are friends and the "inner man" rules. There are all sorts of vices when this relationship is disturbed, because the lion nature prevails or the snake nature, or else the many-headed beastly desires rule. Punishment is when the beast is appeased and the tame nature released. As for the opinion of the many that to escape from punishment is preferable to being punished, what else does it mean but that the many-headed beast is set free at the expense of the "inner man"?

This line of thought corresponds exactly to that of the *Gorgias*.[56] In both cases, it prepares the ground, as we shall see, for the myth of life after death. Did the full-fledged picture of the *Republic* not grow out of the rudiments in the *Gorgias*? The creative impulse in Plato impelled him to represent the structure of the soul pictorially. It is the same impulse that later will create the image of the chariot in the *Phaedrus* and the metaphor of the puppets in the *Laws*.[57] Here it seems to have fixed upon the contrast between tame and wild animals, elaborating the core image into this fantastically magnificent portrait. A trace of it is preserved at the beginning of the *Phaedrus* (230A) in the "monster that is more labyrinthine than the giant Typhon."

This particular matter is less important to us, however, than it is to show the correspondence between this section of the *Republic* and its counterpart in the *Gorgias*, since we are laying the ground here for the preliminary hypothesis that the fantastic portrait in each dialogue is a stage on the way to the myth. It goes without saying that the hypothesis can be confirmed only by following the movement of the *Republic* itself.

There the ratio 729:1 is said, at the conclusion of the survey of corrupt governments (587DE), to be the relative scale of happiness applying to the philosopher-king and the tyrant. The same proportion holds for a year of 364½ days and a day of twelve hours as it does for the "great year" of Philolaos (consisting of 729 months) and a single month.[58] So this numerical expression not only is "true," but also "applies to human life" (προσήκοντα βίοις) unfolding in the temporal sequences of days, months, and years. This is definitely not idle play.[59] Length of life and amount of happiness are related to each other in various ways. Perhaps Plato intends to suggest that we are not dealing here solely with the exceptional cases of philosopher-king and tyrant, but that this struggle for justice determines human life as such. Yet above all, he is saying that the distance dividing one kind of happiness from another becomes negligible when we compare inner order, or virtue, with its opposite, for in the end these are simply opposites, i.e., there is no way of comparing them.

Be that as it may, the conversation at once shifts in a peculiar way. Instead of philosopher-king and tyrant, the just man and the unjust man (588A 1) are now to be compared. Yet, while it was still possible to compare the happiness of the tyrant with that of the philosopher-king, such a comparison is practically meaningless once we come to see the difference between the good and just, and the wicked and unjust. And as the abundance of political types in the *Republic* grew out of this radical contrast in the *Thrasymachus*, so Plato here returns to the point of origin. He returns, in a cyclical movement, to the question raised at the beginning of Book II, whether perfect injustice under the disguise of justice is not advantageous to the individual (588B ~ 360C). In fact, he goes back still farther, to the beginning of the whole work, by addressing himself again to the view proposed by Thrasymachos that a tyrant would exercise his power to harm those over whom he rules. In Book I, Socrates protested against this view in words that pointed ahead toward a "state of perfectly good men if such a state could be realized" (347D 2). Now the picture of the "inner republic" makes it quite clear that the ruling principle, being akin to the divine, cannot possibly intend to harm anybody, and that all other powers submit willingly to the ruling principle or must be subordinated. It is significant that these references to the beginning of the work do not disappear even in the concluding parts. The power of the adversary remains present to the end.[60]

The formal needs of the artist who is here completing his

work would be merely external devices if the content did not correspond to them. Up to the point of measuring the scale of happiness, we had moved in the political domain. After the founding of the ideal city there followed its disintegration. The defective constitutions corresponded, in turn, to defective human types also viewed from a political perspective. After the balance sheet of happiness, however, we return to the more primitive view, as it were, out of which the political view had arisen. It is only in this general perspective that we can study the true laws of human life that are valid for everybody even if one does not recognize himself in the philosopher-king, in the tyrant, or even in any of the in-between types. That is the true meaning of the aesthetic closures, especially the mythical image of the many-shaped monster called "man."

This mythical image shows human nature in its manifold complexity that eludes one's grasp. At the same time, it imposes on man the task—for a Platonic myth also entails a moral imperative—to create an ordered unity out of this complexity. The image is radical because it shows human nature as it is, quite apart from its place in a political community. This radical view of the "inner republic" and its order is made explicit at the end of this section (i.e., the end of Book IX) by means of a twofold outlook, upon the empirical state and upon the ideal state. He who has achieved harmony in his "inner republic" will always remain an alien in the city of his birth (as Plato did in the Athens of his time)—"except by some divine contingency" (a phrase that Dion must have thought referred to him). A man with this inner harmony belongs only to the ideal state. But the ideal state at this moment disappears from earth to be "laid up in heaven," where it remains visible forever as the pattern of high order in the realm of high order.

After the types of government and the corresponding human types, then man himself . . . Thus, the discussion is pulled together by leaving the external aspects of politics behind in order to absorb them, as it were, in the concept of the "inner republic" of man. Let us not forget that the founding of the ideal city was undertaken in order to show justice and its opposite "in large letters" (368D). Even as the mythical image at the end of

Book IX was more radical than what preceded it, so does it contain the seeds for the still more radical expression that will culminate in the concluding myth of the *Republic*.

Two lines point in this direction. First, man has in himself an "inner republic." It is presided over by a "ruling element," the "man within" (589A 7), the "divine" principle (589D 1, 590D 1). What this consists of was shown in the central section of the work—as much as it can be shown in words. There it was called the "best in the soul" (532c) and its goal was said to be the "vision of the best in the realm of being." The path to this goal is recalled briefly now by mentioning the "objects of study" (μαθήματα, 591c 2). The second line begins where the true state disappears from earthly reality in order to be "laid up as a pattern in heaven" (592B 2). The heavens, a system of high order, as the location of this state, and the state itself conceived as the pattern, are features this state has in common with the world of Forms. The divine soul and the ordered system of heavenly bodies as the location for the soul and its vision—both of these elements will be brought together in the concluding myth.

But this myth could not as yet come here. For what is its function? It serves to extend the life of the soul beyond the limits of this life. The many-shaped monster whose "inner republic" had to be set in order was explicitly conceived, however, as being limited in body (precisely because the physical harmony must be subordinated to the harmony of the soul— 591D) and, hence, it is limited in time as well. Nothing great can grow in the short span of time from child to old man 608c–614A (608c). Thus, a new aspect of the soul must be introduced, not BOOK X canceling what has gone before but rather absorbing and raising it, in order to serve as the basis for the concluding myth.

This new aspect of the soul is not developed, as in the *Phaedrus*, from a theory in natural philosophy. Instead, it is derived from the basic position inherent in the *Republic* itself, the opposition of just and unjust. The body has a specific "evil," or its own defective condition (πονηρία)—illness. In the extreme case, illness destroys the body. The soul has its own specific "evil"—injustice, or wickedness (κακία) in general.

But, unlike the body, the soul cannot be destroyed by this evil, even in its extreme form. Hence, the soul is indestructible, immortal, and eternal.

So runs this "proof of immortality." We cannot miss the ironic tone Socrates adopts, at the outset, in asserting that there is "nothing difficult" about it, thereby pointing to the doubts in the mind of his partner—and in our own minds as well (608D). For as a proof *more geometrico,* this deductive argument is absurd. Yet, as an insight into the nature of good and evil, as an insight into the soul, it is most profound. Heretofore the soul had been envisaged by analogy with the body. This still was the case in the image of the many-headed monster. The soul, to be sure, was held in higher esteem (τιμιωτέρα, 591B) than the body, but the parallelism between the health of the body and the "healthy state of mind" called *sophrosyne* seemed to be unbroken. Now, however, we have reached the place—similar to the third and highest level of the *Phaedo* (see p. 57, above)— where analogy breaks down and the soul is sharply separated from the body.

The body has the good fortune that it can be released from its sufferings when it is dissolved after death. The soul is not so fortunate. It is indestructible, and this means something quite different from what fearful minds think it means. Immortality is not an escape from nothingness, but a great, *yes, the only* threat, and a great, *yes, the only* task. We cannot dispose of this threat and this task by saying, Before long it will all be over. When I fix my mind on the fact that there is just and unjust, good and evil, knowledge and ignorance, and when I know from the *Republic* that these terms designate the two fundamental possibilities of the soul (i.e., of man himself), and when I know, again from the *Republic,* that justice and the good are *Ideas,* eternal Forms, then I cannot envisage the soul, indissolubly united with the body, as something that is immortal and that is also concerned with just and unjust, but I must instead envisage the soul as the eternal and indestructible field of battle between justice and injustice. The basic contrast of the *Republic* requires and confirms the eternal life of the soul.

Thus, we have gained the new aspect of the soul. And the

aspect we had seen before is not canceled but is raised to a higher level. The way leading from one level to the other is shrouded in semidarkness, as is suggested (611c *et seq.*) in the mythical image of the sea god whose original nature can hardly be recognized because he has lived so long in the ocean. To return to its original nature akin to the gods—in short, purification—is the task imposed upon the soul. The precinct of the myth describing the rites of purgation for the eternal soul has almost been reached.

Almost, but not quite. Since Glaukon's speech at the beginning of Book II, we have focused on the question of the happiness enjoyed by the just as compared with the unjust. Plato does not intend to evade this question because a natural impulse of life is behind it. In Book VI, where education through the different stages of life had reached the period of old age and we read about the happiness accompanying this educational process, we pursued the theme of happiness, for a moment, beyond the limits of this life. We glimpsed a life after death corresponding to such happiness, and a future rebirth when the philosophical insights gained in the former life would be continued. The same vista again comes into view in connection with the balance sheet of happiness in Book IX, at the conclusion of the section on the defective states. This is where the discussion takes a turn toward a final radicalization. The two aspects of the soul are unfolded, and again, the question as to its "reward," i.e., its happiness, is admitted only after the nature of the soul has been clarified (612AB). Yet now there can be no objection to the question (νῦν ἤδη ἀνεπίφθονον, 612B). And now it can no longer be evaded.

Two stages of reward correspond to the two aspects of the soul, although neither is distinguished pedantically.[61] The second stage where the "soul itself" may confront "justice itself" (612B) is taken over into the myth. The question as to what the soul's rewards and punishments are in the confines of this life on earth is the last link leading to the myth.

"The good man is loved by the gods. Hence, all things must ultimately prove good for him both in life and in death. For the gods do not neglect a man who has pursued the task of becom-

ing like a god as far as this is possible for man." So speaks
Socrates, and his partner replies: "Yes, it is reasonable that
such a man should not be neglected by his like." We cannot miss
hearing in this exchange the literal echo of words spoken in the
Apology (41D). Now, however, their justification is grounded
more deeply, pointing back to the ascent toward the highest
good in Book VII and pointing forward to the "digression" in
the *Theaetetus* (176B). What profound irony that Plato's
Socrates in turning to the earthly rewards and reminding us of
his own fate can ultimately put the prize bestowed by the gods
only into the hands of men!

And what about these human rewards (613B)? Simple
enough. Everything will be fine and great and very respectable.
The just carry off honor and prizes among their fellow men at
the outcome of every action and at the end of life. As they
grow older, they hold offices of prestige in the city as they
wish, and enter into marriage as they like with the best families.
And the unjust in the end suffer the reverse. This is a passage
that could make one lose his taste for all of Plato—if the passage
had to be taken in complete seriousness.[62]

But does not the discussion immediately introduce an ironic
qualification? All will be well for the man loved by the gods—
except in so far as he may have to atone for offenses committed
in a former life (613A). And did we not just hear an echo from
the *Apology?* "The good man will not be neglected by the gods"
—so that we may know, from the perspective of Socrates' own
fate, what the "end" of life is like when the just receive honor
and prizes from their fellow men. A peculiar prize of victory it
was that the Athenians bestowed upon Socrates! Also, the
promise that the just man on reaching the proper age will hold
high office in the city sounds rather funny after we have been
told not long ago (IX 592) that the wise man will have nothing to do with any public life in his community. And, as far
as marriages with the best families are concerned, should this
prospect be taken in dead seriousness—Socrates being the
speaker?

Let us not forget that we have here, especially in what is said
about the final sufferings of the unjust, a reply to the threat

voiced by Glaukon (II 362B). Socrates descends to the level of
the many and returns to them their own verdict in reverse. And
at the end, after so many qualifications, this section is made
worthless in the sentence that leads to the myth of the beyond.
"All these things are nothing in number or magnitude when
compared with the things that await man after death." Indeed,
compared with the *eterno dolore* suffered by the tyrant Ardiaios,
it is as nothing whether he previously ruled on earth "under the
disguise of justice, whether he could marry as he wished and
enjoyed every kind of advantage and gain" (II 362B), or
whether his life was in the bad state that Glaukon predicts for
the just man and Socrates predicts for the unjust.

595A–608B
BOOK X

Between the two views of the soul, there is a section that we
have so far passed by except in survey. This is the struggle
against Homer and the tragic poetry derived from him. In the
concluding part of this work seemingly composed of a series of
interludes—each of which has nonetheless been shown to be an
integral part of the whole—this section is quite appropriately
called an interlude. Those who think it is simply a piece of
polemics are wrong, as they always are wrong when they read
Plato merely in this light. Yet they have felt the strange character of this interlude more deeply than those who think that in
the "arbitrary composition" of this concluding part, it does not
matter whether there is one digression more or less.[63]

As a matter of fact, we are fully prepared for this section. The
speech of Adeimantos in Book II (364CD) had given rise to the
struggle against the poets (Homer in the forefront) because
they propagated the wrong theology. Moreover, a major part
of the educational theory developed in Books II and III consisted in combating the myths of Homer and his successors,
especially the tragic poets, in order to lay the foundations for
the new view of the gods and for the new morality (380C
et seq.). In contrast to the legends told about the gods fighting
with each other and changing their shapes and being the source
both of evil and good, there is presented in the central part of
the *Republic* a view of the unchanging Forms up to the highest,
the *Idea* or Form of the Good. And finally, after the founding of
the "inner republic," in Book IX (591D), we are told that the

harmony of the body must aim at the harmony of the soul if the individual "is to be a truly musical man." These words point backward, to the educational theory in Books II and III, and forward as well. For as Socrates, at the beginning of the *Phaedo*, gives an ironic and puzzling interpretation of the order, received in a dream, to "practice the arts of the Muses," so here in the *Republic* the words referring to the "truly musical man" prepare the ground for the struggle that is fought through in the first part of Book X. Here we see how tragic poetry disturbs the balance of the "inner republic" (605B, 608B) and, at the end of this section, we find that poetry, in its significance and danger, is placed side by side with money, honor, and power —in other words, alongside those forces that previously (591E *et seq.*) had threatened the structure of this "inner republic."

Undoubtedly, the struggle against the poets as agents who foster a false theology and destroy the true one (a struggle originally launched, as we have seen, in the speech of Adeimantos in Book II) still required a final and systematic clarification. This could be done only on the basis of the ontology developed in Book VII.[64] But we cannot say why, in terms of the over-all structure of the work, this final encounter should come here, placed as it is between the two views of the soul and shortly before the concluding myth. There are paintings in which one figure looks out upon the spectator. Does it belong to the painting? Unquestionably, for the whole picture would collapse if the figure were taken out. Yet, indispensable as the figure is for the painting as a whole, it also is removed from the painting, as it were, by virtue of looking out of it. Let us say that Plato's interlude on the poets has a similarly dual status. The "old discord between philosophy and poetry" (607B) that first broke out in the *Ion*, and struggles for a reconciliation within Plato himself, here finds its most powerful expression—*here*, almost at the end of Plato's greatest work, in which philosophy and poetry are combined. For it is indeed here that Plato claims for himself and for his philosophical poetry[65] the very place that he compels the tragic poets along with Homer, their ancestor, to vacate.

The Mythical Line of the Work

Parallel to the critique of traditional mythology runs the construction of the new myth by means of a new poetry. At the end of the work, the new myth makes its appearance, yet not as suddenly as some might think. We have shown how the ground for it is laid in popular conceptions about life after death (heard about from Kephalos in Book I), and how introductory and concluding myth, in their connection as well as in their profound contrast, provide the frame for the tension that stretches from the beginning to the end of the *Republic*. It remains to be shown now that the mythical line also comes into view at crucial places throughout the work.

At the end of Book III (414B *et seq.*), where the founding of the city has been sketched out (ὡς ἐν τύπῳ), we find the fairy tale about human beings fashioned out of different metals, gold, silver, iron, and bronze, in the depths of the earth, and then sent forth into the light of day by their mother Earth. In Book VI, when Adeimantos speaks with the voice of experience against the central paradox of the *Republic* (the thesis that philosophers be kings), we find the fate of the philosopher in actual society illustrated through Socrates' metaphor of a ship's crew rising in mutiny (488A *et seq.*) because they do not understand the true navigator. At the beginning of Book VII, where the *Idea* of the Good is revealed in its copy and its effect and where its "being beyond being" is intimated, we find the simile of the cave. In Book IX (588B *et seq.*), we find the concrete image of the creature composed of a man, a lion, and a many-headed beast, all enclosed in human shape. The figure of the sea god Glaukos, whose original shape is unrecognizable because of the many accretions and mutilations he has undergone, helps to bridge the gap between the first image of the soul and the second image (X 611c) where the soul is shown to be eternal, immortal, and no longer manifold. It is no accident that the simile of the cave stands at the center of the whole work, preceded by the description of the ordered and disordered states and followed by the two images of the soul, with the two myths of life after death standing one at the beginning and one at the end of the whole work.

Yet these mythical components differ from each other. Only the last one is a genuine myth, genuine because—as a whole—it can only be listened to and followed. Except for details, it cannot be interpreted or cast into another form. The story about the metals is presented as a useful deception (γενναῖον ψεῦδος), in the sense previously justified (382CD, 389B). It should serve to persuade, perhaps not the rulers but at least the lower classes, of two things: first, of the necessary unity of the city—this is the meaning of the "Cadmean" element (birth from the womb of the same mother), and second, of the necessary hierarchy—this is the meaning of the "Hesiodic" element (the different metals). And the simile of the cave does not even take the form of a story or a myth. It is rather something like a parable used for the purpose of illustration, and the image (εἰκών) employed is interpreted subsequently (517A et seq.) in its individual features. Similarly, the other elements are "images" (488A 1, 588B 10) or comparisons (611C 7).

But despite these essential differences, all of these elements are infused with the same mythopoeic fantasy, which produces various connections among them. It is probably due to the parallelism between state and soul that the metaphor of the mutinous crew in Book VI evokes the image of the soul in Book IX. In order to depict the conditions in a corrupt state one must proceed like the painters who paint goat-stags or similar mixed creatures, Socrates says (VI 488A), and in the later passage, the image of the many-shaped soul evokes comparisons with just such mythological creatures, like Chimaira, Skylla, and Kerberos (IX 588C). The mutinous sailors in the earlier passage represent the elements of desire in the state. In the later passage, the heads of the animals, both tame and wild, also represent desires. The sailors fight to death to get control of the wheel, for they want to "rule," and, at the same time, eat and drink well (εὐωχουμένους, 488C 6). The many-headed beast wants to grow strong and eat and drink well (εὐωχοῦντι, 588E 5). The animals fight and bite each other

(589A 4). In the first case, there is the "true navigator" whom the sailors call a stargazer, babbler, and good-for-nothing. So, in the later case, there is the danger that the "inner man" will be torn up by the other elements even though his proper task would be to rule over them and create peace and friendship among them.

The images of the soul, in turn, flow into the concluding myth about the fate of the soul after death. The image introduced by the sea god Glaukos shows the contrast between the "pure" state of the soul that is properly its own, and its present state in which "earth, stone, and wild substances have grown around it." This contrast as it applies to the soul itself returns in the concluding myth, but is distributed here among different souls. There are those who arrive "pure" from their heavenly voyage, others "from the earth full of dirt and dust." The choosing of lots in the concluding myth is a reminder of the lion and the heads of the tame and wild animals used in the first image of the soul. Ajax chooses the life of a lion. He is nothing but "courage." In the image, the heads of the animals are exchangeable (588c 9), and if the "inner man" is the ruler, he will cultivate the tame heads and suppress the wild ones (589AB). In the myth, men change into animals and animals change into men, the unjust into wild animals, the just into tame animals. What happens in the imagery to the soul as such happens here in the myth to different souls, and the words at the end that they "undergo mixtures of every kind" (πάσας μείξεις μείγνυσθαι, 620D 5) perhaps describe a process out of which the kind of mixed creature is produced as in the earlier imagery of the soul (μειγνύντες, 488A 7).

Let us look, finally, at the story of the metals, the simile of the cave, and the concluding myth. All three of them employ the spatial contrast of lower and upper spheres, the notion of ascending from one to the other, and the contrast of types of men whose existence moves in these respective spheres. The spatial poles in the story of the metals refer to a contrast in human nature. The lower spheres are the womb of nature out of which human beings grow into various shapes. Thus, the difference between men is rooted biologically and so is their ascent.

Or rather, their ascent is not of their own free will, since the earth "brings them forth" as if they were plants. In the simile of the cave, the spatial contrast between lower and upper spheres as reinforced by the contrast between darkness and light refers to the characteristics of the genuinely human or spiritual existence. Here the ascent—the forming of man—is a genuinely human or spiritual process, and the differences among men, their sympathies and antipathies, are determined by whether or not they partake of this ascent.

The concluding myth preserves the differences among men, but this difference is now expanded to apply to the contrast between just and unjust, pious and impious, good and evil. The notions of ascent and descent still include the contrast between light and darkness and thus between knowledge and ignorance, but what dominates the scene now is the image of judgment, reward and punishment, salvation and perdition. Thus, the mythical line of the *Republic* illuminates the three stages of the work—the foundations of the city in nature (*physis*), the ascent into education (*paideia*), and the culmination in justice (*dike*). *Physis* and *paideia* are absorbed into the realm of *dike*. The power of nature is represented by Necessity (*Ananke*) and her daughters, the Fates. The spindle of the world represents, in a visible image, the highest object of knowledge. And when we are advised in the last sentence of the whole work "to keep to the upward way (τῆς ἄνω ὁδοῦ) and cultivate justice in conjunction with wisdom," we should not try to decide whether this is the way to the judgment in the hereafter or the ascent from the cave. It is both, for the simile of the cave gleams through the myth of the beyond.

The Existential Mode of the "Republic"

After it is recognized that a metaphorical-mythical line runs through the entire *Republic*, there emerges the final question as to the existential status of this political construction.

The ideal state has its place in the *logoi*. It dwells in the "sphere of words," not here on earth (592A). It is "speech" (λέξις), not a "happening" or an "action" (πρᾶξις, 473A). But these characteristics do not deprive the ideal state of reality, as common opinion would have it in Plato's day even as now.[66] *Logos* is not a "mere word," but is a word directed toward the "truth," toward true being. Thought is not a feeble forerunner of action, nor does it weakly straggle behind. On the contrary, as Socrates says—in a paradoxical reversal of the customary view—practice necessarily "partakes less of the truth" than thought does (473A). Whatever truth or reality there is in practice is borrowed from the *logos*.

Myth is a kind of "thought" (*logos*)—a kind, however, that in a narrower and stricter sense is also opposed to thought. Yet, in addition to its being located in the realm of discourse and thought, this ideal state is also a myth, the telling of a story. This dual aspect suddenly was revealed in an untranslatable phrase that combines myth and thought (ἣν μυθολογοῦμεν λόγῳ, 501E), and again in the description of the degeneration of soul and state told on the model of Hesiod's myth of the ages of mankind. It is significant that, just at this point, Socrates— as if he were Homer—invokes the Muses. Moreover, he then proceeds, in the mythical manner of the *Timaeus* and yet in a strict, mathematical fashion, to construct the nuptial number that determines the moment (*kairos*) of the right births which, if missed, causes the initial corruption of human nature.

Every component piece, therefore, is "right" only when it is viewed within the structure of the dialogue as a whole. The censorious criticism of individual institutions, which occurs from Aristotle on, misses the total mythical structure of the work.[67] At the same time, the word "myth" must not be used to cover up all differences. We would in no way deny the importance of realizing that Plato, whether he is showing the rise or the decline of the ideal city, writes not like a learned historian or sociologist but *numine afflatus*.[68] Nevertheless, we also can see, especially by comparison with the myth of creation in the *Timaeus*, how much closer Plato's "tragedy" (τραγικῶς, *Republic* VIII 545E 1) of the disintegration of soul and state is to the actual world of human and historical reality than the miracle of the universe is. The abundance of empirical material contained in this "tragedy" of the *Republic* may be appreciated when we realize that the transition from democracy to tyranny reveals many specific features we have experienced in our own time in Germany, 2300 years later.

So the *Republic* hovers between reason (*logos*) and myth. It is a product of reason, or thought, not only in a general sense but in a strict sense, because it deals with the world of true being. And it has a mythical quality in so far as it describes a realm of possibility transcending all human experience, and in so far as myth may be envisaged "as a curve whose focal point is the Form (*Eidos*)."[69] The *Republic* is not genuine myth, if only because genuine myths always reach into the beyond of human existence—whether the beyond is called death, or love, or the cosmic spheres. Nor is it always and everywhere a product of pure reason, because the state though related to the realm of true being also belongs to the world of becoming in its aspects of growth and decay. It is "play" (536C, 545E) that is at the same time imbued with a profoundly serious spirit, in the genuinely Platonic "interpenetration of seriousness and play which is more impenetrable than steel and granite."[70] What must be combined in an encompassing view of the *Republic* are these two facts: that, on the one hand, Socrates invokes the Muses in the manner of the poets (545D) and that, on the other hand, he asserts emphatically (378E) that "for now" we are not poets but founders of a city. The *Republic* is at once a work of the Muses, the product of philosophical reflection, and political action.

The most paradoxical aspect of this state (ἀδοξία, 473C 8; παρὰ δόξαν, 473E 4) is the fact that its existence is almost impossible—or possible only under circumstances almost inconceivable and absurd from the point of view of common sense. But if these circumstances should prevail—and nobody controls this conditional—this state is not only possible but immediately real, so real that it is the only true state, related as it is to the realm of true being. If realized, this state is the salvation of man. Without it there is nothing but ruin. Yet, this state is indifferent to whether or not it is realized on earth because it represents the true reality in the political domain, whereas the so-called empirical governments are only more or less corrupt copies of this reality. Furthermore, even under the most favorable circumstances, this state could be realized only approximately, because action always is further removed from the truth than theory is. Thus, this state has its proper place in heaven rather than on earth (592B), not in the sense that it should disappear from man's sight, but precisely in order for it to be seen all the more clearly as "example and pattern for those who are determined to see and to constitute their inner republic" in its image. The ideal state is not itself an *Idea*, or Form, since its central structure is based on the knowledge of Forms. Still it acquires features associated with the Forms— eternal being, and the aspect of being a pattern—and it is related to the various states in actual life as the Forms are related to their variously defective copies.

We would avoid any simple formula, then, in characterizing the existential mode of Plato's *Republic*. And we cannot do otherwise, for we are dealing here not with a specific area of Plato's world, but with the central task of his life.

As Cicero assured his son in the opening words of *De officiis*, he "always brought Roman and Greek thought together." This he most certainly did do in his *De re publica*, which became the foundation of Roman philosophy of the state. Moreover, in so Romanizing Plato's *Republic*, Cicero prepared the way for the principate of Augustus, which (according to Eduard Meyer) was "the form of state whose outlines Cicero had sketched in his treatise on the state." Thus, Plato's ideal state—indirectly —has had a very great effect on real political history.

THIRD PERIOD

THE LATE DIALOGUES

PART I

Dialectics

TWENTY-THREE

Theaetetus

THE conversation of Socrates, Theodoros, the mathematician, and the young Theaitetos is conducted as a straight dramatic dialogue without any narrative insertions. This dramatic technique is found in some of Plato's earliest writings, then in the *Cratylus*, the *Gorgias*, the *Meno*, and especially in the late works—in short, whenever the human-spiritual world is presupposed or suggested rather than fully developed. The *Symposium*, the *Phaedo*, and the *Republic* represent the other group of dialogues, where the conversation is narrated in the context of a rich setting. The *Theaetetus*, however, is the only dialogue of the straight dramatic form that is preceded by an introductory conversation of the kind found in the *Symposium* and the *Phaedo*. The actual conversation in the *Theaetetus* is not an oral report but instead is read, the only time this happens in a Platonic dialogue. The introductory conversation sets the stage for this reading; hence, it seems to be easily separated from the main body of the dialogue. In fact, in late antiquity a different introduction was known, and was characterized by a literary critic as "rather chilly" (ὑπόψυχρον). Ancient interpreters of Plato as well as modern ones have often approached the dialogue as if it originally did not include the introductory setting at all.[1]

The introductory conversation has a threefold significance for the work. In the first place, like the opening conversation in the *Symposium*, it serves to fix the (ideal) historical accuracy of the report. Eukleides heard the conversation from Socrates himself and has frequently checked back with Socrates in order

142A–143C

145

to correct any mistakes in the version he had written down.[2] In the second place, this conversation, like those at the beginning of the *Symposium* and the *Parmenides*, serves to reinforce the importance of the main conversation, still completely alive as it is a full generation after the death of Socrates. And a third value of the prelude concerns the portrait of Theaitetos, the chief partner in the conversation with Socrates. In the main conversation, Theaitetos is the intelligent young man, especially gifted in mathematics. But the more his talent (in the course of the dialogue) is shown on the intellectual level, the more important it becomes that, at the very beginning of the report, other things are told about him—that Theaitetos not only has a quick intelligence, but also combines in his character such opposite qualities as a gentle disposition and a courageous spirit (144A). The introductory conversation shows the fulfillment of what in the main conversation must be taken on the word of Theodoros. For Theaitetos himself was fatally wounded while fighting bravely in the battle before Corinth. Plato undoubtedly is setting up a memorial here for that young man who was killed in the year 369, but even this gesture must not be taken in a personal sense only. When the intelligent youth of high character is shown as a man who preserved his courage unto death, this goes beyond praising him as a person. It also is a presentation of what for Plato was a perfect human type.[3]

Still more important for the work is a fourth gain to be derived from the introductory conversation. Without it an unforgettable scene in the main conversation (172c–177c) would be incomprehensible. There Socrates, apparently for no special reason, takes up the subject of how those who have spent a long time in philosophical pursuits make themselves ridiculous when they appear in court. This sudden digression is indeed baffling—if we have forgotten the introductory conversation or dismissed it as a later addition. For in this opening scene, we learn (142c 6) that Socrates "shortly before his own death" had met the young Theaitetos. And at the end of the dialogue, Socrates will say that now he must go to the portico of the King-Archon to answer the indictment drawn up against him by Meletos. These last words of the dialogue refer dramatically to the beginning. Facing his own trial, his own ultimate decision, then, Socrates undertakes this subtle "epistemological" inquiry. Beginning and end of the dialogue support the scene in between. And this scene, rising high above the level of the actual investigation, shows the sublime yet precarious existence of the philosopher.[4] Still, has this dialogue perhaps quite another significance besides its being the "basic text of Plato's theory of knowledge"?[5]

What, finally, does it mean that Plato chose the Megarians, Eukleides and Terpsion, as speakers in the introductory conversation? Was it only because, as you came from Corinth, the city of Megara was a stop on the way to Athens? Or was it also because the Megarian school, practicing a kind of dialectics in the tradition of Parmenides and Zeno, represents a stage leading toward Socrates-Plato, even as the Pythagorean community of Phlius does in the introductory conversation of the *Phaedo?* Perhaps Plato also intended to suggest through the name Eukleides that there *is* a kind of perfect being, "called by many names, thought, God, spirit, etc."[6]—in short, a reality that from the very beginning resists sophistic dissolution.

The introductory conversation unquestionably serves also as an expression of gratitude toward Eukleides, with whom Plato and other disciples of Socrates had taken refuge thirty years earlier, after the death of Socrates. But what does the dedication mean, beyond this personal dimension? Terpsion and Eukleides appear one other time, in the *Phaedo*. There they are the last in the long enumeration of companions cited by the narrator as being present at the death of Socrates. It is inconceivable that Plato would not have remembered this detail when he was composing the introductory conversation of the *Theaetetus*, and it is hardly any more conceivable that he would not wish his readers to be reminded of this connection. (These two works, incidentally, are also the only dialogues in which the scene for the introductory conversation is set away from Athens.) Thus, we must recall the events described in the *Phaedo*, events that took place thirty years back. And from this perspective, the accent on the phrase "shortly before his death" weighs even more heavily. This is another way of realizing that it is too narrow a view to see the *Theaetetus* as concerned only with the theory of knowledge—unless theory of knowledge has something to do with death.

143D–145E   The scene is in the palaestra, though this is not said at the beginning and is just barely suggested later on. First Socrates talks with Theodoros, a mathematician from Cyrene, about the young Theaitetos. Then Theaitetos himself enters as the middle figure among a group of his contemporaries, who will be mentioned occasionally later on (168D 8) as well. The general setting and movement of the scene are reminiscent of the *Charmides*, the *Lysis*, and the *Euthydemus*. There also are similarities in some of the specific features. For example, we find Socrates again asking, as in the *Charmides*, who the most promising young men are (although here in the *Theaetetus* the question is stated in a more complicated way). There is, too, the detail from the *Lysis* that Socrates does not know the name of the young man.[7] Theodoros occupies the same place in the dialogue, at least to begin with, that Kritias does in the *Charmides*. Since he knows the young man, he serves—in the dramatic context—both as mediator between Socrates and Theaitetos and as a mirror reflecting the image of Theaitetos for the reader. These similarities are significant. Furthermore, when we consider that the dialogue's dominant question, soon to be raised, is *What is knowledge (episteme)?*, even as the *Charmides* asked, What is moderation?, and the *Lysis* asked, What is friendship?, and that the answers to all of these questions are inconclusive, then it becomes clear that, with the *Theaetetus*, Plato takes over into the work of his late maturity the structure of the aporetic dialogues in search of a definition.[8]

The somewhat ceremonial conversation between Socrates and Theodoros reveals the personal dimension that will support the later discussion of problems. Socrates asks the mathematician who the most promising young man is, not among the youth of Cyrene, but among the youth of Athens—for it is in Athens that Socrates fulfills his mission. Theaitetos is mentioned as the most gifted. He is said to combine within himself such different qualities as quick intelligence and good memory, as well as firmness and natural poise, or gentleness as well as a brave spirit. To discuss "epistemological" questions with someone who is intelligent yet also cowardly or intemperate might be possible by modern standards, but it is thoroughly anti-Platonic. On the contrary, the reader is supposed to remember that a combination of opposite "virtues" similar to Theaitetos' is called for in the tale of the philosopher-king in the *Republic* (485A *et seq.*), where music and gymnastics serve to prepare the ground for this unified structure of the soul. And at the end of the *Statesman* (309E *et seq.*), Plato still defines the task of the royal statesman as the weaving together into one garment of the two basic dispositions in man, aggressive courage and restraining measure, while in the *Laws* (V 731B *et seq.*), he establishes the rule that the "good" man should combine the opposites of courage and moderation.[9]

Such nobility, then, Theaitetos possesses as a gift of nature. And just as the nature of moderation (*sophrosyne*) could be discussed only with Charmides who possesses this virtue in its natural form, so the inquiry into the nature of knowledge can be conducted only with Theaitetos. From this perspective, the emphasis on Theaitetos' ugliness as resembling that of Socrates is also more than a reminder (as much as it is that, too) of personal traits. This resemblance to Socrates—does it not go beyond such traits as snub nose and bulging eyes? And as far as ugliness is concerned, are we not reminded, on the one hand, of the beautiful youths whom Plato showed us in his early dialogues and, on the other hand, of Diotima's ladder of love on whose higher level "even a feeble blossom of the body" suffices to kindle love if only the soul is beautiful (*Symposium* 210B 8)? Or, more generally, are we not reminded of the irony in the appearance of Socrates (and, here, of Theaitetos also) whereby the external appearance conceals the inner man?[10]

Theodoros, too, is not introduced simply from personal memory and to express Plato's gratitude, though these elements contribute to his presence. Geometry is the propaedeutic for dialectics, as we learn in the *Republic*, and Theodoros will retire when the real philosophical discussion begins. Furthermore, since we will be inquiring into the nature of knowledge, and apparently without success, it is extremely important that Socrates, in his first words, mentions together "geometry or any other science" (γεωμετρίαν ἤ τινα ἄλλην φιλοσοφίαν). We do not know *what* knowledge is; hence, it is all the more important to see *that there is* knowledge. Geometry and the mathematician represent knowledge, not on the highest level, but on a high level and in a concrete form. This fact that there is true knowledge contradicts from the very beginning the attempts to dissolve knowledge and its objects into an indefinite flux.[11]

In the *Charmides*, the line of the conversation moves from the physical beauty of the young man to his inner qualities. Then Socrates asks him whether he possesses *sophrosyne*, the virtue of moderation ascribed to him by his uncle. This gives rise to the question, What is moderation? Similarly, in the *Theaetetus*, the personality of the young man is the point of departure for the inquiry, leading to the question: What is knowledge? The transition is shorter, yet richer in the vistas it opens. Here, too, the conversational line moves from physical to spiritual characteristics, but in place of beauty is Socratic ugliness. The discussion turns to the concept of "likeness" or "resemblance" (ὅμοιον), which will be included later among the general concepts (κοινά) that the soul perceives only by itself (185c *et seq.*). The draftsman (γραφικός) is playfully cited as an expert in judging such "likeness" and is contrasted just as playfully with those who though ignorant in this respect are nevertheless knowledgeable in other areas, like geometry, astronomy, the art of calculation, music, and all the related arts (καὶ ὅσα παιδείας ἔχεται). This kind of reference to experts in the crafts and sciences is familiar to us even if it serves a special purpose here in light of the subsequent analysis of the nature of knowledge. Again we are dealing with concrete forms of knowledge in which there are acknowledged experts. And their unquestioned professional competence guarantees that these are real forms of knowledge even though we have not yet discussed the nature of knowledge as such.

With a view to these special fields of knowledge, then, Socrates asks: What is the general characteristic by virtue of which they are knowledge? Even though the representatives of these disciplines might find such a question superfluous, would not every science betray its own nature unless this nature is examined by such a critical, philosophical, Socratic question? Must we not say then that this question, put in such general terms and addressed here to Theaitetos, is addressed at the same time to all of us who practice a science or an art? (For a Platonic dialogue differs from a pure work of art precisely because, at any time, it may invite the reader to join the discussion.[12]) From the beginning, the question raised by Socrates thus reveals a concern not only with the "theory of knowledge" but with ethics as well—and even with "existence."

As soon as the actual topic for discussion is announced, Theodoros retires from the conversation and leaves it to the young man to be examined by Socrates.[13] Similarly, in the *Thrasymachus*, the old Kephalos retires from the conversation when it turns to the nature of justice itself. And just as Kephalos represents a traditional, inarticulate type of justice, so does Theodoros represent a type of knowledge that is limited to specific subject matter and thus cannot deal with the nature of knowledge itself. It is a kind of instruction that is alien to the Socratic conversation (διαλέγεσθαι, διάλεκτος, 146ΑΒ). Still, Theodoros (unlike the old Kephalos) remains on the scene, as the representative of firm knowledge in a specific field. Thus his science, mathematics, has special meaning for the dialogue's basic query, and we must look forward to the time when he rejoins the conversation.

Socrates asks Theaitetos about a "little thing" that puzzles him: What is knowledge (ἐπιστήμη)? Just before posing this formal question, he had equated "knowledge" with "wisdom" (σοφία), thereby indicating that he was thinking not of some partial branch of knowledge but of the highest kind "which alone, among all the scientific disciplines, may be called wisdom" (*Republic* 429Α). Theaitetos overlooks this hint, however, in replying that things like geometry and other mathematical sciences, together with the crafts, like shoemaking, *all* these things, jointly and individually, are knowledge. Socrates shows him the mistake in his definition. We did not ask, What

PRELIMINARY
APPROACH
145E–147C

are the different fields of knowledge? but "What is this thing—knowledge itself?" The answer of Theaitetos opens up an "in-definite" domain, whereas a "definition" was called for, a "limiting" concept.

The *Theaetetus* belongs to the series of aporetic dialogues in search of a definition. Similar attempts at a first definition by selecting from the experience of the person questioned a specific trait or object, out of a class of things, may be found in the *Laches*, the *Thrasymachus*, and the *Euthyphro*. In the *Hippias Major*, after two such attempts, Plato adds a third definition by way of a long enumeration. The first part of the *Meno* also follows along the lines of these dialogues, for there, too, enumeration instead of delimitation is found, or enumeration instead of a unified concept. Although this structural affinity clearly shows that the *Theaetetus* belongs with the series of earlier dialogues, it will not do to say that Plato is slavishly following a schema,[14] not even his own. On the contrary, the answer of Theaitetos—by no means an ordinary pupil—has a special meaning in several respects. Enumeration fails to meet Plato's logical specifications for a definition, to be sure. Yet, the critique does not aim merely at exposing this approach for lack of trained reasoning or awkwardness. Also implicated is a definite theory (Plato will specifically mention it later on—207c) according to which a definition does consist in the enumeration of individual elements.

This theory, together with its naïve precursors, may be disposed of right away by means of Plato's demand that a definition must express the "one in the many" or the "same in all."[15] As far as the content is concerned, we find (as often elsewhere) that the exact sciences are listed, together with the crafts. It is these sciences that remain the point of reference in what follows and confirm the reality of knowledge (*episteme*) as against any sophistic skepticism. Finally, it is of special significance for the structure of the dialogue that after Socrates' ironic critique and brief analysis of the logical mistake, Theaitetos himself carries the conversation forward on the basis of his own knowledge of mathematics. In order to appreciate this new version of an old theme, we may compare the situation here with that in the *Meno*. Critique and analysis are of the same kind, but there the partner must be painstakingly guided by Socrates (*Meno* 72A *et seq.*), and even an illustration from geometry, it too brought up by Socrates, is used to help him make progress (*Meno* 73E *et seq.*).

In the series of dialogues that is continued by the *Theaetetus*, it is customary, as soon as the critical analysis has exposed the flaw in the original definition, to follow up with a first real definition that satisfies the logical requirement of unity. The *Theaetetus* has a broader structure, however, for here a discussion of two topics is placed between the critical analysis and the first real definition—placed, that is, still in the fore-field. This discussion, departing as it does from the straight path, determines—precisely because it is a digression—the special nature of this dialogue.

The first part of the preliminary conversation, already alluded to, is conducted by Theaitetos himself and deals with the discovery he has made together with his friend, a young man named Socrates. This young Socrates undoubtedly existed. Yet, it must be with more than a personal reference in mind that Plato selected just this name for the youthful companion of Theaitetos. The features of Theaitetos—snub nose and bulging eyes—resemble those of Socrates. Young Socrates bears the master's name. And the discovery reported by Theaitetos had come to them in joint discussion (διαλεγομένοις, 147D 7)—i.e., in a kind of youthful, natural prefiguration of the true Socratic dialogue—after their teacher, Theodoros, had "outlined" (ἔγραφε, 147D 3) for them the problem that became the starting point for their discussion. As Theaitetos describes it, jointly they divided the series of numbers first into two classes, then into four, according to specific criteria, and added the definition appropriate to each class.[16] Theaitetos would like to apply this method to the problem of knowledge, but does not know how. Here we have a concrete example of mathematics as a propae-deutic science in the manner of the educational system of the *Republic*. Moreover, the principle of division (diaeresis) is illus-

147c–148E

trated in a simple model.[17] It also is significant that the pupil displays both an independent spirit and his dependence upon the master.

148E–151D   Corresponding to the model pupil, what is shown in the second part of this preparatory discussion is the model teacher. He knows how difficult it is to inquire into this subject and so informs the young man explicitly that the problem is one of the "hardest" (148c 7)—as is borne out by the fact that the dialogue ends aporetically. At the same time, however, Socrates as teacher instills in the pupil the courage to embark on the difficult undertaking. He interprets the young man's confusion as labor pains and his own role as that of midwife. Midwifery —this is the new formulation adopted here in the *Theaetetus* to describe the method of examination and education practiced by Socrates. Midwifery goes together with the power of the "demonic," for only when the daimonion opens the way can Socrates practice his art.

What is said here in the *Theaetetus* about the sphere of the demonic resumes the line pursued in the *Theages* and the *Alcibiades Major*.[18] The citing of Aristeides, the younger (grandson of the "Just"), as an example of a pupil who failed to benefit from Socratic instruction, reminds us of the end of the *Laches* where Socrates is asked to take care of him. We are reminded again of the same passage in the *Laches* when Socrates adds, here in the *Theaetetus*, that if he does not feel he is the right teacher himself, he serves as matchmaker (a continuation of his profession as midwife) in recommending pupils to other teachers. From this perspective we must look back to all the dialogues in which Socrates' art of midwifery is practiced. For in the *Theaetetus* it is not merely practiced. Here the educational power of Socrates gains the highest degree of self-consciousness and, simultaneously, a consciousness of its own limits set by the demonic.

I
151D–187B   Our interpretation has shown that essential matters have been clarified before we even reach the point where, according to the prevailing conception, the real philosophical line of the work begins—i.e., with the first definition in a strict sense.[19]

This dialogue is never concerned with pure "theory of knowledge" in the sense of Descartes, Locke, or Kant. It is equally concerned with moral norms, with the contrast between dialogue and lecture (or treatise), with education and the demonic, with life and death, with "existence." Furthermore, we have learned that there are the exact sciences, together with the objects they study, and these are to remain concretely present in the course of the discussion (through Theodoros and his pupils). We suspect that knowledge must be sought for in the direction of these sciences, perhaps beyond them, but by no means ever divorced completely from them. So prepared, we now hear the first of those definitions that from now on divide the dialogue into three separate parts. The definition reads: knowledge is perception, nothing else (151E).

There is a tendency to ascribe this "sensualistic" definition to Aristippos or to Antisthenes, or to think of both as responsible for it.[20] Antisthenes cannot be meant if for no other reason than that he did not distinguish at all between perception and knowledge, but intermingled the two fields of consciousness. According to Aristippos, however, only one's inner states of mind, or affects (πάθη), are real. For this reason, Aristippos probably falls into the general group of "subjectivists" whom Plato has in mind. (Of these he will presently mention Protagoras and the Herakleiteans.) But Aristippos quite logically also denied that perceptions are always true.[21] So, strictly speaking, he cannot have equated perception with knowledge. In point of fact, several people from Parmenides and Empedokles on[22] had probably done so, but whether they used this conceptual formulation is a different question.

How do we know that anybody at all devised the formulation before Plato? In pursuing the question of whom he may have had in mind, we tend to underestimate Plato's own creative power for condensing in a single formula a number of tendencies to which he was opposed. Thus, in this definition, he combines all those common beliefs and philosophical views that he considered to be diametrically opposed to his own knowledge of being, and on them puts a general and striking stamp such as perhaps nobody had done before.[23]

Knowledge (*episteme*) is perception—this is the thesis dominating the first part of the main dialogue. The movement that Plato follows is (as always in such cases) antithetical, *first* clarification, *then* refutation. There is need for clarification, since the definition pointedly expresses a certain type of metaphysics, or rather various related types. There is need for refutation, since Plato selected or invented this thesis, so radically opposed to his own view of knowledge, precisely in order to clarify his own view by struggling with and refuting the other. For somebody like Plato to whom integration, or subordination, is the true method of refutation, it was important to clarify the place of perception in the structure of his own epistemology and ontology, precisely because the true knowledge he aims at differs fundamentally from all mere perception.

I 1
151D–160E
I 1a
151D–152c

The thesis is clarified in three stages. In the *first stage*, it is translated into the doctrine of Protagoras that man is the measure of all things, or it is presented as another version of this subjectivist theory.[24] Perception means "feeling cold." Thus, we are dealing just with the most primitive sphere of the senses, and the rather rapid pace of the exchange holds up only to the point where we ask what kind of being this subjective judgment aims at. The answer to this suddenly is clear when we reach the conclusion (152c) that "perception, then, is always of something that *is*, and, as being knowledge, it is infallible."[25] We are almost shocked, and indeed are supposed to be, at suddenly coming up against "what is."

At least three questions arise, and three insights accompany them. (1) Is being cold really something that is? Or is "what is," or *being*, radically different from something like being cold? (2) Hence, does perception really aim at "what is" and thereby become a mode of knowledge? Or do perception and knowledge differ from each other radically because knowledge, but not perception, aims at being? (The words "appearance," "appearing"—φαίνεται, φαντασία, κινδυνεύει—occur constantly in this analysis of perception, and for a good reason.) (3) Is appearance really the same as being, or are not the two radically different? Is appearance perhaps the same as not-being?

In the *second stage*, the perspective is enlarged beyond these
tentative suggestions. Now the world itself is nothing but a
state of motion where neither being nor any definite quality is
found, but only movement and mixture. On this level, the historical perspective is deepened as well. In addition to Protagoras, the names of the philosophers of nature and the poets
(Homer again leading) are now found. All those who thought
about nature are meant.[26] The only exception mentioned is
Parmenides, which suggests immediately, though it receives no
further attention, that there is another world-view opposed to
the doctrine of movement and change. The doctrine itself is
now supported by the proof that movement everywhere is
characteristic of life, and rest is characteristic of death. This is
shown by a survey throughout the universe, from the elements,
to the body, to the soul, and to the heavens (153D).

Moreover, the analysis of the process of perception itself
finds its place in this world-view. According to this analysis,
perceptual qualities arise as a result of the encounter between
the sensory organs and the objects of perception. Color is used
as an illustration. It is not something in itself, either in the
object or in the eye, but rather is a motion in between. Plato
might well have accepted this theory provided it were confined in scope—and also provided we did not fail to see that
there is something beyond it, something "ordered" (ἐν τάξει),
or "fixed" (μένον), or "in and by itself" (αὐτὸ καθ' αὑτὸ ἓν
ὄν). This is mentioned only in passing, however, in order to
be discarded as unreal (153E). But, for the time being, these
predicates would fit the objects of mathematics, astronomy,
and harmonics—the very sciences whose representatives have
been present on the scene from the beginning. It also must come
to our attention that placed next to touch (ἐφαπτόμενον) and
the object of touch (οὗ ἐφαπτόμεθα), we find that which measures or measures itself (παραμετρούμενον), and that by which
we are measuring or measuring ourselves (ᾧ παραμετρούμεθα),
i.e., the standard of measurement, as if these two areas, touch
and measurement, were the same—and as if Plato, from the
Protagoras to the *Philebus* and the *Statesman*, had not always
invoked measurement as the "art" that rescues us from the

world of appearance (*Protagoras* 356D) and as the principle, along with calculation and weighing, that provides the foundation of the sciences (*Philebus* 55E).

So the passing reference again points to the area of the exact sciences. Finally, when a mathematical illustration is used to support the thesis of Protagoras—the number six appears larger when compared with four, but smaller when compared with twelve[27]—Theaitetos, though replying in the affirmative, is uncertain of himself. This is understandable, for as soon as we seriously consider the world of mathematics, it is not easy to apply the doctrine of general flux to it. The illustration itself is taken, however, from the logic of relative terms, a favorite field for sophistic sallies. Against these dangers, Socrates calls for a calm analysis, and sets up three axioms (ὁμολογήματα, 155B 4) in order to cope with the difficulties posed by relative terms. (*1*) Nothing can become greater or smaller, in weight or in number, so long as it remains equal to itself. (*2*) A thing to which nothing is added and from which nothing is taken away is neither increased nor diminished, but always remains the same. (*3*) A thing that was not at an earlier time cannot be at a later time without a process of becoming.

These axioms seem only to confuse matters still more, however, because they appear to justify two diametrically opposed statements: first, the statement that Socrates neither gains nor loses in size, but remains the same, is supported by the first two axioms; second, the statement that Socrates now is taller (than Theaitetos), but soon will be shorter (than Theaitetos), is supported by the third axiom. Theaitetos is thrown into confusion, or a dizzy spell. But Socrates, with the kindness of the true educator, explains to him—and to Aristotle or Goethe— that this "sense of wonder" is the origin of philosophy. Following our own view, i.e., taking the knowledge of mathematics as the hidden constant of the dialogue, we see that numerical magnitudes prove to be constant just when they are supposed to be relativized in sophistic fashion. We further encounter principles that "are in us" (ἔστιν ἐν ἡμῖν, 155A 2) and that we have "in common" (ὁμολογήματα). Hence, their validity refutes the thesis being examined, and even more so does their content refute it in so far as they acknowledge something that "always remains the same" (ἀεὶ ἴσον εἶναι). Thus, the destructive thesis that knowledge is perception is opposed (at the very moment when it is to be grounded in firm logical principles) by the hidden power of these same principles that refute the thesis—or restrict it to the domain where it is valid even for Plato.

The *third stage* develops everything that has preceded into a complete system of "sense-data positivism." In order to evaluate this world-view as an intellectual achievement and to acknowledge its "spiritual" qualities, as it were, Plato employs a favorite device of his. He contrasts the view with the crude and vulgar materialism of those who think only that is real which "they can grasp with their hands" (οὗ ἂν δύνωνται ἀπρὶξ τοῖν χεροῖν λαβέσθαι). This remark does not strike at Antisthenes, let alone at Demokritos. It does not strike at any individual thinker or philosopher. Rather, Plato constructs here the non-philosopher par excellence—the most radical opponent—with whom any discussion, any meeting of minds in the universe of discourse, is impossible.[28] As against these "uninitiated" (ἀμύητοι), Plato feels akin to those more "refined minds" (κομψότεροι) whose world-view he now presents for the third time and in great detail—in order to oppose it.

Everything, then, is motion. In this endless flux, two kinds of motion may be distinguished, one active, the other passive, through whose "intercourse and friction" numerous "offspring" are generated, again falling into two general classes: *sensory perceptions* (αἰσθήσεις), and the *objects of perception* (αἰσθητά) which are co-ordinated with and "related" (συγγενῆ) to the perceptions. A sensation comes into being when the eye sends out its power of vision (ὄψις) while, simultaneously, the object produces the related quality of "whiteness" (λευκότης) and both of them join to produce the color white. There is nothing active, then, unless it joins with something passive. There is nothing in and by itself (αὐτὸ καθ' αὑτό); there is only movement and relatedness. Language deceives us about this state of affairs.

Parallel with this sense-data epistemology, there runs a

I 1c
155D–160E

skeptical critique of language reminiscent of the view that Hermogenes expounds in the *Cratylus*.[29] Not only individual qualities are drawn into this maelstrom, but also assemblages (ἄθροισμα) such as man, stone, living creature or species (εἶδος) in general. It is not without meaning that the term "eidos," though used in a very general sense, occurs here (157c 2). Nor is it without meaning that such concepts as "good" and "beautiful" are cited in passing (157d 8) as being submerged in the seemingly all-powerful flood of becoming. Here the danger is felt more immediately. Yet for the attentive reader it also is suggested that there are breakwaters stemming the flood: language, *Eidos*, and the good.

For the time being, however, Socrates develops the last and most radical consequence of the view (157e). He cites dreams, madness, and sensory illusions in order to show realities that are powerful enough to justify the distinction between true and false in the field of sense perception—but for a moment only. For this refutation of the view Socrates is "delivering" Theaitetos of is derived from the same grounds (biological, one might say) on which rests the original thesis that the argument is intended to refute. So the thesis is powerful enough to absorb this critique with the result that it becomes still more radical. Now Socrates is no more right when he is healthy than when he is sick, no more right when he is awake than when he is asleep. Socrates is viewed biologically. Worse, the Socrates who is sick is a different person from the Socrates who is healthy, the Socrates who is awake, a different person from the Socrates who is asleep.

Thus, the third stage of clarification ends by completely dissolving man, i.e., his existence—and, what is more, Socratic existence. Man is not "soul" as in the *Alcibiades Major* and the *Phaedo*; he is an assemblage, not being for himself, but always being or rather becoming in relation to something else. Man is dissolved into a system of relations, and the section concludes on the note that there is no such thing as "being in itself." These are the frightening consequences of the worldview derived from equating knowledge with perception—all the more frightening when we realize that this same Socrates who here is submitting his own existence to logical annihilation will go, in a few hours, to the portico of the King-Archon to meet the indictment drawn up against him (210D 2).

So far only a keen observer has felt, now and then, the counterforces mobilized against this view. Now the "midwife" turns to an examination of the newly born he has delivered. What is to be examined here has such conceptual power that the position of "Protagoras" speaking through Socrates remains unshaken even after the first two counterthrusts. Only the third thrust destroys it or, more correctly, integrates it with the conceptual universe of Plato's Socrates. As previously the clarification so now the refutation proceeds in three stages.[30] On the two lower levels Theaitetos remains the partner, but on the highest Theodoros takes his place. The beginning of this countermovement, however, is marked in advance by the fact that Theodoros briefly rejoins the conversation (161A). This is more than a dramatic or technical device.[31] The mathematician, by his mere presence, represents the strongest objection against "Protagoras," and yet, the ironic reference to "your companion Protagoras" (161B 8) means something else as well. The mathematician refutes the sophist without knowing it. To know this would require a knowledge that—to use the formal language of the *Republic*—is "noetic," not only "dianoetic."

On the *first level*, the critique deals with "man as the measure," the strongest formulation of the "epistemological" skepticism. Against it, Plato had used an argument *ad hominem* in the *Euthydemus* (286E *et seq.*), where the question was asked: How can anyone who holds this view claim to be a teacher when on this premise every opinion is equally true? And the *Cratylus* (385E *et seq.*) contrasts, in not so personal a way, the "truth" of Protagoras with the generally acknowledged difference between being intelligent and being stupid. Here in the *Theaetetus*, the argument used in the *Euthydemus* is repeated, except that, in addition, Socrates also puts his own case next to that of the wise Protagoras, in the ironic modesty of an aside, or puts his own art of midwifery next to "this whole business of philosophical conversation" (σύμπασα ἡ τοῦ διαλέγεσθαι πραγματεία, 161 E 6).

I 2
160E–187B

I 2a
160E–163A

Here in action is the power by which the thesis of Protagoras is overcome, yet it is silent, below the surface. The polemical question on the surface is: Why only man? Why not pig or baboon? And (after a while) a second question: Why not God? The first question is quite crude,[32] but the second points to something of deep seriousness. Or is it only an accident that the counterthesis, "God as the measure," recurs in a solemn passage of the *Laws* (IV 716c)? There Plato affirms that as long as a community is ruled not by God but by man, there is no escape from misery (713E), and that the man of wanton power who believes he does not need the guidance of God and God's justice is forsaken, and brings ruin to the community (716A *et seq.*). Thus, Socrates is raising a serious matter in the *Theaetetus.* Yet he only hints at it, and therefore "Protagoras or a representative of his" speaking through Socrates can object to this loose manner of arguing and demand instead the kind of precision practiced in geometry. When it is Protagoras who appeals to geometry, however, he must be careful lest it turn against him.

The attack, then, on this first level, is still a preliminary skirmish. It is not systematic enough, and the opponents' front is too broad for the attack to have any effect in depth. It strikes only at the Protagoras-thesis itself (even here not systematically enough) but not against its "Herakleitean" foundations nor against the epistemological consequences derived from it. On I 2b the *second level*, then, we turn to these consequences in a series 163A–168c of brief arguments which raise doubts about equating knowledge with perception, but do not by any means upset the system as a whole. These arguments, too, are not systematic enough, and indeed, they even employ sophistic techniques so transparently that Protagoras speaking through Socrates can rightly object. The whole procedure seems to suggest—and the repeated warnings we hear against purely disputatious verbal arguments (164c 7, 166D 8) make this suggestion still more plausible—that we gain very little by dialectical refutation of the definition proposed by Theaitetos so long as we have not reached any clear understanding of the metaphysical view behind it.

Still, Socrates advances (on this second level) four brief arguments against the definition, or cites four phenomena that do not agree with the definition, knowledge is perception. First (163B), there is a difference between hearing the sounds of a foreign language and understanding them; there is a difference between seeing the letters of a language and knowing what they mean. Second (163D), memory (μνήμη) clearly differs from perception, yet it just as clearly is a kind of knowledge. Third (165c), it is possible both to see and not to see at the same time, but it is not possible both to know and not to know at the same time. Finally (165D), there are qualitative differences in perception, but not in knowledge.

Theaitetos objects to the first argument and, in doing so, earns Socrates' praise—yet not without irony, however, so that we feel his objection may in turn be overcome (163c). Socrates himself criticizes the second argument by calling it verbal eristics and insisting that "Protagoras" is not overcome by it. The third argument is still more transparently sophistic. A "dauntless man" (as Socrates points out) might put his hand over one of Theaitetos' eyes and ask the young man whether he is now both seeing and not seeing at the same time, demanding, in a sophistic spirit—as we know it from the *Euthydemus* (296A)— a clear-cut answer, either yes or no. The fourth argument is described also as an armed attack from ambush. Yet, these retractions do not mean that the arguments have failed to open certain legitimate perspectives for the reader. Even the third argument eristically conceived will be restated later (182E), when knowledge and perception are said to differ in that while we can both see and not see at the same time, we cannot know and not know at the same time.

We have suggested why Plato for now refrains from carrying the attack through energetically, with the result that, at the end, the opponents' position is almost stronger than it was before. In a long and comprehensive speech, Protagoras (speaking through Socrates) rejects the arguments advanced against the original definition. He insists upon the relativity of knowledge to the extreme point of denying the unity of the self; he opposes the argument that was supposed to refute the "man as the measure" thesis; and he insists upon his superiority to others in that he is capable of leading them from a worse opinion to a better. It is most delightful to read how the sophist complains about the philosopher—it is the philosopher, however, who is speaking—reproaching him for engaging in an eristic type of argument. As he previously had insisted on mathematical precision, so he now warns (as only Socrates does elsewhere[33]) against the consequences of this abuse. It will make men haters, instead of lovers, of philosophy. After everything that has preceded, in the end we still have the same threefold doctrine: that all is motion, that man is the measure of all things, and that knowledge is perception. It did no good to attack the second and third parts of this system separately. The whole system must be—we do not say "overthrown," for it cannot be overthrown in some of its essential aspects. The system must be assigned its proper place in order to acquire the validity it does not have as yet. This takes place on the *third level*, as we

ɪ 2c
168c–187ʙ

now shall see.

On the previous levels of analysis, "Protagoras" had insisted on mathematical precision and philosophical dialectics. So, on the third level, where the decision will come, Theodoros despite his reluctance is brought back into the conversation because his profession represents mathematical precision. He is to take over as Socrates' partner (and agrees to do so) until we can find out whether it is true that everybody is equally qualified to judge in such matters as geometry, astronomy, and the other exact sciences. Thus the conceptual theme that, from the beginning, has run through the dialogue, though mostly below the surface, now comes into the open. This is the change marked by the re-entrance of Theodoros into the conversation.[34]

ɪ 2c α
169ᴅ–172c
177c–179ʙ

"Protagoras," we are reminded, had admitted earlier—no, he had in fact vigorously asserted, through Socrates—that certain men whom he called "wise" were superior to others in judging what is better or worse. What else can this mean (for since he is not present Protagoras cannot really concede anything) but that this assertion follows directly from the fact he is a sophist, i.e., a man who claims to be able to teach his pupils? Yet, the discussion is to be placed on broader foundations. We are shown that in the field of judgment, or opinion, which Protagoras equated with reality, it is generally taken for granted that men differ in the "wisdom" they possess. This is confirmed by referring to the reality of human life, where men seek a teacher or a ruler. Actual life, or "existence," is appealed to as proof that human beings do acknowledge the difference between knowing (σοφία) and not-knowing. Thus, we reach the same conclusion whether we set out from the thesis of "man as the measure" or if we look directly at the reality of the human situation.

The discussion takes up the thesis of Protagoras once more in order to demonstrate, very pointedly, its self-destructive consequences.[35] Since it makes everybody the measure of what is true and false, it is not valid for everybody but perhaps is valid for its author only. At any rate, it sets the majority up as judges—the majority, always considered by Plato to be least qualified to decide what is right and wrong (*Laches* 184E;[36] cf. *Cratylus* 437D). Finally comes the most exquisite (κομψότατον) consequence: on the basis of his own theory that every opinion is valid, Protagoras must allow that those people are right who think his theory is wrong. This amounts to a dialectical self-refutation of Protagoras' thesis.

Important as it is to realize these self-destructive implications of the Protagorean view, Plato did not intend simply to dissolve the view into nothing. Protagoras himself, as Socrates points out (171D), would have a few things to say if he were to comment on this discussion,[37] and indeed, Protagoras speaking through Socrates had emphatically asserted that he was not at all prepared to discard differences in intellectual capacities (166D *et seq.*). This is evident from the fact that he called his treatise *Truth*, and advanced his thesis with the claim of deserving to be heard. So it is obvious that the thesis points beyond itself, and calls for delimitation precisely because it has a wide range. It applies, in the most specific sense, to the field of pure sensory perceptions. No one considers it valid, however, with regard to decisions about health and illness in the case of the individual, or with regard to benefit and harm in the case of the community. In other words, it does not apply to areas of life where we can confirm the difference between expert competence and its opposite by the advantages we derive from that very competence. Thus, two areas are separated out of the field of general experience. The next question then leads to a still higher level, for it asks into which of these areas we must put such concepts as beautiful and ugly, just and unjust, pious and impious (concepts which, for now, are treated in their social meaning). These concepts, too, are generally considered by the majority to fall into the class of subjective judgments, as if they did not have an essential nature of their own.

At this point (172B 8), Socrates suddenly departs from the straight path, and the conversation shifts to a contrast of the philosopher with the political orator, as opposing types of men. After this digression, it returns (177c) to the exact point where it had broken off (ἐπὶ τὰ ἔμπροσθεν ἴωμεν): even if we grant— so we read now—that what is "just," and everything else, i.e., what was previously (172AB) called "beautiful" or "pious," is determined by subjective judgments only, nevertheless when it comes to deciding what is advantageous, this decision does not depend on people's opinion or on the enactment of laws in the community. If we now ask what is the general class of things (περὶ παντὸς τοῦ εἴδους) that have such an autonomous status, we come to judgments dealing with the future. When it is a matter of making a judgment about the future, not everybody is qualified to judge according to the same standard (κριτήριον), but only the physician or the husbandman, *in short*, the expert, i.e., Protagoras himself in so far as it is a matter of judging the effect of arguments in court. Finally, the field of legislation is alluded to on a still higher level. And so it is Protagoras himself who helps us discover a domain beyond that in which his own thesis is valid—a domain where judgments are the result not of subjective decisions, but of expert knowledge.

Yet, who speaks for Protagoras? Socrates himself leaves no doubt, at the end of this section in the dialogue, that he speaks throughout as the ironic man. An ignorant person like himself, to be sure, is not the "measure," but since he had to speak in defense of Protagoras he had to make himself the "measure."

In what other sense Socrates is the measure we learn from the
digression here in the *Theaetetus*, and, above all, from his conduct in court.

Let us come back, then, to the digression that intrudes into
this argument with Protagoras as if it were a foreign body.
Faced with one argument after another, Socrates remarks—
and the transition could not be more abrupt—that, as often before, it occurs to him now again that men who have spent a
long time in philosophical studies fail ridiculously when they
appear in a court of law.[38] "Now again . . ." This phrase is
not intelligible unless we remember the introductory conversation, for according to it, this meeting with Theodoros and
Theaitetos took place shortly before the death of Socrates. And
this hint at the fate awaiting Socrates becomes even more significant when we look back on the sudden digression from the
perspective of the dialogue's end (210D), or when, in a subsequent reading, we look forward from the digression to the end.

DIGRESSION
172C–177C

Yet, these personal or biographical allusions only provide
the occasion, as it were, for the digression. They do not clarify
its meaning in the dialogue as a whole. We come closer to this
meaning when we consider what immediately precedes the
digression and what follows right afterwards. Searching for
objective standards that would refute a subjectivist skepticism,
the conversation had turned from matters of practical knowledge
to the political domain (172A). On this higher level, such concepts as "beautiful," "just," and "pious" emerge, and their
meaning, or being, is in danger of being dissolved by the "truth"
of Protagoras. In the *Apology*, Socrates risks his own life to
confirm the objective validity of these virtues. For the reader
must not forget, not even in the midst of the most subtle
"epistemological" analysis, that, in a few days, Socrates will
deliver his defense in court.

Yet the transition is still quite sudden. The digression is to
pose a paradox and then keep the question of its meaning always alive. The ridiculous failure of the philosopher is, as it
were, the corner by which the whole thing is rolled up. The
"whole thing" is the contrast between two ways of life, that
of the philosopher and that of the political orator: the slavish

life of the orator, always subject to external influences and orders, as against the unpolitical, unworldly life of philosophy. For so may philosophy be seen at least among its true protagonists, who are unconcerned about their personal affairs and are deeply immersed in the fate of the soul (τᾶς τε γᾶς ὑπένερθε —we hear Pindar), in geometry, and astronomy, and the discovery of true being.[39] The philosopher looks ridiculous when he appears in a law court or when he must deal with other practical affairs. (Here is the corner again by which the whole thing is rolled up.) Yet to the philosopher, in turn, the stupidity of the others is ridiculous. It is the stupidity commonly displayed in the pride people take in rich possessions or noble birth. For the philosopher, these things are measured by a different and higher standard. And if he finally "drags the others upward"—we are reminded of the simile of the cave in the *Republic*—out of their world of practical competition and legal controversies, upward to thinking about the meaning of "justice and injustice in themselves" and about the meaning of "perfect happiness and misery," then the relationship is reversed. It is the practical man who now fails completely.[40]

After this antithesis has been followed through the human and social world, it is raised to a level beyond man (176A). The opposition of good and evil is revealed as necessary. Good and evil are assigned their cosmic place, as it were. Evil dwells here with us in our mortal nature on earth. The good—or, as is then said emphatically, the just—dwells in its true nature with the gods. Thus, the philosopher's pursuit may be seen as an attempt "to escape from here to there" or, put differently, as an approximation and imitation of the divine. Finally (176E), the two models (παραδείγματα) of life are once more contrasted with each other, not through a glass darkly, but in the light of eternity: divine blessedness as against godless misery. The balance sheet of virtues, therefore, corresponds to the balance sheet of happiness. If the individual chooses a life of injustice, he has simultaneously chosen misery, first in this life and then after death. And as the ridiculous failure of the philosopher was the occasion for embarking on this digression, so the appropriate ending is the ridiculous failure of the political man when he is called upon "to give an account" of his principles.

Before we ask what after all this digression means in the dialogue as a whole, let us note that the contrast between the two ways of life—constantly present in Plato's mind—had been expressed, on a grand scale, in earlier works. This is the same contrast that dominates the conversation with Kallikles in the *Gorgias*.[41] There, too, it culminates in a balance sheet of happiness, and the brief words by which, in the *Theaetetus*, we accompany the soul's fate in its journey beyond this life sound like an echo of the myth of the beyond with which Socrates concludes the conversation in the *Gorgias*. Even beginning and end are comparable in these two contexts, for Kallikles soon reproaches the philosopher (*Gorgias* 485D *et seq.*)—with distinct reference to Socrates himself—for not being able to master the affairs of practical life, and, at the end of the whole discussion, it is Kallikles who no longer is capable of "giving an account" of himself.

The same antithesis that dominates the last part of the *Gorgias* also may be seen to hold the structure of the *Republic* together, by and large. Here the antithesis extends from Book II where the two pure types are put up against each other like two statues (ἀνδριάντες, *Republic* 361D) to the simile of the cave, in Book VII, describing the unworldly philosopher who must appear ridiculous when he returns to the affairs of this life (517D)[42] and, finally, to Book X which contains another balance sheet of happiness and concludes with a myth of life after death. In the *Republic*, it seems as if Plato in an ironic turn is more concerned with the external success of the just man in life— a highly dubious success—whereas in the *Theaetetus*, the emphasis is on such a man's inner blessedness. Still, the path of those practicing virtue is described in the *Republic* (613B), just as it is in the *Theaetetus*, as an approach to the divine so far as this is possible for man.[43] These two great constructions of the contrasting ways of life, then, are condensed in the digression of the *Theaetetus*.

But what do they mean in the context of the *Theaetetus* itself?

We must first note that the digression occurs at a point where the question has arisen, as a genuine possibility, whether one's judgment of what is "just" is purely relative and arbitrary—the most damaging presumption as far as Plato is concerned.[44] When, after the digression, the conversation resumes exactly where it had broken off, doubts about the nature of justice remain what they were before. The concept of the advantageous is alone said to have a definite meaning beyond the sphere of subjective opinion. Per contra, in the digression itself, the two topics of philosophical thought are revealed as justice and injustice, "what they are in themselves and how they differ from each other and from everything else." Then it is shown that what is good dwells in the divine sphere. God is "completely just," and to become like a god means to realize justice so far as this is possible for man. Thus, the digression makes it clear that the good and the just rest on divine foundations, whereas the dialectical analysis in the main conversation does not rise to these heights.

We must keep in mind, further, that Theodoros had agreed (169c 6) to serve as a partner in the conversation until it became clear whether the view of "man as the measure" applied also to the mathematical sciences represented by him. Theodoros soon will quit the conversation, before this question has even been touched. In the digression, however, geometry and astronomy emerge as the pursuits of the philosopher (173E)—preparatory pursuits, it is implied, yet so far above the pursuits of the majority of men that the original question is settled thereby. We must note a peculiar irony. In the context of the conversation before and after the digression, an appeal to the man of practical affairs is made in order to refute the validity of the Protagorean view. The question raised there—and answered in the digression—is whether the mathematician would refute it far above the level of the practical man. The question whether the philosopher, in turn, would do the same above the level of the mathematician is not even raised explicitly. Yet the digression provides an answer to the unstated question—and in order to answer it we need not even compare Theodoros with Socrates.

Furthermore, Socrates has raised the possibility, without voicing any criticism, that judgments concerning even justice and piety might have to be abandoned to the sphere of subjectivity. This possibility is repeated after the digression. Could Plato present such a thrust against the core of his own position, in theory and in life, however, without even hinting at how it is to be resisted? It is in the digression that he shows how the threat can be and must be resisted. And after we have read the digression, we understand the irony behind Socrates' words when he restates the view that judgment of what is just and pious might be purely subjective.[45] Finally, the dialogue poses the question, What is knowledge?, and ends aporetically. But the digression shows the man of knowledge, and explains that all human "wisdom and virtue"—for knowledge and action are inseparable—aims at what is divine and just, far above the ordinary intellectual pursuits in the fields of technical production and political action.

Nobody can miss, throughout this clearly demarcated digression, the traits revealed in the ironic and often sarcastic pictures of the man of intellect and the ordinary politician.[46] "We are not servants of the argument; it is our servant and it must wait until we come to its aid as we choose." So speaks Theodoros (173c), and we are almost surprised that Socrates does not object by replying: You know very well from geometry that the argument is sustained by its own law, that *it* prescribes —we do not—when and where it is brought to a conclusion (*Protagoras* 314c, *Gorgias* 505cd). Again, when Socrates says that the masters in philosophy do not know their way to the market place or the Council Chamber, it does not take long to remember that Socrates often was seen in the market place (*Apology* 17c), that he played his part in the Council with special courage (*Apology* 32b), and that he is on his way even now to the court of the King-Archon (*Theaetetus* 210d). "To take any part in festivities with flute girls would not occur to him in dreams." (But what about the *Symposium?*) All philosophers, so the description continues, deserve the scorn of that Thracian servant girl who mocked Thales for gazing at the stars. And the philosopher does not know his own neighbor, for he is in-

terested only in the question of man in general. In all, what
do we have here but a caricature of the philosopher as seen
through the eyes of the Philistine and ordinary politician? Or
do we simultaneously catch a glimpse of the philosopher in
his highest state? Socratic-Platonic irony conceals the last
truths in pointing to them. Must it not do so here even more
than in the *Republic?* For here the mathematician Theodoros
and his young pupil, not Plato's own brothers, appear as the
partners of Socrates, and the problem is not, here, to know
what is the nature of justice, but to know rather what is the
nature of knowledge itself.

Thus, we may have an inkling of what the digression means
for the work as a whole.[47] Suddenly, the clouds are torn asunder, as it were, and we catch a glimpse of a piercing light. Then
they close in again. The digression is over and the discussion
resumes as if nothing had happened. Yet, all at once, everything has new meaning. If previously mathematics was the
hidden constant, if being was divined once and God as the
measure alluded to once, only to disappear again, now there is
revealed the sphere of the divine and (strictly corresponding
to it) the knowledge and life, in short, *the existence*, of the
philosopher. If, to begin with, the Protagorean thesis threatened to make all speech and conversation impossible, now the
fact of this conversation itself, together with the areas it has
opened up, resists and overcomes the thesis. The question is,
What is knowledge? Here we see what it is in living fulfillment
—and everything that is said later in dealing with this question
must be referred to this glimpse of light from which it all derives
its peculiarly ironic meaning: a gleam leading to the truth.[48]

We had followed the conversation between Socrates and Theodoros to the point where the thesis of "man as the measure"
was refuted, or restricted in its validity (179B). We know,
however, that this thesis does not stand alone, but is intimately
connected with what is called the Herakleitean world-view of
endless flux. (How little this view has to do with the great
Herakleitos himself need not be pointed out here.) This view

must be examined in order for us to see clearly whether the Protagorean thesis applies to the sense impressions (πάθη) of the individual. Here we immediately are suspicious as we read Theodoros' description of these Herakleiteans. They are so much "in flux" themselves, he says, that one cannot conduct a conversation with them; they cannot attend to any argument, and no one of them can be teacher or student of any other. Yet we know that there are such things as dialectics, argument, teaching, and discipleship. We see them in living fulfillment, so their absence must arouse our suspicion about the doctrine even before we have begun to examine it carefully.

After considering the teachers, the discussion then turns to their doctrine. Socrates goes back explicitly to his analysis of sense perceptions, and the system of an extreme sense-data epistemology, outlined in the first major part of the dialogue (I 1c).⁴⁹ Suppose we take "motion" in the general sense and distinguish between two kinds of motion, change of place or local motion (φορά), and alteration (ἀλλοίωσις), that are always present together. Then it is impossible, say, in the case of a color, to call it "white," because it is changing every moment. One cannot even use the word "seeing" without running into a contradiction with the doctrine of flux. One must simultaneously call the same process "not-seeing," so that if perception is the same as knowledge, knowing is at the same time not-knowing. In other words, there is no such thing as knowledge; everything we say is equally true; there is no language, or we would have to invent a new one. Of the words we use, only the expression "in no way" (οὐδ' ὅπως) might be suitable as being "indefinite" (ἄπειρον) enough.⁵⁰

This line of thought does not dispose of the doctrine of flux as such, nor does it settle the validity of judgments of perception (πάθος, 179c). It shows, however, that there are limits to both, for limits are set by the fact that there is reasonable and responsible discourse and by the fact that there is a difference between true and false. While the sense-data epistemology earlier (157ʙ) threatened to dissolve all language, now it is language that resists this process of disintegration, even as the

Cratylus (385B) showed that the distinction between true and false is the indispensable prerequisite for all discourse.[51] And so perception as belonging to the world of change is finally divorced from knowledge. After we have separated these two functions, there remains the task of clarifying their reciprocal relationship.

The part of the dialogue in which Socrates and Theodoros converse with each other yields the following results. The over-all validity of the doctrine of flux has been impaired, the thesis of man as the measure has refuted itself, and the definition by Theaitetos has turned into its opposite. The digression in between has given us a glimpse of the philosopher, wisdom, and the realm of true being. Now Theodoros quits the conversation. Previously there had been a brief appearance of Parmenides and his pupils as opposed to the Herakleiteans (180DE), and so Theaitetos now expects a discussion about the view that "the all is one and immovable." Socrates, however, evades such a discussion. With due respect to Parmenides, as he explains, the abundance of arguments, or thoughts, that would break in upon us would push the present question, What is knowledge?, out of sight (183E). Those who would infer from these words of Socrates, or of the youthfully exuberant Theaitetos, that Plato originally intended to treat the doctrine of being in the same detail as the doctrine of becoming but later changed his mind for external reasons, misunderstand the nature of Platonic irony. We are caught between extremes (ἀμφοτέρων εἰς τὸ μέσον πεπτωκότες), between endless flux and eternal being, as Socrates puts it (180E). And, indeed, in the second part of the dialogue, we shall turn against Parmenides, since the difference between true and false also is obliterated in the rigid Parmenidean contrast of being and not-being, knowing and not-knowing.[52] Yet, while the *Cratylus* is balanced on the scale between "Herakleitos" and "Parmenides," the *Theaetetus* has its own (or, if we like, "one-sided") law of development, and what seems to be lacking here, Plato, strictly speaking, has never supplied elsewhere, not even in the *Parmenides* or in the *Sophist*.[53]

After the withdrawal of Theodoros, the first part of the

dialogue is brought to its conclusion in the conversation be- ɪ 2c γ
tween Socrates and Theaitetos. The identity of perception and 184ᴀ–187ʙ
knowledge has been overthrown. There remains the problem of
the relationship between the two. Plato equated them to begin
with so that he could clarify their true nature and their correct
relationship to each other as they fell apart. Disregarding the
lack of good manners (ἀνελεύθερον) shown, from a social point
of view, by his being overprecise with concepts, Socrates now
distinguishes between what we perceive *with* (ᾧ) and what we
perceive *through* (δι' οὗ). This distinction is still clearer when
we pass to the field of thought (διανοεῖσθαι) where we may say
that we think *with* the mind about the material transmitted
through the senses. While the senses have their own specific
powers that are not interchangeable, there is something in us,
"one single nature, mind, soul, or whatever it may be called"
(184ᴅ), "the soul itself" (185ᴇ), that uses the senses as instruments and thinks in such categories as being and not-being,
similarity and dissimilarity, sameness and difference, and also
in numerical concepts, or about judgments of what is beautiful
and ugly, good and evil.

We have thus established both the difference between perception and knowledge and also their respective order in rank,
for "among the things that are ours we should always prefer
the ruling element to the servant" (*Laws* V 726). A further
indication of this order is the fact that while both animals and
men are born with the power of perception, only men are born
with the power of thought—and then not even all of them.
Thought aims at essence and reality, being and truth (οὐσία
καὶ ἀλήθεια); perception does not. So, as we conclude this part
of the dialogue, we have again refuted the view that knowledge
is perception. Nevertheless, we have learned more than "what
knowledge is *not*."[54] We have grasped some essential truths
about the structure of the mind, and about the relationship between perception and knowledge. On the side of the mind, we
deal with psychology; on the side of the objects, with ontology,
since knowledge aims at "essence" or "being." This seemingly
formal schema is filled with live content. Conjoined with psychology and ontology are ethics and transcendence, if we look

back to the digression where being itself was shown to be the
goal of the philosophical life, from "justice itself" to the "approximation of the divine." At the threshold to the sanctuary,
Plato has his Socrates hold back.

II
187B–201C

The *second major part* of the dialogue is concerned with
formally clarifying and refuting the next definition: knowledge
is true opinion (ἡ ἀληθὴς δόξα ἐπιστήμη, 187B). "Opinion" or
"belief" (δοξάζειν) is a common expression in ordinary language
that Plato frequently uses in place of what, in more precise
language, he would call knowledge. In the *Timaeus* (51D), it
is said that there are "some" who do not distinguish between
true opinion and knowledge, whereas the two concepts should
be separated. In this dialogue, young Theaitetos is one of those
"some." Apparently taking it for granted that knowledge
(*episteme*) is opinion, he formulates his definition by qualifying
with the word "true" the general notion of opinion. Plato introduces this definition in order to further clarify the nature of
knowledge in contrast to true opinion, even as he had previously
clarified it in contrast to perception. The word *doxa*, opinion,
carries the connotation of what "seems acceptable, or plausible,
to me" (δοκεῖ μοι). It is this active component in the concept
of "seeming" that is the focus for the discussion. Hence, the
equation is made between *knowing* and *seeming true*.

II 1
187B–200D
II 2
200D–201C

The strange thing we note in surveying this section as a
whole, however, is that by far the largest part of it deals with
the question of error, and how error is possible. Only at the end
is the definition examined briefly, and refuted. This would be
a lack of proportion except that in the course of dealing with
what seems to be a side issue, or a digression, the discussion is
in fact clarifying the main problem. We know from the *Hippias
Minor*, from the *Euthydemus*, and from the *Cratylus* what it
means to the philosopher to refute the sophistic intermingling
of truth and falsehood and to prove that "error is possible."
It means nothing less than "rescuing" the possibility of knowledge. In the domain of pure sense perception there is no error.
In the domain of pure knowledge there will be no error either.
As for the domain of *doxa*, however, it is virtually defined by
the presence of error and false judgments. This, then, is the

appropriate place for the dialogue to analyze the meaning of error. And probably the word "true" is included in the definition because clarifying the meaning of *true* and of its opposite, *false*, is a prerequisite for understanding the nature of knowledge.[55]

The inquiry into what is error, or false belief, proceeds in a series of futile attempts at catching this elusive thing. There are five such attempts. Of these the first three belong together because they are based on common assumptions and are given similar treatment.[56]

In the *first attempt*, knowing and not-knowing are sharply contrasted with each other, with the intermediary stages of learning and forgetting excluded (for the time being). How, then, is error, i.e., mistaking one thing for another, possible? It is not possible in the case of two things both known, or in the case of two things both not known, or in the case of one thing that is known and another that is not known. So, evidently, there is no room for anything like error.

The radical (Parmenidean) contrast between knowing and not-knowing excludes the sophistic intermingling or denial of both. At the same time, however, this radical contrast without intermediate links or transition apparently leaves the phenomenon of error inexplicable and then puts itself at the service of the sophistic mix-up. Yet Parmenides had dealt with error or the false opinions of mankind in the second part of his philosophical poem. Moreover, the life work of Socrates would be meaningless if there were no error and if it could not be removed. It was no accident that, at the beginning of this section, Theaitetos had taken it for granted that "there is also false opinion" (187B 5: ἐπειδὴ καὶ ψευδής ἐστι δόξα)—no accident, because subsequently the rigid Parmenidean contrast between knowing and not-knowing is retained, and knowledge is all too simply equated with opinion. Do we not immediately find the outlines of a basic schema: on the one hand, knowing and not-knowing in an absolute sense and without transitions, and on the other hand, true and false opinion, i.e., a domain in which error is possible? Certainly this is a kind of polemics against contemporary "Parmenideans," or eristics. Still, in our

II 1a
187B–188c

judgment, it is much more a way of Plato's coming to terms with the Parmenides inside himself.[57]

In the *second attempt*, the problem that seems to be insoluble on these epistemological grounds is now approached from an objective side. Being and not-being are contrasted as sharply as knowing and not-knowing were before. False opinion means to believe something that is not, and so the problem of error may be reformulated to read: How is it possible to believe in what is not? Judgment, or opinion, like any other mental activity (seeing, hearing, touching) seems to refer to something as being.[58] He who believes in not-being believes in nothing; hence, he does not believe, or judge, at all. So, again, from the side of the objects of knowledge, the phenomenon of error cannot be explicated.

Yet—let us add immediately—there is such a thing as error. Apparently it is not going to be intelligible as long as we retain the rigid Parmenidean contrast of being and not-being. Did we not encounter, in the first part, a field of experience that could be called neither being nor not-being? Sense perceptions disclose objects, but it remains to be seen whether they aim at something that exists, and in what sense they do so. Let us look again at the statement that to believe in not-being is to believe in nothing, or not to believe at all. If we do not notice right away that this is a sophistic inference from propositions that are not identical, we should let the *Euthydemus* and the *Cratylus* help us realize what problem is hidden here. To solve this problem, however, we need to overcome—as is done later in the *Sophist*—the rigidity of the Parmenidean concept of being.

In the *third attempt*, error is said to be misjudgment that occurs when one thing is mistaken for another (ἀλλοδοξία, ἑτεροδοξία). In the first attempt, the emphasis was on the side of knowing, while in the second attempt, it was on the side of being (though it goes without saying that in each case the other side was involved as well). Now in the third attempt, knowing and being are both equally involved. A person mistakes two things in his mind; he takes one (ἕτερον) for the other (ἕτερον), a contrast expressed in Greek by the same word. Do we read

too much into this linguistic fact if we say that this identity of
opposites suggested by it contains a temptation to eristic abuse
that is intended by Plato's Socrates?

At any rate, in this case Theaitetos does not follow docilely as
in the two previous attempts, for now, in lively response, the
young man tries to clarify the Socratic formula by giving an example of his own. When we think "ugly" instead of "beautiful,"
he says, then we are "truly thinking what is false." Why does
Socrates cut this contribution off instead of using it for purposes
of clarification? Theaitetos seems to be on the right track. We
need only put the article in front of "beautiful" and "ugly"
(as Socrates presently does himself—190B 3) in order to come
close to a Platonic position. Yet there is a danger: "truly false"
may be meant in a purely factual sense, but it also may lead to
sophistic confusion (as the Greek use of the identical word for
"one" and "the other" did before). That probably is the reason
why Socrates, repeating the phrase, "truly thinking what is
false," calls a halt. He returns to his definition that "false judgment is mistaking" and, elaborating upon this, gives an account
of thinking as a conversation of the soul with itself.

Why this account? It is not only to give a concrete image but,
above all, to make it clear that while in conversation with others
truth may be twisted sophistically, truth cannot be twisted in the
soul's conversation with itself. Nobody hearing both voices
within himself can think that "the beautiful"—using the example cited by Theaitetos, Socrates adds the article, and that
means much—is ugly or the just unjust (we cannot forget that,
on the following day, Socrates will appear in court), or that odd
numbers are even (Socrates is addressing a young mathematician). When we truly know both A and B in this series of opposites, we cannot mistake A for B. Even less can we mistake
them when we know only A or only B. Mathematics and ethics
become visible beyond the field of ordinary experience—ox and
horse (190c 4).

Thus, the criticism of the third attempt (190B *et seq.*) must be
measured by the standards set in these two disciplines, mathematics and ethics. If the soul knows two things (in these disciplines), how can it mistake one for the other? If it knows only

one thing, how can it think that what it knows is something else that it does not know? A counterargument to this last statement would be that one cannot know what is even or what is just unless he also knows what is uneven or what is unjust.[59]

II 1d
191A–196D

In the *fourth attempt*, the metaphor of the mass of wax (κήρινον ἐκμαγεῖον),[60] which is referred to the soul for the sake of the argument, serves to bring learning, remembering, and forgetting into the discussion—after the first three attempts intentionally (188A) employed the radical contrast of knowing and not-knowing. Now the discussion inquires into all possible cases of knowing and perceiving, and also their negations, with respect to their compatibility.[61] Most of the cases are ruled out as impossible. Then there remain three possibilities for making a false judgment: (1) when we mistake *A* (or *B*) that is known for *B* (or *A*) that is both known and perceived, (2) when we mistake *A* that is known for *B* that is not known but is perceived, and (3) when we mistake *A* that is both known and perceived for *B* that is both known and perceived. The analysis shows, therefore, that false opinion or false judgment is to be located where knowledge, in the form of memory, is combined with perception. In the end, the image of the mass of wax also serves to explain differences in human dispositions. This is a kind of empirical confirmation, or expansion, of the epistemological aspects in the psychological domain (194C–195B).

However—so the critique resumes sharply—this attempt cannot account for mistakes in calculating. Here the mistake occurs without a perceptual act's being involved. So the fourth attempt is finished, too, or rather restricted in its validity. The expansion of the empirical field under investigation, as compared with the narrow range of the first three attempts, is unquestionably a gain. Even if we have not discovered what error is as such, we have described a class of phenomena where mistakes may occur. And why should we not recognize that this way leading from perception via learning and remembering to knowledge, or from forgetting to not-knowing, is quite legitimate? It would only be wrong to think that this is the one way leading to knowledge. For the simple example of adding two numbers reveals an area—the area of *dianoia*, or mathematical reasoning, in the language of the *Republic*—where this empirical method of making progress fails, and we are then thrown back to the aporetic conclusions of the first and third attempts. Thus, in the fourth attempt, we have recognized one area—the area of perception and empirical knowledge—where we can easily account for error by using the metaphorical mass of wax. Beyond it, however, there is another area, mathematics, where we find a different kind of error and, hence, a different kind of knowledge, about which we know nothing so far except that it does not belong to the empirical world.

In the *fifth attempt*, the metaphor of the aviary in which the pieces of knowledge, like birds in a cage, fly about in flocks, in small groups, or solitarily, serves as another concrete image in order to explain the difference between possessing and having knowledge, between latent or potential[62] knowledge, on the one hand, and present or actual knowledge, on the other. In the fourth attempt, the impressions were envisaged as stamped into the block of wax without meaningful order, and stamped in such a way that some were more clear and others less clear according to the consistency of the wax, i.e., the individual. Now in the fifth attempt, the pieces of knowledge are shown as ordered, comprising (according to their nature) larger or smaller groups, or being solitary, and moving about in the aviary with the same kind of naturalness as they did outside. The world of knowledge now seems to be an ordered system that operates according to its own rules. Error enters the picture not in the "first catching" of the birds, i.e., in the first acquiring of knowledge, but in the "second catching" of the birds when they are inside the aviary, i.e., in the converting of the knowledge we possess into a knowledge we have. In this second catching we may mistakenly catch "one piece of knowledge instead of another" (ἀνθ' ἑτέρας ἑτέραν). And while, in the fourth attempt, we reached the limit with arithmetic, we find that the illustration here is taken directly from the field of arithmetic, followed by grammar. If Theaitetos were not as young as he is—so we must assume— Socrates would probably have cited other fields of knowledge as well. The metaphor of the aviary shows that a "false catch" can be made. Thus, the difference between latent knowledge and

II 1e
196D–200D

actual knowledge clarifies truth and falsehood on the level of *dianoia*, or mathematical reasoning.[63]

But here, too, criticism presently sets in.[64] How can error come about as a result of the interchange of pieces of knowledge? Or, put differently, how can we get a false result from what is true? With Theaitetos' proposal that, in addition to the pieces of knowledge, we should also include in the aviary "pieces of ignorance" (ἀνεπιστημοσύναι), either we are taken back to the first aporetic conclusion, the incomprehensible mistaking of knowing for not-knowing, or else we are compelled to assume that there is another kind of knowledge that settles this conflict between knowledge and ignorance, and so forth ad infinitum. An infinite regress is the striking aporetic result of this last attempt.

Looking back on the fourth attempt, we note that it failed because of the possibility of mathematical error, which revealed above the realm of empirical knowledge a realm of another kind, that of *dianoia*. With the fifth attempt, we are in this higher realm, where mistakes in mathematical reasoning are explicated by means of a concrete metaphor. Now, however, we are confronted by a new difficulty and, at the same time, a new dimension—a series of knowledges apparently regressing ad infinitum. What is the point of this argument? We know it as the culmination of the discussion in the *Charmides*, and again we may recall that the *Theaetetus* belongs to the thematic tradition of that dialogue. It is clear, then, that the basic form of the *Charmides* re-emerges here in the culmination of the second part of the *Theaetetus*.

In the *Charmides*, we were compelled to admit that all knowledge remains empty until it is subsumed under, and raised to, the knowledge of the good. We cannot seek the solution to the problem in the *Theaetetus* anywhere else. A knowledge must be postulated that is beyond the knowledge and ignorance just encountered in the field of mathematics. If this higher knowledge seemed to go nowhere, into an infinity that would make all knowledge meaningless, then we have forgotten the light cast by the digression in the first part of the dialogue. For from this perspective, may we not say that the regress terminates when knowledge is no longer merely knowledge of knowledge, but is knowledge "of the divine and of justice and truth"? This, then, would be a level of knowledge to which both empirical and mathematical knowledge are subordinated. When Socrates breaks off here, admitting that the argument shows we did not come to any satisfactory results because we sought first to explain "false belief" instead of knowledge, his words must be understood ironically, i.e., as being both true and false. Indeed, there can be no complete clarity "until we have given a satisfactory account of the nature of knowledge." Yet, the aporetic attempts inquiring into the nature of falsehood were not wrong but a right way in the direction toward the goal. These attempts indicated that the field of knowledge can be put into a hierarchical order up to a level that—had we reached it—would show a way out of the impasse.

The specific problem of this part of the dialogue is the analysis of the definition that knowledge is "true opinion," the intention being to show the relationship between these two modes of knowing and to clarify one by contrast with the other. If the analysis of error had not done a great deal of this work of clarification, the organization of this section would show a lack of balance. For the original definition is now refuted very briefly and simply by an appeal to life.[65]

There is a profession whose practice proves that the definition is wrong. What is meant is the profession of orators and, especially, skilled pleaders or "lawyers" (δικανικοί). The very conditions under which they practice show that they aim at persuasion, but never at instruction, and that they may produce true opinion ("true" under the best circumstances), but never knowledge. This is the old argument known to us from the *Alcibiades Major* (114B *et seq.*) and the *Gorgias* (454A *et seq.*).[66] In the *Theaetetus* it has still another meaning. These orators must talk "by the clock" (201B 2). This was said previously, in the digression (172E 1), where this type of activity was contrasted with that of the philosopher, with that of Socrates, or with that taking place here in the dialogue, the inquiry into truth—an activity for which one must "have time," i.e., be free from external compulsion, as we heard then and later on (187E).

II 2
200D–201C

Thus, at the end of the second part of the dialogue, it is not only "opinion" and "knowledge" that are sharply separated. From the digression there is carried over into this separation the radical difference also between orator and philosopher, and indeed, the hostility between these two ways of life. And from the perspective of this hierarchy of ways of life and modes of knowledge, we recognize the superiority of the philosopher and knowledge over the orator and opinion.

In the *third part* of the dialogue, we examine the third definition to be proposed: knowledge is true opinion (or true belief) together with an account (ἡ μετὰ λόγου ἀληθὴς δόξα). Theaitetos has heard this definition from someone else; so has Socrates. It is customary to think of Antisthenes, because the theory that —according to Socrates—lies behind this definition seems to be that of Antisthenes.[67] But this can hardly be the case for the definition itself because, according to Aristotle's explicit statement, the Cynics did not admit that there was any possibility of defining "what is."[68] How much of this formulation here is Plato's own and how much it owes to others can never be completely settled. At any rate, we do well to remember that Plato did not write to preserve some otherwise extinct chapter in the history of philosophy. The only question relevant to an understanding of the dialogue is why this definition is introduced here.

Knowledge differs from true opinion or belief by virtue of the fact that an account, *logos*, is added to the latter. This is not far from Plato's own view.[69] In the *Meno* (97b *et seq.*), Socrates points out that true opinion must be bound to an account of the cause in order to become knowledge. In the *Symposium* (202a), it is said more guardedly that as long as we have true belief without being able to give an account, we do not as yet have knowledge. And so Socrates says, in the *Theaetetus* (202d), it is quite "obvious" that there cannot be any knowledge without an account (*logos*) and true belief (χωρὶς τοῦ λόγου τε καὶ ὀρθῆς δόξης). Thus, *logos* is of highest significance in contributing to knowledge, and it is for this reason that Plato here analyzes the meaning of this term by criticizing a theory with which he does not wish to be identified.

Socrates had developed this theory—one might call it a type
of epistemological atomism[70]—on the first level of the dialogue
(156A–157C) and had touched on it again on the second level
(182AB). Now he presents it a third time as if it were a
"dream." As far as the simplest elements (πρῶτα στοιχεῖα) in
nature are concerned, no conceptual account can be given of
them. They can only be named, and nothing can be added to the
names. They are perceptible and nameable, but inexplicable
(ἄλογα) and unknowable (ἄγνωστα). An account or description
(*logos*) can be given only of the things that are composed, or
combined, out of these elements as a sentence (*logos*) is composed of individual "names" or words. Element and letter correspond to each other, and a syllable is a complex of letters (or
elements). Thus, the theory is compared to the relationship that
holds between letters and syllable, but this relationship also
represents a larger class of phenomena (204A 3, 206B 6).

Plato has two things in common with this theory, which is
generally believed (as we said) to be that of Antisthenes.[71] In
the philosophical part of the *Seventh Letter*, he mentions first
the name and then the *logos* as the two lowest levels on the
ladder leading up toward knowledge of being. A similar ranking, *logos* above mere name, occurs in the *Sophist* (218c).[72]
Furthermore, even in the *Cratylus* (424B *et seq.*), and in the late
works, the *Sophist* (252E *et seq.*) and the *Philebus* (18B *et seq.*),
the system of letters is used by Plato as a symbol for the system
in the world of things. The elements are the last indivisible
"forms" to which everything else is reduced in this system. And
as in this "theory of Antisthenes" the point is that the elements
and the names corresponding to them are "interlaced" with each
other, so is the "interlacing of Forms" the most important
theme in the *Sophist*.

Yet, despite these affinities, or precisely because of them,
Plato intends to show what his own theory is, in contrast to the
other. So, after an initial assent, the "dream" (*Theaetetus* 202c
5) is quickly subjected to Socrates' criticism. This critique
serves to dispose of the radical distinction between letters and
syllable. Either a syllable is the sum of its component parts—
and if so it is incomprehensible how the parts that are "un-

III 1
201c–206c

knowable" can form a "knowable" whole. Or the syllable is one single form, or entity (μίαν τινὰ ἰδέαν, 203C 5; ἔν τι γεγονὸς εἶδος ἰδέαν μίαν αὐτὸ αὑτοῦ ἔχον, 203E 3), an indivisible unity—and this indivisibility is explained by an analysis of the two concepts, "sum" (πᾶν), and "whole" or "entire" (ὅλον).[73] In this case we would have to say that the syllable is unknowable (205E) as the letters were previously. Experience teaches the same lesson as dialectics. In teaching others to read, write, or play an instrument, we begin by teaching them the "elements," which provide a clearer and firmer grasp of the subject than the "combination" does. And other examples might be given to prove this point, Socrates says, before he turns to the examination of the definition as such (206C).

We stop briefly to take another look at these last discussions. The reason for analyzing this "theory of Antisthenes" evidently was to show that the world of being becomes "a-logical" if no account (*logos*) can be given of its elements. And being is atomized if the higher forms are nothing but aggregates of lower forms. Both dangers are avoided if we envisage the higher "Forms" as a unitary entity, or *Eidos*, and similarly envisage the elements themselves, i.e., if we transfer the "logical" character of the higher "Forms" to the simplest, indivisible elements. In this way we may see—though by means of intentionally primitive examples—that the forms of being constitute an ordered system. Just as, at the end of the dialogue's first part, the "one single Form of the soul" (μίαν τινὰ ἰδέαν, 184D 3) emerged, the soul as a whole that is more than the sum of its perceptions and is "occupied with things by itself" (187A 5), so there emerges here on the side of things the "one Form" that can no more than the soul be envisaged as an aggregate of elements. It is left to the reader to co-ordinate these two aspects with each other—the soul as a whole and the "one Form of being" rescued for the *logos*.

III 2
206c–210c

After the theory has been refuted, or rather, after it has been raised to a Platonic level, Socrates turns in conclusion to a criticism of the definition that introduced the third part of the dialogue. He distinguishes three meanings of the word "account" (*logos*). In each case it turns out that the word does not add anything new to the concept of right opinion. Either the word "account" means speech itself—in which case the meaning in speech is simply expressed through the voice by means of nouns (names) and verbs—or else the word "account" means an enumeration of the elements of which a thing is composed. This meaning of "account" that refers to "elements" and their "combination" seems to go back to the theory ascribed to Antisthenes and discussed previously. But even in the case of reading and writing, we must proceed by way of the "elements." Thus, an "account" does not bring right opinion, or true belief, up to the sphere of knowledge; on the contrary, it is indispensable for having a true belief. On the first level, "account" is interpreted physically. On the second level, it is interpreted atomistically and mechanically. On the third level, it is raised to its own characteristic meaning. True belief together with an account no longer means belief expressed in sounds or belief that simply enumerates all the elements of which a thing is composed. Now, on the third level, it is the determination of the specific difference (ᾧ τῶν ἁπάντων διαφέρει τὸ ἐρωτηθέν) that distinguishes a thing from the others in the same class (κοινόν). Again it is shown that the correct notion of anything must include its distinguishing mark. If we say, however, that by "account" we mean a knowledge of this distinguishing mark, instead of a true belief, then it follows that we are going around in a circle trying to explain what is unknown, namely knowledge, by this very thing that is unknown. With this circle the dialogue ends aporetically.

The meaning of the third part was to show, in different stages, the meaning of *logos* as the highest concept to which the dialectical discussion had risen. This was the reason for including this concept in the third definition. Why, then, does the discussion end in a vicious circle? What a peculiar paradox it is that the dialogue constructed as a succession of definitions finally runs aground on the problem of definition! Or does this ending suggest that we cannot know what knowledge is by means of the *logos* (thought) alone, i.e., by following the path of this dialogue? How could we, when, according to the theory of knowledge outlined in the *Seventh Letter*, *logos* occupies the second stage and knowledge is to be found in the fourth stage far above it? How could we, when, to return to the *Theaetetus*, the digression has shown us the philosopher, the man of knowledge, in his "escape from here to another world," in his "approximation of the divine," in his "true wisdom and virtue"? Thus, we see that *logos* even at its highest level cannot explain the specific characteristic of knowledge, indispensable as *logos* is for such a task. Knowledge stands far above the *logos*. This is the insight to which the conclusion of the dialogue leads— by means of the *logos*.

210D   Socrates takes leave by saying that he must go now to meet the indictment drawn up against him by Meletos. Here the setting in which this conversation has taken place comes once more to life. Here we are once more thrown back to the digression where we witnessed the hostile encounter between philosopher and political orator, and we feel the tremendous power of the "despite it all" that is the law of the Socratic existence. From a formal view, Socrates' words remind us of the ending of the *Euthyphro*. And when he continues, "Tomorrow morning let us here meet again," we sense the never-ending task of the seeker of wisdom even as we sense it at the close of the *Charmides* and the *Laches*. Thus we may say once more that the *Theaetetus* displays, in the period of Plato's late maturity, the structure of the early aporetic dialogues. It is the same construction, here as in the early dialogues, by which we follow a series of definitions that are proposed and overthrown, never catching the thing to be defined. The building up in three stages is the same in the *Theaetetus* as in the *Thrasymachus*, and the set of three definitions the same as in the *Charmides*, the *Euthyphro*, and the *Hippias Major*.

Yet, there is one feature that distinguishes the *Theaetetus* from all these dialogues. While they never reach the goal toward which they are moving, that realm is included here in the construction of the *Theaetetus* by virtue of the digression. Thus, for *once* in the writings of Plato, the pattern characteristic of the aporetic dialogues in search of a definition is broken. It is transformed here by the formal structure of the *Gorgias* and the *Republic*. The juxtaposition is rough, but this roughness certainly does not indicate any defective powers on Plato's part.[74] It is a symbol of something else—that the gradual ascent through inconclusive results, indispensable as it is, can never lead to the knowledge of knowledge. In the words of the *Seventh Letter*, the light is "suddenly kindled like a flash by a leaping spark."

Viewed from the distance, the dialogue looks like a pyramid of steps. The area in which knowledge is to be discovered grows more and more restricted as the discussion moves upward in three levels. And at last it becomes clear that the very highest level, true knowledge, lies still beyond the highest step one can climb.[75] What is revealed is the structure of the aporetic dialogues in search of a definition. Moreover, once we have seen that this is interpenetrated by another structure, we realize that, on the lowest level, there is a vast distance between a "knowledge" of white and cold, of which an animal also is capable, and the knowledge of the divine or the just, which only the philosopher can approximate. The layers in between are examined on the second level and the third. On the second level, in the area of "opinion" (*doxa*), falsehood—and, implicitly, truth—is followed in ascending layers. On the third level, it is the area of *logos* that is refined in upward stages. At the height of both the second and the third levels, we catch a glimpse of true knowledge as something that one cannot attain simply by making another move of the same kind as those already made. And so the view from these two levels leads upward to the realm that had suddenly opened up on the lowest level, where it was called the realm of the divine or the just.

Finally, when we look back from the end of the dialogue to the beginning (142c 6), and from both beginning and end to the digression in between, we can see epistemology, ethics, and metaphysics, and beyond them all another dimension: human existence. It is here that we encounter what Jaspers has called the "boundary situation" of life—the struggle against brute force, the acceptance of suffering, and the knowledge of death. All this is present in the living reality called "Socrates." And all this permeates (more than a reader of the *Theaetetus* may suspect) the inquiry into what is knowledge.

TWENTY-FOUR

Parmenides

WHEN he wrote the *Theaetetus*, Plato envisaged his own position as situated between the two fronts, "Parmenides" and "Herakleitos." In the *Theaetetus*, he confronts the representatives of perpetual and all-engulfing flux. At the same time, he must have been thinking of the confrontation with the representatives of the one, unchanging being, that dramatic moment when Socrates "while quite young met Parmenides, who was then quite old." These words of the *Theaetetus* (183E) clearly point to the *Parmenides*, regardless of whether Plato then only planned to write the *Parmenides*, already had written it, or was working on it simultaneously.[1] His own theory of eternal Forms had to be tested—in this test to gain a new clarity—against the radical rigidity of the Parmenidean view of being.[2]

A certain Kephalos is the narrator. He first relates—it is not clear to whom or where, only not in Athens and hardly in his home town of Clazomenae—how he came to Athens with some fellow citizens, "philosophical-minded" men (i.e., desirous of learning), and heard reported the conversation that Socrates had had with Parmenides and Zeno a long time ago, some fifty years back. Kephalos' origin cannot have been accidentally chosen by Plato, as prominent as it is in the opening of the dialogue. According to Proklos, Plato intended to show the meeting in Athens of the two "schools" whose extremes Socrates and Plato reconciled, the "Ionian" philosophers who dealt with the "nature of things," as against the "Italic" representatives of conceptual thought (περὶ τῶν εἰδῶν θεωρία)

190

who denied the reality of the world of appearances.[3] With less strain, the city of Clazomenae must suggest to everybody the name of Anaxagoras, its greatest citizen,[4] who was the first to elevate "mind" to its proper place in and against the world of things and therefore represents a marker on the way to Plato's own goal, including that pursued here in the *Parmenides*.[5] Must we not say that in exchange for what his city has given others, including Athens herself, Kephalos reaps more than ample reward? For Plato, admiringly adopting the "mind" of Anaxagoras, carried this concept far beyond Anaxagoras (*Phaedo* 97c *et seq.*). Those who believe, however, that Plato could introduce "philosophical-minded" men from Clazomenae without thinking of the philosopher who lived in this city will repudiate what we just said as whim or fancy. Against such a spirit of doubt, we can only fall back upon the conviction constantly confirmed anew that Plato, like nature, "does nothing in vain" (οὐδὲν μάτην ποιεῖ).

The transmission of the conversation is reconstructed elaborately, and Plato willingly accepted the pedantic exactness of such transitions as "Antiphon said that Pythodoros had said that . . ." (One might almost say that Plato used this technique here consciously, in ironic contrast to that used and emphasized in the *Theaetetus*.[6]) Kephalos, then, is the narrator. Adeimantos and Glaukon, known to everybody from the *Republic*, serve here only to introduce Kephalos to Antiphon, their (and Plato's) stepbrother. Antiphon, now interested in almost nothing but his racing stable, is as it were the mechanical intermediary of the conversation we are about to hear. (Today his place might be taken by a record or tape.) Only "a certain Pythodoros, a member of Zeno's circle" had actually been present during the conversation itself.

In the *Alcibiades Major* (179A), Socrates reports that Pythodoros, the son of Isolochos, had taken a course of instruction with Zeno—and paid a hundred minae for it—together with Kallias, the son of Kalliades.[7] Pythodoros and Kallias later became excellent commanders under Perikles. In the year 432, Kallias was in command of the Athenian army before Potidaea, and so both Socrates and Alkibiades must have served under him. All this was alive in Plato's mind—as it must have been in the minds of many of his Athenian readers, too—when he wrote the *Alcibiades* and certainly when he wrote the *Parmenides*. The man from Clazomenae, however, knows little more than malicious gossip (127B 5). Still, Pythodoros had been present during the conversation that Parmenides and Zeno had had with Socrates. It would be an artificial construction to say, as Proklos does, that there is an upward movement from the many (represented by the men from Clazomenae) by way of duality (represented by Adeimantos and Glaukon) to unity (represented by Socrates),⁸ but stages of approximation are clearly recognizable. And as in the *Symposium*, the initial intention is to make us see the distance in time.⁹ For what is shown here is the way in which the philosophy of Forms, in a contest with the Eleatic doctrine of being, gains a new clarity about itself. Plato could show this confrontation in a visual manner only by a meeting between Parmenides and Socrates when Socrates was a young man and still had a lifetime before him in which these problems could mature. Just as the difficulties encountered here had arisen a long time ago, so they had also been thought about for a long time.

But this is not all. What does the young Aristotle signify in this circle? His function in the dialogue will be confined to accompanying the discourse of Parmenides by saying yes or no, in various ways. Did Plato choose the name Aristotle because at the time he was writing the dialogue the young man from Stagira had already joined the Academy?¹⁰ The words by which the Aristotle in the dialogue is introduced point in an altogether different direction: "Later he was one of the Thirty" (127D 2). Thus, he was a member of the oligarchy of "Thirty Tyrants" who, as everybody knows from the *Apology* (32D), intended to make Socrates an accomplice in their crimes and who, since he refused, would "probably" have killed him—if there had been time. The conversation itself is seemingly the most abstract imaginable, and yet for a moment the reader is to be reminded of the fate of Socrates. Here, too, *Idea* and existence, the truth of being and the reality of life, being and time, en-

gender a tension that is clearly recognizable, though difficult
to grasp. Presently this will become clearer still.

Zeno has almost finished reading from his treatise to Socrates
and others when Parmenides comes in with a few companions.
The conversation begins as soon as the reading is finished.   1 1
Socrates leads off by raising to a significant level the gossip   127A–130A
about the personal relationship of the two Eleatic philosophers
(128A). It is also Socrates who establishes the genuine philosophical link between the two. He has correctly seen, like a
"hunting dog," that Zeno's arguments complement the thesis
of Parmenides. This Zeno confirms, an admission made more
emphatic by his slight correction. He had written the treatise,
Zeno continues, in the spirit of "love of controversy" (φιλονικία)
characteristic of his younger days, not in the mature spirit of
"striving for honor" (φιλοτιμία), and then—Plato further
invents—the treatise had been stolen.[11] (. . . As if there were no
other motives than those for writing, as if Plato's own writing,
and still more so, the non-writing of Socrates, whose unwritten
conversations nobody can steal, were not inspired by much
higher motives!)

"Love of controversy": this description associates Zeno's
treatise On Nature, or Being, with Gorgias' On Nature or Not-
Being. There always has been a danger of reading Zeno in the
spirit of Gorgias, and even Isokrates (whom Wilamowitz calls
"the high priest of general education") connected them closely.[12]
Plato's Socrates shows, however, that Zeno's dialectic is not
sophistic so long as—but only so long as—it serves the purpose
of Parmenides. Yet the conjunction of the two Eleatics is still
significant in the second part of the dialogue. There, too, the
discussion deals first with the Parmenidean thesis of unity and
then with Zeno's thesis of plurality, even if the two theses are
treated as antinomies and thus seem to cancel each other. Only
later can it be shown that this antinomy inherently contains the
dialectical relationship between the Form (Eidos) and the
plurality of things co-ordinated with it. Yet we may point out
in advance that it is Socrates who—by identifying, at the very
beginning, the two aspects of the Eleatic doctrine—suggests

that the four pairs of antinomies in the second part of the dialogue must be understood as constituting a uniform dialectical structure. Plato would never have had Socrates be silent in listening to this polyphonous dialectic if it did not acquire its true meaning through the power called "Socrates." (This will be shown later.)

It is Socrates, then, who grasps or creates the unity of Parmenides and Zeno. He has hardly done so when his own view of things disturbs the unqualified agreement between the view of "the One" and the negation of plurality. Reality is too complex to be caught in such a simple formula. The view that there is only one being is an essential insight on the part of Parmenides, but he oversimplifies. Zeno is quite right in proving that plurality contains all opposites within itself. He, in turn, is mistaken in the belief that he has shown thereby that the concept of plurality, or "the many," is self-contradictory.[13] Rising above Parmenides and Zeno there is Plato's world-view as represented by Socrates—on one side, "the Forms in themselves," on the other, "the many" partaking in the Forms. Socrates shows, by a number of examples, that the union of opposites is quite possible in the domain of the many, but not in the world of Forms. "Alike" cannot be "unlike," and one cannot simultaneously be many.

Here we must point out what undoubtedly is an intended ambiguity that seems to become more extreme in the course of Socrates' speech. If someone were to show (a) that the like-itself (αὐτὰ τὰ ὅμοια) becomes unlike, or the unlike-itself (ἀνόμοια) becomes like, then this would be quite "surprising" (or even quite "portentous," τέρας). If someone were to show (b) that the one (ὃ ἔστιν ἕν) is many, or that plurality is unity, then that "would astonish me" (θαυμάσομαι). If someone were to show (c) that the "kinds" (γένη) and the "forms" (εἴδη) undergo within themselves contrary conditions of the sort we have just heard about, then that "would be most astonishing" (ἄξιον θαυμάζειν). If, by means of the method of division, someone were to show (d) that contrasting forms when put in opposition have the power of combining with each other and again separating from each other, then "I would be filled with astonishment" (ἀγαίμην ἂν θαυμαστῶς). "I would be still more astonished"—ἀγασθείην ἄν—if (e) the various combinations (or, according to Socrates, "perplexities") proved by Zeno for things in the visible world were to apply also to the Forms in the intelligible world.

It is clear that Socrates' speech, to begin with, restricts the combination of opposites to the field of experiences, or the world of becoming. It is more questionable whether, as the speech progresses, it does not also open up the possibility that there might be corresponding combination and separation of forms in the world of being. We cannot overlook this possibility, because the phrase "combination of forms" (ἐν τοῖς εἴδεσι πλεκομένην, 129E 6) reminds us too much of the "combination" of concepts in the Sophist (πεπλέχθαι συμπλοκήν, 240c 1), and because the "forms" mentioned here—likeness and unlikeness, one and many, rest and motion—remind us of the "general kinds" mentioned in the Sophist. But leaving these matters aside, we see how Socrates develops the dual thesis of the Eleatics and, at the same time, overcomes it by his own view of things—if this "theory" of his can be proved.

The Eleatics are not annoyed, contrary to the narrator's expectation. They listen attentively and exchange glances and smiles in admiration of Socrates. Evidently they do not feel that they have been opposed or refuted, but instead think they have been proved right or perhaps carried beyond themselves. Now the actual analysis commences. Parmenides exposes the difficulties inherent in the view put forth by Socrates. Socrates defends this thesis without being able to completely hold his ground against the critique. But from now on Parmenides thinks "Socratically"—an indication that we have read his smile correctly—and the old philosopher repeatedly admonishes the young man to continue his search along the path he has chosen.[14]

The difficulties exposed by Parmenides are clearly divided into three groups. First, it is necessary to determine the contents of the world of Forms. Socrates is quite sure (as it must have been Plato's own experience about which he had no doubt) that relational terms such as "likeness" and moral concepts such as "justice" represent genuine Forms. He hesitates, how-

I 2
130A–135c

I 2a
130A–130E

ever, in the case of "man" or "fire," and succumbs to utter perplexity in the case of "hair, mud, and dirt." He prefers, therefore, to go back to the Forms mentioned first, since about them he feels certain. Parmenides suggests that the reason for Socrates' hesitation with regard to the last group is that it seems to be "quite trivial and worthless" (ἀτιμότατον καὶ φαυλότατον). Parmenides then concludes by predicting that, in due course, the young man now still dubious will himself come to recognize, independently of what others think, that nothing is to be despised as worthless (οὐδὲν ἀτιμάσεις).

The man who makes this prediction is the discoverer of the concept of the one being in which there are no qualitative differences, but of which are predicated all the attributes of highest value: "unborn, imperishable, and inviolate like a sacred shrine" (ἄσυλον). As in his own philosophical poem, so here too Parmenides warns against the "opinions of mankind." And indeed in the *Seventh Letter* (342D) where Plato, then an old man, speaks for himself, it is clear he has come to expand the world of Forms so that it includes geometric shapes and colored surfaces, moral concepts, all bodies both artificial and natural, the physical elements, living creatures, and all the states of the soul. In the dialogues themselves, moral concepts are found side by side with mathematical concepts; later, there are various additions.[15] And the discussion continues on—with Xenokrates, Speusippos, and Aristotle. Evidently this is a problem that, by its very nature, must not be settled definitely lest the result be dogmatic rigidity.

I 2b
130E–133A   The second group of difficulties deals with the relationship of the Form (*Eidos*) to the many things that partake in it. Parmenides attempts to misinterpret this relationship and Socrates, in turn, attempts to make it intelligible by his own powers. That in this exchange he fails and Parmenides ultimately prevails is no reason to misunderstand the relative merits of the respective arguments. There is abundant evidence, especially in the earlier dialogues, to show how a Charmides, a Lysis, or an Alkibiades may be on the right path only to be pushed in the wrong direction by Socratic irony. Here in the *Parmenides*, Socrates himself is a beginner—but what a beginner!

Three times Parmenides attempts to derive paradoxical or nonsensical consequences from the theory proposed by Socrates. He argues, first (131A), that if the Form is wholly in each of the many things, it is separate from itself (χωρὶς ἑαυτοῦ); second (131c), that if a part of the Form is in each of the many things, it is divisible; third (132A), that for the Form to be linked with the many things, another Form is needed to mediate between Form and things and so on ad infinitum. These three arguments are of different value. The second is purely eristic and, with Socrates assenting, Parmenides himself shows that it is nonsense. The third criticism is the argument of the "third man," much discussed probably in Plato's own circle, then by Aristotle, and again in our own time. All three arguments wrongly conceive of the Form as a thing in space and time, or, in the language of the Neoplatonists, as "co-ordinate with" (ὁμοταγές, σύστοιχον) individual things.[16] Yet, in the third argument, Parmenides explicitly refers the "idea," "vision," or "prototype" to the act of "seeing" or "looking" (ἰδόντι, ἴδῃς, 132A 3 and 7) and explains that this is a mental act, the mind's vision—a conception that Socrates then makes his own.

Three times Socrates attempts to defend his theory. First (131B), he suggests that the Form has the same indivisible unity as the day, which is everywhere at once and envelops each man wholly. Parmenides replies with the much more "thing-like" analogy of the awning a part of which covers each man. In this exchange, the Socratic analogy shows all the more concretely that the Form is indivisible and is of a higher order of spirituality, for the image of the day reminds us, not accidentally, of the light metaphysics in the *Republic*. Second (132B), Socrates argues that the Form must be a "thought" (νόημα) existing "in the mind." Viewed in the context of the *Seventh Letter* (342D), where it is said that "mind is the nearest in affinity and likeness" to the object of knowledge, i.e., the Form, and viewed also in the context of the *Sophist* (249A), where mind, life, and soul are attributed to perfect being, this passage of the *Parmenides* shows how Socrates tries to make it clear that the Form or *Idea* must be envisaged as an incorporeal, spiritual entity, in contrast to material objects in space.

Even in the *Meno* (86B) it was said that the "reality of true being is always in the soul, or mind," and what is called the doctrine of recollection in the *Phaedo* rests on the same conception or experience. Thus, Plato would have accepted this formulation at any time provided that the phrase "in the mind" not be misinterpreted to mean "only in the mind" or "in the mind of the individual." Aristotle resumes this discussion in his *De anima* (III 4 428ᵃ 27). He agrees with those who say that the soul is the "seat of the Forms" (τόπος εἰδῶν), qualifying this statement in two respects. The Forms are not in the soul as a whole, but only in its rational part, and they are present not as actualities, but only potentially. The medieval controversy over the status of universals may be heard far in the distance and, still farther ahead, the *Critique of Pure Reason.* In the dialogue, too, Parmenides' critique reveals the danger inherent in this view. It may reduce being itself to nothing but a thought.

Third (132D), Socrates argues that the Forms (now speaking of them in the plural) are "in nature." In other words, they are not thoughts, as one might wrongly infer from the expression "in the mind." Nor are they artifacts. (*Techne* is the opposite of *physis*.) They belong to the most comprehensive "system of order in nature" that exists independently of human thought and technique.[17] They are the prototypes (παραδείγματα), and the participation of things consists in their being made in the likeness of these prototypes. But just as the previous metaphor raised the danger that the Forms might be nothing but thoughts, so this third attempt to defend them raises the danger that they might be mistaken for material things with spatial relations among them. Again, we may fail to see the essential difference between Forms and individual things. This failure is revealed in the argument of the "third man," the *reductio ad infinitum* frequently discussed in ancient as well as modern times.[18] True, Socrates fails to make his point in this third try as in the previous two. We must not fail, however, to recognize and connect the repeated efforts he makes to explain the nature of Forms—even if Plato's Parmenides does expose the difficulties in the analogies and metaphors employed and, as the better-trained dialectician, emerge as victor in this ex-change.[19]

Finally, the last and worst difficulty (μέγιστον, 133в 4) is shown. The Forms are not "in us" (ἐν ἡμῖν), but "in them-selves." They are related to each other (πρὸς αὑτάς), not to the copies in our world. And these copies, in turn, are related to each other, not to the prototypes.[20] Prototype and copy belong to different realms of being. It follows that "knowledge itself" concerned with true being is of an entirely different order from "knowledge with us" (i.e., an empirical knowledge concerned with the things in actual experience). Prototype and copy be-long to different domains of knowledge. And, at the end of all this, after we compare the master-slave relationship in our world with mastership itself and slavery itself, we realize that prototype and copy also belong to different spheres of action or power (δύναμις).[21] And so we reach the conclusion that the Forms, beauty itself, goodness itself, cannot be known (ἄγνω-στον) by us.

1 2c
133a–135c

The paradox inherent in this line of thought becomes more striking if we carry it further. The prototypes are the objects of knowledge for him who has knowledge itself—and that can only be a god; but then the things in our world cannot be known by him. And so the world is sharply divided into two completely unrelated spheres of being, of knowledge, and of efficient power. If this is the result, we must indeed ask our-selves do Forms (or *Ideas*) exist at all, and are they not com-pletely unknowable, at least for us. If we posit them as real, do they not seem to split up both the unity of the world and the unity of knowledge? Yet, here in the dialogue, it is Parmenides who is so imbued with the doctrine of Socrates that he con-cludes, quite Socratically, that a person who refuses to believe that the Forms exist would destroy the possibility of any mean-ingful discourse (τὴν τοῦ διαλέγεσθαι δύναμιν παντάπασι διαφθερεῖ, 135c).

Let us also consider the most radical implication of this last problem raised by Parmenides. The gods are not our masters nor do they know things human. Human thought, in turn, can-not know anything of divine being, and furthermore—though this is not said explicitly, it is implied by the reference to masters and servants—we human beings are not capable of serving the gods. In reading these words of Plato's Parmenides, and thinking them over, are we not reminded of the indictment against Socrates himself? Great as the distance may be that separates the *Parmenides* from the *Apology* and the *Euthyphro*, we must think of these earlier dialogues in order to realize that there is deep personal and historical significance underlying the protest here expressed by the youthful Socrates: "That would be a strange argument which would deprive the gods of knowledge." What matters here is not ontology alone, nor even theology alone. For a moment it is a matter of life and death, of Socratic existence.

1 3

135c–137c

At this critical point in the conversation, Parmenides informs Socrates that what he lacks is proper training. Socrates has pursued the search for Forms too directly, without first submitting to the kind of logical training that most people despise as idle talk. Then, on being urged by the audience, Parmenides agrees to give a demonstration of such training, using the means of Zeno's dialectic.

The entire second half of the dialogue is given over now to Parmenides and this young Aristotle, who merely says yes or no. It is stated explicitly that he is not supposed to raise any objections. There follows a peculiar and, for Plato, a new kind of dialogue which might just as well be—or so it would seem at first sight—a systematic treatise or lecture.[22] Yet, can we really assume that Plato's creative irony is not at work here too? Parmenides would like to have a moment's rest between exposition and answer. What about the reader? Perhaps he should not take a rest, but should instead think actively about what has been said and often reply quite differently from the young Aristotle. Moreover, should not the reader put himself in the place of Socrates standing by in silence? For Socrates would reply differently, or raise different questions, as far as specific details are concerned. And above all, the entire dialectic of the second part acquires new meaning when it is viewed from the Socratic perspective.

Something else often is misunderstood. It is customary to

read the second part of the dialogue as if the respondent were some young man who, by chance, is called Aristotle. As we pointed out earlier, this will not do. There must have been a reason for Plato's selecting a young man of whom he says explicitly that he later became one of the Thirty. Plato intends to direct the reader to a historical event that occurred decades later, and the difference between the two young men present here is to be understood symbolically. Aristotle says yes and no as the master wishes. Later he will be a member of an autocratic ruling group that is to impose its yes and no upon others. Yet Socrates goes his own way here vis-à-vis Parmenides and Zeno as he will later go his own way, at the risk of his life, vis-à-vis the Thirty.

With regard to the second part of the *Parmenides*, there is an ancient division among interpreters.[23] One group maintains that in calling this part an "exercise," Plato is speaking his mind both clearly and completely. The other group, more "suspicious" (because of his literary ironies) of what Plato says, seeks to discover a substantive content behind the formal exercise. If we were to "trust" Plato's words, these commentators maintain, we would have to interpret the three speeches on love in the *Phaedrus*, too, as no more than oratorical exercises. According to the first group of interpreters, there is no resolution of the difficulties raised in the opening part of the conversation, which alone is of substantive significance, in their opinion. According to the other group, however, we may look for such a resolution precisely in the dialectics of the second part.

The same division of views exists with regard to the dramatic structure of the dialogue. According to the first group of interpreters, the presence of Socrates makes no difference in the meaning of the closing half, and might as well be forgotten. According to the second group, this presence is essential, for it is Plato's Socrates who thinks beyond the dialectics of Plato's Parmenides in the direction of his own philosophical discovery. Now it may be considered probable that Plato, at this stage of his writing, would not go back to the form of the purely aporetic dialogues of his earlier period, especially since he changed the nature of this type of dialogue in the *Theaetetus* with the digres-

sion about the philosopher. It is plausible to maintain, moreover, that at no stage of Plato's writings could the actual conversation come to an end in the middle of a dialogue. Even
when he was writing the *Parmenides*, Plato was still enough
of a creative and ironic thinker, or simply enough of a human
being, not to have Socrates stand by in silence without compelling the reader to discover through this presence the Socratic
meaning in the midst of such un-Socratic exercises.

There are eight proofs divided into two groups of four, one
group positive, the other negative. Each group of four, in turn,
is divided into pairs. The first pair in each case deals with "the
One,"[24] and the second deals with "the many," or "the other"
(τὰ ἄλλα). Each pair of proofs forms an antinomy in which
thesis and antithesis seem to cancel each other. The first antinomy is followed by a synthesis[25] which undoubtedly is meant
to apply to the second antinomy as well if for no other reason
than that the second corresponds, in a diametrical arrangement,
to the first. In schematic outline:

Thesis I:	*Antithesis I:*
"the One" is separated from everything else.	"the One" is connected with everything else.

Synthesis in the
"now" (instant) of time

Thesis II:	*Antithesis II:*
"the many" are connected with "the One."	"the many" are separated from "the One."

Once we have come this far, it may be that we would look for
a synthesis, perhaps, in the case of the third and fourth antinomies also.[26] For if we disregard the fallacies, some certainly
intentional, that are strewn throughout, especially in the second
proof (this is the proof worked out in greatest detail), and if
we simply survey the over-all schema as it presents itself most
clearly in the shorter proofs beginning with the third, we are
bound to be moved to astonishment at the art of counterpoint
displayed in this polyphonous fugue. This is true even for those
of us not particularly talented in these skills to begin with. Yet,

such wonderment does not release anyone from the obligation to understand the composition as a work in which no voice can be missed.[27]

Let us add that though this contrapuntal fugue may seem to be unique, it has its predecessors in Plato's work. We would think of the *Lysis*, where Socrates himself successively develops and destroys four opposite views of the nature of friendship in order to leave the truth hanging in dialectical tension. We would go back even to such an early work as the *Hipparchus*, where a proof of the proposition that "nobody is a lover of gain" is followed by a proof of its opposite, that "everybody is a lover of gain." We may recognize that there are formal similarities even in the antithetical fallacies of the *Euthydemus*, and that behind these fallacies some genuine knowledge is pointed to, although the eristics are not aware of it. Judging from these preliminary stages, then, there is every reason to believe that what appear to be the purely formal exercises in the *Parmenides* have a content beyond the mind of the man who conducts them.

FIRST ANTINOMY—THESIS. The One has no parts, neither divisibility nor extension, neither temporal nor spatial attributes. In this proof, the One is conceived in extreme separation, only as the One and nothing else. This is the most radical conception of the One, as astonishing as it is indispensable—indispensable especially for Socrates who is listening and must recognize in this concept the mode of being of his own Forms. The question soon arises of whether we are cutting off possibilities here that ought not be cut off. Suppose the One has no shape. Does it really follow from this that it "does not partake" (137D 8) of straight or round? Or would Socrates, were he the respondent, remind Parmenides here of what they had agreed upon previously (129A *et seq.*, 130B), i.e., of the difference between the Form (*Eidos*) and the thing that partakes of it? Similarly, even if sameness and difference, space and time, cannot be ascribed to the One—and granted that these distinctions are necessary— it is still an open question whether combining the One with these concepts may also be possible.

Must this question be discussed at all? Had not Parmenides

II 1
137c–157B

II 1a
137c–142A

shown in his poem that there is only the One and nothing else but the One? Plato's Parmenides, indeed, follows the outline of thought in the philosophical poem by the historical Parmenides. Both here in the dialogue and in the poem, the One is said to be without parts, motion, and change. Plato's Parmenides surpasses the real Parmenides, however, in the consequences derived from this thesis. In the poem,[28] being has the attributes of wholeness (οὖλον, 8 4), of imperturbable rest (ἀτρεμές, 8 4; ἀκίνητον, 8 26), of remaining in its own sameness (ταὐτόν τ' ἐν ταὐτῷ τε μένον, 8 29), of limitation (πεῖρας, 8 31; οὐκ ἀτελεύτητον, 8 32). In Plato's *Parmenides*, it is deprived of all these attributes, as of those mentioned previously. It is without beginning and end, i.e., is infinite (137D); it is without shape, neither round nor straight (137DE); it is nowhere, neither in another nor in itself (138A); it is neither at rest nor in motion (138B); it is not the same as itself nor as another (139B). Indeed, if the One is nothing but the One, there is no reason why it should have any attributes. Thus, the Parmenidean "One" carried to its logical conclusions refutes itself. Nothing can be predicated of it; it becomes nothing. It cannot be spoken of or thought, but since we have been speaking and thinking of it all along, the Parmenidean view has refuted itself—". . . if we can trust such an argument," as Parmenides says at the end (141E 12). By this he is suggesting to his own disciples that there might be reasons for doubting the radical consequences of the view developed here. We need not repeat that Socrates would have replied throughout quite differently from the obedient young Aristotle.

To describe the One in all its purity was the merit and necessary task of the thesis. Its self-refutation at the end raises questions: whether the separation of the One might not be responsible for this conclusion; whether we might not preserve its absolute nature but give up the extreme separation; whether we should not acknowledge the principle of "participation" here rejected; and whether this might not be the only correct way toward a solution. For here we are told (138B *et seq.*) that the One is neither at rest nor in motion. In the *Sophist* (245D), however, being combines with both rest and motion. Here we are told (138A) that the One is nowhere. In the *Sophist* (250B), however, being encompasses both rest and motion.

FIRST ANTINOMY—ANTITHESIS. The same thing may be looked at from a different perspective (ἀλλοῖον). The hypothesis "if there is the One" combines the One with another, namely, being. The "one being" is a whole here as it was for the historical Parmenides, but—in contrast to Parmenides—it consists here of "parts" (μόρια), and we need not misunderstand this relationship of whole and parts in a numerical or "thing-like" manner. Since the One has being and each being is a One, the "one being" is unlimited in multitude. The plurality inherent in the "one being" is derived perhaps still more strictly in a different way.[29] The concept of "one being" contains the concept of duality, since the One is "different" from being. With duality comes the concept of "three," and then the whole series of numbers. In short, the "one being" contains the possibility of plurality. The reader must keep this necessary connection in mind in order to cope with the one-sided consequences derived from this thesis. And following Socrates, who is listening, the reader must ask, Does not the thesis contain the possibility of the necessary plurality and combination of Forms, on the one hand, and the equally necessary relationship between a single Form and its manifold copies in the world, on the other?[30]

Yet here, too, confusion sets in immediately. Since not only the whole, but also each part "partakes of being" (οὐσίας μετέχει, 144A)—i.e., not only the One, but also the many—then being is cut up into the smallest possible parts (κατακερμάτισται, μεμέρισται, 144B). And if each part is "one" part, then "the One" *is* also, and it is subdivided like being. In other words, not only the "one being" is many, but the One itself is many.[31] Here the concepts of "one" and "being" are conceived in crudely material terms, and the more refined possibilities inherent in the concept of "partaking" are lost.

The conclusion, then, is most strange and doubtful: "The One is many." It is not shown that there is a necessary connection between the One and the many, or—as will be said with solemn emphasis in the *Philebus* (15D)—that the One and the many are

II 1b
142B–155E

the same in the "act of thought, or speech" (ὑπὸ λόγων). Instead, it is said that the One is simply many. And once we have
come so far, we find that a score of opposite predicates are piled
up on "the One." The One is not only, as Parmenides said in his
poem, limited (8 42), in itself (8 29), at rest (8 4), and identical with itself (8 29); it is also simultaneously unlimited, in
another, in motion, and different from itself. And so the One is
both equal and unequal to itself and the other, both younger and
older than itself and the other. It includes all opposite
predicates, but nothing is said to make us feel that these predica-
tions may be understood in different ways or that there is a
possibility of going beyond this "coincidence of opposites."

  This antithesis, proceeding as it does from the logical failure
exposed in the view of the historical Parmenides, develops the
anti-Parmenidean thesis on an extreme scale. The One here is
something like the *apeiron* of Anaximander, and it also contains
much of the *logos* of Herakleitos in the union of opposites. This
dissolution of the One into an indefinite *all*, full of opposites,
raises the question that this result may be due to hasty and undialectical reasoning with regard to the connection between the One
and the many. (Perhaps it is appropriate here to mention the passage in the *Philebus*—16c *et seq.*—where we are warned that passing too quickly from "the one" to "the limitless," without stages
and intermediaries, is a sign of eristic reasoning.) Can we
preserve the necessary connection without piling up on the One
a heap of contradictory opposites? And would not this be a way
leading out of the confusion, a way that is barred—and yet also
shown—by the antithesis as well as by the thesis?[32]

ii 1c
155ᴇ–157ʙ

First Antinomy—Synthesis. The antithesis proved that the
One participates in everything there is; the thesis repudiated
any such participation. Thesis and antithesis can be maintained
only if they apply to "different modes of time."[33] Thus, to
mediate between them we must find a point in which becoming
and passing away, separation and combination, growth and
decline coincide, i.e., a point that is "in no time." This is the
"now," the instant (τὸ ἐξαίφνης), the moment in which one mode
of being changes into its opposite. This moment reconciles not

only the antithetical propositions of the first antinomy, but also the antithetical attributes (such as motion and rest, likeness and unlikeness) that the first antithesis predicated of the One.

What, then, does this mediation of the antithetical views, their synthesis in the "now," mean for the whole discussion? What is shown here is that thesis and antithesis were advanced not in order to refute each other eristically, but in order to be seen as converging upon each other. The thesis established the absolute nature of the One, but this proof must not be pushed so far that the result is an undifferentiated nothing. The antithesis showed the need for connections, but these connections require mediation. Without intermediates, there is no way from the One to unlimited difference. The synthesis shows that what must be found is something that is absolute and not only admits but demands connection, and, conversely, a connection that not only admits but demands something that is absolute.

Where the Parmenidean formula as well as its opposite failed, the Form (*Eidos*) succeeds—the Form that Socrates had postulated in this conversation with the Eleatics and with their agreement. For the *Eidos* combines, and necessarily so, something that is absolute with a multitude of relations. The thesis serves to make us see the Form, or *Idea*, as something absolute. The antithesis points to the multitude of relations necessarily inherent in the Form. Here is the basis for a twofold view. On the one hand, there are many Forms and they may be combined; on the other hand, there is a necessary relationship between each single Form and the things "participating" in it. The thesis shows that space and time, in the sense of divisible units, do not apply to the Form. The antithesis—the most detailed demonstration, full of intentional fallacies[34]—also helps greatly to resolve the perplexities that had not found a solution in the conversation between Socrates and Parmenides.

Being (so we read in the antithesis, 144B) is "split up" into pieces because it is not absent from anything (οὐδενὸς ἀποστατεῖ). The One also is divided into infinite fragments, in as many pieces as being is, because each part of being is "one" part, i.e., the One is present in it (πρόσεστι). Thus, we quickly reach the conclusion that the One is many (144A–E). Here we must go back to the difficulties that arose in the first part of the dialogue when the Forms seemed to be divisible (μεριστὰ τὰ εἴδη, 131c 5) and "participation" was envisaged as a spatial, material process in which the Form was alienated from itself (131B et seq.). Socrates then tried (unsuccessfully) to counter such false interpretations by means of the metaphor of the day that is indivisible, and by pointing to the relationship between prototype and copy. Now Parmenides shows a dialectical solution to the problem. More accurately put, the Parmenidean dialectics shows, just as it is getting lost in the underbrush, how such a solution is possible. And it shows this both to Socrates who is listening and to the reader who is thinking in a Socratic spirit. What must remain indivisible, i.e., the One and being, was split up. Such nonsensical results were reached because participation was interpreted as if it were a spatial, material phenomenon.

How can the Form (Eidos) be in each individual thing without being "separated from itself"? This was one of the difficulties discussed in the conversation between Parmenides and Socrates (131AB). Socrates proposed a metaphorical solution to the problem by comparing Form and day. Now the Parmenidean dialectics enables Socrates to propose a conceptual solution. The thesis proved that the One cannot be in itself or in another (138AB). The antithesis proved that it is both in itself and in another (145B–E). Applied to the concept of Form (Eidos) this means that, as in the thesis, we must envisage it as pure Form and nothing else and, as in the antithesis, we must see how it can enter into another without losing its own nature, without being alienated from itself. Only if we recognize, on the one hand, that Form is strictly separate and self-enclosed, can we assert, on the other hand, that it enters into the things that "participate" in it, without our losing sight of the differences in rank between Forms and the things in the world. Thus, we preserve the immanence of Forms without surrendering their transcendence.

How can we conceive of the relationship between the Form as a prototype and the individual things that are like it by virtue of their participation, without being compelled to assume that there must be another Form mediating this relationship and so

on ad infinitum? This was another difficulty raised in the aporetic part, there leading to the argument of the "third man"
(132D–133A). The first antinomy replies to this difficulty with
the arguments concerning sameness (139B–E, 146A–147B) and
likeness (139E–140B, 147C–148D). The thesis proves that the
One is neither the same nor different, neither the same as itself
nor as another, neither different from itself nor from another.
The antithesis proves that the One is both the same as itself and
different from itself and it is both the same as another and different from another. (In the thesis, Parmenides uses the singular, in the antithesis, the plural.) Applied to the concept of
Form (*Eidos*)—or, put differently, in the mind of Socrates who
is listening—this means that, as in the thesis, we must recognize
that the Form is something absolute and, as in the antithesis,
we must see that it is outside itself as much as it is in itself, that
it is in many other things as much as it is opposed to them as
something totally "other." We must keep all eight assertions
before our eyes in order to see both immanence and transcendence simultaneously.

The eight propositions in which both likeness and unlikeness
are respectively ascribed to and denied of "the One" and "the
other" do not provide anything new, in so far as likeness is reduced to sameness, unlikeness to difference. In the case of the
first two assertions of the antithesis, however, we find a new and
rather paradoxical argument (147c 2 – 148c 2) according to
which likeness is derived from difference and unlikeness is
derived from sameness. The One is said to be like the others because it stands in the relationship of "difference" to others, which
difference is "like" their relationship to the One. (In Greek this
comes through still more strikingly because the same word
ἕτερον is used for "one" and "other.") Conversely, we conclude
that just as "difference" makes for likeness, so "sameness"
makes for unlikeness.

Applied to the concept of Form, or *Eidos*, this paradox seems
to mean something as follows. Form and the thing participating
in it are not the same or similar, nor are they different and unlike. The interrelationship is much more intimate. In being
different they are like each other; in being the same they are un-

like each other. If we abuse the fact of likeness, as Parmenides did, and derive from it the perplexing argument of the "third man," we may see here that likeness is grounded in difference and vice versa.

Perhaps this knot of paradoxes might or would be untangled —by Socrates—in still a different way, keeping strictly to the realm of Forms itself. A single Form, or *Idea*, and the other Forms necessarily posited along with it are the same and similar qua Forms. They are unlike and different from each other in so far as each is a specific Form. Again, the interrelationship is more intimate than appears at first sight. Only because the Forms are the same qua Forms can they be different Forms. And only because the Forms are completely different from each other can they combine in the single concept of "being Forms." The universe of Forms as a unified structure may be envisaged —by Socrates—beyond the paradoxical consequences derived by Parmenides.

Thesis and antithesis of the first antinomy, though contradictory, meet in a point of convergence, a synthesis symbolized by the "now," or instant of time. In this convergence, the one Form may be seen as related both to other Forms and to the individual things "participating" in it.[35] For two concepts, that of the *one* so absolute that it turns into "nothing" and that of the *one* so rich in relations that it loses itself in the limitless, converge in the *one* that is both absolute and necessarily related to *others*, i.e., in the one Form. Yet the point of convergence, the locus of the Form, also contains the possibility of divergence. It leads, on the one hand, toward an infinite multitude of relations, and on the other hand, toward the realm of not-being and unknowing. We must realize, however, that this not-being is the most radical intensification of absolute being. Just as, in one way, we reach the Forms, the unlimited world of becoming, so, in the opposite way, we reach that highest being, which Socrates characterizes in the center of the *Republic* (VI 509B) by the paradoxical expression "being beyond being."[36] Thus, Plotinos (V 1 8) can appeal explicitly to Plato's *Parmenides* in support of his own concept of the "threefold one": the first one that is pure one, the second one that is also many, and the third one that is one and is many. In this Iamblichos and Proklos follow Plotinos.[37]

SECOND ANTINOMY. The One was separated from everything else in the first thesis, and in the antithesis it was thrown together with everything else. The synthesis provided a reconciliation of these two theses. The second antinomy corresponds to the first as far as "the other" or "the many"—that which lies outside the One—is concerned. Here, too, we find the *contrast between* "the other" that is connected with the One (οὐ στέρεται παντάπασι), containing within itself all the opposites, *and* "the other" that is separated from the One, ultimately dissolving into nothing. Yet this is not merely a repetition of the previous demonstration. The simple fact that the order of the two theses is reversed cannot be without significance since, in this order, the synthesis falls symmetrically between the first two antinomies.

The *second thesis*, therefore, must be put together with the first antithesis. And here we must immediately note a change. There is no sudden leap from the other, or many, to the One as previously there was from the One to everything. On the contrary, the relationship of the many to the One is described in cautious and general terms. The many are not "wholly destitute" of the One; they "partake of it in some way" (μετέχει πη, 157c 2). A communion (κοινωνία) of the One and the many is shown, where the One is the cause of limit (πέρας), the other the cause of the unlimited (ἄπειρον). Thus, "the other" ultimately is the reservoir of all possible states (πάθη).

The One and the many in their necessary combination make up the nature of thought and speech. The One and the many, or, put differently, limit and the limitless, comprise the nature of being itself (so we are told in the *Philebus*). Limit and the limitless, or unlimited, belong to the "general kinds" (γένη, εἴδη) examined in the *Sophist* with respect to their possible combination (κοινωνία). Thus, the second thesis points once more toward this realm of pure being. Moreover, "the One" is occasionally called "one Form" (μία τις ἰδέα, 157D 8), and "the other" is

II 2
157B–160B

II 2a
157B–159B

occasionally called "the nature other than the Form" (ἡ ἑτέρα
φύσις τοῦ εἴδους, 158c 6), so that the eternal Form, the essentially different mode of being of the many, and the participation
of the many in the "one Form" must become still clearer in the
mind of Socrates who is listening. Once more, Parmenides does
not pursue these implications. Instead, as if it were a matter of
course, he interprets *par-taking* again as though it referred to the
relationship between parts and a whole. Is he testing us, perhaps, on whether we have learned—from the aporetic first part
of the dialogue as well as from the first antithesis—to see the
danger inherent in this false interpretation?

II 2b
159B–160B
The separation between the One and the many, which was just
effaced, is now restated in the *second antithesis*. The One and the
many others are "separate" from each other since the One cannot
be in the others without canceling the difference between them.
This makes it impossible to conceive of participation as the
relationship of a whole to its parts. It does not exclude another
kind of participation that would rescue the meaning of the words
"another nature" (158c). But even as the second thesis put
forth clearer distinctions than those found in the first antithesis,
only to have this tension then give way again to an indiscrimi-
nate mixture, so is it here—for everything is soon exaggerated
in the second antithesis. Since participation is conceived only in
terms of the spatial relationship between a whole and its parts, it
must be denied altogether (οὐδαμῇ μετέχει, πανταχῇ στέρεται).
And so the presence of contrary states is denied since a thing
that cannot partake of a single Form cannot partake of two
Forms that are contrary to each other. And so "the other" is
deprived not only of participation in "the One," but of all possible states or characteristics. In short, it becomes nothing. As far
as we are concerned, however, we who have been listening—with
Socrates—to the echoes of the "theory of Forms" that could be
heard in the first antinomy and, more clearly still, in the dialectics of "the One" in the second thesis, we shall refuse to
misinterpret "participation" as a spatial relationship. "Participation" in the thesis and "separation" in the antithesis complement each other meaningfully. Together, in dialectical tension,
they represent the relationship of the Forms (or *Ideas*) to each

other and the relationship of each single Form to the things "participating" in it.

THIRD ANTINOMY. From now on the hypothesis is turned into its negation, at first in a purely formal opposition. How would we have to formulate thesis and antithesis of the third antinomy if they were to correspond to the pattern of the first antinomy? From the thesis that not-being can be known, it would follow that not-being possesses all attributes, and hence would come the conclusion: not-being is everything. Per contra, the antithesis would develop to the extreme consequence: not-being is nothing. This radical antinomy would then lead us to seek a point of convergence. Again we would encounter, first, the Forms which are as separate from as they are in "communion" with each other, and, second, the things "partaking" in them and thus standing in a relationship of both participation and separation. But the first pair of antinomies has partly clarified the concepts of Form, participation, and thing participating. Thus, the *thesis of the third antinomy* is stated not as an exaggeration but in a moderate or appropriate form.

First of all, the nature of negation is examined, as it is later and in greater detail in the *Sophist*. To say that one thing *is not* is not to say that it is nothing, but that there is another (ἕτερον) which this thing is not. From this point of view, if we say, "the one is not," this does not mean that it is a nothing that can be neither known nor spoken of, for it can be known and spoken of and it enters into all possible relations designated by the word "partaking." Thus, we derive the paradoxical implication that not-being partakes of being in numerous ways. The reciprocal relationship between being and not-being is shown to be indissoluble. Being and not-being come together, then, in "the one that is not-being." This would be impossible if there were not some kind of transition and connection between them by way of a "shift" (μεταβολή) from one to the other—something we previously encountered in the "now" (156c *et seq.*). On this basis, it is possible to include all kinds of change (motion, becoming, passing away) in "the one that is not." Yet change cannot be unlimited if we still wish to use the word "something"

II 3
160B–164B

II 3a
160B–163B

at all. It must come to rest, as it were, in order to be spoken of. Thus, "the one that is not" combines all opposites.

Conversely, the *antithesis* derives from the hypothesis, that "the one is not," the conclusion that it is the absence of being (οὐσίας ἀπουσία). It follows that there is no possibility of knowing or speaking about that which is not.

The antithesis develops the view held by the historical Parmenides in his own poem that "nothing is not" (6 15), "for it is unspeakable and unthinkable how not-being could *be*" (8 8). The thesis develops, just as strictly, the anti-Parmenidean view—that of the "mortals"—which Parmenides himself repudiated in his poem as mere words (8 38 *et seq.*). How is it possible to derive these contradictory theses from the same hypothesis of "the one that is not"? The point of convergence may be located where we find something that is not and that is opposed to being, but in such a way that it stands to it simultaneously in the relationship of necessary participation and complete separation. The view of a not-being that partakes of being up to the point where all opposites are combined in it, and that at the same time is completely separated from being, has twofold significance. First, if (as in the *Sophist*) we take not-being to mean what is other, or different, the view refers to the communion of Forms. Second, if we take not-being to mean that which is not true being, then the view refers to the things in this world participating in a single Form, as necessarily related to it as they are separated from it.

We have just shown that only the antithesis, not the thesis, is pushed to the extreme position found in the first antinomy. Similarly, the divergence contained in the convergence of this third antinomy is developed only in one direction—on the side of the nothing. What does this "nothing" of the antithesis mean? The first thesis reached the unknowable by the radical postulate of the absolute nature of being. Here we come to what is unknowable by the radical postulate of the absolute nature of not-being. And just as in the first case we discerned in the unknowable the dimension of being beyond being, so here we catch a glimpse of the opposite—that which is called in the scientific-mythological language of the *Timaeus* the "receptacle, space, or the wet nurse of becoming," and can be grasped only "in a spurious mode of thought" (λογισμῷ τινι νόθῳ).

FOURTH ANTINOMY. The *thesis* here states that if "the one is not," then the other is devoid of any fixed units, numbers or other ordered sequences (beginning, middle, end). It crumbles away (θρύπτεται κερματιζόμενον). What still looks like a unity when viewed from afar dissolves on closer inspection into a plurality and, similarly, is seen to contain—depending upon the degree of inspection—both like and unlike states or characteristics (πάθη). Without the One there is only unlimited possibility.

The *fourth antithesis* states that if "the one is not," then the other has neither unity nor plurality; it is not related to anything; it does not know anything nor can it be known. Without the One there is no other. Without the One there is nothing.

The two theses have moved so close together that the second seems to be but a more striking version of the first.[38] They agree that, without the One, knowledge of the many is either entirely inadequate or completely impossible because, without the One, the many are either entirely indeterminate or nothing. As the third antinomy depicted the combination of Forms, and at the same time depicted the reciprocal relationship between a single Form and the individual things, so the fourth antinomy shows once more that the many can neither exist nor be thought of without the One. Thus, a Herakleitean tension prevails both in the realm of Forms and in the relation between Forms and the world of becoming. The thesis proves that, without the Form (*Eidos*), the world would dissolve into a formless and shapeless mass. The antithesis proves that, without the Form, nothing could exist or be thought. Once again we see that what the thesis calls a chaotic, shapeless mass is rendered more radically in the antithesis as the concept of "nothing." And once again we realize that if we think the absence of Forms to its logical conclusion, nothing remains except the indeterminate something which is called, in the scientific-mythological language of the *Timaeus*, the "receptacle" or "space" and, because of its indeterminateness, is also referred to by other metaphors.

The dialogue concludes as Parmenides sums up (or appears to

Right margin notes:

II 4
164B–166c

II 4a
164B–165E

II 4b
165E–166c

sum up) the artful fugue of antinomies he had previously constructed:

"Whether there is the One—the first two antinomies—
or whether the One is not—the third and fourth antinomies—
the One itself—the first and third antinomies—
and the other—the second and third antinomies:
All this *is* in relation to itself and to each other in all possible
    manner,
and, conversely, *is not* in relation to itself and to each other,
is and appears,
is not and does not appear."

The young Aristotle replies for the last time, using an expression of wholehearted assent he had rarely used before: "Most true." That is the end. For the reader too? Or should he object that the synthesis of the first two antinomies has been forgotten? In other words, can we let it be forgotten that the opposite movements take place in different "sectors of time" and meet, or change from one into another, only in the "now"? Do we not feel here that, ultimately, the dialectical tension is dissolved in a chaotic confusion which only in its verbal structure conforms to dialectical precision? The reader once more is called on to examine the meaning of dialectics by examining the concluding summary to which the faithful pupil has replied: "Most true."[39]

Let us return to a question raised at the beginning, and again venture an answer. Why did Plato choose this Aristotle instead of any other young man—for there were plenty of names to choose from—and introduce him with the explicit statement (127D 2) that "he was later one of the Thirty"? Is this without any significance, or can we no longer grasp its significance? Can we not sense, at the conclusion of the dialogue, that in this intellectual chaos is grounded the political chaos that Socrates will fight against at the risk of his life? And, strange as it may sound, do we then find in the *Parmenides*, at the beginning and —if we listen exactly—at the end, a suggestion of aspects educational, moral, and political? One should pursue these questions, or try to explain in some other way this reference to the political catastrophe of the year 404.

Socrates listens without saying a word to these logical exercises of Parmenides. Anybody who keeps in mind the dramatic form of the dialogue (and Plato counts on such readers), anybody who keeps sight, in the midst of the logical acrobatics, of the human beings who are present, anybody to whom it is inconceivable that Plato, at any time of his life, would have his master Socrates, who died for the cause of truth, stand by merely as a matter of habit while somebody who will later be one of the Thirty takes the role of the respondent—such a reader cannot but ask himself what Socrates gets out of these exercises as far as his own problem is concerned. His own problem is twofold. Theoretically it is the nature of Forms up to the highest Form beyond being, in their relation to each other and to the things in this world. Practically—or existentially—it is the problem of action, or how to act in conformity with this realm of being. If this essential relationship emerges again and again as the *Parmenides* analyzes the One, the many, and "the one that is not" in their various combinations, we may recognize the attempt to rethink the dialectics of Parmenides in the spirit of the listening Socrates.

As far as the relationship between prototype and copy is concerned, the difficulties discussed in the first part of the dialogue are overcome by the interpenetration of "separation" (χωρισμός) and "participation" (μετοχή). There remains the last and most serious difficulty (133B), which divides the world of knowledge and action into two separate spheres—"perfect knowledge" and "perfect mastership" among the gods, and "knowledge" and "mastership" in the human sphere. This difficulty keeps alive the genuine tension that exists between ordinary human experience and the knowledge of Forms. The knowledge of Forms: it always strikes like lightning—in the *Republic*, the *Symposium*, the *Phaedrus*—into this world. And the tension is reinforced from the opposite side by the bewildering paradox that, corresponding to human ignorance about things beyond, the gods have no knowledge of things human nor any effect on them.

The Neoplatonists used to deal with this paradox by the doctrine that the gods know "the manifold in a simple way, the divisible in an indivisible way, the temporal in the way of eternity," and correspondingly, that the gods make human beings know "the indivisible in a divisible way and the eternal under the aspect of time."[40] But this is a refined, dogmatic version of Plato. He himself suggests, in the "ascent" and in the "vision of the highest Forms" in the *Symposium* and the *Republic*, how this gap can be bridged on the part of man—though there is something that is ultimately unknowable. Does not the *Parmenides* itself hint at a solution to this "most serious difficulty" (133B 4)? The function of the dialectical "exercise" was to make us see again and again the necessary relationship between the one and the many, between being and not-being, between the Forms and the world of appearances. Only at the extreme pole did the absolute become something unknowable, being beyond being (in the terminology of the *Republic*), and only at the extreme pole did the world of appearances become a chaotic nothing. By this restriction, the radical split in the realms of being, knowledge, and action, to which the worst difficulty seemed to lead, is overcome—without surrendering the dimension of the beyond. The bond of being, knowledge, and action is the goal toward which the dialectics of the *Parmenides* moves, and for this goal Socrates answers by his life and by his death.

TWENTY-FIVE

Phaedrus

WE KNOW young Phaidros from the *Protagoras* where he is an eager pupil of the sophists, participating in a seminar on astronomy conducted by Hippias. In the *Protagoras*, in the *Symposium*, and in this dialogue named after him, Phaidros is a friend of two physicians, the father Akoumenos and his son Eryximachos, both apparently followers of the fashionable intellectual movement. Since Phaidros appears in this dialogue first as an enthusiastic adherent of the orator Lysias and then inclines toward Socrates, and since the second speech of Socrates (addressed to some fictitious fair youth and dealing with the theme that the beloved should favor the lover) seems to be directed to Phaidros himself (242E), it is clear that here again the struggle between sophistic rhetoric and philosophy is ultimately a struggle for the soul of youth. In this struggle the theme of love—it is sounded first by Phaidros through the words of Lysias and is then raised to altogether different heights by Socrates—is uniquely significant. For according to Plato this is a struggle between genuine and false love. Thus, we are very soon made aware of the polyphonous themes that are written into the *Phaedrus*—rhetoric, soul, love, and philosophy.[1]

"Father of the discussion" is the name given to the young Phaidros in the *Symposium* (177D), since he is responsible for starting the contest of speeches. In the *Phaedrus* (242B), Socrates jokingly pays him the compliment that no one has been responsible for eliciting more speeches than Phaidros. We are expected, then, to remember the speeches on love from the *Symposium* at the very moment when Socrates departs from his

219

"pseudo-speech" to deliver his true speech in the *Phaedrus*. And when, at this same moment, the name of Simmias of Thebes is mentioned in passing—Simmias is said to be the only one who can compete with Phaidros in producing speeches—it is difficult not to think also of the *Phaedo*[2] where Simmias, by raising objections and by proposing the view of the soul as a harmony, helps to prevent the conversation's collapse. What else does this mean but that we must try to combine what is said about the fate of the soul in these two dialogues, and not forget, in the midst of the cheerful serenity of the *Phaedrus*, the ultimate seriousness of Socratic existence?

The unique quality of the *Phaedrus'* setting has always been deeply felt. We may compare this scene with the opening of the *Lysis*—the dialogue, from the early stage of Plato's writings, in which the theme of love, or "friendship" as it was called then, is discussed—so as to bring out the special characteristics of the *Phaedrus* all the more clearly. There are, too, certain similarities to the earlier dialogue. In both cases, the encounter begins with the question, Whence and whither . . . ? And in both cases, the road leads "outside the city wall." In the *Lysis*, however, Socrates takes the shortest road along the foot of the wall from one gymnasium to another, and the aporetic dialogue describes an intellectual wrestling match of youthful athletes. Phaidros, on the other hand, had been sitting for hours in the home of his master Lysias, and now, on the advice of his physician, is taking a walk outside the city for his health. More important is the fact that Socrates, contrary to his habits, is lured outside the city wall into a landscape not known to him. His enthusiasm is aroused by the beautiful and open scene, by the midday hour, and by the sanctuary of the nymphs. These are for Socrates unusual aspects, intended by the poet to convey that this is a rare experience to which the ecstatic mood of the otherwise sober Socrates corresponds or, indeed, by which it seems to be awakened.[3] Yet, all along, it ultimately is the same Socrates we meet. He wants to "know himself," for he is a riddle to himself (229E *et seq.*), and his "strangeness" (ἀτοπία) is as astonishing here (229c 6, 230c 6) to Phaidros as it is to Alkibiades in the *Alcibiades Major* (106A) and in the *Symposium* (215A).

The first and longer part of the dialogue deals with three
speeches on love. About their relation to each other we may simply say, to begin with, that the speech of Lysias (read by Phaidros) marks the opening, and that Socrates then bests the orator on his own ground—only to lead the discussion, in the speech that comes third and is apparently on the same subject, to an entirely different and genuinely Platonic level.

Socrates as orator—this theme is prefigured in the *Menexenus*,[4] a dialogue almost completely given over to a speech of Socrates in which he takes up the challenge of professional oratory on its own ground even as he does in the middle speech of the *Phaedrus*. The seeds of the first and third speeches also are present in the *Menexenus*. What, then, does this formal affinity mean? Aside from the fact that it shows how certain creative motifs may lie dormant in Plato as an artist over long periods of time and then emerge again in more perfected form, evidently it means this: Plato realized that what the orators are talking about may be said more clearly, more instructively, and more strikingly even on their own premises. But this still is not enough. Those professional speeches deal with subjects about which one can and should talk with an altogether different sense of seriousness. The limited value as well as the danger of those speeches is the very fact that they touch on such subjects. And Plato concerns himself with rhetorical speeches here precisely in order to use them on the lowest level and thereby render them innocuous.

The Speech of Lysias

Because of its elegance and sensuous charm (as well as the sophisticated and paradoxical pointedness of the situation), one of Lysias' speeches that Plato had read moved the orator and artist in him to enter into competition, and at the same time aroused his indignation as a philosopher. For in this speech he detected a frivolity that reduced the love relationship among human beings to mere pleasure or mere babble. That this speech of Lysias was incorporated by Plato into the dialogue "as a foreign substance, added from the outside, like leaven to dough" (Vahlen) is more probable than the notion that Plato pasted together, out of dozens of scraps and references, a laborious tract in the style of Lysias.[5] Be that as it may, "the occasion was chosen only to go far beyond it" (Grillparzer).[6]

The speech of Lysias addressed to "a fair youth" purports to prove the contrived thesis "that one should favor the non-lover more than the lover." (What would this oratorical stunt turn up as today? It might take the form of a sophisticated short story in which the seducer hides behind the mask of the cool, reserved friend.) Lysias' reversal of a generally acknowledged norm[7] cannot be taken seriously, as Socrates immediately suggests in the dialogue by replying that the author of the thesis might as well have discussed such contrasts as rich and poor, or young and old (227c). Love, a thing of high value, stands to be frittered away in rhetorical flippancies. Furthermore, rich or poor, older or younger, do not ultimately make any difference—but loving and not-loving make a radical difference, as Socrates knows better and lives more intensely than anybody else. Thus, we are supposed to learn first what the analogy means and then to realize that, with ironic intent, Socrates has thrown into the game an analogy that is only half adequate.

TRANSITIONAL
CONVERSATION
234C–237A

After the speech of Lysias has run its course, Socrates will set out to surpass it. The critique that is suggested in the transitional conversation with Phaidros (234C–237A) but actually given in the second main part of the dialogue shows all the more clearly at what Socrates is aiming. It shows, too, that essential aspects of his philosophic power are hidden behind this effort to surpass Lysias. Yet, the important thing we would also discover for ourselves. In the speech of Lysias, the basic disposition of the speaker was left indefinite, and Lysias might well have counted this indefiniteness an advantage. Socrates, however, clearly defines the situation in an opening summary such as was retained for these fictitious speeches in later rhetoric.[8]

The First Speech of Socrates

37B–241D

The admirer (a "wily flatterer") of a handsome young man who is much loved has falsely persuaded the youth that he does not love him. Thus, the theme taken over from Lysias is not posed paradoxically, for the more clearly delineated description serves a psychologically determined strategy. As Socrates does not fail to emphasize right at the beginning as well as later on in the second part of the dialogue (237c, 263c, 265d), this clarification of what previously was left indefinite aims at the question "about what" (περὶ οὗ) are they talking, i.e., at the essence (οὐσία). Love is to be defined, and the entire discussion must be based on a definition (ὅρος). The same move, sober and direct, is made in the *Symposium*. There Socrates sets himself off from all the other speakers as he does here from Lysias, and in both dialogues he begins with the question, What is love? (οἷός ἐστιν, *Symposium* 199c 7; οἷόν ἐστιν, *Phaedrus* 237c 8.) In both dialogues, too, this search for a definition is separated from the actual speech. In the *Phaedrus*, however, matters are more complicated, for here in the first speech of Socrates, we do not hear his own views and, hence, not his own definition either.

The other requirement laid down by Socrates later (264c) is that a speech, like a living creature (ζῷον), should have a clear structure. And, indeed, we may note the articulate organization of his first speech, explicitly emphasized (238DE, 241D). This aspect also has a deeper meaning.

What is continued here is the clarification of the premises referred to earlier, and this clarification occurs in a context where—as is to be expected—Socrates agrees with certain arguments advanced by Lysias. That love is a sickness Lysias mentioned as one among many other arguments (231D). In this speech of Socrates (238E), the pathological condition of the lover, his bondage to pleasure, is the premise from which his conduct is derived in a logical sequence that is determined by the categories of the harmful (βλαβερόν), the unpleasant (ἀηδές), and the unreliable (ἄπιστον). The harm done is analyzed, in turn, in the context of the three Platonic realms of being as they were worked out with special exactness in the *Alcibiades Major*,[9] i.e., the harm done to the lover is related to his soul, his body, and his possessions. That the lover seeks to separate the beloved from all other company, that he bestows excessive praise on him—these, again, are objections that may be found scattered through the speech of Lysias (232c,

233A).[10] Here they are cited at their proper place, integrated in the over-all construction of the speech made by Socrates (239A–240E).

Lysias might have judged his own speech as more effective than that of Socrates for its specific purpose—the purpose of persuasion[11]—precisely because it was less strictly organized and less logically grounded. Yet Plato's Socrates ultimately pursues an entirely different aim: to gain clear knowledge and necessary order. And the second part of the dialogue will show that this necessary order is not to be understood in a merely formal sense, as in the sense, say, of criticizing and correcting a poorly organized school essay.

In his first speech, Socrates produces only a half of the proof —namely, that one must deny himself to the lover. Despite Phaidros' entreaties he does not deal with the other half, which would show that one must favor the non-lover. He claims, though, that this result would follow from simply converting what he had said about the lover (241DE). The deeper reason for his omission, however, is that Plato was concerned only with the lover, not with the non-lover. And this brings us to the deeper meaning of the "subject" itself. The subject matter was rhetoric. Now, in the definitions and organization of Socrates' first speech, something else seems to come through which transcends the field of rhetorical technique. The subject to be discussed, love, is something that leads beyond oratory into the depths of human existence. If Plato had not seen these possibilities, he would not have chosen Lysias' lecture as the point of departure for his dialogue.

What does emerge, then, from this initial search for a definition, and what is confirmed in the later parts of the dialogue? Love is defined as a longing desire (ἐπιθυμία τις). This definition disposes of the difficulty, still present in the *Meno* (73E *et seq.*), of distinguishing between the general concept of virtue and "a" virtue, or between Forms in general and "a" Form. For Socrates immediately includes love in the general class of desires, citing the different kinds of desire that are competing within the soul (237D)—desire for pleasure, willfulness, or *hybris,* on the one hand, and a reasonable desire for the good, or temperance, on the other (δόξα ἐφιεμένη τοῦ ἀρίστου). The struggle going on within the soul is glimpsed; later it will be raised to Socratic radicalism and Platonic vision in the myth in the second speech of Socrates. There is still a long way to go before we reach these heights, however, for here the struggle is between desire and "opinion" (*doxa*). Later we find the image of the two winged steeds of the soul—desire and "courageous spirit" (θυμός)—and reason, their charioteer. And we know from the central part of the *Republic* (V 477A) how high reason stands above mere opinion.[12]

Now in order for "love" to exist—so it is said here in the *Phaedrus*—the outcome of this struggle must be the victory of the desire for pleasure. This desire must aim at beauty, moreover, and must acquire from the accompanying desires the power of aiming at the beauty of the body. Beauty as the aim of love reminds us of the *Symposium*, especially if we look back (as noted earlier) on the formal affinities between the respective passages that deal with the conceptual clarification of the subject. All the more alarming it must be, for anyone who has learned only a little from Plato, to read now that the reasonable impulses are defeated and that love is restricted to bodily beauty. Love is on a level with hunger and thirst (238AB). It is the naturalistic view of love. In other words, it is not love in general that is defined here, but a very one-sided kind of love—physical love.

Thus, we realize that the first speech of Socrates is by no means simply a new edition of the Lysias speech or a formal improvement. It is at the same time an effort to clarify the human or all too human content of the sophistic product that is all the more dangerous when it is left vague. Only after this danger is plainly shown can Socrates fight against it. Now, with every word, he shows on how low a level love is conceived of here, most clearly at the beginning—especially if we remember that, according to the *Symposium*, love is the guide toward philosophy. Here in the *Phaedrus*, the wily friend (237B) asserts that the lover keeps the beloved away from "divine philosophy." He must know, for he himself is caught up in this kind of love, after all, as much as he conceals it. Thus, it should not be said that a specific mode of life determined by false love is refuted here. What happens, rather, is that this specific mode of life is led to reveal itself in its true nature. This is the substance and meaning of the first speech of Socrates.

TRANSITIONAL
CONVERSATIONS
234C–237A
241D–243E

The brief critical discussion that follows makes it still more clear that the two aspects of the first part of the dialogue are present even in the first speech of Socrates. These aspects, which are so hard for us to reconcile, are the formal, rhetorical, and the substantial, here indicated by the word "love." In fact, for a moment we sensed this tension between form and content as early as the transitional conversation that follows Lysias' lecture. We feel it when Socrates raises the question— only to drop it again in favor of the purely formal aspects of the matter—whether the speaker had said what was "appropriate" or "fitting" (τὰ δέοντα). Phaidros himself is so much the faithful disciple of the rhetorical expert that, as far as Socrates' speech is concerned, he seems to pay attention only to its form. Socrates, however, ordinarily committed to the form of dialogue, experiences the speech he makes as something strange and alien, something that is not his own (242DE). Before speaking he had covered his head in shame because he was embarking on something inappropriate for him (237A). Then, in poetic words and rhythms, he had called upon the Muses and enlisted the help of the distant people of Liguria for the sake of an entirely superfluous etymological connection that is just as forced as the speech is itself (237A 8).[13] Then he had interrupted his speech to ascribe it—ironically—to divine inspiration.

Now that he has concluded, it is the content he is ashamed of. It is an offense against the deity, an offense of which he must cleanse himself (242C). For while the two opening speeches were quite different in formal structure, they are on the same level as far as content is concerned. Both are in conflict with the conviction that love is "a god or a divine being" (242E 2). This would seem a strange disjunction if we did not look back to the speech of Diotima[14] where Eros is not a god but a great demon, an intermediary power, who mediates between gods and men and thus transmits the art of prophecy and other priestly powers from gods to men and from men to gods. It is these powers or types of ecstasy that will be formed into an ordered system in the second speech of Socrates here in the *Phaedrus*.

Poetic references to Ibykos and Stesichoros set the tone for this speech (242c, 243a), which will rise to poetic heights. Socrates delivers the speech bareheaded, i.e., without keeping his head covered. And the speech is not addressed to anybody in particular, even if Phaidros knows that he is the boy whom Socrates is addressing (243e). And although Socrates interweaves play and seriousness here, as he does so often, and although by the term "yielding" he certainly means something quite different from what the many understand by it, Phaidros, at least at this moment, means just what he says to Socrates: "Here he is (the boy you mean), quite close beside you, whenever you want."[15]

The Second Speech of Socrates

The contrast between the first two speeches becomes blurred because the third speech, delivered by Socrates, is a completely new creation both in language and in content,[16] and it also changes the focus of attention. Whereas the speech of Lysias seemed to be concerned merely with the formal theme of rhetoric, and whereas the first speech of Socrates seemed to introduce substantial matters in addition to formal and rhetorical problems, the subject of rhetoric now drops altogether out of sight—for the time being—in the palinode of Socrates. Its only subject is love. From this perspective, we must view the first three speeches as a whole in order to realize that they present a new version of a genuinely Platonic tension—the contrast between noble and ignoble love. This contrast refers to a basic Platonic experience that is expressed even in his early works, in the *Euthydemus*, for example, and then most strikingly in the *Alcibiades Major*. The *Alcibiades* begins with the puzzling question of why, out of an entourage of lovers, only Socrates has remained loyal, and it concludes with the answer that only Socrates, among all the others, has loved the youth himself, i.e., his soul. In the *Symposium*, the tension between earthly love (*pandemos*) and heavenly love (*ouranios*) is the explicit

243e–257b

theme of the speech delivered by Pausanias. Here in the *Phaedrus*, this same tension determines the structure of the entire first part. For in the first two speeches, we cannot but hear the voice of earthly love, whose devotees, as Pausanias says in the *Symposium* (181B), love the body more than the soul since they are looking forward only to the act of consummation. It is heavenly love that is given its full due in the third speech, for here love leads the soul upward to the heavens and to the place beyond the heavens.

Nevertheless, the two speeches of Socrates also belong together. The second part of the *Phaedrus* (265D *et seq.*) will show that the philosopher has a dual task—to discover both the "one Form" (εἰς μίαν ἰδέαν ἄγειν) and the "ordered system" (κατ' εἴδη τέμνειν). At the beginning of Socrates' first speech there was a definition of love. In the critical investigation of the dialogue's second part, it will turn out that this concept of love as "one among the things that are" (ἕν τι τῶν ὄντων) leads to an understanding of the "one Form" (265DE). And the ordered system will be seen (265A *et seq.*) when the two speeches of Socrates are viewed together; for the single concept of madness (mania) is divided, like a body, into a right side and a left side. The first speech of Socrates dealt with the "left" or wrong kind of madness. The second speech will deal with the "right" or good kind of madness.[17] Moreover, it is no accident that the right kind falls into four distinct types (the fourth is the noble passion of love), whereas the wrong kind of madness has "many branches or forms" so that this (ignoble) love is mixed up with similar desires showing no clear demarcation.[18] Since this division must be performed in an "orderly" way and not "in the manner of a crude butcher" against natural growth, the division, if performed correctly, represents the structure of the object itself.

"Divine madness," then, is subdivided in the second speech of Socrates into four types: prophetic, cathartic, poetic, and erotic.[19] This madness is opposed to all "worldly wisdom that keeps a niggardly balance sheet of goods and induces in the friend the kind of ungenerous spirit that the multitude considers a virtue" (256E). And in this portrait, the heights are reached of a movement that had, as early as the *Ion*, granted an equal place to the existence of the poet beside that of the thinker, in the *Meno* (99c) had attributed—however ironically —political action to divine inspiration, and in the *Symposium* celebrated Eros as the demonic intermediary leading upward to the realm of eternal Forms.

Here in the *Phaedrus*, Socrates' second speech outlines the system of this madness. Erotic madness occupies the highest place in the system. As, by comparison, "prophets and divine priests" are cited in the *Ion*, as the "creative (poetic) men" are added in the *Meno*, and as, in the *Symposium*, the "priestess" speaks about the nature of love, so all these aspects are combined in the system of madness in the *Phaedrus*, in a manner of exposition that is at once strict thought and ecstatic exaltation. Because of its careful structure, the speech reads like a contribution to descriptive and analytic psychology, and this impression is reinforced in advance, as it were, by the precise logical distinctions Socrates introduces at the beginning. Soon, however, his speech is lifted up into the realm to which its subject belongs—ultimately transformed into ecstasy and into poetic-mythical sounds and images. Thus, this speech has had the same powerful effect upon poets (like Ronsard and Shakespeare) as upon thinkers and scientists, among the Arab scholars as well as in the West—and probably in modern times also.[20]

The portrait of erotic madness, and with it the speech, is rounded out by a prayer to the god of love, who appears here once more as the guide toward philosophy (257A). Socrates points out in ironic understatement that the speech "necessarily had to employ many poetic words," but nobody who knows his irony will believe that it was done "for the sake of Phaidros." Plato himself was deeply attached to this world of the demonic to which he here makes Socrates the guide. For this bond with the demonic provides, on the one hand, protection against Philistinism and, on the other, the impetus for an ascent into the realm of Forms.

As for the great philosophical myth at the core of the third speech, we may refer to our previous remarks.[21] It rises above the mythical highlands of three lesser legends. It is a myth of

the soul, of love, of the universe, and of the realm of eternal
Forms. As always in Plato, the myth is more than an effort to
put into words and image what is ultimately ineffable. For at
the same time it contains an injunction that is expressed here
in the final prayer—"to live in the search for knowledge, striving toward Eros."

The first two speeches dealt with an assigned topic in rhetoric.
If the subject matter itself took over in the third speech, this is
a digression from the course, as it were, and we are brought
back—immediately after Socrates' true speech on behalf of love
—as Phaidros voices his doubt whether Lysias, the master in
the art of rhetoric, would be able to hold his own in a contest
with Socrates (257B). Thus, almost abruptly, we are forced
back into the domain of formal rhetoric, and the second part
of the dialogue that is now commencing will indeed use these
speeches as the basis for a formal analysis in the field of rhetoric.
Yet the subject matter itself had broken through in the astonishing inner turn taken by the dialogue. Love had risen as a vital
power after being the subject of an academic lecture. From the
domain of rhetorical exercises we had reached to the realm
of eternal Forms and had encountered the cosmic fate of the
soul in mythical images. If, in the second part of the dialogue,
we now seem to return to the level of discussing rhetoric, almost as if we had not gained a vision beyond it, we may be
confident that for Socrates this discussion of rhetoric is not an
end in itself, as it is for his partner. Socrates consents to it only
in order to show the philosophical possibilities inherent in such
a discussion of rhetoric.

There are four main topics in the second part of the dialogue.
The first topic deals with the contrast between written (i.e.,
prepared) speeches and oral (i.e., extemporaneous) delivery.
The contrast was alluded to earlier when it was said that Lysias
was the ablest writer of his time (δεινότατος ὤν τῶν νῦν γράφειν,
228A), and when Socrates feigned reluctance to compete as a
mere amateur (ἰδιώτης) and in an extemporaneous manner with
so accomplished a master (236D). As we have pointed out elsewhere,[22] Plato enters into this technical discussion of a subject
then current not because he was particularly interested in the

II
257B–278B

II 1

subject itself, but in order to raise it to a level where an entirely different oral speech—the educational conversation of
the philosopher—may emerge as the truest form of speech.

The second topic deals with the question of whether a speaker   II 2
should have true knowledge of his subject or whether a general
acquaintance with the subject is sufficient. In the first part of
the dialogue, not only did it become clear that it would be folly
to strive at "deceiving a few poor people and winning their applause" (243A 1–2), but in addition ignorant talk about love
was actually called an offense against the god (242c et seq.).
Now the analysis will unfold the whole relationship between
philosophy and rhetoric, and will culminate in Plato's paradoxical demand for a philosophical rhetoric.

The third topic deals with the contrast between two kinds of   II 3
speech, one that is indefinite and unstructured, and another that
is strictly defined as to subject and is also based on a clear plan.
This contrast also appeared in the first part of the dialogue,
when Socrates criticized the speech of Lysias (235A), and then
avoided its defects by giving a definition at the beginning of
his own speech (237CD) as well as by keeping a clear structure
throughout. If this contrast is now restated, we may safely
assume that it means more to Plato than a school exercise in
definition or division. The conceptual analysis proves to be a
means of directing the mind toward the "one Form" (ἓν εἶδος),
and it leads toward a systematic ordering of the Forms, a task
that Plato had envisaged as necessary from at least the *Cratylus* on.

The fourth topic deals with the contrast between a theory that   II 4
is concerned only with the formal elements of speech and another theory that includes a clear account of the listener's state
of mind and produces a speech appropriate to this state. Even
this topic has roots in the dialogue's first part. For it obviously
is connected with the precise specifications of the "case" that
Socrates, at the start of his first speech, cites, describing the
age, the handsome, attractive qualities of the youth, the flattering and wily nature of the older man, and the moment of their
encounter.

Plato does not present the four topics sequentially as in a

treatise, but combines them in such a way that the third and fourth topics form the center, the second topic (subdivided within) encloses them as if they were the kernel, and the first topic (also subdivided within) surrounds the whole like a shell. This artful, concentric construction puts dialectics and psychology in the center—not as separate disciplines but as the culmination of the philosophical search—and surrounds this kernel with the general questions about rhetoric and philosophy.

II 1a
257B–258D

The first problem, the value of the written word, is raised by Phaidros. He cannot but compare the enthusiastic improvisation of Socrates with the skill of his Lysias, and he is reminded now that Lysias recently was scolded by "one of our politicians" for being a "speech writer" (λογογράφος). And so, to repeat, we are drawn into a contemporary controversy. Instead of pursuing the matter into genuinely Platonic depth, Socrates at first takes the side of Lysias by calling attention to a different kind of speech-writing that is highly honored among politicians—the composing and submitting of laws.[23] A quick glance at the famous lawmakers of Greece and Persia shows that there is nothing dishonorable about speech-writing as such. *How* it is done determines whether it is good or bad. After this crucial question is settled in our minds, the discussion takes a more general turn. Written works may be addressed to the public or to a private circle; they may be poetry or prose. It would be strange if Plato did not also think of the poetic form of his own dialogues—and in the distance perhaps even of his *Laws*. We sense here, and later on even more, the depths into which Socrates will carry these discussions that are taken from political controversy of the time. The question of "how" enables him to open the door for the other problems that follow.

The first problem is put aside rather than analyzed. Now that matters are to be treated more firmly, we find, at the

II 2a
258D–262C

beginning of the second topic, the fairy tale of the cicadas. These creatures, originally men full of musical passion, now in their changed state sing forever, without need of sustenance whether food or drink. The story points to the indefatigable pursuit of conversation, and the names of the Muses cited next, especially Urania, echo the matters of high import that were discussed

previously. Our attention sharpened by this playfully serious
appeal, we then listen to the second question posed by Socrates:
whether a good and successful speech presupposes that the
speaker knows in his own mind the truth about his subject
(259E).

This is the crucial question with which Plato confronts the
art of rhetoric. It was raised before, in the *Gorgias*, when
Gorgias himself—pressed by Socrates—renounced the claim
that his art was based on true knowledge of just and unjust,
admitted to being satisfied with an approximate opinion (455A),
and thus revealed the weakness of his own position. Similarly,
Phaidros remembers he has heard it said that a man intending
to be an orator need not know what is truly just, good, or beautiful, but need only know what is thought to be so by the multitude. The refutation of this view also reminds us of the *Gorgias*
in several respects. First, Socrates uses an argument *ad hominem*.
If the orator, being ignorant of good and evil, should persuade
the many to do evil rather than good, he will reap a bitter
harvest (260CD). This is the argument of the *Gorgias* in disguise. There (519B *et seq.*) it was said that if the people re-
belled against the orator-politician, it was his own fault because
such rebellious spirit is the result of bad education. Second,
there follows an analysis designed to overthrow the claim of
rhetoric or, in the peculiar paradox of the *Phaedrus*, to raise
rhetoric to the level of philosophy. For if, as Socrates argues,
rhetoric should defend itself by claiming to be no more than
the "art of words," leaving a knowledge of good and evil to be
taught elsewhere, then rhetoric loses the dignity of being an
"art" and is satisfied with being an "artless exercise" (ἄτεχνος
τριβή)—because it is in the nature of an "art" to grasp the essence or truth (ἀληθείας ἧφθαι).

Again, we are reminded of the derogatory classification of
rhetoric among the "arts of flattery" in the *Gorgias*. There, too,
rhetoric was excluded from the domain of "genuine arts" and
reduced to a mere exercise (οὐ τέχνη ἀλλ' ἐμπειρία καὶ τριβή,
Gorgias 463B). The place of a rhetoric that has surrendered the
claim of truth along with knowledge of its subject matter is
thus taken over by philosophy. For philosophy does make this

very claim and makes it, moreover, as the presupposition for conversing seriously about any subject.[24] Rhetoric is said to be the "guidance of the soul by means of words" (ψυχαγωγία διὰ λόγων, *Phaedrus* 261 AB). Such guidance may be misguidance, as when the speaker in a court of law makes just appear unjust or the speaker in a public assembly makes good appear evil— and vice versa. As, previously, the "private sphere" (ἐν ἰδίοις, 261A 9) followed upon the public, i.e., the sphere of law and politics, so now the world of law courts and political assemblies gives way to philosophy and dialectics.

At this point in the *Phaedrus*, there seems to be a reference to the *Parmenides* that is not easy to explain. Who is this "Palamedes of Elea" (261D 6) who can demonstrate that like and unlike, one and many, rest and motion are the same? From antiquity on, commentators have tried to solve this riddle by identifying him with Zeno and by interpreting this passage as a struggle against eristic reasoning.[25] If we adopt this interpretation, we overlook the fact that for Plato the mythical Palamedes stood high both as an inventor and as somebody who had been unjustly condemned to death. At the end of the *Apology* (41B), Socrates expressed the hope of meeting after death Palamedes and Ajax, both of whom lost their lives by an unjust verdict. In the *Republic* (VII 522D), Palamedes is praised as the inventor of number, without which Agamemnon could not have become the leader of troops. Political action, therefore, as we are to infer, is based on—mathematics. And Daidalos, Orpheus, and Palamedes are cited even in the *Laws* (III 677D) as the great inventors in ancient times.

Would Plato, then, in the *Phaedrus* really have included Zeno among these original inventors, the same Zeno of whom an ancient source correctly says that he was not an original thinker, but only pursued and developed the ideas of Parmenides?[26] Similarly, in the *Parmenides* Socrates points out that Zeno, in his treatise, had said the same things as Parmenides and, by simply modifying the form, had tried to convey the deceptive impression that he was saying something of his own. Zeno, then, is exactly the opposite of an original inventor in the tradition of Palamedes. Is it not more probable, therefore, that "Palamedes of Elea" stands for Parmenides of Elea? The affinity

in the sound of the two names would support such a view, since
Plato often plays seriously with names—as he has played just
now with the names of the Muses. If this is so as to Parmenides,
then Plato intends here in the *Phaedrus* to refer to the second,
dialectical part of the *Parmenides* where the Eleatic demonstrates that if there is "the One," then it is both like and unlike
(158E), it both is infinite and partakes of the finite (158D,
143A), and it is at once in motion and at rest (145E). These
paradoxes are meant not as eristic exercises—as they might
appear to be in Zeno's treatise (*Parmenides* 127E *et seq.*)—but
as serious moves toward dialectics.

Eristic rhetoric, then, is superseded and surpassed by dialectics, however much these two may resemble each other at times.
This is the meaning of the section here in the *Phaedrus*, and it is
for the sake of this meaning that we are referred to the *Parmenides*. In the background we find the problem of the knowing
deceiver, discussed in the *Hippias Minor*.[27] This problem has
now grown into a confrontation of two basic systems of speeches.
The two powers confronting each other are, however, not equal.
On the contrary, it is inherent in the nature of rhetoric that it
must become philosophy if it does not wish to surrender its
claim to being a serious art. This is in effect the decisive and
paradoxical breakthrough, and the implications will be pursued
later (II 2b). The urgent question here is how we are to understand this transformation of rhetoric into philosophy. The
third and fourth topics are now integrated into the discussion.

It so happens, Socrates says—leaving us to have our own opinion about this "stroke of luck"[28]—that the speeches delivered
earlier provide illustrations of what we must know. The first
thing to note, however, is that when the discussion was about an
ambiguous concept such as love, the speech of Lysias, in contrast
to that of Socrates, failed to define the indefinite subject. This
is the way of rhetoric as it is practiced everywhere in public
life. But the true speaker must compel us to be clear about precisely such concepts on which we disagree not only with others
but in our own minds. The concepts of "just" and "good" are
cited as being different from "iron" and "silver" in that we
do know what we mean by the latter.

Here Plato returns to a critical moment in the *Alcibiades*

II 3
262c–267E

Major, where Socrates explains to the youth that men agree when they talk about "stone or wood," but disagree when they discuss what is "just and unjust." Alkibiades cannot give an account of what is "just and unjust" because he has not learned anything about these concepts. And he now meets a teacher who explains to the prospective politician the "madness" of his undertaking—for Alkibiades is about to throw himself into politics without knowing anything about semantics and ethics. This critical moment must be felt in the background if we are to understand fully the demand made here in the *Phaedrus.* It is the demand that the beginning student of rhetoric should learn the method of definition and division (diaeresis), especially with regard to those terms and concepts that are confused in the minds of the many. Thus, we realize that it is a matter of both semantics and ethics when Lysias is criticized for his logical defects. The true speaker—which Lysias is not—would "compel us to conceive of love as a definite entity and then compose his speech with a view to this specific meaning" (263DE).

There follows the injunction that a speech should not be constructed as an arbitrary sequence of exchangeable parts, but be organized like a living creature. A comparison of the two speeches of Socrates shows what this means. Each speech dealt with a single form of madness, a human sickness in one case and divine ecstasy in the other, thus dividing the subject as a whole into two species. The second speech of Socrates divided divine madness or ecstasy into four different kinds, the last and highest being erotic madness. Now we draw the consequences (τὴν δύναμιν τέχνῃ λαβεῖν) from the rules derived accidentally (ἐκ τύχης), as it were, from these illustrations. We must "bring together a dispersed plurality into a single, visible form, seeing it all together" (εἰς μίαν ἰδέαν συνορῶντα ἄγειν τὰ πολλαχῇ διεσπαρμένα, 265D). Again, we must "divide according to forms, following the joints in their natural growth" (κατ᾽ εἴδη δύνασθαι διατέμνειν, κατ᾽ ἄρθρα ᾗ πέφυκεν, 265E).

Socrates himself points out that these procedures go beyond the practical domain of rhetoric. Division and combination are prerequisites for speech and thought in general, division into many forms and combination into a single form according to natural growth. He who can achieve this is like a divine guide in whose footsteps Socrates purports to follow (266B 6)— while he is the guide himself. As in the second section of this part of the dialogue (II 2a) rhetoric is raised to the level of philosophy, and as in the third section (II 3) semantics and ethics emerge as special fields in philosophy, so now the phi-losopher is concerned with ontology and dialectics, with the "division and combination" of Forms (or *Ideas*). The rules and the technical terminology to be found in treatises on rhetoric (266D–267D) are treated rather cavalierly from this higher perspective.

Yet, while these matters of rhetorical technique are the petty and confused counterpart to the great and simple task of the dialectician, they also lead to something new. The orators have developed their technical apparatus on a sophisticated scale, but the case of the physician, of the poet, or of the musician shows that all this technical training is ridiculous if a person does not know how, when, and on whom to practice his technique. In order to be an expert in the other fields, it is necessary to acquire knowledge that is prior to, and beyond, medicine, tragedy, and harmonics.[29] The same applies to rhetoric. In order to achieve excellence in rhetoric, it is necessary, first, that a person have natural talent, second, that he know dialectics so as to be able to define "what rhetoric is" (269B 6)—and we have just come to see dialectics (II 3)—and, third, that he acquire a knowledge prior to, and beyond, rhetoric (269B 7–8).

II 4
268A–272B

What this means is shown in the case of Perikles, who stands as the example of the perfect orator. Perikles, highly gifted to begin with, acquired a knowledge of nature, and thus a knowl-edge about reason and unreason, from his association with Anaxagoras. For all arts and sciences of high order must engage in a study of "growth and essence," i.e., in a study of the phi-losophy of nature.[30] Here medicine joins rhetoric, distant as these two disciplines are otherwise. That Perikles is put on the same level as Hippokrates shows how much Plato's estimate of the worth of political rhetoric has risen since the *Gorgias*. Medicine studies and analyzes the body; rhetoric, the soul.

The one employs medication and dietary prescriptions; the other, legislation and rules. The one aims at health and strength; the other, at "persuasion (conviction) and virtue."

As far as details are concerned, one must inquire first into the nature of the soul, whether it is a single form or complex (we are reminded of Socrates' second speech on love). Then one must inquire into the soul's capacity to act upon and to be acted upon. Finally, one must study the correspondence between certain kinds of speeches and certain dispositions of the soul. If in the previous section (II 3) dialectics came into view, the philosophical task before us now is to create a "descriptive and analytic psychology," based on a comprehensive science of nature and directed toward the practical goal of rhetoric. It is an enormous task that Plato here sets up and (looking forward) co-ordinates with a system of sciences that are both possible and necessary for his own purpose. Yet we would miss the note of Socratic irony if we were to take completely seriously Plato's saying that he is concerned with the education of the orator instead of with education in general—or with philosophy.

II 2b
272B–274A

The very magnitude of this task raises the urgent question of whether there might be a short cut. Thus, we return once more to the view that the orator perhaps has nothing to do with the truth of what is just and unjust and—as is now said, expanding the last section—with the truth of who are just and unjust. Instead, the orator may have to do only with what is "probable" (εἰκός). This, indeed, was a general principle in rhetorical theory and practice of the day, or rather a basic attitude toward human affairs, for which Plato refers to Teisias, the Sicilian teacher of rhetoric (i.e., he refers to the most ancient textbook on rhetoric).[31] But the decision had gone against "Teisias" and this basic attitude in advance, as it were, when the problem first emerged (II 2a). For it was shown that what is now called "probability" is probable only because of its affinity with truth, or philosophy. With this established, the dual task of philosophy —both psychological and dialectical—became clearer, and is now emphasized once again. The reason why the basic question of the relation between philosophy and rhetoric (which has already been decided) appears anew is that what was previously

said might be understood to mean that philosophy merely provides a deeper and firmer foundation for the superstructure of
rhetoric. Now, however, we have gained sufficient insight into
these two disciplines to realize what an absurd misunderstanding
it would be to conceive of philosophy as a means toward the end
of rhetoric. Means and ends would have changed place and rank.
Speech and action should be measured by the standards not of
men but of gods, by the standards not of our "fellow slaves"
but of the good "masters," as is said here, with echoes of the
Orphic-Pythagorean language in the *Phaedo* (62B).[32] And the
long "cycle," or detour, of which Socrates speaks in a playful
puzzle not only refers to the way through this superior knowledge. It also points to the cosmic myth of the soul where the
image of the soul's "cycles" recurs frequently (*Phaedrus* 247D,
248C, 249A), as it does in the concluding myth of the *Republic*
and in the *Timaeus* as well.

With this broad view in mind, we are in a position to return
to the first question, on the relation between speech and writing, which up to now had remained on the low level of a purely
rhetorical problem. This problem, too, is raised ultimately to
the heights of Socratic reflection.[33] We begin with the Egyptian
legend of the god Theuth who invented the art of writing and
the good king Ammon who recognized the invention to be a
dubious blessing. This beginning also contains the foundation
for the answer to the problem. We hear about the dangers and
defects inherent in written works—in words that literally re-
produce two famous passages in Plato's *Letters* (II 314C, VII
341B *et seq.*). In contrast to the written treatise there is oral
discourse, alive and animate, engraved in the soul of the pupil;
of this the book is but a copy. All that was previously established as the task of philosophy is gathered together now in
order to depict the live philosophical conversation, educational
and productive, as the highest form of human speech.

In the end it is said that Phaidros must now convey this
message, and this appeal, to his beloved Lysias, and Socrates
must convey it to his beloved Isokrates. Here is a wishful picture—if, for the moment, we disregard the actual life situation
—of how a philosophical conversation might spread if it were

(margin) II 1b
274A–278B

(margin) CONCLUSION
278B–279C

sustained in a loving and live human relationship. Viewed more closely, it is philosophy that intends to show rhetoric the way to its own fulfillment. This has been Plato's intention throughout the dialogue. Yet, since Socratic irony is not a garment to be put on and off at will, it is inconceivable that this appeal to the two masters of rhetoric is meant in complete seriousness.[34] Though Plato may have acknowledged that, in contrast to Lysias, Isokrates did have a "philosophical mind" and that his influential school did represent an educational system of rank[35] (of secondary rank, to be sure), there cannot be a moment's thought that either Lysias or Isokrates followed the call here addressed to him.

The prayer that Socrates, in conclusion, offers to Pan and the other gods dwelling in this place awakens once more, after the long discussions, the feeling of closeness to nature that pervaded the first part of the dialogue. Socrates who is ugly prays for beauty, *inner beauty*, to Pan, the god whom he resembles (for if he looks like a satyr or like Seilenos—*Symposium* 215AB— he looks like Pan as well). Perhaps one also may remember that in the welter of etymologies in the *Cratylus* (408D), the name of Pan is interpreted as the one who "shows all (things)" and that, as the son of Hermes, Pan is "Logos or the brother of Logos." Again, the prayer for beauty gains philosophical significance when it is read in the conceptual context of the second speech of Socrates—in the context of the soul that is eternal, of the high rank the Form of beauty has in the life of man, and of the soul's striving toward this Form. And this striving is called "love." The prayer for "friendship" between the outward and what is within seeks to reconcile—in an inner harmony, or well-ordered system—the conflict depicted in the myth of the two steeds of the soul. Plato himself had to struggle incessantly for this very harmony, which he attributed ultimately to an act of grace on the part of the gods. Finally, the natural wish for wealth—already ennobled by Solon in his elegy to the Muses—is acknowledged, but not as an end in itself. What belongs to man is subordinated to man himself (*Alcibiades Major* 131A *et seq.*). It owes its value, and limit, to wisdom and temperance. "Pray this for me, too," Phaidros says, "for friends

have all things in common." Prayer, philosophy, and love—
these belong in a special sense to the intermediary realm disclosed by Diotima.[36]

There has been a dispute, from the time of antiquity on, as to
the actual theme of the *Phaedrus*. According to the commentary
of Hermias, a Neoplatonist, some said that the real subject of
the dialogue is love, others said that it is rhetoric, and still others
that it is the good, or highest beauty.[37] In 1834, Franz Grillparzer wrote: "What is the true main theme of Plato's *Phaedrus*
has been much disputed. Some entitle it: *On the beautiful;* others:
On rhetoric. Schleiermacher believes that it deals primarily with
dialectics. Everybody can see how forced these various imputa-
tions are . . ."[38] No other dialogue of Plato's has suffered from
so many different interpretations. And of no other dialogue has
anybody said what Eduard Norden says of the *Phaedrus*, that it
is a "failure" in composition[39]—although this sounds more like
a renunciation of the search than a solution to the puzzle.

Rhetoric is not *the* theme of the *Phaedrus*, but it is the theme
in the foreground.[40] In the first part of the dialogue, Plato presents some examples of rhetoric which are then examined in
the second part in the light of rhetorical theory just as they,
in turn, are used to refine the theory. Socrates cites them explicitly as "examples" (262cd, 264e)—which is reason enough
to distrust this even if he had not added the ironic remark that
they happen to be available "by chance" (265c 9). Thus, they
are examples of rhetoric, but they are also something altogether
different, for in the ecstatic elevation of the third speech, a view
is opened up into the nature of love, into the universe, into the
realm of eternal Forms, and into the cosmic fate of the soul.

The second part of the dialogue moves beyond the theoretical
discussion about rhetoric to another level where dialectics and
a philosophical doctrine of the soul are set up as postulates and
where the philosophical conversation appears as the highest
form of human speech. Yet this philosophical conversation is
not simply set up as an abstract demand. It is realized in the dialogue itself. Thus, we can see how the unity of the dual nature
of the whole dialogue is achieved, on the one hand, in the personal context of the loving bond between Socrates and Phaidros

and, on the other, in the conceptual context of the ecstatic elevation and the educational ascent upward into the realm of Forms.
This is a unity that reconciles the two distant poles of love and
speech. For *philo-sophy* is at once the highest form of love and
the highest form of speech. From this perspective we need not
speculate how it is possible that the way toward the Forms is
shown first in the ecstasy of madness and then in the strict context of dialectics.[41] These are the two ways that Plato knew
about because he had experienced them both and because he
could not but travel both. That in the *Phaedrus* he pursues these
two paths almost simultaneously and with equal energy characterizes the special tension and the unique quality of this
astonishing work.

TWENTY-SIX

Sophist

WE do not know whether Plato intended, at the conclusion of the *Theaetetus*, to keep the appointment for "tomorrow morning" (an ending similar to that of the *Laches*) by following up on it with a separate dialogue of its own.[1] At any rate, later he used this opportunity in writing the pair of dialogues, the *Sophist* and the *Statesman*. For Plato to come back to the persons, the insights, and the problems left behind in the *Theaetetus* was not a way to save himself the trouble of creating a new spiritual setting for the *Sophist*. On the contrary, this was done precisely in order to show what was new in the later dialogue.[2] The question of knowledge and its object, eternal being, also forms the background of the new conversation, which overtly inquires into the nature of the sophist and implicitly inquires into that of the philosopher. Socrates as the philosopher and counterpart to the sophist stands in the background of this inquiry.

The mathematician Theodoros opens the conversation and, without participating in the dialectical discussion, represents the stage of mathematical existence in the search for being and not-being. It is no accident that Theaitetos is the partner in a discussion in which the method of "division" is practiced—and exaggerated. For it was he who told us in the previous dialogue (*Theaetetus* 147c *et seq.*) how he and the younger Socrates, stimulated by the mathematical demonstrations of Theodoros, had come to divide the system of natural numbers first into two groups and then into four, and to define each group. We also must recall the division of types of being and of knowledge, as we find it in Book VI of the *Republic*, transcribed onto the proportionate sections of the "divided line." We must think, further, of the relation between division and mathematical reasoning as it is suggested once in the *Sophist* itself (251A), and keep in mind, too, the general connection that exists between the system of numbers and the schema of division as such, in order to realize what the presence of the mathematician signifies in this dialogue especially, and later in the *Statesman*.[3]

As the *Sophist* is related to the *Theaetetus* by virtue of the mathematician's presence, so it is related to the *Parmenides* by virtue of the presence of the "guest from Elea."[4] Parmenides and Zeno themselves had come from Elea to Athens in the *Parmenides*. That was impossible in the *Sophist* for chronological reasons if Theodoros and Theaitetos were to participate in the conversation. So an anonymous "stranger from Elea" who was a member of the school of Parmenides had to take the place of the famous philosopher himself. The conversation is conducted only between him and young Theaitetos. This technique is basically the same as that practiced in the second or dialectical part of the *Parmenides*, to which Socrates here refers explicitly (*Sophist* 217c) in asking the stranger whether he prefers to conduct the inquiry by means of a systematic discourse or by means of questions and answers. The stranger opts for questions and answers as the easier method provided that the respondent "be tractable."

In the dialogue *Parmenides*, Plato did not raise the question of whether to conduct a systematic exposition, but Parmenides himself did request as the stranger does here that the respondent not be difficult. Perhaps it is true that this new form of the dialogue is taken from the "actual teaching practice" in the Academy and is designed "to make sure that the partner understands at each moment the course pursued in the conversation" (Stenzel)[5] —though it must remain an open question whether Plato would have wished to have, or would have chosen, only such tractable pupils. (The young Aristotle of Stagira surely was not of this disposition, and the all too tractable young Aristotle in the *Parmenides* later became one of the oligarchy of the "Thirty Tyrants"!) At any rate, we must not fail to see something that is more important. While the dialectical tension between the Eleatic stranger and his partner is reduced practically to zero, another tension is generated between this almost indifferent conversation, on the one side, and Socrates who is silently listening to it, on the other. This tension must be constantly kept in mind if we are to read the dialogue in Plato's spirit, i.e., as a dialogue and not as a treatise.[6] This is another respect in which the *Sophist*—and it goes without saying, the *Statesman*, too—corresponds to the second or dialectical part of the *Parmenides*, the only difference being that Socrates, who stands by silently, here in the *Sophist* is not a young man but a man of seventy. This certainly reinforces the dialectical tension between the sophist's mode of being that is the subject of inquiry and the existence of the philosopher that Socrates—as nobody else—represents.

Socrates himself set the place and time of the conversation reported in the *Sophist*, for at the end of the *Theaetetus* he says: "Now I must go to the portico of the King-Archon to meet the indictment that Meletos has drawn up against me. But tomorrow morning we will meet here again." Thus, the two conversations are separated not only by a fixed number of hours, but by an event deciding the life and death of Socrates. It is inconceivable that Plato did not have this in mind when he connected the opening of the *Sophist* with the ending of the *Theaetetus*. And it is hardly conceivable that he did not intend also to remind the reader of this decisive event in the life of Socrates.

Is it possible to discover a hint of this in the initial remarks of Socrates by which he replies to the opening words of Theodoros in the *Sophist?* Theodoros has introduced his companion, a "guest"—the conventional way of translating the untranslatable ξένος—who has come to Athens from distant Elea. Socrates replies in two brief and compact speeches that are full of Homeric associations[7] and he even refers specifically to Homer in asking whether Theodoros might have brought a god instead of an ordinary "guest." In the *Odyssey*,[8] Athene appears as a guest from a foreign land and then is recognized as a goddess as she suddenly disappears in the shape of a bird. Also, the youthful suitors discuss whether the returning Odysseus, unrecognized in his homeland, might be a god—exactly the same question that Socrates here puts to Theodoros. Moreover, the *Odyssey* twice expresses the moral conviction that Zeus, the protector of strangers, looks down upon the lawless and the rightful conduct of mankind.

What does all this mean coming from Socrates, coming especially at the beginning of a discussion on the nature of the sophist? As for the question of whether the guest might be a god, we cannot but recall the struggle waged against Homer in Book II of the *Republic*. There (381D) Socrates criticizes the Homeric notion that gods may appear in the disguise of strangers, and alludes to the same verses as he does here in the *Sophist* to counter this view with the conviction that a god does not change his shape. Thus, Socrates' question is permeated by irony.[9] All the more unshakable is the serious conviction presently expressed that the god who protects strangers marks the lawless and lawful conduct of men. Do we read too much into these Homeric words, this image, if we remember that, on the previous day, Socrates was called upon to defend himself in the portico of the King-Archon? The indictment, as everybody knew, charged that "Socrates does not honor the gods, but believes in demonic beings of a new kind" (*Apology* 24BC). It is the same Socrates who, in a spirit of deep seriousness, invokes Zeus here as the god who "examines and convicts," the judge of right and wrong. This does more than expose the indictment as senseless, for Socrates also implies that he and his accusers are to be judged before the tribunal of the highest god. Let us ask ourselves, then, whether the critical presence of the man who yesterday defended himself in court, and soon will suffer the death sentence, does not open up a dimension of profound significance beyond the conversations that follow in search of the "sophist" and the "statesman."

The *Theaetetus* had raised some questions without solving them. First, in order to define knowledge, it inquired into the meaning of error. It showed several types of error, but not what error is as such, and so both the inquiry into error and the inquiry into knowledge finally came to an aporetic conclusion. Secondly, the *Theaetetus* dealt with the problem of "Herakleitos," and in the course of the dialogue, becoming and change were assigned their necessary place in Plato's world. For reasons of structural economy, the *Theaetetus* explicitly avoided a confrontation with Parmenides.[10] But do these two threads that were not tied together nevertheless belong together? Put differently, did the search for falsehood and truth in the *Theaetetus* fail because Parmenides was not included in the discussion? By identifying being and knowledge this great predecessor had opened the way to the knowledge of being. Yet, by denying reality to anything but "the One," he also had blocked this way, as was shown by his eristic successors. Thus, a confrontation with the Parmenidean concept of being is necessary to solve the problem raised in the *Theaetetus*. The dialogue *Parmenides* had done much to make this confrontation more meaningful, first because the metaphorical language of the "theory of Forms" was rigorously examined from the logical perspective of the concept of the "one being," and second because the dialectic of "the One" and "the other" led to a zig-zag system as instructive as it was dangerous.

If "truth" refers to beings or being, then falsehood must have something to do with the uncanny problem of not-being. For an intuitive mind such as Plato's, however, the question of truth and falsehood, even though it might eventually lead into rarefied regions, was never simply an abstract problem of logic. For Plato the question was always grounded in a live encounter, or basic experience. From the *Protagoras* on, he never tired of representing it—this confrontation of philosopher and sophist—in ever new ways, as he also did, and from a definite point of view, in the interlude or digression of the *Theaetetus*.[11] In the *Protagoras*, the *Gorgias*, the *Euthydemus*, and elsewhere, the sophist had appeared in various and different guises, but Plato never was deceived about the simple contrast. It is truth and falsehood, *aletheia* and *pseudos*, that confront each other. And now the strange paradox was this, that it was precisely the eristic sophists who were making use of the Parmenidean view denying the reality of not-being (and hence the possibility of speaking about it), and they were doing this precisely in order to destroy the possibility of truth, true speech and conversation, and in order to put over their own distorted image of genuine conversation. They denied that *pseudos* (falsehood, lying, deception) was possible—in order to mislead all the more effectively (*Euthydemus* 285E *et seq.*). For these reasons, it was necessary to clarify the nature of the sophist and thereby the nature of *pseudos* so as to see more clearly the meaning of truth and the nature of the philosopher. As there is no truth without the possibility of falsehood, so the philosopher realizes his own true nature only in the struggle against the sophist—perhaps the struggle even against the sophist within himself.

The new form in which this old struggle is waged here can only be explained by the fact that Plato was obsessed—or perhaps one should say, acted as if he were obsessed—by the method of division (diaeresis). What is new and characteristic of this dialogue as well as of its twin is that both works are completely dominated by this method of division. The principle of division, or systematic ordering, must have been present in Plato's mind as early as the method of dialectics was. If we find now that it is just the sophist, the statesman, and thereby the philosopher who are the subject of this systematic division, we may trace the system itself back to the *Gorgias* (464A *et seq.*):

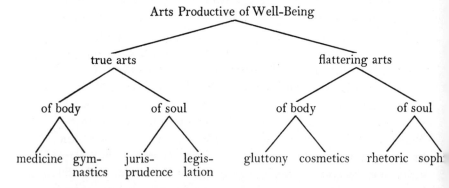

Arts Productive of Well-Being

true arts   flattering arts

of body   of soul   of body   of soul

medicine gym-   juris-   legis-   gluttony cosmetics rhetoric soph
        nastics prudence lation

The left side of this system occurs also in the *Republic* (see pp. 91f., above), except that there, for a good reason, "music" takes the place of legislation (both are forms of "law-making"). The system is resumed in the *Sophist* with more detailed subdivisions:

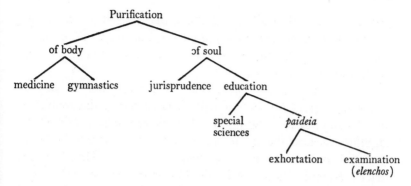

With examination (*elenchos*) we have reached the "sophistic
of high and noble birth" (ἡ γένει γενναία σοφιστική, 231в 8). In
other words, philosophy emerges behind a sophistic made
transparent, as it were. Again, in the last of the systematic
divisions by which the sophist is to be tracked down in this
dialogue, we recognize the diaeresis of the *Gorgias*. Below, we
simplify the elaborate schema worked out in the *Sophist* so that
its affinity with the *Gorgias* may be seen more clearly:

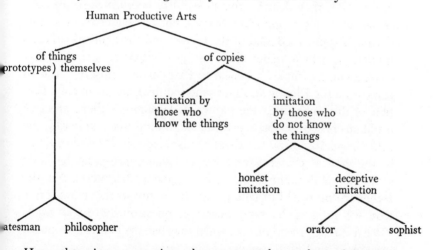

Here, then, is a connection where we see the method of division
applied, even to the same topic, long before the *Sophist*. This
shows clearly that Plato did not create this method in his late
years. He merely carried it to an extreme limit and, we may add,
beyond this limit. For even in his old age Plato had not for-

gotten to view ironically any method that tended to become an end in itself, as in his earlier years he had ironically depreciated the logical hairsplitting of a Prodikos that he nevertheless would not have wanted to be without.[12]

After what we have said, it is not surprising that the subject of the first great division actually carried out is the sophist—and, by implication, the philosopher. Question and method go together because the truth can be obtained, and falsehood be excluded, only by means of a strict division of "kinds" and a strict hierarchical order of levels. Nor is it surprising that it is precisely the "guest from Elea" who must practice this art of division. The original distinctions between being and not-being, being known and not-known, are Parmenidean. Zeno and Melissos then carried this method further by introducing other distinctions: adding and subtracting, less and more, finite and infinite, beginning and end. The fundamental opposites of Parmenides, however, have a peculiar consequence. On the one hand, they make intelligible discourse possible at all; on the other hand, they destroy this possibility because they are conceived of as rigid opposites that cannot be connected. For this reason, a sophistic denial of the *pseudos* and the principle of contradiction, which undermines all possibility of genuine discourse, could ultimately appeal to Parmenides himself.[13] And so it must be the Eleatic stranger who inquires, by means of a system of divisions, into the nature of falsehood—there are two problems posed by Socrates at the beginning, one explicitly, the other implicitly—and the Eleatic must also solve these problems in the critical presence of Socrates, who represents the antisophistic, philosophical existence, genuine discourse, and the ascent to the world of true being. It is only in this perspective that we fully understand Socrates' question (216D *et seq.*): "What do they mean in Elea when they use the names of sophist, statesman, and philosopher?"

The Search for the Sophist

A
218B–236D
264C–268D

What happens in the conversation between the Eleatic stranger and Theaitetos? When we wish "to find the sophist and clarify his nature in discussion," the only thing we have in common, to begin with, is the "name." As to the "thing" itself (ἔργον, πρᾶγμα) each man has his own private meaning, so that we lack understanding. It is the task of a clarifying discussion to reach the goal where we have the thing in common as we previously had the name.[14] This goal is reached, however, not by fixing concepts and by definitions but by attempting to see and to stabilize the thing in a diaeretic system of related and different things. This is easy in the case of "angling," but difficult in the case of the sophist, for he is such a slippery and iridescent being (223c 2, 226a 6) that he always slips through the net we have cast and therefore must be caught by ever new systems.[15] Although the abundance of these systems of division threatens to become excessive, and we are overwhelmed by an avalanche of names coined in an astonishing mixture of play and seriousness, we still must admire again and again the precision with which Plato has observed and ordered various arts even as we admire the power of invention he has invested in this coining of terms.[16] (Diès has pointed out the similarity to Rabelais.) Above all, however, we must realize how this undertaking is to be judged from the point of view of Socrates who is standing by. For variability is part of the realm of not-being in whose darkness the sophist takes refuge (254a). Socratic knowledge, however, is one not manifold, simple not iridescent (*Theaetetus* 146d).

The determination of angling by means of a system of divi- 218D–221c
sion is not simply an illustration of the method. It also outlines, in sarcastic jest, a counterinstance of the actual thing that is to be discovered. It is indeed an ironic accident that three passages in this system subsequently become points of departure for three systems in which the sophist finds his place: "hunting on land" (πεζοθηρική) for the first system, "exchange by gifts, hire, or purchase" (μεταβλητική) for the second system, and the "art of conquest" (ἀγωνιστική) for the fifth system. Above all, the basic division of activity into productive and acquisitive (ποιητική— κτητική) is most important for two reasons. On the one hand, the class of productive activity, though put aside for the time being, is given its due in the seventh and last system of classification, so that the formal structure of the dialogue is held together by this division. On the other hand, producing or making is of crucial

significance from the very outset, for producing means "to bring not-being into being, or existence" (219B). Thus, not-being immediately enters into the discussion, but not in such a way (as it will be later in the dialogue) that its reality is put into question and barely saved. Rather, not-being is seen here as a basic phenomenon of life itself, since producing, making, or creating presupposes not-being. We cannot begin to understand a simple phenomenon like "making" without not-being.

221c–223c   As the *first determination*[17] begins, we learn that sophistic is hunting of tame animals; for Theaitetos kindly had put man into the class of tame animals, even though the Eleatic stranger had left it open whether man should be counted among the tame animals or the wild. Plato here again hints at the opposite traits that he thought were characteristic of human nature itself.[18] According to the *Laws* (VI 766A), it is education that determines whether man will become the tamest or the wildest animal on earth. In the mythical image of the *Republic* (IX 588c), man is depicted as a many-shaped beast with heads of wild and tame animals, and (to change the image) it is his task in cultivating the "inner garden" to curb the growth of the wild impulses and to develop the tame ones. The same contrast is restated in the concluding myth on the transmigration of souls.

According to the classification in the *Sophist*, then, sophistic falls into a general class—hunting of tame animals, hunting of man. It is a hunt by means of persuasion as distinguished from piracy, slavery, tyranny, and war. This persuasion aims at individuals and therefore is distinguished from the kind of persuasion addressed to the public. The public kind is rhetoric, akin to sophistic, and described in the *Gorgias* (452E *et seq.*) as "productive of persuasion." Sophistic is a hunt "bringing in pay" as distinguished from another "bringing gifts." This is a paradoxical formulation to which the young Theaitetos replies, for the first time, "I don't understand." The Eleatic guest explains the second type by comparing it to the art with which lovers hunt—reminding us that, at the beginning of the *Protagoras*, Socrates comes "from a chase of Alkibiades," and that, in the *Symposium*, Diotima describes love as a "mighty hunter."[19] If not before, it now is clear that what distinguishes

Socrates from the sophists here is the same contrast that runs all through Plato's work. The familiar charge against the sophists that they take pay for their teaching is shown once again in its true meaning: they would not do so if they were driven by a daimonion—as Socrates (who is listening) is driven.

Next, the private manhunt bringing in pay is divided, on the one hand, into the art of flattery or the sweetening art (κολακική, ἡδυντική)—one might say, the art of the confectioner—and, on the other, into the art that claims to teach virtue. In the *Gorgias*, rhetoric was one among several arts of flattery; here it is the sister of flattery. Its defective nature is revealed precisely by the fact that it claims to teach virtue. By contrast we see from afar what philosophy must be, especially after our view has focused on Socrates by way of the references to a "hunt bringing gifts" and to the "amatory art."[20]

In the *Protagoras* (313c), Socrates in inquiring into the nature (ὅτι ποτ᾽ ἔστιν) of the sophist called him, maliciously enough, a merchant trading in food of the soul. This description is used now in the *second determination* as the central theme of a new classification. Let us observe especially the aspects that are excluded in this dichotomy. Giving (δωρητικόν) is excluded: the sophist sells, but he does not give presents. The sale of a man's own products (αὐτοπωλική) is excluded: the sophist sells what others have produced. He is a middleman trading in, say, Parmenidean products. This is particularly bad in the intellectual field because in the act of spiritual creation only a live product has any genuine value. Retail trade within the city (καπηλική) is excluded: the sophist is engaged in wholesale trade from one city to another. The sophist (as Plato says everywhere) travels as a stranger from city to city—and indeed is not a petty schoolmaster teaching only in his own home town. 223c–224d

The sophist is a merchant of food not for the body, but for the soul (ψυχεμπορική). His is not an art of display (ἐπιδεικτική), but a trade in objects of learning (μαθηματοπωλική). He sells not specific skills (τεχνοπωλικόν) but *arete*. Again we are reminded of the *Protagoras*. There (313d *et seq.*) the danger of the sophist is said to be that this merchant of food for the soul commends his wares to everybody whether the food will agree with a person or not, and that, while the buyer of ordinary food can carry his things home in a receptacle and examine them at leisure, the buyer of sophistic wares has only his own soul as a receptacle. From the *Protagoras* (312B), we also know the distinction between technical instruction and cultivation of the soul (*paideia*), so that we might raise the question of whether something like virtue can be sold in the same sense that technical instruction can. A glance at Socrates who is listening provides the answer.

Looking more closely at the last branches excluded in this division, we find a peculiar principle of order. Among the arts of display imported from outside are listed music and painting, i.e., the works of Simonides, Pindar, and Polygnotos, artistic works of high rank for Plato, too. Yet rhetoric is ranked above them. Again, among the objects of learning we find special skills whose names suggest mathematics and the technical arts, i.e., sciences of high value for Plato, too (and we recall that here mathematics is represented on the scene by Theodoros and Theaitetos).[21] Yet "virtue" as taught by the sophists is ranked above the sciences. No instrument, however subtle, could register the interplay of irony and seriousness in this classification, but we may say this: If such a superior rank is assigned to sophistic because it teaches virtue, how much more superior is philosophy as represented by Socrates—who, on the previous day, had to defend himself in a court of law against the charge of corrupting the youth!

224D–224E   *The third and fourth determinations*[22] are variations of the second, which presented the type of the sophist as revealed in its most famous representatives, Protagoras, Gorgias, or Hippias. We had read in the *Protagoras* (313C) that the sophist may be a "wholesale merchant" or a "retail peddler" (ἔμπορος ἢ κάπηλος). Now we learn that it does not really matter whether he moves from city to city; he may even reside in the same city. Nor does it matter whether he sells acquired products or those that he has fabricated himself. These variations show that we must not mistake what ultimately are accidental characteristics for the essence of the matter.

In the *fifth determination*, once more we go back to the classifi- 224ᴇ–226ᴀ
cation of angling or, more specifically, to the point (219ᴇ) at
which the area of contest (ἀγωνιστική) was dropped. Sophistic
is located now in this area, not as contest but as fighting (μάχη),
and not as fighting in the physical sense but as a war of words
(ἀμφισβητητικόν). We move into the domain of words (*logoi*),
whose crucial significance immediately is apparent. From this
domain are excluded the long public speeches about just and
unjust, i.e., above all, the battles in law courts. The speech
consisting of short questions and answers is retained, however,
and we become attentive because this division seems to reflect
the contrast between a Socratic discussion and the long speeches
delivered by public orators. This proximity to a Socratic dimension grows in what follows, for now we leave aside the artless
exchange of talk in business dealings and retain another kind of
conversation that proceeds by rules of art and deals with justice
and injustice. Are we not facing the genuine philosophical
dialogue as practiced by Socrates who silently is listening? But,
at the last moment, a radical change in direction occurs. The
kind of argumentation that is conducted for its own pleasure,
and without regard to one's own affairs, and even at the risk of
loss (χρηματοφθορικόν)—this kind of contest is put aside. It is
called not Socratic conversation, but loquacity.[23] We leave it
aside, then, and take up the other type, which makes money out
of private argumentation (χρηματιστικόν). With this step, a
regress to a previous position, we turn away from the Socratic
dimension we had almost reached and are back to sophistic. The
Socratic element, however, is to become still more tangible in
what follows.

In the *sixth determination*, we begin with various household 226ᴀ–231ʙ
activities, winnowing, straining, and so on. All of them contain
the notion of division (διαιρετική) and give rise to the general
concept of the "art of discrimination" (διακριτική). This is a
new departure, different from the classification of angling. Is
it accidental that what the Eleatic stranger does throughout
the dialogue is just such an "activity of division," so that we
actually begin not with random or farfetched activities but

with the most essential? Next, "purification" (καθαρμός) is separated out from the various processes of division, and there follows the system of classification described earlier (p. 249, above).

Even here there is an admixture of the grotesque and of crude joking in the midst of the most serious matters.[24] For example, the Eleatic stranger puts the preparation of bath sponges beside the preparation of medications as subdivisions of purifications, and, returning to the first determination, the art of strategy beside the art of catching lice—the one no more dignified than the other, but generally more pretentious! He is heading toward the method of cross-examination (*elenchos*), as we are about to see. The extreme "foolishness" is now brought out: it consists in supposing to know what one does not know. We are familiar with this formula, for it is Socrates' own.[25] We are also familiar with Socrates' way of dealing with this foolishness, for the goal of "eradicating erroneous belief" (τῆς δόξης ἐκβολή, 230B 1) is reached not by exhortation, but only through examination and refutation, i.e., through the *elenchos*.

It is the Socratic method, then, that is outlined here by the Eleatic guest, the method of compelling a person to admit that he holds inconsistent or contradictory views at the same time about the same things in the same respect. Whereas in the fifth system of classification the sophistic came so close to the Socratic element that at the last moment a violent shift in direction was necessary, an ironic accident turns the discussion now toward the method—or one that seems to be indistinguishable from it— of this very Socrates who opened the conversation and all along has been listening silently. The Eleatic stranger himself fears that here we may be according too much honor to the sophist. That we perhaps may encounter the philosopher is at once asserted and concealed in the strange phrase that refers to a "sophistic of high and noble birth" (231B 8).[26]

Is the eristic of the *Euthydemus* such an examination or purification of the soul? In what sense could it be? What does it have in common with the Socratic method, and what separates one from the other?[27] We are warned of the slippery ground of "similarities" where a man must be cautious not to lose his secure footing—a methodological hint that applies as much to the activities of the Academy in Plato's old age[28] as it does to the conceptual work involved here in the *Sophist*. Yet the stranger does not carry on the process of dividing similarities from dissimilarities, and for a good reason. Socrates himself would have to speak out, but Plato has him remain silent. There is a deeply ironic tension between the formal method of classification, on the one hand, as practiced by the Eleatic stranger, and the kind of philosophy, on the other hand, as conceived by Plato's Socrates and only by him. Such philosophy includes formal rules, but goes far beyond and above them. One does not die for the method of division!

Six times we have tried to catch the changing aspects of the sophist in a system of classification. As the *seventh determination* begins, the results of the first six are summed up. We see that we advanced from such external criteria as the manhunt for pay to ever more internal determinations until, by way of "trade in food of the soul" and the "art of argumentation," we came to the process of "purification." It was more than questionable whether the sophist was capable of this. In fact, we had reached the Socratic level here. For this reason the seventh, last, and decisive attempt at defining the sophist turns all the more sharply away from this level.[29]

231b–236d
264c–268d

The sophist is a "master of controversy" (ἀντιλογικός) who also is capable of instructing others in his art. This art he exercises with regard to all things (περὶ πάντων), from theology and cosmology to politics and even to such special techniques as athletics. But since it is impossible for any single individual to have true knowledge of all things, the sophist can possess only an "apparent knowledge" (δοξαστικὴν ἐπιστήμην, 233c). For this reason his art is the opposite of the *elenchos* that, in the sixth determination, aimed at "eradicating false appearance." Only this contrast enables us to clarify these two kinds of knowledge, and only the contrast between appearance and truth (or true being) that is emerging here enables us to see the problem in its radical aspect.

Sophistic is a counterfeit imitative art, as it was described earlier in the *Gorgias* (464d *et seq.*). This formulation allies it with the imitative, illusionistic type of painting to which Plato assigned a place, consistent with his general view, in the last book of the *Republic* (X 596B *et seq.*).[30] The sophist is a juggler and a wizard (γόης, θαυματοποιός, *Sophist* 235AB), as the imitative Jack-of-all-trades was called in the *Republic* (598D; cf. 602D). Sophistic is not an art of making likenesses (εἰκαστική), i.e., works in which the true proportions of beautiful things are reproduced, but an art of "illusion" (φανταστική) in which apparent proportions, i.e., things that merely appear beautiful and correct, are worked into artistic products.[31]

"Making of illusive appearances"—with this formulation the Eleatic stranger departs from the path of division he has strictly followed up to now. The question about the sophist turns into the questions of whether, and how, it is possible that there be something like appearance, copy, not-being, and falsehood. The remainder of the dialogue is concerned with clarifying these problems until, at the end, it comes back to the question about the sophist and to the method of division as well (265B). It may be said that only now do we penetrate to the real theme, the core of the dialogue, so that what has gone before together with the concluding section is nothing but a "frame." Yet we must realize that Plato does not pose the questions of being and not-being, truth and deception, in a vacuum. On the contrary, these questions have their live counterparts in the opposition of the philosopher and mathematician, on the one hand, as against the sophist, on the other. What "ontologically" is the necessary contrast between being and not-being manifests itself historically and in the reality of life—or "existentially"—in the opposition of sophist and philosopher. Thus, here as elsewhere, what is called the frame and what is called the picture (or content) are related not at all accidentally, nor could one be separated from the other.[32]

Only after we have grasped the nature of not-being, and clarified copy and appearance, do we have the solid foundations for interpreting sophistic as a pseudo-art (264D). In this seventh and last attempt, we go back to the primary distinction between productive and acquisitive arts. The first six determinations had placed the art of the sophist in the class of acquisitive arts. In the seventh determination, however, it is put, as an imitation, in with the productive arts. In this way we return to the phenomenon of making, producing, and creating as the power that transforms not-being into being (265BC, 219B). What at the beginning of the dialogue was derived, without further inquiry, from the conception of ordinary life has now gained its proper depth. This is so because the necessary contrast, together with the complementarity, of being and not-being has been revealed as a basic constituent of the world in its widest and highest sense.

Hence, we must distinguish between two kinds of production, divine and human. Divine production is defended—as in the myth of the *Statesman*, or in the *Timaeus* and the *Laws*[33]—against the false view that it is the effect of blind forces of nature. Rather, it is creation with reason and intelligence. It seems, then, to be interpreted after the human model. Yet, the works of men can be made only "out of" that which divine production has made available (265E). The class of divine and human works is divided next into two parts, the original essences as against their copies, or images. This is an analogy by which divine production becomes intelligible to man and by which human production acquires its dignity as well as its limits. In the realm of divine creation we find, on one side, the living beings and the natural elements of which they are composed, and on the other side, the dreams, shadows, and mirror images. (All this reminds us of the *Timaeus*.) In the realm of human works we distinguish, for example, between the building of a house and the painting of a picture of a house. The analogy between divine and human works is not carried any further, so that the question arises of whether anything in the realm of divine creation corresponds to the distinction between "likeness" and "illusion" (εἰκαστικόν—φανταστικόν), or corresponds to imitation, or even to false imitation (δοξομιμητική). The further we go in these divisions, the more we shall deny that there is any such correspondence. And as for the "concealed (and self-concealing) imitator" (εἰρωνικὸς μιμητής), which includes the popular speechifier and the sophist, it would be blasphemy even to think of divine correspondence. That we should feel this without words is another aim (and not the least) of the method of division.

The principal goal of this method, however, is not to discover a definition that is justified only in the end as a kind of retrospective summary, but rather to reveal the matter itself in an animated and ordered system of classification. It is revealed as it is set apart together with that from which it is set apart.[34] It is no accident that we had to pay as much attention to the discarded members of the division on the left as to the members on the right (cf. 264E 1). And if we have learned that we cannot say, or understand, body without soul, copy without original, arts of flattery without genuine arts, eristic without philosophy —and vice versa—then we have gained a vivid insight into the area to be investigated ontologically in the second part of the dialogue. Even though this insight requires an explicit inquiry, we already know vaguely that being and not-being, too, can only be determined, if at all, in a necessary, reciprocal relation of complementarity. A new and important link is found that connects the ontological investigation with the divisions.[35]

There is another link that is not expressed explicitly. This method of division is by nature such that each part, in so far as it "is" what it is, "is not" the "other" from which it is separated. The meaning of "not-being," therefore, in which the ontological investigation will actually culminate has been conveyed throughout implicitly.[36]

The Ontological Investigation

B
236D–264c
I 1
236D–237c

With words like "seeming" and "appearing" we enter upon the greatest difficulties. How something can "seem" or "appear" to be and at the same time not be, or how (on the level of discourse) we can say "something" and at the same time say something not true—these are obscure and puzzling matters. So they are now and so they were "always." The *Hippias Minor* touched on this old problem so often abused by eristic thinkers, and the *Euthydemus* went further in playing the dangerous game. The *Cratylus* and the *Theaetetus* also struggled for the solution to the problem. Now it is to be analyzed in its logical foundations. In referring to falsehood (*pseudos*), our inquiry (*logos*) itself "dared" to presuppose the being of not-being. In doing this it came into conflict—*logos* against *logos*—with the basic principle of Parmenides, whose successor the speaker is, and consciously so (237A). This contradiction is pursued now to its depths, seriously, without eristic word play (237B 10), and in a manner quite different from that of Euthydemos and Dionysodoros.

We may sound (φθέγγεσθαι) the phrase "not-being," but we cannot apply it to anything that exists, whether to "something" (τι) or to "one" (ἕν) or to many. In short, we cannot apply not-being to number as such. It seems to follow that, in this case, not only do we "say nothing," but we do not even "say" anything, i.e., make a statement that differs from mere "sound" in that it refers to an object. In the *Euthydemus* (284c), the sophists use a similar argument; so does Socrates in the *Theaetetus* (189B). Here it is put into a more radical form. In the case of a thing that exists, another thing may be added to it. We cannot add anything to a non-being, however, not even number since number is something that exists. Thus, not-being cannot be uttered, spoken of, or thought. Here the wording of Parmenides has been reached and his basic thesis demonstrated[37] —except that the phrase "not-being itself and in itself" (τὸ μὴ ὂν αὐτὸ καθ' αὑτό) adds a peculiar radicalization.

At this point, however, with the motivation that now only the "greatest difficulty" is to be exposed, a countermovement gets under way. While the guest from Elea had denied that any attributes apply to not-being, and had even declared not-being to be "ineffable," still he had spoken—"spoken," not merely "sounded"[38]—of it as "a" being. Thus, the proof of Parmenides, as expounded here by his Eleatic disciple, is caught in a contradiction. Lest we think this may be a mere play of words, we immediately are brought back to the initial theme of the dialogue: the sophist is hiding in some impenetrable (ἄπορον) place. He cannot be caught, for his existence requires that there be such a thing as "seeming" and, hence, not-being.

Yet now the Eleatic turns into an eristic thinker—even as it was not accidental that Gorgias, and Euthydemos and his

I 2
237D–238c

I 3
238D–239c

I 4
239c–241c

brother, borrowed the tools they used from the workshop of Parmenides. The stranger here raises the challenging question of what we possibly could mean by an image or phantom (εἴδωλον) as the maker of which (εἰδωλοποιός) we consider him. In eristic fashion, he claims that there are no such images (the better to fish in troubled waters!). But Theaitetos, with good reason, will not let himself be talked out of the experience that there are images and, though at first he enumerates specific instances instead of defining the general concept, he soon is led by his partner to grasp the essence of an image. An image is something that resembles real existence (or truth) and yet is different from it. It is "not real in a true manner" (οὐκ ὄντως), yet it is what it is "in a true manner" (ὄντως). Hence, it has "some sort" (πως) of existence.[39] We may recall how it displeased Euthydemos when Ktesippos defined a person practicing deception as someone whose statement described being "in a certain manner but not as it really is" (τρόπον τινά . . . ὥς γ᾽ ἔχει, Euthydemus 284c). In the Sophist, the meaning of this "some sort" obviously refers to the "intertwining" (συμπλοκή) of opposites (ὄντως οὐκ ὄντως), but it is not clear at this point what this intertwining really means. Thus, at the end of this section, we find the two hostile camps directly confronting each other. On the one side is the sophist who, supported by Parmenides,[40] clings to the view that there is no such thing as deception. On the other side stands the fact that there is such a thing as the sophist and, consequently, that there must be deception and appearance and that the combination of being and not-being must be possible "in some way."

II
241c–250e

PRELIMINARY
REMARKS
241c–242b

The discussion to follow, therefore, must be concerned with the view of Parmenides. We will not overthrow the "powerful" thesis itself, but will be content if we "can pull some part of it over to our side." In other words, it is a matter of transforming the Parmenidean concept of being. We wage this struggle against our "father," the Eleatic stranger explains, out of necessity, not from lack of filial piety—for the Eleatic doctrine of being calls for a modification of the status of not-being if the doctrine itself is not to succumb to empty eristics. And so we enter upon the long-delayed inquiry.

The consideration of not-being necessarily leads back to being, for it makes sense to talk about not-being only in talking about being (and vice versa). Thus, we start out (ἀρχή, 242B 6) by discussing what seems to be self-understood but really is a source of confusion, namely, the doctrines of earlier thinkers about what is, the various kinds of beings (τὰ ὄντα), their number and attributes. The natural philosophers actually told fairy tales about these matters (242c 8), yet we must inquire into what they really meant by "being" and "reality" (τὸ ὄν, 243D 3). And so we embark upon the beginnings of a doxographical account, or a history of philosophy, which Aristotle will continue, he as well as Plato not for historical reasons, but in order to distinguish his own views and at the same time to connect them with the views of earlier thinkers.[41]

First we call up those thinkers who postulated two kinds of reality, say, warm and cold, as the Eleatic stranger puts it. In other words, in the light of the precise concept of being as developed by Parmenides, we now judge the earliest speculative theories (as yet devoid of any clear concept of being) about the "origin" of things. Is being itself (τὸ εἶναι) something in addition to the two kinds of being, so that we would then have three instead of two? Or is it only one of the two, or are both kinds together "being itself," so that we would again have but *one* being? Contradictions arise in the earlier systems of thought when we ask for the meaning of being itself. Evidently, being is not something to be added to warm and cold as something of the same kind, nor something to be restricted to one or the other, nor something designating the sum of both. In thinking about "being" we are concerned with an entirely different concept, but what concept? "We are completely puzzled by these difficulties," as the Eleatic stranger says—the same difficulties, we may add, that are the point of departure in our time for Heidegger's renewed inquiry into the meaning of being.

Now the stranger even puts the Parmenidean doctrine of being up for cross-examination. He exposes the difficulties inherent in this doctrine. "The One" and "being"—are these two different names for one and the same thing as Parmenides claimed? What, then, is the meaning of these two names? More-

II 1
242B–245E

II 1a
243D–244B

II 1b
244B–245E

over, what is the meaning of the "name" as such for someone
who postulates that there is only "the One"? We run into contradictions both with respect to the name and with respect
to the One.[42] So says the Eleatic stranger who reveals the difficulties inherent in his master's system. For did not Parmenides
refer contemptuously to the "names" that ordinary men apply
to the—*unreal*—multitude of things, and did he not himself
use "names" to refer to "the One," the only real being? In
other words, discourse itself explodes the undifferentiated oneness of being that it proclaims, first, by virtue of the fact that
it consists of a multitude of "names," and second, by virtue
of the fact that speech is intentional, speaking *of something*.

Parmenides had also spoken of the One as the "whole" (ὅλον,
πᾶν) and compared it to a perfect sphere. A sphere, however,
has a center and a surface, i.e., parts, and the concept of a
"whole" makes sense only if it is a whole of something, i.e.,
of parts. Thus, what is divided or divisible may be a whole,
and hence, one—but it cannot be the "One as such" or the "One
itself" that Parmenides postulated. To avoid this difficulty there
are the following alternatives. Either we leave the "whole"
as something real outside the One. In this case, the "one being"
loses its perfection and in being defective it becomes a kind of
not-being. Moreover, the "whole" outside or beside the One
would again give us two kinds of being. Or, as the second alternative, we deny that there is such a thing as the "whole." In
this case we not only destroy being itself (because we deprive
it of perfection), but we destroy becoming along with being
(because everything in the world of becoming tends to become
a whole). We must look back to the *Theaetetus* (203c *et seq.*)
in order to see that the distinction between the "whole" or
"sum" (πᾶν) composed of different parts and the "entire"
(ὅλον) representing a unified, indivisible form (εἶδος) provides
the background for the present discussion.

In thinking through the Parmenidean doctrine of being, then,
we encounter these and "numerous other" difficulties, and the
doctrine itself calls for a deepening of the concept of being. But
is not Socrates present, silently listening to this discussion—
Socrates who in Plato represents the path of knowledge into

the world of eternal Forms, who likewise represents the method of ceaseless questioning by which any answers are kept alive, and who vouchsafes all this by his own life? Do not the difficulties here lead us to where this Socrates would see a solution? With the concept of the One, Parmenides meant to discard the "multitude" of things (or, in concrete terms, the colorful abundance of life) as an appearance created through language. But he can achieve this goal only by means of a language that confirms this multitude and helps to create it, and cannot be refuted since only language can refute. Now it was precisely in the realm of speech (ἐν λόγοις) that Socrates—as is said explicitly in the *Phaedo* (99E)—had discovered the knowledge of being. Moreover, that unity and diversity do not exclude but require each other was explicitly shown in the dialectics of the *Parmenides*, although this basic theme may be found throughout Plato's dialogues from the *Protagoras* on. Finally, the *Theaetetus* (204A *et seq.*) established that "wholeness" is a necessary attribute of every Form. In this way, all the lines that are not pursued here in the *Sophist* point toward the *Eidos*.

The inquiry here takes a more radical turn.[43] On the first level, the difficulties about the concept of being were discussed in the context of the opposition between the early philosophers of nature and the ontology of Parmenides. Now, on the second level, a "battle of gods and giants" is to be waged between those who attribute "real existence" only to what is physical and tangible, and despise everything else, on the one side, and those who attribute true being to intelligible and bodyless forms, on the other.[44] In the *Theaetetus* (155E), those "uninitiated" who believe that only what "they can grasp with their hands" is real are contrasted with those whose world-view has everything in constant flux (a view that Plato considered worth analyzing). There the uninitiated only seemed to serve as a foil in order to reveal the non-material and intellectual foundations of the doctrine of flux, though this doctrine nevertheless is opposed. Here the contrast is conceived more radically. On one side we have a world-view that, to say the least, resembles Plato's own "theory of Forms" (expounded in earlier dialogues) to such a degree that it is practically indistinguishable

II 2
245E–250E

from it.[45] On the other side, we do not deal—at least not to begin with, and perhaps not at all—with a philosophical doctrine,[46] but rather have a kind of naïve grasp of reality according to which the real is simply what is tangible and concrete. This view is so naïve that those who subscribe to it do not wish to hear anything else. Viewed from the perspective of the "friends of Forms," the bodies (i.e., that which this naïve attitude takes as the only real things) dissolve into a shifting process of becoming (γένεσις φερομένη).

The two views, opposed as they are, however, paradoxically seem to have one thing in common. Do they not display the same rigidity—on the one hand, the rigidity of bodies clashing with bodies, and on the other, the rigidity of the mind fixed on intelligible objects as the sole source of reality—with the result that, in the first case, we cannot conceive of any intelligible reality at all, and in the second, we must concede that all bodily reality is pulverized (κατὰ σμικρὰ διαθραύοντες, 246 c 1)? Plato intends to examine these two views, at once diametrically opposing and approaching each other, with regard to their understanding of reality. The battle between them is of gigantic proportions. It is not a battle between two philosophical doctrines, but a battle that "has always been going on" (246c 3).

II 2a
246c–248A

Equal understanding is not to be obtained from both parties. In fact, this would be impossible as far as those are concerned who "drag everything down to the level of body" (246c 9). They do not think philosophically at all,[47] because if they were to use rational discourse, they would have to acknowledge that there is something incorporeal. Thus, we must help them to communicate with us. The best thing would be if we could reform them in actual life. If that is not possible, we must reform them by means of words, i.e., by lending them our words and arguments (246D, 247c). This is most significant, showing that there is another dimension behind the ontological inquiry—the dimension of practical conduct, moral demand, actual "existence."

In the ensuing conversation, Theaitetos represents the naïve conception of reality, but in such a way that this conception is raised to a level where it is capable of being discussed. The true "earthborn" (247c)—i.e., those in whom this conception of reality is expressed in its crudest and most uncompromising form—are without shame. (Again, a moral aspect is combined with the ontological investigation, indicating that this is more than a formal feature of the argument.) They hold fast to the conviction that what "they cannot squeeze with their hands" is nothing at all. But if we reform them and lend them our words, they are compelled to make several concessions. There are not only bodies; there are also bodies animated by a soul; hence, there "is" such a thing as soul. Moreover, souls may be just and unjust, wise and foolish; hence, there "is" such a thing as justice or wisdom or their opposites. We are just in so far as we possess justice or in so far as justice is present in, or added to, the soul. Consequently, what "is" must mean what is "capable (δυνατόν) of being present in, or absent from," a thing.

With the concept of soul and most certainly with the concept of justice, we have left the realm of what is tangible. Thus, there is a kind of being, or reality, that is common (συμφυὲς γεγονός, 247D) to what is intangible as well as to physical things. What possesses power (δύναμις)—power to affect or to be affected—is real. In precise formulation, power is the definition (ὅρος) of being. This is as far as one can transform the original "power" of resistance put up by the earthborn. Again, we must not fail to see that the opening for this definition of being was provided by "justice, and the other virtues or their opposites" (247AB). The ethical perspective behind this ontology becomes still more visible than before.

A final question remains. "Power to affect or to be affected" as the, or one, basic determination of being—does not this formula sound in its very words like a famous thesis proposed by Aristotle?[48] Does Plato thus incorporate what young Aristotle, his most gifted disciple, the "Nous," had discovered in the Academy? Or did Aristotle use this Platonic definition as the basis for a philosophical system of universal significance, by expanding the definition in two respects—first, by introducing the concept of "entelechy" coined by him and, second, by reformulating the meaning of the term "energy"?

As the Eleatic stranger leaves these findings with the proviso that later they may be revised, he turns to the opposite party, the "friends of Forms." They speak just as we heard, or thought we heard, Socrates speak in the *Phaedo*, the *Phaedrus*, and the *Theaetetus*. They differentiate sharply (χωρίς) between being and becoming. Our intercourse with becoming takes place by means of the body through perception (δι' αἰσθήσεως); our intercourse with being takes place by means of the soul through reflection (διὰ λογισμῶν). But what do we mean here by the expression "intercourse" (κοινωνία)? This is the crucial question by which the Eleatic stranger puts himself in opposition to the friends of Forms. He is ready to apply the result of the debate with the materialists by interpreting the meaning of this "intercourse" as the power (δύναμις) of affecting and being affected. The friends of Forms wish to restrict this power to the world of becoming, however, and not apply it to the world of being sharply separated from becoming, because it contradicts their conception of being.

Yet this separation, as the stranger shows, is a kind of Eleatic rigidity which the friends of Forms cannot justify. Moreover, it is not compatible with the phenomenon of "intercourse." If perception is "intercourse," so is thinking. Thinking, knowing, is an action. Being known is experiencing an effect, and thus is a kind of "being moved" (248E). And, step by step, systematically, the rigidity of this concept of being is broken down. We must think of the myth in the *Phaedrus* (250c), where we read about the "prototypes that are whole, simple, unshakable, and blessedly perfect,"[49] in order to sense the ironic tension expressed here when the stranger asks whether the "perfectly real" (τὸ παντελῶς ὄν, 248E) "stands solemnly aloof, immutable, and devoid of intelligence." On the contrary, the perfectly real cannot possibly be conceived of as without intelligence; hence, not as without life; hence, not as without soul; hence, not as without movement. This is how far the concept of movement is carried beyond and above the concept of locomotion in space. Conversely, whatever moves must be acknowledged as real. The stranger cannot be more radical in overcoming the Eleatic rigidity both in the doctrine of the friends of Forms and in the

Eleatic doctrine itself as he—apparently—changes over to the camp of the "Herakleitean" doctrine of constant flux.

Here we immediately (249B 8) come up against the argument that we know from the *Theaetetus* (183A *et seq.*). The doctrine of constant change excludes "sameness" (ταὐτόν) from the class of being. There is no identity (τὸ κατὰ ταὐτὰ καὶ ὡσαύτως καὶ περὶ τὸ αὐτό) without "rest" (χωρὶς στάσεως). But he who destroys sameness also destroys intelligence and knowledge which cannot be directed toward what is constantly changing but can be directed only toward what is permanent. So we must fight on two fronts and, for the sake of truth, overcome both Eleatic rigidity and Herakleitean flux (249CD).

We take a step in this direction by "combining" (συλλαβών) the two opposites of motion and rest—i.e., by disregarding what separates them and by concentrating on their "communion with respect to being" (πρὸς τὴν τῆς οὐσίας κοινωνίαν). Being (τὸ ὄν) is a third thing beyond motion and rest (as, at a previous and more primitive stage, it appeared as a third thing beyond warm and cold—250A, 243DE). Being is something that "encompasses" (περιεχομένην) motion and rest. And these concepts now are elevated so far beyond their spatial connotation that this encompassing is located "in the soul." Yet the critical voice is heard again: Is this possible? Must "being" not be one or the other? And so this inquiry into being ends just as inconclusively as the previous inquiry into not-being ended. There we found the suggestion of a possible solution in the notion of the "combination" of being and not-being—if only it were possible to clarify this notion. Here we find the notion of being as "encompassing" the mutually exclusive opposites, or as their "communion" in being—if only it were possible to clarify the meaning of this encompassing and this communion.

We must examine further this either-or, the not-this-but-that, for it was about to help us overcome the rigidity of the two alternatives. We must examine, in other words, the "communion" expressed in the act of thought, or the "dynamic reciprocity of acting and being acted upon" in which the relationships of things are grounded both in the world of bodies as well as in the world of intelligible Forms. Let us never forget that Socrates, prototype of the dialectician, is present, silently listening. As he conquers the rigidity of the Eleatic doctrine of the One by means of the most original kind of human "communion," i.e., by the genuine "dialogical" exchange practiced by him, thus opening up the path into the world of eternal Forms, so his presence here guarantees the "communion" and "power" that will also overcome any "thing-like" rigidity in the world of Forms.[50]

III
250E–264C

The difficulties are now unfolded (διηπορημένον). Not-being and being are equally problematic. (How could it be otherwise when we can talk meaningfully about "not-being" only in contrast to "being"—and vice versa?) Thus, there is hope that light may be thrown on both in a joint investigation. And even if we should not catch sight of either, we shall at least take the investigation as far as possible. We must not fail to hear this warning. It may save us from assuming—as has been done not infrequently, from Hegel on—that the logical structure set up by the Eleatic stranger, important as it is, represents the lonely peak of Plato's philosophical thinking. Even as this logical analysis is conducted with Socrates listening, so must we try to connect it—a daring attempt, to be sure—with what Socrates teaches and represents in the work of Plato and by his own life.

The investigation will deal both with being and with not-being. So it must be put if the theme is to be "communion" or "combination." But since this combination is to be founded

III 1
250E–254B

in "speech," we must first dispose of the opposite view as it is stated in the logic of the Cynics. According to this view, true assertions are only those expressing identities, "man is man," for example—so that all meaningful discourse is destroyed.[51] Here, as well as at the end when this matter of the community of Forms has been clarified (259DE), Plato speaks rather condescendingly about "the young and some of their elders of late learning" and about this wholly "unphilosophical and a-musical attempt to separate everything from everything else." The reference to Antisthenes has generally been recognized, here, for once, correctly. It is not that Plato considered Antisthenes a significant opponent against whom the whole discussion need be directed. It is rather that the doctrine of Antisthenes provides a striking example showing that "communion" must be recognized in order to justify the simple and basic fact of meaningful discourse.

That there is, and must be, such a thing as communion has been clear for a long time. Still, the preliminary inquiry is divided into three parts and is addressed to all those who have ever talked about being and with whom this conversation is concerned. (1) Is there such a thing as communion in the realm of being and, hence, in speech as well? Or (2) can everything communicate with everything? Or (3) can only some things communicate with some other things?

If we were to deny the first question, everybody would oppose us. Herakleitos, Parmenides, and the friends of Forms know about the communion of being and motion, or of being and rest. The representatives of the doctrine of "elements" that separate and mix know about the blending of the many or the one. And the oddest thing is that even our opponent Antisthenes cannot pronounce the very statement in which he is denying the possibility of communion without acknowledging it in the connection of the words used in his own statement. Affirming the second question, however, would lead to the contradictory consequences that motion is rest and rest is in motion. Thus, there remains only the third possibility, and the question arises whether there is an art or a science that would have a knowledge of possible combinations, as grammar or music has a knowledge about the combination of vowels or sounds.

The system of words and sounds (γράμματα) as handled by the expert in writing often had symbolic value for Plato beyond the literal context. In the *Cratylus* (424B *et seq.*), he uses the systematic order of vowels and consonants first as an example for the method of division; next, he considers how the different sounds, each a unity in itself, combine into the higher unities of syllable, word, and sentence, and he raises the problem of whether there may be an ordered system of things corresponding to this system of words. In the *Theaetetus* (203A *et seq.*), he takes the single letters that have sound but no meaning and shows how they combine into a meaningful Form, or *Eidos*, i.e., the "syllable." There we also find the parallel with music:

a sound corresponds to a letter and a melodic figure to a syllable. In the *Philebus* (17A *et seq.*), the system of letters is used as an illustration to show how the passage from the one—here meaning the individual letter or sound (γράμμα)—to the unlimited world of sounds must be traversed not in one leap, but step by step through different grades determined by number and kind.

In the *Sophist* (252E *et seq.*), the main problem is to make us see how division and communion go together and what the different kinds of communion and division are. The grammarian, for example, can show that the vowels serve as a "bond" through all sounds of a language, but that there are some sound combinations which are impossible. Correspondingly, the community of Forms is envisaged, on the one hand, as a pervading, a comprehending, a blending, and on the other, as the separation and isolation of various different Forms.[52] Whether there is any communion between essences and what sort of communion there is can be decided only if the essences are known individually. They are truly known when we succeed, by means of the method of division, in assigning them their definite place in the system. This is the task of the dialectician, or philosopher, the very task we have been accomplishing in our conversation. So in searching for the sophist we have stumbled upon the philosopher.

That happened once before, in the sixth determination, and not accidentally either. There, too, the theme was division, or separation. Now it happens again, as division and combination are joined. The philosopher is the counterpart of the sophist. The respective nature of these two, just like the nature of being and not-being, can be clarified only jointly—and not by a third party (who could that be?). Only the philosopher can gain clarity about his own nature, and only by practicing the philosophical method, the method of division and communion. In the same way, he inquires into the nature of the sophist. But the sophist takes refuge in the darkness of not-being, whereas the philosopher dwells in the thought of true being (τῇ τοῦ ὄντος ἀεὶ διὰ λογισμῶν προσκείμενος ἰδέᾳ, 254A 8). Both natures are difficult to grasp—the philosopher's because in most men "the eye of the soul cannot endure to keep its gaze fixed on the divine."

These words sound strange coming from the Eleatic, but they remind us suddenly of what Socrates said in the central sections of the *Republic* about the ascent from the cave and about the dialectical path. Here in the *Sophist*, Socrates is listening silently, but we would misunderstand Plato if we were to think that the presence of the Eleatic spokesman renders Socrates superfluous. The Eleatic doctrine examined correctly—i.e., uneristically, philosophically—leads to its own refutation. In preserving and even intensifying the purity of the Eleatic concept of being, the stranger overcomes its rigidity as he overcomes the Eleatic rigidity inherent in the doctrine of the friends of *Ideas*. But despite its novelty and importance, and difficult as it may be, the investigation that follows takes us only part way toward the goal. This goal is hinted at here, before the investigation begins, by the words "brightness," "eye of the soul," "divine." Only Socrates, not the Eleatic stranger, could lead us to the goal itself, and Socrates not only by means of a conceptual analysis, but ultimately through his own life and death.

"At him," the stranger says, meaning the philosopher, "we will perhaps look more closely if we are still so inclined." The reference to the alleged dialogue, the *Philosopher*, is unmistakable, but the qualifications "perhaps" and "if" also indicate that Plato never thought of writing such a dialogue. (There are stronger reasons for this view.)

We are ready now to embark upon the inquiry into the "communion (combination) of essences, kinds, or Forms." (Plato apparently uses the words γένη and εἴδη interchangeably.) Five "of the greatest, most important"[53] are selected for the explicit purpose of clarifying the nature of being and not-being "so far as our present discussion permits"—another hint at the future conversation about the philosopher. We must keep the central sections of the *Republic* in mind, as well as the *Timaeus*, to realize that there are other ways of dealing with being and not-being.

"Being itself," "motion," and "rest"—these three concepts, which had emerged from a survey of earlier ontologies, are different from each other. Motion and rest do not combine, but being combines with both. Each of the three Forms is identical

III 2
254B–259C

to itself and different from the others. So we obtain a fourth and a fifth kind: "the same" (ταὐτόν) and "the different," or "the other" (θάτερον), both of them different from motion and rest and different from being as well. Motion "is" (or exists) because it "partakes" of being. Motion is different from "the same" and different from "the other" as well; it combines with both by virtue of "participation" and "communion" (μέθεξις, κοινωνία, 256B, 257A). Motion is something different from "being," but it participates in being. Therefore it is being and not-being at the same time. Thus, we learn that it is "the different," or "the other," that makes it possible for each Form to partake of being and, more so, of not-being. Even being itself is what it is only because it "is not" everything else. In this way, not-being loses its place "opposite" to being and becomes "the other." A negative (ἀπόφασις) like not-beautiful or not-being does not signify contraries, but signifies "something different," both in the realm of discourse and in the realm of things designated by words (257BC). Thus, the concept not-being is, as it were, divested of its horror, as "the different" has found a place in the realm of being (258BC).

A little later (258E), to be sure, there is a hint that the problem of not-being has still another side to it—namely, whether or not there is something simply contrary to being, and whether or not there can be any "account" (*logos*) of it. This question was raised at the beginning of the great ontological investigation (238C), but then disappeared for a long time to make room for an inquiry into the nature of not-being as not-*this*-being. Now, at the end, when not-being paradoxically turns out to be a kind of being or, more specifically, a *single* Form, an *Eidos*, among the many things that are, Theaitetos affirms the results of the discussion by saying, "Most true." Perhaps we should remember that at the very end of the *Parmenides*, the young Aristotle replied with the same superlative affirmation just when a dissent might have been appropriate. There it is left to the reader whether he on his own part would have replied differently. Here the Eleatic stranger, looking back to the beginning of the ontological investigation, concludes: We have said good-by to all questions about not-being as such or as the opposite of being (258E 8). Should we on our part say this means good-by forever, or must we not conclude that Socrates might resume these questions?

Another hint is not to be overlooked. In the midst of what seems like a highly abstract analysis of being and not-being, we are told specifically that this is not merely a matter of "names" or words, but even more, is a matter of the "things" (257c 1–3) designated by words—which must mean, the realities of life. And just at this point, where the nature of "the other" seems to be "cut up into its smallest parts," we encounter moral and perhaps metaphysical opposites: the beautiful and the not-beautiful, the great and the not-great, the just and the not-just. Just and unjust—this is the basic contrast that runs through the life of Socrates and Plato's work. It will reappear once more at the very end of the Sophist (267c).

The energy that Parmenides had invested in the question of being is not diminished. Rather it is intensified when the Eleatic stranger, explicitly correcting the view of his master, refers to the "Form of not-being" (τὸ εἶδος ὃ τυγχάνει ὂν τοῦ μὴ ὄντος, 258D) whereas Parmenides had spoken of "things that are not" (τὰ μὴ ὄντα). Yet the rigid contrast of mutually exclusive opposites has been changed into the rich and manifold structure of community. The next task (here represented by Socrates who is listening) would be, then, to use this knowledge to point the way to the "bright region," to the "divine," the vision of which cannot be endured by the eye of the soul in most people (254AB). Plato only hints at this way; he does not enter upon it. To do so he would have had to write the dialogue Philosopher, i.e., "he would have had to put down in writing the most serious matters, an impossible undertaking for someone who is himself serious" (Letter VII 344c). As for the Sophist, however, with this new knowledge concerning the participation (methexis) and communion (koinonia) of the kinds of things that are, the Eleatic turns downward toward those eristic thinkers who take "the same" for "the different," or vice versa, without asking in what respect this identification holds, or those who do not admit any kind of combination and thereby undermine all meaningful discourse.

The discussion had moved upward from the eristic destruction of rational discourse to a proof of "community." Now in the end it turns explicitly toward those destructive critics. It does so by including discourse itself in the community that has been worked out. Discourse, too, is "one of the kinds of things that are" (τῶν ὄντων ἕν τε γενῶν). "Not-being" in the form of "the different" was discovered to be dispersed throughout all the other kinds of realities. If it is also mixed into thought and discourse, there is error, deception, semblance, copy, and the like. This mixture, then, must be shown last, in order to reveal the nature of the sophist through the nature of falsehood.

As always, the question as to possible "community" presupposes that we know the nature of the things that may or may not enter into such community. The structure of discourse is as follows. It consists of words ("names"), and it corresponds to what has been shown (III 1, above) in connection with the "greatest of the kinds" and by comparison with verbal sounds. Some words fit together; others do not. The criterion as to whether they do or not is whether the sequence of words means or signifies anything (δηλοῦντά τι, σημαίνοντα) or nothing. We can distinguish between two kinds of words, names (ὄνομα) and verbs (ῥῆμα). Verbs refer to a happening or an action (ἐπὶ ταῖς πράξεσιν δήλωμα). Names apply to that which undergoes or performs an action (ἐπ' αὖ τοῖς ἐκεῖνα πράττουσιν).[54] A simple experiment shows that we cannot signify anything, either happening or being, by a sequence of words consisting of only one kind or the other. But the shortest possible "combination" of one kind with the other yields a genuine (i.e., meaningful) statement, as, for example, "Theaitetos sits."

This statement goes beyond mere "naming." It "says something" about a state of affairs. It is a statement "of something" (τινός), and a statement "of this kind" (ποιός τις) may be "true" or "false." True *logos* states "being as it is." False *logos* states "not-being as being" or, as we may say with the knowledge we have gained about not-being, "beings as other than what they are" (ὄντων ὄντα ἕτερα). Along these lines we now can assign a firm place to false and deceptive discourse. Even thinking (διάνοια) may be false and deceptive, as a silent discourse or inward dialogue. The same may be said, therefore, of judgment, or "opinion" (δόξα), as a kind of thinking that involves assertion and denial, and it may be said also of "appearing" or "imagining" (φαντασία), as a judgment that depends upon perception (αἴσθησις). So we understand the nature of error in understanding the nature of discourse, and of discourse in understanding the nature of being as communion. (If Socrates were more than a silent partner to this conversation, however, he would go beyond assent and ask: Can we really place "thinking" and "opinion" so close to each other, on the same plane, once we have grasped the fundamental difference between true being and the world of appearance?)

We know that the task of clarifying the meaning of *pseudos*— falsehood, deception, and lie—occupied Plato from his beginnings as a philosopher. It did not grow out of a special interest in a difficult logical problem. It occupied him because (to speak in the concrete imagery of the *Sophist*) both sophistic and eristic hide in this darkness and confusion—everything, in other words, that is hostile to philosophy and that, because of its dangerously similar appearance, jeopardizes the reputation of philosophy and the life of the philosopher. Even one of the earliest of Plato's works, the *Hippias Minor*, deals with the problem of deception, involuntary and voluntary, sophistic and Socratic deception. Then, with the *Cratylus*, language becomes the instrument of positive enlightenment. There (*Cratylus* 431 BC; cf. 385 BC) discourse is explained as the "juxtaposition" of noun and verb. In the *Sophist*, it is the "combination" of the two, and this change is more than a mere difference in expression. In the *Cratylus*, we are shown that just as the elements of a sentence, the "names," may be used wrongly, so may the juxtaposition of these elements. The *Sophist* derives discourse not simply from "naming"; discourse has a new and autonomous structure. As a unique kind of being it has the structure of being itself, characterized by "communion." In the *Cratylus*, the "names" have the function of revealing (δήλωμα, 433 B *et seq.*); in the *Sophist*, it is the statement that has this function. Hence, the *Cratylus* seeks to discover falsehood in the elements of language; the *Sophist* seeks it more deeply, in the structure of language.

Something else is connected with this. In the *Euthydemus* (284c) and in the *Cratylus*, truth is defined as saying "of the things that they are as they are" and falsehood as saying "something of the things that are, but not as they are." The phrase "not as they are" is understood truly only in the *Sophist* because, on the one hand, the "intentional" structure of discourse is shown, i.e., its necessary relatedness to something else, and because, on the other hand, what follows from the nature of communion is that every kind of being can be combined with not-being, i.e., with "the different." So the struggle against the sophists ends by making it clear what falsehood is and, correspondingly—in a certain sense, at least—what truth is as well.

We tried earlier to probe into the strange structure of this dialogue that, in the end, after a surprisingly long interval, leads to the resumption of the series of divisions interrupted in Part A and concludes the series with the seventh and last division (264c). An important aspect of this conclusion has been disregarded.[55] For suddenly, after the mention of men, animals, and elements, after mirror images, architecture, impressionistic painting, and other things—suddenly the "Form (σχῆμα) of justice and, to summarize, of virtue in general" (267c) emerges in the midst of this logical division as, briefly, the significant theme. It is said that many set about making it appear, in actions and words, that they possess justice and virtue, and many succeed in appearing just although they are not. This is the area of "mimicking appearances," which then is further subdivided into rhetoric and sophistic. Must we not infer that Plato is pointing here beyond dialectics to the basic contrast that determined the life of Socrates and thus his own work?

"Socrates is guilty of unjust action"—these were the initial words of the charge against him in the *Apology*, and Socrates begins his defense by saying that his accusers had talked about his alleged "injustice" with great power of persuasion, but without truth. In the *Thrasymachus*, Socrates debates the nature of just and unjust, first with Polemarchos, a disciple of the sophists, and then with the sophist Thrasymachos himself. In the *Gorgias*,

264c–268d

Socrates is engaged in another controversy about the meaning of justice, first with the rhetorician Gorgias and then with his more radical disciples. In this discussion, rhetoric is classified, by division, in a system of arts which may be recognized, down to its details, as a preliminary version of the system of division developed in the *Sophist*.[56] Plato used the *Thrasymachus* as the introduction to the *Republic*, for Socrates constructs the ideal city in a struggle with the power of injustice personally present throughout in the figure of Thrasymachos.

Must not we keep this background in mind at least in connection with four significant passages in the *Sophist?* In the first place, Socrates himself reminds us at the beginning of the dialogue, in his first words, that, according to Homer, the gods look with favor upon men of reverence and virtue, and that the highest of them, Zeus, watches over the lawless and lawful doings of men. In the second place, we are told, at the beginning of the "battle of gods and giants," that although, if possible, we should bring about a change of heart in the materialists, at least we shall reform them in the context of thought (246D). Then, among the non-material things whose existence they must concede, the contrast of just and unjust soon becomes the dominant theme (247AB). In the third place, almost at the end of the ontological investigation, stands the warning that we are dealing not only with words, but even more, with "things" or "realities" (257C)—and, again, just and not-just very soon are cited among these realities (258A).

The same theme is sounded a fourth time, and with special emphasis, at the end of the whole work (267C). Suddenly, to repeat, the Eleatic stranger begins to talk about the "Form of justice" and he sets up two contrasting types of men: "popular orators" and "statesman"—"sophists" and "wise man." We have often alluded to the fact, for it is easily forgotten, that the wise man has been standing by silently all along and that, on the previous day, he had to present himself in the court of law to defend himself against the charge of injustice. This is the reality of life that permeates, and transcends, the conceptual analyses and ontological investigations of the *Sophist*.

TWENTY-SEVEN

Statesman

STATESMAN and *Sophist* form a pair of dialogues so closely linked that their bond is comparable only to the one between *Timaeus* and *Critias*.[1] The same persons are present in the *Statesman* as in the *Sophist*. Again Socrates and Theodoros, after exchanging a few words in the beginning, remain silent listeners to the end,[2] but now in place of Theaitetos, the "young Socrates" is the partner in the conversation with the Eleatic stranger. Like Theaitetos, this young man also is a student of mathematics. From the *Theaetetus* and the beginning of the *Sophist*, we know that he is a pupil of Theodoros and a companion of Theaitetos.[3] Both of the youths have a "certain outward similarity" to Socrates, the one in looks, the other in name.

We know something more about this younger Socrates. *Letter XI* in the Platonic collection is a part—or, if we wish to be very skeptical, purports to be a part—of the correspondence between Plato and Leodamas of Thasos, mathematician and colonizer. Leodamas, we learn, had informed Plato about his plans to found a colony (on the coast of Thrace).[4] Plato advised him to come to Athens for personal discussion of these plans. Leodamas replied that this was impossible, and he asked Plato either to come himself or to send Socrates. It is generally assumed that this refers to the "younger Socrates" who apparently was a member of the Academy (where, as in the school of Pythagoras, mathematics was combined with political theory and practice). Plato replies in the extant letter that Socrates could not accept the invitation because he was suffering from bladder trouble. This young Socrates' interest in politics undoubtedly is the reason why Plato in this discussion of the statesman or the political man gives him the part taken by Theaitetos in the *Sophist*.

Both dialogues are dominated by the same method: the search for an essential definition by means of division. And both dialogues aim at a goal—the philosopher—that lies beyond the theme treated on the level of the conversation itself. This goal is envisaged differently, however, in that the sophist is the counterpart of the philosopher, whereas the statesman, the true statesman, is essentially the philosopher himself. To believe that Plato ever intended to write the conversation about the philosopher that is promised for "another time" (εἰσαῦθις, 257B 8, 258A 6) means to underestimate his irony. Those who did not make allowance for this irony and thought they could speculate about the content of this "unwritten dialogue" have shown by their efforts that it was impossible to write such a dialogue. For it would have to deal with matters that Plato, according to his confession in *Letter VII*, never could or would express in writing.[5]

In the preliminary conversation of the *Statesman*, Socrates looks back not only to the discussion about the sophist at which he "just" was present, but also to the conversation he had "yesterday" with Theaitetos. Not a word is said about what happened yesterday after that conversation had taken place. It is inconceivable that Plato himself would not have thought of this, or that by the mention of "yesterday" he would not have intended to remind the reader of the last words in the *Theaetetus*. Should the conceptual analysis about the nature of the statesman fall under the shadow of the indictment just brought against Socrates charging him with unlawful actions? We shall even encounter literal allusions to this indictment, and to Socrates' defense, at one of the high points to come in the *Statesman* (299BC, 299E 7–8).

We must weigh the few words spoken by Socrates all the more carefully as he does not participate—or does not seem to participate—in the conversation between his young namesake and the Eleatic stranger. The mathematician Theodoros puts the sophist, the statesman, and the philosopher side by side as if they were all of the same class and rank. Just so had Socrates put them side by side at the beginning of the *Sophist*. Here, however, he objects to the mathematician's ranking. The three types differ so far from each other that they cannot be put into any proportion to each other. One must be Socrates to know about this non-proportion or incompatibility. He who still believes that Plato intended to write the dialogue *Philosopher* as the third member of a trilogy thinks too much like Theodoros.

To start, we take a broad view of the dialogue as a whole. Its construction, in the manner of Plato's late works, is complex

I and entwined.[6] The long introductory part (I) provides a first determination of the statesman in the context of a system of

III divisions. The long section (III) that brings the enterprise to an end provides a second determination of the statesman. Each of these two parts branches off, somewhere in the middle, into a kind of digression. The first of these digressions is the myth of the great cosmic periods. The second digression deals with the doctrine of the various types of government and their respective value. Between these two main, diaeretical parts, we

II 2 are given an example of the method of division by inquiring into the art of weaving (II 2). This example, in turn, is intro-

II 1 duced by a methodological discussion (II 1) on the nature of "example" (or paradigm). It is followed by a discussion (II 3),

II 3 rather loosely connected, on the nature of "measure," which is designed to apologize for the apparently "measureless" structure of the dialogue but seems only to make it still worse. The over-all impression is confusing, and the ironic shifts in emphasis are more pronounced here than almost anywhere else in Plato's works. Nevertheless, we have every reason to be skeptical when any section in this entangled construction is designated as being "only" a digression, "only" an example, "only" a methodological introduction, or "only" an apology.[7]

I In the first determination of the statesman, the system of

258A–277A division as such, to start with, is developed in detail (I 1). Then follows the myth (I 2), and, to end the section, a modification of this first system (I 3).

The task is to find the statesman or the king or the ruler (δεσπότης). Master of the household and manager of an estate (οἰκονόμος) are variations of the same type. It makes no difference, or is a mere accident, whether this statesman is actually in power or whether he is a private citizen (259B). This principle will be restated, not without reason, in the concluding part of the dialogue where it is said (292E) that he who possesses the royal knowledge (βασιλικὴν ἐπιστήμην) must be called a (true) king—βασιλικός—whether he is in power or not. We are reminded of the *Euthydemus* where suddenly, at the climax of the dialogue (291B), the "royal art" comes into view, one does not quite know how. It is the same as the "political art" and it rules over all the other arts. We learned about its being founded on knowledge and about its relationship to the good. At this point, however, we lost sight of the royal art because the nature of the good remained unclear (even if it was quite clear that nobody but Socrates practiced this art). What merely is hinted at in the *Euthydemus* is raised to the level of systematic precision in the construction of the *Republic*. There (580BC) the man "who is best and most just" occupies the highest place in the scale of happiness. "This is the most kingly man who is also ruler and king over himself." So the words in the *Statesman*, expressly repeated, referring to the man "who possesses this art whether he is actually in power or not," must direct us to Socrates standing by silently, the man who is king and ruler of himself.

The first division gets under way by distinguishing between two kinds of knowledge (ἐπιστήμη—τέχνη), one merely theoretical and the other at the same time practical (πρακτική—γνωστική). The practical kind is divided, in turn, into two parts, one critical and the other directive (κριτική—ἐπιτακτική). And so it goes until we come to the rearing of animals (ἀγελαιο-τροφική), which suggests (we need not wait long to encounter some grotesque features) a division between human herds and animal herds (262A). This division is rejected, however, in a methodological digression (262A–264B) to which we shall return later.

Instead, we divide animals into those that live in the water and those that live on land, and then divide the land animals, in turn, into those that fly and those that walk on foot. At this point (265A) the Eleatic stranger, in another methodological comment, distinguishes between a longer and a shorter path. Following the longer path that he purports to favor, he divides the land animals (amusingly enough) into horned and hornless animals; the horned animals into single-hoofed (whole-hoofed) and many-toed; and the hornless into those that are four-footed and those that are two-footed. Thus, we come to man and—lest we forget that we are trying to discover the statesman —the latter is defined as the "shepherd of a hornless herd." According to the shorter path (266E), the land animals are divided immediately into four-footed and two-footed, and the two-footed into feathered and featherless. This is the kind of division that would justify Diogenes' ridiculing it, by the plucked cock he threw into Plato's Academy, if Plato himself did not display a sense of ironic playfulness within a method that is meant quite seriously as well.[8]

The result—so we are told, in case we did not notice it—is not final. The tending of a herd as practiced by a shepherd combines all sorts of activities, and these activities, when transferred to the human world, are distributed among men of different professions, the merchant, farmer, physician, teacher of gymnastics, musician, and others. This objection is intended to keep open to the end the question as to what is the distinguishing characteristic of the statesman. This we have not yet found— and surely will not find as long as we are involved in zoology and the rearing of animals. For the time being, however, the objection serves to introduce the myth of the cosmic periods.

I 2   We have discussed this myth elsewhere.[9] It stands in sharpest
268D–274E   possible contrast (felt even in style and language) to the dialectical parts of the dialogue. The meaning of the myth goes far beyond its immediate function. For, as is expressly suggested later (277B), the essential thing about the myth is not that it brings about a minor change in the definition of the statesman, but that it makes us see the confusion of affairs in the world and in politics as soon as they are measured by a standard of

perfection. Also, the myth brings home to us the realization that whatever order we find in the world of confusion is an outgrowth of this perfection, and that human life as such is possible only in so far as we take these divine gifts over into our own care.

Thus, the myth links order in the state and the true statesman with the order in the universe, that is to say, with the Forms and with God. Also, it opens up a view of the distant goal toward which dialectics painfully leads us part of the way but can never find within itself. The myth is intermingled as "play" in the serious business of dialectics (268D 8), if we are to believe the words of the Eleatic stranger. Sometimes we may well ask whether there is more playfulness in the dialectics and more seriousness in the myth—playful seriousness as, for example, in the passage where the Eleatic stranger leaves it open what the men of the golden age were conversing about with each other and with the animals, whether philosophy or fairy tales. If somebody could tell us this we would know whether the men of that age were truly happy. Here, too, *directio voluntatis* is an indispensable component of the Platonic myth.

The myth, the Eleatic stranger adds, has revealed two flaws in the discussion. One mistake is serious. So far, we have confused the king or ruler with the shepherd of the human flock as it existed in the cosmic period under divine rule. In other words, we have mistaken a mortal for a god. The other mistake is less serious. We have not clearly delimited the sphere of political activity nor determined its manner. Since there are others who have a claim to "feeding" the flock, we must choose a different expression, "tending" of the herd (ἀγελαιοκομική) rather than "rearing," so as to emphasize the aspect of attendant service (θεραπευτική) and care (ἐπιμελητική).

1 3
274E–277A

These seemingly minor changes conceal matters of importance. In the *Euthyphro*, Plato first referred to "tendance" of the gods (θεραπεία, 12E) and then changed the expression explicitly to "service" (ὑπηρετική, 13D). "Tendance" had the sense of "improving" (hence, the word could not be applied to the gods), for there is no care that would harm a person who is cared for. We may realize now what is meant by this change in the definition of the statesman. It takes us back to the struggle waged in the *Thrasymachus* (338c *et seq.*) over the question of whether a ruler would ever harm the ruled. After the words "tending" or "caring" have reminded us now that such harm is not possible, a distinction is made between human and divine tendance. This must mean that while politics is a human affair, it stands in a relation of dependence, or imitation, to divine action, as the myth taught us.[10] This lesson is taken over here into the division, i.e., it is reinforced conceptually. And finally, what was implicit throughout is made explicit: the true king is distinguished from the tyrant by virtue of the fact that he rules over free bipeds, with their consent (ἑκουσίων), not against their will.

What is the result of the discussion so far? It has yielded a system of logical divisions in which seriousness and grotesque playfulness are indissolubly interwoven, and, in polar opposition, a legend of human life in a mythical age. One must be as immature as the young Socrates to think that we have now "completed the definition of the statesman" (277A).[11] The Eleatic stranger does not think so. Yet, before we move on to the second part of the dialogue, we should look back at a number of methodological hints gained in the first part.

The method of division is conveyed in a concrete image. Any being that is to be divided has a natural cleavage (διαφυή, 259D 9; διέστηκε, 260c 7). Cut correctly, it yields to the division (τομὴ ὑπείκουσα, 261A). (A similar image is used in *Phaedrus* 265E, where we read about the man who dissects the parts of the body according to their natural growth and does not cut them up as a poor butcher does.[12]) Also, as far as possible the cut must be made in the middle so as not to slice off a small piece (λεπτουργεῖν, *Statesman* 262B 5); for what matters is that the "section possesses a specific visible form" (τὸ μέρος ἅμα εἶδος ἐχέτω, 262B), or in other words, that it not be a formless fragment. Moreover, a section in the middle is more likely to produce such "insights" (ἰδέαι, 262B). According to this principle, then, a division of mankind into male and female would be more appropriate, though the division into Greeks and barbarians corresponds to Greek one-sidedness (262DE).

It is important that we take small steps (264A, 265A, 266D). The eristic method as described, for example, in the *Philebus* (17A) depends upon skipping the intermediary steps. Here we are told that the more steps there are to be taken in the division, the better it is. In actual application, however, we might well have our doubts whether the most elaborate division, where we start with the distinction between horned and hornless animals, really is better than the simpler division of feathered and feather-less bipeds (or than the simplest division, men from animals). We may have doubts because the "spirit of science and satire here interpenetrate to such a degree that one can hardly know which is the instrument of the other."[13] Similarly, seriousness and playfulness combine in the warning against any insistence on fixed technical terms. "If you avoid this, you will manifest more wisdom in your old age" (261E). This stands as a warning undoubtedly addressed beyond the framework of the dialogue to the members of the Academy to whom Plato would show the way without depriving them of their freedom.[14] It stands also as a warning for us.

At one point (262CD, the objection raised against the division of mankind into Greeks and barbarians), we might wish to ask whether the methodology does not have deeper significance, going beyond the concern for method. This division was taken for granted by many Greeks—by many, but not by all. "This is a division that most people around here (in Athens) would make," as the Eleatic stranger puts it, thereby clearly detaching himself and probably his own people as well from this view.

How seriously Plato meant this objection has been discussed back and forth down to our own time.[15] It is hardly conceivable that he would be unaware of anticipating this discussion. It is possible that he intended by an aside, as it were, to stimulate the discussion, as quite certainly he did do. In a treatise ad-dressed to Alexander, Aristotle advised the future ruler of the world to treat the Greeks as friends and the barbarians as enemies.[16] This view need not be contrary to Plato's, for in the *Republic* (V 570C *et seq.*), Plato himself clings to the radical division between Greeks and barbarians. Yet we find an agree-ment (perhaps not accidental) between this passage of the

Statesman and the polemical critique of Aristotle's view conducted by Eratosthenes, the universal mind of the third century.
Eratosthenes reproaches those who divide the whole of mankind
into two groups, Greeks and barbarians. This is an almost
literal allusion to the passage in Plato's dialogue.[17] If Eratosthenes, called "the Platonist," did not have this very passage in
mind, he was at least steeped in this same discussion that deeply
moved the thinkers of the fourth century and the Hellenistic
period, even as it moves us today.

II   If there are many hints of methodological significance in the
277A–287B first part of the *Statesman*—one of them suddenly going far
beyond a concern with method—we seem to be completely
overwhelmed by method now as the Eleatic stranger begins "to
fill in the outline of the sketch." An example or counterdemon-
stration (παράδειγμα)—literally, something "shown on the
side"—is to be given, and the question, "What is such a
II 1 *paradigm?*" is approached by referring again to the "example"
277A–278E of the system of letters that we know from the *Sophist* (pp.
271f., above). In learning how to read and write, young children learn first how to distinguish (διαισθάνονται) each particular letter in the shortest and simplest syllables and to "say
correctly" what each of them is. In more difficult cases where
they make mistakes, the teacher may place the known and the
unknown syllables side by side (παραβάλλοντες) and then point
to the same elements present in both of the "combinations"
(συμπλοκαί).

Here we encounter a twofold connection with the basic categories of "the same" and "the different" that are known to us
from the *Sophist*. In the first place, the pupil recognizes each
letter in the various syllables as "different" (ἕτερον) from
other letters, and as "identical" to itself (ταὐτόν). A "paradigm" consists then in correctly identifying something that is
"the same" in "the other" that is separate from it,[18] thereby
gaining one correct understanding of the two things, both together and individually.[19] Again, there is a paradigm of the
paradigm. Corresponding to the letters of the alphabet, there is
the "alphabet" of being, and its "large and difficult syllables"
also are composed of "letters" or "elements" (in Greek, the

same word στοιχεῖα means both). Here, too, we must perform the same act of comparing and identifying.

This concludes the methodological digression on the nature of a "paradigm" or "example."[20] Yet, before we turn to the art of weaving as the paradigm for the art of politics, we realize, in retrospect, that the lesson involved much more than "mere method." For we have again heard about the elements reality is composed of and about their combinations. In other words, we have heard about the "way" (*methodos*) of the philosopher, which is something quite different from "method." In short, what seemed to be only an instrumental link in the progression suddenly throws entirely new light on the whole scene. What we are shown is the ontological justification for the method of division—and so also for the work of the philosopher. And in a peculiarly veiled manner we are introduced, when we least expect it, to the nature of the "statesman" who cannot be anything else here but what he is in the *Republic*, "a man who knows," i.e., a manifestation of the philosopher himself.

After we have clarified the structure of "example" by means of an example, we are in a position now to consider the example that is supposed to help us separate the statesman from all the others who have a claim to providing for society. The small paradigm for the great matter at stake is wool-weaving (ἐρίων ὑφαντική).[21] It is different from nailing, felting, sewing. Weaving, in contrast to these activities, is a plaiting together (συμπλοκή, 281A 3), but it must be preceded by the opposite activity of carding (ξαντική), which is a separating process (διαλυτική). Later, after many other divisions—in the midst of which we shall encounter the basic difference between "real cause" and "contributory cause" (281E)—the two types of activity, separating and combining (διακριτική, συγκριτική, 282B), are once more contrasted. The plaiting together in weaving is a combining art. The separating arts fall into a different class, but they nevertheless are closely related to weaving because they "contribute" to it.

We may briefly anticipate the simple point to be made in the concluding part of the dialogue (III 3b, below) where statesmanship is conceived of by analogy to the art of weaving. It is

II 2
279A–283B

the art that weaves together opposite natures in the community. The statesman is not like the man sewing up pieces of leather or patching up quilts or nailing boards together. Instead, he is a person who artfully interweaves (firm) warp and (loose) woof. Yet, as in the case of the previous example where the methodological digression had a deeper significance, so it is here too. "Plaiting together," or combination, refers to the structure of reality itself, as the *Sophist* shows and as we discovered here in connection with the example of "letters" and "elements." Furthermore, we find among the early philosophers, from Anaximander on, a characteristic systolic and diastolic movement that pervades the universe and is designated by various expressions.[22] The terms "separation" and "combination" (διάκρισις, σύγκρισις), though mixed in with others, occur in Anaxagoras. Epicharmos used them (for the first time, as far as we know) as a pair in strict reciprocal relation, which is to be found again later on in Aristotle, as well as in the doxographic tradition. For Plato himself had taken these terms over when, in his later life, he was led to incorporate the doctrines of the pre-Socratics into his own thought. In the *Sophist* (243B), the terms are used with reference to the earlier thinkers. In the *Timaeus* (65c), it is said that "most things (τὰ πολλά) come into being by separation and combination." In the *Laws* (897A), it is the moving soul (the "world-soul") that, with the help of physical motion, "brings everything (πάντα) into growth and decline, into separation and combination." And the terms occur similarly in the *Philebus* (42cD). So far-reaching, then, are the various connections associated by Plato, especially in his late period, with the words "weaving," "separating," and "combining."

Perhaps weaving is not only a paradigm for the art of statesmanship, but a symbol for reality as such.[23] And though earlier in the dialogue we were warned against mistaking our age deserted by God for the golden age ruled by God, or mistaking our statesman for the divine shepherd, what stands here in such sharp contrast expresses a relation between prototype and copy. Is not the art of weaving as practiced by the true statesman a copy of the world "bound together" by the law of proportion

(*Timaeus* 31B *et seq.*), the "living garment of the deity"?[24]

The lack of measure (or apparent lack of measure) in this
dialogue leads to what seems to be a new digression on the
subject of "measure" and the art of measurement. Here, too, the
method of division distinguishes between two types of measuring excess and defect, greatness and smallness, in things:
(*1*) when they are measured relatively to each other, and
(*2*) when they are measured according to the "essentially right
norm" (τὴν τοῦ μετρίου φύσιν, 283E 3; πρὸς τὸ μέτριον, 283E 11,
284A 2). The first type deals with relative terms. The second
type deals with an absolute relation. It goes without saying
that the discussion is oriented toward the second type of measurement. This type is active where it is a matter of marking off
the radical difference between good and evil or—as is said in
order to make it clear that we are concerned here with human
affairs, including our own lives—the difference between "the
good and the bad among us" (283E 5–6). The concept of "due
measure" is the central norm for all the arts, and hence for the
art of statesmanship as well as for this inquiry into the nature
of the statesman. Behind this investigation (μετὰ τοῦτο) there
looms the study of the "royal science" (284B 5) alluded to at
the beginning of the dialogue, where it was placed on the same
level with the art of statesmanship and management of domestic
affairs. Now it is given a higher rank, and this difference of rank
will be clarified further (in the last part of the dialogue, 302c
et seq.) in the discussion of the different systems of government.

The second and true art of measurement deals with "due
measure," with the "fitting" (πρέπον), with what ought to be,
or with standards that refer to a mean between extremes
(284E). Here Plato adds, evidently to clarify his own view, a
critique of the view held by "many of our learned minds"
(285A 1) according to whom the art of measurement "extends
throughout the realm of becoming" (which must mean,
throughout the whole of human life). The phrase "learned
minds" is read correctly as referring to the Pythagoreans, yet
perhaps we are to think not only of the Pythagorean schools in
distant Sicily, but also of Pythagorean tendencies within the
Academy itself.[25] And the critique, like all genuine polemics,

II 3
283B–287B

extends in two directions. On the one hand, the critique points
to that philosophical school to which Plato is so deeply indebted
in his thinking about mathematics and natural science, and about
the nature of measure as well. On the other hand, the critique of
this school reinforces once more the difference between the two
types, measurement and the measurable, previously distinguished.

Perhaps the reader—with a glance at Socrates who silently is
standing by—should raise still another question. The Eleatic
stranger in criticizing the "learned minds" says of them that
they hold that the art of measurement applies to "all things
that come into being" (περὶ πάντ' ἐστὶ τὰ γιγνόμενα, 285A 2).
Shortly before, he had said that "true measurement is based
on the becoming of due measure" (πρὸς τὴν τοῦ μετρίου γένεσιν,
284C 1, 284D 6) and, still earlier, he had used the strange expression, "according to the necessary being of becoming"
(κατὰ τὴν τῆς γενέσεως ἀναγκαίαν οὐσίαν, 283D 8–9). Are these
words which Plato repeatedly puts into the stranger's speech
merely accidental, or are the words intended to remind the
reader of the contrast between being and becoming, between
true knowledge and opinion (Republic VII 534A; Timaeus 29C),
or even to suggest the "coming-into-being as a result of limit
and measure" which in the Philebus (26D 8) is one of the four
kinds of being?

At the end of this section on measure, the question arises
(286B), why this long discussion just about measure? The
answer is, because it was difficult to understand the art of
weaving, difficult to understand the cosmic myth, and—here the
words of the Eleatic stranger go explicitly beyond the framework of the Statesman—difficult to understand the nature of
not-being discussed in the Sophist. We embarked on this digression about the art of measurement and due measure in order to
avoid these difficulties in the future. The main thing of value in
this discussion, as the stranger puts it, is the exercise in the
method of division. However much young Socrates—and
we—may learn from the stranger, shall we really accept his
evaluation? Or shall we try to find out rather how the other
Socrates, the old Socrates who silently is listening, would

evaluate the discussion? Is there not something else that is more essential? For in the midst of the dialectical divisions the goal emerges—"the things without visible embodiment, the things of highest beauty and value, that are accessible only through reason" (*logos*, 286A). So the stranger had just said himself, pointing to "due measure," to the "fitting," to what "ought to be" (284E), and to the true norm of accuracy (αὐτὸ τἀκριβές, 284D 2) in contrast to relative measurements. This is the realm of eternal being toward which Plato's Socrates leads us, the realm of moral imperatives testified to by Socrates in his life and death. This is the goal for which the method of dialectics and division prepares the way.

The Eleatic stranger seems to know on his own that dialectics and division are not ends in themselves. What has been said so far about measure, as he puts it (284D), is sufficient for the present purpose, but someday we will need these results "for an exposition of what is truly exact and essentially accurate." One might say: this is a reference to the unwritten dialogue *Philosopher*—which Plato never intended to write—or an anticipation of the *Philebus* (64D *et seq.*), where "goodness" and "perfection" have the characteristics of measure and symmetry. At any rate, the seemingly measureless digression on the nature of measure leads precisely to the same point that we had reached in the section on the nature of paradigm and in the section on the art of weaving. All lead to the realm of true being that it is incumbent upon the true statesman—the philosopher—to investigate.

Yet, it is not only with these philosophical hints that the *Statesman* points beyond its own framework. For a moment the dialogue even seems to address itself to the contemporary political situation. At the very beginning, shortly after the Eleatic stranger has taken charge of the conversation, he makes an explicit statement (259A), to which he will specifically refer toward the end (292E). His words are, "If there is somebody who can give expert advice to the ruler of a country, shall we not say that this person, though he is a private citizen, possesses as much knowledge as the ruler himself ought to possess?" In this pronouncement, Plato formulates his own relationship to Dionysios II so clearly that his contemporaries must have understood the allusion. Thus, it is likely that the *Statesman* was written in the years (366–361) between Plato's second and third journeys to Syracuse.[26]

It seems as if this dialogue is as devoid of "measure" as it is full of digressions. Yet, what is characteristic of Plato's late style is precisely this—that a coherent conceptual structure is visible behind what looks, if viewed from the outside, like an incoherent juxtaposition of parts.[27] There are ironic displacements in the structure of the dialogue, as is shown now in the

III
287B–311c

third part. While overtly resuming the search for a definition of the statesman, the last part also brings to fruition the results that were gained in the digressions of the central section.

III 1
287B–291c

Not directly so, however. In order to define the statesman, we return first to the example of the art of weaving, and fall back upon the distinction then introduced between arts that are "contributory causes" and arts that are "real causes." From a methodological point of view, it is important to realize that what we witness now is a fanatic of divisions reaching the limits of his craft so that, instead of "cutting through the middle," he begins "carving up the sacrificial victim by its joints."[28] To start with, seven classes of people are lined up as being engaged in the production of things: raw materials, tools, vessels, conveyances, clothing, toys or diversions, and food. They all are "contributory" to the existence of the state; they are not real causes. There follows (289c) the class of those who are not producers, but perform services. They are divided into slaves and free men who are middlemen such as money-changers, merchants, sailors, and retailers. We seem to come closer to the goal, yet still remain far from it, when we turn to administrators and civil servants. They, too, render services, in words and writing. From these administrative middlemen in society, we move upward to the intermediaries between men and gods, soothsayers and priests. Even among them, the statesman is not yet to be found—though in Egypt the king belongs to the priestly caste and though "with you" in Athens (it is the guest from Elea who is speaking) the King-Archon combines the official duties of priest and judge (290E 5).

It has been a long way upward from slaves to these kings, but the "kingly man" for whom we are looking stands even above these priest-kings and King-Archons. In the end, a "mixed crowd" is pressing in on us. They resemble lions or centaurs or satyrs or even beasts that are weak and of quickly changing appearance—as in the *Republic* (IX 588c), where man is depicted as a many-headed and changing monster, or in the *Sophist* (240c), where the many-headed sophist is shown. And, indeed, those in the crowd here are now revealed as the "chief wizards among all the sophists." Why are they given these strange names and such peculiarly changeable appearances? Evidently they are related to the true statesman as, in the *Sophist*, the sophist himself is related to the philosopher. Evidently it is they who call themselves statesmen and are so called by most people, and it is they who are hardest to distinguish from the "true statesmen and kings." That must now be done.

III 2
291c–303D

Again, it is not done in a direct manner. Instead, a new beginning is made by setting up a system of possible constitutions. If, in the *Republic* (Book VIII), these constitutions are almost sublimated into mythical essences, or if they become "pure expressions of spiritual totalities . . . reflected, in a fragmentary or mixed state, in actual systems of government,"[29] what we find here in the *Statesman* is a clearer and simpler classification based on the principle of who rules—one man, a few, or the many—and whether it is rule by force or by consent. Thus, there are six types of constitutions: monarchy and tyranny, aristocracy and oligarchy, and the two types of democracy that have the same name.

III 2a
291c–293E

A similar but still simpler classification of three basic types of government may be found in Pindar, or in Herodotos' account of the debate among Persian nobles on the merits and defects of the three types.[30] In his *Memorabilia*, Xenophon records (in the midst of quite unrelated matters) that Socrates distinguished five types of constitutions: monarchy and tyranny, aristocracy, plutocracy—here mentioned for the first time—and democracy.[31] The first two form a pair, as in Plato, and are distinguished according to the same criteria, namely, whether they are based on consent or on force, whether they are lawful or unlawful. As for the other three types, however, Xenophon seems to have

lost the power of classifying them systematically, and there is
no indication of what this brief section on constitutional matters
has to do with "Socrates." Evidently Xenophon picked up the
material from contemporary sources, perhaps from "Socratic"
circles, and the affinities with Plato's *Statesman* suggest that he
may actually have heard about discussions conducted in the
Academy.

Aristotle, in the *Ethics* and the *Politics*, adopts the system of
the *Statesman*, although his distinction of the three good constitutions and the three defective types is based on different
grounds.[32] Polybios, too, appeals to "Plato and some others
among the philosophers" for his classification of governments,
far as this political historian is from following Plato in his ultimate intentions. Plato indicates the intention guiding his systematic order by a brief remark. None of these constitutions can
be "right," he says, because the criterion they employ for justi-
fying the ruling group is derived either from numbers (large or
small), from consent or force, from lawfulness or unlawfulness,
from riches or poverty, whereas the true state, like the true
statesman, is distinguished from the false by a single criterion—
knowledge. Thus, the system of possible constitutions was constructed in order to show that, except for democracy (which
cannot have anything to do with knowledge because of the number of people who rule in it), the "true state" may be concealed
behind any of the other types. For there is only a single criterion
that distinguishes the true state: the rulers use "knowledge and
justice to improve it as much as possible." This is the same
criterion known to us from Plato's earlier works, from the
Thrasymachus, the *Alcibiades Major*, and the *Gorgias*, the same
criterion which ultimately, in the *Republic*, determines the principle of construction of the state that educates its citizens. If this
criterion is lacking—as it practically always is—the existing
types of government are more or less imperfect "copies" of the
true state. As little as we hear about the true state in this dialogue, it is still, as in Plato's main work, the state constructed on
the foundations of justice.

III 2c
302b–303d

Finally, after a long digression (III 2b) to which we shall
come back, a ranking is made of the defective constitutions. This

ranking is reminiscent of the balance sheet of happiness in the *Republic* (Books VIII and IX). As there we find the imperfect states ranked in progressive decline from the true state and from the happiness prevailing in it, so here we face the question as to which of the defective types is the hardest to live in and which is the easiest. It is asserted rather than proved that the lawful governments are less good the larger the ruling group is, while the contrary is true in the case of unlawful governments. In other words, the pressure of life increases from monarchy to aristocracy and lawful democracy, and it increases, conversely, from a lawless democracy to oligarchy and tyranny. The right form of government here too rises above the classification, even as God rises above everything human. In the spirit of Socrates who is listening we might also say, besides God, perfection, truth, and being beyond being.

Once more we see clearly that those who participate in the defective types are to be marked off from the statesman whom we are seeking. They are not statesmen but—as is said in an untranslatable play on words: οὐκ ὄντας πολιτικοὺς ἀλλὰ στασιασ-τικούς—mere partisans in a community torn by internal conflict instead of members of a well-ordered polis. They administer copies and semblances of the true state. They are themselves copies and semblances; they are imitators and tricksters to the highest degree, and so they are of all sophists the greatest sophists. Again, in a literal reference to what was said earlier (291a–c), the swarm of centaurs and satyrs appears. We understand now why they are called "sophists," for in the companion dialogue (*Sophist* 235a 1), the sophist was called "one of the tricksters, an imitator of being." The significance of this section is, then, that it distinguishes the true statesman from all those who are ordinarily so called. And this is done in such a way that the difference is brought back to the distinction between being and appearance. The ontological contrast between being and appearance is the bridge that links the two dialogues, the *Sophist* and the *Statesman*.

We return to the long digression that forms the center itself of the threefold central part of the third main part of the dialogue. (This is an indication of the secret architechtonic struc-

III 2b
293E–302B

ture hidden behind what seem to be the free-floating twists and turns taken in this late work of Plato's.) In a puzzling statement made more than once (293A 7, 293C 8), it is said that as the true state cannot be judged by ordinary criteria, it also makes no difference whether the rulers hold power with or without a code of laws. This is supposed to sound paradoxical, and it promptly elicits a response of surprise on the part of the young Socrates. His response, in turn, is the point of departure for one of the most astonishing sections in the entire body of Plato's works—the discussion on the relation between the true state and the laws.[33]

The essential point is this, that the law, being simple and general, is not adequate to deal with the manifold variety of life. It is a makeshift as compared with the rule of the true statesman, who is creative and not bound by laws. Similarly, it would make no sense to invoke "laws" against the experience of a captain at sea or a physician or any man of science, including the mathematician. If the true statesman acts contrary to existing laws, he is acting "most truly," i.e., most in accordance with true being (300E). Measured only by this absolute standard, laws are of less value. They are the "second-best course" when the best is not possible. They sum up and are based on long experience. Hence, they must be acknowledged as inviolate and they must be protected by severe penalties as long as we live in a state without the true statesman.

This is the dialectics of the law and the true state without laws. Employing special verbal effects—both scornful and solemn speech, and the young partner's playing of a more active role than elsewhere (299E)—the discussion reaches its climax when it alludes, in the barely concealed words of the indictment, to the fate of Socrates himself (299BC). The reply of the young Socrates at this point is an echo of the defense of the old Socrates (299E). He is the true statesman for he has knowledge of true being, in comparison with which existing laws are but imitations and approximate copies. His fate symbolizes the unavoidable clash between the laws of the state and the man whose existence represents the knowledge of the philosopher-king acting without the help of laws.

Thus, the reader is directed once more toward the presence of him who is merely listening. We must not overlook Plato's dramatic intention, even in his late works, and we must remember that, according to the last words in the *Theaetetus*, Socrates presented himself "yesterday" before a court of law. His presence is the answer to the problem discussed in this dialogue. This entire last section, though appearing to digress again from the straight path, serves a specific function. It assigns the rank appropriate to the true statesman—in the realm of true being far beyond the sublimity of the law.

This is the meaning of the section here within the dialogue itself. Yet, beyond it, this discussion also has a special significance in Plato's work as a whole. The *Statesman* stands between the *Republic* and the *Laws*.[34] It stands, that is, between the work that prepares the ground for the rule of the true statesman governing without laws, and the great book of laws designed for a utopian Crete. The *Statesman* assigns to the *Laws*, Plato's last work (of which many sections must have been written by then), a rank far below the *Republic*, but a necessary place as the "second-best course." In this perspective, we may understand both the solemn statements and the deprecating remarks made here about legislation.

After we come to see, again and again in the various turns taken by the conversation (and especially when we least expected to make this discovery), how the true state and the true statesman are related to the realm of true being, there remain only two lines of thought that must be pursued to a conclusion. We still lack the most subtle distinction between the statesman and the other professions that make a claim (then as now) to this high office, and are indeed significant and akin to it. These others are the art of generalship, the science and administration of justice (δικαστική), and the kind of rhetoric (depicted in the *Phaedrus*) that is related to the royal art.

Here we come back to a theme that preoccupied Plato from the time of his earliest writings. In the *Laches* (195c), we learn that the physician has knowledge with respect to health and illness, but whether it is better for someone to be healthy or sick, this the physician does not know. It is known only to someone

III 3
303D–311C

III 3a
303D–305E

who ranks above the physician, one who, in the context of this early dialogue, is called "the manly." In the *Euthydemus* (290D *et seq.*), where we find the same term, the "royal art," as here in the *Statesman*, the point is developed more explicitly.[35] We are shown a hierarchical system of the arts in which the arts on a lower level "produce" what is then "used" by the art on the next level up. According to this criterion, dialectics is placed above astronomy and the art of calculation, and statesmanship is placed above the art of generalship. Dialectics and statesmanship know how to use what the other arts "provide" for them. Again, in the *Alcibiades Major* (125B *et seq.*), Plato shows an ordered system of ruling arts. Every profession is a kind of "rule," in that the physician has command over the patient, the captain over the crew. Yet there is another art that has command over physicians, captains, and choir leaders, and since they are all members of a political community, this art must be the art of statesmanship, though the name itself is concealed here behind such terms as "good counsel" and "community spirit."

What is shown now in the *Statesman* is very similar to these earlier discussions. In the art of music there are teachers and students, but there must be an art of a higher order that decides whether or not someone ought to learn a particular art. (We are reminded of the place of "music" in the structure of the *Republic*.) Similarly, above rhetoric, or the art of persuasion, there is a higher art that decides whether one ought to persuade. (We are reminded of the defeat of rhetoric in the *Gorgias*, and of its reinterpretation and integration in the *Phaedrus*.) Hence, as statesmanship has command over the art of music, over all other subjects of study, and over rhetoric, so it also has command over the art of war in deciding whether or not it should be practiced. (The art of war is a branch of statesmanship, as we learn even in the *Protagoras*—322B 5. Put differently, in the words of Clemenceau, "War is much too important a thing to be left to the generals.") The office of the judge, who is charged with the preservation of the law, also is subordinate to the art of politics. In the *Laches*, this art of politics vanishes behind the word "manliness," an ambiguous and inappropriate term. In the *Euthydemus*, the nature of the royal art remains problematic, and in the *Alcibiades Major*, it is alluded to but left in abeyance. Meanwhile, however, Plato wrote the *Republic*, and now in the *Statesman*, statesmanship once more is shown to be concerned with true being, with "due measure," or with what is "essentially accurate."

Statesmanship is the art that "weaves everything in the state together perfectly." We return to the analogy with weaving in order to complete the inquiry into the nature of statesmanship. What does it weave together? How is it done? What is the fabric that results from the process? We surmise that there are contrasting strands that must be woven into a unified fabric. Reappearing here is the old theme of the "virtues," known to us from the *Protagoras* and the early dialogues in search of a definition. In the *Protagoras*, in particular, it was difficult to fit manliness, or courage, into the system of the virtues so that Socrates resorted to rather sophistic techniques in order to reduce courage to knowledge and thus demonstrate the unity of the virtues by means of this single virtue. The theme of the *Laches* is education, or *paideia*, and the task there is to assign courage its proper place in the educational process as well as in the over-all system of the virtues. In the *Gorgias*, self-discipline (*sophrosyne*) and courage are placed side by side to test whether Socrates' opponent has been able to grasp even the nature of courage in a Socratic sense. In the *Republic*, finally, the virtues are united in and through the one virtue, justice, and this is the basis for the system of education which, even in its first stage, has the function of harmoniously combining, by means of music and gymnastics, opposite dispositions in man's soul. In the process of selecting the guardians, it is emphasized repeatedly (II 374E *et seq.*) that two opposing tendencies, driving energy and a calm, moderate spirit, inhere in them "by nature." Then, in the education of the guardians, "music" is to balance these opposites, and gymnastics contributes to the same goal.

This basic theme is resumed in the *Statesman*. Here, too, manliness and moderation are the two essential types of virtues, but this contrast in human nature is singled out now for emphasis, and a critical blow is leveled against the view that all parts of virtue are in mutual accord (306c 1). On the contrary,

III 3b
305E–311C

the two basic types can develop into such one-sided extremes that the one turns into slavish cowardice, the other into warlike violence, and either can bring ruin to the state. The task of statesmanship consists not in eradicating this opposition given by nature, for this would be impossible, but in reconciling these two powers in a Herakleitean "bond of opposites." The analogy with weaving shows how the statesman achieves this unity of opposites.

Is it the case, then, as sometimes is alleged, that in the *Statesman*, as compared with the central as well as the earlier works, Plato replaced his "idealism" or "rationalism" or what is called his "doctrine of virtues" by a "doctrine of characters or temperaments"?[36] Those who argue along these lines forget one thing—that the Eleatic stranger is conversing here with the young Socrates while the great educator himself silently is listening. The theme of education is alluded to only now and then in the *Statesman*. The art of statesmanship, it is said, first will separate good characters from bad characters by testing them in "games," and after the bad natures have been eliminated, it will pass the rest on to professional educators (308D). "Music" is mentioned only incidentally and by way of comparison (304B). We should keep in mind how, in the *Republic*, music is combined with gymnastics in order to promote the unity of body and soul in the guardians. In the *Statesman*, the Eleatic stranger mentions music along with the "knowledge of any other craft" as if it were just one of the crafts, i.e., as if it consisted of playing an instrument or of doing rhythmic exercises. This conception is far removed from that of the "musical art" about which Socrates says in the *Republic* (III 401D) that it provides the essential nourishment of the soul because rhythm and harmony penetrate into its innermost being and mold a "well-formed" soul.

If, in the *Republic*, philosopher, statesman, and educator are practically one and the same person, in the *Statesman* educators appointed by law are subject to the royal art of the true statesman (308E). Those pupils who cannot be taught manliness and calm gentleness are to be put to death or expelled from the community. As far as the others are concerned, the statesman joins the immortal elements of their soul by a "divine bond," the mortal elements by a human bond. The divine bond is "right opinion" (ἀληθῆ δόξαν, 309c, 309ε 6) concerning what is beautiful, just, and good. The true knowledge of highest being is alluded to from afar, but Socrates who is listening might well ask whether "right opinion" is enough, even though the stranger underscores its "unshakability" (μετὰ βεβαιώσεως)— or whether we should rather look toward a kind of knowledge that rises high above right opinion.

Still, how is this educational work accomplished? The energetic, violent nature is calmed down to "courage" so that it combines also with "justice." The quiet, gentle nature is made "moderate" and "wise." This is the "divine bond" that unites the opposing natures with each other. Each of them is imbued with two of the four "cardinal virtues," and in this way the opposites are united. Here, too, were Socrates to speak, he might remind the interlocutors that in his ideal state, the guardians and especially the philosophers are educated in such a way that, despite opposite tendencies by nature, each individual combines the four virtues harmoniously in one and the same soul.

The "human bond" to be forged by the statesman refers to the intermarriage between the two opposite types lest a repeated union of members of the same type intensify the difference to an extreme. Marriages also are subject to strict supervision in the *Republic* and in the *Laws*. In the *Republic*, this supervision applies only to the marriages of the guardians. The third class apparently may act more or less freely in this respect as in others. Moreover, in the *Republic*, which makes incomparably higher demands upon the educational process than the *Statesman* does, the regulations concerning marriage remain on a physiological level, as it were. It is no accident that the expression "herd" (ποίμνιον, ἀγέλη, *Republic* V 459ε) is used in referring to the class of guardians whose kind and number must be determined by the right selection. The *Laws*, however, follows the *Statesman* in combining opposite natures into measure and symmetry. And an economic factor is added in the *Laws*, which mentions that in marriage, poor wives are to be preferred to rich ones.

In words of deep feeling the Eleatic stranger brings the statesman's work of weaving to a conclusion, invoking at the end the beautiful phrase, "by concord and friendship," familiar to us from the *Alcibiades Major* as well as the *Republic*.[37] Here it is invoked more comprehensively than ever, since it extends to all members of the community, both "slaves and free men." Thus, it serves as a symbol for the Herakleitean tension which, according to Plato, is the essence of the true state and of the realm of being as such. "Concord and friendship" are the means by which the kingly weaver fashions happiness as far as this is possible in a human community.

One more detail must not be overlooked, especially with a view toward the philosopher who is listening. There is no difficulty, the Eleatic stranger says, in forging the bonds between the two opposite natures provided they both share the community of "opinion" (δόξαν, 310E 7) about what is beautiful and good. Various means must be employed in the process of interweaving, but the first among them is "community of opinions" (ὁμοδοξίαι, 310E 10). This is said well and impressively, but one thing still is lacking—true knowledge rising above right opinion.

"The picture that you have now drawn of the true king and statesman, as previously of the sophist, is quite perfect." Most scholars nowadays attribute these words of grateful assent, on which the *Statesman* concludes, to the old Socrates instead of to the young Socrates.[38] It is forgotten that in the *Sophist*, the young Theaitetos says, in conclusion, "Quite so!" and, in the *Parmenides*, the young Aristotle says, in conclusion, "Most true!" Although it would not occur to anyone to attribute the last words spoken in these two dialogues to anybody except the young men who served as respondents, the desire to let the old Socrates have the last words in the *Statesman* may reflect a modern conception of courtesy. But Plato perhaps intended something other than courtesy—and might not such an assent on the part of the old Socrates introduce a note precisely opposite to that intended by Plato? Should we instead interpret Socrates' silence at the end, as throughout the dialogue, as a silence that both speaks and questions?

At the beginning of both the *Sophist* and the *Statesman*, Socrates promises a conversation about the philosopher to be conducted with the young Socrates after the guest from Elea has finished his discourse. We cannot construct, even in our thoughts, the dialogue that Plato did not write and probably never intended to write. Yet, we may guess what the philosopher must have found wanting as, listening, he contemplated the portrait of the statesman drawn here with the assent of the young Socrates. He would have found lacking everything said about the education of the philosopher-king in the *Republic*. If we keep this in mind, we realize that the philosopher is not satisfied with weaving together opposite natures in the fabric of the state. He, instead, educates and forms into a unity the opposite tensions in the souls of the best and directs their minds toward a view of true being. In the Academy, Plato undoubtedly held fast to the educational ideal of the *Republic*. For Syracuse or Assos, however, the art of weaving as set forth in the *Statesman* would have seemed to him a most appropriate program—as it still is for any state in our own time.

TWENTY-EIGHT

Philebus

IN THE manuscripts, the *Philebus* bears the subtitle, "On Pleasure [Joy, Gladness, Delight]: Ethical Dialogue." Modern scholars have often interpreted the work in the same sense. Yet, even the Neoplatonist Olympiodoros objected strongly to this interpretation.[1] The tenth book of Aristotle's *Nicomachean Ethics* quite rightly is subtitled "On Pleasure." The case of the *Philebus* is different, however, for there are large parts in the dialogue that deal with dialectics and ontology but have nothing to do with pleasure and ethics, or if so, only indirectly. The *Philebus* is a dramatic contest between pleasure and knowledge in the course of which a third state, beyond both pleasure and knowledge, carries off highest honors. Pleasure, or enjoyment, is represented by Philebos and Protarchos. Socrates represents knowledge. It goes without saying that Socrates advocates his own view in quite a different sense from the way in which the two young men represent theirs. This difference becomes clear at the very outset when Socrates considers it possible, or rather anticipates (11D 11), that a third view might win highest prize.

It is customary to say that in the *Philebus*, Plato enters into a discussion started in the Academy by Eudoxos, the great mathematician and scientist, who held that the good is pleasure (a view subsequently opposed by Speusippos). Perhaps even Aristotle understood the dialogue in this sense, for in the *Nicomachean Ethics* he cites the *Philebus* immediately after mentioning the doctrine of Eudoxos. Yet Plato had discussed— that is, opposed—the pleasure theory as early as in the *Protagoras*,[2] and disputes it even more vigorously and more explicitly in the *Gorgias*, and in the central part of the *Republic* (VI 505AB), where the *Idea* of the Good or the "prototype of perfection" is made visible as the highest object of knowledge. Thus, Plato himself must have stimulated discussion in the Academy on the respective merits of hedonism and intellectualism rather than just "entered into" the discussion by writing the *Philebus*. And as to Eudoxos, before he left Knidos and joined the Academy he is likely to have thought more about the stellar spheres and geometrical proportions than about the question of the highest good.[3]

The contrast between a hedonistic and an intellectualistic ethics had been anticipated by the opposing camps of the Cyrenaics and the Cynics. And even earlier, a generation before, Prodikos had depicted the same conflict in the famous allegory of Herakles at the crossroads where the choice is between two women, of whom one represents virtue while the other—sometimes called evil, sometimes happiness—promises all the pleasures of life.[4] Older still than this allegory dressed up as a myth, which on its own part has had a lasting influence, is the genuine myth of the judgment of Paris. Sophocles dramatized this in the satyr-play called *Crisis*, apparently simplifying the ancient epic tradition in such a way that Paris is shown choosing between Athene and Aphrodite, between reason and pleasure. Also, the two diverging paths in the allegory of Prodikos had been anticipated in the famous verses where Hesiod distinguishes between the smooth and short path of evil and the long, steep path of virtue.

Plato, then, was heir to a rich tradition which he had been absorbing over many decades by the time he decided to write the *Philebus*. This alone suggests that he does not simply continue the tradition. And there is something beyond the simple question posed at the outset, and beyond the simple answer (that the truly good and perfect is above both reason and pleasure, but thought and intelligence are incomparably closer to perfection than pleasure and enjoyment can ever be). Rising above and beyond both question and answer, the dialogue opens onto perspectives and insights which make it clear that "the initial question is by no means the only and perhaps not even the main tendency of the conversation" (Schleiermacher).[5]

How little most modern readers grasp the dialogical spirit of the *Philebus* may be shown by the peculiarly significant characteristic of punctuation adopted in our texts. This conversation more than any other in Plato's entire work is full of exchanges in which Socrates stops for a moment in order to resume his line of thought after an interruption (as a question or an assent) by his partner. One should indicate these stops and interruptions by a colon, a comma, or a series of ellipsis points, depending on the context. Instead, the editors, in uniform consensus, use only periods and question marks.[6] Once we become aware of this and introduce a more lively system of punctuation, we may wonder if it would not be better, after the last words of Protarchos at the very end of the dialogue—"I will remind you of what remains to be said and done . . . "—to use ellipsis points instead of a period, in order to suggest that the conversation continued without interruption, but that the reporter, as it were, no longer recorded what was said.[7]

Thus, the *Philebus* is, after all, not "without any artistic attraction," and perhaps it cannot be "transposed so easily into a formal lecture" as many interpreters seem to believe.[8] The conversation is to be envisaged as a segment cut out of a larger setting.[9] A group of young men have gathered, most likely in a gymnasium for wrestling, as the wrestling motif is carried jokingly into the intellectual discussion. They have been exchanging views on a popular question—which of the human goods is the best?—and they have drawn Socrates into the discussion at a moment when two opposing views have emerged. At the point where the conversation breaks off, then, it will be continued, perhaps tomorrow, most likely right away. The youths have threatened jokingly not to let Socrates go home until the discussion has been completed. The ending, "Will you let me go?" alludes to this threat. There are, too, the earlier words (50D): "Will you relieve me or will you keep me up until midnight?" The erotic atmosphere is also hinted at. "Philebos, our handsome friend," Protarchos says in taking his place at the beginning (11c 7). "Fair Philebos"—so Socrates chides him mockingly later on (26B) when Aphrodite is shown to be the goddess of law and order and not, as Philebos thinks, the goddess of pleasure. Even the name *Phil-hebos* itself was chosen, and probably coined, by Plato in order to express this very atmosphere.[10]

Socrates is the one we know from the early dialogues, especially in the company of young men.[11] Defending a specific thesis, as he does here at the beginning of the *Philebus*, would be "un-Socratic" only if he were not willing to examine it critically. But this he begins to do immediately and soon participates in its defeat. Thus, the statement, the good is knowledge, is presented not as a dogma but as a preliminary basis for discussion, and it is left behind once we see both the inadequacy of the initial thesis and its partial justification. It is worth noting that Dionysius of Halicarnassus, an intelligent literary commentator, in a rather critical analysis of Plato's stylistic form singles out just the *Philebus*, praising it as an example of a dialogue in which Plato "preserves the Socratic characteristics."[12]

Philebos himself stands completely aside. More correctly, he seems to be lying aside, for there is every reason to take Protarchos at his word when he says, modifying a common saying, that perhaps it is best not to disturb Philebos with questions since he is "well bedded down"[13] (μὴ κινεῖν εὖ κείμενον, 15c 9). It may be asked, then, why the person after whom the dialogue is named hardly participates in the conversation. The few exceptions when he does provide a key to the answer. Twice Philebos breaks into the conversation. As the discussion has moved beyond the initial question to the more distant and abstract problem of the one and the many, he asks angrily what all this has to do with the matter (18A–E). Later he speaks up once more (27E), to assert emphatically that pleasure is "unlimited" in every respect.

Now it seems quite clear why Plato introduced this Philebos and even named the dialogue after him. Philebos represents the "pure" pleasure principle, "unlimited" in its essence. It is not a minor detail either that he is lying down, whereas the participants in the conversation itself are thought of as either standing around or sitting. Philebos has "refused to go on" with the discussion (11c 8). Pleasure cannot be expected to "give an account" of itself—cannot be expected to because engaging in controversy is not pure pleasure. If it does so engage itself, it enters into a pact with its adversary, reason (*logos*), and in this contest is necessarily defeated. Pure hedonism and dialectics exclude each other. For hedonism is essentially hostile to any dialogue, which means it is non-human. The dream of the hedonist will ultimately reveal itself as the life of an oyster (21c). We may remember how, in the *Gorgias*, Kallikles—prophet of the violent ego or, as Socrates interprets him, prophet of pleasure—must be defeated as soon as he ceases to be merely violent and permits his thesis of the "unlimited" pleasure principle to be analyzed dialectically. Thus, it is clear what the silent presence of Philebos "means."[14] He is not the "weakest element in the dramatic structure." For what is always silently present—through Philebos—is the rigid resistance of pure hedonism.

Similarly, it is clear why the Philebos-thesis must be presented by somebody else.[15] The name "Protarchos" does not conceal a philosophical doctrine, say, for example, the hedonism of Aristippos or of Eudoxos.[16] Protarchos rather represents the average view that is inclined toward hedonism without—in contrast to Philebos—shutting off all other powers in life. Undoubtedly, this "son of Kallias" was a real person. Perhaps he really was a pupil of Gorgias (58A), but whether he was or not, the reason for bringing Gorgias into the conversation must be found within the matter, or topic, itself. True knowledge, Socrates says, aims at eternal being. Rhetoric, Protarchos replies (citing Gorgias), being the art of compelling persuasion, is the supreme, the most powerful art. And in so far as the true representative of pleasure is incapable of joining the conversation, pleasure can engage in discussion only by way of rhetoric as, conversely, pleasure is the basic principle of rhetoric.

Socrates had raised the question of hedonism to the sophists earlier, in the *Protagoras* (315B *et seq.*). There he makes Protagoras (the most powerful mind in that sophistic circle) distinguish, though somewhat uncertainly, between the two concepts, "good" and "pleasant." Then in the course of the conversation, Socrates makes sure that the decisive power is recognized to be knowledge and, within the field of knowledge, the art of measurement and calculation. Yet Socrates goes this far only to conclude—with the sophists' applause assured—by again identifying "pleasant" and "good." Thus for Plato, from his early period on, sophistic rhetoric and pleasure are closely related. Both of them aim ultimately at power, not at truth. In the *Gorgias*, Polos is a pupil of the great sophist, and Kallikles is a follower of both Gorgias and Polos. Similarly, here in the *Philebus* the implications of hedonism are suggested when Protarchos appeals to his master, Gorgias. Put differently, the problem of the *Gorgias*, or the mortal combat that is fought out there, emerges here once more at the margin of the *Philebus*.

Thus, we have to go back to the *Protagoras*, or more particularly to the *Gorgias*, to see how deeply the *Philebus* is rooted in Plato's works.[17] In the *Gorgias*, Socrates fights in two moves against the thesis of the right of the stronger. First, he exposes it as the view that the pleasure principle has primacy in life, and second, he destroys this view by compelling his opponent to concede (*Gorgias* 499B) that pleasures are not all alike. There are noble and vulgar pleasures. Hence, there is a standard of judging pleasures, and this standard is the good. The same concession will be wrung from the opponent here in the *Philebus* (13A, 14A). In both dialogues, too, the discussion descends to the level of relieving itches (*Gorgias* 494D; *Philebus* 46A). In both dialogues, pleasures mixed with pain as, for example, in the quenching of thirst (*Gorgias* 496D; *Philebus* 31D *et seq.*) play an important part—in the *Gorgias* because these phenomena show that pleasure is different from the good, which is never mixed with evil, and in the *Philebus* because it is in a move upward from these mixed pleasures that the level of pure pleasures is attained. In both dialogues it is shown that the opponent, to begin with, is impartial enough to acknowledge differences in the order of pleasures, but for the time being is prevented from making any breakthrough because of his commitment to the radical thesis (*Gorgias* 494E *et seq.*, 499B; *Philebus* 13AB, 14AB). And in both dialogues it is clear that we are concerned not with verbal controversy or abstract principles, but with basic attitudes toward life itself (πῶς βιωτέον, *Gorgias* 492D 5, 500C 4; βίου, *Philebus* 11E 2).

In recasting the basic structure of the *Gorgias*, the *Republic* also reformulates the pleasure theme. It is reasonable to expect that this reformulation stands, as to substance and as to time, between the views developed in the *Gorgias* and those in the *Philebus*.[18] In the *Republic*, pleasure no longer is at the center of controversy as it is in the *Gorgias*. Essentially this struggle has been won, inasmuch as the state is erected on the principle of justice, with the victory made complete by the balance of happiness drawn up in the ninth book. But though the theme of pleasure recedes to the periphery, it acquires new depth in the *Republic*. Even as the theme of knowledge, which was peripheral in the *Gorgias*, becomes of central concern in the *Republic*, so does the relationship with knowledge give to the concept of pleasure new depth, in two respects. First, the highest pleasure is the pleasure of knowledge. Only the "philosopher," the man of knowledge, can determine that his pleasure is superior to that of others, because he alone knows the other pleasures as well as his own and because he alone is capable of judging by means of reason (IX 580D–583A). In the second place, pleasure itself is infused with an element of knowledge: one kind of pleasure not only may be "better" than another, as in the *Gorgias*, but it also may be more or less "true" (*Republic* 583B–588A).

In the *Philebus*, we find this new connection between pleasure and knowledge. We find the same struggle (as in the *Republic*) against the mistaken view that identifies true pleasure with a state of equilibrium between pleasure and pain.[19] And we find the same hard struggle to recognize the difference between true and false pleasures. Though the field of observation in the *Philebus* is greatly expanded, we even find a recurrence in detail (beautiful odors are cited as a case of unmixed pleasure: *Republic* 584B, *Philebus* 51B). In the *Philebus*, too, pleasure is sublimated when it is attached to the highest objects of knowledge.

Let us also note the differences. In the *Gorgias*, the opposite of pleasure is called "justice." This moral and political aspect is preserved in the *Republic*, except that the political aspect becomes the central theme and the aspect of knowledge (hidden behind the search for "justice") is developed to a degree of autonomy not previously achieved. The ascent to the realm of Forms fills the central part of the *Republic*. The question of pleasure is raised only toward the end and marginally, as it were (IX 580D *et seq.*). Yet, new light is thrown on it from the perspective of the knowledge just won.

In the *Philebus*, the political dimension has practically disappeared. The moral conflict—a matter of life and death in the *Gorgias*, and still so vital as to marshal all the forces in the *Republic*—seems to have spent itself. Yet, for a moment, Socrates refers to the "danger" and "impiety" of making a false decision (28A)—strangely emphatic words that Plato would not have chosen had he not had in mind, despite the lapse of years, Socrates' indictment and the *Apology* (28B, 34C). But this disappears again, and in the ensuing controversy over the basic attitudes of human life we hear only an echo of what was previously a struggle charged with intensity and mortal danger.

For in the *Philebus*, the main theme is the connection (established in the *Republic*) between pleasure and the ultimate questions of ontology. It is this tension more than anything else that determines the specific characteristic of the *Philebus*. And the peculiarly anacoluthic structure of the whole is paralleled, in many cases, by the sentence structure of Plato's late style[20]— the gliding transitions that force the "analytic" interpreter to be even more severe in his divisions here than elsewhere,[21] the leaps (hardly understandable) from one level to another and completely different one. For even here Plato, ultimately, is not concerned with a psychology of the affects, and however much he puts into the observation and description of pleasure and pain, this study is but another approach to what was always his true concern.[22]

In *Part I, section 1*, the two opposing views are immediately presented and then elaborated. The question is, What is "good"? or as is soon said (14B) more precisely, What is "the good"? Philebos had defined it (before the beginning of this conversational section) as "pleasure" or "enjoyment." Socrates had defined it as "thought" or analogous acts of the mind. We are familiar with this contrast from the central part of the

I 1

11A–18D

Republic (VI 504DE) and we know that it expresses the conflict between the natural striving of man's physical existence as against his spiritual life. Socrates is so impartial in putting the two views side by side that his opponent assents to the formulation. Yet, an incipient critique is noticeable in the way the views are formulated. The pleasure theory derives its claim from the principle of generality—pleasure is good for "everything that is alive" (πᾶσι ζῴοις, 11B 5)[23]—whereas the "thought theory" posits a good that is unique and not accessible to everybody: thought is good for all those beings who are capable of participating in it (σύμπασιν ὅσαπερ αὐτῶν δυνατὰ μεταλαμβάνειν, 11B 9; cf. 22B 5). More precisely, thought or knowledge in all its variations proves "more sublime and better." The language is solemn, for Socrates is using a ritualistic formula derived from the language of the law.[24] And he is using a comparative, i.e., he is comparing. Only for the conclusion does he use a superlative, "the most profitable," and so we sense that this decision is the result of comparison and conflict.

The question as to what is "good" is somewhat ambiguous, depending on whether we are referring to the good in human life or referring to goodness or perfection as such. At the beginning, it would seem that we are entering the larger domain. "Everything that is alive" and "all beings that are capable" are expressions referring to levels below human life and possibly beyond it. We shall have to watch whether this larger domain comes into view again later. For the time being, however, the field is reduced to that of human life. It is a matter of dealing with "states of the soul," and "good" refers to what makes human life "happy." Whether this be pleasure or knowledge, then, is the question.

Still, there is more to the ambiguity inherent in the initial question as to what is "good." Socrates again formulates the contrasting views: according to Philebos, good is enjoyment, but according to his own view, it is thought or knowledge. And once again he expresses the view, represented by Protarchos (13A 8), that all pleasant things are "good" (ἀγαθά), whereas, according to his own view, many pleasant things are bad and some are "good." In continuing the discussion, Pro-

tarchos (in passing, as it were) changes his language from
"good" to "the good"—as if there were no difference between
the two expressions. For a while, Socrates retains the adjectival
expression without the article (13E 5). Only after he has finished describing the contrast between the two views does he
adopt Protarchos' expression, "the good" (14B 1), as he refers
to "the good as I understand it and as you understand it."[25]
This change in expression from "good" to "the good" cannot
be accidental. Protarchos has picked up a catchword that must
have been current in Platonic circles at least from the time
the *Republic* was read and discussed. Socrates resists for a while.
If he were talking not to Protarchos and the group of young
men here but, say, to Glaukon and Adeimantos, he would say
that "the good" is beyond being and, hence, beyond knowledge
as well (*Republic* VI 509B).

Using language appropriate to wrestling, Socrates makes a
remark that anticipates something to come later on. Neither
view might be correct, he says, but a third state might be "the
good." In this case both opponents would have to secure victory
for what is "most true," a clear allusion to the subsequent
course of the conversation. But if "the good" has this transcendent status we just have described, it would seem likely
for us to sense some reference also to the transcendent status
of "the truth," which then would raise the question of whether
"the good" is not at the same time "the true." For the time
being, however, the conversation returns to the conflict over
the two initial definitions.

Protarchos withdraws to a defense of the nominal (or conceptual) unity of "pleasure." Pleasure is pleasure wherever it
may come from; qua pleasure there is no difference among
pleasures. Socrates points out that color or shape is, as a genus,
a unity, which may contain a variety of different species, like
white or black, square or circle. If we were to take Protarchos'
position, we might as well assert that two things that are most
unlike are most alike because they both belong to the genus of
the unlike (13D). An eristic thinker in the tradition of Zeno—
or Socrates depicted in the *Euthydemus*—might be amused to
spin ingenious fallacies from this likeness of the unlike. But

here Socrates quickly brushes aside even the attempt at such identification. (That would be most foolish, he says.) Just as there are opposites within each class, so there must be pleasures that are opposed to each other—good and bad pleasures. Hence, pleasure cannot be the good. In replying, "Perhaps" (13A 6), Protarchos had half conceded that there might be differences in the class of pleasures. That is, he had taken the naïve point of view of the ordinary man. Now, realizing that he is jeopardizing his position, he withdraws to the pleasure principle as such even though it had been surrendered in part by that earlier "Perhaps."

Socrates lures the opponent from his seemingly secure hideout. In agreeing to submit his own principle, knowledge, to an examination that is designed to bring out differences or opposites which may be concealed within it, he persuades the other to submit pleasure to the same kind of examination. Protarchos, then, is ready to agree there is a "motley" (ποικιλία) of pleasure as long as there is a "motley" of knowledge as well. In short, pleasure hopes it can drag knowledge down to its own confusion, without noticing that knowledge is what compels the pleasure principle to reveal its own confusion —provided we mean human pleasure and not only a principle that is common to "everything alive" (11B 5).

This is the way the conflict presents itself in conceptual terms. In human terms it means that a life oriented purely toward pleasure is essentially meaningless, i.e., without *logos*, and hence, not human. As soon as it is called upon to give an "account" (*logos*) of itself it is lost, or it can escape shipwreck only on a raft of "nonsense" (σῴζεσθαι ἐπί τινος ἀλογίας, 14A 4), which is but another form of defeat.

So, basically, pleasure has lost its claim. In fact, it lost when Protarchos agreed to join the conversation. If Plato had been interested only in the old problem as posed in the context of the *Gorgias* or even in the context of contemporary discussion, he might have completed this defeat of the pleasure principle here and now. But these old struggles lie far behind him, and he is aiming now at something else. At this point, therefore, of a motley of pleasure and knowledge, Socrates breaks the

discussion off, only to suggest once more as he had earlier
(11D 11) that the good might be a third possibility beyond both
pleasure and knowledge. He will return to this possibility later
(I 2). For now, however, he begins pulling the discussion
sharply upward to an altogether different level.

Before we follow him there, let us come back briefly to a
detail in the present section. As Philebos withdraws from the
conversation, he calls upon the "goddess herself" (12B 1–2).
He means Aphrodite, as Socrates points out, adding that, to
Philebos, her true name is Hedone, Pleasure, and expressing
his own "fear" of the names of the gods. Fear of the gods is
the note struck here by Socrates. We are reminded of what is
said in the *Cratylus* (400D *et seq.*) about the importance of the
gods' names, and we cannot but recall what Socrates—faced
with his own indictment—says about fear and reverence of the
deity (*Euthyphro* 12A *et seq.*). But now the aged Plato has Socrates speak with an even more deeply veiling reverence. What
he is first of all concerned with is this, that pleasure is a thing
of variety and, hence, is not a god. Then follows an elaboration
on the theme of the variety of pleasure. This cannot be an insignificant ornamental figure of speech when we are dealing
with so elevated a term as the "goddess herself" and when
the nature of this goddess is in doubt. The word "god"—as
we know from the "theology" of the *Republic* (II 380D *et seq.*)
—designates an exalted being whose nature excludes a motley
variety. This negative conclusion is all that we learn here, but
we shall have to take note when this theological leitmotiv is
sounded again—theology in a dialogue that allegedly deals
with "pleasure."

Pleasure is pleasure is the position to which Protarchos had ɪ 1b
withdrawn. It might reflect, as in the case of Philebos, the 14B–18D
original obstinacy of the pleasure principle. It might also reflect, as in the case of Protarchos, the principle in Cynic logic
(though this is not articulated here) according to which each
thing should be designated only "by its own name" and not
by any other predicate (Aristotle, *Metaphysics* 1024b 32).
Pleasure, then, is neither good nor bad; pleasure is pleasure.
Socrates had not accepted this proposition, but he had com-

pelled his opponent to acknowledge that there are differences within the seeming unity of this class.

Instead of continuing to explore the central question, or what seems to be the central question, Socrates turns to the logical problem (λόγος) itself that is posed by the difference within unity—a troublesome problem (14c 4). To counteract the dialogically destructive tendencies inherent in the position taken by Protarchos, the discussion rises to a completely new level with Socrates' questioning: Can the one be many and the many be one? And how is this possible? A great distance separates the two problems before us. On the one hand, there is the question as to which has priority, pleasure or knowledge. On the other hand, there is the problem of the one and the many. And the connection between the two problems seems arbitrary in the sense that we might have come upon the second from any other direction just as well. Yet, for this very reason, the connection is not accidental, for the problem of the one and the many is the fundamental problem of philosophical reasoning itself. It is no accident that, in the *Parmenides* (129B), this is one of the first in the series of problems confronting Socrates in his encounter as a young man with the Eleatics.

Protarchos immediately begins to exploit the problem fallaciously. If "the one"—he cites himself as an example: "I, Protarchos"—had opposite predicates, it would be many and would be dissolved in plurality. (What was noted earlier in passing is quite clear here, the generally recognized reference to the logic of the Cynics, i.e., to what Plato considered sophistic logic.[26]) This, however, as Socrates says, is not a genuine problem for us, nor is it a problem how "one thing" can be a plurality of parts or members. We have long since passed beyond these pseudo-problems. In the context of the early dialogues, this controversy would have engaged us in a struggle between eristic and Socratic logic. Now it is hardly hinted at, because altogether different and genuine problems confront us. In brief, we are not concerned with cases of the one and the many that belong to the world of becoming and passing away. We are concerned with conceptual or ideal unity, *oneness*. Now three questions arise:

(*1*) Are these unities, or monads (μονάδες), really to be posited as being?

(*2*) How can we envisage these true unities (or monads), eternal and unchangeable as they are, as parts of the one (or unity) itself? Put differently, how are the separate monads (Forms) at the same time one monad (Form)? Or, in still other words, how are unity and plurality compatible with each other in the realm of pure being?

(*3*) How is the unity of the monad, or Form, compatible with the plurality of things in the world of appearances, since the Form cannot be divided and cannot separate from itself to enter into plurality?[27]

A great and difficult battle, Socrates says (15D), rages over these questions. Where to begin? With a common experience. It is characteristic of the *logoi* (of thought, of speech, of sentences) that they combine the one and the many. Here the combination is obvious because the possibility of any responsible speech is based on it. Thus, this characteristic (πάθος) of sentences is marked by the Homeric attributes, "immortal and never aging," words of high significance. Yet this very significance entails the danger of eristic abuse. Young men, especially, are guilty of such abuse (16AB)—words of warning reminiscent of a similar passage in the *Republic* (VII 539B), and referring here in the *Philebus* to the group for whom Protarchos is spokesman. Viewed in this perspective, it surely is no accident that the same Protarchos turns out to be a pupil of Gorgias later on (58A). Youthful, eristic, and rhetorical, then, is the abuse of this characteristic of speech. The proper use is "dialectical." Again, the possibility of a conflict is suggested here without being carried out dramatically. There is merely a sketch of the opposing forces, and then Socrates, quite undisturbed, goes on developing the "dialectical path" that is the fairest but also the most difficult—easy to show, but very difficult to traverse.

All the arts have been discovered by following this "dialectical path." (We know that this broad concept of "art," *techne*, includes all technical disciplines and sciences.) A mythical introduction, which had a far-reaching effect on later ages,[28] shows that this path leads into the high regions. It is said to be a gift of the gods, a spark of Prometheus, as a message from the ancients who dwelled nearer to the gods than we do. Everything that exists, so the message says, consists of the one and the many, and combines both the limit and the limitless. Plato is not quoting from a Pythagorizing treatise of the Academy or from (or not only from) the book of the Pythagorean Philolaos that he had bought in Italy. What he has in mind is the half-mythical figure "Pythagoras," as is shown by the solemn words used to introduce this doctrine of the union of opposites.[29]

The dialectical path of the Platonic Socrates is based on this antithetical structure in the realm of being. In each case, then, we must posit "one Form" and search for it, since it is "contained therein."[30] Then we must go on to search for plurality, a definite plurality that is encompassed by "the one." The same process is repeated in the case of each of the unities included in this plurality. In this way we cover, step by step, and not by leaps, the progression from the one to definite higher number-Forms —until, at the very end of this series, we do take a leap, as it were, from the limited to the limitless or unlimited (ἄπειρον). The same process in reverse leads from the limitless by way of the higher number-Forms to the one.[31]

This process is illustrated by reference to the system of musical sounds (as in *Republic* VII 530D *et seq.*) and to the system of linguistic sounds (as in the *Cratylus*). Each system consists of a collection of parts, notes or letters, that are numerically determined and are in a necessary relationship of super- and sub-ordination. This systematic bond (δεσμός, 18c 8) is expressed in the name "music" or "grammar," and the fact that there is such a thing as "music" or "grammar" confirms that we are dealing with realities. When Protarchos retreated to his insistence that "pleasure is pleasure," there was a danger that the conversation might collapse, and this danger was present again here and there. At the end of this first section, however, the *logos* is firmly grounded. It is seen as the clearest revelation of the principle recognized by Pythagoras as permeating the universe—the union of the one and the many, the limit and the limitless. Dialectics derives from this principle and rises above it. The realm of eternal Forms comes into view in the "one Form" (16D 1) and in the ordered plurality of Forms. At the same time, we realize that this discussion has a direct, pragmatic significance as well. The sophistic eristics is opposed to dialectics. So it is the task of the philosopher to wage a battle against sophistic eristics, as Plato does from the *Protagoras* on through the dialogues of his late period, the *Sophist* and the *Statesman*.

As *Part I, section 2* begins, the discussion has moved so far from its point of departure that Philebos is justified in asking what is the point of it all. The question is justified, to be sure, but not in the sense Philebos means. For viewed from the perspective of pure pleasure, every attempt at exploring the problem more deeply must make "no sense" because there is "no pleasure" in it. Socrates and Protarchos, however, consider the question a real one. An answer would require that the respective rank of pleasure and of knowledge be determined by inquiring into the nature of each, i.e., by examining the ordered system of pleasures, on the one hand, and the ordered system of knowledge, on the other. This, then, would have to come next, but our expectations are not fully satisfied. Protarchos, to be sure, succeeds in compelling Socrates by a playful threat[32] to continue the conversation—as if this were needed where Socrates is concerned! Yet he also suggests that the question (to him it is a purely practical one: what is the best of all things possessed by man?) might be resolved by a simpler method (19c 2, 20A 6). In yielding to Protarchos Socrates postpones, for the time being, at least, the examination that should come next. Even later it is actually carried through only with respect to the domain of pleasure, not with respect to knowledge. The project of constructing an ordered system of knowledge remains a task pointing far beyond the limits of this dialogue. Here, then, the conversation returns to where it stood near the beginning. Socrates "remembers" a theory he once heard long ago, maybe in a dream.[33] We expect to hear something extraordinary, but

I 2
18D–27c

I 2a
18D–23B

learn only what was hinted at previously (14B)—that the good may be neither pleasure nor knowledge but a third thing different from both.

To be more precise, the good is now defined as that which is perfect and self-sufficient (τέλεον, ἱκανόν). According to this criterion, each of the two ways of life would have to be completely free of any ingredient of the other in order to qualify as the good of the highest order. Considered in its pure form, neither can pass this test. Suppose we take the life of pleasure without any admixture of judgment, without memory of the past (i.e., without memory also of past pleasures), and without expectation of the future (i.e., without expectation also of future pleasures)—as Aristippos restricted pleasure to the mere present or to "momentary time" (μονόχρονον).[34] Such a life of pure pleasure, Socrates concludes, would ultimately be the life of an oyster. But the life of pure knowledge, without any pleasure and, hence, without any pain—in other words, a life of "a-pathy"—such a life would not be desirable either.

In fact, reason, being "reasonable," does not even make the same kind of claim that is made by pleasure (22E 6 et seq.). A life of pure pleasure would be subhuman; a life of pure reason inhuman, or perhaps superhuman. Pleasure requires an intellectual ingredient in order to be human pleasure, even as knowledge requires an ingredient of pleasure and pain in order to be human knowledge. In this way, we discover that the "mixed" life must be the most desirable state, and the contest between pleasure and knowledge is now for second prize. More correctly, the question now asks whether pleasure or knowledge is "more akin to and like" the good (i.e., mixed) life, or, put differently, which of the two is to be considered the "cause" (αἴτιον) making the mixed life the good life. Socrates claims that reason will deserve second prize whereas Protarchos continues to defend the claim of pleasure.

When, at the beginning of the dialogue, the contest of pleasure and knowledge raised the issue hidden behind the simple contrast between unity and plurality, we could not anticipate the ontological heights to which this issue would be carried in the first section. Now, in the second section, Socrates develops the concepts of mixture, the good mixture, and cause of the good mixture, quite naturally in the course of his exposition. The ontological significance soon to be assigned to these concepts cannot be foreseen. Nevertheless, there are a few hints pointing toward a new level. When Protarchos comforts himself at the defeat of his "goddess," Hedone, by reminding Socrates that his "reason" did not win first prize either, Socrates replies mysteriously (22c): "Not *my* reason, to be sure—but there is yet a higher reason, the true and divine reason." Thus, true reason becomes visible, from afar, beyond human reason. The exchange refers expressly and playfully to the earlier passage (12B 10) when a "truer deity" came into sight above the goddess whom Philebos called Aphrodite but should have called Hedone, or Pleasure. The theological leitmotiv is heard again.

The same tension, although between two quite different levels, is present in the second section as it was in the first. The contest for second prize requires new tactics—and with this statement, the discussion again rises to the higher level of ontology. In fact, in saying that we need "new weapons," though some may possibly be the same as before, Socrates explicitly refers to the previous logical and ontological level (i.e., of the first section, I 1b, above) both in method and in content. First, in method: "I am sort of ridiculous," he says ironically (23D), "in first separating things according to Forms, or classes (εἴδη), and then adding them up again." But this was precisely the method sighted there as the dialectical path. And later, after he has distinguished (i.e., "separated") the "four Forms, or kinds" (εἴδη, γένη) of being, he applies the method of separating and combining even more explicitly among them.

Second, in content: here again Socrates refers to what was established earlier. The two basic Forms of the limited (defined) and the unlimited (limitless, or undefined) are taken over. The Form of the mixture, too, was suggested earlier (16c 10). Now, however, it is co-ordinated with the other two on the basis of experience, since (in the second section, dealing with the three ways of life) the mixed life was shown to be more meaningful or valuable than either of the unmixed ways of life (22A). Even the fourth kind of being was anticipated in

I 2b
23B–27c

the search for the cause of the mixture (22D). These are the sources that now yield the system of the "four kinds" of being. It is in these four ways, and no more, that being as such manifests itself. When asked whether he might not need a fifth kind, Socrates brushes the question aside half jokingly (23DE), perhaps in order to give more weight to the fourfold division, and perhaps in order to warn against taking this division as a matter of dogma.[35] At any rate, a "cause of separating" is not to be assumed in addition to the "cause of mixing," since— as is said in the *Timaeus* (32C)—only that which combines can effect separation.

Let us consider the nature of the "four kinds" of being. The *first kind*, the limitless, refers to everything that is designated as indefinite by comparisons such as "more" and "less" or by adverbial expressions such as "very." The *second kind*, the limit, refers to everything that admits of measurement and number. It is briefly put, and this brevity later (25D 5) is criticized as defective from a systematic point of view.[36] The *third kind* refers to the mixture of the first two. This mixture is produced in such a way that it is the task of the limit to create out of the conflict of opposites in the limitless, by means of numbers, something that is sym-metrical and sym-phonic. Mixture, then, is just the opposite of an aggregate, which, according to Plato, would belong instead to the first kind. Mixture means "right communion" (ὀρθὴ κοινωνία), the mastering of excess and conflict by law and order. Thus, "coming-into-being as a result of limit and measure" (γένεσις εἰς οὐσίαν ἐκ τῶν μετὰ τοῦ πέρατος ἀπειργασμένων μέτρων, 26D) is the most general formula for the plurality of things that fall into this third category. The world of becoming belongs here—and not any arbitrary or aimless kind of becoming, but only the genuine kind that aims at being, since it is determined by limit and measure.[37]

If we were to translate the ontological language of this dialogue into the "physical-mythical" language of the *Timaeus*, we would have to say that the first kind corresponds to the "receptacle of all becoming" (usually called "space" by modern interpreters though Plato uses this term only once and at that among several others). The second kind would corre-

spond to the Forms. The third kind would include everything
in the cosmos that is meaningful, i.e., good and intelligible.
Now we also may understand why Socrates is critical of his
treatment of the second kind. "We should have combined the
members of the class of the limit, but we did not," he exclaims
(25D 6–7). If one were to make clear the nature of limit, not
by means of a few examples, but systematically—i.e., in a system of division and combination—one would have to undertake
something like the construction of a system of Forms. This is
hinted at as a task as yet unrealized and perhaps unrealizable.

Finally, the *fourth kind*—cause (αἰτία). What has been missing
up to now is the causal agent (αἴτιον), the element that makes
things (ποιοῦν) and, therefore, leads (ἡγούμενον), the agent
that "fashions" all things (δημιουργόν).[38] The last word reminds us of the mythical "demiurge" in the *Timaeus*. Again,
we see how the ontological schema of the *Philebus* comes to life
in the physicalistic and mythical images of the *Timaeus*. Yet,
we need not go outside of the *Philebus* itself to find this spirit
of life. As we surveyed the products of mixture (25E *et seq.*),
we came upon health, beauty, and strength in the context of
the body, upon music in the field of sounds, upon the sequence
of the seasons in nature, and upon the mastering of excess
(ὕβρις) and evil through law and order in the realm of the soul.
And now, "fair Philebos," says Socrates, it is the "goddess
herself" who establishes order (26B). We must look back, especially since Philebos suddenly is addressed again, to the earlier
playful banter (12c)—to be resumed later (28B)—on the nature
of the "goddess" and her true name.[39] If we wish to give
the right name to this foundress of all order, we should call her
Aphrodite, not in the sense of Philebos who equated her with
his Hedone, but in the sense of Socrates.

Let us also look back to the *Symposium* where Eryximachos,
the physician, develops the view that health in the body, rhythm
and harmony in music, and the orderly sequence of the seasons
are produced by the right combination of opposites. These are
the same examples as here (except that the physician does not
mention the order of the soul), and as it is Aphrodite in the
Philebus, so it is Eros in the *Symposium* to whom we are in-

debted for the right mixture. In the *Philebus*, however, the union of opposites has a more profound significance since it refers to the mastering of excess through form and measure, i.e., beauty and perfection. Hence, the playful address, "fair Philebos," and hence, Aphrodite. Now we realize why we did not have to call upon the *Timaeus* in order to see the divine order of the *Philebus'* fourth kind in live form. It is recognizable from the hints to be found in the dialogue itself. What ontologically is called the "cause" of the right and beautiful mixture is called the "goddess" in the language of myth and theology.[40]

I 3

27c–31b   In *Part I, section 3*, the discussion for the third time returns to the level beyond which it has twice risen. We are ready now to enter the contest for second prize. No matter how far or how high ontology may carry us, it starts from the most basic questions of human life and returns to the basic question of Plato's "pragmatism": How to live? The four kinds of being are now used to answer this question.

The life that proved to be the most desirable, a "mixture" of knowledge and pleasure, belongs to the third kind of being. It is the conquest of the limitless by limit. Pleasure—the pleasure of the pure pleasure seeker—by its very nature is opposed to any limit. At this point Philebos joins the conversation and for a good reason. He speaks up in order to protest against limiting pleasure and in order to defend it as the good, the only good, precisely because it is unlimited in quantity and degree. The hostile position is by no means overthrown; in fact, on its own grounds it is irrefutable. A brief and sharp exchange ensues. Socrates shows—though Philebos does not see it—that being limitless applies to pain as well, and that it is this very characteristic which makes pain the greatest evil. This, in turn, shows that being limitless does *not* give pleasure a share of the good (μέρος ἀγαθοῦ), as Socrates is willing to concede while repudiating the claim that pleasure is *the* good. Although it remains an open question why some pleasures in contrast to others belong to the good, both pleasure and pain, for the time being, fall into the category of the "limitless."[41]

Where, then, does reason belong? The question is raised in a solemn spirit. It is a "dangerous" question, and we would be committing an act of "impiety" if we were to give a wrong answer. Impiety and danger . . . Does Plato, after so many years have passed, mean to evoke for a moment the indictment of Socrates, so that we may sense the human decision at stake behind this seemingly abstract discussion? Philebos also renews the half-playful and half-serious banter concerning the right name of the goddess (12b, 28c). But then Socrates cites the consensus of "all the wise" that "reason is king of heaven and earth." There follows a more concrete explication, distinguishing between those who believe that the universe is controlled by chance and those who believe that it is governed by reason or intelligence.

Plato had tackled this question once before in the pseudo-biography of Socrates' philosophical development in the *Phaedo* (96a *et seq.*). As described there, the first period of his development is occupied with mechanistic principles of explanation, and the second period with the principle of "mind," or reason, which is attributed solely to the work of Anaxagoras. Yet Socrates is dissatisfied with the limits of this particular principle of mind and hopes to find a teacher who will show him that intelligence is really the cause of the universe. The conflict between these two principles of explanation is carried through now in the *Philebus*. The view previously proposed (but defectively so and only by Anaxagoras) now becomes the view on which "all the wise" agree.[42] Hence, it is incumbent on us to join the conflict on the side of reason as opposed to the principle of a chance mechanism. And so the conversation for the third time recedes from the material in the foreground to lift itself up to the level of a mythical physics and metaphysics whose connection with the matters of immediate concern is only gradually revealed.

The same four elements of which the human body is composed are present also in the universe, only on an incomparably larger scale with respect to extension, power, and unity, as is best shown in the case of "fire." Every element in the human body is produced, sustained, and ruled[43] by the corresponding element in the universe, not vice versa. The union of the elements in us we call "body." Correspondingly, the universe is a body, too, of the same composition of elements that produce, sustain, and rule the human body. This alone accounts for the high degree of order that is denied by the spokesmen of blind chance. Now since the human body, in addition to the physical elements contains also a soul, or life, that is the highest principle in man, it is clear that the body of the universe, too, must be endowed with soul and life, and that this soul of the universe must be more perfect and beautiful than that of man (30A).

If we return now to the four kinds of being in order to clarify the nature of this mixture, of its components, and especially of mind, what we clearly see, both in man and in the universe, is this. "Wisdom and reason" is the cause (*fourth kind*), the living, ordering, and healing principle, that combines the limitless (*first kind*) and the limit (*second kind*) into an ordered unity (*third kind*). Different stages within the domain of wisdom and reason are suggested, with the highest stage represented by the names of the gods. Zeus means royal reason, and the rank of the other gods corresponds to their right name. Again, we are reminded not only of the host of gods in the *Phaedrus* (246E *et seq.*, 253B), but of the controversy over the true Aphrodite in this dialogue itself. Aphrodite might have been mentioned here beside Zeus as the prototype of "wisdom and reason" that is the "cause" of all beauty and order.

The problem is solved. As pleasure has found its place in the domain of the limitless, so reason is settled in the domain of cause. And although it is not explicitly said, we realize that, since reason is the cause that masters the limitless by means of the limit and produces the best possible mixture, it has a secure place ruling above pleasure. To see this we have had to move into the realm of a mythical physics and metaphysics far transcending the dimensions of human life. Yet we may remember that this transcendence seemed to be hinted at earlier: first, at the very beginning when we heard of "all such beings who are capable of participating in knowledge" (11B 9 *et seq.*), and again when Philebos addressed the "goddess" and Socrates asked for her true name—or her nature (12BC). Then Aphrodite was elevated above pleasure; now it is reason that rules all things (30D 8). Thus, in co-ordinating the structure of man with the structure of the universe, we gain insight into both of them and see more clearly what action is called for corresponding to this insight. We must not overlook this "pragmatic" aspect, particularly since suddenly, in the midst of the seemingly abstract discussion, the arts of gymnastics and medicine are mentioned as products of "reason" (30B 2–3).

Before we turn to the second part of the dialogue, let us briefly summarize Part I in its three sections. In the first section, reason is conceived of as that which combines the limit and the limitless. The second section deals with the four kinds of being and inquires into their relation to each other. In the third section, reason is settled in the domain of cause and is recognized, therefore, as the power that rules the universe and human life. Did Plato, then, really begin with the rather simple question as to the respective ranking of pleasure and knowledge in the good life so that later he could rise far above this question in an ironic shift of balance?[44]

As *Part II, section 1* begins, we are still far from the end of the winding path. Has not Socrates insisted, from the very beginning, that there are good and bad pleasures, noble and vulgar pleasures, in order to combat the opposing view that pleasure is always the same? Yet now he himself has classified —and thereby devalued—pleasure as a whole with his system of kinds of being. Must we not say, then, that this classification, important as it may be, is only a preliminary step? For we remember something else—that just when Socrates repudiated the view advanced by Philebos that unlimited pleasure is the good as such (28A), he suggested that we must find something other than the limitless in order to give pleasure a share of the good (μέρος τοῦ ἀγαθοῦ). Such a share, then, is its due. How can we reconcile this view with the inclusion of pleasure as a whole in the class of the limitless, a class that acquires value only through "mixture" with "limit"? At the beginning of the first part of the dialogue, the emphasis was on the differences among pleasures or kinds of pleasures. These differences then were intentionally disregarded in order for us to grasp the unitary nature of pleasure. Now the theme of differences, which has been waiting on the sidelines, as it were, since the first exchange

II 1

31B–55C

between Socrates and Protarchos, becomes a central problem.
We are told explicitly that there is to be a change in direction. With regard to each of the two objects of our investigation, pleasure and knowledge, we now must see where (ἐν ᾧ) they are to be found and under what conditions (πάθος) they come about. It is expressly said (31B 5) that we cannot examine pleasure without examining pain. Earlier (27E 5), we recall, Socrates (in contrast to Philebos) spontaneously put pleasure and pain side by side, a parallelism that is of great significance for the entire investigation to follow.[45] Thus, the different varieties of pleasure and knowledge are to be examined after the essential nature of each has been established. This is to be done first with respect to pleasure, so that consideration of the varieties of knowledge remains in abeyance until later (55C et seq.).

The initial question, soon to be repeated (32D), guides the inquiry into pleasure. Must everything that is called pleasure be affirmed as good, or are pleasures and pains sometimes good and sometimes bad? In other words, since the unity of pleasure has long since been discarded, the task now is to show the differences among pleasures and their respective order.

To begin with, there is a theory of pleasure and pain, both physiological and psychological, to which we are referred constantly in what follows. Yet, while new problems are taken up and examined in this second part of the dialogue, the basic orientation remains the same as in the first part and the question itself of where (ἐν ᾧ, 31B) pleasure and pain are to be found is taken over directly from Part I. But while pleasure as conceived of by Philebos, and pain too, were assigned to the class of the limitless and thus abandoned, as it were, pleasure and pain are now included in the domain of "mixture." This mixture, however, quite in contrast to the class of the limitless, should not be thought of as a chaos devoid of order. Therefore, it is described now, as it was earlier (25E), in terms of such visible characteristics as health and harmony, structure, or balance. Looking back to the controversy over the name of the goddess, we may recall that Harmonia was the "daughter of golden Aphrodite," as Plato and his readers would have known from Hesiod's *Theogony*.[46]

The simplest cases of thirst, hunger, and frost are cited to show that pain is due to a disturbance of harmony, or equilibrium, in the organism, and that pleasure is due to the restoration of this harmony. In contrast to these affects derived from organic processes, there is another pleasure, arising solely from expectation (προσδόκημα) of the future. This resides in the soul only, and not the body. The difference between these states of the body and of the soul is that in the bodily states pleasure and pain are necessarily conjoined whereas in the soul each may occur pure (εἰλικρινής) and unmixed (ἄμεικτος). Right here, then, we find an order among pleasures, in that there are physical and mental pleasures, or mixed and pure. All this still is quite tentative, or, as Socrates points out explicitly, this is a brief and rapid statement of an important subject (31D 9). Soon the analysis will be expanded and refined.

For the time being, however, the discussion branches off again.[47] The physiological basis is broadened beyond the field of pleasure and pain. If pain reflects the disturbance of a state of equilibrium, and pleasure its restoration, then there must be a state beyond disturbance and restoration, a neutral condition in between pleasure and pain. To this state belongs the life of mind or reason, as we saw earlier in the basic comparison of the two ways of life (21D). It is the divine life—a life to which it would be inappropriate to attribute such states as disturbance and restoration, pain and pleasure. Following this statement, the topic is dropped with one further remark that we may come back to this if it should be relevant to the discussion (πρὸς λόγον). And indeed, later on (44C *et seq.*) the discussion will make use of this point when it is a question again—as it is in the treatment of pleasure in the *Republic*[48]—of defining the positive characteristics of pleasure in contrast to the neutral in-between state. The physiology here prepares the ground for the later struggle. It also does something more.

From the intentionally low level of physiology, there is a rise upward to a view in which the life of the pure spirit, the divine

32D–33c

life beyond pleasure and pain, in a state of sublime *ataraxia*, is visible for a moment.[49] Preceding and immediately following this moment, pleasure is the topic of discussion. Yet, at the right time, we are reminded that there still is such a thing as spirit opposed to pleasure—and not only opposed. At the moment when we first are shown that there is an order among pleasures, the divine spirit is revealed as rising above pleasure, even in its highest aspects. Thus, the departure from pleasure is most significant for a decision, or "judgment" (κρίσις, 33A 4), on the subject of pleasure. This must be kept in mind in what follows as the conversation, in repeated thrusts, turns to the project of constructing an ordered system in the domain of pleasure.

33c–34c   Returning to the subject of pleasure, the discussion focuses on "memory" (μνήμη) and "recollection" (ἀνάμνησις). To be exact, memory had come into view before (32c) when we heard about expectation, for it seems that it is not possible to expect without remembering. From a physiological-psychological point of view, there are some experiences (παθήματα) that affect only the body, others that penetrate through the body into the soul, and still others that affect only the soul. The first state may be called "insensitivity" or "unconsciousness" (ἀναισθησία) as far as the mind is concerned. The second state referring to processes which body and soul have in common may be called "sensation" or "consciousness" (αἴσθησις). In the third state, something that was previously experienced is lifted by the soul out of forgetfulness, or out of the unconscious, into memory by means of recollection.[50] Thus, strictly speaking, there are no purely physical sensations of pleasure. In short, all pleasure is at least also pleasure of the soul.[51]

This does not mean that the degrees within pleasure are abolished. A more careful analysis shows merely that there is a connection between higher pleasures, on the one hand, and such essentially mental acts as memory through recollection, on the other. (May we go further without succumbing to excessive subtlety? For we would suggest that while Plato here is keeping to a level that is comprehensible to Protarchos and his companions—or to the young students in his own

Academy—still, on his own part, he could not touch on the problem of "memory" and "recollection" without thinking, and without reminding at least some of his readers, of the metapsychology and metaphysics developed in the *Meno* and the *Phaedo*.[52]) As we just have heard about "expecting" the future and now learn about "remembering" the past, we may well ask whether it is possible to expect without remembering.

After considering the significance of memory and recollection for the problem of pleasure, the discussion breaks off again. "Desire" (καὶ ἅμα ἐπιθυμίαν, 34c 7) is suddenly introduced along with "pleasure" as a phenomenon that also may be clarified by reference to "memory." The examination of the broad field of pleasure is postponed. Instead, the inquiry now concentrates upon the nature of desire and its origin (τί ποτ' ἔστιν καὶ ποῦ γίγνεται). In following this inquiry, we must not lose sight of two things. First we must ask, Why this digression (or what seems to be another digression)? Second, we must watch for the resumption of the discussion of pleasure that is here dropped.

34c–35d

The analysis of desire leads to the following phenomenon. Being thirsty aims at something. It is desire for drink, as Protarchos says. Or, as Socrates puts it more precisely, it aims at replenishing by drink what is empty. Desire, then, has as its object something that is opposite to the physical state of the body. *I desire this something*—namely, drink. Yet, desire cannot aim at this opposite through sensation, which obviously is directed toward what is present; it can apprehend it only by means of memory directed toward what is absent. Thus, desire is not a physical affect. It is, instead, a part of the soul, and so is indissolubly linked with memory, whose significance as a basic function of the soul has just been made clear (33c *et seq.*).[53] In this way, the soul also establishes its position as the ruling power in the organism as a whole.

This section on desire—a phenomenon closely related to pleasure and pain, though not identical with them—points both backward and forward in peculiarly associative links.[54] It points backward by virtue of the function of memory, and forward, as we shall see, by virtue of the fact that the conversation turns here for the first time to the "mixture" of pleasure and pain that is to become increasingly significant in what follows.[55] This section on desire also has its own unified structure and meaning, which we may recognize from its direction and goal. Desire, as we know, ranks low on a comparative scale. In the *Phaedrus*, desire is the worse steed, and in the *Republic*, the appetitive soul ranks lowest. Yet, even so lowly a phenomenon as thirst is not simply emptiness, as it appeared before in a superficial perspective (31 E 6 *et seq.*).[56] There hunger and thirst referred to a state of dis-equilibrium and, connected with it, dis-pleasure in the body. Now we see that thirst is a phenomenon of the soul connected with something as high as memory.

Thus, the analysis of desire leads to the same conclusion as the previous analysis of pleasure did. The body by itself is not even capable of desire; it needs a soul even for desiring, and so high a function of the soul as memory. All this is aimed at establishing the soul as the ruling element in the organism as a whole (ἀρχὴ τοῦ ζῴου παντός). The second half of the dialogue, as we said, is concerned with the ordering of pleasures. To discover degrees of order among pleasures, it seems one first must recognize that there is a system of order and rank in the human organism as a whole. Self-discipline is the concept generally employed by Plato to refer to such a system (*Republic* IV 430E; *Laws* I 626E). Here the analysis of desire, so important in the context of the whole dialogue, serves the same purpose. An exercise in descriptive and analytic psychology leads us precisely to the same point we already had reached in the context of a mythical physics and metaphysics of the cosmos.

The structural function of this section on desire was to direct us to the mixture of pleasures and pains as they are variously encountered in life. The problem of mixture, however, will be the topic of a serious psychological analysis much later on (46B). For the time being, it remains in the background—though reappearing now and then—and serves as a transition to another question: Can we apply the predicates "true" (ἀληθής) and "false" (ψευδής) to various pleasures and pains? Or, are pleasures and pains true and false like "opinions"?

35D–40E

Over this question, a battle ensues, waged by Protarchos
with exceptional stubbornness until he admits that he is representing a view that he heard elsewhere (ἅπερ ἀκούω λέγω,
38A 5)—a specific pleasure theory, undoubtedly that of
Aristippos.[57] We are reminded of the resistance Protarchos put
up at the beginning of the dialogue, and rightly reminded, for it
is essentially the same resistance. Protarchos insists that pleasure is always pleasure, in waking, or dreaming, or in a deranged
state of mind (36E), and that it is only "opinion conjoined with
pleasure" that can be called true or false (37E). According to
this view, pleasure would be autonomous and devoid of differences, whereas Socrates is concerned with working out the
marked contrasts within pleasure itself, as well as with placing
pleasure under a law beyond itself.

Socrates tries to show that even as "opinion," though remaining the same qua opinion, still may be right or wrong, so
pleasures and pains, too, may be of different qualities: they may
be great or small, and they may be wrong or right. Protarchos
admits this, and so by implication admits that all these differences are part of the common conception of pleasure and pain.
(Let us add that as a result of this admission, especially the
admission that there is "bad" or wrong pleasure, a powerful
blow already has been struck against the unity of pleasure, and
a standard beyond it is won.) Thus, Protarchos' attitude (of
excluding the predicates "true" and "false" from pleasures, and
attributing them only to the "opinions" accompanying pleasures—37E) reveals itself as unjustifiably rigid and also as an
artificial construction, though it is still widely held today.[58]

Even so, Protarchos must concede that it makes a difference
whether pleasure is associated "with right opinion and knowledge" or associated "with false opinion and nonsense."[59]
Socrates is concerned with rescuing "sense" in the realm of
pleasure, and so the inquiry moves on to examine falsehood as
it was examined in the *Theaetetus* in connection with the simile
of the mass of wax. Similarly, the soul is compared here in the
Philebus to a book, and its activities to those of a writer and a
painter who jointly produce an illustrated volume. Memory and
perception combine to write sentences, or thoughts (λόγους),

true or false, into the book of the soul and to paint pictures
(i.e., concrete, not conceptual objects), which also can be true
or false.[60]

Thus, we see that error is possible: first, when perception
and memory meet, and next, when the product is transcribed
into the book. This schema is enlarged by explicitly adding the
dimension of time. That is, all this refers not only to the past
(memory) and the present (perception), but to the future
quite as much. Pains and pleasures referring to the future are
expectations, or hopes, and here (39D) we are directed back to
what was said previously (32C). These expectations are
pleasures and pains that belong only to the soul, in contrast to
those that belong to both body and soul and refer to past and
present.

The possibility of error—a problem that lies outside the
scope of the *Philebus*—need not be explicated here as it was in
the *Theaetetus* and the *Sophist*. It is enough to say that, while
opinion is always opinion, this opinion may aim at something
that was not, or is not, or will not be. In these cases we have
false opinion. Applying the same principle to pleasure and pain,
we may say that while pleasure is always pleasure, and pain
always pain, each of them may aim at something that was not, or
is not, or—as happens most frequently, in the case of expectations—will not be. The same applies to fear (φόβος), driving
spirit (θυμός), and similar affects. They all may be false—or
true, as is understood though not expressly stated.

We have passed by two strange offshoots in this section on
true and false pleasures. What is inscribed in the book of the
soul concerns things past and present. In addition, there are
hopes and fears concerning the future, and these are only in the
soul. As this becomes clear, Socrates—suddenly, unexpectedly,
and quite emphatically—injects a moral note by describing the
difference between two types of men (39E–40A): on the one
hand, the man who is just, pious, and in every way good, and
on the other, the man who is the opposite, unjust and altogether bad. Moreover, Socrates calls the first type of man "dear
to the gods," and the second type, the opposite. Then we go on

as if we had not witnessed this breakthrough into the moral and religious dimension.

The second offshoot appears just as suddenly. In referring to 40E–41A the difference between bad and good opinions, Socrates explains that this difference corresponds to the difference between false (deceptive) and right opinions. Are we to take this distinction in a moral sense or in a logical sense? Socrates, we cannot doubt, has both in mind, both at the same time. As he is about to apply this distinction to pleasures and pains, however, Protarchos protests vigorously and cannot be swayed from his own position. Bad pleasures, he claims, are bad not because they are false, but for some different reason. Hereupon Socrates pretends to be satisfied. He continues with the discussion of "false" pleasures, while the examination of "bad" pleasures is postponed until later, "if we should then still feel inclined to talk about them." This promise is partly redeemed later on (45A *et seq.*).

But why this departure here from the direct path? It must serve an immediate purpose, and indeed does so. For the analysis deals with the question of "false" pleasures, a question as difficult as it is unfamiliar. While everybody is acquainted with the concept of bad pleasures, it is not customary to call pleasures "false." The intention, therefore, is to contrast this unusual procedure with what is customary, but, again, for what purpose? If we read this digression alongside the earlier one, it becomes clear that Socrates is concerned with establishing a much more radical point—the ultimate convergence of the true and the good, and of the false and the bad. The "virtues," as a matter of course, belong to the realm of the true, and their opposites belong to the false. And as the realm of the true is "loved by the gods," so is the other realm (we may confidently add) "hated by the gods."

We hardly can fail to see re-emerging several lines we have been following: the playful exchange over the right name of the goddess at the beginning of the dialogue (12BC), the One-Good (15A, 20D), divine reason (22C), and later, in the more systematic presentation of the "four kinds" of being, the characterization of the fourth kind as the creative, causal, and effective power in the world (27B), and, finally, the agreement of all wise men that reason rules heaven and earth (28c). These are the great lines, ontological, cosmological, metaphysical, and religious, that are pursued here, high above the simple, boyish question about pleasure and knowledge posed at the beginning of the *Philebus*.

41A–42c   Protarchos still doubts that there are any false pleasures, and so the contest—as Socrates says jokingly—must go into the next round. Two positions are taken over from the previous discussion. In the first place, the analysis of desire had shown (34c *et seq.*) that purely physical states of pleasure and pain may penetrate into the mind, or consciousness, whereas the soul by itself simultaneously "desires" a state in accordance with its own and remote from physical states. In the second place, it was shown much earlier, in Part I of the conversation (27E), that pleasure and pain admit of "more" and "less" and, therefore, belong to the class of the limitless. Just as in the field of vision distance deceives us about the true size of objects, so—or even more so—must distance deceive us in our comparative judgment about the magnitude of pleasures and pains existing side by side. A new source of error, then, is uncovered. Whereas earlier (37A) the predicates "true" and "false" were attributed to pleasures and pains by analogy with right and wrong "opinions," now it is the feelings themselves that may be deceptive, owing to their distance or to their comparative strength side by side. Thus, while before these predicates could be applied to the accompanying "opinions," they now are to be applied, irrefutably, to the feelings themselves.

42c–43D   With a new move forward (τούτων ἑξῆς), we turn to another phenomenon to see still more clearly what is meant by "true" and "false" as applied to affects. Socrates returns to the earlier physiological discussion (31D *et seq.*). Pain results when there is a disturbance in the equilibrium of an organism; pleasure, when the equilibrium is restored. In between there is a neutral state in which neither pleasure nor pain is experienced. We may leave aside the view of the "Herakleiteans," who would insist that such states of rest do not occur. We are not concerned with these states themselves, however, but are concerned with their conscious perceptions. And from this point of view, it is clear that small changes in the organism are not perceived at all. It is only major changes that cause conscious feelings of pleasure and pain. Thus, three kinds of life come into view: the pleasant, the painful, and that which is neither one nor the other.

This schema is not elaborated on immediately. Instead it is 43D–44D defended—and here the conversation again branches off a little —against a theory of natural philosophy that is clearly stated but left indefinite as to its supporters. According to the people holding this theory, there are not three but only two kinds of life. That is, there is no positive pleasure, since "pleasure" refers to the neutral state—the absence of pain. These people are enemies of Philebos, i.e., enemies of pure hedonism. Their theory contradicts the insight just gained in the conversation. But the purpose in mentioning these thinkers is not simply to clarify the Socratic insight by contrast. In a sense, they are our allies, as Socrates says, for they know something intuitively. A certain "dourness" (δυσχέρεια) of character has made them hate the "power of pleasure." Evidently they have studied pleasure where it is strongest, or most extreme, and we must follow them along these lines.[61]

Let us look ahead. In an extended discussion, the analysis will deal first with "mixed" pleasures and then with "pure" pleasures. Only the latter are "true" pleasures, for to be true means to be essentially and completely that which is designated by the name. Hence, strictly speaking, a pleasure mixed with pain does not deserve to be called "pleasure" at all. Now evidently these thinkers (still anonymous) in studying the most extreme kinds of pleasure have found them to be impure. In this respect—we shall presently see—they are right, as against Philebos. But in refusing to admit that there are any positive pleasures at all, they have exaggerated, so that in this respect Socrates takes the opposite view.[62] Thus, this strange minor digression serves the purpose of anticipating the structure of the two long sections on pleasure that follow in the dialogue. It is no accident that Socrates once more takes issue with this rigoristic point of view (51A) after he has dealt with mixed pleasures and makes the transition to pure pleasures.

44D–50E   The analysis of mixed pleasures starts with cases of pleasure that are strongest or most extreme. In these cases—so it seems to Protarchos, representing the ordinary naïve view of things— we see the nature of pleasure most easily. It then is shown that pleasures are stronger in a sick person, say, who is feverish, than in the healthy. In other words, the strength of pleasure depends upon the strength of the antecedent desire. Pleasures are also stronger in the life of the irrational and intemperate person than in the life of the temperate man who avoids every kind of extreme. Thus, the strength of pleasure and pain is a function of a "bad" or defective state in body and soul. This conclusion immediately deprives the strongest pleasures of any claim to priority. Nevertheless, the main theme of the dialogue is not the question of good and bad, though this remains in the background and was alluded to earlier (40E et seq.), but the question of true and false. For this reason, another character- istic aspect of these extreme cases of pleasure is singled out. An example is the case of a skin itch, when the person scratching himself does not experience pure pleasure, but rather experi- ences a mixture of pleasure and pain. The problem of mixed feel- ings, already encountered here (35BC), now becomes the topic of discussion.

Three possible mixtures are distinguished in a strict division. These are (1) the mixture of physical pleasures and pains, (2) the mixture of pleasures and pains in the soul, and (3) the mixture of physical pleasures and pains with those in the soul. As far as the first mixture is concerned, it is possible that pain outweighs pleasure (as in the case of the skin itch) or that pleasure outweighs pain (as in the case of the sexual act). The third mixture was analyzed earlier in connection with the phenomenon of desire (34C et seq.). Thus, there remains the second mixture, which we find in life but above all in art. There follows a long section (48A–50B) on what nowadays might be termed the psychology of art. This section is justified on the grounds that because the subject matter is quite obscure, the analysis might make it easier for us to find our way in still more complicated cases. Yet we may surmise that in making these comments on tragedy and comedy, Plato, a dramatist himself, is also thinking of his own work, which transcends both categories. And it is certain—because he says so himself—that he is looking beyond the poetic categories at the "whole tragicomedy of life" (50B).

Life itself, then, is a mixture of pleasure and pain—"however much one may strive in the opposite direction" (50B 6), as Philebos does. Again let us note, in particular, the precision employed in making distinctions. Ignorance and ineptitude[63] are shown in three areas (τριχῇ τέμνειν, 48D 4), known to us in advance from the *Alcibiades Major*. These areas are possessions, body, and soul. The ignorant, in turn, fall into two classes (διαιρετέον δίχα, 49A 7): they are either strong or weak. Accordingly, their ignorance is either harmful and hateful, or ridiculous and funny. Then the analysis shows that we laugh at harmless defects, i.e., we experience pleasure, yet the laughter also expresses malice (φθόνος), which is a source of pain. In order to discover what Schiller called the "reason why tragic subjects are pleasing" or, in Plato's language, to analyze the mixture of feelings experienced in witnessing tragedy, we would have to start off from the ignorance, or blindness, of the powerful man who is harmful and hateful. But this analysis is not carried through, nor are other mixed feelings analyzed.

Instead, the discussion will turn to the unmixed pleasures. Looking back, however, we may say that even in the class of mixed experiences, the various cases cited are not to be put on the same level. There is a great difference between the mixed pleasure derived from scratching an itch and the feelings aroused by a stage play and, finally, the feelings aroused either by observing the tragicomedy of life from a distance or by actively participating in this play. It is an ascent from the level of physiology to the aesthetic level and thence to the realm of human existence.

From the mixed pleasures we turn to the pure—again in a 50E–52B physiological context. Whenever the want is imperceptible and painless but its fulfillment perceptible and pleasant, we have pure pleasure as, for example, in the case of simple geometrical figures, clear colors, pure musical notes, beautiful odors. What these have in common, and what distinguishes a circle and a sphere from an organism or distinguishes a single note from a melody is this: the circle, or sphere, or note is beautiful not in relation to something else (πρὸς ἕτερον),[64] but in its very nature (αὐτὰς καθ' αὐτάς). This expression shows how close we are to what Plato otherwise calls *Eidos* (Form, or *Idea*). Even in this class of pure pleasures there are differences in rank. Odors are "less divine," apparently because they are not as sharply "limited" as the other experiences. Yet, the pleasures of knowledge (τὰς περὶ τὰ μαθήματα ἡδονάς, 51E) are added to the list—and this addition must mean that this series, too, is envisaged in ascending stages. The pleasures of knowledge also are devoid of pain. What may appear to be pain—either before from lack of knowledge or afterwards from forgetting—is not an immediate experience (οὐ φύσει) but one derived from reflection, and hence it does not count. The pleasures of knowledge belong to the very few only (τῶν σφόδρα ὀλίγων). This alone shows that they represent the extreme in this series, especially as we look back to the beginning of the dialogue (11B) where pleasure stakes out its claim to be good for "everything that is alive."

Three brief passages now deal with the conclusions to be drawn from this analysis of pleasures. In the manner of Plato's late style, these simply follow each other successively,[65] and it is up to us to discover their connection.

52c–53c   (1) Pure and impure pleasures are separated from each other. The impure (albeit strong) pleasures belong—in terms of the "four kinds" of being distinguished earlier (I 2b)—to the class of the limitless; the pure pleasures exhibit measure (ἐμμετρία).[66] This classification in terms of the kinds of being shows all the more clearly what differences, or distinctions of value, are to be found in the allegedly uniform realm of pleasure. The "truth" of pleasure was under discussion. In the end an illustration settles this question. Even as a small quantity of pure white is whiter, fairer, truer than a large quantity of mixed white, so a small quantity of pure pleasure is pleasanter, fairer, and truer than a large quantity of pleasure mixed with pain. (Let us not fail to hear the moral imperative implicit in this.)

(2) There are certain "subtle thinkers" who maintain that 53c–55a pleasure is always a becoming, and hence has no being. Is this consequence still to be attributed to those "subtle thinkers" or is it Platonic? And who are these thinkers—the Cyrenaics, the Megarians, some others? While we would like to know the answers to these questions, we cannot say anything for sure.[67] Nor does this matter as far as the *Philebus* itself is concerned. Plato evidently uses a theory current in contemporary thought because it provides an opportunity to raise his own discussion to an entirely new level. (In *Nicomachean Ethics* 1152^b 12 *et seq.*, 1153^a 15 *et seq.*, Aristotle uses the same theory in order to clarify the meaning of his own concept of "energy" in contrast to what ordinarily is called "becoming.") In any case, Plato constructs here a number of opposites:

that which is in itself—that which wants something else
that for the sake of which—that for the sake of another
the goal, or that which is intended—that which is aiming and intending
the good and the perfect—becoming and passing away.

In this schema of opposites, being belongs to the "in itself," while becoming belongs to want or desire. Hence, only being is good, not pleasure. As far as the choice of life is concerned, this means that, as among the three kinds of life previously distinguished, one must choose the third kind—a life that is neither pleasure nor pain, but is thought, or pure thought to the extent that this is humanly possible.

The line of reasoning in this second passage, in which pleasure is again envisaged (or seems to be envisaged) as a unity, has a different aim from the first. It is meant to show—by means of being, the goal, the beloved, and the good—the direction in which we shall move in the "progress of the conversation" (53e 9). Here it remains to inquire into the connection between this second discussion and the passage immediately before it in the dialogue. There, degrees of purity within the class of pleasures were expressly distinguished, whereas here this class is treated again as a unity. Yet, obviously, we are not returning to the conflict that was fought out earlier between Socrates and Philebos-Protarchos and long since has been overcome. Instead, we are dealing with two different aspects of the same phenomenon. Pleasure is a unity stamped with the seal of becoming and thus of imperfection as compared with the good and the perfect. Yet, this does not prevent us from recognizing that within the realm of pleasure there are levels of value, stages upward to the realm of being. And if pleasure is now called "becoming" (γένεσις), and each becoming is becoming for the sake of being, and becoming as a whole becomes for the sake of being as a whole, we may recall that, in the ontological part of the dialogue (26D), the realm of the mixture was distinctly labeled as a "coming-into-being" (γένεσις εἰς οὐσίαν). There is no better name for the highest kinds of pleasure.

55A–55C   (3) The third passage again deals explicitly with differences in the realm of pleasure. Since good pleasures are those of the soul only, pleasure itself directs us to the soul. Now, as far as the soul is concerned, we cannot possibly fail to see that, in addition to pleasures, it contains other things as well, namely, virtues and knowledge. The same point may be stated more sharply. For if the highest kinds of pleasure are those accompanying the process of learning (μαθημάτων ἡδονή), this process itself must be something that is still higher. Pleasure itself, therefore, when followed step by step to its highest kinds, leads us to the threshold of the realm of knowledge.

These are the three brief discussions that follow in simple succession upon the analysis of the different kinds of pleasure. All three pursue a common goal, as was to be expected. The first discussion separates out of the many pleasures those that are beautiful, pure, and true, and in doing so, points to beauty, purity, and truth as modes of being. The second discussion recognizes that pleasure itself is a graded progression of coming-into-being, and in doing so, points to the realm of being beyond becoming. The third discussion, finally, points from the pleasures of learning and knowledge to the realm of knowledge itself. Being and the knowledge of being emerge from the analysis of pleasure and will guide the discussion to follow.

II 2   In *Part II, section 2*, an investigation of "reason and knowl-
55C–59E   edge" is undertaken. It is much more brief than the analysis of

pleasure. Why? Is this only because the problem of knowledge occupies so large a place in the total body of Plato's works? Or rather is it not the case that—in a strangely ironic twist—the inquiry into pleasure itself was an exemplar of "inquiring," i.e., of knowledge? Did not the dialogue begin with the concept of "the good"? Did it not contain a great amount of both logic and ontology? The method of division, the four kinds of being, the question of classifying pleasure and reason in terms of these categories—what else is this but scientific, or philosophical, analysis? One cannot seriously inquire into the nature of pleasure without using knowledge as the guiding instrument. Philebos, restricting himself to pleasure, is condemned to silence.

In this section the method of division is applied even more strictly than in the previous section. Also, opposition to the eristics again is expressed in the course of this division (57D). The first division distinguishes between technical knowledge (δημιουργικόν, 55D) and education or culture (περὶ παιδείαν καὶ τροφήν)—a distinction earlier made in the *Protagoras* (320D *et seq.*). Practical knowledge is divided into those studies (like the art of music[68]) that are based on experience and skill, and those studies (like the art of building) that are based on mathematical precision. Mathematics, in turn, is divided into applied and pure mathematics. Thus, analogous to the division of pleasures, there is a graded order among the sciences, according to the principle of purity (56D, 57AB). And even as pure, or philosophical, mathematics rises above applied mathematics (μετρητική), so it is itself superseded by dialectics which, as the science of eternal and unchanging being, is the truest knowledge (ἀληθεστάτη γνῶσις).

When this system of the sciences has been constructed, though in outline only, the voice of opposition is heard. Protarchos cites Gorgias, according to whom the "art of persuasion" is the "best" of all arts, the best in the sense of the most powerful. (Once more there is a hint of the kind of battle that Plato waged passionately when he wrote the *Gorgias*, while here the issue is smoothed over gently by Socrates.) We are talking about two different things, is Socrates' reply to Protarchos. The claim of the orator is based on the practical use of his art. We, however, are seeking the truth and, as in the analysis of pleasures (58c;

II 2a
55c–58A

II 2b
58A–59E

cf. 53A *et seq.*), we are concerned not with the question of which science (or art) is the most powerful, but which is the most precise and true. As a matter of fact, we are not concerned at all with such incidental matters as usefulness and fame. The decision is to be made on the ground of the inner structure of the questioner: "In our soul there is a power of loving the truth" (58D). In other words, as our questioning itself reveals, the soul in its very nature strives toward true being.[69] Even this is not to be understood in purely theoretical terms, however sublime. "Loving the truth and . . . " (as Socrates adds in the same breath) "doing everything for the sake of the truth"—this is the nature of Socratic "pragmatism," opposed, on the one hand, to a desire for usefulness and power, which is the aim of rhetoric, and on the other, to a purely theoretical existence.

The ontological and epistemological aspects are summed up briefly and clearly at the end of the second section. They are firmly secure now against any attack by Gorgias. Still, there is something of his desire for usefulness and power in all of us— Socrates includes himself (59B 10)—and it is precisely for this reason that Plato introduced, and refuted, the attack. Now, immune to this danger, the realms of being and of thought stand before us. Each is divided into three ascending levels. The levels of being are strictly co-ordinated with the levels of thought: *first*, the realm of "opinions" and the technical knowledge corresponding to it; *second*, the world of nature, both becoming and passing away, and the scientific studies corresponding to it; *third*, the realm of true being and the pure thought of reason corresponding to it.

The analysis has provided all the material we need concerning both pleasure and knowledge. Since we already know that the good life is a mixture of the two, the only remaining task is to achieve this mixture—or so it seems as viewed from the foreground, or, one might risk saying, from the dramatic level of the dialogue. Ultimately and essentially, however, what remains to be done is something quite different. The first (ontological) part of the dialogue shows how the world of "coming-into-being" is a mixture of the two modes of being, the limit and the limitless. The second (empirical-pragmatic) part shows how the good life is a mixture of knowledge and pleasure. The first

part takes us to the point where reason, in its most general significance, becomes visible as the highest sphere of being and as
the cause for the mixture. The second part takes us to the point
where dialectics becomes visible as the science of pure being beyond all the other sciences. The concluding part, then, must
bring these two lines of inquiry, as yet separate, together into a
unity.

The prayer to the gods in charge of mixing and the cautious
procedure adopted in *Part III* show that mixing is a difficult and
important process even when all the ingredients are ready. Indeed, what else is to be understood by the metaphor "mixture"
than the reality of our own life: how are we to live? First, the
truest knowledge (i.e., knowledge of true being) and the
truest pleasure (i.e., the pleasure of this knowledge) are put
in. On the side of knowledge, to pure mathematics are then
added the highest applied sciences and, finally, all scientific
studies—not as such, let us note, but only after the highest disciplines are present. (Without this qualification, the sciences
may well be harmful: see the business of science today!) On the
side of pleasure, not all of them are added, but first the "true"
pleasures, then those that are "necessary," and finally a selection of those that are compatible with health in the body and in
the soul.

III 1
59E–64B

The final choice is left to the pleasures and sciences themselves. For their own sake the pleasures decide that all kinds of
knowledge are desirable. Reason and intelligence, however, are
selective with regard to the pleasures. To complete the mixture,
a third ingredient must be added: "truth." For it alone makes
everything that becomes, and everything that is, into *true becoming* and *true being*. Actually we must say that truth—although
in different degrees—was already present in the sciences (61E)
and that the pleasures, too, were selected according to the principle of truth (62E). Still, it is not enough for human life to
partake of the truth by pursuing knowledge and the pleasure of
knowledge. Life must itself possess truth in order truly to *be*. It
must itself be the truth, or in the truth, as we might say. And
perhaps, though this is not stated explicitly, man can experience
true knowledge and true pleasure only in being the truth.

We are still dealing with human life and with the ingredients (analyzed in the second part of the dialogue) that enter into its mixture. This mixture of knowledge and pleasure was not affected at first by the mixture of the limit and the limitless that was distinguished in the ontology of the dialogue's first part. Yet the one mixture cannot be independent of the other. Unity must prevail—and the structure of good life must be coordinated with the basic structures of being itself. And we see, indeed, how the larger domain gradually becomes visible through the matters of immediate concern. We are seeking a mixture that is the most beautiful and peaceable (ἀστασιαστοτά-την, 63E 9) and we wish to discover what is good (or, "the good") in man and in the universe and what form (ἰδέαν) we should divine this good to possess.[70] What the logos has established, through the symbol of mixture, is an incorporeal ordered system, or cosmos, as it were, in rightful control over a body endowed with soul. We are reminded of the Gorgias (505E), where we learn about the order, or cosmos, of the soul, and where the larger "cosmos" soon appears in the background (507E). We also are reminded of the Timaeus, where the universe is called "a living being endowed with soul and intelligence" (ζῷον ἔμψυχον ἔννουν, 30B), and where we soon read about the "body of the world" (τὸ τοῦ κόσμου σῶμα, 32c).

Thus, here in the Philebus, we catch a view of the world at large through and beyond the world of man. Moreover, now we can rightfully say that we stand at the threshold of the good (ἐπὶ τοῖς τοῦ ἀγαθοῦ προθύροις, 64c),[71] which completes the view through and beyond the sphere of human life (61A). The next question asks what is of highest value (τιμιώτατον) in the mixture, and what is to be considered its cause (αἴτιον) in the highest sense (64c). We are taken back to the ontological part where reason was the cause, occupying a place above the other kinds of being. Finally, we arrive at the "mixture itself," and its "cause" (συμπάσης μείξεως τὴν αἰτίαν, 64D). And so the first two parts of the dialogue are joined. On the one hand, the view of the best life, in the dialogue's second part, is seen in the ontological perspective of the first part. On the other hand, the life mixed of pleasure and knowledge of truth (clarified in the second part) and the kind of being mixed of the limitless and the limit (clarified in the first part) are made to coincide.

After the fusion of the first and second parts is acknowledged, III 2
the question is: What is the "cause" of the "mixture" as such? 64B–66D
Put differently, what is it that makes any mixture good, i.e.,
ordered, i.e., real? At once let us note that what we have is not
a chaotic aggregate,[72] but a real mixture in a unique sense. The
cause of such a mixture, then, is measure (μέτρον) and proportion (σύμμετρος φύσις = συμμετρία). So "the good" that we are
tracking down has taken refuge in "the beautiful." For proportion and symmetry are the marks of beauty or, as Socrates puts
it, of "beauty and virtue" (lest we take beauty as a merely
"aesthetic" phenomenon and virtue as a merely "moral" phenomenon).

Here, as in a symbol, we come up against a basic fact. We cannot hunt down the good "in single form" (μιᾷ ἰδέᾳ τὸ ἀγαθὸν
θηρεῦσαι). This explains the earlier allusion to "divining" it
(μαντευτέον), and also explains why we stood "at the threshold
of the good." Remembering the prototype of the good in the
Republic, we could not expect anything else. Yet, even as there
we came to see only its offspring, so here we shall have to be
satisfied with grasping it concretely (refracted through a prism,
as it were) in three Forms—beauty, proportion, and truth.[73] It
is not granted to us to enter into the interior of the house in
which the Perfect-Good dwells. Transcendence remains transcendence—but we can divine it.

After we have risen so high, the contest is resumed: "whether
it is knowledge or pleasure that is more akin to the good and
more highly esteemed among the gods and among men" (65A 8
et seq.). This question long ago was decided against pleasure.
Thus, what matters here is ultimately not a decision for or
against, but something else. Since reason is examined in relation to the three modes of being, a new harmony is envisaged.
First, reason is akin to truth or even identical with it. So—after
reason was revealed as a sublime power in the ontology of the
first part—it now moves definitely into the sphere of the good.
Second, reason is akin to measure and proportion. Wherever
there is form and order, it is the work of reason or intelligence.
And so, *third*, reason is part of beauty. That pleasure is the
opposite in every respect the young Protarchos knows from his
own experience. The stronger the pleasure the more inclined it

is to deceit; pleasure is devoid of measure; pleasure often is ugly and hides in shame. Are we not reminded once more of the controversy over the false and true Aphrodite, which was a significant ornamental motif throughout the first part of the dialogue?

In conclusion, the highest Forms of being, knowledge, and pleasure, which have been clarified here in the *Philebus*, are classified in a five-stage system.[74]

(*1*) The domain of measure. This is the seat of all "limit" and all "form."[75]

(*2*) The domain of proportion, symmetry, beauty, and perfection. Here are situated communion, multiplicity in unity, the world of the limited.

(*3*) Reason and thought. This is the seat of truth in three respects: as the correctness of thinking, as the "disclosure of being" (Heidegger), and as the truth of human existence.

(*4*) The knowledges of the soul. There is a descending order from the special sciences to the arts and crafts and, finally, to right opinions.[76]

(*5*) The pure pleasures of the soul. Again, there is a descending order from the pleasures accompanying pure knowledge to the pleasures accompanying the clearest perceptions. The pleasures mentioned earlier (63E 4–5) as associated with health, self-discipline, and virtue in general may also have their place in this group.

This system of five stages is not to be inscribed as a dogma in a textbook. (In Plato, this goes without saying, everywhere, even if he does not add an occasional remark such as "you won't be very wide of the truth . . .") Yet in this system we see once more the highest domains of being, reason, and pleasure in a graded order. It acquires its ultimate human—or existential—significance by virtue of the moral demand implicit throughout: *Thus thou shalt be.*

III 3
66D–67B
When the system has been described, the dialogue is rounded out into a unified whole by returning to the initial theme of the wrestling match. The winner is announced. Philosophical "divination" has prevailed over the assertions of the multitude dedicated to pleasure.[77] And if the conclusion thus "sinks back" from the heights to the level of the dialogue's beginning, this is not

only for formal reasons. What it suggests is that ontology and metaphysics return to the "pragmatism" of the daily life from which they arose. The question, How shall I live?, as simple as it is decisive for everybody, leads necessarily upward to an investigation into the kinds of being and to the threshold of the good. Yet, this ascent makes sense only if we come back—with an answer—to the question from which we set out.

PART II

Cosmic Law and State Law

TWENTY-NINE

Timaeus

THE *Timaeus* perhaps always will be called the incomparable one among Plato's works, even as for a long time it was considered to be his main work. This mixture of priestly solemnity and grotesque playfulness, of highest abstraction and broadest empiricism, of mathematics and fantasy, did not exist before nor did it ever come again. Still, if we ask of what possible use this "scientific myth" is today when scientific experience has grown so much wider and scientific method so much more strict, we do well to remember the words with which August Boeckh, in 1807, concluded his treatise on the world-soul in the *Timaeus*. "No mortal man has ever beheld chaste Artemis, and she has put horns on many, not on Aktaion alone; but until nature does not blush to appear in her nakedness to mortal eyes, why would you not wish to behold her image, mirrored in the mind of divine men, with pleasure and enjoyment?"[1]

Today we realize, however, that such a poetizing view of things is not enough. No genuine science of nature can exist without inquiring into its own history, and in this history there probably is no single work that has had as deep and wide an influence as the *Timaeus*. To write the history of this influence would be a great undertaking combining research in the classics, history, the natural sciences, and medicine. At the time of Boeckh's writing, the *Timaeus* was taken very seriously in the circle around the philosopher Schelling. In 1804, it was translated into German by the Mainz court physician Windischmann as "A Genuine Document of True Physics." Somewhat later (in 1826), Lichtenstaedt, a professor of medicine in Breslau, wrote a book on "Plato's doctrines in natural science and medicine."[2] Goethe read both of these works and, in his *Geschichte der Farbenlehre*, he refers to Plato in words that we might well adopt again and again in what follows: "It is still more welcome to see how in Plato we encounter every earlier type of doctrine in a purified and elevated form." Otherwise the nineteenth century was not favorably disposed toward the *Timaeus*. And it remains to be seen whether the physics of the twentieth century is indebted to the *Timaeus* in passing beyond the seventeenth-century type of atomism founded by Gassendi. There are some astonishing analogies—the stereometrical shape of the atoms, their destructibility, the correlation between each element and the specific stereometrical shape of its atoms, and the principle of elemental indeterminacy.

What must be shown first is that Plato intended to write a trilogy—*Timaeus*, *Critias*, and *Hermocrates*—and not a tetralogy opening with a revised version of the *Republic*. The first pages of the *Timaeus* seem to lend credence to the mistaken view of such a tetralogy.[3] What is the significance of the strange summary of the conversation about the state that is supposed to have taken place "yesterday"? The summary is confined almost entirely to the "natural" (κατὰ φύσιν, 17c 10; φύσιν, 18A 4) foundations of the city state and to gymnastics and music, the preparatory subjects of education. Comparatively speaking, it deals rather extensively with the theme of communal ownership of property and women, but it breaks off where the education of the philosopher—i.e., the core of the *Republic*—would have to begin.

Nobody any longer seems to believe that Plato is here recapitulating an original version of the *Republic* that thus might be reconstructed from this sketch.[4] If we can say anything about Plato's utopia with any degree of certainty, it is this: the "theory of Forms" was not superimposed afterwards as a "soul" upon a political machinery that was more or less practical and more or less fantastic—for it was this "soul" that gave birth to the body of the state. It would be another mistake, as we said, to take Socrates literally and to believe that Plato intended to submit a new version of the *Republic* as the first part of a tetralogy. That he ever had planned to embark on such a thankless task becomes quite inconceivable when we consider that the state sketched here would have preserved the machinery of the ideal state without its soul.

As the text now stands, however, everything is meaningful. Plato invents, at the beginning of his projected trilogy, a conversation about the state. This is not the conversation that took place, on the nineteenth of Thargelion, in the house of Kephalos between Socrates and the two brothers, Glaukon and Adeimantos. Nor is it the record of this conversation—i.e., the *Republic* as we have it—that Socrates reports on the following day, the twentieth, to some unknown listeners. This is evident because the scope of what he is supposed to have said is so different here, as is the day on which this alleged conversation is said to have taken place—the day before the Panathenaia, or about the twenty-seventh of Hekatombaion. Obviously Plato invented another, shorter report about the earlier conversation or, more likely, an altogether different and shorter conversation about the state conducted with different participants.[5]

Enough. In the *Timaeus'* short report, it is meant to appear that the conversation dealt mainly with external features of the organization of the state. Why there is no mention of the philosopher-kings, or their education, or of the *Idea* of the Good, we would be able to understand fully only if Plato had completed the trilogy, and not just the first part of it and the beginning of the second part. Yet even what we have of the trilogy seems to indicate that nowhere in it would we have pursued a path leading to the highest knowledge, for apparently the *Eidos* was to be represented only in the form of myth. This is the reason—we are inclined to believe—why there was no place here for the theory of knowledge as it is developed in the *Republic*.[6]

"One, two, three . . . but where is the fourth who was among the companions of yesterday?—He is not here today; he was taken ill." Why this opening theme?[7] It has been said that Plato may have wished to keep the way open for expanding the trilogy into a tetralogy. On the contrary, should we not decide rather that this opening distinctly points to the trilogy in which Timaios, Kritias, and Hermokrates are to be the speakers? A

dialogue called *Hermocrates* was to be expected after the *Critias,*
but nothing more. This is why the nameless "fourth" is introduced as absent. Just to understand the Socratic report about
the construction of the state and then the trilogy itself requires
strength—and how much more to write it!—as seems to be indicated by the "weakness" that keeps the fourth from being
present.

As Cicero, in explicitly following Plato, opens his work *De
re publica* with a conversation on an astronomical topic and concludes with the world-view disclosed in the dream of Scipio, so
here the backward glance upon the ideal state that precedes the
construction of the cosmic system serves the purpose, in a more
original way, of combining state and universe. But why did
Plato add to this preliminary conversation the prehistory of the
myth in the *Critias,* tracing its ancient tradition back beyond
Solon to the priests of Egypt, providing the geographical and
geophysical foundations of the myth, casting a glance ahead to
the war between Atlantis and Ur-Athens, and finally, citing the
geological upheavals separating that period of prehistory from
the present period of the world?

At first all this seems quite strange here. Yet strangeness
would reach the point of incomprehensibility if we were to assume that Plato included the material here only when he realized
that he would not complete the *Critias.* On the contrary, such a
detailed account makes sense only if that for which it is a preparation actually follows.[8] And if, looking still more closely, we
see that this preparation is intentionally divided so that Atlantis
is described at the beginning of the *Timaeus* and Ur-Athens at
the beginning of the *Critias,* then the interlocking design of the
two works becomes clear. Yet, it would not be enough to regard
this merely as technical skill of the experienced master builder.
Rather, the dual myth grows out of the common root of the system of the state, on the one hand, the system of the universe as
a "larger state" (Proklos), as the *Idea* of the Good unfolding in
the universe, as a high object of education leading to this *Idea,*
and as an image providing (as earlier the concluding myth of
the *Republic* did) the space for the life of the soul in the hereafter.
On the other hand, original Athens is a symbol representing in

time and in a concrete image what the *Republic* had shown as the education leading upward toward the realm of pure being.

Why the creation of the world in the *Timaeus* had to be depicted as a myth, what the precursors are for this mythical cosmogony in other works of Plato and elsewhere, and what place this creation occupies in Plato's own myth-building—these matters we discussed earlier, in the chapter on "Myth."[9] While a separate book would be required to offer any detailed interpretation of the *Timaeus'* construction of the universe, we shall discuss here at least a few basic features of the work.

Final Cause and Material Cause

The *Timaeus* is not a treatise, on natural philosophy, that was 42E–48E later cast into the form of a dialogue. We cannot do justice to this work if we forget, as we invariably do, that it was Socrates who yesterday charged the Pythagorean to undertake this work and who today is one of the listeners. Socrates' listening—we know how essential this is to the meaning of the *Parmenides*, the *Sophist*, and the *Statesman*. In the *Timaeus* it is perhaps even more essential inasmuch as it is Socrates himself who begins by giving the retrospective report about his construction of the state. Then Kritias announces (27A), looking forward to what is known to us as the dialogue bearing his name, that he will take over from Timaios the subject of men as they are and from Socrates men as they are formed and instructed according to the educational system of the *Republic*. Yet to appreciate the presence of Socrates, must we not also look back to the wish he expressed in the *Phaedo* (99C) that he would gladly learn from anybody who would show him that the world was constructed according to the principle of the "good and imperative"? Put differently, the demand that Plato put to himself in the *Phaedo* he satisfied in the *Timaeus*.

In the *Phaedo*, Plato distinguished the two types of causes applicable to an explanation of the world. These are, on the one hand, the cause (τὸ αἴτιον) in the strict sense, or more precisely, the final cause or the principle of the "good and imperative" (τὸ ἀγαθὸν καὶ δέον), and on the other hand, that "without which the cause would never cause" (ἄνευ οὗ τὸ αἴτιον οὐκ ἄν ποτ' εἴη αἴτιον), or in other words, the material cause. He recognized that all previous "physics" was concerned only with the second, which did not satisfy him. But since the material cause is a precondition without which the final cause cannot operate, Plato must have realized—before he began to compose his myth of the universe—that however much the things in the world are ordered according to the *Idea* of the Good, they do not simply reflect this *Idea*. He must have realized that in this world, final (or teleological) causes *and* material (or mechanical) causes must co-operate.[10] When these two types of causes confront each other in the *Phaedo*, the contrast serves to clarify the true basis on which Socrates acted in the main decision of his life, and for this reason there is only a passing glance at the universe. The *Timaeus* is dedicated to the universe, and only at its beginning is there a passing glance at the construction of the state, i.e., at human life. Yet the interlocking of physics and ethics, of cosmic structure and human existence, is suggested in both works. This is what the presence of Socrates means in the *Timaeus*—and it means still more.

It was impossible for Plato to put the two principles of explanation, final cause and material cause, simply side by side as, say, Aristotle did in Book II of his *Physics*, where he has a chapter (ch. 3) on causes, "how many there are and of what kind." To put the two side by side Plato would have had to give them equal weight, whereas he actually recognizes (even as he did earlier, in the *Phaedo*) only *one* truly creative cause—postulating in addition, as a new terminology now puts it, "accessory causes (συναίτια, 46c) which the god uses as servants in executing the idea of the best as far as possible." Thus he began and could begin only in the spirit of teleology. Still, the principle of material causation had to assert itself somewhere. If we consider the passage where this happens, we must admit that it could not have happened at a better place than here, where the head becomes the dwelling of the soul and where, with the presence of the senses, the joining of the physical and the mental also occurs. Here, too, the mechanical and the teleological explanations of nature are joined.

This artful joining is worth noting throughout the passage.

Timaios describes the creation of living beings, animal and human. The head, resembling a sphere (i.e., the perfect form), is the abode of the immortal soul in man, while the body and its limbs serve the head as instruments of locomotion.[11] The foremost organ of the head is the eye. Timaios outlines a detailed psychophysical theory of the act of vision, to be followed by a detailed theory of the mirror image. In the course of this discussion he slips, unawares, deep into the domain of "accessory causes" (45B–46C). He pauses and then, as if after a moment of self-reflection, proceeds to discuss the essential nature of the two types of "causes."

This is not all, however, for in order to make clear this essential nature, he then reviews the sense of sight according to the principle of the "best," and to sight he adds the sense of hearing. From sight he derives philosophy, and he praises hearing as the instrument of harmony and rhythm in the order of the soul. An explanation of hearing according to mechanical, material causes will follow much later, along with the other sensory perceptions (67B). For the time being, Timaios develops an all the more purely teleological point of view, after slipping into the material cause and after a first pause for reflection. As soon as he has put the two principles side by side, there follows a renewed and more emphatic distinction between the action of reason and the effects of material necessity (47E). It is in this domain of material necessity that the discussion is to remain centered for a long time now. The construction is so skillful and so firm that we cannot fail to appreciate the dialectical interrelationship of the two principles of explanation, on the one hand, and yet the supremacy of intelligence, on the other.

Parmenides, with an inconsistency due to reality itself, had placed physics in his philosophical poem beside ontology, the world of appearance and opinion beside the truth—a paradoxical act without which this magnificently consistent thinker would be an Indian rather than a Greek. The *Timaeus* corresponds to the second part of Parmenides' poem, for while it is within the richer creation of Platonic thought, it nonetheless reflects Parmenidean patterns of thought constantly. Even as Parmenides envisaged the world as a mixture of light and darkness (ulti-

mately a mixture of being and not-being), so Plato constructs
the world of becoming out of being—i.e., the *Eidos*—and that
which ultimately is not-being and which, corresponding to its
indefinite nature, or its not-being, is called by various names,
including "space." Essentially the same thing is meant as when
it is said that the "creation of this world results from the combined work of intelligence and blind necessity." Here, however,
where Plato concentrates upon the realm of necessity, assigning
it a place below intelligence, he moves closer to the older philosophies of nature that he has Socrates repudiate in the *Phaedo*.
It is a common but nevertheless mistaken view of old that the
great Plato is debating here with his great antipode Demokritos.[12] For Plato Demokritos was one in a series of philosophers of nature. What Plato re-created and incorporated into
his own world of thought was not a single doctrine, but the
whole tradition of natural science before him, including the
doctrines of medicine.[13]

Intelligence as the principle of order combines with blind,
inert necessity to create the world of the *Timaeus*. In the *Phaedo*
(77B *et seq.*), Socrates explains that Anaxagoras differed from
all other philosophers of nature because he used "mind" as the
basic concept, but then failed to make proper use of it in his
theory. With Parmenides, unshakable being itself, called *Ananke*, rules as a half-mythical demon over what seems to be a
cosmogony. That "all happens according to necessity" is a doctrine attributed to Herakleitos and Anaxagoras, and confirmed
in the one extant fragment of Leukippos. It also seems that
Empedokles, who called his two basic principles "Love" and
"Strife"—sometimes naming the first Harmony, Joy, or Aphrodite, and the second Wrath—elsewhere refers to them as *Charis*
(Joy) and "*Ananke* that is hard to endure."[14]

It goes without saying that Plato did not adopt and assemble
various doctrines. In the speech of Agathon (*Symposium* 195c)
it is said that *Ananke* ruled over the earliest times when there
was chaos in the world and that *Eros* rules over the present
times in which we live. How much sarcasm Plato puts into this
speech of the poet and polished orator may be appreciated from
the fact that he describes the present as a period ruled by "peace

and friendship"—a characterization given at the halfway mark of the Peloponnesian War which destroyed the power of Greece! In the *Timaeus*, Plato speaks with solemn seriousness. The two principles, intelligence and necessity, do not rule successively, but together. They combine to create the world. With a view to nature and to history Plato realizes that, opposed to Form, there is a "something" responsible for the fact that things in this world never approximate the eternal pattern. In strict ontological language, he refers to this contrast as the opposition between being and not-being. In the language of the myth appropriate to the creation of the world, he falls back upon the demonic powers of the older philosophers of nature to express the same contrast.

Cosmogony

This is the form in which the ancient myths of creation, and, from Thales on, the theories of nature as well, were developed by the "physiologists" of old—whether they indicated by their language their mechanical approach to the processes of separation and combination or whether they actually attributed the work of creation to a shadowy *Ananke* or a not much more substantial (or a spiritual) principle called "mind." As stated in the *Republic* and in the *Laws*, Plato considered it one of his main tasks to reverse this process of de-deification. So while apparently following an old tradition, he differs from it in a decisive respect—for the demiurge in the *Timaeus* creates the world after the highest pattern, "interweaving the mortal with the immortal" (41D 1), so that it becomes a "visible god" (92c 7).

The paradoxical language points to the extraordinary nature of this world-order. With the exception of the Atomists, it was probably common to all earlier philosophers of nature, after Anaximander, to conceive of the universe as a sphere. Parmenides took over this conception even into his ontology so that pure being itself "resembles a sphere." Anaximander also had conceived of the earth as floating in the center of the universe, as a disc, however, not as a sphere. The view of a spherical earth in the center of a spherical universe is attributed to

33ʙ–34ᴀ
55ᴄᴅ

Parmenides and the Pythagoreans. Plato had taken over this view of the earth and the universe into the myth of the *Phaedo.* Here in the *Timaeus,* he interprets it as the outcome of a teleologically perfect and beautiful creation.

From cosmogony Plato turns to the elements, only to return once more (in the second part of the work) to the universe as a whole, by means of a sudden and puzzling move. With a pun —as in *Philebus* 17E, not a good one, although here in the *Timaeus* it makes his negative attitude all the more emphatic— he cites, and opposes, the view that there are an indefinite number of worlds (*Timaeus* 55CD). The doxographic tradition mentions Anaximander, Anaximenes, Xenophanes, Archelaos, Diogenes, Leukippos, and Demokritos as representatives of this many-worlds view. Thales, Pythagoras, Parmenides, Empedokles, and Anaxagoras are cited as representatives of the one-world view. It may be left open whether the same formula does not actually cover a variety of different views. Yet the survey itself shows that one is not on very safe grounds in supposing that here in the dialogue is another specific reference to Demokritos.[15] It seems more likely that Plato is taking sides in an ancient controversy among the philosophers of nature. To be sure, he does not take sides in order to be classified henceforth as one name beside others in the list of contestants. That there is only one world follows for Plato from the fact that this world resembles the perfect living being (τῷ παντελεῖ ζῴῳ, 31B). Thus, its uniqueness is for him a deeply systematic and, ultimately, religious necessity to which he alludes once more, with strong emphasis, in the concluding words of the *Timaeus*— "the greatest and best, the most beautiful and perfect, the one, only-begotten heaven."[16]

One detail we have so far passed by. At the sudden digression (55CD) which raises the question, "one world or an indefinite number?" it is asked just as suddenly, "one world or five?"— apparently in order to consider the number five at least as a reasonable hypothesis which somebody must have advanced. Timaios does not approve of it, but neither does he reject it as firmly as he rejects the hypothesis of an indefinite number of worlds. The entire line of thought is concerned with the idea of perfection. Thus, in order to understand approximately what is meant here, we only need imagine how five such worlds might be arranged in a regular figure or system. What matters, then, is the opposition to an indefinite number of worlds, for this is the view that is sharply rejected in favor of one world. Even five worlds would be more perfect than an indefinite number.[17]

Creation of the Soul

The universe as constructed so far would not be perfect without a "soul" pervading and animating the whole. The "world-soul" —as it later was called, though not by Plato himself—is a concept or construction particularly foreign to modern man,[18] and it evoked opposition and lively discussion even among Plato's successors. According to this concept, the world has a soul or life: it is alive, for this is what ψυχή means. And the belief that the human soul is immortal rests essentially upon the conviction that "life" cannot die. This is different from the view of most modern students of nature who suddenly find living beings— one knows not how—in the midst of a material world-machine, so that a leaf of grass or a caterpillar makes a miraculous appearance in the universe of mechanical solar systems.[19] Plato, on the contrary, envisages the universe as a whole endowed not only with a perfect body but also with "soul," with life infused into the body. And this soul itself is shaped like a perfect being.

We must look back once more to the passage in the *Phaedo* where Plato's Socrates gives an "account" of his intellectual development (96A *et seq.*). After the materialistic stage, a radical turn is brought about by reading of Anaxagoras' treatise, in which "mind" as the cause orders everything in the world according to the principle of the "best." Then comes the bitter disappointment of realizing that Anaxagoras does not make use of mind, but everywhere falls back upon material causes. From the experience of his own life Socrates knows the difference between two types of causes—the true cause as distinct from that "without which" the true cause could "not" be effective. He would like to learn from anybody who would show him that the world is ordered according to the principle of the "best." Mean-

34B–37C
41D–44D

while, his "second-best" course is to take refuge in the investigation of concepts, as he puts it in ironic understatement. Now in the *Timaeus*, Plato's Socrates who discovered the world of Forms listens as the Pythagorean puts a soul into the world he is constructing. The demiurge created the world of bodies in the shape of mathematically perfect figures. Now—the sequence is not temporal, but mythical—he puts soul-life into this world of bodies from the periphery to the center.[20]

Let us follow this construction of the soul, not in all its difficult details, but as to its main features. Let us remember, first, that Timaios does not say "world-soul," but says simply "soul." Thus, it is quite natural to ask how my own soul is related to this all-soul, how much or how little they resemble each other, and whether it is a task imposed upon the individual soul to approximate, at least from afar, the image of the perfect soul. The ingredients that the demiurge employs in mingling the soul (35A) are, first, the being that is indivisible and forever the same, and second, the being that is divisible and comes into being in bodies. That would be enough, but in order to emphasize the difficulty of the mixture, and how its ingredients are inextricably intermingled, he adds as a third component the mixture of the previous two—or, as it may be put differently (35A 3–4), the mixture of "the same" and "the different."

Let us pause to compare. In the *Phaedo* (78C *et seq.*), Socrates distinguishes the "being that is forever the same" (the eternal Forms) from "compound being" (the world of becoming and passing away). The soul perceives the eternal Forms by means of reason, which is akin to them; it perceives the world of becoming by means of the senses. In the *Phaedo*, then, what is lacking is only the third (or artificial) ingredient employed in the mixture described in the *Timaeus*, whereas the first two components are present in very much the same words. Yet what Socrates is expounding in the *Phaedo*, namely, the knowledge of Forms through the soul, is stated as a more general formula in the *Timaeus* because here the speaker is a Pythagorean, not Socrates. As readers, however, we cannot but recall the *Phaedo* passage, to which there are verbal allusions, and we may be quite sure that the exposition of the Pythagorean is rethought by the listening Socrates in his own sense. We may be all the more sure if we remember that in the *Sophist* (238A) —again with allusions, in exactly the same words, to the *Phaedo* and the *Timaeus* passages—the Eleatic stranger attributes to the "friends of *Ideas*" the firm conviction that the soul is always directed in its pure thought toward true being, "that which, as you say, is forever the same."

An essential element still is missing in this account of the total mixture: the Pythagorean (or seemingly Pythagorean) number scheme. This is added to the mixture in the form of the "second tetractys" which the ancients used to arrange in the shape of a lambda.

$$
\begin{array}{ccccc}
& & 1 & & \\
& 2 & & 3 & \\
& 4 & & 9 & \\
8 & & & & 27
\end{array}
$$

The intervals in this series are filled by two intermediary numbers corresponding, respectively, to a "harmonic" mean and an "arithmetic" mean. The stellar spheres move according to this skillfully constructed number system. So strict is the lawfulness inherent in the world-soul or world-life.

Whether this mathematical system is a musical system as well is a question still much debated. For Aristotle and for Plutarch, the correlation with a musical system is practically the most essential aspect of this Platonic construction.[21] In our time, Frank and Cornford have rejected any such correlation. In contrast to them Ahlvers, on the basis of the works of Albert von Thimus and Hans Kayser, has argued that there is a harmonic world-view in the *Timaeus*. I am far from competent to judge this issue as an expert. Yet Ahlver's conclusion "that Plato's universe is permeated by musical laws" so closely corresponds to what is found in the *Republic* as to suggest that one would miss the harmony of the spheres if it were not an aspect of the *Timaeus*. As Plato's spiritual eye perceived the world as a spheric system, so his spiritual ear must have heard a harmony of the spheres. "Astronomy and music . . ." Socrates says in the *Republic* (VII 530D), where the education of the future philosopher-kings is brought to its culmination, "astronomy and music are kindred sciences, as the Pythagoreans say, and we agree with them, Glaukon."

Thus music, together with gymnastics, is not the exclusive province of the education of young citizens in the ideal state. Even there it is the "most royal and effective nourishment of the soul" (*Republic* III 401D). In its highest form, however, music belongs to mathematics and astronomy. Like astronomy, the highest musical art studies the question "which numbers are concordant and which not and why in each case" (VII 531C). This highly difficult study is useful in the search for the beautiful and the good. Dialectics lies ahead (532B), and music is one of the sciences that prepare us for discovery of the Forms. And in the concluding myth of the *Republic*, we hear the music of the spheres since, on each stellar circle, there is a siren giving forth one sound, and all these sounds are attuned in the single harmony of the world.

We must keep these features of Plato's *Republic* in mind as we listen, with Socrates, to the creation of the soul as told by Timaios, the Pythagorean. In many details his construction goes beyond what Socrates says in the *Phaedo* and the *Republic*. To be sure, the Pythagorean has nothing to say about things of a still higher order than the world of stars and sounds. Yet this realm of eternal Forms has not paled, as some believe, in Plato's late period. It is alive and made manifest in the *Timaeus* by the presence of Socrates.

The Elements and Elementary Polyhedra

31B–33B We have investigated this subject in an earlier chapter.[22] Ques-
55D–61C tions that must be asked in any such investigation are (1) how Plato "purified and elevated"—to speak with Goethe—the older theories which are combined here, (2) whether and to what extent Plato's ideas are comprehensible in the light of modern theories, and (3) whether Plato has had any influence on modern theories.

(1) Viewing all the earlier speculations about the elements, Plato combines and reformulates them according to a mathematical principle. Fire and earth are the primitive elements out

of which he constructs the others according to the law of proportion (31B *et seq.*). Parmenides similarly used the contrast of two basic principles, one called "fire," and the other called "night, thick and of heavy shape." In fact, according to Aristotle, Parmenides used fire and earth as primary substances out of which everything else, air and water, originated by "mixture."[23] Plato's point of departure is essentially the same. His own intention, or, perhaps one should say, the Pythagorean aspect of his thought, is seen as substituting geometrical proportion for physical mixture. The theory of four elements, as is well known, was anticipated by Empedokles, except that he took the four elements as given, whereas Plato derives them by means of a geometrical construction. Also, Plato gives a deeper and more precise meaning to the Empedoklean concept of "friendship" to which he clearly alludes. This becomes, in Plato's thought, the geometrical principle according to which the universe "coming into unity with itself remains indissoluble by anybody except him who bound it together" (32c).[24]

In contrast to Empedokles, Plato views the elements as changing into one another. Water, it seems, solidifies to earth. Stones dissolve into vapor and air, burn up into fire, solidify again to air, clouds, and fog, and these, in turn, to water, so that the cycle of becoming seems to be complete. There are well-known precursors for this conception, which is modified later on in the *Timaeus* (54c) only in that the earth, as a true element, is said to be indissoluble.[25] There is a report—it is also a warning about the degree to which the *Timaeus* has colored the doxographic tradition—about a doctrine of Herakleitos concerning "evaporation." According to this doctrine, water is solidified to earth and everything else is originated from water by the process of evaporation.[26] As Herakleitos taught, "The way up and the way down are one and the same" ("and not the same," he probably added in his own fashion). The circle is the appropriate symbol for this movement, since the circle represents a line "where beginning and end meet."[27] Still, we find also in Anaximenes and Anaxagoras the principle of "evaporation," or "condensation," of air into clouds, or the change of water into hail and snow. Epicharmos, too, emphasizes a cycle of air, wind, clouds, rain, cold, and then back to air and wind. And the basic schema of *this turns into that if* . . . may be found in Plato as in the doxographic reports about the earlier philosophers of nature.

Yet, despite these points of agreement, Plato's view also differs from all those earlier speculations about the elements. For Herakleitos, "fire" was the primitive substance, despite all change, while for Anaximenes, Archelaos, and Diogenes, it was "air." According to Empedokles, the four elements were sharply separated from each other. But Plato is a more radical thinker. The elements, instead of being separate substances, become qualities of one basic substance that manifests itself in these various modes. This basic substance is at the same time space and energy. Here the contrast to Empedokles is most striking, but there is divergence from the other thinkers as well. As far as the unified and indeterminate nature of the primitive substance is concerned, Anaximander is the only predecessor who might be cited.[28] Nonetheless, what mattered to Plato was the tension between such a radical indeterminateness of the primary substance, on the one hand, and the precise structure of this material, on the other, and this he could not find in the work of any predecessor.

Within the physical myth, Plato invents as an expression of this strict formal principle the theory of elementary particles. This is altogether his own.[29] With this theory, he joined the number of thinkers who constructed the world out of the smallest atoms. Yet Plato was by no means concerned only with Leukippos and Demokritos; he also was arguing against Anaxagoras and Empedokles.[30] What he has in common with the Atomists, strictly speaking, is the neutral character of the basic substance he posits (though even here he has a different objective in mind). They, however, postulated atoms whose shapes were essentially haphazard, or, in Plato's sense, atoms that were devoid of shape. As far as Plato was concerned, blind necessity could not produce an ordered universe out of such disorder. Empedokles provided the concept of four elements sharply separated from each other, which appealed to Plato's sense of clarity. He did not think of these elements as ultimate substances, however, but as qualities of something beyond them. Anaxagoras conceived of mind as the moving principle, and the world in motion as an infinitely manifold and infinitely divisible continuum. For Plato, too, the "demiurge mind" (Νοῦς δημιουργός) is the moving cause, but his creation of the world is not an indefinite process of separation and combination. He forms according to the laws of geometry: ὁ θεὸς ἀεὶ γεωμετρεῖ.

It is known that Plato here incorporated four of the five regular polyhedra, the "Platonic bodies," into his theory of elementary particles in order to give a concrete demonstration of the geometrical structure of the elementary bodies. Far removed as he is from entering into controversy with any single one of his predecessors, he combines their theories about elements and atoms, and rethinks and recasts them into a conception of his own. Mythical and fantastic as this conception may appear at first sight, after closer study it begins to look like a vague anticipation of the most recent atomic theory.

(2) We tried to indicate, in the earlier chapter on "Plato as Physicist," some of the affinities between Plato's construction and modern theories of physics, and the way in which his ideas ultimately become comprehensible and meaningful when viewed in this perspective—provided we do not conceal or overlook the danger of reading modern ideas into ancient material. Plato's theory of elements and particles probably dominated medieval thought down to the Renaissance. It became incomprehensible when, with Pierre Gassendi in the seventeenth century, the atomism of Leukippos and Demokritos came to dominate the intellectual scene. And now once again, in the light of recent physics, Plato's view has become meaningful.

For the following basic propositions of modern physics, we find unmistakable analogies in Plato. According to Prout, the elements are reducible to one primary element. According to Dalton, there are as many atomic forms as there are elements. According to Rutherford and Bohr, atomic models have a geometrical structure—though these modern astronomical models are again quite different from Plato's polyhedra—and the atom may be split. According to Heisenberg, the principle of "elementary indeterminacy" affects all laws of nature reaching down into an inconceivable substratum that is the ultimate ground for all processes in nature.

(*3*) Did Plato's theory of elements and particles influence modern developments? Although the question can only be stated here, it still deserves to be raised. To provide an answer, physics and history would have to combine in a joint project.

Circular Movement—Empty Space

33B–33D The four elements or, more correctly, the four atoms of stereo-
58A–79B metric structure are encompassed by the circular motion of the whole universe (58A). There must be motion, for the elementary particles differ from each other. Difference and motion go together as do sameness and rest. Timaios returns to what he said previously about the perfect sphere of the universe (33B), and now says that the perfect circular motion comprehends everything, leaving no room for empty space. This rejection of the concept of the void is stated suddenly and briefly. Later on, it is taken up again and clarified in the statement (79B) that there is no empty space into which any one of the moving (particles) could enter.

This rejection of the void has been interpreted—as so often is the case where the *Timaeus* is concerned—as a polemic against Demokritos or, let us rather say, against Leukippos and Demokritos. Again, this does not do justice to what Plato really had in mind. That there is empty space is a common opinion supported by superficial inspection. The Eleatics opposed this superficial view on ontological grounds; they rejected the void as not-being. Anaxagoras repudiated it as a consequence of his conception of the continuum of being. The Atomists, in contrast, needed the concept of the void in order to let their atoms move in it. In rejecting the void, therefore, Plato follows Parmenides, Zeno, Melissos, Anaxagoras, and Empedokles.

In fact, as we realize after closer scrutiny, Plato does not even deny the void as such.[31] How could he fail to notice what Aristotle had objected to—namely, that the doctrine of regular polyhedra implies that there must be minutely small interstices between them? These interstices only must be smaller than the smallest polyhedron so that, for all practical purposes, there is no empty space, i.e., no space that might be, but is not, occupied by a polyhedron. And even if we assume that there are such minutely small interstices, nobody can say whether they are really "empty" in the strict sense of the word or whether they may be filled with the indefinite which modern commentators prefer to call "space," although Plato referred to it by many names of which "space" was only one. A void that had an independent status, as in the theory of the Atomists, would have meant for Plato that here reason had failed in its work of "persuading" *Ananke*. The minimum of unformed space between the polyhedra is, as it were, a constant reminder of the fact that what is formed comes out of chaos, and becoming comes out of not-being. Moreover, as the destruction and re-creation of the polyhedra is a perpetual process, it follows that the triangles will form a spatial body out of what was previously just an interstice between them.

The Senses

Plato's theory of sensory experience has various points in common with earlier doctrines. It probably goes beyond them, however, in its intention of relating these processes "to the soul" (μέχρι τῆς ψυχῆς, 45D 2, 64B 5, 65A 5, 67B 3)—of going beyond mechanics to the mind.[32]

45B–46C
61C–68D

The *act of vision* Plato describes as follows (45B *et seq.*). The pure fire in the interior of the eye combines with the same element outside. This ray of vision striking upon an object transmits the motions set up by this encounter throughout the whole body to the soul. Demokritos' view is not unlike Plato's, only more materialistic. According to Demokritos, an effluence from the object and another from the eye meet in between. In this encounter the air is compressed into an image, and then this compressed image is reflected in the moist parts of the eye, i.e., as a kind of mirror image. It might be said that Plato spiritualizes the theory of Demokritos. Yet, we must not overlook the fact that Empedokles precedes both of them in time, and stands between the two in his treatment of the problem. He is on Plato's side in that he also conceives of the eye as a filter which keeps out all coarser stuff and permits only the finest,

45B–46C

i.e., fire, to filter through. As to Demokritos, Empedokles anticipates him in his theory of "effluences."[33] Thus, here again it is not probable that Plato is engaged in polemics against one specific theory. Such a polemic intent seems especially unlikely when we add that Alkmaion derived the act of vision from the fire and water in the eye, or from the shining and the transparent and, moreover, that a theory of rays of vision is attributed (though in somewhat vague rumors) to Pythagoras and to Parmenides.[34] In short, Plato had various theories before him in opposition to which he developed his own more spiritual version.

Above all, to Plato sight is the source of the "world-view" (47AB). The god has given us sight so that we may see the heavenly motions. Without these motions we would not have the concept of time, which is the source for the study of nature —i.e., for what Timaios is expounding here. And from this study of nature, in Timaios' opinion, we have in turn derived philosophy, "than which no greater good ever was or will be given by the gods to mortal man." This sounds—if we keep in mind, as we must always, that Socrates is present—like a praise of the philosopher and his work. Moreover, when Timaios finally turns to the ethical implications of astronomy, explaining that we should as far as possible approximate to the "unerring" (ἀταράκτοις) motions of the heavenly bodies the "perturbed" (τεταραγμένας) motions within ourselves, we cannot but remember what is said in the *Phaedo* (79D). The highest task of the soul, as Socrates says there, is to behold pure being by means of reason and, through this contact, to assuage its own confusion or perturbation (τοῦ πλάνου). Thus, the eternal Forms did not pale in Plato's late work nor were they even pushed aside by astronomy. It is in his spirit if we think that sublime astronomy, as taught by Timaios, is superseded by the theory of Forms for which Socrates is the witness by his life and his death.

67C–68D   Let us briefly touch upon Plato's treatment of *colors*. Although to go into details is difficult, it would be worth while, among other reasons because, in Goethe's argument against Newton as regards the "theory of colors" in opposition to "optics,"

Plato's views have an important place.[35] In his *Geschichte der Farbenlehre*, Goethe refers to these views with special admiration. He also mentions how difficult it is to translate the Greek terms συγκρίνειν and διακρίνειν into a modern language, and gives a translation of the treatise *On Colors* ascribed to Aristotle.

The *Meno* and the *Phaedo*, in particular, show that for decades and with a keen eye and active interest, Plato was occupied with the phenomenon of colors. In the *Meno* (76CD), he refers to Empedokles' theory of colors in order to demonstrate the nature of a definition. There are "effluences" (ἀπορροαί) and "passages" (πόροι) through which these effluences "make their way" (πορεύονται) if they fit, but not if they are "too large or too small." Thus "color is an effluence from bodies proportionate to sight (ὄψει σύμμετρος) and, hence, perceptible." In very similar words, the section on colors in the *Timaeus* begins by referring to light as "streaming off" (ἀπορρέουσαν) bodies, and "proportionate" to sight (ὄψει σύμμετρος), whereas other particles do not fit because they are "sometimes too large, sometimes too small."

In the concluding myth of the *Phaedo*, Socrates moves in an entirely different sphere. There he describes the true earth, the "earth itself," reaching upward to pure ether, and, in contrast to this, what we call the "inhabited earth," a layer that is sunken in a hollow of the true earth. The true earth differs from our inhabited earth there at the bottom of the hollow primarily because its colors are so much brighter and purer than the colors around us. There is a purple, a gold, and a white in the region above, a white that is much whiter than alabaster and snow, and other colors that are more beautiful than any we have ever seen. Yet, though but by reflection, even our inhabited world provides a colorful sight throughout. The surface of the true earth, however, is a "sight for the eyes of the blessed." We are reminded of this passage in the *Phaedo* as the section on colors in the *Timaeus* concludes by referring to the difference between human nature and divine. God has the power to blend the many into one and to dissolve the one into the many, but no man, now or ever, is capable of performing either task.

In between these links—with the *Meno* at the beginning and

with the *Phaedo* at the end—this section on colors in the *Timaeus* gives a detailed analysis of the colors themselves: the primary colors, the opposite colors, the mixed colors, and the effect of colors on the human eye.

The earlier thinkers held different views also on the nature of
67A–67C *sounds.* According to Empedokles, sound is produced when air currents strike against the solid, whereas according to Alkmaion, hearing is due to the empty space in the ear. Diogenes and probably Anaxagoras believed that sound reaches the brain through the air currents in the ear. In this Diokles, the physician, apparently concurred, and he also referred to the effect of the cranium as enclosing and perhaps amplifying the sound.[36] Plato distinguishes more sharply between the production of sounds and the occurrence of hearing. The path of the motion is longer than that envisaged by the earlier thinkers (from the head to the liver, the organ connecting the rational and the appetitive soul), but for Plato, too, the motion goes back again "to the soul." For, as in the case of sight, the human goal of hearing is to grasp harmony and rhythm and to assimilate to this high order what is devoid of harmony and rhythm in our soul.

65C–67A *Tastes and odors* Plato explains by means of the small veins ($\varphi\lambda\acute{\epsilon}\beta\epsilon\varsigma$), in the respective sense organs, through which the particles penetrate. In general, this corresponds to Empedokles' theory, which explains all sense perception by means of passages; it corresponds, in particular, to the explanation of the sense of taste by Diogenes.[37]

61D–62A In order to explain the phenomena of *warm and cold*, Anaxagoras identified warm with the loose and fine ($\mu\alpha\nu\grave{o}\nu$ $\kappa\alpha\grave{\imath}$ $\lambda\epsilon\pi\tau\acute{o}\nu$) and cold with the opaque and thick ($\pi\upsilon\kappa\nu\grave{o}\nu$ $\kappa\alpha\grave{\imath}$ $\pi\alpha\chi\acute{\upsilon}$). The Atomists held that hot bodies originate from atoms that are sharper ($\acute{o}\xi\upsilon\tau\acute{\epsilon}\rho\omega\nu$), composed of finer parts ($\lambda\epsilon\pi\tau\omega\mu\epsilon\rho\epsilon\sigma\tau\acute{\epsilon}\rho\omega\nu$), and situated on an equal plane. Of Demokritos, in particular, it is reported that he explained the sensation ($\sigma\upsilon\nu\alpha\acute{\imath}\sigma\theta\eta\sigma\iota\varsigma$) of warmth by processes of separation and division ($\delta\iota\alpha\kappa\rho\iota\tau\iota\kappa\grave{\alpha}$ $\kappa\alpha\grave{\imath}$ $\delta\iota\alpha\iota\rho\epsilon\tau\iota\kappa\acute{\alpha}$), and cold by processes of combination and condensation. Here in the *Timaeus* (61D *et seq.*), Plato emphasizes the fineness ($\lambda\epsilon\pi\tau\acute{o}\tau\eta\varsigma$) of the edges, the sharpness ($\acute{o}\xi\acute{\upsilon}\tau\eta\varsigma$) of the angles, and the swiftness of the movement, and explains the phenomenon "warm" by the sharpness and cutting (σφοδρὸν καὶ τομόν) and by the separating (διακρίνουσα) and piercing of the particles. In this respect, he belongs to the group of thinkers represented by Anaxagoras and Demokritos. Yet, Plato is more consciously concerned than they were to explain not only the objective phenomenon, but at the same time the subjective occurrence of the sensation. This is especially apparent in his graphic analysis of the sensation of cold.[38]

Finally, it is worth noting that the problem of *pleasure and pain* is treated as part of the problem of sensations both in the *Timaeus* and in the doxographic reports. Plato's analysis, however, is much richer and more subtle, having little in common with what Empedokles, Anaxagoras, and Diogenes are reported to have taught. Though Plato, like Diogenes, describes pleasure as a phenomenon "according to nature," and pain as an occurrence "against nature," he goes his own way in every other respect and here, too, carries the phenomena through "to the soul" itself.[39] 64c–65b

Medicine

As in the case of Plato's physics, here too an interpretation of the text would have to take into consideration several basic questions. (*1*) Who were Plato's predecessors? (*2*) What is Plato's own contribution? (*3*) What was his influence in the ancient world, in the medieval world, Latin, Greek, and Arabic, in the Renaissance, and so on? (*4*) What does Plato's medicine mean when viewed from the perspective of modern medical science—and vice versa? In our brief space here, we can at best say a few words about the first two questions.[40] 81e–90d

It is understandable that Plato would adopt a medical theory based, like his physics, on the Empedoklean theory of elements. A representative of such a theory, perhaps the main representative, was Philistion of Syracuse, whom Plato, according to the *Second Letter* (314e), knew personally. It is the general view today that Plato followed Philistion—and to a far greater extent than we are justified in claiming on the basis of the actual records.[41] There is something to be said for this view, although, as with Plato's physics, here again we must be careful not to exaggerate the influence of any single source. In addition to Philistion, Menekrates (whose epithet was "Zeus") and also Diokles had a theory essentially of the four elements.[42] Furthermore, between Empedokles and Philistion there must have been several other representatives of this theory.[43] Significantly enough, Timaios himself points out in the first sentence of this section in the dialogue that there is general agreement on the origin of diseases.

There is another consideration, still more important. Plato does not copy; he rethinks. From the four elements, Philistion extracted the four "powers" (δυνάμεις) always co-ordinate with them—hot and cold, moist and dry. He then explained the first of his three types of diseases as the result of too much or too little of one of these powers. The *Timaeus* also employs these contrasts, but in addition to these two pairs it postulates "light and heavy and a variety of other changes." This abundance of opposites corresponds to Alkmaion's characteristically Pythagorean derivation of health from the "equal rights" of these powers (ἰσονομία τῶν δυνάμεων) and disease from the "tyranny" (μοναρχία) of any single power. Plato employs a similar political metaphor in referring to the "excess" (πλεονεξία) of a single power, from which arise "disorders and revolts" (στάσεις).[44]

If Plato here combines certain ideas of Philistion's and Alkmaion's, he also substitutes something quite different for Philistion's third type of diseases, those caused by external factors (παρὰ τὰ ἐκτός). For Plato there are three varieties of externally caused diseases, depending on whether they are caused by air (πνεῦμα) or phlegm (φλέγμα) or bile (χολή). What the varieties have in common is this, that a diseased state occurs and grows worse when these materials remain locked up in the body, whereas relief or health occurs when there is a way out for them (διεξόδους, 84D 3; ἔξω πορευθῆναι, 84E 4; ἔξω τοῦ σώματος, 85A 2). Now breath, or *pneuma*, has a special significance in Philistion's system, where health depends upon a "good airing of the body" (ὅταν εὐπνοῇ). Plato's etiology of pneumonia long has been compared to that of Diokles, and here, too, Philistion has been surmised to be Plato's true teacher.[45] With regard to Plato's procedure in this section of the *Timaeus*, it might be said, then, that he takes phlegm and bile from a two-juice theory of the sort that may be found in many—it is believed "Knidic"—writings of the Hippokratean tradition and transfers them into the system of Philistion.[46] When we discover, however, that according to ancient medical theory in India, "wind, bile, and phlegm" are the three "defects" responsible for the origin of diseases,[47] we may well wonder if there are connections about which we have learned only the merest beginnings.[48]

Whether we prefer to call Plato, in his medical theories, an eclectic or rather a synoptic thinker depends on whether we assign him a place in the history of medicine or regard him as a philosopher of nature who is seriously concerned with the theory of medicine. Suppose we compare the few lines he writes about epilepsy (*Timaeus* 85AB) with the treatise, *On the Sacred Disease*, written by Hippokrates himself or one of his earliest disciples.[49] In this treatise, the medical scientist objects to the popular name "sacred disease," arguing that epilepsy is no more sacred than any other disease. In his opinion, the false name only serves to strengthen the widespread superstition according to which magical remedies are to be used in treating this disease. On the contrary, it has a perfectly natural origin, he states, since it is caused by phlegm's entering the brain in addition to blood and air. Plato adopts this natural etiology for epilepsy except that, in addition to phlegm, he theorizes that "black bile" also is responsible for onset of the disease. His contribution, however, consists in defending the popular name—against Hippokrates— and in giving it new meaning. Epilepsy is justly called the "sacred disease," according to Plato, because phlegm and bile throw the "most divine circuits" (περίοδοι) in the head into confusion.

This circular movement, so important for the whole view of nature developed in the *Timaeus*, is referred to earlier in these sections of the work that deal with medicine (82c *et seq.*). The normal course of nourishment is said to run from the blood to the flesh and to the fibers—sinews and nerves are not yet distinguished—and thence to the bones and finally the marrow. The disturbance or, worse, the reversal of this course is the cause of one type of disease in which the "order of the natural circuits" (τάξις τῶν κατὰ φύσιν περιόδων, 83Α) no longer is preserved. The seriousness of the disease then depends upon whether the reversal reaches as far as the marrow or only goes to the bones or the flesh. While it remains to be shown from which medical theory this view is derived, clearly there are Platonic features in it, in detail as well as on a larger scale. Plato's physics is present in the reference to the "triangles of the purest and smoothest kind" that penetrate through the bones into the marrow (82D). And the courses or "periods" according to nature and against nature remind us, not by accident, of the cosmic periods in the myth of the *Statesman*, the period of divine sovereignty and the period of drifting and distance from God—an indication that Plato's sublime view of the macrocosm also enters into his conception of the human body.

What is said about the diseases (following upon the structure of the human body) culminates, as is to be expected, in the diseases of the soul, which Plato adds to the transformed system of Philistion (86B *et seq.*). Here psychiatry and ethics are combined. And when, in a countermovement (ἀντίστροφον, 87C), therapy is discussed after the diseases, there emerges the image of a man whose body and soul are in the state of proportion and symmetry, the perfect image of man. A new expression—"should" or "ought" (δεῖ, -έον)—otherwise missing in the *Timaeus* makes its appearance here. The perfect image "ought" to be realized. The means toward this realization is the perfect co-ordination, as far as possible, of the motions in the body with those in the soul. Perfection in this respect means that the motions approximate, again as far as possible, the self-motion of the universe, cosmic motion. The body achieves this by gymnastics (89A), the soul by unison with the motions of the universe (90CD). Now it becomes clear what the "ought" really means. Imperfection in the world is due to the power of *Ananke*. To transform a part of this imperfection into perfection is within the power of man. More than that, it is his specific task in this world to do so—as is pointed out once more in the *Laws* (X 905C *et seq.*). Thus, the final passage on animals, quite fantastic and grotesque, serves to show, in the metaphorical context of the transmigration of souls, what may befall the man who does not live up to this task. Yet, even as imperfections are said to be only spots on the perfection of the whole, so the dialogue itself concludes with an encomium to the universe. And in this we are reminded once more of the beginning of the creation myth (31B 3).

Let us look back on the work as a whole from the perspective of the two kinds of "causes" (pp. 360ff., above) on which the composition of the *Timaeus* is based. The theory of sensations had taken us to the point where the body determined the mind and where material causes crossed teleology (47E). Then the entire middle part of the dialogue pursues the course of material causes. It is concerned mainly with the doctrine of the elements as characteristic of the domain of nature, in which the rule of *Ananke* is most powerful and the action of the mind is just barely perceptible. Sensations, treated earlier from a teleological point of view, are analyzed next in terms of material causes. This section concludes (68E–69A) with a retrospective summary of the two "causes," even as it began with their analysis.

The first part of the dialogue breaks off as it becomes clear, in the discussion on the joining of body and soul, that the phenomenon of sensation cannot be dealt with in terms of one cause only (47E). The middle part constantly carries the material type of explanation back "to the soul" itself. Now the third part continues where the first broke off (69A). The human body is constructed "in order to" serve as the mortal conveyance of the soul. The characteristic connective "in order to" now predominates even though the material cause retains its indispensable, but subordinate, place. We can appreciate this fantastic biology only if we keep in mind the theoretical foundations upon which Plato is constructing it. Even so, it is clear that there is much room for grotesque and ironic play in the midst of these teleological speculations.

Between diaphragm and navel, the gods fasten the appetitive part of the soul to a manger, as far away as possible from the organ of thought, with the intention that it should cause the very minimum of confusion and noise (70E). The liver they fashion in order to mirror what happens in the soul, and they make the spleen a sponge for the purpose of keeping the mirror of the liver always shiny (71B *et seq.*). The bowels wind in many coils in order to keep food for a long time and in order to prevent the human race, insatiable in its desire for food and drink, from losing its appetite for philosophy and music (73A). Through the medium of this play Plato indicates, as it were, that only the creator-god himself could tell us in all seriousness the meaning of the "in order that." At the same time, however, the play derives its own meaning from the serious moral demand with which it confronts us. And so let it once more be appreciated how much would be missing in this whole discussion if Socrates were not listening—he who fulfills this demand both in his life and in his death.

A scientific-minded philosopher of nature would have proceeded quite differently from Plato's way in the *Timaeus*. He would have stated, to begin with—as, for example, Aristotle does in his *Physics*—the basic principles, i.e., the doctrine of causes, and would follow this with the theory of elements and then with the construction of the physical world on these foundations. We have seen why Plato did not begin in this way. Looking back on the whole work, we see even more clearly how the realm of *Ananke* is placed at its center, enclosed by the realm of intelligence and purpose into which the "accessory causes" barely enter and at that without any claim to equal consideration. The work concludes with the creation of the universe and an encomium to it. Within this universe we are shown the living beings, both immortal and mortal. With respect to the mortal beings, we begin again with the most perfect, the reasonable soul whose place is in the head, and conclude on a note of perfection—for once more to attain the perfect motion is the task imposed upon human reason. Still, in the middle part of the work, this perfection is impaired since, ultimately, we descend to the level where we encounter the absolutely indefinite. Called by various names, the indefinite represents the power of unreason, chaos, and the anti-divine. This middle part remains surrounded, then, by perfection that comes to dominate as it moves outward toward the periphery. In its very structure, the *Timaeus* is a copy of the ordered system of the universe that it re-creates interpretatively.[50]

THIRTY

Critias

PLATO included in the beginning of the *Timaeus* the fantastic foundations for the myth of Atlantis which Kritias is called upon to tell in the dialogue named after him. We learn in the *Timaeus* that Kritias had heard his grandfather tell the story of these ancient events at the feast of the Apatouria—an "April Fools' Day." We expect to hear the rest of the story after this preliminary report. Then Plato has Kritias suddenly change the (alleged) plan of procedure.[1] Timaios is to speak first, since the creation of the universe must take precedence. If this is a surprise it is nonetheless meaningful. For it enables Plato to join the two dialogues, the *Timaeus* and the *Critias*, to each other and to link their themes that seem so far apart—mythical philosophy of nature and mythical philosophy of history.[2] Some rough spots undoubtedly remained after Plato made this connection, which was not originally planned in this way. He did not achieve a final integration. Moreover, the fact that Hermokrates, the Sicilian, says a few words in each dialogue (*Timaeus* 20A *et seq.; Critias* 108A *et seq.*) also points to the third dialogue in this trilogy. This would be the *Hermocrates*, which Plato did not even begin to write.

We know that Kritias was one of the Thirty. As to Hermokrates, the man who was the predecessor of Dionysios I, we find a clear picture of him in the works of the historians Thucydides and Ephorus. In Thucydides, Hermokrates makes two speeches, in which he appeals to "all of Sicily," and also advocates an alliance "of all who are called by the *one* name Sicilians," an alliance, in short, against the danger threatening them from both Carthage and Athens. He points out that the Athenians have been weakened because they dare to wage an aggressive war so far from home—they should have learned their lesson from the Persian Wars! From these hints we may at least guess at what Hermokrates was supposed to represent in the third dialogue of the trilogy. Plato conceived the myth of Atlantis and the invasion of the Atlantides after the model of the Persian Wars. At the same time, he also had in mind the power of Carthage extending throughout the western Mediterranean, and Athens' disastrous campaign against Syracuse. As little as we can surmise what Plato really intended, it is likely that these matters would have found a place in the dialogue *Hermocrates*. And that he did intend to write such a dialogue completing the trilogy is as certain as it is that he never intended to write the *Philosopher*.

It cannot be accidental either that for these two closely linked dialogues, the *Timaeus* and the *Critias*, Plato chose as main speakers two men who were killed in the civil wars of their respective cities. Did he mean to suggest, among other things, the fate that might have threatened him had he not withdrawn from the political affairs of Athens? That he was not siding with the Thirty when he chose Kritias, his relative, as the speaker in this dialogue goes without saying—whether or not Plato's enemies among the historians and sociologists of today exploit this case against him. For the *Apology* (32CD) makes it quite clear what Plato thought of this oligarchic regime that would have put Socrates to death had it but lasted long enough.

We have previously discussed the story of Atlantis in its nature as a myth.[3] The earlier chapters on "Plato as Geographer" and "Plato as City Planner"[4] show how precisely Plato constructed the geography of the continent of Atlantis and also envisaged the imaginary city and landscape. It remains to say something about how this myth grew out of Plato's work.

In its origins, this imaginary reconstruction of primitive Athens is related to the praise of Athens reported in the very un-Socratic speech delivered by Socrates in the *Menexenus*. The first half of that speech, as well as the speech of Kritias here, follows the basic pattern of an encomium—praise of the country and its inhabitants, praise of their constitution, praise of their heroic deeds. This correspondence extends to details which sometimes modify what was said earlier. The country is "dear to the gods" (θεοφιλής), and to this love the strife (ἔρις) among the gods testifies. In the *Menexenus* (237c), Plato leaves this innermost contradiction as a sting. Now (*Critias* 109b) he states expressly that the gods obtained the share dear to them (τὸ φίλον λαγχάνοντες) not by strife (οὐ κατ' ἔριν) but by righteous allotment. In both works, Athens is contrasted with the rest of the world (ἡ πᾶσα γῆ, *Menexenus* 237d 4; πᾶσα γῆ, *Critias* 110e 3). Her fertility is praised, and "good evidence" (μέγα τεκμήριον) is adduced for her excellence.

Furthermore, it is shown in the *Menexenus* (238c) that the constitution of Athens is a government of the best. In the *Critias*, the construction of Plato's own ideal state is presupposed, and it is attached to the Athenian landscape, to the Acropolis and the surrounding plain. Also, both works cite the many heroic deeds of the city (πολλὰ καὶ καλὰ ἔργα, *Menexenus* 239a; μεγάλα καὶ θαυμαστὰ ἔργα, *Timaeus* 20e; πολλὰ καὶ μεγάλα ἔργα, *Timaeus* 24d; cf. *Critias* 112e). If in the *Menexenus*, the Persian empire is the most important enemy, here in the *Critias*, the empire of Atlantis is the only adversary. And even as in the *Menexenus* (239d *et seq.*) the Persians, protagonists of the whole of Asia who are on the verge of subduing Europe, are stopped by the Athenians, so it is Athens here (*Timaeus* 24e) that puts an end to the power of the Atlantic empire as it mobilizes its forces against all of Europe and Asia. Atlantis had to become a sea power as opposed to the land power of Athens, and not Salamis but Marathon had to serve as the historical model for this mythical battle, because Plato incorporates into the historical myth the conviction that a city situated by the sea is hopelessly incapable of acquiring virtue (*Laws* IV 704d). All in all, it becomes clear once more that an ideal Athens is contrasted to an ideal non-Hellenic world, not to say an ideal Orient. This is the same conclusion we reached previously in analyzing the composition of the myth and the picture of the city and land of the Atlantides.

A great distance separates Ur-Athens and Atlantis from the encomium in the *Menexenus*. Yet—strange as this may sound

—it is in the *Menexenus,* which blends both praise and criticism in an irritating fashion, that the historical myth has at least one of its roots. For myths, too, combine criticism of the present with a wishful image of what ought to be, or with a frightening view of the future. So all later utopias have followed Plato's model, beginning with Thomas More and ending—for the time being—with Orwell's *Nineteen Eighty-Four.*

THIRTY-ONE

Laws

FOR THE Greeks and for Plato legislation was one of the highest human tasks. In the *Symposium* (209D), Diotima mentions Lykurgos and Solon along with Homer and Hesiod because of their works, their spiritual children who earned them fame and memory for all time. As Plato there ranks the greatest lawgivers and the greatest poets on the same level, so in his old age he sets up books of law as the standard by which even all poetry is to be measured (*Laws* IX 858E) and recommends his own laws as the best thing that one can give young boys to learn by heart (VII 811CD). There is, to be sure, a basic tension between what Plato inherited as a member of his family and class, on the one hand, and his deeply rooted suspicion of the written word, on the other—a suspicion which prevented him from believing that the utmost seriousness of a genuinely serious person could ever be expressed, even in legislation (*Letter VII* 344CD).[1] This tension that runs through his statements here reflects, ultimately, the tension between the Solon in him and the Socrates in him.

When Plato was called to Syracuse he could not be simply the philosopher; he had to be legislator as well. Yet he added "preambles" (προοίμια) to his laws, as we learn from one of his letters.[2] This means that even the legislation for Syracuse, whether much or little of it was written down, was intended to be a work of education. The power of a Solon in him joins the Socratic power for the sake of common action. It must be the case, therefore, that the *Laws*, Plato's last work, in which the author specifically claims the "preambles" as his own contribution (IV 722D *et seq.*), contains a great deal of the spirit, substance, and form that went into the legislative drafts for Syracuse.[3] That this attempt at political action was not realized either, but crystallized in a work of art, corresponds to a deep inner law in Plato's life. At times he undoubtedly felt pain at producing "nothing but words and never undertaking a concrete task" (*Letter VII* 328c). Nevertheless, it was more in keeping with his nature to affirm a fate that would bestow upon this work, too, the higher reality and permanence of the written form. What would have remained inadequate as the actual legislation of Syracuse and forever lost for posterity is now preserved as the final work in the series of Plato's spiritual creations. Even so, the *Laws* did have some effect upon Plato's own time, and the influence it has had on Hellenistic and Roman law as well as on later systems, directly and indirectly, remains to be investigated.[4]

The symbolic location for this conversation on the laws is the island of Crete, the mythical *Urland* of Greek legislation, from which all later legislative work, including Plato's, derives its dignity.[5] The walk taken by the three old men leads (like the climb once made by Minos) from Cnossus to the mountain shrine of Zeus, a symbol that "every great *nomos* of the Greeks is infused with the living breath of the great lawgivers."[6] Kleinias and Megillos represent the two Doric states, Crete and Sparta, to which the new legislation is deeply indebted— though it must go beyond them. When Plato, many decades earlier, personified the laws of Athens in the *Crito*, he had then reminded Socrates of the "compact" between the laws of the state and its citizens. They also point out (*Crito* 52E) that while Socrates had always highly praised the laws of Sparta and Crete, he had demonstrated by his own life that, above all other Greek cities, he preferred Athens and, hence, the laws of Athens as well. In this spirit, an Athenian is the leader of the conversation because only Athens has the intellectual power for this task. This is shown in the beginning (I 642B *et seq.*) when the Spartan and the Cretan join in paying tribute to the Athenian (641E *et seq.*).[7]

It is not surprising that this Athenian does not have a name,

even as the characters in Goethe's *Natürliche Tochter* are nameless. The reason for not introducing Socrates is by no means
the distance from Athens, but rather the distance from what
Socrates represents in Plato.[8] That Athens is distant, however,
and that Socrates is absent have the same symbolic meaning. To
put himself into the dialogue would have gone against Plato's
deepest conviction. It would also have been quite false,[9] for
there are moments in the dialogue when Plato's Athenian descends to the level of the "all-too-fond-of-divinations" (φιλο-
μαντευτάς, VII 813D) and yields to popular beliefs to the point of
recognizing ghostly voices and demons attached to specific
localities.[10] Moreover, Plato's highest ideal does not come into
the dialogue at all, for he still clings to the ideal state founded
by Socrates as the best (*Laws* V 739A *et seq.*, VII 807B). The
state in the *Laws* is the "second-best," even though as a second
(ἡ μία δευτέρως, 739E 4), it is unique as is the first.[11] In Plato
the Socratic power is closer to the core of his own being than
the Solonic power, also a part of him; yet the Athenian legislating here has much less of Socrates than of Solon.

The Struggle about the Meaning of Legislation

"God" is the first word of the dialogue, spoken by the Athenian.   624A-632D
It is twice repeated by the Cretan, with the difference that the   BOOK I
Athenian means the word in the highest sense, whereas the
Cretan's invocation seems directed to "a God" one might call
Zeus or Apollo. According to Cretan belief, Zeus was the
source of the laws of Crete. In the course of the conversation,
when the new constitution is to be founded but before the actual
legislation begins (IV 712B), "God" is invoked to "share in
the ordering of the constitution." And "God" is again invoked
in Book X (893B), when it is a matter of convictions about the
universe and the presence in it of divine powers. This is also
when the religious laws are about to be established. "God"
is invoked so that the faith in a divine being shall be secure
among the citizens. The sophists had de-deified the "laws." To
deify them again is the task that Plato set for himself.

The Athenian opens the conversation with a direct reference   624A-626D
to the "laws" of Crete. It is immediately clear that the word

"laws" is used in a very general sense, inasmuch as the institution of common meals, schools of gymnastics, and the special use of weapons are cited as peculiarities of Cretan laws. The next question concerns the meaning of these institutions, at what (κατὰ τί) do they aim? Kleinias, the Cretan, replies that the lawgiver instituted them, like everything else, with a view to war, as anyone can easily see from the general conditions in Crete. From this, however, he immediately draws his own, and as he thinks, more profound, conclusion with regard to the nature of the state. The normal relationship between states is a constant and inexorable (undeclared) state of war. Peace is a mere name. In real fact there is a perpetual *bellum omnium contra omnes*, not only—as Hobbes and Spinoza will say—in a primitive state, but permanently by nature (κατὰ φύσιν). This insight guided the Cretan legislator, Kleinias continues, and he does not indicate the least opposition when he states the legislator's conviction that military supremacy alone guarantees an advantage with respect to possessions and institutions, and that all possessions of the vanquished belong to the victor.

The Athenian makes this point still more explicit, for in his words, a good state must be so organized, then, as to be victorious over others in warfare. Kleinias easily wins Megillos' assent to this basic proposition because it expresses what "every Spartan" believes. The Athenian, however, in order to overcome this view to which he is opposed, pursues it further. The same state of war would hold between village and village, household and household, one individual and another, and even within the same individual.[12] As the Athenian had praised Kleinias (626B) for having a good insight (διειδέναι) into the nature of legislation, so Kleinias now reciprocates in praising the Athenian by praising Athens and its goddess. For the Athenian, so says Kleinias, has reduced the discussion to the basic "principle" by showing that victory in a universal struggle is the common goal pursued everywhere.

626D–627c The Athenian has led—or misled—his partners to where the principle of victorious struggle culminates in the struggle within the individual and in a victory over himself. Yet at the very point where Kleinias is pleased to see his own view stated in its purest form, the view is also undermined. Victory over oneself, or self-mastery (κρείττω ἑαυτοῦ εἶναι), is the principle that guides the discussion in this passage. It is easy to see that the expression "self-mastery," often used at the time, was also much abused in sophistic controversies. He who is master of himself must also be a servant to himself, as is said in the *Republic* (IV 430E). Such eristic reasoning is only barely alluded to here. Does not Plato employ the concept of self-mastery in the *Republic* (430E *et seq.*) in order to show, against such eristic reasoning, that self-mastery is the basis of the true order in the individual and in the state? Thus, the Athenian now declines (*Laws* 627B) to descend to the eristic level. Instead, he points out emphatically that it is a matter not of wrangling over words, but of deciding the basic question as to what is right or wrong about laws "by nature." If self-mastery in the case of the individual means that the better part rules over the worse, then we may apply the same meaning to groups and associations, including the state. (The parallelism between individual and state, we observe, is a guiding principle here as in the *Republic*.) In this way Kleinias concedes—almost without noticing it—that the objective of a state is not victory as such but victory of the better, or victory of the just (as the Athenian puts it, restricting the ambiguity of the Greek word "better").

Thus, the view the Athenian opposes is merely restricted so far; it is not yet overcome. The Athenian now selects a small group for the purpose of analysis, a family of unlike brothers, "just and unjust," or in other words, hostile brothers. A "judge" is introduced into this situation. Either he can exterminate the bad brothers, or he can set up the good brothers as rulers over the bad, or—this would be the best solution—he can reconcile the hostile brothers and make them friends by means of permanent "laws." Similarly, in the larger area of the state, the lawgiver must be concerned not so much with external warfare as with internal warfare, civil war. To prevent civil war or, if it should break out, to restore peace as quickly as possible, must be his main objective. And the best course would not be the victory of one faction, but the reconciliation of the hostile factions. Thus, the opposing view is overcome. The best thing is

627c–629A

not war. Even victory belongs not to the best things, but only to the "necessary." The aim of legislation can only be to promote internal peace and concord (φιλοφροσύνη).

629A–632D   The peaceful struggle—for a struggle it is—among the three old men is continued on a still more basic level against the background of a contrast between the poets Tyrtaios and Theognis. While Tyrtaios praised most highly those who showed courage in war against external enemies, Theognis would weigh in gold the worth of a loyal man in internal warfare. Civil war makes higher demands on men than external war. In external war, courage—a part of virtue and the least part of it at that—is enough. Civil war requires in addition to courage the virtues of justice, moderation, and reason. In short, civil war requires the "whole" of virtue. Therefore, the lawgiver must aim at "arete as a whole" or, as we might say, the "supreme virtue," the "highest justice." Hence, Lykurgos and Minos, who were counseled by the gods, framed their legislation with a view not to a "part of virtue," but to virtue as a whole.[13]

Three stages of possible legislation may be discerned. On the lowest level, the laws are framed singly—and so it is customary "today"—as the need arises.[14] On a higher level, the principle of legislation is based on *one* virtue, and the least virtue at that. This is the stage at which Kleinias and Megillos envisage the work of their legislators. The Athenian demands the highest stage, adding (with proper irony) that if we but look closely, we must be able to find it in Crete. The aim of legislation on the highest level is to promote happiness or, put differently, to provide "all good things."

Now there are two types of "good things," things human, of which there are four kinds, praised since Solon's time[15]—health, beauty, physical strength, and wealth—and things divine, which are the Socratic-Platonic virtues of wisdom, moderation, justice, and courage. Things human depend (ἤρτηται) on things divine, without which they are not "goods." Yet he who possesses the divine goods, possesses the human goods as well. This system of goods—elaborated earlier, in the *Euthydemus* (278E *et seq.*) and the *Meno* (78C *et seq.*)—is essentially prior (ἔμπροσθεν) to all legislation. Hence, it must also be given priority by the legislator. All his statutes must be framed "with a view" to this system, and in it the human goods must be ordered with a view to the divine, the divine with a view to the "leader reason." Here for a moment, as the end of the entire process (631D 5), reason emerges. And reason, according to the *Philebus* (28C), "is the king of heaven and earth, as all the wise agree." At the very end of the *Laws* (963A), we are referred again to this system of virtues and its "leader reason." This, then, is the frame that holds the whole work together.

The laws themselves must begin with marriage and procreation, nourishment, and education. They must end with burial and honoring the dead. It is the life process itself that determines the order of the laws, and even within these limits of life, the order is determined by human rather than legal considerations. The human beings we have seen here born and raised we now encounter in their social relations (ἐν ὁμιλίαις). We see them as natural creatures subject to pleasure and pain, desires, and the passions of love. We see them in states of anger and fear, of inner confusion and passions (παθήματα). We see them acquiring and spending, entering into social relations and dissolving them. It is the task of the laws to supervise the citizens in the midst of this movement of men and circumstances, intensified by good fortune and misfortune, sickness, war, poverty, and their opposites, to supervise the citizens and establish the norms of human action, to honor what is just and fair and to punish the opposite. And at the conclusion of the work as a whole—after the honors due the dead are established, to crown the completed life—there follows the institution of the custodians of the law. They represent in human form *reason*, evidently the "leader reason" just mentioned, binding the whole work of legislation together and placing it under the principles of self-discipline (*sophrosyne*) and justice (632C).

What kind of legislation is instituted here, on a grandiose scale and in noble if sometimes obscure words (631B–632D)? You should have explained, says the Athenian (632D), how all these merits are contained in the laws of Minos and Lykurgos if their claim of being divinely inspired is to be honored, since to us this is by no means visible. The irony in these words must be heard and understood, for the demand raised here ("Even now I expect you to explain . . .") is not and cannot be fulfilled. Only with this understanding does the reader realize what this controversial model of legislation actually intends to do.[16] It looks both backward and forward. As it shows that the highly praised laws of old are inadequate when judged by the standard of the "leader reason," it also provides a first glimpse of what a rational work of legislation would have to look like.

And, indeed, Plato will later frame his own laws in such an order, and will look back to this order once again at the end (XII 958CD). As his laws are framed, they accompany—as an educational force—the whole life process from procreation to death, or rather from before procreation to after death. All specific statutes are to have their place in this lifelong education, and at the end the body of legislation is to be guarded by special custodians (XII 963A). So much does the order of Plato's legislation differ both from the accidental element dominating the laws of Gortyn and from the systematic conceptualization of Roman law and consequently of many modern systems of law as well. Plato's legislation aims at being an education of man throughout his life.

This preliminary sketch of a legislative project concludes the contest. The Athenian says expressly (629A) that it was a struggle, though conducted in a mild form. Yet, what is the contest about? It is about the meaning of legislation as such. And against whom is it waged? Not against those who frame laws as the occasion demands, but against a relatively high principle of legislation existing in reality. This is represented in Crete and Sparta and is characterized by the fact that all individual statutes are framed according to a unified conception. Plato praises these systems for having such a conception, yet for him this conception is not enough. He intends to erect his own laws over those of Crete and Sparta. This is the purpose of the struggle.

In the struggle for the pure idea of the state and in the overcoming of a principle of legislation based entirely on courage (i.e., on a "part of virtue" and not on "virtue as a whole") we recognize, although in sublimated form, an old and deep conflict that had occupied Plato before. The Cretan asserts that war of all against all is the natural state of affairs, that peace is a mere "name," that the only real thing is victory, and that the possessions of the vanquished belong to the victors. Do not these statements ultimately amount to the view of natural law as expounded by Kallikles in the *Gorgias* (483E)? There we are told that justice means that the stronger "have more" than the weaker, that it "has been called" (λέγεται) injustice to desire to have more than the many. Or, according to the words of Glaukon in the *Republic* (II 359A), men made a compact to terminate the universal state of war, the situation in which everybody was inflicting injustice upon everybody else, and this compact is the law—or rather it "has been called" (ὀνομάσαι) the law.

Yet, the view in the *Laws* is still more radical. The state of war is not terminated at all; it continues unabated, but is concealed behind the deceptive name of peace.[17] Furthermore, when we learn that the laws of Sparta and Crete are framed according to the ideal of courage, we must remember that Kallikles also linked the greed-for-more with courage (*Gorgias* 490A), and that Socrates then also opposed the singling out of a particular virtue which, in isolation, is no longer a virtue. The decisive question of Socrates (*Gorgias* 491B), which the opponent did not understand, was whether a person striving for power must also be able to master himself. Here in the *Laws*, too, the turning point in the conversation comes with the concept of self-mastery. Kleinias still thinks this confirms his own point of view, whereas the Athenian conceives of it as transforming the ordinary concept of courage into something higher.

In calling attention to the *Gorgias* let us not forget the *Thrasymachus*, the first book of the *Republic*.[18] There Thrasymachos defends the principle of unlimited *pleonexia* (which can conceal itself so easily, however, behind the name of courage) and Socrates launches his decisive counterthrust by showing (351C *et seq.*) that a city, an army, and even a gang of thieves —in short, any kind of community—can act only if "justice" prevails in it, producing a communal spirit and friendship. The

same applies to the individual, whose soul is a small "republic."
So speaks the Socrates in Plato. But the "Athenian"—or one
might say, the Solon in Plato—transforms this concept of "justice" into a legislation which would reconcile conflicts in a
community so that its members would be on permanently
peaceful terms (διαλλάξας, 628A 1). In other words, it would
not cover up a state of undeclared internal warfare with the deceptive name of peace.

In the broad structure of the *Republic*, the opening conflict
with Thrasymachos serves to remind us of the victory that
must be won over the hostile forces in society—won not once,
but again and again—if the ideal state is to exist. The opening
conversation in the *Laws* serves the same function in the quieter
style characteristic of Plato's old age. Here, too, the work of
true legislation can commence only after its meaning has been
established in opposition to a false principle. This shows to
what a degree even this late work still is a dialogue, no matter
how often we may meet the prejudiced view that in the end,
Plato clung to the form of the dialogue only out of respect for
his own past.

634C 5–638B 3   The contest which is waged at the beginning of Book I,
culminating in a victory of the new legislation over the Doric
idea of the state, runs in several episodes through the sections
that follow. Along with his criticisms of the systems of Crete and
Sparta, the Athenian singles out for praise a Doric law that
forbids younger men, and likewise older men when in the
presence of younger men, to pass judgment on any existing
law. For himself, however, and for his partners he claims the
right to friendly, cautious, and constructive criticism, and
the Cretan agrees. When there is no malice (μὴ φθόνῳ) in the
critique, or when one's attitude is not simply reproachful
(ἐπιτιμῶν) but inquiring (ἀπορῶν), then criticism is not destructive, but rather is the attempt to penetrate beyond what
has been criticized, though in the same direction, to that which
is higher.

The Athenian criticizes the Doric laws on the following point,
that while they put highest emphasis on the struggle against
pain and fear, they fail to do the same for man's struggle

against pleasure. Before the Athenian makes his own puzzling proposal to employ wine-drinking as a means of education, there follows another conflict over existing customs. The Athenian points out that even such excellent Spartan practices as physical exercises and common meals are fraught with danger in that they may be the seat for revolutionary conspiracies and the practice of pederasty. The Spartan, resenting this critique, counters by scorning the licentiousness prevalent at Athenian drinking parties as well as at the festivals of Dionysos. The Athenian, with superior calm, replies by pointing to the license of Spartan women, but adds that nothing is accomplished by such criticism. For what matters is not the general practice here or there, but whether the legislator himself is any good. Evidently the Athenian means that criticism must be concerned not with the success or failure of some specific item, but with the principle of legislation as such.

There is a third mild encounter. It seems as if the Athenian wants to derive a lesson from peoples among whom there is no drinking, a lesson that cannot be learned from the Spartans. The Spartan counters proudly: these people we beat with the power of our arms. This argument appeals again, however, to the kind of "courage" whose limits were defined at the beginning of the whole work. The Athenian once more warns against overestimating victory and, somewhat later (641c), warns even against the dangers of victory. Victory often leads to loss of education. Yet what counts is education, which is ultimately synonymous with the balance of the virtues. Again, then, education is counterposed to strength, or we might say the Attic ideal to the Doric. 638AB–641C

The Doric resistance has already subsided. Presently it ceases altogether, and the Dorians surrender to the Athenian. An impressive moment in the dramatic structure of the work[19] is reached when the Athenian expands the strange topic of "drinking as an educational device" into a discussion of "education as a whole" (παιδείας τῆς πάσης). Should we keep away from a subject of such scope? Megillos and Kleinias here combine (though usually only one of them speaks) to say emphatically: no Sparta and Crete bow their heads in homage to 642A–643A

Athens. The words spoken by Megillos are particularly significant: "Those among the Athenians who are good (ἀγαθοί)
are exceptionally good. For they alone are excellent without
constraint, by their own growth, and by a divine gift of fate—
truly (ἀληθῶς) excellent and not only seemingly so (πλαστῶς)."
We must look ahead to the conclusion of the whole work (XII
968E *et seq.*), where the two Doric partners agree: however
much the Athenian may praise the state-building power of
Crete, it would fail without his spiritual co-operation.

What does all this mean? Only the Doric states have institutions that reflect a genuine political will and set a goal for political action. Hence, the founding of the new state must be pat-
terned after Crete and Sparta. Yet it must go beyond them by
eliminating their one-sidedness and thus shaping a system of
true education. This can be done only by an Athenian, for while
Athens as a state ranks far below Crete and Sparta, in the
spiritual capacity of her most excellent citizens she is unsur-
passed. Only an Athenian—only Plato—is capable of penetrating, purifying, and surpassing the intellectual foundations of the
Doric states. This happens in the first book of the *Laws* and is
echoed at the end of the last book. The whole work, therefore,
is conceived in this spirit.

In the *Republic*, the analysis of the defective constitutions
comes after the construction of the true state because they are
intelligible only as departures from this ideal. Yet the true
state is not simply a rank above the empirical states, not even
above the best of them. It is a creation *sui generis*. In the *Laws*,
however, we are dealing not with the pure ideal, but only with
an excellent creation in reality. This being so, the state in the
Laws can and must grow out of a historical context. And this
process of growing out of and beyond is what we witness at the
beginning.

The Test of Virtues as the Foundation of the State

632D–650B
BOOK I
It was no accident that the conversation of the three old men
began with the subject of *courage*. Even though the one-sided
Doric view (according to which all rightful legislation aims at
this one virtue) was rejected, the conversation nonetheless rein-

forced the conviction that all true legislation must be based
on clear insight into the structure of "goods" both human and
divine, i.e., the system of virtues leading upward to the "leader
reason." With this new insight, the conversation returns now   632D–635E
to the initial subject of courage, which is to be treated as one
virtue within a system of virtues. What we find here is a discussion like that in Book IV of the *Republic*, but transformed,
as it were, in the style of the *Laws*. This characteristic style
shows itself, in the first place, in an extraordinary enlargement
of the content, due, in part at least, to an interweaving of several
different lines of thought. The most important of these, the
one we have followed, is the struggle of Athens with Sparta and
Crete. In the second place, the discussion remains fragmentary.
It deals only with "courage" and "self-discipline" instead of
with the four virtues. But meanwhile, the lively give and take
of the conversation pursues a different course so that we notice
the omissions only in retrospect. In the third place, we find,
instead of systematic and conceptual analysis, a discussion that
stays close to the concrete facts of life. The discussion of self-
discipline grows into an exemplary discussion about the educational value of drinking, and also points out the damage that
total abstinence does to education.

The discussion of courage, the first topic, is to be carried
through as a model (632E 4). While Doric institutions apparently aim at cultivating this virtue, it turns out not only that
courage functions in isolation against all the other virtues but
that it is not even practiced in all respects. In short, courage is
practiced only with respect to fear and pain. Where is the hidden
courage displayed in the struggle against desire and pleasure
that we know from the *Laches* and from Book IV of the *Republic?* It is missing. Yet a perfect legislation should (ἔδει,
635c 4) see to it that courage does not remain "lame" (χωλήν,
634A 2).

We proceed to the second virtue, *sophrosyne* (temperance, or   635E–650B
self-discipline), and discover to our surprise that its nature has
already been treated as one aspect of courage, in connection
with the victorious struggle against the passions and pleasure.
Some interpreters criticize as a "logical flaw" the fact that al-

though it is expressly said we are proceeding to something new, the discussion still continues along the same course. To these critics this "flaw" indicates that the text was revised by some later editor.[20] Yet, if we go back to the system of virtues in the *Republic*, we find that the temptations overcome by courage, or manliness, are called "pleasure and pain, fear and desire" (IV 430AB). Self-discipline (*sophrosyne*), in turn, consists in the mastery of certain pleasures and desires (430E). Thus, the two virtues are practically indistinguishable—even though Plato may also separate them as parts of a whole.

The close connection between courage and self-discipline should not surprise us here. In the popular mind, these two virtues are so far removed from each other that Plato, from his earliest period on, regarded it as his task to reconcile them in the context of a unified theory of education. The means he employs toward this end differ. In the *Republic*, he establishes the ordered system of the virtues, a preliminary version of which he set up in the *Protagoras*. In the *Statesman*, he visualizes the art of weaving practiced by the royal statesman. In the *Laws*, he employs the "illogical" procedure—rightly observed, but wrongly criticized—in the course of which first he endows courage with those characteristics that the popular mind attributes to self-discipline, and then he turns, in a new move, to discuss self-discipline as if he had not just called the struggle against pleasure by the name of courage.

The close conjunction in which these two virtues are envisaged shows up also in the following parallel. Two kinds of fear are distinguished (646E *et seq.*). We are afraid of evil, of some danger, say; we also are afraid of a bad reputation. The first is fear in the general sense, while the second is modesty or shame (αἰδώς). The first must be avoided, the second cultivated. In the case of fear we prove ourselves against danger, and in the case of shame, against pleasure. In the first case, courage is opposed to cowardice, and in the second, self-discipline is opposed to shamelessness. The parallelism could not be carried through more strictly.

Instead of the systematic treatment of *sophrosyne* as in the *Republic*, we find here—and this is characteristic of the difference between the two works—an institution designed to test the virtue. This is the institution of banquets (symposia) as an instrument of political education. It is indeed a strange instrument, yet not so strange to an Athenian of those days as to modern man.[21] Evidently the Spartan custom of common meals was developed as just such an instrument. For this reason Plato incorporates it in the founding of his city (IV 780D *et seq.*) and, fully conscious of the strange innovation he is proposing, even opens the banquets to women. In Sparta the drinking of wine was forbidden, but in Athens convivial customs were all-pervasive, as vases, festivals, and the origin of tragedy and comedy may remind us. And the words of Theognis (vss. 499 *et seq.*), that as fire tests rare metals so wine tests man's mind, were widely accepted as valid beyond the aristocracy of Megara. As a political and educational force the Greek banquet cannot be overestimated. So Plato merely adopted what was widely practiced, even if he went on to seriously examine its moral significance.

If Plato spends more time on this subject of drinking parties than seems justified, the reason—aside from the style of his old age—is to be found in its paradigmatic significance. Pleasure and pain, so we read at the beginning of the discussion on self-discipline (I 636D), are like twin fountainheads. Whether they are drawn from in due measure or beyond reason determines whether the individual, or a community, will be happy or unhappy. In framing laws, therefore, we must concentrate on these affects. We recall the importance attributed earlier (I 631E) to pleasure and pain, desire and passion, as far as human life and the project of legislation are concerned. Here we deal with self-discipline, the mastery of pleasure. Drinking parties, as instruments of political education, provide opportunity for testing and practicing self-discipline.[22] And so we realize why Plato included this institution in his state in the *Laws*. It is a practice in which pleasure is aroused and self-discipline tested.

It is no accident that, in the very middle of this section about drinking, we encounter the great image of man as a puppet made by the gods, whether as a plaything or with some serious purpose (I 644D). The metaphor is another concrete expression of a reality which Plato described by the term, as paradoxical as it was popular, "self-mastery." This is a reality of highest importance in his so-called "psychology" and "ethics," and he expresses it in various images. In the *Phaedrus* (246A *et seq.*), Plato shows the charioteer-reason struggling with the steeds "spiritedness" and "desire." In the *Republic* (IX 588B *et seq.*), he shows the "inner man" in contrast to the lion and the many-headed monster. Now, in Plato's last work, man is a puppet pulled in opposite directions by various strings and threads. One string is golden, "reason," or the "general law of the city" as a manifestation of reason. The other strings are of various kinds, and some of them—i.e., desires and pleasures—are hard and ironlike. It is man's task to follow only the pull of the golden string, the "most noble guide."[23]

While we must admire the creative power of the poet in inventing new images over a period of decades, we cannot read without emotion of the low level to which man has sunk in the estimate of the aged Plato. "Man is a toy in the hands of the god and this is, in fact, still the best thing about him" (VII 803c). Such language, to be sure, is justified when one looks toward the highest being and more-than-being. Yet when, admonished by the interlocutor, one looks back again on the human race, he must concede that man is "something not insignificant but worth a kind of serious effort" (804B)—a conviction without which Plato would never have written the *Laws*.[24]

Let us note still another peculiar detail in this variously interwoven texture that is characteristic of Plato's late style. In that highly stressed episode where both the Cretan and the Spartan pay homage to the Athenian (I 642A *et seq.*; pp. 397f., above), the Athenian expatiates on the basic nature of education, "what it is and what power it has" (643A), in order to justify why banquets are an important aspect of political education and why they must be discussed at such surprising length. But beyond this general explanation a specific detail is worth noting. In discussing how banquets are to have a meaningful function, we must deal with "music," and this we cannot do without dealing with the whole field of education (642A).

Why music? Here the mention of this subject is puzzling. Yet
in Book II, we will hear about choirs and musical education in
general, and this discussion in turn will be loosely connected to
the theme of drinking—at the beginning (642A) and at the end
(II 673E) as well as elsewhere (666A, 671A *et seq.*). No editor
has interconnected different drafts here.[25] Plato himself conjoined these subjects artificially and not with complete harmony,
even as banquets, music, and education were variously conjoined
in Greek life itself.

Wine, Education, and Music

Book II, then, is artfully linked with Book I and is also a separate entity, as may be further seen from a minor detail: the later
reference to the "beginning of the argument" (κατ᾽ ἀρχὰς τῶν
λόγων, 664E 3) may refer to the beginning of Book II (671A 2),
but also to a passage in Book I (640c). Book II is rather clearly
divided into two fairly equal parts. The first part (652–664B)
deals with education in general. The second part applies this
discussion to an institution—the tripartite male choir.[26]

652–674c
BOOK II

The Athenian constantly comes back to the concept of education (I 643A *et seq.*, II 652E *et seq.*, 659C *et seq.*).[27] Plato excludes from it, on the one hand, any practical training that is
"vulgar and not worthy of a free man" (644A) and, on the
other hand, the kind of scientific training culminating in dialectics that we know from the *Republic* (παιδεία, VII 534D 8).
Paideia, according to its linguistic associations, is linked not
only with the word for "boy" (παῖς), but also with the word for
play (παίζειν, παιδιά).

To educate, then, means to lead the boy, in play as well as in
earnest pursuit (643B 6), to the point where he will love the
work he is expected to excel in as a man (643D). Education
shows the boy the way to virtue. It awakens in him the desire to
become a perfect citizen trained in the capacity for both ruling
and serving properly (643E). Education is concerned, therefore,
with the preliminary stage of virtue appropriate to a boy. Thus,
it is clear that education must appeal to the emotions, not to
reason. The boy's soul must learn to experience pleasure and
affection, pain and aversion, in the right manner so that later,

"when his soul takes in reason," there will be a concord between it and the acquired habits—and this concord we call "virtue" (II 653B). "When reason comes": so it is said in the *Republic* (III 402A) where, too, the subject is education in music, i.e., the nourishment the young soul must receive in order to delight in what is beautiful and to reject and hate what is ugly. And there, too, "music" (along with gymnastics) is the means for this kind of education.

But let us immediately note a difference. What is "reason" (*logos*) in the *Republic?*—the mathematical sciences and dialectics. Yet of these we find only traces in the *Laws*. The young boys are to have elementary instruction in arithmetic, measurement, and astronomy (817E *et seq.*). Their mathematical instruction, "as in Egypt," is to be practical and concrete. If it should progress to astronomy, that science should demonstrate the order of the stellar system. All this is far removed, say, from what Plato and Theaitetos had learned from Theodoros of Cyrene or from what Eudoxos taught at the Academy. At the very end of the *Laws* (XII 965B), there is a hint that the custodians, or guardians, must "receive an education of a more exact kind than we have so far described." They must learn to fix their view upon the "one *Idea*." They must have knowledge about the gods, and this knowledge they acquire—as shown in the theology of Book X—by means of a study of the stars above them and of the soul within.

Compared with the *Republic's* description of the stages of education, this is a mere sketch, as may also be appreciated from the fact that Philippos of Opus considered it necessary to include in the *Epinomis* what is missing in the *Laws*.[28] As a matter of fact, the "reason" which later comes to the soul does not primarily refer to the sciences at all. Instead, it refers to the "right word embodied in the law and affirmed as true by the oldest and most distinguished men on the basis of their experience" (*Laws* 659D). Thus, reason in this context does not mean scientific knowledge even though this knowledge is integrated in the structure of the state. Reason here means the order and wisdom of the state itself, embodied in the law. The system of knowledge is the nucleus of the *Republic* without which the state would be an empty shell, even if the nucleus can exist by itself and is ready, as it were, to break out of the shell at any moment. In the *Laws*, however, this contrast is hardly felt, for Plato consciously avoids anything that might disturb the omnipotence of his moderate ideal state here.

"When reason comes . . ." Both in the *Republic* and in the *Laws*, this phrase points to systems of order (albeit systems of unequal rank)—in the *Republic*, to the sciences of mathematics and to dialectics, together with their respective objects of knowledge, and in the *Laws*, to legislation. Thus, music as a preparatory discipline is also not treated in quite the same way in the two works.[29] In the *Republic*, the institutions have already begun to be shaped. Poetry must serve them—hence the critique of the myths, the restriction of "imitative" poetry, and the selection of noble rhythms and modes. In the *Laws*, to this point, there is no such preliminary construction. Here we proceed from immediate experience. All young beings have a natural desire to practice bodily movements and vocal sounds incessantly. Yet, order in these movements, i.e., rhythm and harmony, occurs only in human beings, and along with it comes the pleasurable experience of such order. Now it is precisely this aspect of pleasure that—quite in the spirit of the *Philebus*—is not rejected, but rather is used as the foundation because it is a basic drive of life. "It is inevitable that a man who enjoys something should become similar to what he enjoys." This is reminiscent of the passage in the *Republic* according to which a man becomes like that to which he is lovingly attached.[30]

The more immediately and generally experience is expressed here in the *Laws*, the more evident it becomes that pleasure, or enjoyment, is of enormous significance in the education of young boys. Enjoyment is the criterion for judging music now and always. From this point of view, however, it is all the more important to make sure that the criterion is not some arbitrary, accidental state of pleasure that would make any valid judgment impossible. It is for this reason—always Plato's concern—that he rejects the common view that some experiences might be both bad and pleasant (656A). For this reason, it is not the pleasure of Tom, Dick, or Harry that sets the standard, but the pleasure of the best and the most educated (658E). For this reason, the poets "must be compelled" to base their works (661A *et seq.*) on the hierarchy of goods—already outlined in Book I (631B *et seq.*)—and to show in their works the kind of life in which perfect justice and perfect pleasure converge (the kind of life shown, in contrast to the common view, at the end of the *Republic*—IX 580B *et seq.*). As immediate as Plato's approach is to the phenomenon of pleasure, as much as he elevates it and seeks to establish its convergence with other standards of value, the mere fact that there are such other standards indicates that art cannot be understood from pleasure alone.

667B–669D   Like pleasure, imitation (mimesis) also is treated differently here in the *Laws*. In the *Republic*, imitation was the ground on which Plato waged his battle against the poets,[31] for imitation meant distance from the truth. But as pleasure acquires a positive value in Plato's late work, so does imitation. What "music" and other "arts of imitation" (εἰκαστικαὶ τέχναι) have in common is that they essentially aim at something quite different from mere pleasure. They wish to copy and to copy correctly. In other words, they aim also at the truth. Just as Plato, in his early period, considered only the evanescent aspect of "pleasure" and then recognized, in the *Philebus*, that pleasure contains a component of truth as well, so in the *Republic* he viewed imitation only in its distance from truth, whereas in the *Laws* he now views it in its necessary relation to truth.

In neither the *Republic* nor the *Laws* does the concept of imitation lead to a pure theory of art—as in Aristotle. The concept of imitation is used in the *Republic* as a weapon against the contemporary drama. Here in the *Laws*, it protects the poetry of the state from succumbing to arbitrary standards; it distinguishes between right and wrong. "Right" music is not that which aims at pleasure, but that which reproduces a likeness of the original, ultimately, of the beautiful.[32] Thus, the best poetry must be not only enjoyable, but "right." As with every work of art, the first question asks what is represented, the second asks if it is right, and the third asks if it is represented well (εὖ). Music as the highest of the arts is the most difficult in all these respects. Word, melody, and rhythm must agree with the original and with each other, for they are imitating a unity (669E). Here begins the struggle against mixture and dissolution.

Integrating "music" into the founding of the state—in the *Republic* this task was impossible without a struggle, a struggle against the poets. This struggle is taken over into Plato's late work and is seen, in repeated thrusts, through Book II of the *Laws*. Against the craving for novelty on the part of the individual artist, we are told about the praiseworthy custom in Egypt of preserving gestures and melodies that were once   656c–657B
found beautiful. "Theatrocracy" (III 701A) is criticized—the sovereignty of the mass audience in the theater, which imposes its taste upon the poets instead of permitting its taste to be improved by the poets. The Doric states are put beside the model of Egypt, whereas on the other side Athens is mentioned along   659A–660D
with Sicily and Italy. The emphasis on sheer virtuosity among the poets is criticized, for such virtuosity leads to heaping up   669D–670A
and mixing artistic devices as well as to dissolving the structure of the work of art in favor of one-sided talents.

Finally, another peculiar feature must be noted, as it is characteristic of what Plato in his late years means by education and it also is significant for the over-all structure of the *Laws*. At the very beginning of Book II, education—strangely enough—is practically identified with choric art (χορεία), and an etymological pun confirms the correspondence between chorus and enjoyment (χορός ~ χαρά, 654A 4 and 5). Choric art combines song and dance (654B) or, more exactly, combines gesture, melody, song, and dance (654E). Soon rhythm and harmony are scrutinized more closely within this artistic totality (655A), and toward the end of the book (II 672E) it is shown, in retrospect, that choric art as a whole and education as a whole are one and the same.

Here we see the meaning of this paradoxical identification, designed evidently to emphasize the unity of educational process and goal. For the bodily movement involved in choric art shows that this art is a preliminary stage of gymnastics. Music and gymnastics, therefore, intersect. And the discussion of dancing already dealt with the aspect of gymnastics (673B).

This interlocking is analogous to the treatment of courage and self-discipline in Book I, where even as we seemed to be talking about one thing, we were already discussing the other. As far as average attitudes are concerned, gymnastics and music are separated from each other, assigned respectively to body and to soul. In the *Republic*, on the contrary, Plato assigned to the two of them a joint goal, education of the soul (see pp. 84f., above). The peculiar intersection of gymnastics and music here in Book II of the *Laws* is another way of expressing the same thing.

One aspect of gymnastics already has been dealt with, we are told. The other we will try to deal with "next" or "in the sequel" (ἐφεξῆς, 673D 8). This does not follow here, however, but is taken up only in Book VII, where we are referred to Book II and are explicitly reminded that this is a "continuation" (ἑξῆς, 796E 4 and 8).[33] As the work stands now, i.e., probably as Plato intended it to be, the preliminary discussion expressly points to the systematic body of legislation to follow.

Book II ends with a "finale." (Does even the division into books go back, at least in part, to Plato himself?) The "finale" we would expect to deal with the subject of music. Instead, the topic of wine-drinking recurs and is concluded here. This is the paradoxical intermixture of such seemingly incongruous subjects as wine-drinking and "musical" education, to which we have alluded earlier (pp. 402f.). Is this perhaps a manifestation of irony in the aged Plato? We think we are through with music at the end of Book II, only to be told that we are through with the discussion of drinking, so that we are reminded how closely these two themes are intertwined—in the first two books of Plato's *Laws* as well as in life. And yet, how far apart from each other they are!

On the Origin, Stability, and Decline of States

676A–702A
BOOK III

Book III opens, without any transition, on a distinctly new theme: What is the origin or principle (ἀρχή) of a state? From the perspective of being or ideal being we now move to the dimension of becoming, or development, yet again with the objective of discovering something about being. We may look back to Book II of the *Republic*. There as here the state is shown to grow out of modest beginnings. There as here the principle underlying all later forms of the state is revealed in, or built into, these earliest beginnings. There as here the original state is described with cheerful irony—in the *Republic* (372 *et seq.*) enjoying a kind of rustic comfort, and in the *Laws*, an intellectual and moral simplicity as yet devoid of any real knowledge. And in both works, the later forms of the state develop organically from this model.

We must not overlook the differences. The objective pursued in each work is entirely different and so is the direction taken to reach that objective. In the *Republic*, the goal is the true state; here in the *Laws*, it is Sparta. In the *Republic*, the goal is an ideal reality. Here it is a historical reality, and for this reason, time and place of origin are stated—after the last great flood, high in the mountains—and the Athenian reports in the temporal mode of the past, referring to ancient dates (683c 8). In the *Republic*, where there is no reference to the past or to a definite place, we witness events in the present (369A)—and even over long stretches in the future (370E *et seq.*)—stamped with the seal of necessity and essential being (see pp. 79f., above). Here in the *Laws*, Homer is cited as a historical witness to supplement the general discussion. There, however, pure reason is responsible for showing what is necessary, and it is able to do so.[34]

The historical development of the states, as outlined by the Athenian visitor, proceeds in four stages. The first stage describes the mountain settlement of simple shepherds without any culture, living far from the pernicious effects of the sea, distantly removed from the next settlement and with no opportunity of coming into contact with it, living without internal strife and external war, a simple life without evil and knowledge. Their form of the state—or rather the "pre-formation" of a state—is shown as a patriarchal dynasty (δυναστεία, 680B 2; πατρονομούμενοι, 680E 3), a mode of life that Homer attributes to the Kyklopes. (It is not likely that here we are supposed to remember the cannibalism of Polyphemos.) Individual families of this kind unite naturally like flocks of birds into the "most

677A–680D

just form of a kingdom." This is apparently meant to refer to the first in the series of actual forms of the state.[35]

680D–681D   In the second stage, several of these settlements combine to form a "city." Agriculture predominates in place of the herd culture. The union of different ethnic groups with different customs requires conciliation and thus the beginnings of legislation. This state is called an aristocracy or a monarchy, depending on the type of authority set up by the legislator.

681D–682E   In the third stage, all sorts of communities and constitutions are found. The city has now moved to a low hill in a plain. Cities are closer together. War breaks out—the Trojan War is used as the great example—and internal strife greets the returning warriors.

682E–693D   In the fourth stage are found the Doric states of the Peloponnesian peninsula: Sparta, Argos, and Messene. Here we are completely in the historical domain, for Megillos belongs to the one state of the three that is a reality in the present. A specific question arises and is evidently of highest significance for our own enterprise. Despite the most solemn oaths, or covenants, by which the ruler and the ruled in these three states swore allegiance to their respective constitutions, and the princes as well as the peoples swore to come to each other's aid from state to state, of the three only Sparta was preserved with its ancient laws. How can we explain this strange fact (685A)? To explain, we must answer the question of what kinds of laws preserve the stability of the state and what kinds of laws undermine it (683B).

Let us look back. In Book I, the original point of departure was a discussion of Doric customs, revealing their merits and defects and moving upward to institutions—banquets and choirs—that might be called "hyper-Doric." With a completely new start, Book III shows the Doric state as the fourth stage growing out of the three previous forms of the state, and we are now to learn something about the nature of the state as such by analyzing the conditions responsible for the stability and decline in the three Peloponnesian states. The new beginning in Book III, then, is expressly tied in with the first two books. We had digressed and now we have come back to the laws of Crete and Sparta (682E et seq.).

Why, we may ask, does Book III (unlike Book I) not immediately take up the Doric laws? Why is there this slow
progression through the three preliminary stages? What is
gained by the procedure, inasmuch as Plato never pursues such
inquiries for the sake of a purely historical or "sociological"
interest? We must even note that what separates the fourth
stage from the third is quite unlike what separated the first
stage from the second and the second stage from the third.
In the first three stages, the differences referred to types of
settlements and the corresponding differences in their laws. Yet
the type of settlement shows no change, or practically none,
between the third stage and the fourth.[36] Here the only fundamental difference refers to an institutional characteristic: the
covenant, or oath, between rulers and ruled and among the
states. As we can see, there is no even progression from stage to
stage. So once more, why deal with the preliminary stages at all?

Here we encounter a problem that is much discussed—and
may perhaps come to our aid. "No monarchy, nor any other kind
of government," says the Athenian (683E), "has ever been dissolved (κατελύθη) by any forces except its own. This was our
position a while ago (νυνδή, ὀλίγον ἔμπροσθεν) when we embarked upon this discussion. And can we have forgotten it now?"
Interpreters have advanced the most diverse views about the
meaning of the words "a while ago," for nothing like this was
explicitly said.[37] But must it be said explicitly? "This was our
position." What these words can possibly refer to is the question
here. Earlier we were concerned with the question of what is to
be learned from the origin and development of states. Now, can
these two questions answer each other? Where did we take "this
position"—if not in this very history of the development of
states? And what is the meaning to be derived from this history,
if it is not the general proposition that governments are sub-
verted, changed, or overthrown never from the outside, always
from the inside?

In the *Republic*, the only true state is created with an essential necessity—before the eyes of pure reason, as it were—
out of its most primitive origins in nature which are also preserved in the perfect state. Decline and disintegration set in

when the law inherent in the original state is violated. In the *Laws*, however, the form of the Doric state is developed in a historical perspective that aims at being through the world of becoming, at "nature" (or "essence") through history. This state is developed out of primitive, natural origins in various stages of growth. It is a high but by no means perfect form, and as a whole it disintegrated early, so that only one part of it remained. It is this form of state that we must examine in order to discover the principle of its stability and of its decline, and in order to raise the founding of our own state beyond it (688BC).

Before advancing his own views, the Athenian rejects a false theory commonly held about the causes of decline, and generally put into some such form as this: If these states had only had sufficient power to preserve their own freedom, to rule over others as they pleased, and to do as they desired with respect to all mankind, they would still be in existence. What is the point of this theory? It is characteristic that the word "desiring" is used again and again next to "willing,"[38] along with the expression of the wish to exercise great power among Greeks and barbarians. Thus, the battle waged in the *Thrasymachus*, in the *Alcibiades Major*, and in the *Gorgias* is visible in the distance. There is an echo of the *Lysis* as well,[39] where the father out of love for his son resists the son's wishes and desires. One gets the impression, here as elsewhere in Plato's late works, that an encounter or struggle which is just sketchily suggested would have been expressed concretely, in one of his earlier works, through the clash of two partners.

Behind the common view, therefore, that the collapse of states is due to a lack of power, the Athenian discerns—and fights against—the greed-for-more, the will-to-power, the thesis of Kallikles, in contrast to which he holds up reason (φρόνησις, νοῦς) as that for which one must pray (687E). This struggle, which is only intimated, calls forth the real struggle—concerning the aim of the state—at the beginning of the whole work. This was basically the same struggle as here, yet in a different disguise. Then it was said that the laws of Sparta, i.e., of the best state as such, were based on the *one* virtue of courage. Here it is said that the two other Doric states fell because of a lack of power—from which it would follow that only power has preserved Sparta. In Book I, the struggle concluded with the new table of values culminating in the concept of the "leader reason." Here we are explicitly referred (688AB) to this earlier discussion as we are referred to what was said in Book II about the affects. For, in addition to intelligence and reason, we now hear about "opinion (δόξα) that is attached to love and desire and that follows intelligence and reason." The opposite, there-fore, must have caused the downfall of the Doric states and must cause the downfall of states in general—unknowing, un-wisdom (ἀμαθία, 688D 1, 688E 4).

This is more precisely defined not as a lack of theoretical knowledge but, in line with the theory of emotions, as a "dis-sonance between pleasure or pain, on the one hand, and reasoned opinion, on the other" (τὴν διαφωνίαν λύπης καὶ ἡδονῆς πρὸς τὴν κατὰ λόγον δόξαν, 689A 7). How important it is to achieve consonance and how dangerous is the dissonance is shown by an analogy which is familiar from the analogy employed in the *Republic* between the state and the individual soul. The large mass of people in the state corresponds to the part of the soul that experiences pleasure and pain. And even as a state in which the people do not obey their rulers is without reason, so is the individual who hears the voice of reason without acknowledging its claim. From all this there follows the conclusion for all future legislation that only those in whom this consonance exists should be appointed rulers. The highest and most beautiful consonance is rightly called "highest wisdom" (689D 7).

If, then, the cause for the decline of Messene and Argos was to be found in the "dissonance" or "discord" of the rulers, we must next turn to Sparta. There the people were saved from the excessive power of the individual. A god gave them the institu-tion of the two kings, and the council of elders (senate), and the office of ephors elected by the people. This division of powers preserved Sparta. From this institutional system the legislator must learn something—and the repeated use of "must" (ἔδει, δεῖ, 693B) indicates that it is not merely a matter of recording what happened once. The legislator must learn not to establish "unmixed governments" (ἀρχὰς ἀμείκτους, 693B) if he is to achieve the goal that may be called self-discipline, or reason, or freedom, or friendship, all these expressions being identical (693CD). We know from Polybios' portrait of the Roman constitution how much he had learned from Plato; we also know how much Cicero learned from them both, and how much Montesquieu learned from all these predecessors.[40]

693D–698A   The lesson derived from Sparta is supplemented by a review of the history of Persia and Athens, the two paradigm forms of constitutional government that may be called monarchy and democracy, respectively. The history of Persia and Athens shows that the two forms must be mixed if the state is not to fail in promoting freedom, friendship, and reason. They were mixed in Persia under Cyrus, but the defective education of subsequent rulers—the word "education" becomes a kind of leitmotiv in what follows[41]—permitted the tyrannical element to grow more and more powerful. This is something to be considered (σκεπτέον, 696A 4) by the legislator, to make sure that the hierarchy of goods, of honors and dishonors (which we know from the list in Book I), is observed. (The word "honor" and its cognates dominate the discussion for a time.[42]) Athens, too, was not devoid of genuine constitutional forces at the time of the Persian Wars. It degenerated only gradually into a state of unchecked freedom destructive of fear and respect as well as of "friendship." This decline of political standards exactly corresponds to a decline in the modes of music. From the strict separation of the sacred modes, music degenerated to a dissolution of all fixed standards. In the theater, the judgment of the educated was replaced by that of the mob; aristocracy was replaced by "theatrocracy."

The relation of Persia and Athens to Sparta is similar to that described in the *Republic* between the worst of the defective states, democracy and tyranny, on the one hand, and the true state, on the other. The *Republic's* description of tyranny here and there, and its description of democracy over a long stretch, remind us of what is said here in the *Laws*, often in the same words, about Persia and Athens.[43] If the decline of Athens is shown not in its institutions but in its music, we must think of some features in the *Republic:* of the profound insight of Damon,

the famous theoretician of music, that a change in music is always accompanied by a change in the state (*Republic* IV 424cd);
or of the inception of political disintegration that is first of all a
disintegration of music (VIII 546d); or of the thrust (VIII
568b) against tragedy—aimed at Euripidean tragedy—as being
appropriate to the democratic and the tyrannical forms of government.

What we may say by way of a general summary is this. In
showing how the hitherto most perfect state, the Doric state,
had grown out of the simplest origins and in showing its subsequent decline, and, finally, in showing the decline of a moderate
monarchy and a democracy into extremes, Book III of the *Laws*
describes a curve similar to the much larger one arching between Book II and Book IX of the *Republic*. This similarity must
be grasped in order to note the differences. In the *Republic*, we
have an ideal-typical construction, though subject to processes
of becoming and passing away. In the *Laws*, we have the natural
development of actual historical states, though the account includes a considerable amount of construction. In the *Republic*,
the construction itself is all-comprehensive, while in the *Laws*,
the historical account serves to clarify the structure of what
follows.

And, indeed, at the close of Book III (702a), the entire discussion is summarized and is said to be subservient to the same
end. The summary includes not only the historical account just
brought to a close but also the discussions in the first two books,
which had taken their own course practically separate from the
third book.[44] All this is summarized into a common meaning,
which should serve the purpose of showing how the life of the
state and the life of the individual are best conducted. The original question of what is "good" and the old parallelism between
state and individual again come to the fore. Here, however, we
are at a crucial juncture in the whole work.

The New Founding

How can we test what we have said, the Athenian asks. At this
point the Cretan discloses to his partners what he has held back
so far—on purpose, one is supposed to think. It is the plan of

702b–702e
BOOK III

founding a new city on Crete, an undertaking for which the previous discussion "by a fortunate coincidence" seems most opportune. And he invites his partners to found this city with him. To those critics[45] who do not find this "coincidence" natural enough, Plato might have mockingly replied that they ought rather consider the question of why, here as elsewhere, he employs the device of such a coincidence. For surely it would have been easy to start out with the new founding on the first page of the work. In that case, however, Plato could not have shown the ascending line that leads toward this founding of a new city. It is an ascent through the Doric states, and an ascent symbolized in the dialogical "space" by the walk to the shrine of Zeus on Mount Ida. Without the first three books, it would not have become clear that this new foundation—however central a place it occupies in this last work of Plato's—is only an example of something more general. It is not the sole answer, though a most impressive one, to the basic question that Plato asked and has already dealt with in various ways in the first three books of the *Laws*. For the question is: what is the best life for the state and for the individual? Yet, again, the general inquiry into what the best state is, and the critical examination of existing states, ultimately make sense only if they are of use (εἰς χρείαν, 702B 6), somewhere and sometime, in the actual founding of a state.

General theory about the state and the specific founding of a city (the twofold objective of the whole work, as Plato says explicitly at 702D 3) must coincide sometime, at an opportune moment (κατὰ καιρόν, 702B 7)—and this is the symbolic significance of the "coincidence" so wisely designed. It is not surprising, then, that even in the first books, the language of legislation (νομοθετήσομεν, 666A 3) is frequently used, or that later (VII 812E *et seq.*) the educational system of the new colony on Crete includes those choirs that were planned in Book II for an as yet indefinite founding, as it were. These things are not surprising because, from the very beginning, Plato himself is legislator and so are the figures created by him in the dialogue. It is more than probable that in his own mind he conceived of the educational system as a unity, parts of which he included in the propylon of the work. The rest of the actual legislation Plato saved, however, for his colony on Crete.[46]

The Conditions of the New Founding

Let us never forget that Plato is not reporting an actual event, but is poetically imagining the founding of a new city. Hence, the reader must always ask, "Why?" or "For what purpose?" even when Plato does not say anything—although he often enough does[47]—about this "view toward an end." The name of the colony is left to the future. Later on, Plato calls it the city of the Magnesians, thereby linking it to an actual tradition on Crete.[48] That he may have decided to do so only in the course of the writing is possible, but not very likely. For even later he does not definitely have a proper name in mind, and refers to it as the "city of the Magnesians or whomsoever God may have named it after" (XII 969A 6). Perhaps Plato refrained from mentioning the Magnesians in the beginning so that we would not fasten on a definite location. For evidently the location of this new city corresponds not to any geographical reality, but to a philosophical purpose. This city on Crete is a utopia—though less distant from reality than Atlantis and Ur-Athens.

". . . Or whomsoever God may have named the city after." One should ponder for a moment on the name of this Cretan city. Did Plato perhaps intend that when he mentioned the city of the Magnesians the magnetic lodestone should come to our mind? We might then remember that many decades earlier, in the *Ion* (533D), he had described how the lodestone imparts its power to iron rings so that a chain of magnetic rings forms. This served him as a symbol for the way the Muse renders the poets "full of the god" and how the divine power spreads from them. Is it too much to assume that Plato wished to endow his model city of the Magnesians with the power to become such a magnetic city, attaching to itself a chain of magnetized and further magnetizing rings?

The first specific question is whether the city should be located on the coast or inland. The question is decisive, because a coastal city would be "incurable" (704D 3). Thus, Plato puts the city eighty stadia (ten miles) inland, but also gives it a

704A–715E
BOOK IV

704A–707D

good harbor. While the mountainous soil provides everything that is needed, the land is rugged and does not produce too much. Plato, therefore, has carefully mixed "natural" benefits in the founding of this city.[49] The "true state" of the *Republic*, however, is not situated on earth at all. While its inhabitants are subject to conditions of "nature" in a general human sense, the city itself is not. If we think of its location, we perceive that it would have to be without a harbor—but even this is not said, and only later do we realize that the ideal state has no fleet.

By contrast, the very location of the Cretan colony determines its human fate. Precisely because Plato directs it toward a definite "goal"—to virtue, *arete* as a whole, and not to any part, like courage, as is said explicitly with a view back to the struggle in Book I—for this very reason he raises the old hostility of the Athenian aristocracy to "the horrible fleet"[50] to the level of principled consideration, and moves the city away from the sea. Yet at the same time, he gives it a harbor, thereby exposing the city once again to those threats from which he had just removed it. From its very inception, then, the city is not perfect, but is subject to a number of natural conditions both advantageous and threatening.

707E–709D   The so far unknown composition of the group of settlers is one of these conditions. And, for a moment, the conditions of the new founding loom as such formidable factors that the work of the legislator is reduced to practically nothing. Let us ponder what it must mean for Plato, just as he is embarking on his program of legislation, to have the Athenian say with great emphasis: "There is no human legislator at all, but chance and turns of fate are, by and large, our legislators." Thus, God is exalted as the guide of all things, and together with God, chance and circumstance and the right moment (709B 7). They are the guides, and it is even a great thing when man can co-operate in taking the ship's wheel in a tempest. Or, to change the image, man is like a puppet with strings, as was said earlier, the best thing about him being that he is a puppet in the hands of the gods. Now even legislation, which Plato esteemed so highly and pursued as the last task of his life, is reduced to almost nothing. It derives its dignity from being somewhat helpful in human affairs.[51]

Location, composition of the group of settlers, and then largely *tyche* and *kairos*—these are the conditions to which the founding of the new city is subject. They lead to a last condition expressed in the question: How is such new legislation possible at all? Or, what conditions must we give you, legislator, so that you can best do your work? What are the most favorable preconditions for such a constitutional change reaching down to the roots of the state? We can easily see that this line of thought is concerned with an issue more general than the settlement on Crete,[52] and we soon realize that another aspect of the *Republic* has been transposed and is transformed here in the late work. We recall the three waves that break in upon us at the great turning point of the *Republic* (pp. 102ff., above). With the third wave comes the question of how the ideal state is possible (*Republic* V 471c). The answer is that such a change presupposes another kind of change, that this other change is not easy but is possible, and that it is easier in one person than in two, easier in two than in several (473bc). This change, upon which the renewal of the state is conditioned, is the union of political power and philosophy. This central proposition of the *Republic* states the condition for the possibility of the ideal state. Later on (*Republic* VI 502bc), it is stated once more. This union, if possible, is the very best; it is difficult to attain, but not impossible, provided there is but *one* person who is capable and is in charge of a city that obeys him.

Now let us look at the passage in the *Laws* (709D *et seq.*). What must the city be like to be in the most favorable condition for the change?[53] It must be ruled by a tyrant—a tyrant, to be sure, who is young, of good memory, quick to learn, bold and brilliant, and who also practices self-discipline. These traits are the ones that Plato praised in Dion and prescribed as requirements for the philosopher-kings in the *Republic*.[54] Then a fortunate coincidence must bring this "disciplined tyrant" (τύραννος κόσμιος, 710D 7) together with a legislator. When this occurs, the god has done his utmost to bestow benefits upon the city. The situation is less favorable if there are two rulers of this kind as, for example, in the Spartan institution of two kings, still less favorable in the case of a democracy, and most unfavorable in the case of an oligarchy where there are the greatest number of power holders. The ideal case is difficult to attain but not impossible,[55] and when this improbable situation does occur, it brings the greatest happiness to the state.[56] Toward the end of the passage, this possibility is expressed again in one condensed sentence that reminds us immediately of the central proposition in the *Republic*. "When supreme power is combined in one person with reason and self-discipline, this is the only condition—and the necessary one—that makes it possible for the best constitution and the laws that correspond to it to come into being" (*Laws* IV 711E *et seq.*).

Let us look still more carefully at the decisive passage in each dialogue. In the *Republic*, the crucial moment occurs when the movement—in the metaphor of the biggest wave—carries us to the highest level. There is no such ordered structure in the *Laws*. Here the process of legislation unfolds, as it were, in a single dimension. For this reason, the central statement (corresponding to that in the *Republic*) occurs as the work of actual legislation is about to commence.

The statement itself is noticeably modified here in the *Laws*. It does not contain the word "philosopher,"[57] in the *Republic* the crucial word, which, as soon as it is pronounced, carries the discussion to its highest level. Its place is taken in the *Laws* by "reason and self-discipline" (φρονεῖν καὶ σωφρονεῖν), expressions that stay more within the field of empirical reality. This is especially so as to self-discipline, or temperance, which was expressly restricted (710A) to its popular meaning and thus loses—not without irony—the deeper meaning that Plato had associated with it from the *Charmides* on. But if the *Laws* is more modest than the *Republic*, the intervening years have added to Plato's experience, as is reflected in the new ordering of the governments, *tyranny, monarchy, democracy*, and *oligarchy* (*aristocracy*). It is not that Plato's judgment as to the respective worth of these forms has changed,[58] but that the point of view has shifted. The only question of concern now is which of these forms is best fitted for the special purpose of realizing the state. In this connection, we must note the peculiar paradox suggested by the expressions "tyrannical state" (τυραννουμένη πόλις, 709E 6) and "tyrannical soul" (τυραννουμένη ψυχή, 710A 1).

In the *Republic* (IX 577DE), the situation described by these
expressions represents the extreme opposite to virtue, especially to the virtue of self-discipline. Plato took these expressions over into his last work, together with the parallelism
between state and individual soul,[59] but in doing so he re-
adjusted the meaning of the expressions so that tyranny again
corresponds to the popular conception. It is a form of absolute
rule free from tradition and not curbed by laws. The paradoxical
phrase "disciplined tyrant" calls attention to this shift.

Yet the transformation of the central thesis of the *Republic*
goes still further. We are now about to begin the actual work   712B–714A
of legislation, so we are told, and the god is invoked as our
aid, even as "God" was the first word spoken in the whole
dialogue. The question now before us is this: What constitution
do we propose for the new state? A traditional constitution such
as democracy or monarchy? Sparta and Cnossus are neither,
but have constitutions that are beneficial mixtures of both (an
insight already worked out in the historical account of Book
III). Thus, they are genuine constitutions, whereas the types
that ordinarily are so called are nothing else but communities
in which one component exercises domination by enslaving the
others, so that, in fact, such governments get their names from
the party that exercises domination. Our state, then, must be
different. It can be named after only *one* sovereign—the god.
The myth of Kronos consecrates this insight, and there follows
a restatement of the *Republic*'s central proposition in its last
and highest form, solemn as an oracle: "For a community ruled
not by God, but by a mortal man, there is no escape from
misery and evil" (*Laws* IV 713E). Yet the next sentence shows
that even the aged Plato has little to do with any kind of mystical
theocracy. We are enjoined to order our own affairs in obedience
to "what is immortal within us," i.e., the "leader reason"
(I 631D). This name is alluded to by a play on words, a deeply
serious play, in which the law is described as that which is
"posited by reason."[60]

After the law has risen to such heights of dignity and before   714A–715E
the actual legislation begins, we encounter another episodic
struggle against something of a lower order. Like the other

struggles of Plato's late period this one, too, is only suggested. In contrast to the genuine rulers who follow reason, there are those whose souls are constantly set on new pleasures and desires,[61] like leaky vessels that cannot keep their contents. Language and imagery remind us of the *Gorgias* and the *Republic*, and present to us the form of life based on the pleasure principle, to which Plato in those works had reduced the highly praised life of the man of power. While we cannot fail to note that, in his old age, the philosopher finds new positive features in the pleasure principle, neither can we deny that his essential attitude remains the same.

As early as in the *Thrasymachus*,[62] it is the man of pleasure and power who formulates the dangerous thesis that, according to the law of nature, justice is the advantage of the stronger. Those who hold such a view not only have not advanced to the conclusion, established at the beginning of this work, that laws must aim at "virtue as a whole." They are at an even more primitive stage than the Doric conception, criticized at the beginning, that all laws must be framed from the standpoint of war. Strictly speaking, those who hold such a view are concerned not with laws at all, but with party interests. And, in a virtually untranslatable play on words, they are "not citizens, not *politai*, but factionalists, *stasiotai*" (715B), a term connoting factionalism and civil war and reinforcing the significance of its opposite: community. We realize why the old struggle of the *Thrasymachus* is here renewed. There the construction of the true state followed; the new legislation follows here. Plato's form-creating impulse has changed, but it is not extinguished.

Prelude

715E–734E
BOOKS IV–V

The Athenian imagines himself to be addressing an assembly of the new settlers and he speaks in words of solemn proclamation. He first invokes the god, who, according to the ancient Orphic poem, holds in his hands beginning, end, and center of all that is, and completes the cycle on the right course according to his inborn nature.[63] The lofty image of eternal, ordered being rises before the listeners, and—as we know from the *Gorgias* (507E *et seq.*)—the order of justice and the order of the universe

715E–725B

are related, so that "Justice" (Δίκη) punishes any violation of this order.[64] And we soon hear (716c) that God is the measure of all things, not—as Protagoras had affirmed in a famous sentence—man. Just as earlier the central proposition of the *Republic* was reformulated to proclaim the rule of God in the state, so here "man as the measure" is surprisingly transposed into "God as the measure." Why? Because, in Plato's mind, the "man as the measure" proposition was the symbol for all disintegrating, destructive tendencies in life. Hence, as in his earlier works, it is again repudiated, here for the last time.

This contrast between order and confusion is shown by human examples. Alkibiades appears for the last time—unnamed, but easily recognized[65]—as a symbol of destruction. The final judgment is that "he brought utter ruin to himself, his house, and his state."

Losgerissen vom heiligen Feuer zerstörst du in Freveln
Prächtig ein irrender Brand dich und die Grösse Athens.[66]

("Torn loose from the sacred hearth and splendid in sacrilege,
You destroy, like a raging fire, yourself and the greatness of Athens.")

In contrast stands the man who is similar to God and therefore dear to him, for, "as the wise men of old say, the like is dear to the like." So it was said in the *Lysis* (214c) and in the *Gorgias* (510b). Here in the "prelude" of the *Laws*, the likeness theme is transferred, boldly and solemnly, to the relation between man and the deity.

"God as the measure"—this principle, first alluded to in the *Theaetetus* (162c), is impressively made clear now. God is the measure: he who is similar to him has measure, and he who is dear to him is integrated in the great order of the universe. In this way, worship of the gods here acquires a new foundation, toward which the *Euthyphro* in its aporetic manner was a first move. Worship of the gods is based on measure and order, which, as shown in the *Philebus*, are synonymous with perfection. It therefore becomes a good man to be pious; it is useless for him who is impure, or evil. We can now say who is to be worshipped and honored: first, the Olympians, next, the other gods, demons, and heroes, and, finally, the parents (to whom pious reverence is due in their lifetimes as well as after their death).

And so we have come to the work of actual legislation—and yet not quite, for we are told that the laws themselves, which are evidently to deal with the mutual relations among men in society (718A 6 *et seq.*), will begin only later (718B 2, 718C 2). Now we are still in a domain of life about which the legislator has important things to say, things that cannot be fitted, however, into the form of laws (718B 5 *et seq.*). This presents a strange conflict. It is not easy to talk about it in a few words (718C 4) and, indeed, the matter will become clear only after various detours. What is commencing here are the "preambles," a most important means toward the fulfillment of Plato's legislative task. We must try to explain their function.

Legislation is education. "The legislator will aim in his whole work at teaching, or persuading, the people to accept a life of virtue" (718CD). The laws in the strict sense, it will turn out, cannot perform this task by themselves and, for this reason, the preambles are needed to help. This is the objective Plato has in mind, though it is strange how he goes about it all. For he begins with the saying of Hesiod that the path to perfection is long and rough. This saying could serve as a motto for the whole work of legislation, but that apparently is not the aim here. Instead, the theme of poetry emerges anew.

Whereas a little while ago, music had been severely criticized for its radical decline (700A *et seq.*), the Athenian now speaks on behalf of the poet (719B 9)—and presently the poet speaks through him (719D 7). The manic and therefore irresponsible aspect of poetic life is conjured up in the spirit of irony, known to us from the *Ion* and the *Phaedrus*, in which Plato's old enchantment with poetry and the inevitable battle he wages against it are strangely mixed.[67] The poet, being a "re-presentative" artist, is not concerned with "presenting" the truth which is necessarily *one*. He may represent the same subject in two or three different ways. On these grounds, imitative poetry was condemned in the *Republic* (III 394E). Here, by contrast, it is the poet who compels the legislator to set himself apart. For the legislator is asked to make only one pronouncement on any

subject and not, as he had just begun to do, to make a pronouncement that is more or less general (719D; cf. 718A). His
statements are to be explicit and numerically precise—if they
are to be laws. While the commanding legislator and the ad-
monishing Hesiod seemed to join hands as leaders toward
virtue, the poet, now reflecting upon the nature of his own art,
detaches himself from the legislator and—in an ironic paradox
—admonishes him to observe precision.

Yet, in this exchange, Plato has shown only one side of the
problem. His legislation also, as we shall see, must speak in
two ways, not only one, about the same subject, although this
double form has a meaning different from the double talk of
the poets. Thus, a countermove presently follows, employing
the analogy of two types of physicians. The "physician of the
slaves" gives only brief "tyrannical" prescriptions based on his
own practical experience. The "physician of free men," who is
himself a free man and a free spirit and who has truly scientific
knowledge, uses a different procedure. He consults with the
patient and does not order a prescription until he has convinced
the patient that it is right.[68] This example is then applied to the
case of marriage laws (with which all true legislation must
begin) in order to show the two possibilities—on one hand,
the "simple" form of a law,[69] a brief and precise enactment, and
on the other hand, the "double" form of a law in which a rational justification (διανοηθέντα, 721B 7) is added to the enactment. In the case of marriage, this justification consists of
Diotima's insight into the connection between procreation and
immortality.[70] For us only the second type of legislation is right
and possible, because it is the only legislation that educates or,
in other words, persuades the soul to accept the law. No previous legislator ever has practiced this method (722B 5, 722E 2).
Yet every law in our city is to consist of these two things, a
prelude, or preamble, and the law itself, as has always been
the rule in the "nomos" of music.

Noon has come, and the wanderers rest in a delightful arbor.
Here we learn a strange thing: "The whole forenoon we have
done nothing else but converse about laws. Yet we are only now
beginning to formulate actual laws; all we have said before has

been but preambles to laws" (722CD). The new method that
will be applied to what follows is, therefore, also retroactive.
Not only will every law in the future have a preamble, but all
we have said heretofore becomes, in its general outlines, a
prelude to the whole work of legislation. In particular, what
was said in the casual course of the conversation about the
honors due to the gods and to one's ancestors receives retro-
actively the firm status of a preamble.

The legislation—or, as we now know, the prelude—had begun with the honors due to the gods and after them to one's
726A–730A   parents. This line is continued. Honor is also due to one's own
BOOK V   soul (726A 6) and to one's own body (728D). A sense of honor,
instead of money, should be bequeathed to one's children
(729B 1). Kinship (729C 5) and friendship (729C 8) are to be
honored as are the laws of one's city (729D 4). And, finally,
the aliens are to be honored (729E 5) and, above all, the sup-
pliants (730A 5), whose violation will be most severely punished
by the god who is their protector.

The list, to be sure, presents a strange assortment, and its
meaning is intelligible only in the light of the tradition it
follows.[71] To honor the gods, and after the gods, one's parents
—these are the "sacred laws" of old, the "unwritten laws,"
the "unwritten law of custom," the "laws of Triptolemos." In
addition to honoring one's parents, there are other obligations,
such as to benefit one's friends and to pay respect to the alien.
Euripides (frag. 853) combines the gods, the parents, and the
laws of Greece. Plato is following ancient precepts in adopting
these "honors" as preambles for his legislation. We see immediately, however, that he has expanded the traditional list,
and in a rather striking manner, by inserting between parents
and friends such different topics as soul, body, and youth. Also,
as we soon realize, he has completely transformed the traditional concept of "honor." And it remains to be seen whether
the expansion of the list is due to the transformation of the
concept.

Again the Athenian imagines himself addressing the people
gathered together.[72] To them the entire fifth book is addressed
as a continuous speech. After the gods and one's parents, honor

is due to "one's soul" or to man himself in his true nature.[73] In order to explain what this means, the word "honor" must be given a new meaning in depth. We recall that according to the two tables of values (I 631E, III 697B), the state was charged with the explicit task of rightly dispensing and withholding honors. Piety, or worship of the gods, has already been given a new meaning; only he can honor the gods who improves himself. Thus, we are prepared for the new meaning that is attributed here to honor, or esteem, or dignity (τιμή).

A person does not do honor to others or to his soul by means of fine speeches or gifts—as if he could decorate them or himself by external ornaments. On the contrary, this is a way of dishonoring and disfiguring instead of paying true honor and homage.[74] To do honor means that I follow the lead of the better and that I improve, as far as possible, what is worse. Thus, honoring the gods and honoring one's own soul are reduced, as it were, to the same common denominator. I must change myself after the model of the better, lest honor become dishonor. Now it is clear why honor is called a "divine good" (727A 3), and not only a good (which would be admitted even by the person who misunderstands its nature). For truth and being must reach their highest possible expression in this concept.[75] In this sense, the state in the *Laws* is a true "timocracy" without being so called—and in a purer form than in the *Republic*, where timocracy is the name for the best of the defective forms of government.[76]

An analysis in more detail would have to show next what Plato means by honoring the body after the soul—the body that "belongs" to the soul, i.e., is subordinate to the soul or to "oneself." Plato's directive would please neither those who despise the body nor those who glorify it as the highest good. Again, a detailed analysis would have to show the meaning of Plato's attitude toward youth. For the idea (so often repeated, from Juvenal on, and abused, too) that older men should respect the young is first stated here as a paradox, then to be linked with the theme of the *Phaedrus* that every education is at once a form of self-education. Finally, such an analysis would have to show the different emphasis that Plato places on the ancient

custom of protecting the alien by making this custom a part of
his list.

730B–731D After this series of basic precepts reformulated in a Platonic
sense, there follows a section on "what kind of a person a man
should be in order to pass through life in the best manner."
This question cannot be regulated by the laws to be enacted
since they themselves require the kind of person who is "amena-
ble" to them. We recognize that the list of desirable qualities
has undergone a transformation from the *Republic* to the *Laws*.
As is the case with the future guardians in the *Republic* (II
374E *et seq.*), so here the future citizens must combine courage
and self-discipline. In the *Republic*, the guardians must be selected in such a way that they are equally fit to protect the state
against external war and to promote internal peace, and so
that they are able to develop a love of "wisdom" out of their
union of a spirited and a gentle disposition (375E). The *Laws*,
however, omits these aspects that are characteristic of the caste
structure of the true state. Now it is the citizen himself who
must be manly in the struggle against the incurable evils and
gentle in his attitude toward those evils that are curable and
(according to the old Socratic view) involuntary.

Thus, the qualities that benefit a community are selected,
and the same holds everywhere. A person should possess justice, measure, and intelligence—the old virtues—and he should
not keep them to himself but rather pass them on to others.
It is a contest for virtue "without envy" (ἀφθόνως). Such a
contest is of benefit to the community, whereas the "envious"
or jealous man in contesting with others weakens the powers
of the state.[77] Truth, veracity (ἀλήθεια, 730C), has the same
effect these virtues have, since truth makes a person trustworthy
whereas the opposite of truth isolates him. In this "ethical"
context, we might not be cognizant of the ontological meaning
which Plato ordinarily attaches to this concept, the "truth"
of being, were it not for the solemn words that truth "occupies
the highest place among all the goods for gods as well as for
men." So the highest level is just barely alluded to, while the
actual discussion takes place on a level not so high but enriched
by the wisdom of broadest experience.

While these demands were designed to benefit the community, there now follows a warning against the greatest of 731D–732D
the evils that threaten the community—self-love.[78] Self-love is opposed to the truth and justice that we just found praised. It leads to the worst folly in that a person thinks he knows, when in fact he is ignorant. And in practice, it leads to the worst distortion in that a person acts without understanding what he is doing and refuses to let others act who know what they are doing. Yet, this warning against self-love must be read also in the context of what preceded it a while ago—the demand to honor one's own soul, i.e., oneself. Demand and warning delimit each other mutually. Self-love is the false mode of self-honor.

All the previous considerations about a man's right character and what he must do are summed up as "divine." They are now followed by considerations that are purely "human," 732D–734E
and this will conclude the great prelude. Pleasure, pain, and desires are essentially human. If legislation for the sake of education were to disregard these feelings, it would, so to speak, go above the heads of people. This is avoided here, however, inasmuch as a comparison between two ways of life makes it clear that a life aiming at virtue, in both body and soul, is also more pleasant than the opposite way of life. Beauty, rightness, virtue, and fame combine with pleasure to form the kind of perfection that to the Greeks was eudaemonia.

Again we encounter a problem that in its nature goes back to Plato's beginnings, and finds its fullest expression in the concluding part of the Republic: in the balance sheet of happiness between the life of the philosopher and the life of the tyrant.[79] As always, the material that is transposed from the Republic into the Laws is also treated differently. What is lost here are the different stages and the marked reference to the highest level of philosophical knowledge. In the Republic, the philosopher-king is the extreme opposite of the tyrant, separated by the intermediate types, and his pleasure and pursuit aim at the knowledge of true being. There is nothing comparable in the Laws. Instead, two kinds of lives confront each other directly. On the one side is the life of discipline, reason, courage

—and health. On the other side are all the opposite conditions of life. Physical health side by side with the "virtues"—this is an intentional sacrifice of philosophical precision. It is now shown, strictly on the basis of experience, that the licentious and the sick kinds of life are ever so much more painful than their opposites.

And so we have reached the point where the actual legislation can begin. It is not by accident that the scale of happiness comes here in the *Laws*. In the *Republic*, the "balance sheet of happiness" comes almost at the end and looks back almost to the beginning of the work, so that it has a peripheral position. In the *Laws*, it concludes the prelude as a necessary supplement without which everything else would be unsuitable for human beings. The scale of happiness serves here as a last persuasion before the legislation itself commences.

The Settlement, the Officials, and the Code of Law

735A–969D
BOOKS V–XII

We cannot undertake a detailed interpretation of the solid body of laws here in this dialogue any more than we ventured on such an interpretation of the body of natural science in the *Timaeus*. As with that work, so here a thorough interpretation of the text would have to be combined with some basic considerations. (*1*) Who were Plato's predecessors? (*2*) What is Plato's own contribution? (*3*) What effect has Plato had on Greek and Roman law and—directly or indirectly—on later legislation? (*4*) What does Plato's legislation look like from the perspective of modern jurisprudence (and vice versa)? This last question is even more difficult than the corresponding question as regards the *Timaeus*. For while there are hardly any national boundaries in the natural sciences, constitutions and laws differ from nation to nation in the contemporary world.

After the prelude comes, in the well-known musical play on words, the composition itself, i.e., the composition of the laws of the state. Just as—in another analogy—a web is woven together out of the firm material of the warp and the soft material of the woof, so the state is woven together out of rulers and ruled, magistrates and citizens.[80] In the *Statesman* (305E *et seq.*), the analogy with the art of weaving served to show the moral and political task of the statesman: to unite the opposite natures within the community and prevent their clash. In the *Laws*, the same analogy serves as a concrete image for the institutional task confronting the lawmaker: to create the unity of rulers and ruled despite their natural differences. From this point of view, there are two aspects (εἴδη) that are relevant to the constitution. Who are the officials? Under what laws are they to exercise their authority?[81] Yet, before the first question can be taken up, the actual settling of the city must be regulated. Thus, what follows in the *Laws* falls into a logical order. *The settlement* is taken up from V 735A to the end of the fifth book (747E). *The officials* are described in Book VI, from its beginning through 771A. *The laws* begin in VI 771A and occupy the work to the end (XII 969D).

Education

Since the code of law in its enactments follows the natural course of human life (see pp. 393f., above), we find—after the marriage laws—the comprehensive precepts on education, and these follow in turn upon regulations with regard to the growth of the child, starting even before birth.[82] His care is at first purely physical, in terms of movement. Yet the control of the emotions comes very early; they must not be repressed, but be developed toward a mean. The actual "subjects of instruction" (794C, 795D) begin in the child's sixth year. As in the *Republic*, the subjects still are gymnastics and music, except that gymnastics is now concerned with the body, while music is concerned with the soul. In this respect, the late work of the *Laws* returns—as so often—to the popular view, which was superseded in the *Republic* by a higher perspective.

BOOK VII

As in Book II of the *Laws*, gymnastics is divided here in Book V into *dance* and *wrestling and boxing*. After a few scattered remarks, however, it is said (796D) that the treatment of gymnastics promised earlier (II 672E) is now completed.[83] There follows the subject of music, and here the Athenian, going into greater detail, frames actual laws (799E *et seq.*). Yet here, too, we are referred (797A, 798D) to something said earlier (in Book II), i.e., to the doctrine of imitation. Here, too, we are reminded (799A) as in Book II (656D) that Egypt provides a model for the arts that have remained unchanged since ancient times. And this unchangeability with regard to our sacred hymns is now expressed specifically in the form of a law.[84]

When we consider that the actual legislation is systematically organized, but that only the framework of the subject of gymnastics appears here because its content was discussed earlier, and that, as far as music is concerned, many details were also treated earlier, the following conclusion suggests itself. Out of the total body of his theory of education—whether it was complete in his own mind or even written down—Plato selected certain parts to incorporate in the dialogical introduction to his *Laws*.[85]

What does this mean? The dialogical and the legislative principles, or as we may call them the Socratic and the Solonic principles, are two original forces in Plato. Just as he quite early achieved a dynamic equilibrium between the dialogical force and other forces in him—the mythopoeic, the rhetorical, the political—so in his last work, he balanced the dialogical force against the force of the legislator. We cannot expect that this union of forces perhaps most alien to each other should grow into a perfect harmony. Even as in a rock only some parts form crystals whereas others remain crystalline or amorphous, so the rigid body of laws enacted in Books V through XII is permeated only now and then by the live power of dialogue. The theory of education in the seventh book is treated dialogically, and so is the question of voluntary and involuntary actions in the ninth.[86] Again, the theology in the tenth book and, finally, at the end of the whole work, the institution of the nocturnal council as the representatives of this new theology are subjects also cast in dialogue form. All these matters are of deep significance for the work as a whole, and all of them must have strongly challenged the aged Plato to enter into dialogue because he saw in them problems still to be solved or counterforces still to be subdued. Yet, in now and then interrupting the closed circuit of the laws, he is in fact only continuing what he had initiated in the conversations of the first books. Beginning with what seemed to come most readily to hand, the cus-

toms and laws of Sparta and Crete, he opened for himself and
for the reader a way into the dialogical domain—even though
the material, as we have seen, he took at least in part from the
legislation itself.[87]

Theology

The section at the end of Book IX and the beginning of Book BOOK X
X deals with laws concerning acts of violence committed against
a person and against real property. Book XI begins with the
violation of property again. The natural connection between
these topics[88] is interrupted by Book X, which is loosely inserted. Here we find, cast in dialogical form, the major section
about the gods.[89] The section is first called an "admonition"
(παραμύθιον, 885Β 3), then a preamble (887Α 3), and is connected with what precedes because the violation of sanctuaries
and the robbery of temples are singled out as the most blas-
phemous acts of violence. The Athenian says himself (887C,
907BC) that he is speaking with passion and in anger, adding,
however, that one must try to control these impulses.

No man—so the Athenian begins—who believes in the existence of the gods has ever of his own free will (ἑκών) committed
an impious act or made a lawless remark. (The problem of free
will was discussed earlier, in Book IX.) In this way he immediately affirms the connection between a belief in the gods, on
the one hand, and lawful action, on the other. In the end he
sees himself as having triumphed over his argumentative adversaries whose victory would but reinforce their boldness to
act wrongly, whereas their defeat might lead them to the path
of right action (907BC). Three propositions are stated at the
outset and are then declared to have been refuted in the end
(907B): first, that there are no gods; second, that they do not
care about mankind; and third, that they can be swayed easily
by sacrifice and prayer. In the *Republic* (II 365D *et seq.*), Adeimantos formulated the view of the many in similar words and
in a similar context, and called upon Socrates to refute it. Thus,
another old conflict seems to re-emerge here in this last work.[90]

Still, let us not overlook the difference. It is true that in the
Republic we find a struggle against the disintegration of norms.

We also find that the poets are exposed as the most dangerous representatives of a false view of the gods, and that in the course of this struggle, new "basic modes of right discourse concerning the gods" are set up. But we do not find the reasoning of the adversaries spelled out and refuted, explicitly and in great detail, as in the *Laws*, nor do we find the belief in the existence of the gods grounded in a knowledge of the soul within and a vision of the starry sky above. Why is there nothing like this in the *Republic?* Evidently because there, in the center of the dialogue, the soul itself rises upward, through the sciences, including astronomy, to the realm of Forms and to the Form or *Idea* of the Good. In the *Laws*, theology—or religion—takes the place of the dialectical path in the *Republic*. It is the "noblest and best prelude to the laws" (887B 8), while dialectics is the heart of the ideal state itself. In this distinction, both the affinity and the difference between the two works are revealed.

In order to emphasize that the struggle here is difficult, the Cretan at first underestimates it. He tries to dispose of unbelief (to put it briefly) by means of the cosmological proof of God and by the argument *ex consensu gentium*. The matter is not as uncomplicated as this, replies the Athenian. It is also too simple, too "Doric," as it were, to assume that an irreligious life is due to the licentiousness of impulses. Looking further we see that an impulse of knowledge has here gone astray (ἀμαθία). Past and present have contributed to this misguidance. First, there are the ancients, i.e., the poets with their stories about the origin of the world and of the gods, and their accounts of the quarrel among the gods, to which men appeal when they mistreat their parents. What we see re-emerging is the *Euthyphro* theme, which was pursued in the struggle with the poets in the *Republic* (see pp. 72f., above). Here, however, this conflict is dismissed rather lightly. "It is not easy to criticize these stories, since they date from the remote past" (886c).

The real struggle is concerned with "the young and intelligent" among us who deprive the universe of soul and deity—and now we understand why the Athenian spoke with such passion. He sees before his eyes the good old times when the

stability of domestic worship impressed on children from their
earliest years a faith in the gods, and he sees this old order
destroyed by the new enlightenment. "To support the old
ordinance with the (written) word"—this, as the Cretan says
later, is the task of the legislator.[91]

There are three propositions to be opposed here successively.
The *first round* attacks the view of pure atheism. (Yet, as the   888D–899D
Athenian said earlier—888c—he never had found anybody who
held this view throughout a lifetime into old age.) What does
this view represent? In order to understand it, we have to
reach far.

"All things (πάντα τὰ πράγματα) . . ." These are the first
words here, as they were in Anaxagoras (ὁμοῦ πάντα χρήματα)
and in Protagoras (πάντων χρημάτων).[92] ". . . that become,
have become, and will come into existence . . ." "All is becoming," as Herakleitos said almost at the beginning, or "has
become, is, and will be," as Parmenides said. Or, in the words
of Melissos, "all things are by nature." In short, we are in the
midst of the pre-Socratic theories of nature. The strange thing,
however, is that according to the view of some intelligent
men, "nature" here is at once equated with "chance" and
"necessity." It means, in other words, the blind necessity of
chance as in the *Timaeus* (48A), not the lawfulness of nature,
and it is contrasted with "art," i.e., with the purposeful production of the artist or craftsman. "Nature," therefore, is entirely devoid of "art" and, likewise, of "spirit" and "God."
As compared with nature, art is a secondary, human, and insignificant matter. Law and custom belong to art, and, indeed,
the gods themselves are a product of art and convention. Now
we have reached the point where we grasp the old sophistic
contrast in its true depth—the struggle, waged in the *Gorgias*,
over the contrast between the law of nature and law by convention. Nature here means what is devoid of reason and God;
moreover, it has no counterpart that is truly reasonable and
divine (890A).

Stripping nature of soul and God—this, viewed in an over-all
perspective, had been the effect of the older philosophies of
nature (τῶν περὶ φύσεως ζητημάτων, 891c). Sophistic subversion

of human norms was the final consequence of this development. The task that Plato sets himself here—it was the central task of his life—is to reverse this trend as far as possible, i.e., to ground law and art again in nature and thus to respiritualize nature (890ᴅ). For the ultimate source of all this unreason (πηγὴ ἀνοήτου δόξης, 891c) is the false view about the nature of soul. Whereas it was thought to be derived from the previously existing physical elements, it is in truth the most original principle in nature, the cause of "becoming and passing away."

An analysis of "motion" reveals ten different kinds. The highest kind is that which moves itself and all that is, the "beginning" or "origin" of motion everywhere (895ᴀʙ). This is the "soul" (895ᴇ). Hence, soul is the first-born and most exalted of all that is (τῶν πάντων πρεσβυτάτη, 896ʙ), and the "soul-like," i.e., spirit, art, and law, is "prior" to the hard and the soft. Soul is the source of the beautiful and the ugly, the just and the unjust. Soul pervades the universe, too, whose motion is akin "to the motion, revolution, and calculations of the mind" (897c).

In the earliest of the philosophical studies of nature, Thales had affirmed that "all things are full of gods." Then the course of thought progressively deprived nature of God, and soul, and spirit. Even Anaxagoras had not been able to counter this trend. On the contrary, it seemed as if his discovery that "mind" rules in nature only served to reduce the sun all the more cruelly to a "fiery ball" and the stars to "stone and earth" (Laws XII 967ʙc; cf. Apology 26ᴅ). Only Plato's new knowledge about the soul succeeded in recasting the old type of natural philosophy —and to this fact the myth of the universe in the Timaeus is most magnificent testimony. Here in the Laws, however, the symbol for this victory at the end of the final struggle is a reaffirmation of what Thales had said: "All things are full of gods" (899ʙ 9).

We have called attention to the general affinity between Book X of the Laws and the heart of the Republic. It remains to show where the two works approximate each other most closely. In the Laws, in the course of the groping analysis of "motion" as a problem in nature, we gradually reach the highest point in

asking (897D), "What is the nature of the motion of mind?"
—a difficult question, as is said right away. Yet the thought is
immediately expressed again in stronger terms. We cannot at
all behold the mind with human eyes. We must beware of being
overcome by darkness as we are when we look directly at the
sun at noontime. It is safer, therefore, to look at an image
(εἰκών) instead of the object itself that we are seeking.

We are at once reminded of the central part of the *Republic*.
The search for the *Idea* of the Good hardly has been posed as a
problem when it is diverted to its offspring, from the sun to
what is sunlike. In the simile of the cave, the prisoner climbs
upward toward the light, yet at first he is blinded and must ac-
custom his eyes by looking at shadows and images (εἴδωλα),
then at the things themselves and at the starry sky, and only in
the end at the sun. The language in the *Republic* is dialectical
and mythical. Here in the *Laws*, it is the language of natural
philosophy, so that while the level is lower, the scope is wider.
Yet the target ultimately is the same. In the language of the
Laws, the language of natural philosophy, the movement of the
sphere of the universe is the image for the movement of the
eternal mind. Mind and universe "move in the same manner
and in the same course and around the same center and toward
the same goal, according to a *single* law and order."[93]

We may briefly touch on the part of the conversation when
the Athenian stipulates that there must be a variety of "souls"
and, for a moment, speaks of two kinds—a soul that has beneficial effects and its opposite kind, which produces evil in the
world. The contrast is actually between the power of a soul
that is associated with reason and guides all things in the right
direction, and the power of a soul that is associated with unreason and is the cause of disorder. In his treatise *On the World-
Soul in the Timaeus*, Plutarch refers to this passage of the *Laws*
and, boldly enough, equates the soul that is the cause of disorder with what is called "matter" (among other names) in
the *Timaeus*. Plutarch also refers to the myth in the *Statesman*,
to the reversal of cosmic periods when God is at the world's
wheel during one cycle whereas blind fate rules in another.
And, indeed, we can hear echoes of these myths—as far as their

896E–899B

religious and natural philosophy is concerned—in this passage of the *Laws* where it is Plato's aim to affirm, against a materialistic conception of nature, that there is a cosmic order. Whether this struggle, and opposition, of good and evil also reflects Persian influences is a question still debated in our time.[94] Plato knew something about Zoroaster when he wrote the *Alcibiades Major* (122A), and he undoubtedly learned a great deal more later on when Eudoxos was a teacher in the Academy and a Chaldean was one of its members. Yet little or nothing can be proved about these influences on Plato's theology, as may be seen both from the continuing controversy just mentioned and from the genuinely Platonic goal of divine order pursued in this episode of the *Laws*.

899D–905c   The *second round* attacks the assertion that the gods do not care about human affairs.[95] This view still is based, as it was in the speech of Adeimantos in the *Republic*, on alleged experience, i.e., the good fortune enjoyed by evil men and the misfortunes visited upon the good. The initial rebuttal makes the simple point that this view ascribes a defect to the gods, but then the critique goes deeper. Since the separation of nature and art was overcome in the previous struggle, we know that God is the greatest artist who—like any good artist—is equally concerned with the greatest as with the least aspects of his work. The universe is a work of art and, hence, a coherent structure of forms and meanings—a coherent structure and a necessity that does not exclude, but includes, man's will. In this coherent structure in which the individual serves the whole and its blissfully perfect being (εὐδαίμων οὐσία, 903c), reward and punishment also have their necessary place. They are subordinated to the great natural lawfulness of change (μεταβολή).[96] "Right" is what leads like to like and unlike to unlike. Thus, reward and punishment, here or beyond, no longer are accidents or parts of a myth; they are special cases of a universal law. Here is the cosmic dimension of what was said in looking at the human domain in the *Crito* (53D) and was repeated in the *Laws* (728B) —namely, that the punishment of evil men consists in having to live with evil men.

905c–907B   The *third round* is simple and brief. The belief that the gods would be open to bribes from criminals attributes to them a kind of conduct that would place them below the level of human rulers, whereas they are in truth the highest rulers, "presiding unshakably over the heavens."[97] For the last time our view is directed toward the universe as the eternal battlefield between good and evil—and we must join the battle as helpers of the gods. It is the same connection that justifies the moral aspects' intruding into the myth of nature in the *Timaeus* (see pp. 380f., above). Human evil, just like sickness or plague, is a cosmic disturbance. It transgresses the limits set for each thing. *Pleonexia* is its common name, applied either to the human soul or to elements in nature. The third view that is here repudiated would have meant that the guardians of the universe neither punish such a violation of the great order nor wish to restore the limits transgressed. "The right justice, however, is to bring the man who is out of tune back into harmony" (*Critias* 106B).

Once we realize how Plato here co-ordinates the moral and political aspects with a belief in cosmic order, then we may at least understand—although we may not approve—the laws of a severe inquisition that are now incorporated in the code (907D *et seq.*).[98] This is a deeply serious, violent attempt "to come to the aid of the god." And even if these laws look alarming, it is to be remembered that Plato frames statutes for the state in his *Laws* that he would no more have decreed in Syracuse or in Athens than he would have instituted the chorus of old men or military training for women.

It is also inconceivable that as Plato discusses, with such frightening rigor, the different forms of impiety and establishes the corresponding kinds of punishments, he would not have thought of the trial of Socrates, who was accused of impiety. Plato here in the *Laws* envisages three prisons, the first of them located near the market place (908A 1–2). While in the *Phaedo* (59D 3–4) we read that the Athenian courthouse was close to the prison, we know that the courthouse of the Eleven was located in the market place of Athens.[99] Thus, Plato took the institution of the first prison in the imaginary city on Crete from his own native city. In writing this detail into his *Laws*, Plato could not have forgotten his *Phaedo*. How, then, is this legislation against impiety propounded by the Athenian here in the *Laws* related to the historical trial of Socrates, indicted on the charge of impiety?

In Book V of the *Laws* (739A *et seq.*), the Athenian distinguishes three kinds of constitutions. The best of these is a society of perfect communism. (If Socrates were the speaker, instead of the anonymous Athenian, he would say that the best society is that in which philosophers are kings.) The second-best state is the one we are constructing here in words. The third-best is the state we shall found on Crete according to this model. To the question, "Where would Athens rank in this scheme?" we would have to answer, "Far below the third-best state." In the perfect state there are no written laws, and such a thing as impiety is least likely to occur when the traditional gods are spoken of only in the language of myth and when philosophy reveals the highest being in the realm of transcendence. In Athens the legal procedures in matters of impiety are in such deep confusion, however, as to permit the judicial murder of the man most just. Perhaps one reason why Plato's legislation on impiety is so frightening is that it makes us see that a judicial murder such as Athens committed against Socrates would be impossible in the lawful state on Crete. On Crete, we might imagine, Socrates would be one of the custodians of the law or a member of the nocturnal council.

The Custodians of the Law and the Nocturnal Council

960B–969D
BOOK XII

The legislative sketch that is part of the great plan in Book I (see p. 393, above) provides at the end for custodians to guard the laws (632c). They should embody the principle of the "leader reason" as the inner bond and highest goal in the state. They are to guarantee that all the laws aim at self-discipline and justice, not at wealth and ambition. This means that the true order of values is guaranteed only by the institution at the top of the whole structure. From Book VI on, therefore, where the officials are chosen and the legislation begins, many separate references to the custodians occur.[100] The difficulty in selecting the custodians is mentioned, as are their duties, their length of office, the occasions when they are entitled to issue enactments and mete out punishment alone or jointly with priests or civil officials. Much of what cannot be spelled out in the actual laws is left to the custodians. Yet, after the suggestion made in Book I, we expect to hear more about the custodians than merely this abundance of details.

And, indeed, after the law code itself is completed with the rites for burial and honors for the dead (XII 960B 5), we come at the end of Book XII to the institution that is to guarantee the "irreversibility" of all these laws (960D 4–6). Yet, with close attention we realize that this very high magistracy is not occupied by the "custodians of the law"—that group whose strange numerical composition of thirty-seven men $(1 + 17 + 19)$ was quite carefully constructed in Book VI (752E *et seq.*). Whether Plato so intended it or whether this is a flaw due to a final revision, there is, somehow still above the body of custodians, the "nocturnal council" that is to meet in the hours between daybreak and sunrise (951D). It is composed of the ten senior custodians and a number of other men who have won highest distinction, as well as some who have traveled abroad for the sake of serious study, and some younger men, in their thirties, who are included to provide continuity.

It is strange yet hardly accidental that in this concluding section, the work suddenly and for the last time is broken up into dialogue after so many books of uninterrupted legislation. The necessity for the institution of this council can be demonstrated only in conversation. For "it is no easy matter to discover nor can we find out from others" what subjects are to be studied by the members of the council. And "it would be futile to write down regulations" (ἐν γράμμασιν, 968D) as to when and how long subjects are to be studied. We cannot fail to observe that even after so many books on legislation, Plato in the end is still cognizant of the fact that there is something unsatisfactory about the rigidity of the written word.[101]

We cannot fail, too, to see[102] that the name "custodians of the law" (νομοφύλακες) only slightly varies the name of the "guardians" (φύλακες) in the *Republic*, who also are charged primarily with "guarding the laws" (φυλάξαι νόμους, *Republic* 484B). In the central section of the *Republic*, we may remember, it is stated exactly how many years those who are selected to be rulers must study various subjects (VII 539D *et seq.*). Thus, at the end of the *Laws* is an echo of what was said at the center in the *Republic*.

Let us note the leading themes of this concluding section as Plato impresses them on us in frequently repeated key words. The nocturnal council, the "anchor" of the ship of state, is its "protector" and "savior" (σῴζειν, σωτήρ, σωτηρία). To succeed in this "rescue," we must come to see the "goal" or "object" (τέλος, τὸν σκοπόν) of the pursuit. Not many aims must be pursued, but "one" or "the one" (ἕν, τὸ ἕν). The moral pursuit has a single goal. Here (963A) we are expressly turned back to Book I, so that this moral theme provides the frame for the work as a whole. The four virtues are one, namely, virtue. The eye must be capable of discerning the "single Form" in the realm of the many and the unlike (965c 2). The beautiful-and-good is not many, but is one (966A). So this is the "one *Idea*," ultimately the same as the *Idea* of the Good at the center of the *Republic* (VII 540A). Thus, here at the periphery of the *Laws*, Form and transcendence briefly come into view, whereas the work as a whole had for the most part remained within empirical reality and the realm of traditional Athenian and Doric piety.[103]

Also remarkable is the way in which this view of the "one *Idea*" is introduced here. For this is done in the simplest possible manner—that is, by harking back to the early dialogues, the *Protagoras* and its satellites, and then to Book IV of the *Republic*, where Plato treated the problem of the one in the many, the relationship of "virtue as a whole" to the various single virtues which, in addition to being courage, justice, temperance, and wisdom, are also one, namely, virtue (*Laws* XII 965c *et seq.*).

What is impressed on us here, with strong ontological-metaphysical hints that unmistakably call up the central part of the *Republic*, is carried into a theological dimension with an explicit reference to Book X of the *Laws* (966c *et seq.*). "Soul is the most sublime and divine thing in the realm of being and becoming." (These two concepts, being and becoming, are linked in what is for Plato a paradoxical conjunction—not unlike the "coming-into-being" in *Philebus* 26D or the "necessary being of becoming" in *Statesman* 283D.) "Mind" is the power of order in the universe. Here where the divine in the soul and in the universe become visible, then, a struggle ensues against those who see only blind necessity instead of the order of reason. The old conflict between philosophy and poetry—reminiscent of the last book of the *Republic*—is heard once more. Indeed, inasmuch as literal quotations from Sophron's book of mimes (which Plato, according to tradition, bought in Sicily) seem to be strewn throughout the discussion in the *Republic*, it would be strange if Plato did not also remember, from reading Sophron, the portrait of the "philosophizers" who bark foolishly like dogs.[104] That the name "philosophizers" refers to the spokesmen for a mechanistic and materialistic world-view, and that Plato takes sides against them in favor of the poets, must be emphasized in order to appreciate Plato's often misunderstood attitude toward poetry.

Even as the nocturnal council cannot be completely integrated in the institution of the magistrates and in the constitution of the laws, because it is something beyond both, so the function assigned to this council, to contemplate the "one *Idea*," goes beyond the spiritual domain characteristic of the *Laws*. We have seen (p. 437, above) how the theology in Book X, in general, corresponds to what is described in the ascent to the realm of Forms in the *Republic*. The custodians of the law are charged with guarding this theology, which is based on a study of the heavenly bodies and the soul (*Laws* XII 966B *et seq.*). Yet, for a moment, the search for the "one Form" rises above the study of the soul and astronomy. To attain this ultimate goal, a much stricter and more complete kind of instruction would be necessary than has been outlined in the *Laws* heretofore, especially in the first two books. The way to the ultimate goal by means of higher mathematics and dialectics is suggested in the briefest words (964D 4, 965C 1). Yet these few words, in retrospect, as it were, give the entire enormous work of legislation direction by transcending it.

That is the meaning of this institution, leaving aside its institutional aspects. It is no accident, then, that at the end of the whole work, the highest level of Plato's thought is once more cast in the form of dialogue—a dialogue that, for a moment, even takes the form of a genuine contest. For at the very time the Athenian points to the "one Form," his Cretan partner, wanting to leave in abeyance what has been glimpsed, replies with a "maybe" (ἴσως). At this moment, this goes so much against the grain that the Athenian corrects his partner sharply: "Not 'may be,' but truly (οὐκ ἴσως ἀλλ᾽ ὄντως)—there is no surer path of study for any man" (965c). Thus, when the "one Form" comes to the fore after so many books of uninterrupted legislation, and when Plato, at the conclusion of his last work, returns to a section written in the form of dialogue, for the reason that these matters cannot be treated in any "fixed" type of discourse, this is an indication, however slight, that he is still conscious of old struggles and conquests. The Socrates in Plato still wins out over the Solon in him. Rigid discourse is sublimated in dialogue. And above the laws there rises the world of Forms.

AFTERWORD

On the Order
of the Dialogues

W E MAY SAY that today we are no longer preoccupied
with "the Platonic question," which for decades almost
obscured the view of Plato himself even as the Homeric question
hid the view of Homer. As to the authenticity of Plato's works
and their chronological sequence, there are, in general, hardly
any serious differences of opinion. Thus, if it no longer is permissible to constantly rearrange the order of the dialogues on
the basis of an alleged development of Plato's thought or doctrines, we owe this result to the achievements of linguistic
studies that began with Lewis Campbell in 1867. He placed the
late dialogues in one group—the *Sophist*, the *Statesman*, the
Timaeus, the *Critias*, the *Philebus*, and the *Laws*. Later on, Blass
and Janell observed that the hiatus is avoided in these very
dialogues.[1] The two observations fit together, for in his late
period Plato chose and avoided certain verbal expressions because he had adopted the rule of Isokrates against the use of the
hiatus.

Campbell's studies were continued and extended into the
whole body of Plato's works by Dittenberger, Schanz, Ritter,
Łutoslawski, and von Arnim. The statistical method of von
Arnim put the final touch to these linguistic studies for, despite
various objections to verbal statistics, the fact remains that this
method is invaluable precisely because its results are not new.
In short, it does what was to be expected.[2] Even radical doubters
should pause to think that von Arnim succeeded in arranging
together the books of the *Republic* (with the exception, however,

of Book I), the books of the *Laws,* the group *Sophist, Statesman,* and *Philebus,* and the group of early aporetic dialogues.

It is nonetheless appropriate to add that these calculations must not be allowed to coagulate into dogma. The linear conception, according to which each dialogue has its definite dating before or after another dialogue, suffers from a lack of dimensions since the body of Plato's work presents a cosmos of forms. It is within this universe that we perceive—looking at once at the form and the content of each work—various groups of dialogues which exhibit affinities. That the order adopted cannot but reflect some personal characteristics of the observer is no objection in the field of the *Geisteswissenschaften.* What we must try to determine is the relative stableness of such groupings of dialogues.

Verbal statistics alone cannot distinguish the great periods of work. This is indispensable in all efforts to understand Plato's work as a whole, even as it is all the more important to evaluate again and again whether, and how much, the ordering of the dialogues according to periods and groups helps or harms the understanding of the works themselves. Thus, while the grouping of Plato's dialogues attempted in these volumes must not be overrated, it may be conceded that the attempt itself is more meaningful than the refusal to adopt any kind of order—more meaningful, in other words, than a strictly linear pattern.[3] We must at least try to transform this linear view into an organic, three-dimensional conception, and to see groups rising above the individual dialogues, periods above the groups, and, above the periods, Plato's work as a whole.

In the center of Plato's work as a whole is the *Republic.* There are few dialogues of the earlier period that do not lead, in one way or another, toward the *Republic,* and few works in the later groups that do not hark back to it. Only the *Symposium* and the *Phaedo* can claim a place beside the *Republic,* whereas the *Gorgias* and the *Meno* clearly are works preparatory to it. The *Symposium* and the *Phaedo* point to the two other ways, in addition to the way of knowledge pursued in the main work, that lead to the world of Forms. Beside the way of knowledge are the way of love and the way of death. This trinity expresses the symbolic meaning that gives the division into periods its real value.

Preserving this, we have included the *Theaetetus* in the third period, although according to verbal statistics it belongs closest to the *Republic*.[4] It would be hard to justify separating the *Theaetetus* from the pair of dialogues, the *Sophist* and the *Statesman*, which continue its line as to participants and in other respects as well. In its essence, too, the *Theaetetus* would seem to belong closer to the *Parmenides*, the *Phaedrus*, and the other late dialogues. The characteristic tension in the *Theaetetus* between the aporetic course of the whole work, on the one hand, and the digression about the philosopher, on the other, is similar to the tension in the *Phaedrus* between love and rhetoric, the tension in the *Parmenides* between the aporetic first part and the dialectics of the second, and, again, the tension in the *Sophist* between the systems of division and the dialogue's central ontology. In contrast to this movement by "leaps," as it were, is the carefully ordered series of stages in which a work ascribed to the middle period unfolds. Thus, if the *Theaetetus* and the *Republic* are really "contemporaries," this becomes a place where our division into periods would be justified more on systematic grounds than chronologically.

The reasons for dividing the late works into the two groups adopted here are strictly systematic, not chronological. It is quite possible that the *Timaeus* and the *Critias*—both works being linked with the *Republic*—preceded the *Statesman*. This cannot be known but neither is it particularly relevant. The work on the *Laws* must have been in progress over many years, and it is hard to believe that Plato had completed all his other dialogues before he began the last.

Now back to the beginning—where the aporetic dialogues in search of a definition have always stood out as a separate group. The findings of the statistical method agree entirely with what must be concluded from analysis of the aesthetic structure and the conceptual movement of these dialogues. What is particularly characteristic of this group is the human encounter, together with the statement of the problem, the series of definitions, the aporetic conclusion, and the tension between the very pointed dialectics and a rich vitality of action. Within this group, four dialogues—the *Laches*, the *Thrasymachus*, the *Charmides*, and the *Euthyphro*, each inquiring into a single virtue—form a subgroup. In formal terms, the problem they have in common is that of the one and the many or, as it might also be said, the problem of division. This problem is hidden, yet only because its nature is so clear to Plato can he guide each of these dialogues, with such unerring grasp, toward an aporetic conclusion. Within this group of four, an unfolding may also be sensed. While Plato leads the *Eidos* expressly to the fore in the *Euthyphro*, he seems to hold it back in the three other works so as not to release the tension prematurely.

That the *Lysis* follows this group is shown both by linguistic analysis and by study of its structure. This placing is consistent also with the relationship of the *Lysis* to the *Symposium*. For the *Lysis* represents on the level of the early aporetic dialogues the same vital force that Plato will give shape to again in the *Symposium* at the central stage of his work and in the *Phaedrus* at the late stage.

In form and content the *Hippias Major* also belongs in this early group. Here, however, the statistical and the structural analyses disagree. Thus, for the time being, it must remain an open question whether one dialogue of this group actually extends into the second period or whether the statistical approach is misleading here—or whether there is some other way to resolve this conflict.

As we have indicated by the title of the first group of dialogues, the *Protagoras* occupies a special position. Its affinities with the other aporetic dialogues on *arete* are just as evident as the fact is that it overlaps each of them. It also unifies them by setting up a first system of the "virtues" that is similar to the way the virtues are unified in Book IV of the *Republic*. The *Protagoras*, to be sure, accomplishes much more than this. In its basic struggle between two kinds of discourse and in its contrast between true and false education, it anticipates the *Euthydemus* and the *Gorgias*. Yet the abundance of characters, forms, and relationships displayed in the *Protagoras* makes it possible to say either that it is a relatively late work (if we assume that Plato progressed from simpler to more complex works) or that it comes at the beginning—if we assume that Plato might have wished to launch his literary career with a work as comprehensive and many-faceted as possible.[5] The statistical method leads to the strange finding that the *Protagoras* is related closely to the *Ion*, but not related to any other dialogue. Thus, von Arnim places the *Protagoras* at the very beginning. Its development of the problem of the virtues, too, is at an earlier stage than in the *Laches.* We should at least try to explain why Plato, in the *Protagoras*, stopped short in his analysis of "courage" if he had already written the *Laches.* Be all that as it may, let the place we have given the *Protagoras* indicate primarily that it represents the unifying work among the four aporetic dialogues on *arete.* For here, too, our order is intended to be systematic rather than chronological.

Part II of the first period was originally made up mainly to give clearer shape to Part I. It then turned out that the dialogues in Part II have a genuine unity of their own. In the *Hipparchus*, the image of the "lover of wisdom" shines through the existence of the "lover of gain." The *Ion* develops the contrast between poet and philosopher, and in the *Hippias Minor*, the contrast between deception and truth is the occasion for contrasting sophist and philosopher. In the *Theages*, we catch a glimpse of the demonic limits imposed on the work of loving education. Nowhere else can we find a portrait of the philosopher, the poet, and the sophist that is so unburdened by any intruding problems as here in these early dialogues of Part II.

Yet, separating the first two groups does not say anything about the chronological relationships of the works. If the *Hipparchus* is genuine—and there is no proof to the contrary— it undoubtedly is one of Plato's earliest works. This also is generally said of the *Ion*, and here statistical analysis at least does not disagree. The *Hippias Minor* is placed unexpectedly late by von Arnim, however, so that its position remains questionable. And in the case of the *Theages*, there is the quite expected opposition of those who consider the work spurious because they find it "uncanny."

As to the works of the middle period, aspects of the *Republic* are anticipated in a number of the early dialogues, and the theme of love treated in the *Symposium* is anticipated in the *Lysis*. Even the theme of death developed in the *Phaedo* is not entirely absent in the works of the early stage. For while the *Idea* of the Good is not yet explicitly present in the *Apology*, its proximity must unfailingly be sensed by a mind trained in the works of Plato's maturity. It is impossible to set a more precise date than we have for the *Apology*. The unity of the virtues—a theme constantly present in the *Apology*—is also the theme that dominates the *Protagoras* and the aporetic dialogues, up to the *Republic*. The *Apology* must find a place somewhere in this chronological line. Perhaps this place should be after the *Euthyphro*, on the following reasoning. The *Euthyphro* directs us to the trial to which the *Apology* is (or seems to be) given over in its entirety. Also, the *Euthyphro* analyzes the nature of piety by showing what it is not, whereas the *Apology* shows this same piety to be the center of Socratic *arete*. Thus, there seems to be little prospect of fulfilling the wish (expressed repeatedly) that the *Apology* might be Plato's first work. Yet, in suggesting that the *Apology* comes somewhere between the *Euthyphro* and the *Gorgias*, we may say that its inclusion here in Part III is intended to be far more a typological than a chronological ordering.

At first sight, the *Apology* seems to occupy a place that is unique in Plato's work, as is the moment in the life of Socrates there recaptured. Yet the *Apology* as a Platonic work is not without connections. The *Menexenus*, too, is given over almost completely to a speech of Socrates which is so long that the frame dialogue is reduced to practically nothing. Both of these works fall into one group because in them Socrates employs a form of discourse that is alien and unnatural to him. Within the group, however, the two works represent opposite poles. For in the *Apology*, the philosopher reveals himself with an openness shown nowhere else, whereas in the *Menexenus*, he conceals himself more thoroughly than almost anywhere else.

The *Crito* belongs to the *Apology*. As much as we may try to break away from the old tradition linking these two works, we will always come back to it. But if, in a παλίντονος ἁρμονίη, we regard the *Apology* as the self-portrait of the philosopher and the *Menexenus* as a form of self-disguise, and if we put the *Crito* beside the *Apology*, we may not be unwilling to include the *Euthydemus* and the *Cratylus* in the same group. For in these works, too, Socrates conceals himself, if only for rather long stretches, behind a form of thought that is basically alien to him —etymology in the *Cratylus* and eristics in the *Euthydemus*. Yet genuine philosophy breaks through both of these un-Socratic forms just as it breaks through the alien form of a public speech in the *Menexenus* and in the *Apology* above all. In the *Euthydemus* and the *Cratylus*, the veil covering the true image is lifted again and again with masterly playfulness, so that here through the disguises of eristics and etymology, more of the true aim of the philosopher is revealed than in any other work of the first two groups.

The *Gorgias* belongs to a new stage. For the first time, "the *logos* takes a stand." By this very fact the *Gorgias* is distinguished from all the works we have placed earlier. And for the same reason, it is impossible—quite aside from any statistical analysis—to place even such dramatically rich works as the *Protagoras* and the *Euthydemus* after the *Gorgias*. The *Gorgias* takes the struggle against rhetoric from the *Protagoras*, the struggle against injustice from the *Thrasymachus*. Both contests are more radical in the *Gorgias* because this dialogue fuses the themes of sophistic and injustice, on the one hand, and the symbol of Socrates and justice, on the other. Now the constructive forces are so powerful that they cannot be exhausted in the process of struggle and critique. After the opposing forces are overcome, then, something new is shown, to be stamped at the end—through the myth—with the seal of true being. This is so different from anything in the preceding works that there can hardly be objection to separating Part IV from the first three groups of dialogues. Similarly, in our chapter (IX, in *Plato* 1) on "Myth," the myth of the *Gorgias* was set apart from that of the *Protagoras* as belonging to a different group. Whether this fourth group of works is considered to be in the first or the second period is not of great moment. Yet, when Part IV is designated as the last and highest group of the first period, as it is here, the direction of the dialogues themselves is brought out most clearly.

The *Alcibiades Major* grows out of the elenctic dialogues but grows also beyond them. For it brings into view the unity of opposite tendencies that is hard to achieve—the nature of man striving for knowledge, on the one hand, and the nature of the state, in its unity of contrasting tendencies, on the other. As the struggle between Socrates and Alkibiades contains in a hidden form what later breaks out into the open in the struggle with Gorgias, Polos, and Kallikles, so the dialogue anticipates the *Gorgias* and, more distantly yet, the *Republic*. In this sense the *Alcibiades* seems to fill the gap between the *Gorgias* and the earlier dialogues.

That the *Meno* belongs to the *Gorgias* we may learn from verbal statistics, but the same connection has often been felt on other grounds as well. The two dialogues are linked by the question of whether statesmen can educate, and by the myth of a life hereafter. The new tone in which the great Athenian statesmen are spoken of in the *Meno* justifies the view that this dialogue looks back to the *Gorgias*. The *Alcibiades Major* may be said to turn the aporetic characteristics of the early dialogues into something positive. The first part of the *Meno*, too, reads like an aporetic dialogue in search of a definition (Part I). The question of whether virtue can be taught, and therefore, the question as to the connection between teachability and knowledge, the *Meno* takes over from the *Protagoras*. The *Euthydemus* depicted the contrast between a destructive eristic and a true dialectic, with the ironic twist that the conflict—seemingly —was won by eristics. True knowledge, moreover, had become visible as the royal art, but its nature was lost in *aporia*. The *Meno* overcomes this *aporia* by showing the transcendence of knowledge in mythical imagery, and it also overcomes the Eleatic-eristic dichotomy of knowledge and ignorance by giving opinion (*doxa*) a place between the two poles. Thus, both the *Alcibiades Major* and the *Meno* go beyond the dialogues of the earlier groups by not only including their aporetic method but transforming it—the *Meno*, to be sure, in a much more extensive and decisive way. (Later on in the *Theaetetus*, Plato once again, this time most boldly, constructs an aporetic dialogue in three stages and transforms it in its depths. This he does by inserting in the first stage the digression on the philosopher.)

Looking back once more on the relationships among the four groups of dialogues of Plato's early period, we may make certain observations. Part I and Part II may be roughly contemporary with each other. It is quite possible, however, that in the *Hipparchus* and the *Ion*, included here in Part II, we have Plato's earliest writings. Part III probably takes us far beyond the chronological boundaries of Parts I and II since the *Menexenus* is dated about the year 386, whereas the *Apology* and the *Crito* belong close to the *Euthyphro* in content and, hence, probably in time as well (and the *Euthyphro*, as we have seen, is an aporetic dialogue of definition that falls into Part I). In Part IV, at least the *Gorgias* and the *Meno* are later than almost any work of the first three groups. But no attempt is made here to set up an absolute chronology of Plato's works. For definite statements with great probability can be made only about the first decade of his writing of dialogues, the third decade of his life. It was a well-known anecdote of antiquity that Socrates on reading Plato's *Lysis* shook his head at the inventiveness of the young man.[6] The ancient world, therefore, did not share the view quite widely accepted today that Plato began to write Socratic dialogues only after the death of the master. Wilamowitz rejected this view at the price of setting apart the *Ion*, the *Hippias Minor*, and the *Protagoras* as pure satires differentiated from the works with philosophical content, since only in this way did he think it was possible to date these dialogues before the year 399. Our interpretation has shown that these works of Plato's early period cannot be set apart on such grounds. But as to the chronology, it may be said that while many commentators find it satisfying to think that Plato did not begin to write in the new form of dialogue until after the death of Socrates,[7] nobody can prove that this was actually the case.

For in addition to the ancient anecdote, the following consideration must be allowed to speak. Wilamowitz[8] argued that the *Hippias Minor* must be dated before the year 399 on the grounds that after that year no member of the Socratic circle would dare let Socrates represent immorality—in however transparent a veil—as is done in the *Hippias Minor*. And another consideration that points in the same direction may conclude this afterword on the order of the dialogues. If the order we have adopted with regard to the early dialogues is acceptable at least in general, the works that obviously reflect the impact of Socrates' death are by no means the first ones.[9] Now it is hard to imagine that Plato *after the year 399* would have begun to write such dialogues as the *Ion*, the *Laches*, and the *Charmides*, and not approach until later—in the *Euthyphro*, the *Apology*, the *Crito*, and the *Gorgias*—the subject of Socrates' death. It makes much more sense to assume that Plato's first writings date from before the end of the fifth century. For in this case, the year 399 would mark the great break not in the development of the form of Plato's writing, but in the feeling of life behind his works. And we would better understand why to Plato's dialogue creation, too, may be applied Aristotle's word: ἀπεσεμνύνθη.

NOTES AND ABBREVIATIONS

ABBREVIATIONS

Books and Periodicals Cited

AbhLeipz = *Abhandlungen der Sächsischen Akademie.* Leipzig.

AdP = *Archives de Philosophie.* Paris.

AfGP = *Archiv für Geschichte der Philosophie.* Berlin.

Aichroth = Richard Aichroth, "Schauspiel und Schauspielervergleich bei Platon." Tübingen dissertation, 1960.

AJP = *American Journal of Philology.* Baltimore.

Allen = R. E. Allen, ed., *Studies in Plato's Metaphysics.* London, 1965.

Apelt, *Aufsätze* = Otto Apelt, *Platonische Aufsätze.* Leipzig and Berlin, 1912.

Arnim, *Sprachliche Forschungen* = Hans von Arnim, *Sprachliche Forschungen zur Chronologie der platonischen Dialoge.* Sitzungsberichte der Wiener Akademie, 1911.

Arnim, *Jugenddialoge* = Hans von Arnim, *Platos Jugenddialoge und die Entstehungszeit des "Phaidros."* Leipzig, 1914.

Ast = Friedrich Ast, *Platons Leben und Schriften.* Leipzig, 1816.

Barker = Sir Ernest Barker, *Greek Political Theory: Plato and His Predecessors.* 3d edn., London, 1947.

Barth = Heinrich Barth, *Die Seele in der Philosophie Platons.* Tübingen, 1921.

Bekker = Immanuel Bekker, *Platonis Scripta Graece Omnia.* London, 1826. 9 vols.

Bonitz = Hermann Bonitz, *Platonische Studien.* 3d edn., Berlin, 1886.

Bruns, *Porträt* = Ivo Bruns, *Das literarische Porträt der Griechen.* Berlin, 1896.

Buccellato = Manlio Buccellato, *La retorica sofistica negli scritti di Platone.* Rome and Milan, 1953.

Bull. Budé = *Bulletin de l'Association Guillaume Budé.* Paris.

CB = *Classical Bulletin.* St. Louis.

Cherniss, *Aristotle's Criticism of Plato* = Harold Cherniss, *Aristotle's Criticism of Plato and the Academy.* Baltimore, 1944.

Cherniss, *Riddle* = Harold Cherniss, *The Riddle of the Early Academy.* Berkeley and Los Angeles, 1945.

Cherniss, *Lustrum* = Harold Cherniss, "Plato 1950–1957," *Lustrum: Internationale Forschungsberichte*, IV (1959), V (1960). Göttingen, 1960–61.

Classen = C. Joachim Classen, *Sprachliche Deutung als Triebkraft platonischen und sokratischen Philosophierens.* Zetemata, XXII. Munich, 1959.

Cousin = *Oeuvres de Platon*, tr. Victor Cousin. Paris, 1822–39. 13 vols.

CP = *Classical Philology.* Chicago.

CQ = *Classical Quarterly.* London and Boston.

Crombie = I. M. Crombie, *An Examination of Plato's Doctrines.* London and New York, 1962–63. 2 vols.

de Vries = G. J. de Vries, *Spel bij Plato.* Amsterdam, 1949.

DGrA = Paul Friedländer, *Der Grosse Alcibiades.* Bonn, 1921–23. 2 pts.

Dickinson = G. Lowes Dickinson, *Plato and His Dialogues.* New York, 1932. (Penguin reprint, 1947.)

Diès, *Platon* = Auguste Diès, *Autour de Platon.* Paris, 1927.

Dodds = E. R. Dodds, *The Greeks and the Irrational.* Berkeley, 1951. (Beacon reprint, 1957.)

Doxogr. = Hermann Diels, *Doxographi Graeci.* Berlin and Leipzig, 1879.

Eckert = Wilhelm Eckert, *Dialektischer Scherz in den früheren Gesprächen Platons.* Nürnberg, 1911.

Festugière, *Révélation* = A.-J. Festugière, *La révélation d'Hermès Trismégiste.* Vol. II. Paris, 1949.

Festugière, *Contemplation* = A.-J. Festugière, *Contemplation et vie contemplative selon Platon.* 2d edn., Paris, 1950.

Frank, *Pythagoreer* = Erich Frank, *Platon und die sogenannten Pythagoreer.* Halle, 1923.

Frank, *WWG* = Erich Frank, *Wissen, Wollen, Glauben.* Zurich and Stuttgart, 1955.

Freymann = Walther Freymann, *Platons Suchen nach einer Grundlegung aller Philosophie.* Leipzig, 1930.

Friedemann = Heinrich Friedemann, *Platon: Seine Gestalt.* Berlin, 1914.

Gauss = Hermann Gauss, *Philosophischer Handkommentar zu den Dialogen Platons.* Bern, 1952–61. 3 vols., 6 pts. (References are to pages, not to paragraphs.)

Geffcken = Johannes Geffcken, *Griechische Literaturgeschichte.* Vol. II. Heidelberg, 1934.

Gigon = Olof Gigon, "Platon," *Bibliographische Einführungen in das Studium der Philosophie*, No. 12. Bern, 1950.

Goldschmidt = Victor Goldschmidt, *Les dialogues de Platon.* Paris, 1947.

Gomperz = Theodor Gomperz, *Greek Thinkers*, tr. Laurie Magnus and G. G. Berry. New York and London, 1901–12. 4 vols.

Greene, *Moira* = William Chase Greene, *Moira: Fate, Good and Evil, in Greek Thought.* Cambridge, Mass., 1944.

Grote = George Grote, *Plato and the Other Companions of Socrates.* London, 1865. 3 vols.

Grube = Georges M. A. Grube, *Plato's Thought.* London, 1935.

Hermann, *Geschichte* = Karl Friedrich Hermann, *Geschichte und System der platonischen Philosophie*. Heidelberg, 1839.

Hildebrandt, *Platon* = Kurt Hildebrandt, *Platon: Der Kampf des Geistes um die Macht*. Berlin, 1933. (2d edn., 1959; unless otherwise indicated, the first edition is cited.)

Hirzel = Rudolf Hirzel, *Der Dialog*. Leipzig, 1895. 2 pts.

Hoffmann, *Platon* = Ernst Hoffmann, *Platon*. Zurich, 1950.

Jachmann = Günther Jachmann, *Der Platontext*. Nachrichten der Akademie der Wissenschaften in Göttingen, No. 11. 1941.

Jaeger, *Paideia* = Werner Jaeger, *Paideia*, tr. Gilbert Highet. Oxford, 1939–45. 3 vols.

Jaeger, *Aristotle* = Werner Jaeger, *Aristotle*, tr. Richard Robinson. 2d edn., Oxford, 1948.

JHistId = *Journal of the History of Ideas*. New York.

JHS = *Journal of Hellenic Studies*. London.

Joël = Karl Joël, *Geschichte der antiken Philosophie*. Tübingen, 1921.

Jowett = *The Dialogues of Plato*, tr. Benjamin Jowett. Oxford, 1924. 4 vols.

JPhilol = *Journal of Philology*. London and Cambridge.

JPhilos = *Journal of Philosophy*. New York.

Koyré = Alexandre Koyré, *Introduction à la lecture de Platon*. New York and Paris, 1945.

Krämer = Hans Joachim Krämer, *Arete bei Platon und Aristoteles: Zum Wesen und zur Geschichte der platonischen Ontologie*. Abhandlungen Heidelberger Akademie, Phil.-hist. Kl., No. 6. 1959.

Kranz, *Philosophie* = Walther Kranz, *Griechische Philosophie*. 4th edn., Bremen, 1958.

Kucharski = Paul Kucharski, *Les chemins du savoir dans les derniers dialogues de Platon*. Paris, 1949.

Leisegang = Hans Leisegang, "Platon," in *Real-Encyclopädie der classischen Altertumswissenschaft*. Vol. XX, Stuttgart, 1950. Cols. 2341ff.

Lesky = Albin Lesky, *A History of Greek Literature*, tr. James Willis and Cornelis de Heer. London, 1966.

Levinson = Ronald Bartlett Levinson, *In Defense of Plato*. Cambridge, Mass., 1953.

Lodge = Rupert C. Lodge, *The Philosophy of Plato*. London, 1956.

Loeb = Loeb Classical Library. London and Cambridge, Mass.

Luccioni = Jean Luccioni, *La pensée politique de Platon*. Paris, 1958.

Łutoslawski = Wincenty Łutoslawski, *The Origin and Growth of Plato's Logic*. London and New York, 1897.

Meyer = Eduard Meyer, *Geschichte des Altertums*. Stuttgart, 1889–1902. 5 vols.

MusHelv = *Museum Helveticum*. Basel.

Natorp, *Ideenlehre* = Paul Natorp, *Platos Ideenlehre*. Leipzig, 1903. (2d edn., 1921; unless otherwise indicated, the first edition is cited.)

Neue Jahrbücher = *Neue Jahrbücher für das klassische Altertum*. Leipzig.

ParPass = *La Parola del Passato*. Naples.

Perls = Hugo Perls, *Platon. Sa conception du kosmos*. New York, 1945.

PhB = Philosophische Bibliothek. Leipzig.

Plato 1 = Paul Friedländer, *Plato: An Introduction*, tr. Hans Meyerhoff. New York (Bollingen Series LIX:1) and London, 1958.

Plato 2 = Paul Friedländer, *Plato: The Dialogues, First Period*, tr. Hans Meyerhoff. New York (Bollingen Series LIX:2) and London, 1964.

Platon Budé = *Platon*, Collection des Universités de France, publiée sous le patronage de l'Association Guillaume Budé. Paris, 1920– .

Pohlenz, *Werdezeit* = Max Pohlenz, *Aus Platos Werdezeit*. Berlin, 1913.

PR = *Philosophical Review*. Ithaca, N. Y.

Raeder = Hans Raeder, *Platons philosophische Entwicklung*. Leipzig, 1905.

Raven = John Earle Raven, *Plato's Thought in the Making*. Cambridge, 1965.

R-E = *Real-Encyclopädie der classischen Altertumswissenschaft*, ed. August Pauly, Georg Wissowa, Wilhelm Kroll. Stuttgart, 1894– .

Reinhardt, *Mythen* = Karl Reinhardt, *Platons Mythen*. Bonn, 1927.

Reinhardt, *Vermächtnis* = Karl Reinhardt, *Vermächtnis der Antike*. Göttingen, 1960.

RevÉtGr = *Revue des Études Grecques*. Paris.

RevFil = *Revista de Filosofía*. Madrid.

RevInPh = *Revue Internationale de Philosophie*. Brussels.

RevPhilol = *Revue de Philologie*. Paris.

Rey = Abel Rey, *La science dans l'antiquité*. Vol. III. Paris, 1939.

RhM = *Rheinisches Museum*. Frankfurt a. M.

Ritter, *Untersuchungen* = Constantin Ritter, *Neue Untersuchungen über Plato*. Munich, 1910.

Ritter, *Platon* = Constantin Ritter, *Platon*. Munich, 1910, 1923. 2 vols.

Robin, *Théorie des idées* = Léon Robin, *La théorie platonicienne des idées et des nombres d'après Aristote*. Paris, 1908.

Robin, *Théorie de l'amour* = Léon Robin, *La théorie platonicienne de l'amour*. Paris, 1933. (2d edn., with Preface by P.-M. Schuhl, 1964; unless otherwise indicated, the first edition is cited.)

Robin, *Platon* = Léon Robin, *Platon*. Paris, 1935.

Robin, *Pensée* = Léon Robin, *La pensée hellénique des origines à Épicure*. Paris, 1941.

Robin, *Rapports* = Léon Robin, *Les rapports de l'être et de la connaissance d'après Platon*. Paris, 1957.

Robinson, *Dialectic* = Richard Robinson, *Plato's Earlier Dialectic*. Ithaca, N. Y., 1941. (2d edn., Oxford, 1953.)

Rosenmeyer = T. G. Rosenmeyer, "Platonic Scholarship: 1945–55," *Classical Weekly*, Vol. L, Nos. 13–15 (1956).

Ross = Sir David Ross, *Plato's Theory of Ideas*. Oxford, 1951.

Rudberg = Gunnar Rudberg, *Platonica Selecta*. Stockholm, 1956.

Salin, *Utopie* = Edgar Salin, *Platon und die griechische Utopie.* Munich and Leipzig, 1921.

SBBerl = *Sitzungsberichte der preussischen Akademie der Wissenschaften,* Phil.-hist. Kl. Berlin.

SBHeidelb = *Sitzungsberichte der Heidelberger Akademie der Wissenschaften,* Phil.-hist. Kl. Heidelberg.

SBWien = *Sitzungsberichte der Akademie der Wissenschaften in Wien,* Phil.-hist. Kl. Vienna.

Schaarschmidt = Karl Max Wilhelm Schaarschmidt, *Die Sammlung der platonischen Schriften.* Bonn, 1866.

Schaerer = René Schaerer, *La question platonicienne: Étude sur les rapports de la pensée et de l'expression dans les Dialogues.* Neuchâtel, 1938.

Schleiermacher = Friedrich Schleiermacher, *Platos Werke.* 2d edn., Berlin, 1817–28. 6 vols.

Schuhl, *Fabulation* = Pierre-Maxime Schuhl, *Études sur la fabulation platonicienne.* Paris, 1947.

Schuhl, *Platon* = Pierre-Maxime Schuhl, *L'oeuvre de Platon.* 2d edn., Paris, 1958.

Schuhl, *Études* = Pierre-Maxime Schuhl, *Études platoniciennes.* Paris, 1960.

Shorey = Paul Shorey, *What Plato Said.* Chicago, 1933.

Shorey, *Unity* = Paul Shorey, *The Unity of Plato's Thought.* Chicago, 1903. (Chicago Reprint Series, 1960.)

Sinclair = Thomas Alan Sinclair, *A History of Greek Political Thought.* London, 1952.

Singer = Kurt Singer, *Platon der Gründer.* Munich, 1927.

Socher = Joseph Socher, *Über Platons Schriften.* Munich, 1820.

Solmsen = Friedrich Solmsen, *Plato's Theology.* Cornell Studies in Classical Philology. Ithaca, N. Y., 1942.

Stanka = Rudolf Stanka, *Geschichte der politischen Philosophie.* Vol. I, *Die politische Philosophie des Altertums.* Vienna, 1951.

Stefanini = Luigi Stefanini, *Platone.* Vol. II. 2d edn., Padua, 1949.

Steinhart = Karl Steinhart, *Platons sämtliche Werke,* tr. Hieronymus Müller, with Introduction by Karl Steinhart. Leipzig, 1850–73. 9 vols.

Stenzel, *Platon* = Julius Stenzel, *Platon der Erzieher.* Leipzig, 1928.

Stenzel, *Metaphysik* = Julius Stenzel, *Metaphysik des Altertums,* in *Handbuch der Philosophie,* ed. A. Baeumler and M. Schröter. Munich, 1929.

Stenzel, *Studien* = Julius Stenzel, *Studien zur Entwicklung der platonischen Dialektik von Sokrates zu Aristoteles.* 2d edn., Leipzig, 1931.

Stenzel, *Zahl und Gestalt* = Julius Stenzel, *Zahl und Gestalt bei Platon und Aristoteles.* 2d edn., Leipzig, 1933.

Stenzel, *Kleine Schriften* = Julius Stenzel, *Kleine Schriften zur griechischen Philosophie.* 2d edn., Darmstadt, 1957.

Susemihl = Franz Susemihl, *Die genetische Entwicklung der platonischen Philosophie.* Leipzig, 1855–60. 2 vols.

TAPA = *Transactions of the American Philological Association*. Hartford.
Taylor, *Plato* = Alfred Edward Taylor, *Plato, the Man and His Work*. 2d edn., New York, 1927.
UCalPCP = University of California Publications in Classical Philology. Los Angeles and Berkeley.
Ueberweg = Friedrich Ueberweg, *Untersuchungen über die Echtheit und Zeitfolge platonischer Schriften*. Vienna, 1861.
Ueberweg-Praechter = Friedrich Ueberweg and Karl Praechter, *Grundriss der Geschichte der Philosophie*. Vol. I, *Altertum*. 12th edn., Berlin, 1926.
Vanhoutte = Maurice Vanhoutte, *La méthode ontologique de Platon*. Paris and Louvain, 1956.
Vorländer-Metzke = Karl Vorländer, *Geschichte der Philosophie*. 9th edn., supervised by Erwin Metzke. Hamburg, 1949–55. 2 vols.
Vorsokr. = Hermann Diels, *Die Fragmente der Vorsokratiker*. 6th edn., ed. Walther Kranz. Berlin, 1951–52. 3 vols.
WienStud = *Wiener Studien*. Vienna.
Wilamowitz = Ulrich von Wilamowitz-Moellendorff, *Platon*. Berlin, 1919. 2 vols. (2d edn., 1920; unless otherwise indicated, the first edition is cited.)
Wolff = Hans M. Wolff, *Plato: Der Kampf ums Sein*. University of California Publications in Philosophy, Vol. XXX. Berkeley, 1957.
Zeller = Eduard Zeller, *Die Philosophie der Griechen*. Pt. II, Vol. 1. 4th edn., Leipzig, 1889. (In some cases, reference is made to the fifth edition supervised by Ernst Hoffmann [1922].)

NOTES

with Bibliography

A bracketed reference of the style [I²] indicates a previous note where the citation in question is given fully. See also the foregoing list of abbreviations.

xx: *Symposium*

RECENT EDITIONS AND TRANSLATIONS: A. Hug and H. Schöne (3d edn., Leipzig, 1909); K. Hildebrandt, PhB 81 (1920); L. Robin, *Platon Budé*, IV/2 (1929); R. G. Bury (2d edn., Cambridge, 1932); J. Sykutris (Athens, 1934); J. D. García Bacca (Mexico, 1944); U. Galli (2d edn., Turin, 1944); G. Calogero (2d edn., Bari, 1946); M. Meunier (Paris, 1947); W. Hamilton (London and Baltimore, 1951); E. Salin (Basel, 1952); R. Rufener (Zurich and Stuttgart, 1958); O. Apelt, PhB 81 (2d edn., Hamburg, 1960); D. Loenen (Amsterdam, 1963).

RECENT INTERPRETATIONS: J. Hirschberger, "Wert und Wissen im platonischen *Symposion*," *Philosophisches Jahrbuch der Görres-Gesellschaft*, XLVI (1933), 201ff.; Hildebrandt, *Platon*, pp. 201ff. (2d edn., pp. 185ff.); Geffcken, pp. 95ff.; E. Hoffmann, *Über Platons "Symposion"* (Heidelberg, 1947); K. Schilling, *Platon: Einführung in seine Philosophie* (Wurzach, 1948), pp. 169ff.; H. Koller, *Die Komposition des platonischen "Symposions"* (Zurich, 1948); G. Krüger, *Einsicht und Leidenschaft* (2d edn., Frankfurt a. M., 1948); A. Levi, "La teoria dell' Ἔρως nel *Simposio* di Platone," *Giorn. di Metafisica*, IV (1949), 290–97; F. M. Cornford, *The Unwritten Philosophy and Other Essays* (Cambridge, 1950), pp. 68ff.; G. Galli, *Due studi di filosofia greca* (Turin, 1950), pp. 58ff.; Gauss, II/2, 81ff.; A. Valensin, "Platon et la théorie de l'amour," *Études*, CCLXXXI (1954), 32ff.; R. A. Markus, "The Dialectic of Eros in Plato's *Symposium*," *Downside Review*, LXXIII (1955), 219ff.; Vanhoutte, pp. 48ff.; Wolff, pp. 159ff.; H. B. Mattingly, "The Date of Plato's *Symposium*,"

Phronesis, III (1958), 31ff.; H. H. Bacon, "Socrates Crowned," *Virginia Quarterly Review*, XXXV (1959), 415ff.; H. Reynen, "Platon: *Symposion* 183A," *Hermes*, LXXXIX (1961), 495ff.; K. Vretska, "Zu Form und Aufbau von Platons *Symposion*," *Serta philologica Aenipontana* (Innsbruck, 1962), pp. 143ff.; Lesky, pp. 524f.

ADDITIONAL BIBLIOGRAPHY: Shorey, p. 542; Geffcken, Notes, p. 82; Sykutris, *Plato's "Symposium"* (Athens, 1934), pp. 252ff.; Leisegang, cols. 2441ff.; Gigon, pp. 17f.; Rosenmeyer, pp. 189f.; Cherniss, *Lustrum*, pp. 189ff.

1. See J. Martin, *"Symposion," Die Geschichte einer literarischen Form* (Studien zur Geschichte und Kultur des Altertums, Vol. XVII, Nos. 1–2, Paderborn, 1931).

2. Bruns, *Porträt*, pp. 328ff.

3. R. G. Bury, *The "Symposium" of Plato* (2d edn., Cambridge, 1932), pp. xxi f., finds in the fact that only a selection of the speeches is given (*1*) a literary device for heightening probability, and (*2*) a possible reference to "another author." The first argument is not wrong, but neither is it adequate. The second argument is based on the common practice of referring to an outside *x* what one cannot explain from the matter itself.

4. The report given by Apollodoros is to be dated around the year 400. See the Hug-Schöne (3d edn., Leipzig, 1909) Introduction, § 7; Bury's edition, p. lxv; L. Robin, *Le banquet* (*Platon Budé*, IV/2, 1949), pp. xx ff.; Leisegang, col. 2441.

5. The variant reading ᾽μανικός instead of μαλακός is found in most editions, but Burnet and Robin are correct. ἀεὶ τοιοῦτος εἶ does not refer to the epithet, but to what follows. μαλακός as an epithet was perhaps not very rare. It was applied, for example, to Apollonios of Alabanda (see *R-E*, II, col. 140). Robin points with good reason to *Phaedo* 59A, where the characterization of Apollodoros does fit the epithet even though he is not actually called μαλακός. / It is strange that Wilamowitz (II, 356) should call the preliminary dialogue a "dedication to Apollodoros."

6. Cf. L. von Sybel, *Platons "Symposion"* (Marburg, 1888), p. 115.

7. Karl Jaspers, *Philosophie* (3 vols., Berlin, 1932), II, 60ff.

8. Similarly, the change of physical position at the beginning of the *Protagoras* (310C, 311A), and of the *Phaedo* (60B, 61CD), delimits a conversational section. See Olympiodoros' *In Platonis Phaedonem Commentaria*, ed. W. Norvin (Leipzig, 1913), pp. 7, 12. / The seating at the banquet table is made clear in the drawing shown in J. Sykutris, *Plato's "Symposium"* (Athens, 1934), p. 31.

9. See further P. Friedländer and H. B. Hoffleit, *Epigrammata: Greek Inscriptions in Verse* (Berkeley and Los Angeles, 1948), pp. 108f.

Ποικιλομήχαν' "Ερως has an echo in the speech of Diotima (203D): "Ερως ἀεί τινας πλέκων μηχανάς. Also see U. von Wilamowitz, *Der Glaube der Hellenen* (2 vols., Berlin, 1932), II, 180ff.; W. Kranz, "Platonica," *Philologus*, CII (1958), 81.

10. The interpreters are wont to take sides. Hug and Schöne as well as Wilamowitz follow the interpretation in the first sense, while L. von Sybel—in "Nietzsche," *Philologica* (Leipzig), III (1913), 261—and Hildebrandt go in the direction of the second. The second way seems more fruitful than the first, although to me neither is in accord with Plato. Robin, Stenzel, and Krüger are in the direction of my interpretation. See also the fine presentation in Reinhardt, *Mythen*, pp. 53ff.

11. See *Plato* 1, pp. 160–61, and Reinhardt, *Mythen*, p. 63; cf. the criticism by de Vries, pp. 275f.

12. Cf. Wilamowitz, I, 362. / The organizational plan derives originally from the hymn to the gods; see, for example, the prooemium of the *Theogony*. It occurs oratorically in Isokrates' *Busiris* and the *Encomium on Helen*. And as to its theory, it lives on in the rhetor Menander; see L. von Spengel, *Rhetores Graeci*, III (Leipzig, 1856), p. 333. Menander, to be sure, refers to the *Symposium*.

13. Jachmann (p. 304), following Badham, wants to retain in the text only the words θειότερον γάρ of this substantiating sentence—and how much it substantiates!

14. Surely the simple and correct explanation of the Xenophon parallel is that Xenophon's *Symposium* 8 32 follows Plato almost word for word—even though one may concede that this is not the first time the motif occurs in Plato. On this see further F. Lasserre, "'Ερωτικοί Λόγοι," *MusHelv*, I (1944), 174; see also Lasserre's references to the older literature.

15. The ὑπεραποθνήσκειν is, of course, taken up by Socrates himself—in *Symposium* 207B.

16. See H. Neumann, "On the Sophistry of Plato's Pausanias," *TAPA*, XCV (1964), 261ff. / The twofold Eros does not have its model in Euripides (Hug-Schöne [XX⁴], pp. 42f.; Wilamowitz, I, 362 = I², 365). Euripides speaks of the δίδυμα τόξα or the δισσὰ πνεύματα of the one Eros and thus aims at the god's success, not his nature. It is more useful to think of the twofold Eris of Hesiod, which might have led Plato to seize upon two cultic names of Aphrodite as contrasting forms of her nature.

17. Friedemann, p. 52.

18. διὰ βίου μένει ἅτε μονίμῳ συντακείς. Some translations may be quoted. Schleiermacher: "*bleibt zeitlebens, denn mit dem Bleibenden hat er sich verschmolzen.*" Franz Boll: "*bleibt sein Leben lang treu, weil er sich mit etwas Dauerndem verbunden hat.*" Hildebrandt: "*beharrt sein lebelang, weil er mit dem Beständigen verbunden ist.*" Salin: "*bleibt er zeitlebens,*"

da mit Bleibendem verschmolzen." Jowett: "the love . . . is lifelong, for it becomes one with the everlasting." Calogero: *"riman tale per tutta la vita, come congiunto e saldato a una realtà che non muta."* Robin: *"est, pour la vie, constant dans son amour: c'est en effet avec quelque chose de constant qu'il se fond."* García Bacca: *"es firme de por vida, puesto que se fundió en uno con lo firme."* Sykutris: *"σταθερὸς μένει ἐπὶ ζωῆς, συγχωνευμένος ὅπως εἶναι μὲ κάτι σταθερόν."*

19. See *DGrA*, I, 38f.; II, 26f.

20. In plain fact, without "pederasty" neither Greek athletics, physical beauty, sculpture, national feeling, myths, religion, Pindaric poetry, nor Greek philosophy can be understood. Only a little of the recent literature need be cited here: Grote, II, 206ff.; Erich Bethe, "Die dorische Knabenliebe," *RhM*, LXII (1907), 438ff.; Shorey, p. 544.

21. Thus, I should like to consider ἀλλ' ὁτιοῦν διώκων καὶ βουλόμενος διαπράξασθαι πλὴν τοῦτο φιλοσοφίας as the correct reading for 182E (despite J. Vahlen, *Gesammelte philologische Schriften*, Leipzig and Berlin, 1911, I, 389). This, to be sure, does not follow Schöne in construing φιλοσοφίας as accusative appositive with τοῦτο, but rather interprets "this region of mental endeavor" wherewith the noble love of boys would be designated. Robin puts a comma between τοῦτο and φιλοσοφίας and connects φιλοσοφίας with ὀνείδη. Yet surely, in order not to be misunderstood, the reading would have to be παρὰ φιλοσοφίας.

22. See also Ludwig Edelstein, "The Role of Eryximachus in Plato's *Symposium*," *TAPA*, LXXVI (1945), 85ff.; W. Kranz, "Platonica" [XX⁹], pp. 74ff.; Krämer, pp. 232ff. / For an example of this excessively rigid disposition in some writings of the Hippokratic corpus, see Περὶ τῶν ἐν κεφαλῇ τρωμάτων.

23. In particular, compare *Symposium* 187CD with *Republic* 403A–C and *Timaeus* 47DE.

24. See Friedemann, p. 58.

25. Cf. 180E: ἐπαινεῖν μὲν οὖν δεῖ πάντας θεούς, and 181A: καὶ τὸ ἐρᾶν καὶ ὁ Ἔρως οὐ πᾶς ἐστι καλὸς οὐδὲ ἄξιος ἐγκωμιάζεσθαι. Inasmuch as the terms ἔπαινος and ἐγκώμιον are used throughout the dialogue without distinction of meaning by Plato (differing from Aristotle; see his *Rhetoric* I 9), the contradiction must be recognized and its cause inquired into. / See Robin's edition [XX⁴] for the various attempts at emendation.

26. See G. K. Plochmann, "Hiccups and Hangovers in the *Symposium*," *Bucknell Review*, XI/3 (1963), 1ff. "The *Symposium* is neither a statement of philosophy with a delightful background . . . nor is it a drama of persons who happen to be talking theory, but rather it is a new form, which makes the two sorts of drama wholly integral with one another." These words agree with my way of interpreting Plato.

27. See *Plato* 1, pp. 178f., and Robin, pp. lvii ff. Empedokles' relevance

to the myth may be even less than E. Bignone (*Empedocle*, Turin, 1916, p. 579) estimates—although Bignone expresses his view very cautiously: "*può far pensare, mi pare possa recollegarsi.*" / The motif of primitive man cut asunder on account of his arrogance has its analogy (and perhaps its origin) in the beast fable: the flounder got its flat belly because it was torn apart by God as punishment for its pride. On this, see O. Dähnhardt, *Natursagen* (Leipzig and Berlin, 1910), III/1, 35. What perhaps was the origin of the Aristophanes-myth goes on echoing as simile: ἅτε τετμημένος ὥσπερ αἱ ψῆτται (191D 4).

28. For some peculiarities of style, *Protagoras* 320c *et seq.* may be re-called; see also E. Norden, *Agnostos Theos* (Leipzig and Berlin, 1923), p. 368. / The especially numerous atheteses in this speech—as as-sumed, for example, in the editions of Schanz (1882, 1899) and of Hug (1884, 1909)—are due primarily to misjudgment of the repetitious style.

29. *Politics* II 4 1262ᵇ 11.

30. With the speech of Agathon, according to L. von Sybel ("*Symposium*" [XX⁶], p. 21), a new act begins. This view is shared by Friedemann (p. 55), who has Aristophanes "begin the great drama" with the first of the "three sublimer speeches." Juan D. García Bacca (in *Obras Completas de Platón*, Mexico City, 1944) groups the first four speeches as Part I, and the speeches of Agathon and Socrates as Part II. Cer-tainly Plato shaped Agathon's speech in such a way that Socrates can link his to it. Nevertheless, Agathon belongs with the preceding speakers on one level, whereas Socrates—as always—ascends to a higher one. / Bury (pp. liii f.) reviews what has been said about the arrangement of the first five speeches and rejects both the view (like Susemihl's, for example) of a line rising as to importance and the view (like Reinhardt's) of a grouping in pairs. Cf. Reinhardt, *Mythen*, p. 55; G. Calogero, *Il Simposio* (2d edn., Bari, 1946), pp. 11ff.; Robin's edition, pp. xxxvi ff., lxx ff.

31. *Plato 2*, pp. 101ff.

32. Wilamowitz (I, 358 = I², 360) sees cruel mockery in the portrait of Agathon. On the other hand, Friedemann (p. 56) and Hildebrandt (*Gastmahl*, 5th edn., Leipzig, 1920, p. 11) take Agathon much too seriously—i.e., just as seriously as he takes himself. See also Robin, *Le banquet*, pp. lxv ff.; G. Krüger, *Einsicht und Leidenschaft: Das Wesen des platonischen Denkens* (2d edn., Frankfurt a. M., 1948), pp. 80f.; J. and G. Roux, "A propos de Platon: Réflexions en marge du *Phedón* 62ʙ et du *Banquet*," *RevPhilol*, XXXV (1961), 210ff.

33. On Diotima, see *Plato 1*, pp. 148ff., 365 (n. 14); W. Kranz, "Pla-tonica" [XX⁹], pp. 74ff. / Robin's view of Diotima is quite correct, except that he overestimates the social aspect: ". . . c'en serait fini de la cordialité du banquet . . . sans manquer à la courtoisie . . ." (*Le banquet*, p. xxii). Similar overstatement is found in F. M. Cornford,

The Unwritten Philosophy and Other Essays, ed. W. K. C. Guthrie (Cambridge, 1950), p. 71: "By a masterpiece of delicate courtesy . . ." See also J. Wippern, "Eros und Unsterblichkeit in der Diotima-Rede des *Symposions*," in *Synusia: Festgabe für W. Schadewaldt* (Pfullingen, 1965), pp. 123ff.

34. Calogero, loc. cit.: "*Tutti gli altri* μεταξύ *sono posizioni statiche, intermediari; l'eros è funzione dinamica, mediazione.*" Krüger (p. 152) says that Diotima's teaching "amounts to depriving the world of gods," but one is inclined to consider the opposite correct.

35. On the myth of Eros, see further *Plato* 1, pp. 179f.

36. At 208B 3, most editions have adopted Creuzer's conjecture of ἀδύνατον rather than ἀθάνατον. On the other hand, P. Maas ("Textkritik," in *Einleitung in die Altertumswissenschaft*, ed. A. Gercke and E. Norden, 3d edn., Leipzig and Berlin, 1922–27, I/2, 16) cites this passage as an example of an old corruption and an evident improvement. Both are erroneous. It is true that ἀδύνατον produces a powerful, effective close rhetorically, but philosophically it is altogether empty. Yet ἀθάνατον once more—paradoxically—drives through to the substratum of the whole discussion, namely, to the ἀεὶ εἶναι (208B 3): "the immortal on the contrary has a share in ever-being in quite a different way," not by striving for it, but by always *being* it. (Similarly, Aristotle's *De anima* II 4 415ᵃ 29 *et seq.*—referred to by F. A. Wolf in his edition of the *Symposium* [Leipzig, 1782]—keeps returning to the ἀεὶ ὄν: ἵνα τοῦ ἀεὶ καὶ τοῦ θείου μετέχωσιν . . . ἐκείνου ὀρέγεται . . . ἐκείνου ἕνεκα πράττει . . . τοῦ ἀεὶ καὶ τοῦ θείου . . . ταὐτὸ καὶ ἕν. . . .) Robin rightly prints ἀθάνατον in his *Platon Budé* text, but in his commentary wavers between this reading and the emendation. Among those in favor of the emendation are E. Bickel, *RhM*, XCII (1943), 148; and G. Müller, *Studien zu den platonischen "Nomoi"* (Munich, 1951), p. 172, who calls it a "wonderful conjecture of Creuzer." On the opposing side, see R. Hackforth, *Plato's "Phaedo"* (Cambridge, Mass., 1955), p. 21.

37. At 209c 5, the reading πολὺ μείζω κοινωνίαν τῆς τῶν παίδων is correct, and Marianne Koffka's substitution of γάμων for παίδων—see *Hermes*, LIX (1924), 478—is not acceptable; cf. P. Maas, loc. cit. [XX³⁶]. What the soul is pregnant with (κυεῖ) is φρόνησις and ἀρετή (209A 3). This ἐγκύμων or pregnant soul, on meeting another beautiful soul, overflows with λόγοι περὶ ἀρετῆς (209B 8) because of its desire to educate that other soul. So it brings forth what it was pregnant with earlier (ἃ πάλαι ἐκύει, 209c 3), and what is born (τὸ γεννηθέν) of this union must also be ἀρετή, which they bring up in common. If the παίδων κοινωνία is compared now, it is in all respects in sharp contrast to the foregoing, the more so since there it is a question of man-to-man and hence childless relationships. To reject γάμων all we need is the consideration that there are childless

marriages too, but that a marriage is concluded ἐπὶ παίδων ἀρότῳ. Thus, the κοινωνία παίδων stands in contrast to the κοινωνία ἀρετῆς. After the word παίδων has been used once in its proper sense, it subsequently is used imprecisely; this is the "laxness" of living speech. Compare Euripides, *Phoenissae* 16, where Laios requests παίδων ἐς οἴκους ἀρσένων κοινωνίαν, with Plato, *Laws* 772D: εἰς παίδων κοινωνίαν. / Wilamowitz (II, 359) brackets the words τῆς τῶν παίδων because they "are intolerable." But this comes about only because Wilamowitz translated the preceding τὸ γεννηθέν as "their children," instead of leaving it neutral and singular.

38. It is unthinkable that in writing οὐκ οἶδ᾽ εἰ οἷός τ᾽ ἂν εἴης (210A 2) Plato "was indicating the bounds of the Socratic." (These are the words of Stenzel, *Platon*, p. 225, but similar views are found in Cornford, *The Unwritten Philosophy* [XX³³], p. 75, and Krüger, *Einsicht und Leidenschaft* [XX³²], pp. 175f.) Diotima speaks through the Platonic Socrates; her words are the strongest expression of his irony, of his most personal "ignorance." Cf. *Plato* 1, pp. 149f.

39. Stenzel (*Platon*, pp. 243f.) correctly—if one-sidedly—sees Alkibiades as representative of *phthonos*, "jealousy."

40. Cf. Bury's *Symposium* [XX³], p. lx.

41. *Plato* 2, p. 136.

42. See Shorey, *Unity*, p. 82, n. 626.

43. Cf. Robin, *Le banquet* [XX⁴], p. viii.

xxi: *Phaedo*

RECENT EDITIONS AND TRANSLATIONS: R. D. Archer-Hind (2d edn., London, 1894); O. Apelt, PhB 147 (3d edn., 1923); J. Burnet (Oxford, 1925); L. Robin, *Platon Budé*, IV/1 (1926); F. Dirlmeier (Munich, 1949); M. Meunier (2d edn., Paris, 1952); R. Guardini (4th edn., Munich, 1952; English edn., New York, 1948); M. Faggella (3d edn., Rome, 1954); G. Capone Braga (3d edn., Florence, 1955); R. S. Bluck (London, 1955); R. Hackforth (Cambridge, Mass., 1955); M. Valmigli (16th edn., Bari, 1956); O. Gigon (2d edn., Bern, 1959); J. Olives Canals (Barcelona, 1962).

RECENT INTERPRETATIONS: Barth, pp. 1ff.; Shorey, pp. 169ff.; Hildebrandt, *Platon*, pp. 178ff. (2d edn., pp. 164ff.); Robin, *Pensée*, pp. 337ff., 349ff.; B. H. Bal, *Plato's Ascese in de "Phaedo"* (Weert, 1950); Gauss, II/1, 14ff.; Robinson, *Dialectic*, ch. 9, "Hypothesis in the *Phaedo*"; Vanhoutte, pp. 42ff.; R. S. Bluck, in *Phronesis*, II (1957), 21ff.; W. J. Verdenius, in *Mnemosyne*, 4th ser., XI (1958), 193ff.; Schuhl, *Études*, ch. 15, "Remarques sur la technique de la répétition dans le *Phédon*"; P. Kucharski, "L'affinité entre les idées et l'âme d'après le *Phédon," AdP*, XXVI (1963), 483ff.; E. Gaudron, "La théorie des idées dans le *Phédon," Laval Théologique et Philosophique* (Quebec), XX (1964), 50ff.; Allen, ch. 4, "Participation and Predication in Plato's Middle Dialogues"; R. L. Patterson, *Plato on Immortality* (Pennsylvania State University, 1965); Raven, pp. 79ff.; Lesky, pp. 525f.

ADDITIONAL BIBLIOGRAPHY: Shorey, p. 523; Geffcken, Notes, p. 87; Leisegang, cols. 2431ff.; Rosenmeyer, pp. 186f.; Cherniss, *Lustrum*, pp. 127ff.

1. It is typical of his manner that Bonitz (p. 294), "passing over everything that refers to the artistic composition of the dialogue," confines himself "exclusively to the presentation of its didactic content." (Yet, compare his p. 313.) The work is viewed quite differently by Wilamowitz (I, 353 = I², 356): "Although they are in close contact, still it is different topics that the dialogue unites with each other and with the story of Socrates' death; despite all the skill, the fusion would seem not completely successful. But . . . perhaps Reason should not cavil." Shorey's view (p. 169) is similar. In contrast, Schleiermacher (II/3, 9) rightly says: "But everyone will probably see that in no other dialogue is the mimical element . . . so completely grown together with the subject as here. . . ."

2. See J. Burnet, *Plato's "Phaedo"* (Oxford, 1925), Notes, p. 1.

3. See F. J. E. Woodbridge, *The Son of Apollo* (Boston and New York, 1929); C. Kerényi, "Unsterblichkeit und Apollonreligion: Zum Verständnis von Platons *Phaidon," Die Antike*, X (1934), 46ff.

4. Especially significant are the *Pythian Odes* I, V, and VIII. In *Pythian* V 65, Apollo δίδωσι Μοῖσαν οἷς ἂν ἐθέλῃ, ἀπόλεμον ἀγαγὼν ἐς πραπίδας εὐνομίαν in the twofold sense of the νόμος.

5. See A. Westermann's Βιογράφοι (Brunswick, 1845), pp. 383ff.

6. On the double meaning of φρουρά as *praesidium* and *custodia* in 62b, see Burnet's commentary [XXI²] on this passage. He cites the equally ambiguous translation "in ward" of Archer-Hind, and collects quotations for both meanings. Cf. also Frank, *Pythagoreer*, pp. 291ff. Per contra, Hackforth, Bluck, and Robin allow only the meaning *custodia;* so also the note on *Vorsokr.* 44 [32] B 15, l. 23. A probable explanation is this: Originally φρουρά is (*a*) in the main military (cf. φρουρός, φρουρεῖν) and means the advanced outpost from which someone maintains a lookout. Such a military φρουρά can be at the same time (*b*) passive, if the outpost is surrounded by foes (κύκλῳ φρουρούμενος ὑπὸ πάντων πολεμίων, *Republic* 579b). In the Pythagorean tradition, the word may have the sense of (*a*) or of (*b*) or of both. Thus, it is used in the sense of (*a*) in Cicero, *De senectute* 20 73: "*vetatque Pythagoras iniussu*

imperatoris, id est dei, de praesidio et statione vitae decedere." It is used in
the sense of (*b*) in Philolaos, *Vorsokr.* 44 [32] B 15: καὶ Φιλόλαος δὲ
ὥσπερ ἐν φρουρᾷ πάντα ὑπὸ τοῦ θεοῦ περιειλῆφθαι λέγων. . . . Yet,
it remains for Socrates, in the *Phaedo*, to endow the Pythagorean
statement with another nuance: the meaning of (*c*) "prison." This
third interpretation (*c*) then gains ascendancy in the tradition, but
without displacing the original meanings (*a*) and (*b*). Cf. J. and
G. Roux, "A propos de Platon . . ." in *RevPhilol*, XXXV (1961),
207ff. (Of a different opinion is W. Kranz, "Welt und Menschenleben
im Gleichnis," in G. Eisenmann, ed., *Wirtschaft und Kultursysteme*,
Stuttgart and Zurich, 1955, pp. 175ff.) / As in this case the three
meanings of φρουρά are fused together, so the two meanings "tomb"
and "sign" are fused in the Pythagorean σῶμα σῆμα. See Wilamowitz, II, 363.

7. Cf. M. Heidegger, *Sein und Zeit* (Halle, 1927), p. 261: "The questionable being-unto-death can evidently not have the character of an
active concern for its realization. . . . For in that way existence
would deprive itself of the basis for an existential being-unto-death."

8. Cicero, *Tusculanae disputationes* I 30 74: "*Tota enim philosophorum
vita, ut ait idem [Socrates], commentatio mortis est.*" A long series of
quotations from late antiquity is found in Johannes Davisius' commentary on this passage (in the Oxford 1805 edition, p. 67). In the
words of Montaigne (*Essais* I 19), "*Que philosopher c'est apprendre à
mourir.*" Hugo Friedrich, *Montaigne* (Bern, 1949), p. 330, calls this
". . . in late antiquity and in the Middle Ages one of the definitions
of philosophy."

9. From this it follows that Bonitz was thinking too formalistically when
he completely separated this first course of proof from the authentic
"proofs of immortality." Per contra (and in good Kantian formulation), Zeller, p. 825, correctly states that the "belief in immortality
is first exhibited as a general presupposition of philosophic endeavor,
a postulate of practical consciousness." Zeller also appropriately
designates the three levels of discussion.

10. Thus, the very obvious criticism of this proof (e.g., by Wilamowitz, I,
329 = I², 332) would apply only to its dogmatization, and not to
what the proof may have meant in Plato's sense. Instructive as it is,
for the rest, that the meaning "life" was present (as Wilamowitz
shows) in the Greek word ψυχή from Homer on, and granted that
thinking owes much to language, still one cannot start out from here
to make Plato's "paralogisms" understandable. Indeed, it is not at all
proper to speak of "false conclusions" on the assumption that Plato
was deceived as to the strength of the proofs he has Socrates put forward here. A penetrating interpretation shows how little this is the
case.

11. *Vorsokr.* 31 [21] в 115.

12. Cf. Aline Lion, 'Ανάμνησις *and the A Priori* (Oxford, 1935); Emilio Lledó, "La *anámnesis* dialéctica en Platón," *Emerita* (Madrid), XXIX (1961), 219ff.

13. It is these Platonic discoveries of "associative psychology" that for Gomperz (III, 47) are ultimately the substance of the *Phaedo!*

14. Concerning this much discussed passage, see Ross, pp. 22ff.; Dorothy Tarrant, "Plato's *Phaedo* 74A–B," *JHS*, LXXVII (1957), 124ff.; K. W. Mills, "Plato's *Phaedo* 74B7–C6," *Phronesis*, II (1957), 128ff.; III (1958), 40ff.; J. M. Rist, "Equals and Intermediates in Plato," *Phronesis*, IX (1964), 23ff. / The word "equal" is not meant here solely in the mathematical sense. Two stones or sticks can appear both alike and unlike, for example, in form, structure, color. (Ross thinks of the effect of perspective. That is but one possibility among many.) Why does Plato begin with the concept "like"? One reason is the extensiveness of the experience thus designated, and another is the (apparent) simplicity. That Plato finds it necessary to take the step to the αὐτὸ τὸ ἴσον via the stage of the αὐτὰ τὰ ἴσα is founded in the relational character of "equality."

15. Bonitz, p. 306, is essentially correct in saying that the two courses of proof are joined together as integral halves into a single proof. But he is not correct in dogmatizing this, as if Plato were "finally in earnest" in thus joining the proofs. The words following ἀποδέ-δεικται in 77D show the contrary.

16. 66D: (τὸ σῶμα) θόρυβον παρέχει καὶ ταραχὴν καὶ ἐκπλήττει. . . . 66E: αὐτῇ τῇ ψυχῇ θεατέον αὐτὰ τὰ πράγματα.   καὶ τότε . . . ἡμῖν ἔσται οὗ ἐπιθυμοῦμεν . . . φρονήσεως. ~ 79CD: (ἡ ψυχή) ἕλκεται ὑπὸ τοῦ σώματος . . . καὶ αὐτὴ πλανᾶται καὶ ταράττεται . . . ὅταν δέ γ' αὐτὴ καθ' αὑτὴν σκοπῇ . . . καὶ τοῦτο αὐτῆς τὸ πάθημα φρόνησις κέκληται.

17. The question of whether Plato gives three proofs of immortality on this level, or whether the first two are to be taken as one, or whether all three are but one, has been much discussed (Bonitz, pp. 303ff.; cf. R. D. Archer-Hind's *Phaedo*, 2d edn., London, 1894, Introduction, § 2, pp. 8ff.). I think I have settled this dispute by the demonstration that in truth Plato gives no proof of immortality at all, but first gives two halves, which cannot be seriously combined into a unity, and then gives an approximate proof, which cannot be taken seriously as a proof.

18. It is known that Plato visualized the emotions in a system of four: *Laches* 191D, *Symposium* 207E, *Republic* 429CD, *Theaetetus* 156B. It is possible that in *Phaedo* 83B, where he sets up the system twice, once substantively and once verbally, he may have left out καὶ φόβον the first time, ἢ λυπηθῇ the second time, to avoid systematic rigidity. Yet this is by no means certain (despite Burnet; Jachmann, p. 248;

E. Bickel, *RhM*, XCII, 1943, 124ff.). It is to be noted that the *Phaedo* manuscripts differ not only in the number of the emotions, but also in their order—and in the substantive series as well as in the verbal series.

19. If one takes the relation of 84B to 70A as exactly as it must be taken, then the words οἴχηται διαπτομένη in 70A 5 are Platonic—despite the view of Schanz; Wilamowitz, II, 339; Jachmann, pp. 241ff. On the other hand—and contra Burnet and Robin—the doubling οὐδαμοῦ ἔτι ᾖ in 70A 2 alongside καὶ οὐδὲν ἔτι οὐδαμοῦ ᾖ in 70A 6 can hardly be Platonic. For there surely is no trace of a plan on Plato's part to characterize Kebes by repetitious speech. Probably the last five words shifted from 84B 8 to 70A 6.

20. August Boeckh, "Ueber die Bildung der Weltseele im *Timaios*," *Gesammelte Kleine Schriften* (7 vols., Leipzig, 1858–74), III, 109ff.; Frank, *Pythagoreer*, pp. 287, 337; R. S. Brumbaugh, *Plato's Mathematical Imagination* (Bloomington, 1954), pp. 220ff. / It does not follow from *Vorsokr.* 68 [55] A 167 that Demokritos designated the soul as harmony of the body. Hence, another supposed reference by Plato to Demokritos may be denied. On this, see Arthur Ahlvers, *Zahl und Klang bei Platon* (Bern, 1952), ch. 4, "Die Pythagoreer oder Demokrit?"

21. In his dialogue *Eudemus*, Aristotle remodeled the Platonic proof. See Jaeger, *Aristotle*, pp. 40ff.

22. See H. Bonitz, *Index Aristotelicus* (Berlin, 1870), *s.v.* μεταφορά and μεταφέρειν.

23. Cf. W. Kranz, *Wortindex zu den Vorsokratikern* (in *Vorsokr.*, Vol. III), *s.v.* γίγνεσθαι, γένεσις, φθείρεσθαι φθορά, ὀλλύναι, etc. One should recall the agreement of the Platonic formulation with that of Aristotle; compare *Phaedo* 95E 9, 96A 9 *et seq.* with *Physics* II 3 194b 16 *et seq.*

24. *Laws* XII 966D *et seq.* See Jaeger, *Aristotle*, pp. 161f., on the continued historic working of this aspect.

25. R. S. Bluck, *Plato's "Phaedo"* (London, 1955), p. 114, n. 4, sees a "change of tone (almost magisterial, even if there is a touch of humour in it) as Socrates begins to set forth Platonic doctrine." Cf. P. M. Huby, "*Phaedo* 99D–102A," *Phronesis*, IV (1959), 12ff. Also see E. Boodin, in *Mind*, XXXVIII (1929), 495: "What Plato did was what Descartes did. He tried to arrive at an idea which seemed indubitable—clear and distinct. Then he developed the implications of that idea. It is the method of geometry, to which both Plato and Descartes contributed."

26. 100B: ὑποθέμενος εἶναί τι καλὸν αὐτὸ καθ' αὐτὸ καὶ ἀγαθὸν καὶ μέγα καὶ τἆλλα πάντα. Here the deviation of the Marburg school begins: that the *Idea* itself is the hypothesis (Natorp, *Ideenlehre*, p. 151). There is no basis for this in Plato's wording. Cf. H.-G. Gadamer, *Platos dialektische Ethik* (Leipzig, 1931), pp. 52ff. See further Robin-

son, *Dialectic*, ch. 9, "Hypothesis in the *Phaedo*," and my review in
CP, X (1945), 255ff.; R. S. Bluck, "ὑποθέσεις in the *Phaedo* and
Platonic Dialectic," *Phronesis*, II (1957), 21ff.

27. 100D: εἴτε παρουσία εἴτε κοινωνία εἴτε ὅπῃ δὴ καὶ ὅπως προσγενομένη. /
The discussion by Wilamowitz (II², 348) illuminates this passage
admirably. Just for that reason it remains doubtful whether the alteration to προσγένοιτο is necessary (despite the agreement of L. Reinhard, *Die Anakoluthe bei Platon*, Berlin, 1920, p. 74). "Plato helps
himself," says Wilamowitz. Can one prescribe how Plato "helped
himself"? And could he not manage the third, indefinite "accession,"
for which he had no name, by attaching it as our text has it, i.e., with
the participle whose gender is determined by the prefixed article
ἡ and the two substantives in -ία?

28. A good survey of the three main interpretations of this (seemingly
or really) autobiographical section is given in Hackforth's edition
[XX³⁶], pp. 127ff. Also see P. Plass, "Socrates' Method of Hypothesis
in the *Phaedo*," *Phronesis*, V (1960), 103ff.

29. The emphasis is on "always," "consistently." Hence, E. Rohde (see
Psyche, tr. W. B. Hillis, London and New York, 1925, p. 465) cannot
be right in saying that apparently the soul's share in an *Idea*, the
Idea of life, is no different from the share that other phenomena have
in their *Ideas*. Quite the contrary, today there is hardly any remaining
support for the developmental history into which Rohde converts the
dialogues' manifold utterances concerning the soul. The Plato chapter
is in general one of the weakest portions of Rohde's work. / Léon
Robin, *Phédon* (*Platon Budé*, IV/1, 1949), p. lvii, is correct in seeing
here *"une anticipation de la doctrine de la 'communion des genres.'"*

30. Certainly Natorp (*Ideenlehre*, p. 158) does not do justice to the conception, since he obviously falls back to the level of natural philosophy
when he adduces for comparison the "sum total of vital energy." A
similar view is in Archer-Hind's *Phaedo*, p. 23. The counterarguments of Straton are excerpted in Olympiodoros, *In Phaed. Comm.*
[XX⁸], pp. 221ff., and F. Wehrli, *Die Schule des Aristoteles*, Pt. V,
Straton von Lampsakos (Basel, 1950), frags. 120-27. For the modern
criticism, consult Natorp, *Ideenlehre*, pp. 138ff.; Archer-Hind's
Phaedo, pp. 23ff.; Robin's edition, pp. lxviii ff.; Hackforth's, pp.
16ff., 161ff.; Bluck's, pp. 18ff., 188ff. See also D. S. Scarrow, *"Phaedo
106A-106E,"* *PR*, LXX (1961), 245ff.; D. Keyt, "The Fallacies in
Phaedo 102A-107B," *Phronesis*, VIII (1963), 167ff.

31. Reinhardt, *Mythen*, pp. 94ff.

32. Frank, *WWG*, esp. the chapter, "Wissen, Wollen, Glauben," pp.
342ff.

33. See *Plato* 1, pp. 182ff.

34. In truth, then, this is just the opposite of what a widespread dogmatizing conception of Plato claims. See, for example, A. H. P. de

Ridder, *De l'idée de la mort en Grèce à l'époque classique* (Paris, 1896), p. 122: "Plato is, by his very principle, compelled to assume a kind of metempsychosis. He was thus obliged to fall back into contradictions and the arbitrary. . . . How should one conceive of the gradual purification of the soul? How should the trials and the punishments be assessed? How should one imagine . . ." Per contra, Singer, p. 52: "Purification itself is, in the mind of Socrates, the world- and soul-power which is expressed here in many shapes, in pictures and teachings."

35. Robin (*Phédon*, p. x) directs a somewhat strange polemic against the "widespread interpretation" of this scene.

XXII: *Republic*

RECENT EDITIONS AND TRANSLATIONS: J. Adam (Cambridge, 1902; 2d edn., with Introd. by D. A. Rees, 1953); P. Shorey, Loeb (1930, 1935); É. Chambry and A. Diès, *Platon Budé*, VI–VII (1932–34); O. Apelt, PhB 80 (7th edn., 1941); F. M. Cornford (Oxford, 1941); J. M. Pabón and M. F. Galiano (Madrid, 1949); R. Rufener (Zurich, 1950); B. Jowett and L. Campbell (4th edn., Oxford, 1953); F. Sartori (Bari, 1956); K. Vretska (Stuttgart, 1958).

RECENT INTERPRETATIONS: Salin, *Utopie*, pp. 1ff.; H. Kelsen, "Justice platonicienne," *Revue Philosophique*, CXIV (1932), 364ff.; B. M. Laing, "The Problem of Justice in Plato's *Republic*," *Philosophy*, VIII (1933), 412ff.; J. Moreau, *La construction de l'idéalisme platonicien* (Paris, 1939), pp. 204ff., 298ff.; K. Marc-Wogau, "Der Staat und der Begriff des Guten in Platons *Politeia*," *Theoria*, VII (1941), 20ff.; H.-G. Gadamer, "Platos Staat der Erziehung," in *Das Neue Bild der Antike*, ed. H. Berve (Leipzig, 1942), I, 317ff.; R. G. Hoerber, *The Theme of Plato's "Republic"* (St. Louis, 1944); Koyré, pp. 56ff.; G. Brown, "The Alleged Metaphysics in the *Republic*," in *Analysis and Metaphysics*, Aristotelian Society, Suppl. Vol. XIX (1945), pp. 165ff. (also G. C. Field, pp. 193ff.; S. S. Orr, pp. 207ff.); Jaeger, *Paideia*, II, 198ff.; III, 250ff.; E. Cassirer, *The Myth of the State* (New Haven and London, 1946; Anchor reprint, 1955), ch. 6; Barker, chs. 8–10; H. W. B. Joseph, *Knowledge and the Good in Plato's "Republic"* (Oxford, 1948); Festugière, *Contemplation*, pp. 400ff.; G. Krüger, "Der Staat. Über das Gerechte," as Introd. to Rufener's trans. (Zurich, 1950); E. Paci, "Lo stato come idea dell' uomo nella *Repubblica* di Platone," in *Studi di filosofia antica e moderna* (Turin, 1950), pp. 71ff.; N. R. Murphy, *The Interpretation of Plato's "Republic"* (Oxford, 1951); Stanka, pp. 146ff.; Gauss, I/2, pp. 117ff.; II/2, chs. 3–5; D. R. Grey, "Art in the *Republic*," *Philosophy*, XXVII

(1952), 291ff.; Sinclair, pp. 143ff.; K. Vretska, "Platonica," *Wien-Stud*, LXVI (1953), 76ff.; LXXI (1958), 30ff.; P. Piovani, "L'antinomia della città platonica," *Giorn. Crit. Filos. Ital.*, ser. 8, III (1954), 481ff.; Vanhoutte, pp. 54ff.; E. G. Ballard, "Plato's Movement from an Ethics of the Individual to a Science of Particulars," *Tulane Studies in Philosophy*, VI (1957), 5ff.; D. Pesce, *Città terrena e città celeste nel pensiero antico* (Florence, 1957), pp. 11ff.; Wolff, pp. 152ff.; W. C. Greene, "The Paradoxes of the *Republic*," *Harvard Studies in Classical Philology*, LXIII (1958), 199ff.; Luccioni, pp. 1ff.; J. B. Skemp, "Comment on Communal and Individual Justice in the *Republic*," *Phronesis*, V (1960), 35ff.; F. Mayr, "Freiheit und Bindung in Platons *Politeia*," *WienStud*, LXXV (1962), 28ff.; E. A. Havelock, *A Preface to Plato* (Oxford, 1963); R. C. Cross and A. D. Woozley, *Plato's "Republic": A Philosophical Commentary* (London, 1964); F. Solmsen, "*Republic* III 389B2–D6: Plato's Draft and the Editor's Mistake," *Philologus*, CIX (1956), 182ff.; N. Cooper, "The Importance of ΔΙΑΝΟΙΑ in Plato's Theory of Forms," *CQ*, n.s., XVI (1966), 65ff.; Lesky, pp. 526ff.

ADDITIONAL BIBLIOGRAPHY: Shorey, pp. 557f.; Geffcken, Notes, pp. 93ff.; Leisegang, cols. 2450ff.; Rosenmeyer, pp. 188f.; Cherniss, *Lustrum*, pp. 153ff.

1. See *Plato* 2, pp. 50–66. Franz Dornseiff, "Platons *Politeia* Buch I," *Hermes*, LXXVI (1941), 111ff., is opposed to this view. He says, "Book I is taken up among the early dialogues"—*yes, for it has the form of an early dialogue*—"and the discussion of the *Republic* begins with Book II"—*not so in our work.* / "No decision possible," says Shorey, in *The Republic* (Loeb, 2 vols., 1930, 1935), I, xxv.

2. Cf. von Arnim, *Jugenddialoge*, p. 73; Dorothy Tarrant, "Plato as Dramatist," *JHS*, LXXV (1955), 85. On the symbolism of the setting, Proklos' thoughts are well worth pondering; see *Procli Diadochi in Platonis Rem publicam Commentarii*, ed. W. Kroll (2 vols., Leipzig, 1899–1901), I, 17.

3. W. Müri, "Das Wort Dialektik bei Platon," *MusHelv*, I (1944), 162, sees in *Republic* I 354B—i.e., "in those sentences which link the first book of the *Republic* with the following ones"—the "first example of the naming of a Platonic work, the so-called *Thrasymachus*, as a διάλογος."

4. *Plato* 2, pp. 63, 307 (n. 15).

5. Pohlenz (*Werdezeit*, p. 209) and von Arnim (*Jugenddialoge*, pp. 73ff.) show, respectively, that at this point "a slight alteration of the structural plan" has occurred, a "joint in the composition has remained visible, at least to the well-trained eye." For Glaukon's criticism at the beginning of Book II is not wholly justified.

6. See *Plato* 2, pp. 259f. Cf. H. Maier, *Sokrates* (Tübingen, 1913), pp. 243ff. It is true that once we grasp the sequence in which these speeches are stratified within Plato's work, some things begin to look quite different. / In the years of our collaboration, Friedrich Kling-ner helped me to clarify the relationship of the three works, *Thrasy-machus*, *Gorgias*, and *Republic*.

7. *Republic* II 361E: κἂν ἀγροικοτέρως λέγηται ∼ *Gorgias* 486C: εἴ τι καὶ ἀγροικότερον εἰρῆσθαι. *Republic* II 362A: στρεβλώσεται, δεδήσεται, ἐκκαυθήσεται τώφαλμώ, τελευτῶν πάντα κακὰ παθὼν ἀνασχινδυλευ-θήσεται καὶ γνώσεται ὅτι οὐκ εἶναι δίκαιον ἀλλὰ δοκεῖν δεῖ ἐθέλειν. ∼ *Gorgias* 473C: ἐὰν . . . στρεβλῶται καὶ ἐκτέμνηται καὶ τοὺς ὀφθαλμοὺς ἐκκάηται καὶ ἄλλας πολλὰς καὶ μεγάλας καὶ παντοδαπὰς λώβας . . . λωβηθεὶς . . . ἀνασταυρωθῇ.

8. *Republic* IX 577E: ἥκιστα ποιήσει ἃ ἂν βουληθῇ ∼ *Gorgias* 466D: οὐδὲν γὰρ ποιεῖν ὧν βούλονται.

9. Compare, for example, *Republic* II 378C: πολλοῦ δεῖ γιγαντομαχίας τε μυθολογητέον αὐτοῖς καὶ ποικιλτέον with *Euthyphro* 6BC: οἷα λέγεταί τε ὑπὸ τῶν ποιητῶν καὶ ὑπὸ τῶν ἀγαθῶν γραφέων τά τε ἄλλα ἱερὰ ἡμῖν καταπεποίκιλται, καὶ δὴ καὶ τοῖς μεγάλοις Παναθηναίοις ὁ πέπλος μεστὸς τῶν τοιούτων ποικιλμάτων ἀνάγεται εἰς τὴν ἀκρόπολιν.

10. *Plato* 1, pp. 118ff. On this see further Jacques Maritain, *Creative In-tuition in Art and Poetry* (New York, 1955), p. 64.

11. On mimesis, see Hermann Koller, *Die Mimesis in der Antike* (Bern, 1954), and the criticism by G. F. Else, " 'Imitation' in the Fifth Century," *CP*, LIII (1958), 73ff.; W. J. Verdenius, *Mimesis* (2d edn., Leyden, 1962); M. Heidegger, *Nietzsche* (Pfullingen, 1961), I, 198ff.

12. Cf. Aristotle, *Politics* I 2 1252ᵃ 24 *et seq.*, and the comment by W. L. Newman, in *The "Politics" of Aristotle* (4 vols., Oxford, 1887–1902), II, 103f. The concept of φύσις also dominates the discussion by Aris-totle which Plato stimulated. / The importance that *physis*, as a guiding word, has for Plato in this section was observed by Aino Krohn, *Der platonische Staat* (Halle, 1876), pp. 59ff. She, however, interpreted φύσις wrongly as "specific energy of the soul" and based on her sound observation the unsound thesis of a naturalistic phase in Plato's philosophy, when Plato had "not yet" devised his "theory of *Ideas*." / On the connection between φύσις and οὐσία, see for example *Cratylus* 386D *et seq.*—which is in the direction of Aristotle's *Metaphysics* IV 4. / Also note the following: χρεία in *Republic* II 369c 2, 10; 371D 4. (προσ)δεῖσθαι in 371A 14, 371B 1; 373C 5 and 6. ἐνδεής in 369B 7. δεῖ in 369E 2; 370C 7; 371A 4; 373B 2; etc.

13. Taylor (*Plato*, p. 273) cautions that "we must not take the descrip-tion . . . as meant to convey any speculations about the beginnings of civilisation." See also F. M. Cornford, *Plato's Cosmology: The "Timaeus" of Plato translated with a Running Commentary* (London, 1937), p. 27; Koyré, p. 125.

14. On this whole section, see further W. Üxkull-Gyllenband, "Grie-

chische Kulturentstehungslehren," *AfGP*, Suppl. Vol. XXXVI/3-4 (1924). / According to Zeller, p. 893, Plato's depiction is intended "to refute the false ideal natural state." For an opposed view, see Adam's excellent note on 372c in his edition of the *Republic* (2 vols., Cambridge, 1902). Adam's conclusion, which cannot be overthrown but merely supplemented, is this: "The πρώτη πόλις is not of course Plato's ideal republic . . . but it is nevertheless the foundation on which his city is built. . . . It remains on the whole, and as far as it goes, a not unpleasing picture of the life of the lowest stratum in Plato's city and is nowhere expressly cancelled or abolished." / What I call the "broad stream of reflection" is narrowed or neglected if one seeks a definite "source" for Plato's construction, finding it either in Antisthenes (the hypothesis of Zeller *et al.*), or in Demokritos (K. Reinhardt, *Hermes*, XLVII [1912], 492; M. Pohlenz, *Hermes*, LIII [1918], 418; Ueberweg-Praechter, p. 270), or in a lost comedy (Wilamowitz, II, pp. 214ff.). We note the remarkable verbal agreement pointed out by Reinhardt (op. cit., p. 504) between a Demokritos quotation in Philodemos (*Vorsokr.* 68 [55] B 144) and *Republic* 373AB: the origin of musical art belongs in the beginning of an age of abundance, when concern no longer need be felt for the "merely necessary." It is possible that this idea impressed Plato when he read Demokritos. It seems just as possible, however, that Demokritos and Plato both found the idea in the same source, perhaps in Damon's *Areopagiticus.* (This is merely suggested as one good possibility.) On Damon, see further n. 19, below.

15. Aino Krohn, *Der platonische Staat* [XXII¹²], p. 12, sees at this point the signs of an altered structural plan. I agree with Adam on 376E. And see also J. Hirmer, "Entstehung und Komposition der *Politeia*," *Jahrbücher für klassische Philologie*, Suppl. Vol. XXIII (1897), 612ff.

16. Cf. *Plato* 1, pp. 173f., 209.

17. "The man who coined the word 'theologia' was Plato. St. Augustine rightly praises him as the true father of theology, and Meister Eckart calls Plato 'der grosse pfaffe' " (W. Jaeger, *Humanism and Theology*, Milwaukee, 1943, pp. 45f.).

18. Cf. Steinhart, V, 159; Susemihl, II, 121. See also Adam (I, 115) on *Republic* 379B: "Read in the light of Book VI, the theology of this and the following chapters gains, no doubt, in significance and depth." But then follows the strange restriction that "in point of fact, Plato might have written the end of Book III even if he had never thought of the Ideas at all."

19. On Damon, see *Vorsokr.* 37 [25] A; also U. von Wilamowitz, *Griechische Verskunst* (Berlin, 1921), pp. 59ff.; H. Ryffel, "Eukosmia," *Mus-Helv*, IV (1947), 23ff.; W. D. Anderson, "The Importance of Damonian Theory in Plato's Thought," *TAPA*, LXXXVI (1955), 88ff.; F. Lasserre, *Plutarque, "De la musique"* (Bibl. Helv. Rom.,

Lausanne, 1954), ch. 6, "Damon d'Athènes"; Lesky, pp. 305f. /
Damon may be the source for what is said in the *Republic* (397BC) on
the μεταβολαί of harmonies and rhythms, and perhaps also the source
for *Republic* 373AB (on the origin of music; cf. n. 14, above).

20. Πανταχοῦ περιφερόμενα (*Republic* 402c 4). Compare this with πανταχοῦ
φανταζόμενα in 476A, where it is said that the εἴδη appear everywhere
as images through the κοινωνία with the πράξεις and the σώματα, and
each "one" (476A 7) appears as "many."

21. Debate has gone back and forth regarding these εἴδη. Adam, in his
commentary [XXII¹⁴] on Book III 402c, calls them "a harbinger of
the ideal theory of Books VI and VII—a sort of halfway house between the Socratic λόγοι and Plato's Ideas." As soon as we put aside
the aspect of historical development in this formulation, we find
something in it that is correct. / The closest resemblance to these
"forms" is found in *Charmides* 159A: ἀνάγκη γάρ που ἐνοῦσαν (*scil.*
τὴν σωφροσύνην) εἴπερ ἔνεστιν αἴσθησίν τινα παρέχειν. Compare this
with *Republic* 402c 5: ἐνόντα ἐν οἷς ἔνεστιν αἰσθανόμεθα.

22. *Symposium* 210B 8 shows that *Republic* 402DE is not to be understood
as merely biographical (Wilamowitz, II, 192).

23. *Gorgias* 464B–465c; also see *Plato* 2, p. 253. In connection with this
discussion about physicians and judges in the *Republic*, commentators
have traditionally referred to the *Gorgias*. See, among others, Steinhart, V, 173; Susemihl, II, 138; and Adam's comment on 405c.

24. This irony often is not recognized. For example, see Koyré, p. 148:
"*Notre cité, désormais, est achevée. Elle est telle qu'elle doit être.*" Similar
to this is Adam's view, and Shorey's as well.

25. On 424c, see E. R. Curtius, *Kritische Essays zur europäischen Literatur*
(Bern, 1950), p. 153.

26. Obviously this intention was one of those that had to be misunderstood in order to support the hypothesis of the chorizontes. Hirmer,
"Entstehung und Komposition der *Politeia*" [XXII¹⁵], p. 611, has
correctly commented, opposing Krohn.

27. See n. 19, above.

28. See von Arnim, *Jugenddialoge*, p. 150; Shorey, p. 79.

29. Concerning the virtues as viewed in the older speculative ethics, see
Adam's comment on 427E. Of special importance is Aeschylus, *Seven
against Thebes* 610, and the comment on it by Werner Jaeger, in *Die
Antike*, IV (1928), p. 163. Cf. also Erwin Wolff, *Platos "Apologie"*
(Neue philologische Untersuchungen, VI, Berlin, 1929), p. 77.

30. See *Plato* 2, pp. 241f., and *DGrA*, II, 63ff. / On the *Gorgias*, see also
Plato 2, pp. 269ff.

31. Adam (I, 239) remarks that "This has not been said in the *Republic*"
—*but see* 370A 4—"nor (so far as I know) in any of Plato's earlier
dialogues (if we except *Alc. I* 127c), so that εἰρήκαμεν refers to ordinary conversation." More correctly: Plato formulates as a reference

to earlier utterances of Socrates that which in his literary work is a reference to an earlier dialogue. A preliminary form of the system of political virtues occurs in the *Alcibiades*. Moreover, in the *Republic* the *Alcibiades* is "quoted"—as specifically as Plato in any of his dialogues "quotes" another one. See *DGrA*, I, 23ff.; II, 62ff.; also *Plato 2*, pp. 241f.

32. Hirzel (I, 237) shows insight as to the levels of justice.

33. Cf. Barth, p. 14, where there is also a good polemic against the "wooden interpretation," i.e., the clumsy dogmatization, unmindful of sense and connection, of Plato's trichotomy of the soul.

34. Gauss (II/2, 160) objects to my presentation—but in order to do this he has Plato request the "institution of gymnasia for women."

35. I am leaving these lines of the text unchanged in spite of the criticism by de Vries, p. 65.

36. See H.-G. Gadamer, *Platos dialektische Ethik* [XXI[26]], pp. 52ff.

37. Stenzel (*Studien*, p. 49) attempts methodically to differentiate what is meant in *Republic* 454A and 476A from the diaeresis of the later dialogues. Nevertheless, it still cannot be denied, first, that the dichotomous procedure is practiced here in the *Republic* (ἄνδρες—γυναῖκες. φαλακροί—κομῆται. σκυτοτομεῖν—μὴ σκυτοτομεῖν); second, that there is the same contrast of eristic and dialectic here as in *Philebus* 16E (cf. Stenzel, *Zahl und Gestalt*, p. 13); and third, that Plato can derive the opinion to be combated from a false diaeresis only because he is fully clear as to the nature and importance of the correct diaeresis. In the late dialogues this procedure will take on an ironically heightened form, to be sure, but it still is not a question of something wholly new. The articulated system of the *Ideas* or Forms is symbolized as early as the *Cratylus* by the system of the letters. And in the last analysis, the system of Forms has been present in the problem of the one and the many ever since the *Protagoras* and the group of the aporetic dialogues of definition. Cf. Shorey, pp. 50f.

38. Reference to the comedy has frequently been made (see, for example, Adam's comment on this passage). Yet, it must be made clear that Plato is suggesting not the comedy so much as the sort of "lynch law" as is depicted, for instance, in the *Acharnians*.

39. φύσις: 485A 5, 486B 3, 486D 10, 487A 3. δεῖ: 485D 3, 486B 3. The same connection is involved as in the origins of the *polis*. See n. 12, above.

40. *Republic* VI 487D 5; 489A 1, c 6, D 4, D 7; and see Bekker, I, 170; Adam, II, 12. Cf. also Euripides, frag. 913; in an enlarged version, in B. Snell, "Euripides-Fragmente," *WienStud*, LXIX (1956), 91.

41. It is frightening to see how thoroughly Toynbee, world historian of our epoch, misunderstands the "paradox"—as he rightly recognizes it to be—of the philosopher-king. Toynbee depends for his understanding of Plato on Machiavelli, and he finds in the "brutal words"

of the Italian theoretician of power politics the means of ferreting out "a sinister feature in the strategy of the philosopher-king which Plato discreetly keeps in the background." (This is the wording found in the abridged edition of *A Study of History* [2 vols., New York and London, 1947], I, 543. In Toynbee's original, six-volume version [1939], the wording is even more bitter [VI, 256]: "a sinister feature . . . which Plato almost disingenuously slurs over.") The radical difference of even the best state on earth from the ideal state, which "is laid up in heaven as the prototype" (*Republic* IX 592B), eludes Toynbee so completely that he can continue (I, 543), "If the philosopher-king finds that he cannot get his way by charm, he will throw away his philosophy and take to the sword," or, in the original version (VI, 256), "If ever the philosopher-king finds himself at a point at which he is no longer able to gain his end by the exercise of charm or bluff, he will throw away his copy-book of moral maxims and proceed to enforce his will. . . ." Now, one may prefer reality to the *Idea*. One may (and who should not, again and again?) feel closer to Marcus Aurelius than to the ideal philosopher-king. And one may even assert that "the philosopher-king is doomed to fail." What is *not* allowed the responsible historian is this: to confuse Plato with insidious strategists and in so doing to forget entirely what *philo–sophia* meant to Plato. / If Toynbee can make such a blunder, the attacks on Plato by other sociologists and historians—Fite, Winspear, Crossman, Popper, Rüstow—are less surprising. On this see Ronald B. Levinson, *In Defense of Plato* (Cambridge, Mass., 1953). See also Gauss (II/2, 124ff.), who believes, however, that in Plato's thought the enduring should be separated from the passing, and assumes in Plato's political writings more or less of a concession to the *philosophia cotidiana*. See, in contrast, *Plato* 1, ch. I; A. Boyce Gibson, *Should Philosophers Be Kings?* (Melbourne, 1939); E. Lledó Iñigo, "Philosophos Basileus," *RevFil*, XIX (1960), 37ff.

42. *Republic* 492E. Adam (II, 76) is right in understanding παρὰ τὴν τούτων παιδείαν to mean "against the education practiced by the masses," not, as it is usually understood, "in accordance with education." Yet, on the other hand, he is wrong in taking ἀλλοῖον to mean "different from the many." The fact is rather that ἀλλοῖον γίγνεσθαι can only mean ἀλλοιοῦσθαι (cf. *Symposium* 189D 7, *Republic* X 598A 9, *Theaetetus* 160A 3). This is correctly reflected in the translation, for example, of H. Müller (who, however, takes παρά wrongly). On the whole, Schleiermacher is close to the correct sense.

43. *Republic* 494C 5: μεγάλης πόλεως ∼ *Alcibiades* 104A 7: πόλει οὔσῃ μεγίστῃ. *Republic* 494C 6: εὐειδὴς καὶ μέγας ∼ *Alcibiades* 104A 5: κάλλιστός τε καὶ μέγιστος. *Republic* 494C 6: πλούσιός τε καὶ γενναῖος ∼ *Alcibiades* 104A–C: νεανικωτάτου γένους . . . τῶν πλουσίων.

44. *Republic* 494C 7: ἀμηχάνου ἐλπίδος ∼ *Alcibiades* 105A: ἐπὶ τίνι ἐλπίδι

ζῆς. *Republic* 494c 8: καὶ τὰ τῶν Ἑλλήνων καὶ τὰ τῶν βαρβάρων ἱκανὸν ἔσεσθαι πράττειν ~ *Alcibiades* 105b: οὐ μόνον ἐν Ἕλλησιν ἀλλὰ καὶ ἐν τοῖς βαρβάροις.

45. See G. Méautis, in *RevPhilol*, V (1931), 97ff.; also J. Bernays, *Phokion und seine neueren Beurteiler* (Berlin, 1881), pp. 32ff.

46. See Adam's commentary on this passage.

47. See *Plato* 1, pp. 119, 359 (n. 21).

48. *Plato* 2, pp. 262f.

49. See my remarks on Platonic irony in *Plato* 1, pp. 147f. / On what follows, note that a portion of the problem discussed in the text is indicated in the play of the two compounds ἀπο- and παρα-λείπειν, and in the ἑκών which is set beside ἀπολείψω.

50. In *Republic* VII 536c 7 there is an express reference to III 412c. Furthermore, 537e 4 is an unexpressed verbal reference to 424d 3.

51. Singer, p. 141. See also the comprehensive presentation by H. Ryffel, Μεταβολὴ πολιτειῶν: *Der Wandel der Staatsverfassungen* (Bern, 1949); cf. K. Vretska, "Platons Demokratenkapitel: Untersuchung seiner Form," *Gymnasium*, LXII (1955), 407ff.

52. Compare *Republic* II 363d with *Gorgias* 493ab.

53. See *Plato* 2, pp. 28ff.

54. See *Plato* 1, pp. 177f., 184.

55. W. Jaeger ("A New Greek Word in Plato's *Republic*," *Eranos*, XLIV [1946], 123ff.) conjectures ὀργῶδες instead of ὀφεῶδες in 590b 1. But ὀφεῶδες (~ δρακοντῶδες) describes exactly what was expressed more generally in 588e 6 by τὰ περὶ τὸν λέοντα (Schleiermacher). Adam (II, 365f.) is in opposition to the conjecture ὀχλῶδες (Nettleship). For a statement against ὀργῶδες, see Classen, p. 29.

56. On this agreement compare, for example, *Gorgias* 516ab with *Republic* IX 589b, and *Gorgias* 507d with *Republic* IX 591ab.

57. One should also be reminded of the θηρίον Τυφῶνος πολυπλοκώτερον in *Phaedrus* 230a. Evidently the heads of the beast in the *Republic* imagery derive from Typhon. Cf. Hesiod, *Theogony* 824 *et seq.*

58. See August Boeckh, *Philolaos des Pythagoreers Lehren nebst den Bruchstücken seines Werkes* (Berlin, 1819), pp. 133ff.; Susemihl, II, 133ff. Also consult Adam on 588a, and Brumbaugh, *Plato's Mathematical Imagination* [XXI[20]], pp. 151ff.

59. Schleiermacher's (III/1, 607) term is "*Spielerei*," "meaningless trifling." Opposing this, K. Schneider (*Platonis Opera Graeca*, 3 vols., Leipzig, 1830), III, xli, interprets the connection thus: a year in the life of the king corresponds to one day of happiness in the life of the tyrant, and so on. Susemihl (II, 242ff.) accepts this and adds a reference to the number speculation in Book VIII: the great time-periods that emerged there now have the smaller ones attached to them, and we are taught that the internal soundness of the several constitutions as well as their duration declines *gradatim* more and more sharply.

/ Brumbaugh draws a comparison with the nine levels of the soul in *Phaedrus* 248c *et seq.*

60. Compare X 612B with II 367D, 363A, 359C *et seq.*; 612c 7 with 361B; 612E with II 365c and I 352B; 613D with II 361E.

61. 613A 7 (ἢ καὶ ἀποθανόντι) does not properly belong in this section.

62. It is surprising that the interpreters are so little disturbed by this passage. Actually there is a wholly different wording in *Laws* X 899D *et seq.*, 905B. / "*Hier is veel conformistische ironie,*" says de Vries (p. 175), and also refers to R. L. Nettleship's *Lectures on the "Republic" of Plato* (2d edn., London, 1901), pp. 352f. Gauss (II/2, 232ff.) seems to misunderstand me. I do not object to the "principle of reward" in itself, but it hardly seems possible to me that Plato intended as altogether serious this all too human reward of which Socrates speaks. Neither do I agree that "P. F. would be of another opinion if he had known his Kant better." Rather I believe that Gauss would have perhaps judged differently if he had had a clearer grasp of the nature of Plato's irony.

63. See *Plato* 1, pp. 118ff., 358f. (nn. 19–22).

64. See pp. 37f. of the text. / G. A. Borgese, "Goethe—Mythos und Sendung," *Die Neue Rundschau* (1949), p. 338: "Socrates' condemnation, by no means directed unconditionally against poetry as such, only against poetry in so far as it is an escape from the *kalokagathon* . . . did not have a deterrent effect. To Virgil and Dante it served as warning and guide . . ."

65. See *Plato* 1, pp. 118ff.

66. This is pointed to by κἂν εἰ μή τῳ δοκεῖ (473A). Cf. Adam, I, 323. The popular superordination of action over the word is reflected in Plato's *Letter VII* 328c 6.

67. Shorey, in *CP*, IX (1914), 353, quotes Emerson: "All [Plato's] painting in the *Republic* must be esteemed mythical, with intent to bring out, sometimes in violent colours, his thought. You cannot institute without peril of charlatanism."

68. Cf. Susemihl, II, 110, 216; Singer, pp. 68, 76, 117.

69. *Plato* 1, p. 208.

70. Singer, p. 101.

xxiii: *Theaetetus*

RECENT EDITIONS AND TRANSLATIONS: A. Diès, *Platon Budé*, VIII/2 (1924); F. M. Cornford (London, 1935); E. Salin (Basel, 1946); G. Zannoni (Florence, 1948); A. Russo (Milan, 1955); O. Apelt, PhB 82 (6th edn., 1955).

RECENT INTERPRETATIONS: Shorey, pp. 269ff.; M. Dercsényi, "Exegetische Bemerkungen zu Platons *Theaetet*," *Hermes*, LXX (1935), 404ff.; E. Grassi, *Vom Vorrang des Logos* (Munich, 1939), pp. 71ff.; H. Bischoff, in *Hermes*, LXXIV (1939), 104ff.; Kucharski, pp. 232ff., 360ff.; J. W. Yolton, "The Ontological Status of Sense-Data in Plato's Theory of Perception," *Rev. Metaphysics*, III (1949/50), 21ff.; Festugière, *Contemplation*, pp. 408ff.; Buccellato, ch. 6; Gauss, II/2, ch. 6; III/1, ch. 2; A. Guzzo, "Il concetto di 'scienza' e il *Teeteto* platonico," *Filosofia*, V (1954), 562ff.; J. Moreau, "Platon et le phénoménisme," *RevInPh*, IX (1955), 256ff.; Annemarie Capelle, "Bemerkungen zu Platons *Theaetet*," *Hermes*, LXXXVIII (1960), 265ff.; W. G. Runciman, *Plato's Later Epistemology* (Cambridge, 1962), pp. 6ff.; R. S. Bluck, "Knowledge by Acquaintance in Plato's *Theaetetus*," *Mind*, LXXII (1963), 259ff.; Lesky, p. 532.

ADDITIONAL BIBLIOGRAPHY: Shorey, pp. 571f.; Geffcken, Notes, p. 106; Rosenmeyer, p. 190; Cherniss, *Lustrum*, pp. 198ff.

1. For this view, see the *Anonymer Kommentar zu Platons "Theaetet*," ed. H. Diels and W. Schubart (Berliner Klassikertexte, 1905, Vol. II), p. 5, col. 4, 11. 37ff. Jachmann (p. 317) calls this account in the *Kommentar* "the most important testimony we possess in the history of Plato's text." More cautious and more correct is H. Langerbeck's view, in *Gnomon*, XXII (1950), 378.

2. I mention the fact that this historicity is to be taken in a purely ideal sense because Steinhart (III, 30) and H. Schmidt ("Kritischer Kommentar zu Platos *Theätet*," in A. Fleckeisen, ed., *Jahrbücher für klassische Philologie*, Suppl. Vol. IX [1877–78], 433) are of the contrary opinion.

3. See Eva Sachs, *De Theaeteto Atheniensi mathematico* (Berlin diss., 1914), pp. 16ff., 62ff. Her third chapter, "De homine," is of particular importance.

4. This is to refute the hypothesis of Wilamowitz (I, 520 = I², 525) that originally Plato had planned this differently. ("How it was meant to be cannot be guessed.") That Socrates has already been indicted by Meletos can be "a great surprise" (Wilamowitz, I, 509 = I², 515), and the conclusion can seem "patched on without connection"

(Wilamowitz, I, 520 = I², 525), only if we have completely forgotten the words ὀλίγον πρὸ τοῦ θανάτου (142c 6) for the sake of a modern hypothesis.

5. Stenzel, *Metaphysik*, p. 139. Also see F. M. Cornford, *Plato's Theory of Knowledge: The "Theaetetus" and the "Sophist" of Plato* (London, 1935)—where, however, in the "running commentary," under the section he calls "introductory conversation" in the *Theaetetus*, Cornford discusses only the episode concerning the maieutic. Ernesto Grassi (*Vom Vorrang des Logos*, Munich, 1939, p. 72) is against this restriction to the theory of knowledge. Shorey (pp. 269, 572) reveals another biased conception in stating that the dialogue's "theme is psychological."

6. Diogenes Laërtius II 10 106. One will have to agree with what Cicero, *Academica priora* II 42 129, states about the Megarians: "*hi quoque multa a Platone.*" Cf. Wilamowitz, II, 246.

7. *Theaetetus* 144c 8: τὸ δ' ὄνομα οὐκ οἶδα ～ *Lysis* 204e 2: τοὔνομα οὐκ ἔγνων. *Theaetetus* 143d 2: ἀνηρώτων, εἴ τινες αὐτόθι περὶ . . φιλοσοφίαν εἰσὶ τῶν νέων ἐπιμέλειαν ποιούμενοι ～ *Charmides* 153d 3: ἀνηρώτων . . . περὶ φιλοσοφίας ὅπως ἔχοι τὰ νῦν περί τε τῶν νέων, εἴ τινες . . .

8. The fact that the *Theaetetus* belongs to the aporetic dialogues in search of a definition, which Natorp (*Ideenlehre*, p. 88) recognized, obviously has no bearing on the chronology of the dialogue, Natorp notwithstanding. Besides, it will become evident that even in the dialogue's form, the aporetic type does not at all remain constant.

9. *Theaetetus:* εὐμαθής, μνήμων, ἐμβριθής, πρᾶος, ἀνδρεῖος. *Republic:* εὐμαθής, μνημονικός, ἥμερος, μὴ δειλός. Dion's nature, according to *Letter VII* 328b, is φύσει ἐμβριθές, as Schmidt, *Kritischer Kommentar* [XXIII²], p. 436, recalls. *Laws:* θυμοειδής, πρᾷος. In regard to the *Statesman*, one must recognize that its approach is different from that of the *Theaetetus*, and that each approach originates from a completely different point of view. In the *Statesman* ἀνδρεία is a natural disposition; in the *Theaetetus* it is the ἀρετή. Thus, it becomes clear that to the ἀνδρεία ψυχή in the *Statesman* correspond the ὀξεῖς in the *Theaetetus* of whom it is said (144b 1) that they μανικώτεροι ἢ ἀνδρειότεροι φύονται.

10. Cf. *Plato* 1, ch. VII. Somewhat primitive is the statement in the *Anonymer Kommentar* [XXIII¹], p. 8, col. 9, ll. 6–23: Ὁ Θεόδωρος τὸν καλὸν κατὰ τὰ ὑπὸ τῶν πολλῶν νομιζόμενα τὸν ἐκ τῆς μορφῆς τοιοῦτον. . . . ὁ δὲ Σωκράτης μᾶλλον οἶδε καλὸν τὸν καλῶς λέγοντα, τοῦτ' ἔστιν τὸν φρόνιμον. . .

11. Wilamowitz (I, 509 = I², 514) holds the contrary view: "Only a penetrating examination reveals that the controversial issue regarding the theory of knowledge has nothing to do with the two mathematicians." Schleiermacher (II/1, 186) maintained that the question of why Theodoros is introduced here cannot be answered satisfactorily

from the conversation itself. A view that more or less approaches what I have stated in the text is found in Steinhart, III, 23.

12. *Plato* 1, p. 235.

13. The boundary between the parts I have distinguished as "introductory conversation" and "preliminary attempt" is not sharply drawn.

14. Thus Wilamowitz, I, 512 = I², 517. Quite rightly, however, he also refers to the later passage, *Sophist* 239D.

15. ἐν πᾶσι . . . ταὐτόν, *Laches* 191E 10. ἐν ἐπὶ πᾶσι, *Sophist* 240A 5.

16. For the mathematical problem I can only refer to the technical literature: Sir Thomas Heath, *A Manual of Greek Mathematics* (Oxford, 1931), pp. 54ff.; C. Mugler, *Platon et la recherche mathématique de son époque* (Strasbourg and Zurich, 1948), pp. 191ff.; O. Toeplitz, *Die Entwicklung der Infinitesimalrechnung* (Berlin, 1949), p. 6; Brumbaugh, *Plato's Mathematical Imagination* [XXI²⁰], pp. 38ff.; G. H. Hardy and E. M. Wright, *An Introduction to the Theory of Numbers* (3d edn., Oxford, 1954), pp. 42ff. See further Stenzel, *Zahl und Gestalt*, p. 89; Leisegang, col. 2489; A. Wasserstein, "Theaetetus and the History of the Theory of Numbers," *CQ*, n.s., VIII (1958), 165ff.; R. S. Bluck, "The Puzzles of Size and Number in Plato's *Theaetetus*," *Proc. Cambridge Philol. Soc.*, n.s., VII (1961), 7ff.

17. Compare *Theaetetus* 147E 5: τὸν ἀριθμὸν πάντα δίχα διελάβομεν with the following. *Philebus* 23C 4: πάντα τὰ νῦν ὄντα ἐν τῷ παντὶ διχῇ διαλάβομεν. *Sophist* 221E 2: δίχα που νυνδὴ διείλομεν τὴν ἄγραν πᾶσαν. *Sophist* 267A 1: τὸ τοίνυν φανταστικὸν αὖθις διορίζωμεν δίχα . . . τὸ μὲν . . . τὸ δὲ . . . Many other passages in the *Sophist* and the *Statesman* also are germane.

18. See *Plato* 1, p. 35. / Bruns (*Porträt*, pp. 292f.) attempts to understand what he calls this "most interesting survey of Socrates' pedagogic experiences" in an exclusively historical sense, i.e., "placed within the historical continuity of the Socratic life." For Plato, however, a purely historical view like that of Bruns—i.e., typical of the late nineteenth century—does not exist at all.

19. See, for example, Schleiermacher, II/1, 173: "Therefore, the dialogue begins by showing that the Protagorean denial of a common standard of knowledge . . ."

20. For *Aristippos*: Schleiermacher, II/1, 183f. Opposed: Zeller, p. 350. See H. Langerbeck (Δόξις ἐπιρρυσμίη: *Studien zu Demokrits Ethik und Erkenntnislehre*, Neue philologische Untersuchungen, X, Berlin, 1935, pp. 14ff.), who states: "The Aristippos-thesis has been decisively refuted by Peipers, *Die Erkenntnislehre Platons* (Leipzig, 1874)." For *Antisthenes*: Karl Joël, *Der echte und der xenophontische Sokrates* (2 vols., Berlin, 1893–1901), II, 842ff. Opposed: Kurt von Fritz, "Zur antisthenischen Erkenntnistheorie und Logik," *Hermes*, LXII (1927), 465. Joël, *Geschichte*, p. 946, combines the two theses.

21. Diogenes Laërtius II 93.

22. Theophrastus, *De sensu* 3, 10, 23, 25 (in *Vorsokr.* 28 [18]A 46; 31 [21]A 86).

23. The contrary view—that this was "a definition which was at least current"—is expressed by W. J. Alexander, "The Aim and Results of Plato's *Theaetetus*," in *Studies in Honor of B. L. Gildersleeve* (Baltimore, 1903), p. 170. For my interpretation I can refer in general to Shorey, *Unity*, p. 8 ("that in the case of many doctrines combated by Plato there is no evidence that they ever were formulated with the proper logical qualifications except by himself"); and in particular I refer to Schmidt, *Kritischer Kommentar*, p. 447, and to Gomperz' (III, 158) view of the formula as "probably of Plato's own coining." Cf. A. Diès, *Théétète* (*Platon Budé*, VIII/2, 1924), p. 150: "Plato here synthesizes tendencies perhaps more than doctrines."

24. See K. von Fritz, "Protagoras," *R-E*, XX, cols. 913ff.

25. The manuscript version of 152c 5 is confirmed by the *Anonymer Kommentar* [XXIII¹], p. 44.

26. E. K. W. Stoelzel, *Die Behandlung des Erkenntnisproblems bei Platon* (Halle, 1908), p. 23, correctly points out the "generalizing character of the epistemological substruction." / On Epicharmos, the "Master of Comedy," see M. Gigante, "Epicarmo, Pseudo-Epicarmo e Platone," *ParPass*, VIII (1953), 161ff.

27. Cornford emphasizes that the concern is not about mathematical relations between pure numbers, but rather about things that can be perceived: such and such a number of dice. Socrates makes the example visual for the boy. Would anything be changed at all, however, if instead of the dice, Socrates had used pure numbers?

28. The related passages are *Phaedo* 81B: οὔ τις ἂν ἅψαιτο, and *Sophist* 246A *et seq.* (cf. 247c: ὃ μὴ δυνατοὶ ταῖς χερσὶ συμπιέζειν εἰσίν). Paul Natorp, *Forschungen zur Geschichte des Erkenntnisproblems im Altertum* (Berlin, 1884), pp. 195ff., has refuted Schleiermacher's opinion that the reference here is to Demokritos. Lewis Campbell's Introduction to his commentary (*The "Theaetetus" of Plato*, 2d edn., Oxford, 1883) is instructive; for although his investigation points first to Demokritos, ensuing difficulties force him later to assume "degenerate followers" of Demokritos instead of the master himself (pp. xli ff.). See also Campbell's Introduction to his "*Sophistes*" *and* "*Politicus*" *of Plato* (Oxford, 1867), p. lxxiv. / The Antisthenes-hypothesis (Zeller, p. 297; Joël, *Geschichte*, p. 892) is not satisfactory either, as is evident from the passage in the *Phaedo* (81B) in which the primitive materialistic interpretation of matter is related to a similarly coarse and at best unphilosophical "hedonism": γεγοητευμένη (ἡ ψυχή) ὑπὸ τῶν ἐπιθυμιῶν καὶ ἡδονῶν. Antisthenes' attitude toward pleasure, however, is well known. The agreement with Stoic philosophy—upon which F. Dümmler, *Antisthenica* (Bonn diss., 1882), pp. 51ff., with Zeller's concurrence, based his evidence—will not suffice.

For it is not so that in the *Sophist* "the βελτίους γεγονότες already recognized the necessity (after 247BC) of breaking the principle that all reality is matter" (whereby they supposedly—but, again, not necessarily—move closer to the Stoic doctrine). One must not overlook the fact that those "sprung from the earth" (γηγενεῖς, σπαρτοί τε καὶ αὐτόχθονες) use Theaitetos as their mouthpiece; that is, they themselves would not answer at all since they are unphilosophic and undialectic. And in the passage (*Sophist* 247B) in which Theaitetos allows inconsistency to emerge within their pure materialism, it could very well be Plato himself who wants to show us: even the most coarse unphilosophical materialism, in so far as it lends itself at all to a λόγον διδόναι, breaks down before phenomena like δικαιοσύνη and φρόνησις. On the κομψότεροι who oppose this materialism, see further the hypothesis of Annemarie Capelle, "Zur Frage nach den κομψότεροι in Platons *Theaetet* 156A," *Hermes*, XC (1962), 288ff. / Cornford, *Theory of Knowledge* [XXIII⁵], p. 49, refers to H. Jackson, *JPhilol*, XIII (1885), 250ff., and to J. Burnet, *Greek Philosophy* (London, 1914), I, 242, for his view that "the theory must be Plato's own." This conception probably is too dogmatic, however, and it also remains unclear in what sense Plato can both develop and then attack "his own theory."

29. In his translation, Schleiermacher (II/1, 214f., 503) "has turned the white into red everywhere, in order to be rid of the un-German whiteness." / On what follows in our text (on 157D 8) it may be noted that Ludwig Heindorf (*Specimen coniecturarum in Platonem*, Halle, 1789) remarked: "Mira haec ἀγαθὸν καὶ κακόν, *quum supra non nisi formas rerum in sensus cadentes adhibuerit ut* μέγα, βαρύ, θερμόν, λευκόν. . . ." Ever since, these terms have been subject to extensive criticism. They have been correctly understood by Bonitz (p. 90), by Apelt (see the note on this passage in his annotated edition of the *Theaetetus*, 4th edn., Leipzig, 1944), and by Cornford (*Theory of Knowledge*, p. 51), among others. Plato has the terms emerge beside each other similarly to the "measuring" in 154B. The context here does not seem to make it clear, however, whether the words are to be regarded as substantives (the good and the beautiful), as Schleiermacher, Bonitz, and Diès regard them, or as adjectives, as Apelt does. Could Plato have intended this ambiguity? Cornford, p. 51, is correct.

30. Bonitz (by combining I 2a and 2b, and separating them from I 2c) does not divide Part I into two parts as we have done, but into three parts (see his p. 52)—thus contradicting the Platonic metaphor of the delivery (I 1) and the examination (I 2) of the newborn infant. One should reject Bonitz' arrangement, then, and for the same reason reject the three-part structure of Schmidt (*Kritischer Kommentar*, p. 408), who separates Part I into (1) presentation, (2) proof, and (3) refutation of the doctrine, and places the break between (1) and

(2) in 154A. But this difference, after all, is not very important. It is much worse to relate Parts I 2a and 2b to I 1, and say that something altogether different begins in I 2c—as Apelt does (see his Introduction [XXIII²⁹], p. 17).

31. This should not be understood simply in a biographical sense either, as Cornford (*Theory of Knowledge*, p. 60) seems to understand it when he says that Theodoros "is here drawn into the discussion, to mark that the first objection will be made against his personal friend, Protagoras."

32. It is not even necessary to regard this—as some interpreters do (e.g., Natorp, *Ideenlehre*, pp. 104f.)—as a parody of misplaced attacks on Protagoras. The baboon is a foil for the God who has for Plato (as will soon be evident) a very serious, systematic meaning. Moreover, Plato admonishes the reader not to consider this polemic easily disposed of—an appropriate warning regardless of whether or not such misplaced attacks, certainly possible, had actually occurred. Yet, as usual in Plato, this would not explain the admonition sufficiently.

33. Campbell pointed out the relationship between *Theaetetus* 168A and the passage about the μισόλογοι in *Phaedo* 89D–90D.

34. The difference in levels, which is also stressed by Wilamowitz (I, 515 = I², 520), is obvious. But it is not fitting to reduce this difference to the levels of "instructor" and "researcher" since a dialogue consists of instructive research and searching instruction. Also, it is not quite understandable why Socrates should now, according to Wilamowitz, "for the refutation draw upon new principles, i.e., erudition." If this refers to the discussion about the Herakleiteans and the Protagoreans, we should remember (as Wilamowitz himself mentions) that such a discussion had already begun in the conversation with Theaitetos, and is therefore not especially characteristic of the part in which Theodoros speaks. And is it possible to speak of "erudition" or a "scientific character" just because philosophical tendencies defined by name are used? Surely, Zeller's conducting research into the historical relation between Herakleitos and Protagoras is an altogether different matter from Plato's Socrates' disputing in an argument and creating a hostile front united in opposition to himself. / Cf. the scholium to 168c.

35. The "once more" is not expressed in 170D 1; however, the development of thought probably requires a pause here. The passage 170D–171D seems to express in a different way what 169E–170c had already stated.

36. R. G. Hoerber, in his review—see *CP*, LXII (1967), 54ff.—of *Plato 2*, drew my attention to an error in my interpretation of the *Laches*. The word *episteme* does not occur for the first time in the *Laches* at 184E 8. Thus, the text of *Plato 2*, p. 40, ll. 2ff., should be corrected in the following way: "Instead, Socrates pulls the discussion up to his

own level, where decision is not a matter of majority vote but is attained through *episteme*. Here (184E 8) *episteme* is used, for the first time, in the Socratic sense that true knowledge or genuine understanding brings about the decision, whereas Laches and Nikias, the two officers, militarists, had previously understood ἐπιστήμη and ἐπίστασ-θαι as merely professional and technical skill (182c 7, 184B 4, 184c 1 and 3). To emphasize the new element . . ." Thus, Hoerber's criticism in pointing to my oversight has led me to a new insight. / In regard to Hoerber's criticism of my interpretation of the words *xenos* and *hetairos* (*Meno* 90B, 92D), the following may be said. The word *xenos* clearly indicates that Menon is staying with Anytos as his guest. *Hetairos*, it is true, does not imply the fact, but it shows the background by which Anytos and Menon are *xenoi:* Anytos is or was a friend of Menon's father.

37. For a critique of Socrates' conclusions, see Natorp, *Ideenlehre*, p. 106. / Cornford's view (*Theory of Knowledge*, p. 80) is different: "Socrates' last words probably do not mean that Protagoras would, in Plato's opinion, have had any valid answer to make."

38. Theodor Bergk, *Fünf Abhandlungen zur Geschichte der griechischen Philosophie und Astronomie* (Leipzig, 1883), p. 11, suspected—and Schleiermacher (II/1, 182, 509) had already alluded to something similar—that these words reflect Plato's personal experiences. Erwin Rohde (*Kleine Schriften*, Tübingen and Leipzig, 1901, I, 317) also favors this hypothesis, and Natorp (*Ideenlehre*, pp. 92f.) is not very far removed either. I oppose everywhere this kind of interpretation that searches for relations outside of the dialogues themselves instead of within them. Here it is quite clear that Socrates speaks of his own experience. Plato also speaks about himself—on a completely different level of reality, apart from the biographical one. Bruns (*Porträt*, pp. 296ff.) argues forcefully against Bergk and his followers, but without doing justice to the philosophical significance of the digression.

39. Werner Jaeger (in *Aristotle*, pp. 13ff., and in "Über Ursprung und Kreislauf des philosophischen Lebensideals," *Scripta minora*, Rome, 1960, pp. 352f.) probably exaggerates the contrast between Socrates the pure scholar estranged from the world, and Socrates of the earlier dialogues. Even here in the *Theaetetus*, the fate and appearance of Socrates still stand out clearly, although now, of course, those "theoretical" traits have become his own. τᾶς τε γᾶς ὑπένερθε at least does not refer to physics only, but refers as well to Hades and to the fate of the soul. The myth of the *Phaedo*, moreover, shows the two united. Cf. Emma Edelstein, *Xenophontisches und platonisches Bild des Sokrates* (Berlin, 1935), pp. 55ff.

40. Here one should recall the discussion that arose in connection with Cornford's commentary [XXIII⁵]: whether references to the "theory of Forms" are or are not present in the *Theaetetus*. Richard Robinson,

"Forms and Error in Plato's *Theaetetus*," *PR*, LIX (1950), 3ff., has denied such references, as has Taylor (*Plato*, p. 348), who seems to sense nothing of the world of true being in the *Theaetetus*. Robinson is rightly opposed by R. Hackforth, "Platonic Forms in the *Theaetetus*," *CQ*, n.s., VII (1957), 53ff.; Winifred F. Hicken, "Knowledge and Forms in Plato's *Theaetetus*," *JHS*, LXXVII (1957), 48ff.; and Allen, pp. 185ff. Still, the expression "theory of Forms" shifts everything into the realm of doctrine. Setting out on this level of the discussion, one would have to object that there can be no "Form of injustice-itself." Plato surely wanted to pose this question to the reader.

41. Cf. Bruns, *Porträt*, p. 301; Festugière, *Contemplation*, pp. 381ff.

42. Lewis Campbell pointed out earlier that ἑλκύσῃ ἄνω in *Theaetetus* 175B is reminiscent of this episode in the *Republic*.

43. ὁμοίωσις θεῷ κατὰ δυνατόν (*Theaetetus*); εἰς ὅσον δυνατὸν ἀνθρώπῳ ὁμοιοῦσθαι θεῷ (*Republic*). / Cf. Hubert Merki, O.S.B., Ὁμοίωσις θεῷ: *Von der platonischen Angleichung . . . bei Gregor von Nyssa* (Fribourg, 1952), and the review by W. Jaeger in *Gnomon*, XXVII (1955), 573ff.

44. Apart from the obvious fact that the reply of Theodoros makes the digression possible, it is not quite easy to say what the nature is of the λόγος ἐκ λόγου μείζων ἐξ ἐλάττονος in 172B 8. According to Socrates, it is not in any event the digression that is first brought on by σχολὴν ἄγομεν. To Campbell it is about "the question of Justice and Injustice." Yet, instead of this discussion, the "episode" or digression appears. In a very special manner, however, does not the digression fulfill just what was intended for the *logos*? Does not Plato—in a certain characteristic and ironic manner—nevertheless aim, through λόγος μείζων, at that episode which "had not really been the goal"? Cf. Cornford, *Theory of Knowledge* [XXIII⁵], p. 82; H. Bischoff, "Die drei Λόγοι des *Theaitet*," *Hermes*, LXXIV (1939), 104ff.

45. Basically, I follow Bonitz (p. 73) who designates the section under discussion as an "episode" and defends this interpretation against others. In tracing the motives that connect this episode or digression to the rest of the dialogue, I go beyond Bonitz, however, and concur with those against whom he disputes. Susemihl is quite correct in stating that Plato cannot disregard the relativity of the just, while Bonitz is correct in stating that Plato does not mention the connection by a single word. Yet, it is not by chance that Plato leaves this unheard-of thesis without any criticism, and that just then the digression occurs in which that thesis is in fact overcome.

46. Cf. de Vries, pp. 340ff.

47. Schleiermacher, II/1, 180: "Indeed, this digression seems to be placed purposely near the beginning, so that at least the attentive reader has a light by which he will be able to find his way in the twisted labyrinth of the conversation." Yet Diès (*Théétète, Budé* edi-

tion, p. 149) points out that the digression appears almost in the middle of the whole dialogue. Schleiermacher's "near the beginning" shows how without careful checking the precise location may be easily overlooked.

48. Whether or not this digression has an added polemical purpose—as Rohde, *Kleine Schriften* [XXIII³⁸], I, 256ff., attempts to prove, particularly for the passage on the twenty-five ancestors of Herakles—does not seem significant when held against the importance of the internal artistic and systematical relations. (So it always is in Plato.) And Rohde has apparently carried his interpretation too far (see esp. pp. 268ff.) for the sake of his thesis that in 174D *et seq.* definite eulogies were intended for a definite king. Nevertheless, Rohde (p. 318) has refuted Bergk, who mistakenly regarded this, too, as an attack upon Isokrates. One should also remember that Rohde's chronology has endured.

49. See also Diès' edition, p. 216; Cornford, p. 97.

50. In 183B 4 Burnet and Diès print οὐδ' οὕτως, according to Codex *W*. This, however, would only repeat what has already been stated in 183A 9 − B 1. Thus, Cornford (p. 100, n. 2) is correct. οὐδ' ὅπως is the ultimate intensification possible. To this, however, Cornford adds that "οὐδ' ὅπως (*BT*) is not Greek for 'No-how.'" But if οὐδ' ὅπωσ(τι)οῦν is Greek, then how can οὐδ' ὅπως be "not Greek"? Plato chooses (one could say: coins) the shortest expression possible. / Probably it is impossible to decide with any degree of certainty whether in what follows, Plato wrote εἰ μὴ ἄρα τὸ οὐδ' ὅπως μάλιστ' ἂν αὐτοῖς ἁρμόττοι (thus *W*) or εἰ μὴ ἄρα τὸ οὐδ' ὅπως. μάλιστα δ' οὕτως ἂν αὐτοῖς ἁρμόττοι (thus *BT*). The second version, which repeats οὕτως, is perhaps even more witty.

51. On this see E. Hoffmann, *Die Sprache und die archaische Logik* (Heidelberger Abhandlungen zur Philosophie und ihrer Geschichte, III, Tübingen, 1925), pp. 48f.; *Plato 2*, p. 199.

52. Cf. Stoelzel, *Erkenntnisproblem bei Platon* [XXIII²⁶], pp. 71, 89.

53. Wilamowitz (I, 510, 518 = I², 515, 523) misconstrues this in his hypothesis concerning the sudden discontinuation of the *Theaetetus*. "This discontinuation has its external reason, which we know. Otherwise it would be inexcusable."

54. Were that *all* we have learned, then indeed this final section would merely be "an important corollary," as W. J. Alexander ("The Aim and Results . . ." [XXIII²³], p. 173) labels it. Natorp (*Ideenlehre*, p. 108) discovers here "in the form of a mere postscript the central point of the whole discussion." Yet, the importance that this final section does in fact have explains why Stoelzel (p. 24) divides the first major part of the dialogue into only two sections: (1) 151E–183B and (2) 183C–187B. Still, he exaggerates a correct thought.

55. Zeller (p. 590) regards this discussion about error as an apagogic

proof against the identification of ἐπιστήμη and δόξα. Bonitz (pp. 86f.) misses any reference to such apagoge in Plato's work and does not consider it proper to burden the dialogue with this train of thought, in itself justified. This view is not without some semblance of truth. Nevertheless, within Part II 1, we will encounter a movement that renders the discussion about error more than what Bonitz calls a "mere question related to the definition put forth." For I doubt precisely that on which Zeller and Bonitz agree: that Plato's real concern is the refutation of the definition. If this refutation, however, is only the form in which the relation of δόξα and ἐπιστήμη is clarified, then one cannot doubt that much of this clarification is contained in Part II 1. Also see Stoelzel, p. 113.

56. For this reason, no real objection should be raised against the division made by Bonitz (pp. 59ff.), who distinguishes three subsections in all. It is misleading, however, to assume that parts *a*, *b*, and *c* under section *A* mean something completely different from parts *a*, *b*, and *c* under section *B*—i.e., three parallel attempts under *A*, and three differently directed steps in the fourth attempt under *B*. Therefore, it is clearer to arrange the five attempts beside each other.

57. The *Euthydemus* shows that the polemic against Parmenides here, as well as later on, in the *Theaetetus* is directed especially against the kind of eristic that makes use of the Parmenidean antitheses. On this, Stoelzel (pp. 85ff.) is correct, although here too, little as we need to restrict ourselves to the name Antisthenes, we should not overestimate Plato's polemic against outsiders.

58. Stressing the ὄν four times sharply would be strange, if its purpose were not to call attention to the fact that sensations, strictly taken, really do not lead to the ὄντα.

59. Neither Burnet, Diès, nor Cornford seems to have correctly understood the difficult passage 190c 8 *et seq*. The starting point should be 189E 1–2. There the main division appears as (*1*) ἤτοι ἀμφότερα and (*2*) ἢ τὸ ἕτερον, with subdivisions (*a*) ἤτοι ἅμα and (*b*) ἢ ἐν μέρει. (To attribute these words to Theaitetos, as though they were an exposition of what had been stated before, will be shown to be a mistake.) Section *1* is then carried out to 190D 6; section *2* is carried out to 190D 10; and the words in 190D 11 serve as a summary. Section *1* seems to be further divided into parts *a* and *b*, *a* being the part up to 190c 8, and then *b* beginning with ἐατέον δὲ καί σοι τὸ ῥῆμα ἐπὶ τῶν ἐν μέρει. "You must, however, agree also with the thesis of the sequence." (According to the meaning, καί does not belong to σοί, but to τῶν ἐν μέρει.) In part *b*, too, the refutation is carried out similarly to that in part *a*: λέγω γὰρ αὖ[το] τῇδε (according to Schleiermacher), or τό[τη]δε at the utmost (according to Ast). The words ἐπὶ τῶν ἐν μέρει are preserved only in the Bodleian manuscript. They are no less appropriate since the same manuscript adds the gloss ἐπειδὴ τὸ ῥῆμα

. . . ταὐτόν ἐστιν. The interpretation of ἐν μέρει seems to me irrefutable, and from this position one should attack the interpretation of Hoffmann (*Die Sprache* . . . [XXIII⁵¹], pp. 45ff.) who understands by τὰ ἐν μέρει the "things of the world of senses." This goes against the Greek language in general, and in particular against the relation to 189ε 3 shown here. Does anything still remain of the polemical relation to Megarian logic which Hoffmann affirms? (Cf. Campbell's Introduction to the *Theaetetus* [XXIII²⁸], p. xxxvii.) Such a relation should then be discovered at least in part *a* also.

60. On the metaphor, see J. Ortega y Gasset, "Las dos grandes metáforas," *El Espectador* (Madrid), IV (1925), 180ff. The metaphor of the wax—it is not a tablet but a mass (like dough), capable of being formed—has been considered by Dümmler and Joël (and most recently by von Fritz, in *Hermes*, LXII [1927], 481) to be an invention of Antisthenes, and therefore Plato's fourth attempt at defining error is considered to be a mocking of Antisthenes. Stoelzel refutes this in *Erkenntnisproblem bei Platon* [XXIII²⁶], pp. 99ff. / Ernst Hoffmann, in his penetrating essay "Sokrates," *Jahresberichte des Philol. Vereins zu Berlin*, XLVII (1921), 56ff., has traced the wax image back to Demokritos. Against this view there is much to be said. (1) First of all, it is generally doubtful whether Demokritos used the picture. Theophrastus' *De sensu* 51 (*Doxogr.*, p. 514; *Vorsokr.* 68 [55] A 135) has οἷον εἰ ἐκμάξειας εἰς σκληρόν, not εἰς κηρόν—a fact surely to be considered even though the change would be only slight. (Cf. Plutarch, *Moralia* 15ᴅ.) Demokritos is concerned with making us visualize how the perceptual picture imprints itself upon the air. Thus, by means of a simile (παραβάλλων), yet nevertheless quite generally, he may have alluded to the imprinting on something "solid." The σκληρόν has a part in Demokritos' explanation of the sense phenomena. In *De sensu* 62, it is identified with the πυκνόν. In *De sensu* 73, it is contrasted with ψαθυρὸν καὶ εὔθρυπτον. And the second sentence of *De sensu* 51, the passage in question, begins δεῖ γὰρ ἔχειν πυκνότητα καὶ μὴ θρύπτεσθαι τὸ τυπούμενον (as a criticism by Theophrastus but with Demokritean overtones). Thus, the simile (καθάπερ κηρός) which follows could have originated with Theophrastus and could differ substantially from that of Demokritos, whose exact wording escapes us. (2) In the second place, it is not evident from Plato's words that he derived the image from elsewhere. (Stoelzel saw this correctly.) The somewhat belittling tone in *Theaetetus* 197ᴅ (οὐδ' οἶδ' ὅτι πλάσμα) is characteristic of the manner in which Plato's Socrates treats his sudden thoughts wherever they occur. Similarly, φασίν in 194ᴄ (to which Dümmler, *Antisthenica* [XXIII²⁸], p. 46, referred) must be understood to mean ". . . say those who go along with my fairy-tale-like image." This refers not to what preceded but to what is coming. Had Plato wanted to designate this image as a derived one, we

would expect him to have expressed this at the beginning. In 191c, however, nothing of the kind is found. (*3*) The third and most important consideration is that even if Hoffmann's hypothesis were accepted as to the first and second points, it still remains certain that Plato's simile is completely different from anything Demokritos could possibly have intended. Demokritos does not have the ἔμφασις originate in the eye. Rather, from the eye and from the object he has an ἀπορροή emanate then to be pressed and formed between them. As a simile for this material process, he chooses a material but more concrete process—perhaps that of the imprinting on wax, or perhaps only that of the imprinting on something "solid." Plato's concern is to make us able to visualize not only perception, but also—and particularly—reminiscence, oblivion, and error. These phenomena in *Theaetetus* 191c *et seq.* are not in any event pictured as materialistic processes (where is this mentioned by a single word?). Rather, Plato makes the spiritual evident by means of a material image. Even if the similes employed here and previously were the same, the subject of the comparison is for Plato very different. Thus, it also becomes evident that Aristotle, in *De anima* 424ᵃ 17, follows Plato's *Theaetetus* (as Bonitz and Diès assume) rather than Demokritos (as Hoffmann claims). (*4*) It is clear that at least in the image, there is nothing to support the claim that Plato intended to strike at any outside doctrine —least of all at what Hoffmann calls "pure materialism." An examination of the over-all structure of the dialogue demonstrates this. / Hoffmann's hypothesis has nevertheless become the basis for further combinations; see M. Warburg, *Zwei Fragen zum "Kratylos"* (Neue philologische Untersuchungen, V, Berlin, 1929), pp. 32ff.

61. In the older literature, note K. F. Hermann's "De arte combinatoria Platonis," and also see the much more recent article by W. Deicke, "Platon, *Theaetet* 192c 10," *Phronesis*, IX (1964), 136ff.

62. 197c 7: δύναμιν . . . αὐτῷ . . . παραγεγονέναι . . . λαβεῖν κα σχεῖν ἐπειδὰν βούληται. Cf. Bonitz, p. 62, n. 18; A. E. Taylor, *Philosophical Studies* (London, 1932), p. 252.

63. According to Hoffmann, *Die Sprache* . . . [XXIII⁵¹], pp. 42ff., the aviary image, like the mass of wax (see n. 60, above), is borrowed. His arguments for tracing the aviary image back to Antisthenes are much weaker, evidently, for Hoffmann must first of all reinterpret Plato's text (the "birds" supposedly are "essentially words") in order to hit at all on Antisthenes, the "verbalist." Then this question comes up. Is it really true that anyone is attacked in the metaphor of the aviary? The metaphor justifies one type of error and therefore of knowledge, while a higher form (the highest, the one really sought after) is thus not justified and is therefore above this justification. This is the meaning. And nothing is more plausible than that the image of the aviary as well as that of the wax mass originated in

Plato's own imagination—not as a means of attacking certain philosophic theorems, but as a way to picture different forms of error and thereby clarify different stages of the road to knowledge.

64. It is the opinion of Bonitz and Hoffmann, for example, that the criticism here in the fifth attempt, as also in the fourth, destroys what had been stated previously, and that thus the thesis allegedly overcome must consequently become a hostile thesis. This is rightly opposed by Stoelzel (*Erkenntnisproblem*, pp. 100, 110) who goes too far in the other direction, however, and fails to recognize that in the series of attempts, the criticism leads each time to a higher stage.

65. The relationship between Parts II 1 and II 2 probably belongs to what in *Plato* 1, p. 150, is termed the "ironic shift of balance in a work of art."

66. Cf. *DGrA*, I, 35.

67. Thus Bonitz, Zeller, Joël, Stoelzel, von Fritz, Oehler. H. Diels, *Elementum: eine Vorarbeit zum griechischen und lateinischen Thesaurus* (Leipzig, 1899), p. 19, advises us to practice resignation. His advice can be expressed still more fundamentally, however.

68. Aristotle, *Metaphysics* 1043b 25: ὅτι οὐκ ἔστι τὸ τί ἐστιν ὁρίσασθαι. On the Cynics' theory of knowledge, see Zeller, pp. 292ff. Note that Steinhart (III, 204, n. 20), using the same argument stated in our text, had earlier opposed attributing the definition to Antisthenes.

69. Otto Apelt, in the Notes to his translation of the *Theaetetus* (4th edn., Leipzig, 1944), p. 182, correctly refers to the *Meno* and the *Symposium*. His interpretation is too superficial, however, in claiming that in the *Theaetetus* Plato rejects the previously recognized definition. Plato's final concern is not with definitions, nor simply with the antithesis of agreement and rejection. / How difficult it is to translate *logos* and *logoi* into a modern language is evident, for example, from the discussion of R. C. Cross, "Logos and Forms in Plato," *Mind*, n.s., LXIII (1954), 433ff. Cross opposes Jowett's "thought" and "world of mind," and selects "statement" for his own translation besides admitting Cornford's "discourse." But does not every one of these terms suffer from a lack either of sharpness or of depth? / Cf. Diès, *Théétète* [XXIII²³], p. 145.

70. I use this term following Wittgenstein's "logical atomism." On this and in general the question here discussed, see Hans Meyerhoff, "Socrates' 'Dream' in the *Theaetetus*," *CQ*, LII (1958), 131ff.

71. See Zeller, 299ff.; K. von Fritz, in *Hermes*, LXII (1927), 462ff.; Diès, *Théétète*, p. 153; Cornford's edition [XXIII⁵], p. 144.

72. As to the further discussion of this by Aristotle and Sextus Empiricus, see Diès, p. 146. Aristotle, in *Physics* I 1 184b 10, points out the contrast of ὄνομα and λόγος by using the circle as an example somewhat as Plato uses it in *Letter VII* 342B.

73. The discussion in 204A–205A arrives at an identification of πάντα =

πᾶν = ὅλον. But Theaitetos "fights like a man" against this identification—and the whole deduction seems to be meaningful only if the reader puts up an even better fight. Something that lacks something is neither ὅλον nor πᾶν, but this does not entail the freedom to exchange one concept for the other. See Aristotle, *Metaphysics* V 26 1024ᵃ 1: ἔτι τοῦ ποσοῦ ἔχοντος ἀρχὴν καὶ μέσον καὶ ἔσχατον, ὅσων μὲν μὴ ποιεῖ ἡ θέσις διαφοράν, πᾶν λέγεται, ὅσων δὲ ποιεῖ, ὅλον.

74. No one can be prevented from holding the view that Plato had originally devised an aporetic dialogue of definition without the digression. Yet if on this basis one assumes a revision, i.e., the insertion of the digression at some later time (thus A. Chiappelli, in *AfGP*, XVII, 1904, 320ff.; cf. Diès, *Platon*, pp. 317ff., for the opposed view), then one may be disregarding the fact that Parts II and III of the dialogue obtain their essential meaning only by being connected to that "digression."

75. This is approximately the view of Schleiermacher, II/1, 177. / As one again and again recognizes the perfect structure of the *Theaetetus*, it is increasingly difficult to understand how Wilamowitz (I, 510 = I², 515) is able to speak of "false proportion" and "negligence," or how he can conjecture that the dialogue was concluded hurriedly before Plato had to embark on his journey to Syracuse. Against that opinion, see also Diès, *Théétète*, pp. 148f. Diès' own observation that the digression about the philosopher divides the dialogue into two almost equal parts deserves notice. Whether or not Plato really intended "to balance the two areas of the text," although the two parts bear no recognizable conformity to each other, is questionable. / If one wishes to pursue the error in Natorp's analysis, which as always is excellent in its manner, one must begin with the fact that for Natorp (*Ideenlehre*, p. 113), the positive analysis concludes with the end of the first part of the dialogue. / Leisegang's misunderstanding of the *Theaetetus* is revealed when he says (col. 2490) that "the dialogical form has been forced upon the thought like a garment that no longer fits."

xxiv: *Parmenides*

RECENT EDITIONS AND TRANSLATIONS: O. Apelt, PhB 83 (1919); A. Diès, *Platon Budé*, VIII/1 (1923); A. E. Taylor (London, 1934); F. M. Cornford (London, 1939); J. Moreau (in L. Robin, *Platon Oeuvres Complètes*, Paris, 1940–42); E. Turolla (Milan, 1942); F. Acri and M. F. Sciacca (2d edn., Naples, 1942).

RECENT INTERPRETATIONS: D. S. Mackay, *Mind in the "Parmenides"* (Los Angeles, 1924); J. Wahl, *Étude sur le "Parménide"* (Paris, 1926); Stenzel, *Metaphysik*, pp. 125ff.; G. Calogero, *Studi sull' eleatismo* (Rome, 1932), ch. 5; Shorey, pp. 287ff.; K. Riezler, *Parmenides* (Frankfurt a. M., 1934); A. E. Taylor, *Philosophical Studies* (London, 1932), ch. 2; M. Wundt, *Platons "Parmenides"* (Stuttgart and Berlin, 1935); W. F. R. Hardie, *A Study in Plato* (Oxford, 1936), pp. 80ff.; A. Speiser, *Ein Parmenideskommentar* (Leipzig, 1937); E. Paci, *Il significato del "Parmenide"* (Messina, 1938); G. Ryle, in *Mind*, n.s., XLVIII (1939), 129ff. (reprinted in Allen, pp. 97ff.); R. Robinson, "Plato's *Parmenides*," *CP*, XXXVII (1942), 51ff., 159ff.; R. Scoon, "Plato's *Parmenides*," *Mind*, n.s., LI (1942), 115ff.; Chung-Hwan Chen, in *CQ*, XXXVIII (1944), 101ff.; J. Moreau, "Sur la signification du *Parménide*," *Revue Philosophique*, CXXXIV (1944), 97ff.; M. Beck, in *JHistId*, VIII (1947), 232ff.; E. Karlin, "The Method of Ambiguity," *New Scholast*, XXI (1947), 154ff.; Kucharski, pp. 285ff., 335ff., 382; K. Reidemeister, *Das exakte Denken der Griechen* (Hamburg, 1949), ch. 5; A. Speiser, "On Plato's *Parmenides*," *Proc. 10th International Cong. Philos.*, Vol. I, Fasc. 2 (Amsterdam, 1949), pp. 1088ff.; de Vries, pp. 88ff., 146ff.; G. Colli, *Il "Parmenide" platonico* (Pisa, 1950); G. Huber, *Platons dialektische Ideenlehre nach dem zweiten Teil des "Parmenides"* (Vienna, 1951); L. Lugarini, "L'unità dell' idea nel *Parmenide*," *Acme*, IV (1951), 347ff.; J. Moreau, *Réalisme et idéalisme chez Platon* (Paris, 1951), pp. 100ff.; Robinson, *Dialectic*, ch. 13; A. L. Peck, "Plato's *Parmenides*," *CQ*, n.s., III (1953), 126ff.; IV (1954), 31ff.; R. Schaerer, in *RevInPh*, IX (1955), 197ff.; A. Capizzi, "L'uno e i molti nel pensiero di Platone," *Giorn. di Metafisica*, XI (1956), 86ff.; Vanhoutte, pp. 86ff., 103ff.; K. F. Johansen, "The One and the Many," *Classica et Mediaevalia*, XVIII (1957), 1ff.; Robin, *Rapports*, pp. 36ff., 89ff., 122ff.; W. F. Lynch, *An Approach to the Metaphysics of Plato through the "Parmenides"* (Georgetown University, 1959), ch. 13; W. G. Runciman, "Plato's *Parmenides*," *Harvard Studies in Classical Philology*, LXIV (1959), 89ff. (reprinted in Allen, pp. 149ff.); Gauss, III/1, ch. 3; E. A. Wyller, *Platons "Parmenides"* (Oslo, 1960); R. S. Brumbaugh, *Plato on the One* (New Haven, 1961); K. H. Volkmann-Schluck, "Das Wesen der Idee in Platos *Parmenides*," *Philosophisches Jahrbuch*, LXIX (1961), 34ff.; W. G. Runciman, *Plato's Later Epistemology* (Cambridge, 1962), pp. 1ff.; J. Moreau, "Eidos y noema en Platón," *Actas del II Congreso español de estudios clásicos* (Madrid, 1964), 331ff.; E. A. Wyller, "La philosophie de l'instant chez Platon ou la troisième hypothèse du *Parménide*," *Revue de Synthèse*, LXXXV (1964), 9ff.; Lesky, pp. 531f.

ADDITIONAL BIBLIOGRAPHY: Shorey, pp. 583f.; Geffcken, Notes, pp. 106f.; Leisegang, cols. 2479ff.; Rosenmeyer, pp. 185f.; Cherniss, *Lustrum*, pp. 118ff.

1. The literature about the *Parmenides* is vast—so vast and varied that a critical history of the interpretations would be of value for understanding the dialogue itself. (See G. Calogero, *Studi sull'eleatismo*, Rome, 1932, p. 254.) Such a history would have to go from Xenokrates, Speusippos, and Aristotle's *Metaphysics* on up to the present time. It would also have to consider such judgments about the *Parmenides* as these: "the most puzzling of all Plato's works" (Gomperz), "a bewildering and depressing work" (Robinson), "the most mysterious Platonic dialogue" (Calogero).

2. I shall more or less leave aside the much discussed question of whether the *Parmenides* contains a polemic against the Megarians (*"die megarische Ideenlehre," "l'Eleatismo Megarico"*). Recently Calogero (*Studi*, pp. 223ff.) has written in favor of this thesis; against it are A. E. Taylor, *Philosophical Studies* [XXIII⁶²], pp. 52ff., and F. M. Cornford, *Plato and Parmenides: Parmenides' "Way of Truth" and Plato's "Parmenides"* (London, 1939), pp. 100ff. I am convinced that it is of no real help to assume such a polemic if this merely is a way of projecting outside the Platonic dialogue those problems that remain difficult to resolve from within. Otto Apelt (in *Untersuchungen über den "Parmenides,"* Weimar, 1879, pp. 40ff., and also in the Introduction to his translation of the *Parmenides*, Leipzig, 1919, p. 23) resorts to the same polemic hypothesis where he is unable to make the two halves of the dialogue truly relate. Calogero treats only the dialectical part of the dialogue. Nevertheless, as Jean Wahl, *Étude sur le "Parménide"* (Paris, 1926), p. 8, states correctly: "Any interpretation of the dialogue that leaves the two parts separate will not be able to satisfy us."

3. Proklos, *In Platonis Parmenidem Commentarium*, ed. V. Cousin (*Procli Philosophi Platonici Opera Inedita*, Paris, 1864), col. 660. This is a transformation of the historical construction of the two philosophical διαδοχαί, as it appears in Diogenes Laërtius, Prooemium 13.

4. Strabon (XIII 645) considers Anaxagoras the only "well-known man" from this city.

5. To indicate in a preliminary manner the possible influence of Anaxagoras here, we may point to R. D. Archer-Hind's Introduction to *The "Timaeus" of Plato* (London, 1888), p. 12: "The One of Parmenides and the Many of Heraclitus must be united in the Mind of Anaxagoras: that is to say, unity and plurality must be shown as two necessary and inseparable modes of soul's existence, before a philosophy can arise that is indeed worthy of the name." Also see Wahl, *Étude*, p. 54: "The doctrine of Anaxagoras . . . was to contribute to developing the Socratic idea of the Νοῦς and, on the other hand, the idea of communion and the negation of the χωρίς."

6. Concerning this *"narration à cascades,"* see Diès' *Parménide* (*Platon Budé*, VIII/1, 1923), p. 7. Because of this difference in technique and

form, Wilamowitz (II, 228f.) places the *Theaetetus* after the *Parmenides*. For a correct opinion, see Cornford, *Plato and Parmenides*, p. 63.

7. It is worth mentioning that the author of the *Alcibiades Major* (119A) not only knows the name of the father (Πυθόδωρος ὁ Ἰσολόχου—cf. Thucydides III 115 2, and J. Kirchner, *Prosopographia Attica*, Berlin, 1901–3, II, 12399), but also makes more definite comments about the discipleship with Zeno. (See Kirchner, I, 7827: Καλλίας ὁ Καλλιάδου.) It would be too much, however, to claim that Plato was able to introduce Pythodoros so easily in the *Parmenides* because he had already provided more precise information about the same person in the *Alcibiades*. Nonetheless, one can claim the abundant reports in the *Alcibiades* as support for an early dating of the dialogue, a time at which these matters would still be alive. To attribute the reports to the painstaking learnedness of a later author seems much less probable (contra Wilamowitz, II, 222: "One cannot judge what this fact meant to the later author").

8. Proklos, *In Parm. Comm.*, Cousin edn. [XXIV³], col. 662.

9. See A. E. Taylor, *The "Parmenides" of Plato* (Oxford, 1934), pp. 124ff. The authenticity of this encounter does not seem as overwhelmingly plausible to me as it apparently does to Taylor. Also see his *Plato*, p. 352; *Philosophical Studies* [XXIII⁶²], pp. 38f.

10. In favor of this thesis is M. Wundt, *Platons "Parmenides"* (Stuttgart and Berlin, 1935), p. 5—and see the reference there to his *Geschichte der griechischen Ethik* (Jena, 1911), II, 90. Also in favor are Singer (p. 187), and Hildebrandt (*Platon*, p. 313 = 2d edn., pp. 290f.). Further, see R. Klibansky, "Ein Proklos-Fund und seine Bedeutung," *SBHeidelb*, 1928/29, p. 8, n. 4, and the reference there to E. Hoffmann's article in the (*Berliner*) *Philologische Wochenschrift*, XLIV (1924), p. 519. / Nowhere do I find a discussion of reasons why Plato made this Aristotle—who historically is a completely different person—a participant in the discourse.

11. It is generally accepted that the story of the theft of Zeno's treatise (128D) contains hardly any historical truth. Apelt—see his Introduction [XXIV²], p. 37—cleverly interpreted the story by postulating for Zeno and his text Plato and an earlier version of the dialogue. This remains a guessing game that cannot be resolved either way. See Cornford, *Plato and Parmenides* [XXIV²], p. 67, n. 1. For a Neoplatonic interpretation, see Proklos, *In Parm. Comm.*, col. 718.

12. Isokrates, *On Helen* X 3. / Regarding Zeno, Cornford's interpretation (p. 67) is probably too simple and undialectical: "Plato seems to have thought of [Zeno] as a mere Sophist." According to A. Speiser, *Ein Parmenideskommentar* (Leipzig, 1937), p. 11, "The young Socrates treats Zeno's investigations in a much too superficial manner." Quite the contrary, Socrates gives them their proper rank.

13. Natorp (*Ideenlehre*, p. 222 = 2d edn., p. 228) is one-sided when he

bases Plato's participation in the Eleatic doctrine "only on the method, the determination of fundamental concepts, and the working with them." Rather, Parmenides is venerable to Plato as the discoverer of the reality of being; this is sufficiently shown in the *Theaetetus* (180E *et seq.*, 183E). Moreover, Natorp is mistaken in believing that Zeno in his treatise had not seriously intended to defend Parmenides' thesis, but rather had plainly abandoned it. On the contrary, Zeno subordinates his own writing to that of Parmenides (τό γ' ἀληθές, *Parmenides* 128c 6).

14. Natorp (*Ideenlehre*, pp. 219ff. = 2d edn., pp. 225ff.) strangely misinterpreted the relationship of the persons, seeing Socrates "as a youth on the wrong path." Rather, young Socrates is on the proper path, as Parmenides expressly declares. Natorp also says "young Socrates defends the mistaken opinion that takes ideas as things." On the contrary, Socrates struggles to maintain his own view against Parmenides' arguments, which are based on that false opinion. And according to Natorp, "The two Eleatics stand for Plato here." Instead, Plato remains above or beyond the discussion that takes place between the Socrates and the Eleatic within him.

15. Cf. Natorp, *Ideenlehre*, p. 228 = 2d edn., pp. 234ff.

16. See Proklos, *In Parm. Comm.*, col. 879: αὕτη ἡ ζήτησις ὑπέθετο τὸ εἶδος ἐν τοῖς μετέχουσιν εἶναι καὶ ὁμοταγὲς αὐτοῖς, and col. 906: μήτε ὁμοταγῆ εἶναι τὰ εἴδη τοῖς τῆδε.

17. Cf. R. Wiggers, "Die grosse Natur: Ein Beitrag zur Platonforschung," in *Natalicium Johannes Geffcken gewidmet* (Heidelberg, 1931), pp. 176ff.

18. See G. Vlastos, "The Third Man Argument in the *Parmenides*," *PR*, LXIII (1954), 319ff. Vlastos, who works with the tools of symbolic logic, has stimulated a lengthy discussion. His article also includes a bibliography of the older literature. For the more recent thought, see Rosenmeyer, pp. 185f.; Allen, pp. 231–91. N. B. Booth ("Assumptions Involved in the Third Man Argument," *Phronesis*, III, 1958 p. 149) concludes: "I see no evidence that Plato ever really came to grips with the fundamental difficulties involved in the theory of Ideas." Cf. J. M. E. Moravcsik, "The 'Third Man' Argument and Plato's Theory of Forms," *Phronesis*, VIII (1963), 50ff.

19. See Natorp, *Ideenlehre*, p. 229 = 2d edn., p. 236: "Since Socrates is completely without defense against this criticism, he shows that by 'participation' he has understood nothing but such a material relation." The opposite is true. Thus, in what follows, Natorp finds he must take back something of his former claim: "not at all clumsy . . . ," "in any event, great progress . . ."

20. The meaning in 133D 4 has been misunderstood by Taylor, *Parmenides* [XXIV⁹], p. 57, and also by Cornford, *Plato and Parmenides* [XXIV²], p. 96: ". . . [the names] have reference to one another, not

to the forms." Correctly understood, however, it is not the names themselves but rather the objects carrying these names (ὅσα αὖ ὀνομάζεται οὕτως) that stand in a relation to each other. Proklos, *In Parm. Comm.*, col. *939*, is correct, as is Diès, for example, among the modern writers (see his *Parménide*, p. *65*).

21. Cornford (p. *98*) comments as follows on 133c–134e: "Formally, at any rate, this argument is almost grossly fallacious. It confuses the Form (Mastership or Knowledge) with perfect instances of the Form." Cornford seems to disregard the fact that in the *Parmenides*, Plato first establishes the higher or more universal Form: (*1*) the ideal Form of mastership and servitude, and then, second, establishes the less high or less universal Form: (*2*) the ideal Form of master and servant. Only after these are established does Plato consider examples from our world of appearances: (*3*) master and servant as we know them. In the world of appearances, however, Plato could have differentiated further: between (*3*) mastership and servitude, and (*4*) master and servant. But why consider at all a distinction between (*1*) and (*2*)? The distinction is made in order to suggest that the ideal Form of mastership and servitude includes numerous ideal Forms of which the ideal Form of master and servant is only one instance. This is an example of the graduated system of Forms and the system of diaeresis co-ordinated with it.

22. Cf. Stenzel, *Studien*, pp. 45ff. Gilbert Ryle, in "Plato's *Parmenides*," *Mind*, n.s., XLVIII (*1939*), p. *132*, comments: "Liveliness and dramatic qualities, not to speak of humour [irony probably is meant], vanish from the very beginning of the second part." *Not at all.* M. Beck, "Plato's Problem in the *Parmenides*," *JHistId*, VIII (*1947*), p. *233*, finds in the whole dialogue "not the slightest sign of that humour of which Plato always proves himself the great master." *Nothing could be more mistaken*, if one understands "humour" to mean irony. / In his translation [XXIV²], Cornford has left out the answers of the young Aristotle. This does seem to facilitate the task for the modern reader, but nevertheless it is possible only because Cornford inserts his own titles and interpretations between the sections. His idea that "the speakers might as well be labelled *A* and *B*" is not quite intelligible, since it is obvious that *A* hardly could be Zeno and certainly could not be Socrates. (See R. Schaerer, "La structure des dialogues métaphysiques," *RevInPh*, IX, *1955*, p. *197*: "Before long, Socrates lets the young Aristotle, his double [!], continue the argument.") I shall attempt to demonstrate that *B* is, not accidentally, that Aristotle who belonged to the Thirty around the year *404*. / On this section of the dialogue, Dickinson, p. *75*, remarks: "The form of presentation, I think, in this case is clearly a mistake; for when science arrives it expels literature." (*Yet not completely!*)

23. This division has been discussed fundamentally at least twice: by

Proklos, and, in modern times, by Zeller. Proklos, *In Parm. Comm.*
[XXIV³], cols. 633f., sees it as a battle τῶν πραγματειώδη (factual) τὴν
πρόθεσιν εἰπόντων καὶ τὴν μέθοδον τῶν πραγμάτων ἕνεκα γυμνάζεσθαι
λεγόντων against those who εἶναί φασι γυμνασίας τὴν πρόθεσιν. Zeller,
influenced by Hegel, discusses it in *Platonische Studien* (Tübingen,
1839), against Schleiermacher. Wilamowitz (II, 222ff.), without considering these earlier discussions, and without adding new arguments, has taken his position with those who are attacked by Proklos
and Zeller. He refers belittlingly with the term "schoolroom ped-
antry" (*Schulfuchserei*) to the second part of the dialogue—the same
part that was to Hegel (*Werke*, Berlin, 1833, XIV, 240) "the famous
masterpiece of Platonic dialectics," and was to K. F. Hermann (*Geschichte*, p. 507) "one of the great masterpieces of speculative acumen."
For only without serious consideration of the discussions and arguments could Wilamowitz have imagined the origin of the *Parmenides*
to be as follows: that Plato had first written a formal, dialectical exercise which he then expanded into a dialogue by placing *aporias* in front
of it, and by prefacing those *aporias* with an introduction. Apelt, in his
translation [XXIV²] Notes, p. 140, arrives at similar conclusions from
similar presuppositions. / The discussion properly continues: Taylor
finds in the *Parmenides* (see his edition, p. 39) a *"jeu d'esprit"*; Robinson (*Dialectic*, 2d edn., pp. 264ff.) "an exercise or gymnastic." To
Diès (*Platon*, p. 303), it is a *"drame métaphysique,"* and so also to
R. S. Brumbaugh, *Plato and the One: The Hypotheses in the "Parmenides"* (New Haven, 1961). Beck, in *JHistId*, VIII (1947), 232, attempts to provide a third "logical" interpretation as an alternative
to the two main views. Also see Ross, pp. 94ff.

24. I translate this thus, although the word ἕν surely includes "the unity"
as well as "the One." Perhaps the possibility of Plato's dialectics stems
from the lack of differentiation in this fundamental concept. See Cornford, *Plato and Parmenides*, pp. 109ff.

25. The significance of what is here termed "synthesis" is often under-
rated. Cornford (p. 194) calls this section "Hypothesis II A, Corollary
on Becoming in Time." Chung-Hwan Chen, "On the *Parmenides* of
Plato," *CQ*, XXXVIII (1944), 107, says, "The intermediate passage
neither tries [*sic*] to reconcile the two previous arguments, but is appended to the second argument alone." Schaerer, in *RevInPh*, IX
(1955), p. 200, states: "Argument III is only a corollary of II."

26. Wundt, *"Parmenides"* [XXIV¹⁰], p. 42, is against this. I express myself cautiously, and would not be able to construct such a synthesis.

27. On the interpretation of the dialectical part: The (Neoplatonic) attempts that preceded Proklos' work are critically discussed by him
at the beginning of Book VI of his commentary. Zeller, *Studien*
[XXIV²³], pp. 159ff., is influenced by Hegel, whom Kuno Fischer, *De
Parmenide* (Heidelberg, 1851), follows even more systematically.

Natorp's interpretation is (as always) instructive in its details, even if his fundamental conception here is not satisfactory. It seems to be a basic error of Natorp (see *Ideenlehre*, p. 239) to assume that Plato decides "in favor of the relative, against the absolute [non-relative] thesis," i.e., in favor of the antithesis and against the thesis. A similar error is found in H. Jackson, "Plato's Later Theory of Ideas, II," *JPhilol*, XI (1882), 330. Kurt Riezler, *Parmenides* (Frankfurt, 1934), p. 92, calls the dialectical part "the main section of the dialogue." Cf. Chen, p. 107: "In Plato's opinion, only the consequence of the second argument is ontologically valid." This at once disagrees with the symmetrical plan of the whole. And since a reconciling deduction is immediately provided, it becomes impossible to evaluate thesis and antithesis differently on purely formal grounds. Therefore, all attempts made since the Neoplatonists—who took the position of the first thesis—must be mistaken in finding *"le coeur du platonisme"* (Wahl, *Étude*, p. 245) in one of the nine deductions. As Diès, *Parménide* [XXIV⁶], p. 45, correctly observes, "It is obvious that to attempt to choose . . . among the various sections of this dialectical argument is to go against its declared intentions." Does not this from the outset refute the ingenious interpretation of A. Speiser, who, with the Neoplatonists, decides in favor of the first thesis? For like the Neoplatonists, who saw in "the One" of the thesis "all gods and the divine souls and the higher powers" (Proklos, *In Parm. Comm.*, col. 1243), Speiser, *Ein Parmenideskommentar* [XXIV¹²], pp. 25ff., finds here a "refutation of lower concepts of God," and concludes, "Thus, Plato has become the pioneer of Christianity." (See Cornford, pp. 131ff., for a critique of the Neoplatonic interpretation.) / Speiser, pp. 18ff., provides an accurate survey of all the dialectical steps. According to his computation, there are seventy-eight of them. In my opinion, there seems to be an error in his first step. "Only one predication may be made about 'the One': 'is one' where the 'is' is only the copula and not a predicate of being." This interpretation can only be explained by the fact that modern editions print ἓν ἐστιν instead of the more correct ἓν ἔστιν, or better yet (even against common usage) ἕν ἔστιν. The different word order εἰ ἓν ἔστιν (in 137c 4) and ἓν εἰ ἔστιν (in 142ʙ) makes the antithetical dialectic between the thesis and the antithesis more forceful than would have been the case had the same word order been chosen at both starting points. / Stenzel, *Metaphysik*, p. 131, and Calogero, *Studi* [XXIV¹], p. 232, still depend on the customary accentuation for their arguments. On this, however, Cornford (p. 116) is correct.

28. Parmenides' philosophical poem, referred to here and elsewhere by verse number, is printed in *Vorsokr.* 28 [18] ʙ 8.

29. This deduction runs from 143ᴀ 4 to 144ᴇ 7. Here, one could start a new paragraph, although the sense immediately continues. The para-

graphs, however, that Burnet starts after 143B and 144A are not only wrong but also disturbing. One should not make the climb along such difficult trails more difficult by faulty leads. (I find similar criticism of Burnet's paragraphing in Cornford, p. 137, n. 2.)

30. See Wahl, *Étude* [XXIV²], p. 245: "What is the subject matter of this second section [meaning, of the whole dialogue]? Relations of the perceptible to the *Ideas*, as Natorp believes, or relations that exist among the *Ideas*, as the majority of other commentators hold, among them Burnet? In our opinion, for Plato the two problems should not be separated."

31. 144E 5: τὸ ὂν ἕν, in contrast to the immediately following αὐτὸ τὸ ἕν. The latter had already been proved, in 143A. The fact that we find in 143A 2 τὸ ἓν ὄν, but here in 144E 5 the less common construction τὸ ὂν ἕν, is explained by the designated contrast. (It is necessary to draw attention to this point since textual changes have been attempted.) / On what follows in the text as to the conclusion, and esp. the "coincidence of opposites," see Natorp, *Ideenlehre*, p. 245 = 2d edn., p. 251: "One should further consider that the designations [predicates] are to be understood in various respects." Just this fact, however, is indicated only a few times (from which we realize that Plato here does not "accidentally" go astray), and almost everywhere that the fact would have mattered, it is purposely suppressed. Cf. Apelt's Introduction [XXIV²], p. 13: "For in many passages [Plato] requires that the relations be mentioned, although in other passages, he displays small concern for this."

32. Julius Stenzel, "Der Begriff der Erleuchtung bei Platon," *Die Antike*, II (1926), 242 (in *Kleine Schriften*, p. 157), is in line with this interpretation.

33. 155E 10: ἐν ἄλλῳ χρόνῳ μετέχει καὶ ἐν ἄλλῳ οὐ μετέχει. This does not seem to correspond to the evidence within the first thesis: οὐδὲ ἄρα χρόνου αὐτῷ μέτεστιν, οὐδ' ἔστιν ἔν τινι χρόνῳ (141D 5). Apparently "time" must signify something different there and here. "Time" in the first thesis refers to the time period in which becoming and ceasing take place. In the synthesis, temporal differentiation is a symbol for the fact that τἀναντία οὐχ ἅμα. On this see Natorp, *Ideenlehre*, p. 253 = 2d edn., pp. 260f., even though here (as always) he writes in a "criticistic" manner about "placement on various levels of thought," instead of using the ontological approach.

34. Cf. Natorp, *Ideenlehre*, p. 241 = 2d edn., pp. 247f.

35. To that extent, Fischer, *De Parmenide* [XXIV²⁷], p. 73, is correct in stating, "In the 'moment' of Plato, the dialectical nucleus for his *Idea* cannot be disregarded."

36. Wahl, *Étude* [XXIV²], p. 72: "Plato . . . unites the ἐπέκεινα τῆς οὐσίας of the *Republic* to what will be the κοινωνία τῶν γενῶν of the *Sophist*."

37. Cf. E. R. Dodds, "The *Parmenides* and the Neoplatonic 'One,' " *CQ*, XXII (1928), 129ff.; Klibansky, "Ein Proklos-Fund" [XXIV¹⁰], disc. 5; Wundt, "*Parmenides*" [XXIV¹⁰], pp. 7ff.; Cornford, *Plato and Parmenides*, pp. 131ff.

38. Cf. Zeller, *Studien* [XXIV²³], p. 178: "Moreover, thesis and antithesis are here not basically opposed to each other." See also Fischer, op. cit., p. 100, for a similar view.

39. Speiser considers the closing sentence as the seventy-eighth dialectical step and mistakenly calls it "summary" instead of "chaotic confusion." E. A. Wyller, *Platons "Parmenides" in seinem Zusammenhang mit "Symposion" und "Politeia"* (Oslo, 1960), p. 178, calls it "die Hauptkonklusion." Cornford, p. 244, correctly sees it as "ostensible conclusion."

40. See Proklos, *In Parm. Comm.* [XXIV³], col. 950, 11. 28–30: ἐπιστήμης . . . ἡνωμένως μὲν τὰ πεπληθυσμένα πάντα, ὁλικῶς δὲ τὰ μερικὰ συλλαβούσης. Also Iamblichos, as quoted in *Ammonius in Aristotelis De interpretatione Commentarius*, ed. A. Busse (in *Commentaria in Aristotelem Graeca*, IV/5, Berlin, 1897), p. 136: τὰ μεριστὰ . . . ἀμερίστως καὶ ἀδιαστάτως γινώσκειν . . . καὶ τὰ πεπληθυσμένα ἑνοειδῶς καὶ τὰ ἔγχρονα αἰωνίως καὶ τὰ γεννητὰ ἀγεννήτως. Correspondingly, from the point of view of man, see Proklos, *In Platonis Timaeum Commentaria*, ed. E. Diehl (3 vols., Leipzig, 1903–6), I, p. 202, 1. 26: διότι καὶ ὁ ἄνθρωπος μικρός ἐστι κόσμος πάντα ἔχων μερικῶς ὅσα τὸ πᾶν ὁλικῶς, and also Proklos, *In Platonis Cratylum Commentaria*, ed. G. Pasquali (Leipzig, 1908), p. 51, 1. 18: ὅτι τὸ ἀμέριστον τῆς τῶν θεῶν ἐνεργείας μεριστῶς ἡ ψυχὴ ἡμῶν γιγνώσκει καὶ πεπληθυσμένως τὸ ἑνιαῖον. Cf. F. Klingner, "De Boethii *Consolatione*," *Philologische Untersuchungen*, XXVII (1921), 110.

xxv: *Phaedrus*

RECENT EDITIONS AND TRANSLATIONS: C. Ritter, PhB 152 (2d edn., 1922); L. Robin, *Platon Budé*, IV/3 (1933); J. D. García Bacca (Mexico, 1945); J. N. Theodorakopoulos (Athens, 1948); R. Hackforth (Cambridge, Mass., 1952); E. Salin (Basel, 1952); K. Hildebrandt (Kiel, 1953); M. B. Marinucci (Rome, 1954); L. Gil Fernández (Madrid, 1957); A. Richelmy (Turin, 1959); M. Meunier (Paris, 1960); G. Galli and A. Plebe (2d edn., Florence, 1964).

RECENT INTERPRETATIONS: C. Murley, "Plato's *Phaedrus* and the Theocritean Pastoral," *TAPA*, LXXI (1940), 281ff.; Jaeger, *Paideia*, III, 182ff.; I. M. Linforth, in UCalPCP, XIII (1946), 163ff.; F. Pfister, "Der Begriff des Schoenen und das Ebenmass," *Würzburger Jahrbuch*, I (1946), 341ff.; H. Gundert, "Enthusiasmos und

Logos bei Platon," *Lexis*, II (1949), 25ff.; Stefanini, pp. 19ff.;
Hoffmann, pp. 176ff.; E. Paci, "Sul Fedro," in *Studi di filosofia antica
e moderna* (Turin, 1950), pp. 56ff.; O. Regenbogen, in *Miscellanea
Academica Berolinensia*, II/1 (1950), 198ff.; Dodds, pp. 64ff.; W. C.
Helmbold and W. B. Holther, *The Unity of the "Phaedrus,"* UCalPCP,
XIV (1952), 387ff.; G. A. Levi, "Il bello nel *Fedro* platonico,"
Humanitas (Brescia), VII (1952), 479ff.; F. Ruiloba Palazuélos,
Epilogo al "Fedro" (Madrid, 1952); P. Von der Mühll, "Platonica,"
MusHelv, IX (1952), 58f.; W. Kirk, "*Protagoras* and *Phaedrus*:
Literary Techniques," *Studies . . . Robinson*, II (St. Louis, 1953),
pp. 593ff.; H. L. Hudson-Williams, *Three Systems of Education: Some
Reflections on the Implications of Plato's "Phaedrus"* (Oxford, 1954);
W. J. Verdenius, "Notes on Plato's *Phaedrus*," *Mnemosyne*, 4th ser.,
VIII (1955), 265ff.; L. Gil Fernández, "Notas al *Fedro*," *Emerita*,
XXIV (1956) 311ff.; H. W. Meyer, "Das Verhältnis von Enthu-
siasmus und Philosophie bei Platon im Hinblick auf seinen *Phaidros*,"
Archiv für Philosophie (Stuttgart), VI (1956), 262ff.; Rudberg, pp.
27ff.; G. E. Mueller, "Unity of the *Phaedrus*," *CB*, XXXIII (1956/
57), 50ff., 63ff.; R. G. Hoerber, "Love or Rhetoric in Plato's *Phae-
drus*," *CB*, XXXIV (1957/58), 33; also *Phronesis*, IV (1959), 27f.;
Gauss, II/2, 238ff.; Hildebrandt, *Platon* (2d edn.), pp. 253ff.;
Aichroth, pp. 61ff.; H. Koller, "Die dihäretische Methode," *Glotta*,
XXXIX (1960), 6ff.; M. Heidegger, *Nietzsche* (Pfullingen, 1961),
I, 218ff.; W. J. Verdenius, "Der Begriff der Mania in Platons *Phaidros*," *AfGP*, XLIV (1962), 132ff.; J. Pieper, *Enthusiasm and Divine
Madness*, tr. R. and C. Winston (New York, 1964); Raven, pp.
188ff.; Lesky, pp. 532f.

ADDITIONAL BIBLIOGRAPHY: Shorey, p. 549; Geffcken, Notes, pp. 100f.;
Leisegang, cols. 2473ff.; Rosenmeyer, pp. 187f.; Cherniss, *Lustrum*,
pp. 133ff.

1. The question of an early dating for the *Phaedrus* need nowadays disturb only those concerned with shifts in the understanding of Plato
in ancient and modern times. Writing in 1839, K. F. Hermann came
out against the early dating; see his "Über Platons schriftstellerische
Motive," *Gesammelte Abhandlungen und Beiträge* (Göttingen, 1849),
pp. 299f. The hypothesis of a revision (see, for example, Otto Immisch, "Neue Wege der Platonforschung," *Neue Jahrbücher*, XXXV,
1915, pp. 295ff.; Natorp, *Ideenlehre*, 2d edn., pp. 489, 529) was a
δεύτερος πλοῦς, when one had to give up the early dating and did so
only reluctantly. / The tendency to move the *Phaedrus* and the *Symposium* close to each other (see, for example, Jowett, I, 421; Reinhardt, *Mythen*, pp. 77, 97; Shorey, pp. 198ff. 549ff.) is understand-

able, but is nevertheless opposed by the verbal statistics and the much reduced frequency of hiatuses in the *Phaedrus* as well as by the dialogue's formal structure. / Otto Regenbogen, "Bemerkungen zur Deutung des platonischen *Phaidros*," *Miscellanea Academica Berolinensia*, II/1 (1950), 198ff., has offered the most extensive arguments in favor of the contrary tendency: to place the *Phaedrus* among the dialogues of Plato's latest period. This attempt also fails, because of the fact that the latest dialogues avoid the hiatus much more radically than the *Phaedrus* does. Correct views are those of Rudberg, p. 139, n. 19; H. Cherniss, "The Relation of the *Timaeus* to Plato's Later Dialogues," *AJP*, LXXVIII (1957), 231ff. Other advocates of the late dating are cited in Cherniss' article, p. 233, n. 22. Also see Cherniss, *Aristotle's Criticism of Plato*, p. 433, n. 368; Jaeger, *Paideia*, III, 182f.; Stenzel, *R-E*, III A, cols. 859ff.

2. See Robin's *Budé* edition [XXI²⁹], p. xiv: "*l'allusion au* Phédon *saute aux yeux.*" Also see Robin's *Phèdre* (*Platon Budé*, IV/3, 1933), p. 27; E. Salin, *Phaidros* (Basel, 1952), p. 209.

3. Dickinson, p. 12: "the Ilissos, in a sense, is more important than the Mississippi, for it was the scene of Plato's dialogue, the *Phaedrus.*" Cf. Alain (Émile Chartier), *Idées* (Paris, 1932), p. 10: ". . . *ce grand baptême du fils de la terre.*"

4. Cf. *Plato* 2, pp. 218f.

5. On the history of the problem, see Robin, *Phèdre*, pp. lx ff.; Stefanini, p. 25; R. Hackforth, *Plato's "Phaedrus"* (Cambridge, Mass., 1952), pp. 16ff. / Johannes Vahlen ("Ueber die Rede des Lysias in Platos *Phaedrus*," *Gesammelte Schriften* [XX²¹], II, 675ff.) filled several pages with parallels from the orator Lysias. Most of the subsequent judgments are either emphatic in agreement (e.g., see Salin's edition, p. 208) or skeptical, but no one has taken up the matter with anything like the accuracy of Vahlen. Nor has Vahlen's proof been seriously shaken by even the most detailed critique: H. Weinstock, *De erotico Lysiaco* (Münster diss., 1912). Hackforth quotes and assents to the statement of Robin: "Until the partisans of authenticity have brought proofs which are not at bottom mere opinions, we will be entitled to oppose others which at least do not claim to be anything else. . . ." From this it would seem that neither Robin nor Hackforth read Vahlen's article carefully. / In favor of the derivation from Lysias: François Lasserre, " 'Ερωτικοὶ Λόγοι," *MusHelv*, I (1944), 169ff.; Stefanini, p. 25; Regenbogen, "*Phaidros*" [XXV¹], pp. 199f. Against the derivation: J. Pieper, *Enthusiasm and Divine Madness*, tr. R. and C. Winston (New York, 1964), ch. 2.

6. Franz Grillparzer, *Sämtliche Werke*, ed. A. Sauer (5th edn., Stuttgart, 1893), XVI, 91.

7. See *Dialexeis*, *Vorsokr.* 90 [83], ch. 2, § 2. The text cannot be restored

with certainty. χρηστῷ is indispensable. Can one venture on κακῷ instead of καλῷ?

8. Since the *Hypotheseis* (Summaries) of Antiphon's *Tetralogies* were not written by Antiphon himself, the *Phaedrus* becomes our earliest example of this practice, to be encountered also in the *Controversiae* of the rhetor Seneca, later on in the Τυραννοκτόνος of Lucian, and in the Παιδοκτόνος and Τυραννοκτόνος of Chorikios (in the Boissonade edition, Paris, 1846, pp. 49, 205).

9. *Alcibiades* 128ε *et seq*. Cf. *Plato 2*, pp. 236f.

10. Agreements between the speech of Lysias and the speech of Socrates are noted by Vahlen, "Ueber die Rede des Lysias" [XXV⁵], p. 701.

11. Such is the judgment of Vahlen, loc. cit., whose characterization of the speech of Lysias (pp. 685f.) is worth reading.

12. Thus, the distinction between *Phaedrus* 237D and Book V of the *Republic* is not, as Hackforth thinks, "that Plato is here [in the *Phaedrus*] using non-technical language," but that Socrates is intentionally leaving the *episteme* out, in order that the attentive reader may ask for it. In Hackforth's remark (*"Phaedrus,"* p. 42) that δόξης ἐπὶ τὸ ἄριστον λόγῳ ἀγούσης is a phrase "we should read without the Platonic overtones which it inevitably carries to our ears," the word "inevitably" itself shows that we cannot but hear these overtones and thence proceed to criticize the "pseudo-speech" of Socrates. For even if we tried at first to read the speech disregarding the "overtones," then surely on a second reading this would no longer be possible. See also Robin, *Phèdre*, pp. lxviii ff.

13. This is an answer to the criticism of Hackforth (p. 36, n. 1), who calls this "one of those etymological jests in which Plato often, and sometimes rather pointlessly, indulges."

14. Hackforth, p. 51, n. 1: "It is just possible that ἤ τι θεῖον is a verbal concession—it can be no more [*it is much more!*]—to the δαίμων-Eros view." On the contrary, it is precisely as a pointer to this δαίμων-Eros view that the words ἤ τι θεῖον acquire their sense.

15. See R. Boehringer, *Mein Bild von Stefan George* (Munich, 1951), p. 169.

16. Cf. Wilamowitz, I, 456, on the "new style" of this speech. When von Arnim (*Jugenddialoge*, p. 165) calls the palinode "an *epideixis* serving as a model of style," and (p. 215) "a test example of the highest oratorical presentation, such as can thrive only on a philosophic foundation," he is in a certain sense correct. Yet on the other hand, the palinode is an astonishing exception, no example for learners, and the highest type of philosophic rhetoric is for Plato not an ecstatic oration but—to express it in his own paradox—the educational dialogue. Jowett (I, 404) grasps the dialectics of the matter more thoroughly, and sees Socrates' second speech as "an illustration of the higher or

true rhetoric . . . [where] the example becomes also the deeper theme of discourse."

17. On this see Hermias' scholium on 266A (*In Platonis Phaedrum Scholia*, ed. Paul Couvreur, 2d edn., Paris, 1901, p. 235): ἀπὸ τῶν Πυθαγορείων δὲ ὁ Πλάτων ὠφεληθεὶς τὰς συστοιχίας οὕτως ἔλαβεν ἐνταῦθα.

18. In *Jugenddialoge*, p. 207, von Arnim calls attention to the agreement, instructive also for our problem, of *Phaedrus* 238A 2 with *Republic* IX 580D 11, where there is mention of the πολυειδία of the ἐπιθυμητικόν. The comparison is also decisive against the textual reading of Burnet in *Phaedrus* 238A 3, which to be sure is still more plainly refuted by the words that follow in the dialogue itself: τούτων τῶν ἰδεῶν points back to πολυειδές. πολυμελές—instead of πολυμερές—is made certain by the quotations in Stobaeus and Hermias, but primarily by the case itself. See Hermias on 237B (*In Phaedr. Scholia*, p. 53, 11. 9f.: αὕτη ἡ ὕδρα καὶ τὸ πολυκέφαλον θηρίον ὡς καὶ ἐν Πολιτείᾳ (588c) εἶπεν. In fact this picture is envisaged; cf. *Phaedrus* 230A, θηρίον Τυφῶνος πολυπλοκώτερον, and then again, at 265E, κατ' ἄρθρα τέμνειν. / See also the edition of Hackforth, p. 39, and of Robin, pp. 19f.

19. Modern anthropological and psychological research has greatly helped the interpretation here. See Wilamowitz, I, 407, n. 1, and in contrast: Rohde, *Psyche* [XXI²⁹], pp. 282ff.; F. Pfister, "Der Wahnsinn des Weihepriesters," in *Festschrift Cimbria* (Dortmund, 1926), pp. 55ff.; I. M. Linforth, *The Corybantic Rites in Plato* (UCalPCP, Vol. XIII, 1946, No. 5), and *Telestic Madness in Plato, Phaedrus* 244DE (No. 6); Dodds, ch. 3.

20. On the historical impact, see W. A. Nitze, "*A Midsummer Night's Dream* V i 4—17," *Modern Language Review*, L (1955), 495ff.; R. Walzer, "Al-Farabi's Theory of Prophecy and Divination," *JHS*, LXXVII (1957), 142ff.

21. See *Plato* 1, pp. 193ff., on the myth in the third speech, and particularly on the fusion of the two symbolic motifs: that of the chariot and that of the wings. The soul as a chariot without wings is found in the *Katha Upanishad* of India. Wings on the horses, on the charioteer, and on the wheel hubs are encountered in Greek art in manifold variations and combinations. The winged Eros in particular may have become the prototype for the winged Psyche. / Otto Immisch, loc. cit. [XXV¹], thought he could recognize the reworking of the *Phaedrus* in the combining of these two pictorial motifs. Immisch correctly sensed the double root of the imagery, but his inferences were refuted by Max Pohlenz, in *Göttingische gelehrte Anzeigen*, 1916, pp. 272ff.

22. *Plato* 1, pp. 110ff. Cf. Hackforth, "*Phaedrus*," p. 162.

23. On the systematic meaning of this argument, see *Plato* 1, pp. 116ff.

24. The relationship between the *Phaedrus* and the *Gorgias* is discussed

by von Arnim, *Jugenddialoge*, pp. 186ff., and, so far as his problem (the dating of the *Phaedrus*) is concerned, with complete pertinence. He also is in a way correct in seeing that "the idea of a philosophic rhetoric, carried out later by Aristotle, is already set up here [in the *Phaedrus*] as a postulate." And yet the *Phaedrus* is handled too gently, as it were, for von Arnim does not appreciate sufficiently the very ironic paradox which for the art of rhetoric requires psychic knowledge and dialectics, i.e., the ascent to the *locus intelligibilis* (the realm of *Ideas*). What is involved is much more than merely that rhetoric "needs logical and psychological foundations." Natorp (*Ideenlehre*, pp. 54ff.) penetrates more deeply.

25. See the scholium on 261D, and Diogenes Laërtius IX 25. Another ancient interpretation appears in Quintilian, *Institutio oratoria* III 1, 11: "*quem Palameden Plato appellat, Alcidamas Elaites.*" Cf. M. J. Milne, *A Study in Alcidamas* (Bryn Mawr diss., 1924). / Hackforth ("*Phaedrus,*" p. 129, n. 1) correctly says that "the sobriquet of Palamedes recognizes his ingenuity," but Hackforth adheres to the identification with Zeno—who is lacking precisely in "ingenuity," in Plato's view. See *Parmenides* 128A: ταὐτὸν γὰρ γέγραφε (Ζήνων) τρόπον τινὰ ὅπερ σύ (ὦ Παρμενίδη), μεταβάλλων δ' ἡμᾶς πειρᾶται ἐξαπατᾶν ὡς ἕτερόν τι λέγων. One might object that Aristotle's ἐν τῷ Σοφιστῇ (frag. 65) makes Zeno the inventor of dialectics. But the point here is *Plato's* judgment of Zeno. / Note that von Arnim (*Jugenddialoge*, p. 193) thinks he sees here, in addition, an incidental thrust at the Megarians.

26. *Doxogr.*, p. 581, l. 5 = *Vorsokr.* 29 [19] A 23: Ζήνων ἴδιον μὲν οὐδὲν ἐξέθετο. . .

27. See Wilamowitz, I, 480 = I², 485.

28. Cf. Thomas Mann, *The Beloved Returns*, tr. Helen T. Lowe-Porter (New York, 1940), p. 80: ". . . it is the merest, most arbitrary chance that made me choose just this and nothing else out of that rich, that infinite store."

29. On harmony, see Archytas, *Vorsokr.* 47 [35] B 1: περὶ γὰρ τᾶς τῶν ὅλων φύσιος καλῶς διαγνόντες. . . . / On Hippokrates the literature is copious. Only the following need be cited here: W. Capelle, "Zur Hippokratischen Frage," *Hermes*, LVII (1922), 247ff.; L. Edelstein, Περὶ ἀέρων *und die Sammlung der Hippokratischen Schriften* (Berlin, 1931), pp. 118ff.; Rey, pp. 435ff.; F. Steckerl, "Plato, Hippocrates, and the 'Menon Papyrus,'" *CP*, XL (1945), 166ff.; W. Kranz, "Platon über Hippokrates," *Philologus*, XCVI (1944) 193ff., and also *Kosmos* (Archiv für Begriffsgeschichte, II/1, Bern, 1955), pp. 41ff. Capelle (p. 250, n. 2), citing the Littré edition of Hippokrates' works, correctly says that Plato "makes it easy to see (as Littré earlier emphasized, pp. 305ff.) that he is developing further in complete independence an idea of 'Hippokrates.'" / It has been much discussed whether in *Phaedrus* 270c 2 Plato means by

ἄνευ τῆς τοῦ ὅλου φύσεως the entire form or entire field, or rather the universe. That the extension to the universe should at least *also* be understood is indicated (*1*) by this very discussion, (*2*) by the way in which Plato generally uses τὸ ὅλον, and (*3*) by the comparison with the τῶν ὅλων of Archytas.

30. The words in *Phaedrus* 269E 4 *et seq.* (προσδέονται ἀδολεσχίας καὶ μετεωρολογίας φύσεως πέρι) are paralleled in *Apology* 18B 7, *Cratylus* 401B 7, *Republic* VI 488E 4, *Statesman* 299B 7, as well as in Aristophanes, *Clouds* 333, 360. Thus, Plato again is using derisive words that were current at the end of the fifth century. De Vries reads Platonic self-irony into the words, and perhaps there is something of this. Yet, the principal element is mockery of the despisers of natural science who had coined these words.

31. *R-E*, V A, cols. 139ff., *s.v.* Teisias.

32. Cf. Ast, p. 109.

33. See *Plato* 1, ch. V. Also see J. A. Notopoulos, "Mnemosyne in Oral Literature," *TAPA*, LXIX (1938), 476ff.; W. C. Greene, "The Spoken and the Written Word," *Harvard Studies in Classical Philology*, LX (1951), 23ff.

34. Failure to recognize this has persisted since Schleiermacher's time (see his Vol. I/1, pp. 73f.), and has often led to false conclusions as to the date of composition of the *Phaedrus* and as to the relation of Plato to Isokrates. On this, von Arnim (*Jugenddialoge*, p. 191) is completely right when he reckons the mention of Lysias as contributing to the "dramatic accouterment and economy of the dialogue," thus cutting off the question as to whether Lysias was still alive and how old he was when the dialogue appeared (see Pohlenz, *Göttingische gelehrte Anzeigen*, 1916, p. 280). / Wilamowitz, II, 122—in the chapter on "Platon und Isokrates," to which reference is here made—remarks that in the *Phaedrus* passage there is "not a trace of irony" (Stefanini, p. 57, Hackforth, p. 167, Jaeger, *Paideia*, III, 98, agree)—but Wilamowitz virtually takes this back in his very next sentence. Robin, *Phèdre* [XXV²], p. clxxi, makes the rejection by Isokrates even sharper than the present work does. "A satire" is seen by de Vries (pp. 240ff.). Cf. also de Vries' "Isocrates' Reaction to the *Phaedrus*," *Mnemosyne*, 4th ser., VI (1953), 39ff.

35. With the words ἔτι τε εἰ αὐτῷ . . . in 279A—cf. Vahlen, *Gesammelte Schriften* [XX²¹], I, 360—the additional point is made that in Plato's judgment elevated Isokrates above Lysias in particular. / On the textual criticism, see E. Bickel, *RhM*, XCII (1943), 151.

36. On the meaning of the prayer, see E. Bickel, in *AfGP*, XXI (1908), 535ff.; W. Kranz, "Platonica I," *Philologus*, XCIV (1941), 332ff.; T. G. Rosenmeyer, "Plato's Prayer to Pan," *Hermes*, XC (1962), 34ff.; A. Motte, "Le pré sacré de Pan et des nymphes dans le *Phèdre* de Platon," *L'Antiquité Classique*, XXXII (1963), 460ff.

37. See Hermias, *In Phaedr. Schol.* [XXV¹⁷], p. 8, Δόξαι τοῦ σκοποῦ, and p. 10, Τίς ὁ ἀληθὴς τοῦ διαλόγου σκοπός. Cf. Hackforth, *"Phaedrus,"* pp. 8ff.

38. Grillparzer, *Sämtliche Werke* [XXV⁶], XVI, 91.

39. Eduard Norden, *Die antike Kunstprosa* (Leipzig and Berlin, 1898), I, 112. "Bad composition," says Raeder, p. 267; Stefanini (pp. 24ff.) opposes this.

40. Jaeger (*Paideia*, III, 257) sees only the foreground subject: The *Phaedrus* "derives its unity from its concern with the subject of rhetoric."

41. Paul Natorp gave much thought to this question in his later years, when he no longer remained content to see in love "a metaphor of the philosophic urge." The dialogue again seemed to him to fall apart into disparate constituents, although previously (*Ideenlehre*, 1st edn., p. 58) he had thought he did understand the inner unity of the work. I quote the following from a note in his handwriting: "The soul rises upward in the *mania*. Apparently there is no methodical way upward. . . . It is true that Charioteer-Mind guides the chariot, he holds it on the steep curve to the point of a supraheavenly view, but not by virtue of a method, only in an enthusiastic gaze upward to the abundance of light on high. . . . How this fits together with the unique emphasizing of dialectics in the concluding part remains a puzzle. . . . So I cannot get over my uncertainty as to whether two levels of Platonism do not 'tangle' here. I should be grateful to him who would solve this problem for me." Although we shall not follow Natorp in the direction to which he here points, we view with special respect the never-wearied energy of his searching. (See also his *Ideenlehre*, 2d edn., pp. 489, 529.) On the necessity of both approaches (mania and dialectics), see *Plato* 1, chs. I and X.

XXVI: *Sophist*

RECENT EDITIONS AND TRANSLATIONS: (Among the older editions, that of L. Campbell, Oxford, 1867, is especially useful.) A. Diès, *Platon Budé*, VIII/3 (1925); F. M. Cornford (London, 1935); V. Arangio-Ruiz (Bari, 1951); A. Zadro (Bari, 1957); A. Tovar (Madrid, 1959); A. E. Taylor (ed. R. Klibansky and E. Anscombe, London, 1961); O. Apelt and R. Wiehl, PhB 150 (2d edn., 1967).

RECENT INTERPRETATIONS: (While working on the first German edition of the present study, I had the advantage of consulting notes of a course on the *Sophist* given by M. Heidegger at Marburg in 1924/25.) Diès, *Platon*, pp. 305ff., 343ff.; É. de Strycker, in *Revue Néo-Scolastique*, XXXIV (1932), 42ff., 218ff.; Shorey, pp. 294ff.; E. M.

Manasse, *Platons "Sophistes" und "Politikos"* (Berlin, 1937); K. Dürr, "Moderne Darstellung der platonischen Logik," *MusHelv*, II (1945), 166ff.; R. Hackforth, "False Statement in Plato's *Sophist*," *CQ*, XXXIX (1945), 56ff.; Stefanini, pp. 177ff.; Kucharski, pp. 147ff., 325ff.; R. Robinson, in *PR*, LIX (1950), 3ff.; A. L. Peck, "Plato and the μέγιστα γένη of the *Sophist*," *CQ*, n.s., II (1952), 32ff.; Maria Rezzani, "I problemi fondamentali del *Sofista* di Platone," *Sophia*, XX (1952), 298ff.; K. Riezler, "Das Nichts und das Andere, das Sein und das Seiende," in *Varia Variorum: Festgabe für K. Reinhardt* (Münster, 1952), pp. 82ff.; Buccellato, pp. 71ff.; J. Ackrill, "Συμπλοκὴ εἰδῶν," *Bull. Inst. Classical Studies Univ. London*, II (1955), 31ff.; R. Schaerer, in *RevInPh*, IX (1955), 197ff.; M. Grondona, "La dialettica nel *Sofista* di Platone," *Atti Accad. Scienza Torino II* (Cl. Scienza Mor. Stor. Filol.), XCI, (1956/57), 261ff.; R. S. Bluck, "False Statement in the *Sophist*," *JHS*, LXXVII/2 (1957), 181ff.; A. de Muralt, "De la participation dans le *Sophiste* de Platon," *Studia Philosophica* (Lvov), XVII (1957), 101ff.; L. Malverne, "Remarques sur le *Sophiste*," *Revue de Métaphysique et de Morale*, LXIII (1958), 149ff.; A. R. Lacey, "Plato's *Sophist* and the Forms," *CQ*, n.s., IX (1959), 43ff.; J. Xenakis, in *Phronesis*, IV (1959), 29ff.; E. Gaudron, "Sur l'objet du *Sophiste*," *Laval Théologique et Philosophique* (Quebec), XVI (1960), 70ff.; Gauss, III/1, ch. 4; J. M. E. Moravcsik, "Συμπλοκὴ εἰδῶν and the Genesis of λόγος," *AfGP*, XLII (1960), 117ff.; J. A. Philip, "Mimesis in the *Sophistes* of Plato," *TAPA*, XCII (1961), 453ff.; M. Raschini, "La dialettica del *Sofista*," *Giorn. di Metafisica*, XVI (1961), 693ff.; J. M. E. Moravcsik, "Being and Meaning in the *Sophist*," *Acta Philos. Fennica*, XIV (1962), 23ff.; K. Oehler, *Die Lehre vom noetischen und dianoetischen Denken bei Platon und Aristoteles* (Munich, 1962); A. L. Peck, "Plato's *Sophist*: The συμπλοκὴ τῶν εἰδῶν," *Phronesis*, VII (1962), 46ff.; W. G. Runciman, *Plato's Later Epistemology* (Cambridge, 1962), ch. 3; W. Kamlah, *Platons Selbstkritik im "Sophistes"* (Munich, 1963); R. Marten, *Der Logos der Dialektik. Eine Theorie zu Platos "Sophistes"* (Berlin, 1965); Lesky, pp. 533f.

ADDITIONAL BIBLIOGRAPHY: Shorey, pp. 590f.; Geffcken, Notes, pp. 107ff.; Leisegang, cols. 2492ff.; Rosenmeyer, p. 189; Cherniss, *Lustrum*, pp. 177ff.

1. See Bonitz, p. 152. To accept such an ἐποχή is more appropriate than to decide on *yes* (with Paul Deussen) or on *no* (with Eduard Zeller, p. 545).

2. A. E. Taylor, "Parmenides, Zeno and Socrates," in *Philosophical Studies* [XXIII[62]], p. 31: "The *Sophistes* and *Politicus* are carefully attached to the *Theaetetus* in such a way as to date them [he means the

dating of the dramatic happening] immediately after the filing of the accusation against Socrates in the year 400/399."

3. Cf. O. Toeplitz, *Das Verhältnis von Mathematik und Ideenlehre bei Platon* (Quellen und Studien zur Geschichte der Mathematik, I/1, Berlin, 1929), p. 17; Stenzel, *Zahl und Gestalt*, pp. 30ff.

4. René Schaerer, in *RevInPh*, IX (1955), 206.

5. *Studien*, p. 47.

6. Cf. *Plato* 1, p. 152; Frank, *WWG*, p. 97, agrees. For the opposing view, see Jaeger, *Aristotle*, p. 26: ". . . the dialogue form is nothing but an unessential stylistic ornament." Also see Robinson, *Dialectic*, p. 88 = 2d edn., p. 84: "All [!] students of Plato remark how, in the *Sophist* and the *Statesman*, the pretence of question and answer misfits the form, which is really a continuous torture." In contrast, E. M. Manasse, *Platons "Sophistes" und "Politikos": Das Problem der Wahrheit* (Berlin, 1937), p. 56, says, "the dialogical form is still of basic philosophical importance."

7. Burnet and, following him, Diès pick out in the text only the two words ἐπιστρωφῶσι πόληας (*Sophist* 216c 6) as quoted from Homer. But the preceding παντοῖσι is a part of the same Homeric line, *Odyssey* XVII 486, in which Plato replaces polemically the Homeric τελέθοντες by his own φανταζόμενοι διὰ τὴν τῶν ἄλλων ἄγνοιαν. Also, *Sophist* 216B 2–3 contains literal reminiscences of *Odyssey* XVII 486 et seq. and IX 270 et seq. The nominal συνόπαδος (as against the Homeric ὀπηδεῖ) must have been in Plato's mind from the ancient epic. Apollonios Rhodios, *Argonautica* IV 745, has ξείνῳ συνόπηδος ἐοῦσα.

8. *Odyssey* IX 270 et seq., XVII 485 et seq., XIV 283 et seq.

9. Manasse, p. 173. Also see de Vries, p. 157: "Theodoros seems to notice something of the irony. . . . Plato was still able to write at the time he composed the *Sophist*."

10. See above, p. 174.

11. Cf. Campbell, *"Sophistes"* [XXIII²⁸], xlviii: "The present inquiry . . . is restricted to the consideration of the Sophist in the highest and most technical sense, in which he is distinguished from the rhetorician and other artists, as the professor of knowledge and the teacher of virtue."

12. Cf. *Plato* 1, pp. 151f. (where, incidentally, reference should have been made to Schleiermacher, II/2, 252f., Susemihl, I, 292, and Bonitz, p. 183). / Stenzel (in "Logik," *R-E*, XIII, cols. 1006ff.) is at pains to show that standards of value govern the diaeresis of the *Gorgias*, whereas, in radical contrast, "standards of value are no longer allowed to play a part" in the late dialogues. But one need only read the close of the *Sophist*, from 267B on, to *see* standards of value. Indeed, the entire diaeretic system is dominated by the contrast in values presented by sophist vs. philosopher. Stenzel's differentiation is rightly

opposed by Shorey (p. 295), who points out "this exaggeration—caricature, we may almost say," but then undervalues the procedure in suggesting that "the process of dichotomy is only a mechanical aid to exhaustive search. . . ." É. de Strycker, "Le syllogisme chez Platon," *Revue Néo-Scolastique*, XXXIV (1932), 231, follows Stenzel.

13. *Euthydemus* 286c: οἱ ἀμφὶ Πρωταγόραν καὶ ἔτι παλαιότεροι.

14. Here, too, Steinhart (III, 443) and Susemihl (I, 294) sense a polemic directed against the Megarians and Antisthenes. Yet, even though topics of current discussion may enter in, it is above all Plato himself for whom the way of knowledge ascends from the ὄνομα to the λόγος: *Letter VII* 342B.

15. Bonitz, p. 183, is not correct in designating the first six dichotomies as unsuccessful and thus setting them over against the seventh. It is true that the seventh dichotomy finally hits the central characteristic, but this does not mean that the first six contribute nothing at all to the final definition. (Cornford, *Theory of Knowledge* [XXIII⁵], p. 173: "Division VII is the only one that goes to the heart of the matter and starts from the right genus.") It is evidently characteristic of the sophist that he is not to be pinned down in only *one* diaeretic system. See also Campbell, *"Sophistes,"* p. 63; Manasse, *Problem der Wahrheit*, pp. 182ff.

16. On the technical precision, see P.-M. Schuhl, "Remarques sur Platon et la technologie," *Estudios de Historia de la Filosofía en homenaje al Professor Rodolfo Mondolfo*, I (Tucumán, 1957), pp. 227ff. Schuhl recognizes in Plato *"un intérêt véritable pour l'objet, la méthode, la structure des plus modestes techniques."* Cf. C. J. Classen, *Untersuchungen zu Platons Jagdbildern* (Berlin, 1960), pp. 39ff.

17. The numbering followed here in the text is set up according to the summary of the first six determinations which Plato gives in 231D *et seq.* He himself had previously counted only five, taking the third and fourth as variants (224D). This shows how little Plato himself cared about the matter. (Cf. Bonitz, p. 184.)

18. Here, then, as often elsewhere, Plato touches on the criticism that is expressly made by Aristotle. See *De partibus animalium* I 3 643ᵇ 3 *et seq.*, as against τῷ ἀγρίῳ καὶ τῷ ἡμέρῳ διαιρεῖσθαι . . . πάντα γὰρ ὡς εἰπεῖν ὅσα ἥμερα καὶ ἄγρια τυγχάνει ὄντα οἷον ἄνθρωπος [!] ἵπποι βόες. . . .

19. See also *Lysis* 206A. Cf. Diès' *Le sophiste* (*Platon Budé*, VIII/3, 1925), pp. 269f.

20. It seems hopeless for us to reach any certainty as to the text of the recapitulation at 223B, since it is obvious that Plato had no intention of giving a precise recapitulation. See S. Benardete on *Sophist* 223B 1-7, in *Phronesis*, V (1960), 129ff.

21. 224B 6: μαθημάτων. 224B 9: μαθηματοπωλικῆς. 224C 1: μαθήματα.

22. On the difference in the numbering, see n. 17, above.

23. Susemihl (I, 291) mistakenly sees the Megarians hinted at here. Campbell is correct; see his commentary [XXIII²⁸] on 225E.
24. The grotesque jest that follows must have escaped Cornford, who says (*Theory of Knowledge*, p. 177): "In the sixth Division satire is dropped. The tone is serious . . ."
25. An especially exact correspondence occurs in *Alcibiades Major* 117E et seq. For other parallels, see Campbell's commentary on this passage.
26. Cf. G. B. Kerferd, "Plato's Noble Art of Sophistry," *CQ*, n.s., IV (1954), 84ff.; J. R. Trevaskis, "The Sophistry of Noble Lineage," *Phronesis*, I (1955/56), 36ff.
27. Campbell's insight may be correct when he remarks (in his Introduction to "*Sophistes*," p. lii): "We have here perhaps the most striking appreciation of a contemporary phase of thought which is to be found in ancient philosophy. For it is the simple truth that Protagoras and Gorgias did imperfectly and unconsciously a part of the same work which Socrates did thoroughly and consciously." We would agree— except that Plato's "objectivity" is probably overestimated, his belligerence underestimated.
28. See *Plato* 1, pp. 94f.
29. Certainly the seventh attempt is distinct from the first six. Yet the difference in method that Bonitz (p. 179) stresses, as did Schleiermacher before him, is only external. To be sure, Plato does start out in the seventh attempt from a characteristic feature of the sophist. But then he nevertheless assigns to this feature a place in a dichotomic system, just as he did in the previous determinations. The fact that he proceeds differently in the seventh diaeresis is to be understood purely as a matter of technique and is connected with the insertion of the ontological middle section.
30. Consult the literature listed in *Plato* 1, p. 358, n. 20. Also see Diès' Budé edition of *Le sophiste*, p. 271.
31. On the problem of perspective in ancient art, see the bibliography in George Karo's *Greek Personality in Archaic Sculpture* (Cambridge, Mass., 1948), p. 327, n. 81, and the reference to "the Greek *locus classicus*, Plato's *Sophist* 236."
32. Schleiermacher, II/2, 131ff.
33. Esp. *Laws* X 885B et seq. Cf. Campbell, "*Sophistes*," pp. lvii f., 183.
34. Toeplitz, *Das Verhältnis von Mathematik* . . . [XXVI³], p. 17, says with respect to *Sophist* 250E that Plato does not conceive the diaeresis "as a formal subdivision, but that for him the mutual relation of the parts is all important, and that this can perhaps provide a clearer evidence than the parts and their sum themselves." What Stenzel (*Studien*, pp. 47f.) has to say about analysis into concepts and definition as the objective of this dialogue is corrected by Stenzel's own later inquiry (*Zahl und Gestalt*). / On διαίρεσις, cf. Classen, pp. 78ff.

35. See *Laws* 816D: ἄνευ γὰρ γελοίων τὰ σπουδαῖα καὶ πάντων τῶν ἐναντίων τὰ ἐναντία μαθεῖν οὐ δυνατόν, with which, as is well known, Aristotle's sentence τῶν ἐναντίων μία ἐπιστήμη agrees. Cf. Apelt, *Aufsätze*, p. 204.

36. Cf. Stenzel, *Studien*, p. 16.

37. *Sophist* 238C 8: οὔτε φθέγξασθαι δυνατὸν ὀρθῶς οὔτ᾽ εἰπεῖν οὔτε διανοηθῆναι τὸ μὴ ὂν αὐτὸ καθ᾽ αὑτό, ἀλλ᾽ ἔστιν ἀδιανόητόν τε καὶ ἄρρητον καὶ ἄφθεγκτον καὶ ἄλογον. Cf. Parmenides, *Vorsokr.* 28 [18] B 8, ll. 8f.: οὐ γὰρ φατὸν οὐδὲ νοητόν ἐστιν ὅπως οὐκ ἔστι.

38. τὸ μὴ ὂν γὰρ φημί in 238E 2 looks back to the initial position τὸ μηδαμῶς ὂν τολμῶμέν που φθέγγεσθαι in 237B 7, and outdoes it. Cf. the play with φθέγγεσθαι in *Cratylus* 429E *et seq.*

39. The deduction at 240B 7 *et seq.* is not easy to follow in its technical refinement. The ἀληθινόν = ὄντως ὄν is wholly negated; Plato expresses this by οὐκ ὄντως οὐκ ὄν. At this point, οὐκ ὄντως ὄν as in Codex *T* would be possible, except that the double οὐκ recurs again in B 12 (οὐκ ὂν ἄρα οὐκ ὄντως) and thus the two passages support each other mutually. Here one must not follow Badham in deleting the second οὐκ, since Plato evidently intended the paradoxical contrast of οὐκ ὄντως ἔστιν ὄντως. Only in this way does this συμπλοκή of not-being with being come out in a linguistically appropriate style. Only in this way, too, does one understand the adverb πως (240B 9, C 5) linguistically as a coincidence of οὐκ ὄντως and ὄντως. On this passage and the Neoplatonic imitation, see F. W. Kohnke, "Plato's Conception of τὸ οὐκ ὄντως οὐκ ὄν," *Phronesis*, II (1957), 32ff. / That the term συμπλοκή recurs with the Atomists is shown by Stenzel, "Platon und Demokritos," *Kleine Schriften*, p. 67, where he proves a certain correspondence, somewhat like a mirror image, between Platonic and Atomistic trains of thought. Also, the strange passage *Sophist* 253D might become clearer if viewed from this perspective. Nevertheless, on συνημμένην see Herakleitos, *Vorsokr.* 22 [12] B 10 (συνάψιες), and on περιεχομένας see Kranz, *Wortindex* [XXI²³], s.v. περιέχειν. From 254D on, the dominant term is μειγνύναι with its derivatives—and this too is a "pre-Socratic" term which is by no means merely Atomistic. (Cf. Kranz, s.v. μεῖγμα, μειγνύναι, μίσγειν.)

40. See n. 37, above. Madvig's rejection in 241A 5 weakens this support.

41. Cf. W. Dilthey, "Einleitung in die Geisteswissenschaften," *Gesammelte Schriften* (8 vols., Leipzig and Berlin, 1914–29), I, 179f.; R. McKeon, "Plato and Aristotle as Historians: A Study of Methods in the History of Ideas," *Ethics*, LI (1940), 66ff.; H. Cherniss, "The History of Ideas and Ancient Greek Philosophy," in *Estudios . . . Mondolfo*, I (Tucumán, 1957), pp. 93ff.; K. von Fritz, *Aristotle's Contribution to the Practice and Theory of Historiography* (UCalPCP, Vol. XXVIII, No. 3, 1958), pp. 113ff.

42. The passage at 244C *et seq.* is hard to understand as the editions show

it because—as seems to be standard practice in printing Plato's texts —the interrupted sentences are not so indicated. *Sophist* 244c 9 should be printed (using ellipsis points to show the interruption): καταγέλαστόν που . . . , and c 11 should begin with a small initial letter: καὶ τὸ παράπαν. Similarly, 244D 3 should be: λέγει πού τινε . . . , and D 6: καὶ μὴν. 244D 9 should be: οὐδενὸς ὄν . . . , and D 11: καὶ τὸ ἕν γε. And so on . . . / Burnet's reading in 244D 11–12 is wrong. The preceding τὸ ὄνομα ὀνόματος ὄνομα μόνον has an exact correspondence in τὸ ἕν γε ἑνὸς ἓν ὂν μόνον. (The fact that "the One" is only "the one of a one" is even more subtle than that the name is only the name of a name, but this is exactly what corresponds to Plato's intention.) What follows καὶ τοῦτο ὀνόματος αὖ τὸ ἓν ὄν probably is parallel also to the preceding ἄλλου δὲ οὐδενὸς ὄν. If we have ἓν ἑνὸς ἕν, then we must also have ὀνόματος ἕν. Cf. Schleiermacher, II/2, 505. / To complement our observation at the beginning of this note, a matter of principle should be mentioned. Our usual—much too Eleatic— punctuation is far from being any match for the vivacity of the Platonic dialogue. Several substantiating examples may be given. An ἄνω στιγμή (according to our type of punctuation) would be necessary in *Republic* 475E 7, 493A 4; in *Sophist* 241D 1, 242B 8, 246D 2, 247D 6, 250D 5, 255E 9, 257c 5, 257D 12, 258D 3, 262B 3; in *Statesman* 269D 3, 284c 8, 287E 2, 290c 6 (on account of τε in c 4), 309B 7; in *Philebus* 39c 7, 39E 8, 41D 6, 46A 3 *et seq.*, 48D 9, 52D 4, 58B 3; in *Laws* IV 711D 4, 715c 4, 715A 6. No punctuation—neither comma, dash, nor suspension points, as a sign of a sentence broken off—is necessary in *Sophist* 258c 10, 259c 5, 262c 7, or in *Statesman* 257A 8, 290A 8, 294D 8, 297B 5. Such examples are especially numerous in the *Philebus* (see below, ch. XXVIII, n. 6). / How lacking in independence even the good new editions are as to punctuation—i.e., how little they follow the vivacity of the dialogue—has become clear to me through a comparison of Diès and Burnet. And it is no accident that the examples assembled in the present note come almost entirely from Plato's late period. What is shown is the conversational vivacity of these same late dialogues, a characteristic often not recognized (see nn. 6 and 9, above).

43. Bonitz differentiates the two sections as (*1*) philosophemes which have established a definite number regarding being, and (*2*) philosophemes which have definitely established the quality of being. Even if we admit that these headings are not exactly wrong, still we may suggest that this contrast is not at all important—as indeed Plato himself did not expressly make it anywhere. Also, Bonitz (see the note on his p. 162) is mistaken if he thinks he can derive the interpretation of this contrast from the relation between 243c 10 *et seq.* and 245E 6 *et seq.* These two passages do not refer to the same thing at all.

The first passage concerns the contrast of the many, some of whom have previously been spoken of, and the one Parmenides. The many are to be discussed further, ἂν δόξῃ—but this is evidently not done. The second passage separates the two sections without looking back to that earlier passage. In saying ἄλλως λέγοντες, Plato means the two opposed positions about which the discussion is now carried on. The πολλοί in the first passage, however, are the philosophers of nature in contrast to Parmenides. / In 245E 7, by the way, one must not write πάντας μὲν οὐ, as even Burnet does (and Wilamowitz, II, 239, approves). One should follow the manuscripts and write πάνυ μὲν οὐ. Campbell's reference—in his *"Sophistes"* [XXIII²⁸], pp. 116f.—to *Protagoras* 238E 3 carries weight. Besides, πάνυ is in contrast to ἱκανῶς. "We have not developed the *aporias* to the ultimate. But enough!" Yet it must be added that τοὺς διακριβολογουμένους ὄντος τε πέρι καὶ μή fits only those who were last considered, the Eleatics; from this standpoint, then, πάντας becomes altogether impossible. The transition being made is from the Eleatic problems, about which much more could be said, to the discussion that follows. It is by no means requisite (as Bonitz thinks, to whom Zeller concedes too much) that those concluding and transitional words "must comprehend the two philosophic trends treated in 243D-245E."

44. B. Schweitzer, *Platon und die bildende Kunst der Griechen* (Tübingen, 1953), pp. 61ff., sees in the "gigantomachy" a reference to Pheidias' shield of the Athene Parthenos—quite possible.

45. The verbal similarity of *Sophist* 248A to *Phaedo* 78DE, *Phaedrus* 247DE, and *Theaetetus* 184CD is striking. Thus, in this case Plato is referring to Plato. This fact can still be variously interpreted, however, without any need for the different interpretations to exclude each other. Where Plato modifies or seems to modify the views of the "friends of *Ideas*," one can see him aiming at an earlier stage of his theory, or see a trend of thought within the Academy, or see both. In particular we do well not to adopt a historicizing form of thinking that divides up the contrasts by periods. Rather we would comprehend them as antithetic points of view within the one creative human being. / Diès, *Le sophiste* [XXVI¹⁹], p. 292, n. 1, in a very commendable manner culls out of the superabundant literature the main answers proposed to the question, Whom did Plato mean by the "friends of Forms"? Diès distinguishes six groups of answers (with variations). Cherniss (in *Aristotle's Criticism of Plato*, p. 439, n. 376) distinguishes a "seventh," for Cherniss thinks Plato is designating a trend against Eudoxos within the Academy. / Diès in fact considers it impossible that in this passage Plato could mean himself. It is Diès' error to think that the words κίνησιν . . . τῷ παντελῶς ὄντι μὴ παρεῖναι apply to the movement of the cosmos—whereas what Plato does mean is "true being"

(Schleiermacher), "that which is perfectly real" (Cornford), and therefore not the cosmos. (Cf. Grube, p. 296.) / Cherniss, loc. cit., observes: "It is not a 'new development' either for Plato in the *Sophist* to posit as ideas the actions which are the meanings of verbs (*Sophist* 261D–263D); πράξεις had been declared to be ὄντα in the *Cratylus* (386E–387B)." Only this contra: In the *Cratylus*, Socrates shows that the objects (τὰ πράγματα) have a certain being (οὐσίαν τινά), and therefore that one cannot trifle with them at will. The little word τινά shows that right here Socrates is not talking about ὄντως ὄντα. From the πράγματα he then goes over to the πράξεις. These, too, have their own growth. The πράξεις as well as the πράγματα are "one Form of being" (ἕν τι εἶδος τῶν ὄντων), so that they must be cared for in accordance with their nature or their character. Since the πράγματα "are," to be sure, but are not truly being, then—in spite of the word εἶδος—the same must hold true for the πράξεις. / According to Stefanini (1932 edn.), I, xvi: "When the critics read in the *Sophist* a fierce attack by the *philosopher of Ideas* against the *friends of Ideas*, they tried—in order to avoid the scandal of a self-criticism—to identify the *friends of Ideas* with another school which would not be the Platonic. Yet they could not attempt a similar salvaging of Platonic coherence in the presence of the pressing objections with which the *Parmenides* demolishes the doctrine of *Ideas*." (Against the word "demolishes," "*demolisce*," I would, however, raise an objection.) / See also Wilamowitz, II, ch. 18, "Εἰδῶν Φίλοι"; Grube, pp. 295ff.

46. It is correct that in *Hippias Major* 301B the sophist takes possession of this thesis as a weapon with which to fight Socrates; cf. F. Dümmler, *Akademika* (Giessen, 1889), p. 204. But this does not entitle us to call the thesis Antisthenian. See Wilamowitz' remarks (II, 245) on "Antisthenes the Unavoidable."

47. See p. 159, above.

48. Cf. esp. *Metaphysics* IX 1 1046ᵃ 19: δύναμις τοῦ ποιεῖν καὶ πάσχειν, and V 14 1021ᵃ 15: κατὰ δύναμιν ποιητικὴν καὶ παθητικήν.

49. Susemihl (I, 301) refers to "reconsideration of the *Ideas*, seen as motionless as late as the *Phaedrus*, mythically personified into images of gods." The words "reconsideration" and "as late as" are based, however, on the concept that there is this "doctrine" of Plato's developing from dialogue to dialogue. Yet, the dialectics of the *Sophist* does not overcome the myth of the *Phaedrus*. There exists instead a παλίντονος ἁρμονίη between the two. / How far astray this "development theory" can go is shown, for example, in Sir James George Frazer's *The Growth of Plato's Ideal Theory* (London, 1930), p. 99: "The ideal world has collapsed; the sky has fallen and down tumble the *Ideas*." Or, in the words of Gomperz (III, 176): "The aged thinker shivers in the heaven of his ideas." Ross (pp. 107f.) also

views the matter too much in terms of development when he states: "The 'Friends of Forms' are Plato's earlier self and those who have accepted his earlier view."

50. See Stefanini's discussion (pp. 204ff.) of the *"dinamismo e staticità delle idee nel 'Sofista.'* "

51. Cf. Zeller, p. 293.

52. On this and esp. the difficult passage 253D, see Schleiermacher, II/2, 505ff.; Bonitz, pp. 170ff.; Stenzel, *Studien*, pp. 62ff.; Gadamer, *Platos dialektische Ethik* [XXI²⁶], p. 74; Cornford, *Theory of Knowledge* [XXIII⁵], p. 267; Stefanini, pp. 188ff.; J. L. Ackrill, "Plato and the Copula," *JHS*, LXXVII (1957), 1ff.; Allen, pp. 207ff.

53. Not "the five greatest," as in Cornford, pp. 273ff.

54. It has been stated several times that the distinction between substantive and verb, subject and predicate, is not yet established. See the comments of H. Steinthal (*Geschichte der Sprachwissenschaft*, Berlin, 1863, pp. 136ff.), who combines misleading criticism with good analyses. Also see Stenzel, *Studien*, p. 88; M. Heidegger, *Einführung in die Metaphysik* (Tübingen, 1953), pp. 43f.

55. As to the ethical and existential component of the *Sophist*, emphasized once more here in the text, I have found nothing in the critical literature.

56. See pp. 248f., above.

XXVII: *Statesman*

RECENT EDITIONS AND TRANSLATIONS: O. Apelt, PhB 151 (1922); A. Diès, *Platon Budé*, IX/1 (1935); J. B. Skemp (London, 1952); G. A Roggerone (Turin, 1953); A. Gonzáles Laso (Madrid, 1955); A. Zadro (Bari, 1957); F. Adorno (Turin, 1958).

RECENT INTERPRETATIONS: M. Schröder, *Zum Aufbau des platonischen "Politikos"* (Jena, 1935); E. M. Manasse, *Platons "Sophistes" und "Politikos"* (Berlin, 1937); H. Zeise, *Der Staatsmann* (Leipzig, 1938); Annemarie Capelle, *Platos Dialog "Politikos"* (Hamburg, 1939); Barker, ch. 12; Schuhl, *Fabulation*, pp. 89ff.; Kucharski, pp. 147ff.; Stefanini, pp. 215ff.; G. A. Roggerone, "La funzione del 'politico' nella dottrina platonica dello stato," *Sophia*, XVIII (1950), 239ff.; J. H. M. M. Loenen, *De "Nous" in het Systeem van Plato's Philosophie* (Amsterdam, 1951), pp. 158ff.; Stanka, pp. 158ff.; Sinclair, pp. 173ff.; Vanhoutte, pp. 128ff.; Luccioni, pp. 162ff., 246ff.; Gauss, III/1, ch. 5; P. Kucharski, "La conception de l'art de la mesure dans le *Politique*," *Bull. Budé* (1960), pp. 459ff.; S. Benardete, "Eidos and Diaeresis in Plato's *Statesman*," *Philologus*, CVII (1963), 193ff.; Lesky, p. 534.

ADDITIONAL BIBLIOGRAPHY: Shorey, p. 598; Geffcken, Notes, pp. 107f., 115f.; Leisegang, cols. 2498ff.; Rosenmeyer, p. 187; Cherniss, *Lustrum*, pp. 146ff.

1. Schleiermacher (II/2, 251) regards the *Statesman* and *Sophist* "more as counterparts than halves of a whole." Less to the point is Ritter, *Platon*, II, 134: "The *Statesman* is actually nothing but the disconnected second half of the *Sophist*." Hermann (*Geschichte*, pp. 500f.) goes to the other extreme in exaggerating the differences between the two works.

2. Many writers, among them Schleiermacher, Hermann, Stallbaum, H. Müller, Steinhart, Wilamowitz, Diès, and Skemp, ascribe the last answer to the old Socrates rather than to the young namesake. Burnet disagrees—as does Campbell, in *"Sophistes" and "Politicus"* [XXIII²⁸], p. 191. The question probes deeper, however, than even Campbell realized. See p. 304, above.

3. See E. Kapp, in *R-E*, III A, cols. 890f.

4. See Meyer, V, § 988; J. B. Skemp, *Plato's "Statesman"* (London, 1952), p. 25. Franciscus Novotny, *Platonis Epistulae* (Brno, Czechoslovakia, 1930), p. 275: *"Pro certo dicere non possumus idemne fuerit Leodamas Thasius . . ."*

5. Wilamowitz (I, 564 = I², 570) speculates: "Had the 'Philosopher' been written, not only would we have been shown the philosopher whose mind is always directed toward the *Idea* of being . . . but this divine itself would have been shown to us . . ." Diès agrees; see his *Platon Budé* edition of the *Theaetetus* [XXIII²³], p. 137. / My opinion about the third dialogue of this supposedly planned trilogy is like that of Schleiermacher (II/2, 511; cf. II/2, 252, 369). The same view was sharply stressed by K. F. Hermann, *Gesammelte Abhandlungen* [XXV¹], p. 30, and more thoroughly substantiated by Ritter, *Untersuchungen*, pp. 66ff. Nevertheless, the position is still in need of more radical foundation. See *Plato* 1, pp. 152f. / We need not mention the attempts to find the third dialogue in the *Parmenides*, in the *Phaedo*, in the *Symposium*, or even in the *Republic*—except to recognize that there could not be a particular dialogue about the philosopher because he is present in all of them. Had Salin carried his considerations further in *Utopie* (see p. 57), they would have led him to a denial of the dialogue *Philosopher*. / Cornford says, in *Theory of Knowledge* [XXIII⁵], p. 169: "Why the *Philosopher* was never written, we can only conjecture." Stefanini, pp. 188f., finds the *Philosopher* unnecessary because the *Sophist* and the *Statesman*, even if only indirectly, "had exhausted [!] the subject matter." A similar view is in Geffcken, Notes, p. 135.

6. See A. Diès, *Le politique* (*Platon Budé*, IX/1, 1935), p. viii, and the

"diagrammatic plan" on p. lxviii; also see Skemp's edition, p. 113. The five-part division (Steinhart, III, 588ff.; Susemihl, I, 314) is rather arbitrary.

7. Schleiermacher (II/2, 256) finds "in what is *merely a parenthetic digression*, the most profound disclosures . . ." (italics added). Cf. Susemihl, I, 329.

8. The anecdote about Diogenes in *Diogenes Laërtius* VI 2 40 alludes even in its wording to *Statesman* 266E. Cf. Schleiermacher, II/2, 253.

9. *Plato* 1, pp. 204ff. Cf. Reinhardt, *Mythen*, pp. 113f.; Diès, *Le politique*, pp. xxx ff. (ch. 4, "Le mythe"). / P.-M. Schuhl, "Sur le mythe du *Politique*," *Revue de Métaphysique et de Morale*, XXXIX (1932), 46ff., draws attention to the model character. A model of this kind probably did exist in the Academy. / According to J. E. Boodin, *Three Interpretations of the Universe* (New York, 1934), p. 300, "the myth of creation in the *Statesman* exhibits the relation of the Creator to the world by showing what would happen if the Creator withdrew." / Grube, p. 278, has strangely misunderstood the mixture of playful irony and deep seriousness: ". . . awkwardly introduced . . . inartistic . . . two images are incompatible . . ." Grube seems neither to recognize the relation to the topic of the dialogue (cf. *Plato* 1, pp. 204ff.), nor to recall the myths of the *Timaeus* and the *Critias*.

10. Taylor (*Plato*, p. 297) finds here rather an attack against the "autocrat or dictator paternally managing the rest of mankind without the need of direction or control by the law." That Taylor even misunderstands the purpose of the whole is revealed in his statements (see pp. 393, 403) that "Plato means to decide definitely for constitutionalism and, in particular, to commend a limited monarchy." Evidently the political tradition of England has biased Taylor's interpretation of 294A *et seq.*

11. Therefore, the contradiction between 276E and 296B *et seq.*—which Skemp, p. 16, emphasizes (referring to Barker, p. 278)—is not to be taken seriously either.

12. Cf. Campbell's commentary on the *"Politicus"* [XXIII²⁸], p. 17, and the reference there to *Philebus* 14E and *Republic* IV 445D. Strangely unPlatonic is the remark: "It is difficult to say how far the 'form' here spoken of is objective, and how far subjective."

13. Campbell, p. 34. Cf. Schleiermacher, II/2, 252f. / I fail to understand how parts of the *Statesman* can be considered boring, a frequent criticism (see, for example, Ritter, *Platon*, II, 135). To judge the dialogue dull, one cannot have recognized, beyond the structure of the whole, the abundance of playfulness or the creative power of Plato's language, a power that "spooks" even in what Steinhart (III, 588) calls the "comically contrived terminology." The *Statesman* and also the *Sophist* remind Diès (*Platon*, pp. 306f.) of Rabelais. The false punctuation so frequently found in modern editions contributes to

this misjudgment. (On this see above, ch. XXVI, n. 42.) Wilamowitz (I, 555 = I², 561) regrets that Plato "has not abandoned the form of the dialogue." / In these divisions one somehow senses Aristotle's method and at the same time his criticism as practiced in *De partibus animalium* I 2–3. See esp. the passage at 642ᵇ 10: ἔτι δὲ προσήκει μὴ διασπᾶν ἕκαστον γένος, οἷον τοὺς ὄρνιθας τοὺς μὲν ἐν τῇδε τοὺς δ' ἐν ἄλλῃ διαιρέσει, καθάπερ ἔχουσιν γεγραμμέναι διαιρέσεις (of the Academy). ἐκεῖ γὰρ τοὺς μὲν μετὰ τῶν ἐνύδρων συμβαίνει διῃρῆσθαι, τοὺς δ' ἐν ἄλλῳ γένει. In general, see 643ᵇ 14: τὸ αὐτὸ γὰρ εἰς πλείους ἐμπίπτει διαιρέσεις καὶ τὰ ἐναντία εἰς τὴν αὐτήν.

14. See *Plato* 1, pp. 93f.

15. Julius Jüthner, *Hellenen und Barbaren* (Leipzig, 1923), pp. 22ff.; K. J. Vourveris, Αἱ ἱστορικαὶ γνώσεις τοῦ Πλάτωνος. Α: Βαρβαρικά (Athens, 1938), pp. 27, 58; Shorey, p. 600; Diès, *Le politique*, p. 10; Skemp, *Statesman*, pp. 131f. Skemp's evaluation seems to me particularly thorough and cautious.

16. See *Aristotelis . . . fragmenta*, ed. Valentinus Rose (Leipzig, 1886), frag. 658; cf. Strabon I 66.

17. Compare Strabon I 66: οὐκ ἐπαινέσας (Eratosthenes) τοὺς δίχα διαιροῦντας ἅπαν τὸ τῶν ἀνθρώπων πλῆθος εἴς τε Ἕλληνας καὶ βαρβάρους . . . with *Statesman* 262CD.

18. My earlier interpretation of διεσπασμένῳ (see the first German edition of *Platon*, II, 544, n. 1) was mistaken. Cf. V. Goldschmidt, *Le paradigme dans la dialectique platonicienne* (Paris, 1947), p. 65, n. 7.

19. συναχθέν in 278c 5 seems to mean συνάγειν εἰς ἕν: see *Philebus* 25D 5, *Sophist* 267B 1. It is probably more correct to connect περὶ ἑκάτερον to what follows. / I read περὶ ἑκάτερον καὶ συνάμφω (as in *BW*), and compare *Sophist* 243E 1: λέγοντες ἄμφω καὶ ἑκάτερον εἶναι. In agreement with Codex *T*, the editions print ὡς instead of καί. But what does this mean? Goldschmidt (p. 66) and Skemp (p. 160) give penetrating interpretations. Both are close to my interpretation (as stated above in the text), but neither of them wants to give up ὡς in favor of καί. Yet the formulation ἑκάτερον καὶ συνάμφω becomes meaningful against the background of *Hippias Major* 300E *et seq.* and *Republic* VII 524BC—we are facing a problem that was much discussed and eristically exploited in Plato's time.

20. Cf. Robinson, *Dialectic*, pp. 224ff. = 2d edn., pp. 212ff.

21. Cf. Ritter's schema, in *Untersuchungen*, p. 71. See also Diès, *Le politique*, p. xvii.

22. In the indexes to the *Doxographi Graeci*, the *Vorsokratiker*, and the works of Aristotle, see entries under σύγκρισις, διάκρισις, etc. For the complexity with which the archaic language expressed these matters, see Empedokles, *Vorsokr.* 31 [21] B 17. συγκρίνεσθαι: Anaxagoras, *Vorsokr.* 59 [46] B 4. διακρίνεσθαι: Anaxagoras, *Vorsokr.* 59 [46] B 12, 13. In the preserved fragments, however, these terms are always

used with other expressions and not in sharp opposition. For the latter purpose, Anaxagoras used rather συμμίσγεσθαι and διακρίνεσθαι (*Vorsokr.* 59 [46] B 17). Also see Epicharmos, *Vorsokr.* 23 [13] B 9: συνεκρίθη καὶ διεκρίθη.

23. Stefanini, p. 227, agrees.

24. Once we have followed up to this point, we are reminded of the "world fabric," whose importance in the beliefs of different peoples has been shown by Robert Eisler in *Weltenmantel und Himmelszelt* (Munich, 1910). Plato was familiar with Pherekydes' Zas (*Vorsokr.* 7 [71] B 2) who, for his wedding with Chthonie, made a φᾶρος (ποικίλλει). And Plato almost certainly was acquainted also with the Orphic Kore: ἱστουργοῦσα, ὑφαίνουσα τὸν διάκοσμον τῶν οὐρανίων (see in Otto Kern, *Orphicorum Fragmenta*, Berlin, 1922, pp. 192-94; cf. also p. 33). In Pherekydes' account, the woven or embroidered pictures are of great importance (as is generally true of the *Weltenmantel*), but primary significance is attributed to the symbol of weaving itself. It would fit what we know about Plato—whose *Statesman*, incidentally, Eisler's study does not include—to assume that he assimilated this primitive image to suit his own purpose. The Platonic motif occurs again in the Περὶ βασιλείας of Diotogenes, the Pythagorean; see Stobaeus IV 1 (ed. C. Wachsmuth and O. Hense, 2d edn., Berlin, 1954, p. 265): ἁ μὲν γὰρ πόλις ἐκ πολλῶν καὶ διαφερόντων συναρμοσθεῖσα κόσμω σύνταξιν καὶ ἁρμονίαν μεμίμαται. Cf. Campbell, *"Politicus"* [XXIII²⁸], Introduction, pp. xxv ff.

25. See Campbell, p. 107; Singer, p. 229; Diès, *Le sophiste*, p. 46, n. 1; and Skemp's edition, p. 173, n. 1.

26. Wilamowitz, I, 551f. = I², 557f.; Diès, p. lxii ff.; Skemp, pp. 16f. Skemp refers to Barker, p. 278, for the thesis that between *Statesman* 276E and 292A *et seq.* (and esp. in 296B *et seq.*), there is an unresolved contradiction. Plato actually did intend this contrast: that within the order of the six empirical constitutions, better constitutions are distinguished from worse ones on the basis of the approval of the ruled. In the best state, however, such approval is unnecessary— since it has to be taken for granted. / On 286B-287B see Schuhl, *Études*, pp. 75ff.

27. Gomperz recognizes only the external aspect when he says (III, 179–80) that Plato's "mastery over his thoughts is gradually losing in strictness."

28. One realizes again how closely Aristotle (*De partibus animalium* I 2-3) approaches the true Platonic intentions when he criticizes the dichotomy. Note esp. the passage at 643b 23: διὸ πολλαῖς τὸ ἓν εὐθέως διαιρετέον . . . ὅτι δ᾽ οὐκ ἐνδέχεται τῶν καθ᾽ ἕκαστον εἰδῶν λαμβάνειν οὐδὲν διαιροῦσι δίχα τὸ γένος, ὥσπερ τινὲς [!] ᾠήθησαν, καὶ ἐκ τῶνδε φανερόν . . . On the subject in general, see Stenzel, *Studien*, and Diès, *Le politique*, pp. xv ff., "Dichotomies et dialectique."

29. Singer, p. 141.

30. Pindar, *Pythian* II 86; Herodotos III 80 *et seq.*, and also VI 43.

31. Xenophon, *Memorabilia* IV 6 12. Plato lists five constitutions for the reason that *democracy* is the name for the good as well as the bad system of government. But it appears that Xenophon simply snatched up the number five. / Barker (pp. 289f.) is hardly justified in finding a difference between *Statesman* 291D *et seq.* and 302c *et seq.* According to Barker, the first classification follows a theory that was current at the time and was related, he thinks, to Xenophon's theory. Barker claims, then, that Plato's own classification starts only with 302 *et seq.*

32. Aristotle, *Nicomachean Ethics* VIII 12 1161b 11 *et seq.*; *Politics* III 4 1279a 8 *et seq.*; *Politics* VI 1 1316b 30 *et seq.* Cf. W. L. Newman, *The "Politics" of Aristotle* [XXII¹²], I, 214ff.; III, xxvii ff. Also see Polybios VI 3–5; and E. K. Rand, *The Building of Eternal Rome* (Cambridge, Mass., 1943), p. 10.

33. This section is more extensively interpreted in *Plato* 1, pp. 115ff., because of its very fundamental significance. Concerning this, see further Diès, *Le politique*, pp. li ff., on "L'illégalité ideale."

34. Erwin Rohde, *Kleine Schriften* [XXIII³⁸], I, 275, sees the *Statesman* as the "bridge from the *Republic* to the *Laws*."

35. Cf. Schleiermacher, II/2, 262f.; Campbell's *"Politicus"* [XXIII²⁸], Introduction, p. xviii.

36. Gomperz (III, 184) lets himself be deceived, in so far as he actually regards this as a "memorable self-correction" of Plato's. Ueberweg-Praechter (p. 301) also find that "in the *Statesman*, the theory of temperaments has completely replaced the intellectualism." But the customary concept of intellectualism is not valid here (Singer, p. 32, has rightly opposed it). Even in the *Protagoras*, courage was difficult to unite with the other virtues since it alone often seems to depend more on temperament than on insight.

37. See *DGrA*, II, 64ff.

38. See above, p. 525, n. 2, and in the text, p. 304.

XXVIII: *Philebus*

RECENT EDITIONS AND TRANSLATIONS: R. G. Bury (Cambridge, 1897); O. Apelt, PhB 145 (1912); A. Diès, *Platon Budé*, IX/2 (1941); R. Hackforth (Cambridge, Mass., 1945); A. E. Taylor (ed. G. Calogero, R. Klibansky, and A. C. Lloyd, New York, 1956); A. Zadro (Bari, 1957).

RECENT INTERPRETATIONS: H.-G. Gadamer, *Platos dialektische Ethik* (Leipzig, 1931); Shorey, pp. 316ff.; W. Szilasi, *Macht und Ohnmacht des Geistes* (Bern, 1946), pp. 19ff., and the review by E. M. Manasse in *Philos. Rundschau*, V/1 (1957), 36ff.; A. Tovar, "Observationes aliquot in Platonis *Philebum," Orientalia Christ. Per.*, XIII (1947), 656ff.; Stefanini, 227ff.; P. Kucharski, *Les chemins du savoir* (1949), and also "La musique et la conception du réel dans le *Philèbe*," *Revue Philosophique*, CXLI (1951), 39ff.; H. J. M. Broos, "Plato and Art," *Mnemosyne*, 4th ser., IV (1951), 113ff.; J. H. M. M. Loenen, "De ontwikkeling van Plato's teleologische natuurbeschouwing," *Tijdsch. Philos.*, XV (1953), 179ff.; G. E. Mueller, "The Unity of Plato's *Philebus*," *CJ*, L (1954/55), 21ff.; M. Vanhoutte, "La genèse du plaisir dans le *Philèbe*," in *Mélanges Diès* (Paris, 1956), pp. 235ff.; Stenzel, *Kleine Schriften*, pp. 342ff.; J. Gosling, "False Pleasures. *Philebus* 35c–41B," *Phronesis*, IV (1959), 44ff., and also "Father Kenny on False Pleasures," *Phronesis*, VI (1961), 41ff.; Fr. A. Kenny, "False Pleasures in the *Philebus*. A Reply to Mr. Gosling," *Phronesis*, V (1960), 45ff.; J. R. Trevaskis, "Classification in the *Philebus*," *Phronesis*, V (1960), 39ff.; S. MacClintock, "More on the Structure of the *Philebus*," *Phronesis*, VI (1961), 46ff.; P.-M. Schuhl, "Cosmos asômatos," *RevÉtGr*, LXXVI (1963), 52ff.; Lesky, p. 534.

ADDITIONAL BIBLIOGRAPHY: Shorey, p. 603; Geffcken, Notes, pp. 116f.; Leisegang, cols. 2502ff.; Rosenmeyer, p. 187; Cherniss, *Lustrum*, pp. 141ff.

1. Olympiodoros, *In Platonis Philebum Scholia*, ed. G. Stallbaum (2d edn., Leipzig, 1826), p. 237; cf. L. G. Westerink, *Damascius: Lectures on the "Philebus" Wrongly Attributed to Olympiodorus* (Amsterdam, 1959). Also see A. Diès, *Philèbe* (*Platon Budé*, IX/2, 1941), pp. xc ff.

2. See *Plato* 2, pp. 28ff. / The remark of Wilamowitz (I, 623 = I², 630) that "it is still embarrassing to [Plato] that he once had, in the *Protagoras*, considered the pleasant and the good to be equally high" is based on Wilamowitz' interpretation (I, 147ff. = I², 149ff.) of the *Protagoras*, against which many objections must be raised. Cf. Werner Jaeger, in *Gnomon*, IV (1928), 5.

3. See H. Karpp, *Untersuchungen zur Philosophie des Eudoxos von Knidos* (Würzburg, 1933), and also the still-important article of R. Philippson, "Akademische Verhandlungen über die Lustlehre," *Hermes*, LX (1925), 444ff. Diès, *Philèbe*, p. lxii, correctly objects to the assumption that there is a "duel" here between Eudoxos and Speusippos. See further Diès, pp. liii ff., "Le *Philèbe* et les théories contemporaines du plaisir."

4. J. Alpers, *Hercules in Bivio* (Göttingen diss., 1912); E. Panofsky, *Hercules am Scheidewege* (Studien der Bibliothek Warburg, XVIII, Leipzig and Berlin, 1930).

5. So writes Schleiermacher (II/3, 128), recognizing the particular tension of the dialogue more clearly than most of the later interpreters, who do not sufficiently grasp its artistic and philosophical irony.

6. Only in one single sentence of the *Philebus* (namely, in 57D 4) do the editions—in total agreement at least since Bekker (1826)—punctuate the interruption. (One could, however, use a colon or a series of points here just as easily as the dash, as also in *Phaedrus* 273C 10.) In the first group below, I list twenty-four passages in the *Philebus* that are completely similar to 57D 4, *with the difference* that in these passages no edition punctuates the interruption in any way. These are places where Protarchos interjects (τό) ποῖον; or (τά) ποῖα; or τό(ν) ποῖον δή; or something similar. Socrates usually precedes this with τόδε or τοιόνδε and often premises it with a request like λαβέ or λάβωμεν or σκεψώμεθα. (Therefore, one should write ἀπροκρινώμεθα in 57D 4 according to Stephanus.) This *first group* includes: 11D 2, 13E 2, 14C 2, 20C 8, 23C 7, 29B 4, 34B 4, 34C 4, 36C 4, 39C 8, 41D 6, 42C 7, 46A 3, 46A 6, 52D 4, 54A 3, 58B 7, 59B 11, 59E 8, 60B 8, 63A 10, 63B 5, 64A 8, 64D 7. The *second group* of passages are those where the question or consent of Protarchos stands between a μέν and a δέ of Socrates: 17C 2, 30D 8, 42A 9, 48E 2, 65E 7, 67A 15. In the *third group*, a ὧδε or τῇδε or ἐν τούτοις or ἐκεῖθεν of Socrates is separated from what it points to by an interjection from Protarchos: 27E 3, 28D 3, 34E 7, 38C 7, 38C 10, 41C 9, 43A 8, 43C 2, 55A 12, 60A 5, 60B 10. A *fourth group* may be made up of passages that differ only slightly from the preceding examples and from each other: 16B 7, 48C 9, 48D 9, 56B 6. / Also see above, ch. XXVI, n. 42.

7. That they are "through" (Wilamowitz, I, 621 = I², 628) is true only in a restricted sense. The dialogical motif, that the discussion will go on, recurs—*not by chance*—throughout the *Philebus*: 19E, 50D, 67B.

8. See, for example, Wilamowitz, I, 622 = I², 629; Jaeger, *Aristotle*, pp. 26f. This view is opposed by R. Hackforth, *Plato's Examination of Pleasure: A Translation of the "Philebus"* (Cambridge, Mass., 1945), p. 8: ". . . Plato could still write a Socratic dialogue." / Concerning the "articulation" through "interrupting questions" and answers, see Stenzel, *Kleine Schriften*, pp. 341 ff.

9. The fact that even in his first sentence Socrates uses the address Πρώταρχε, rather than the ὦ Πρώταρχε he almost always uses elsewhere, characterizes the suddenness of this beginning. (The reason for omitting ὦ is not in order to avoid the hiatus. Indeed, the opposite is true. Plato could have Socrates say δή if he purposely intended to omit ὦ.) Philebos informally says Πρώταρχε (in 12A 8, 28B 6). Protarchos definitely differentiates in saying ὦ Φίληβε (12A 9, 28B 4). As far as I can see, Πρώταρχε without ὦ is used by Socrates only once again—in 21A 8. Is there perhaps an original ω hidden in

the συ or σοι of the manuscripts here? None of the youths would ever omit the ὦ before Σώκρατες.

10. Wilamowitz (I, 622 = I², 629) observes that "the name does not occur in Athens." (This is still the case today, we may add.) Neither does the name seem to occur outside of Athens (as verified in personal communication with B. D. Meritt). The author of the donkey novels, whose tradition Apuleius and Lucian (or Pseudo-Lucian) follow, gave the name "Philebos" to his sharply caricatured priest of Kybele. It is very unlikely that in choosing this name he did not think of Plato—regardless of how much his "lover of youths" may differ from Plato's. / G. Rudberg, "Zur Personenzeichnung Platons," *Symbolae Osloenses*, VI (1928), 29, comments: "At first glance the scene is more lively than in the preceding dialogues . . . but the whole is only seemingly so." This is not quite clear to me. Cf. Hackforth's edition, p. 6; de Vries, p. 168.

11. The remarks that follow in the text are directed against Wilamowitz (I, 621 = I², 628), with whom Philippson, "Lustlehre" [XXVIII³], p. 462, agrees. See also Stenzel, *Studien*, p. 135, who regards Socrates —but without his individual features—as moderator of the discussion.

12. *In Demosthenem* ch. 23 (in *Dionysii Halicarnasei Opuscula*, ed. H. Usener and L. Radermacher, V/1, Leipzig, 1899, p. 178, 11. 21ff.); cf. Shorey, *Unity*, p. 63. / Wilamowitz (I, 622, n. 3 = I², 629, n. 3) attempts to discredit the opinion of Dionysius. Yet, we would do better to learn from it. Dionysius seems to know the *Symposium*, the *Phaedrus*, and the *Philebus* especially well—well, that is, for his purpose of stylistic criticism.

13. H.-G. Gadamer, *Ethik* [XXI²⁶], p. 83. / Diès' translation [XXVIII¹], "*Philèbe est défaillant*," does not catch the right nuance in 11c 8. "The mental deafness of Philebos" (Stefanini, p. 226) is perhaps too strongly expressed. Nonetheless, one should remember that the proverb is really μὴ κινεῖν κακὸν εὖ κείμενον. / On this passage further, consult the scholia.

14. Gomperz, III, 186: "To have assigned Philebos a more active part in the dialogue would have been to impress upon it the character of a real conflict of opinion, for which the author lacked the inclination perhaps still more than the strength." A more accurate statement is found in Susemihl, II, 2. Singer (p. 234) characterizes Philebos as "an effeminate libertine who does not even prove strong and attentive enough to defend his own doctrine." This conception is too psychological, and even from the psychological point of view, it is not correctly stated. Far more to the point is Schaerer, p. 204: "Philebos is at the same time both attentive and unconcerned." See also Diès, *Philèbe*, pp. vii f.

15. Wilamowitz (I, 622) insists, however, that "one does not see why." Philippson ("Lustlehre," p. 461, n. 1), having misunderstood the

first few words of the dialogue, consequently misunderstands the whole situation. The question is not "which of the two theses Protarchos wants to take over," but rather, how to formulate the thesis that Protarchos is about to take over from Philebos. Thus, the attempts to alter the text here become meaningless.

16. Zeller considers Protarchos to be almost identical with Aristippos. Arno Mauersberger, "Plato und Aristipp," *Hermes*, LXI (1926), 209ff., correctly opposes this view. / After Diès' discussion (in *Platon*, pp. 332ff.), no further comments need be made about the *roman à clef* which J. Eberz found in the *Philebus* and other dialogues of this period.

17. Schleiermacher (II/3, 135) stated this much earlier, although he considered the *Gorgias* and the *Theaetetus* together. See further Susemihl, II, 1ff.; Singer, pp. 232, 234; Diès, *Philèbe*, pp. xxxv ff.

18. On the relation of the *Philebus* to the *Republic*, see Wilamowitz, II, 267ff.; Diès, *Philèbe*, pp. xxxvii ff.

19. Wilamowitz (II, 268f.) attempts to prove that in the *Republic* "nothing points to a polemic against another opinion," while the *Philebus* "refers to a philosopher who was not at all considered in the *Republic*." It is true that μὴ ἄρα πειθώμεθα (*Republic* 584c) does not necessarily contain a polemic against a definite person. Yet, since in addition to the great similarity in thought there is also verbal correspondence (πότερα πείθεσθαι συμβουλεύεις occurs in *Philebus* 44c), one cannot acknowledge this kind of difference between the two works.

20. Friedrich A. Trendelenburg, *De Platonis Philebi consilio* (Berlin, 1837), p. 5, bases on this peculiarity the lost work of Galen, Περὶ τῶν ἐν Φιλήβῳ μεταβάσεων.

21. This holds true for any attempts at structural analysis. One might nevertheless compare our analysis with Ritter's (in *Untersuchungen*, p. 95), and ask whether Ritter—apart from his excessive schematization—has not failed to recognize the major links. And Susemihl (II, 1ff.), with his six divisions, offers no improvement either. Much more appropriate is Apelt's analysis in the Introduction to his translation (Leipzig, 1912). His designation of the first section as "preliminary investigation" and the second section as "main investigation," which others also favor, is questionable, however, because it fails to recognize the "ironic shift of balance" (see *Plato* 1, pp. 150ff.). / Cf. the analysis of Gadamer, *Ethik* [XXI²⁶], pp. 81f.; Hackforth, "*Philebus*," p. 10; Diès, *Philèbe*, pp. x ff., and cxiii f. ("Plan schématique du dialogue").

22. Nevertheless, Jaeger (*Aristotle*, pp. 375f.) probably is correct *only conditionally* in asserting that "the problem of ἡδονή becomes independent in the *Philebus*. Granted that the Academy may have read the *Philebus* in this sense, for Plato himself it was only a new road toward his one goal.

23. The thesis of Eudoxos is well known. See Aristotle, *Nicomachean Ethics* X 2 1172b 9: πάντα . . . καὶ ἔλλογα καὶ ἄλογα. Cf. Epicurus, frag. 397, "Omne animal . . ." Aristotle's criticism of an objection raised against Eudoxos (*Nicomachean Ethics* X 2 1172b 36: οἱ δ' ἐνιστάμενοι ὡς οὐκ ἀγαθόν, οὗ πάντ' ἐφίεται, μὴ οὐθὲν λέγωσι) would not constitute a countercriticism directed against Plato's objection as we have established it before. For Aristotle is right in claiming that something desired by all must be ἀγαθόν. And one will easily agree with Plato that it cannot be τἀγαθόν. / Concerning the extensive discussions on pleasure that preceded Plato's *Philebus*, see Philippson, "Lustlehre" [XXVIII³], pp. 444ff.

24. See Wilhelm Dittenberger, *Sylloge Inscriptionum Graecarum* (3d edn., Leipzig, 1915-24), inscr. 204, l. 25; 398, 40; 977, 25; 1044, 5.

25. In 14B 1 τοῦ ἀγαθοῦ is considered spurious by Bury, Burnet, and Diès. Hackforth correctly opposes this. The discussion in our text points out the emphasis with which here, for the first time, Plato has Socrates express τὸ ἀγαθόν as a noun. For, in 13E 5, Socrates says ἀγαθά. And in 13E 6 one should probably write ἀγαθόν (as Burnet does), and not τἀγαθόν (as Bury and Diès do, following Codex *T*). But even if one leaves the last problem undecided, nothing stated in our text would need to be altered. / As to 11B 4, R. G. Bury says (in his edition of the *Philebus*, Cambridge, 1897, p. 2): "I have no doubt that the omission of the article here is intentional." Bury does not see the reason for this clearly enough, however, and later (p. 215) changes his opinion. / Hackforth translates: *the good*. Diès correctly says: *"qu'est bon pour tout ce qui vit la jouissance, le plaisir . . ."*

26. Cf. *Parmenides* 129CD, *Sophist* 251A *et seq.* On the question of a reference to Antisthenes, see E. Zeller and W. Nestle, *Grundriss der Geschichte der griechischen Philosophie* (13th edn., Leipzig, 1928), II, 131; Gomperz, II, 142-43; Wilamowitz, II, 162; Cornford, *Theory of Knowledge* [XXIII⁵], pp. 143f.; Hackforth, *"Philebus,"* p. 17.

27. The difficult passage at 15B has been treated in different ways, in my opinion correctly only by Archer-Hind (in *JPhilol*, XXVII, 1901, pp. 229ff.). / That there are three parts (see *In Phil. Schol.*, Stallbaum edn. [XXVIII¹] on this passage; also Susemihl, II, 9) is evident first of all from the structure of the sentence; the words εἶτα πῶς αὖ . . . μετὰ δὲ τοῦτο . . . αὖ . . . introduce a second and a third part. The contrast is intensified through μήτε γένεσιν μήτε ὄλεθρον προσδεχομένην in the second part, and ἐν τοῖς γιγνομένοις αὖ καὶ ἀπείροις in the third part. No one would have interpreted this contrary to the impression gained from the language, had not the second part appeared to resist interpretation; see Gadamer, *Ethik* [XXI²⁶], pp. 93f. Yet, though this second part is only briefly formulated, it is completely intelligible. ταύτας stands for μονάδας. They are differentiated in the well-known form of the individualizing apposition in

the singular. Then they are said to be μίαν ταύτην, i.e., μονάδα. The following ὅμως (which Apelt, Badham, Bury, Susemihl, Stenzel, and Diès all assail without foundation) gives a concessive sense to the preceding participle. In spite of their individualization, the μονάδες are at the same time also μονάς. The following consideration determines the matter only negatively. A common procedure is to reduce the second and third parts to one part—or, like Stenzel (*Studien*, p. 98), the first and second parts to one part—and thereby establish altogether only two problems: *first*, whether there are these unities, and *second*, how the unity of the Form, or *Idea*, is related to the multiplicity of the appearances. But this procedure disturbs the connection between the point here in question and the discussions that ensue in the dialogue about the one and the many. What matters most of all is the gradual transition—and this transition is present only in the realm of the unchanging unities, rather than between the *Idea* and the world of becoming where the sudden leap from the one to the infinite is necessary (16E 2). / Wilamowitz' attempt to insert ἐν δὲ τοῖς πολλοῖς φαινομένην after προσδεχομένην destroys the distinction between the second and third parts, as does the rearrangement in Natorp's *Ideenlehre*, p. 297, and in Schleiermacher's translation. / G. Schneider (*Die platonische Metaphysik*, p. 51, as quoted by Ritter in *Untersuchungen*, p. 102) recognizes the three-part structure, but incorrectly interprets the second part as "how, while each single one always remains the same and is unable either to become or to cease, it is nevertheless the one, *scil.*, which we believe it to be, i.e., through which we arrive at the cognizance of the single *Idea*, since the *Ideas* are beyond the sphere of becoming and ceasing within which we find ourselves." Schneider has overlooked the plural ταύτας in its contrast to the singular μίαν ταύτην, and therefore has wrongly interpreted ὅμως (as has Adolfo Levi, *Il concetto del tempo nella filosofia greca sino a Platone*, Milan, 1919, p. 76). Schneider's addition of "which we believe it to be" is unjustified, as also is the quite subjective turn by which he introduces the theory of knowledge. It is evident how little use this interpretation is to Ritter himself (see *Untersuchungen*, p. 107). See also Bury's discussion of this passage as further evidence that the issue is still not clarified. A. E. Taylor's translation (annot. edn., New York, 1956, p. 411) reads, "how we are to reconcile their *unity* with their reality or *being*"—as if in reference to the problem of the ἐν ὄν in the *Parmenides*. But how can one derive this from the wording of the *Philebus?* A sentence from Wilamowitz (I, 631) also sounds very strange: ". . . but the existence of the *Ideas*, their relation to each other, and their effect on the world of senses creates difficulties." When Wilamowitz wrote this sentence, he must have understood the passage in question in the sense of my interpretation. Susemihl (II, 9) was close to the correct interpretation.

It appears that neither Archer-Hind's nor my discussion of the matter has had effect. Hackforth follows Bury's quite artificial conjecture of βεβαιότατα α (=πρῶτον) μὲν ταύτην ("this gives a clumsy, but not impossible sentence . . ."). Diès prints ὅλως, as Badham does. Ross (p. 131) considers ὅμως to anticipate the contrast, but none of the parallels he cites for an anticipating ὅμως seems to be without a participle. / Against Archer-Hind's and my interpretation, Hackforth raises the following objections: (1) "I cannot see any relevance in μήτε γένεσιν μήτ' ὄλεθρον προσδεχομένην," (2) "or any meaning in the word ταύτην." To (1) I reply: these words state in a negative manner once again what just before had been worded as μίαν ἑκάστην οὖσαν ἀεὶ τὴν αὐτήν. And as for (2): on this I have said enough in the text and here in the notes.

28. Karl Reinhardt, "Poseidonios von Apameia," in *R-E*, XXII, cols. 572ff.

29. Cf. F. M. Cornford, *Plato and Parmenides* [XXIV²], pp. 1ff., where the false thesis is taken over from Tannery that Zeno's proofs are directed against the Pythagoreans. Frank (*Pythagoreer*, pp. 302ff.) ascribes the book of Philolaos to a Platonist of Speusippos' generation. / On the doctrine itself, see further P. Wilpert, "Eine Elementenlehre im platonischen *Philebos*," *Studies . . . Robinson*, II (St Louis, 1953), pp. 573ff.

30. Here it is evident how Natorp (*Ideenlehre*, p. 300 = 2d edn., p. 317) gives to the Platonic words an almost Kantian turn: ". . . so one will find therein just that which one has posited oneself."

31. A similarly sudden transition should appear here too at the beginning of the series, as before at the end. The infinite multiplicity of the accidental single objects is not grasped at all by the *logos*.

32. For 19E (λέγομεν καθάπερ οἱ παῖδες, ὅτι τῶν ὀρθῶς δοθέντων ἀφαίρεσις οὐκ ἔστι), *Gorgias* 499B (ὥσπερ τὰ μειράκια) does not constitute a very clarifying comparison, Bury notwithstanding. One senses a verse, perhaps like ὀρθῶς δοθέντων οὐκέτ' ἔστ' ἀφαίρεσις. When we were children, we knew a corresponding rhyme: *"Was geschenkt ist, ist verbrannt, kommt nicht mehr ins Haus gerannt."* As an analogy to this passage, Diès (*Philèbe*, p. 14) quotes the proverb, *"Donné est pire que vendu"* ("To give something is worse than to sell it").

33. See Wilamowitz, II, 266f., for some apparent "quotations." Also see Hackforth's *"Philebus,"* p. 31, n. 1, and Diès' edition, p. 14, n. 2.

34. See Athenaeus XII 544A, and compare esp. *Philebus* 21c.

35. Rey, p. 263, probably takes the fifth kind somewhat too seriously.

36. Regarding this difficult passage at 25D 5 *et seq.*, see Bekker, V, 469; Vahlen, *Gesammelte Schriften* [XX²¹], II, 62ff.; Wilamowitz, II, 354f.; Bury, *"Philebus"* [XXVIII²⁵], Appen. A; Diès, *Philèbe*, p. 23; R. Hackforth, in *CQ*, XXXIII (1939), 24ff. / The hiatus in Vahlen's

conjecture δράσει ⟨εἰ⟩ is contrary to Plato's style in this late period. (Add to this also the objection of Wilamowitz, loc. cit.) Against Badham's ταὐτὸν δράσασιν, we would raise this point: what then would be the identical that we undertake? Therefore, the sentence may be correct as printed in Bekker's edition (. . . δράσει τούτων . . .) and translated by Schleiermacher to mean approximately this: "Perhaps now too the result will be the same: if one connects both kinds, then the limited one will become clearer than it has been until now."

37. Hackforth agrees with Grube (p. 305) that "γένεσις εἰς οὐσίαν need not mean anything more than γένεσις alone." But the unusual expression must mean something particular. Richard Heinze, *Xenokrates* (Leipzig, 1892), p. 23, objects that "the stress should be on οὐσία." Rather, the emphasis is on the synthesis of the contrasting states. / Diès, *Philèbe*, pp. xxviii ff., attempts to level as much as possible the tension between γένεσις and οὐσία. He is certainly correct in stating that (1) "Plato frequently employs the less rigorous language of common life and calls 'to be,' or 'being,' what according to strict philosophical usage should be 'to become,' or 'becoming,'" and that (2) it is unjustified to find here "a promotion of 'becoming' to a higher degree of ontological value." Nevertheless, one should not overlook this tension, but should instead attempt to discover its meaning. / M. Gentile, *La dottrina platonica delle idee numeri* (Pisa, 1930), p. 39—where reference is made to Ritter, *Platon*, II, 183—is mistaken, in my opinion, in the view that "all four kinds belong to the world of *Ideas*."

38. It is noteworthy that Natorp, *Ideenlehre*, pp. 311ff., actually reduces only the first three γένη from the ontological to the logical level. For the fourth, however, he is forced to identify αἰτία κοινωνίας with κοινωνία itself, and only afterward does he differentiate artificially what he had identified before.

39. ἡ ⟨σὴ⟩ θεός, the conjecture of C. Badham (2d edn., London, 1878) in 26B 8 would be wrong, for it is the goddess just of Socrates, and not of Philebos. But αὕτη does not really make sense; rather, it should be αὐτή. Thus, the reference to 11B 2 (αὐτὴν τὴν θεόν) and 11B 7 (αὐτῆς τῆς θεοῦ) becomes still more sharp. It is strange that Diès (*Philèbe*, p. 24) retains the customary αὕτη and yet translates correctly as "*la déesse elle-même.*" / Only thus does one understand the address ὦ καλέ fully with its ironic undertones.

40. Thus, the goddess is not ὑγίεια and μουσική, as Bury thinks, nor is she the κοινωνία (as Wilamowitz, II, 354, writes). The goddess is the αἰτία of all this. She might be called Ἀρμονία—if one thinks of Empedokles, *Vorsokr.* 31 [21] B 18, and B 122, l. 2. Perhaps for this entire cryptic exercise one should consult Empedokles, who called

his *Philia* also Γηθοσύνη and 'Αφροδίτη (*Vorsokr.* 31 [21] β 17, l. 24). And, as Diès (p. 24) notes, Plato read in Hesiod that Harmony is the daughter of Aphrodite.

41. Perhaps one should write in 28A 3: τούτων δή σοι τῶν ἀπεράντων τὸ γένος (instead of γεγονὸς) ἔστω.

42. To isolate a single writer as "model" would be contrary to Plato's intention. Actually, one should go back to Homer (*Iliad* XVI 688, *Odyssey* IX 176). As Diès (*Platon,* p. 536) observes: "We can trace the origin of the eternal and divine soul as a principle of universal movement by going back from Anaxagoras and Diogenes of Apollonia at least to Alkmaion of Croton." Thus, it is unjustified to limit this "argument" to Diogenes of Apollonia—as Jaeger, for example, does in his *Theology of the Early Greek Thinkers* (Oxford, 1947), pp. 167–68, 244. Diès' qualifying phrase "at least" is justified; see also Kranz's *Wortindex* [XXI²³], pp. 296ff. In the δεινὸς ἀνήρ (29A 3) Bury searches for a reference to sophists like Gorgias or Kritias. For Zeller-Nestle, *Grundriss* [XXVIII²⁶], II, 174, n. 4, it is "undoubtedly Demokritos." A similar view is in H. Usener, "Organisation der wissenschaftlichen Arbeit," *Vorträge und Aufsätze* (Leipzig, 1907), p. 90.

43. To write αὔξεται in 29c 5 (as Jackson does) next to τρέφεται would be a tautology. But ἄρχεται becomes meaningful in 30D 8.

44. On this shift of balance, see *Plato* 1, p. 150.

45. See Gadamer, *Ethik* [XXI²⁶], p. 121.

46. *Theogony* 937, 975; cf. *Phaedo* 95A. Also see Diès, *Philèbe,* p. 24, n. 1.

47. πρῶτον μὲν in 32D 9 is misleading, because it creates the impression of being a first step to be followed by others. This, however, is not the case. On closer examination, we notice that with καὶ μὴν in 33c 5, the connection is made to the point from which the digression began with πρῶτον μὲν. It is peculiarities of this nature that make the *Philebus* so difficult to understand.

48. See above, pp. 121ff.

49. Schaarschmidt, p. 301, declared the *Philebus* to be unauthentic because of the short duration of this moment. Cf. Bury's "*Philebus*" [XXVIII²⁵], p. lxiv; Stefanini (1932 edn.), I, xx.

50. In 34c 1: καὶ ταῦτα σύμπαντ' ἀναμνήσεις καὶ μνήμας που λέγομεν, reminiscences and objects of recollection. [καὶ μνήμας] is the reading of Gloël and of Burnet. Diès prints οὐ μνήμας. Bury: καὶ ⟨ἀναλήψεις⟩ μνήμης. All three readings are in agreement that the word μνῆμαι must not be printed following ἀναμνήσεις. But then that from which the discussion proceeded is really lacking—namely μνήμη—and the discussion in this section ends with the ἀνάμνησις. Should the text be understood in the following sense: ". . . and all this we call 'acts of recollection' and—to return to the beginning—'objects of reminiscence' "?

51. Nevertheless, there is reference later (in 50D 4, for example) to pleasure and aversion which the "body without soul" experiences. This is stated in an ordinary, less stringent manner, however, without the strict distinction just established.

52. Cf. Shorey, *Unity*, pp. 43f.

53. Cf. Hackforth, *"Philebus,"* p. 66, n. 1.

54. Notice 34c 7: καὶ ἅμα ἐπιθυμίαν, and 35D 8: ἔτι δὴ καὶ περὶ ταὐτὰ ταῦτα κατανοήσωμεν.

55. Later (in 41c and 47c) there are references again to this analysis of "desiring," when it is a question of bringing in examples for the "mixture" of desires and aversions.

56. See also *Republic* IX 585A. / The answer (ἀληθέστατα) which Plato has Protarchos make to Socrates' words (οὐδαμῇ ὁ λόγος αἱρεῖ, 35D 6) is at least very careless, even if it is not as far from the point as the concluding ἀληθέστατα in the *Parmenides*. More precisely expressed, the answer should probably be this. There is purely physical thirst; this we have discussed before (31E). And there is also physical-spiritual thirst, as has become clear just now.

57. See Diès, *Philèbe*, p. 45, n. 1.

58. Stenzel (*Platon*, p. 261) mistakenly takes the thesis of Protarchos in 38A as expressing Plato's own opinion. / A. Bremond, "Les perplexités du *Philèbe*," *Revue Néo-Scolastique*, XIII (1911), 472, congratulates Protarchos for his resistance. But is it actually an "irrefutable principle: pleasure cannot err since it is not cognitive"—or is it rather a prejudice? Bremond's other "perplexities" are based perhaps on the fact that he considers as dogmatic what is meant dialectically. Compare Gadamer's view (*Ethik*, p. 9, n. 1) to Bremond's.

59. Almost all editors replace ἄνοια with ἄγνοια in 38A 8 and in three successive passages at 48c *et seq.* This replacement is made against the agreement of the manuscripts; it is a change contrary to all probability. Karl Friedrich Hermann is the only one who has—rightly —objected, but since he did not convince even Bury or Diès, we must express his opinion still more sharply. ἄνοια and ἄγνοια are not used *"promiscue"*; rather, the stronger generic concept is used where the concept of the species would have sufficed. Cf. *Timaeus* 86B: δύο δ' ἀνοίας γένη, τὸ μὲν μανίαν, τὸ δ' ἀμαθίαν (=ἄγνοιαν). Also, the significance of the νοῦς in the dialogue should be considered in evaluating the ἄ-νοια correctly. It seems that Hackforth and Diès have not understood 38D 9 – D 10 correctly. The meaning probably is this: that someone sees what is actually a statue but takes it as something made by shepherds, perhaps a haystack or a bundle of straw.

60. One must follow the words and their parallelism very closely in 39A. Who does the writing? Not ἡ μνήμη but ἡ μνήμη ταῖς αἰσθήσεσι συμπίπτουσα εἰς ταὐτόν. To make certain that the subject is not taken as ἡ μνήμη alone, isolated from αἰσθήσεις, κἀκεῖνα ἃ περὶ ταῦτ' ἐστὶ τὰ

παθήματα is added, whereby the conjunction of μνήμη and αἴσθησις is again implied. Because of this, whenever such a single case is considered later on, the subject can be designated as τοῦτο τὸ πάθημα. Immediately thereafter we read, with reference to the acting person, ὁ τοιοῦτος παρ' ἡμῖν γραμματεύς. One could call this, with Bury, "a curious change of horses when crossing the stream." Yet, this is the text, and as such it is completely consistent. Stallbaum—who, for support of his opinion, referred to Tennemann—viewed the matter correctly. Badham created havoc in the sentence, however, and Burnet followed him in considering spurious the words τοῦτο τὸ πάθημα (which Schleiermacher had incorrectly separated from γράφῃ by a comma). Diès and Hackforth are correct.

61. There is no need to discuss who is meant here; cf. Bury's edition, p. 95, and Diès', p. lvii. We know that at least Speusippos also advocated this thesis; see P. Lang, *De Speusippi Academici scriptis* (Bonn diss., 1911), frags. 60A *et seq.* (cf. frag. 57). For a bibliography of the older literature, see Philippson, "Lustlehre" [XXVIII³], pp. 444ff. / The identification is insignificant so far as the *Philebus* itself is concerned. Nevertheless, for the sake of Platonic interpretation, the following should be stated: If Wilamowitz (II, 271), after protesting correctly against the Demokritos-hypothesis, leaves room for the possibility that the unceasing attempts of Demokritos to explain nature could appear to Plato as δυσχέρεια, then it must be said that, according to Plato, this δυσχέρεια relates to nothing other than the attitude toward pleasure (44c 6). Thus, Demokritos is definitely out of the question.

62. In 44D 3 one should write αἵ γ'ἐμοὶ δοκοῦσιν ἡδοναὶ ἀληθεῖς εἶναι instead of the customary αἵ γέ μοι . . . Only in this way is the contrast to τούτοις μὲν οὖν brought out. (Cf. 44E 4: καθάπερ ἐμοί.) Hackforth concurs, but not Diès. / In 44D 1, I would prefer ἀλλ' οὐχ (*TW*) to the simple οὐχ in Codex B. (For the textual history, see Diès, *Philèbe*, pp. cx f.) One does well to read this passage aloud: ὥστε καὐτὸ τοῦτ' αὐτῆς τώπαγωγὸν γοήτευμ' ἀλλ' οὐχ ἡδονὴν εἶναι.

63. The simple expression would be ἄνοια καὶ ἀβελτερία. This becomes ἄνοια καὶ ἦν δὴ λέγομεν ἀβελτέραν ἕξιν (48c 2) in the late Platonic style, which Jackson fails to recognize in his emendation ἀβελτερίαν. Cf. *Laws* 666A: τὴν ἐμμανῆ ἕξιν τῶν νέων with *Cratylus* 404A: τὴν τοῦ σώματος μανίαν—or σύμμετρος φύσις in *Philebus* 64D 9 with συμμετρία in *Philebus* 64E 6.

64. How is this to be understood? In 51c 6, ταῦτα γὰρ οὐκ εἶναι πρός τι καλὰ λέγω καθάπερ ἄλλα is said of the σχήματα. Therefore, according to the wording, the facts of the relation refer to the whole reproduced form, i.e., to a painted image of man. (It is not an "uninterested delight.") On the other hand, the situation differs perhaps in the example (see 51D 7) taken from the realm of sounds: τὰς (ἠχὰς) ἕν τι

καθαρὸν ἱείσας μέλος οὐ πρὸς ἕτερον (*scil.* μέλος) καλάς. The meaning could be that within a melodic measure there exists a relation between one tone and another, whereby the one and the other in themselves may be injured in their particular being.

65. One should notice the transition at 53c 4: τί δὲ τὸ τοιόνδε and at 54ε 1: καὶ μὴν αὐτὸς οὗτος.

66. The sentence 52c is so badly corrupted that it can be reconstructed only approximately. On the whole, one may read it as Burnet edits it, except that τῆς in c 6 has to be bracketed, as Étienne has done (see Diès' edition). And τῶν ἐμμέτρων in D 1 is hardly correct (thus also Hackforth). The strong desires have ἀμετρία, while the opposite ones have ἐμμετρία. Therefore, the first group belongs to the mode of being of the ἄπειρον, and the second group belongs to . . . one expects: the mode of being of the mixed (since they are not pure πέρας). Rather than τῶν ἐμμέτρων, which would be tautological, should something like τοῦ μεικτοῦ be written? This would not be too daring, considering the sorry state of the text. Or does Plato perhaps leave it to the reader to remember the μεικτόν, and does he intend ἔμμετρον to refer only to the πέρας of the mixture, since the ἄπειρον has just been pointed out?

67. Diès (*Philèbe*, pp. lxii ff.) is the most recent in deciding for Aristippos, while Mauersberger—see "Plato und Aristipp" [XXVIII[16]], 208ff.— decides for the Megarians. For the older literature, see Stenzel, "Kyrenaiker," in *R-E*, XII, cols. 137ff. One should take note of Stenzel's fundamental remarks concerning sources, as for example this: "The more a particular author lives in his own essential philosophical movement, the less relevant for him will be any possible 'occasion' leading to his thought, or any actual step preceding it."

68. Here, scientific music is expressly not implied as it is in the *Republic*. Rather, music as an entertaining exercise is meant, as in the *Statesman* (268B, 306D). Cf. *Philebus* 62c. / The text of 56A 3 *et seq.* cannot be reconstructed with certainty. μουσική as the embracing concept in the diaeresis must precede the particular concepts—probably αὐλητικὴ καὶ κιθαριστική. που αὐτῆς does not fit into this style, which avoids the hiatus. (These objections are directed against Diès; see his edition, p. 75.)

69. In Natorp's opinion (*Ideenlehre*, p. 327 = 2d edn., p. 345), the thoughts in 59A–D return to a stage in Plato's philosophy that has otherwise been overcome. Natorp finds a direct contradiction between 59A (in this world one is not supposed to look for reason and insight), and the view expressed earlier, in 28B *et seq.*, according to which man's reason is derived from the reason of the cosmos. But the contradiction only appears to exist. For in 59A (περὶ τὸν κόσμον τόνδε ὅπῃ τε γέγονε καὶ ὅπῃ πάσχει τι καὶ ὅπῃ ποιεῖ), as in the *Timaeus*, we are concerned with philosophy of nature; and in 28B *et seq.* (τοῦ κόσμου

καὶ ἡλίου καὶ σελήνης καὶ ἀστέρων καὶ πάσης τῆς περιφορᾶς), as in the seventh book of the *Republic*, we are concerned with mathematical astronomy.

70. For 64A (τί ποτ' ἐν τἀνθρώπῳ καὶ τῷ παντὶ πέφυκεν ἀγαθόν, καὶ τίνα ἰδέαν αὐτὴν εἶναί ποτε μαντευτέον), I have translated as if the text had αὐτοῦ. This was my original conjecture. Because of the hiatus alone, however, the reading is impossible, although the meaning is surely right. Diès translates (p. 88): ". . . *et quelle nature nous lui devons supposer.*"

71. καὶ τῆς οἰκήσεως τῆς τοῦ τοιούτου in 64C 2 is a strange expression. If one deletes καὶ, as Badham does, the result is a construction characteristic of Plato's late work, where a genitive placed after a phrase still modifies it, although the reader might have thought the meaning already clearly established. But this requires here that one also delete the words τῆς τοῦ τοιούτου. And strange as these words may be, no one will venture to delete them without falling victim to Badham's hyper-Cobetism. What is said about the *Agathon* must naturally sound strange.

72. It is difficult to translate the pun συμπεφορημένη συμφορά in 64E. Schleiermacher: "*ein zusammengewehtes Weh.*" Apelt: "*ein verworrenes Wirrsal.*" Bury: "a mere mass of mischief instead of a mixture." Hackforth: "a miserable mass of unmixed messiness." And Diès: "*un vrai pêle-mêle, une réelle misère.*" συμφορά is the unfortunate chance event, and it retains this meaning even after Plato with his penetrating feeling for language had observed in it the sense of irregular drifting or being blown together. Also, the word carries more overtones than we perhaps realize. Kranz's *Wortindex* [XXI²³], p. 410, lists under *Vorsokr.* 22 [12] c 5 an imitation of Herakleitos in Lucian: λέγω δὴ τὰς ἐκπυρώσιας καὶ τὴν τοῦ ὅλου συμφορήν. Thus, Herakleitos may have used the word with a new meaning, and Plato may have then continued the play with words. And compare Euripides, *Alcestis* 802: οὐ κρᾶσις . . . ἀλλὰ συμφορά with *Philebus* 64DE: οὐ βίος . . . ἀλλὰ συμφορά. What is behind this similarity? / See further Classen, p. 3.

73. A more exact reading clarifies the following: First of all, in 64D 9, μέτρον καὶ σύμμετρος φύσις (= συμμετρία) stand beside each other. Then, in 64E 6 *et seq.*, μετριότης and συμμετρία are identified with κάλλος. And further, in 65A 2, there are placed next to each other as three ἰδέαι: κάλλος καὶ συμμετρία καὶ ἀλήθεια. It seems that the number *three* is more important than the exact designation of the three ἰδέαι. Also, this inconsistency might have been intended expressly as a warning that this trinity must not be frozen into dogma. Surely it is not the case that "the dithyrambic fervour of the concluding speeches . . . destroys the effect of the strictness in thought which Plato has so carefully endeavoured to observe," as Gomperz (III, 197) claims.

A similar inconsistency is found in the *Sophist;* see above, ch. XXVI, n. 17.

74. For more than abundant discussion of the five-stage system here in the *Philebus,* cf. Bury's edition, Appen. B, and Diès' edition, pp. lxxxiv ff. Also see J. Xenakis, "Plato on Ethical Disagreement," *Phronesis,* I (1955/56), 50ff.

75. 66A 7: καὶ πάνθ᾽ ὁπόσα χρὴ τοιαῦτα νομίζειν τὴν ἀΐδιον ἡρῆσθαι φύσιν. Wilamowitz (II, 355) has proved that φύσιν—be it original text or a Byzantine conjecture—is correct; it is the subject of the infinitive. Thus also Jowett (III, 207): ". . . in measure, and the mean, and the suitable, and the like, the eternal nature has been found"—where the contrast between "nature" and "attribute" is not completely adequate. But the thought becomes false if one deletes τοιαῦτα. Not only the first genus, but also the second and the third, belong to what divine nature chooses. Thus, whatever eternal nature chooses for itself from this genus, namely, the τοιαῦτα, is therefore as necessary as the corresponding γενεᾶς αὖ ταύτης is to the second part. (That τοιαῦτα occurs in the manuscripts both before and after the χρή is irrelevant. The same holds true for the lack of the ὄντα.) / Diès' view differs radically. Yet his χρὴ νομίζειν τινὰ ἥδιον ἡρῆσθαι sounds weak, even if one considers τιν᾽ ἥδιον to be permissible.

76. In 66B 8 τέταρτα may not be deleted or removed through any conjecture (as of Jackson or Diès), since the foregoing as well as the following numbers always appear at the beginning, as is natural. In this case, the second τέταρτα in 66C 1 could be deleted; τέταρτα . . . τὰ πρὸς τοῖς τρισίν, with a great distance between these words that belong together, would conform perhaps to Plato's late style. Or would this late style be characterized more by a double τέταρτα at the beginning as an enumeration, and then once again at the end after the long intervening clause τὰ πρὸς τοῖς τρισίν? In colloquial language, this is probably most natural.

77. Concerning the inner μαντεύεσθαι in Plato, see Jaeger, *Aristotle,* p. 159, n. 1.

XXIX: *Timaeus*

RECENT EDITIONS AND TRANSLATIONS: O. Apelt, PhB 179 (2d edn., 1922); A. Rivaud, *Platon Budé,* X (1925); A. E. Taylor (Oxford, 1928); F. M. Cornford (London, 1937); J. Moreau (in L. Robin, *Platon Oeuvres Complètes,* Paris, 1940–42); C. Giarratano (with notes by G. Manacorda, Bari, 1950); R. Kapferer and A. Fingerle (Stuttgart, 1952).

RECENT INTERPRETATIONS: W. Theiler, *Zur Geschichte der teleologischen Naturbetrachtung bis auf Aristoteles* (Zurich and Leipzig, 1925), pp. 68ff.; Shorey, pp. 329ff.; J. Moreau, *L'âme du monde de Platon aux Stoiciens* (Paris, 1939), pp. 3ff.; G. Vlastos, "The Disorderly Motion in the *Timaeus*," *CQ*, XXXIII (1939), 71ff. (reprinted with added section in Allen, pp. 379ff.); T. Negro, *La concezione platonica della scienza* (Milan, 1940); H. J. Pos, "De Kosmologie in Plato's *Timaios*," in W. B. Kristensen, *et al.*, *Antieke en Moderne Kosmologie* (Arnhem, 1941), pp. 29ff.; Robin, *Pensée*, pp. 231ff.; J. B. Skemp, *The Theory of Motion in Plato's Later Dialogues* (Cambridge, 1942), pp. 31ff.; Solmsen, ch. 6; Cherniss, *Aristotle's Crit. of Plato, passim*; R. C. Taliaferro, *Plato: The "Timaeus" and the "Critias," The Thomas Taylor Translation* (New York, 1944), pp. 9ff.; J. F. Callahan, *Four Views of Time in Ancient Philosophy* (Cambridge, Mass., 1948), pp. 3ff.; Festugière, *Révélation*, ch. 5; Stefanini, pp. 256ff.; G. R. Morrow, "Necessity and Persuasion in Plato's *Timaeus*," *PR*, LIX (1950), 147ff. (reprinted in Allen, pp. 421ff.); A. Olerud, *L'idée de macrocosmos et de microcosmos dans le "Timée" de Platon* (Uppsala, 1951); A. Ahlvers, *Zahl und Klang bei Platon* (Bern and Stuttgart, 1952), esp. pp. 63ff.; W. Heisenberg, "Platons Vorstellungen von den kleinsten Bausteinen der Materie und die Elementarteilchen der modernen Physik," in *Im Umkreis der Kunst* (Wiesbaden, 1953), pp. 137ff.; J. Moreau, "L'idée d'univers dans la pensée antique," *Giorn. di Metafisica*, VIII (1953), 88ff., 324ff.; G. E. L. Owen, "The Place of the *Timaeus* in Plato's Dialogues," *CQ*, n.s., III (1953), 79ff. (reprinted in Allen, pp. 313ff.); H. Cherniss, "A Much Misread Passage of the *Timaeus* (49C7–50B5)," *AJP*, LXXV (1954), 113ff.; G. S. Claghorn, *Aristotle's Criticism of Plato's "Timaeus"* (The Hague, 1954); W. Kranz, *Kosmos* (Bonn, 1955), pp. 5ff.; A. Rivaud, "Espace et changement dans le *Timée* de Platon," *Mélanges Diès* (Paris, 1956), pp. 209ff.; H. Cherniss, "The Relation of the *Timaeus* to Plato's Later Dialogues," *AJP*, LXXVIII (1957), 226ff. (reprinted in Allen, pp. 339ff.); H. Herter, "Bewegung der Materie bei Platon," *RhM*, n.s., C (1957), 327ff.; H. W. Miller, "The Flux of the Body in Plato's *Timaeus*," *TAPA*, LXXXVIII (1957), 103ff.; F. M. Brignoli, "Problemi di fisica celeste nel *Timeo* di Platone," *Giorn. Ital. Filol.*, XI (1958), 97ff.; W. Kranz, *Die griechische Philosophie* (4th edn., Bremen, 1958), pp. 209ff.; Hildebrandt, *Platon* (2d edn.), pp. 346ff.; Reinhardt, *Vermächtnis*, pp. 274ff.; Gauss, III/2, ch. 3; H. Morin, *Der Begriff des Lebens im "Timaios" Platons* (Uppsala, 1965); Raven, pp. 235ff.; D. J. Stewart, "Man and Myth in Plato's Universe," *Bucknell Review*, XIII (1965), 72ff.; Lesky, pp. 534ff.

ADDITIONAL BIBLIOGRAPHY: Shorey, p. 612; Geffcken, Notes, pp. 119ff.; Leisegang, cols. 2505ff.; Rosenmeyer, pp. 190f.; Cherniss, *Lustrum*, pp. 208ff.

1. August Boeckh, *Kleine Schriften* [XXI[20]], III, 175. / On what follows,

see Shorey, pp. 347f.; R. Klibansky, *The Continuity of the Platonic Tradition* (London, 1939).

2. K. J. Windischmann, *Platons "Timaios": Eine echte Urkunde wahrer Physik* (Hadamar, 1804). J. R. Lichtenstaedt (*Platons Lehren auf dem Gebiete der Naturforschung und der Heilkunde*, Leipzig, 1826) is critical of Windischmann for his praise of Plato's mathematical corpuscular theory. / On what follows, and esp. the analogies to modern physics, see *Plato* 1, chs. XIV and XV.

3. See, for example, Wilamowitz, I, 584; II, 255ff. On the contrary, if one considers the instructive proportion, *Theaetetus : Sophist + Statesman = Republic : Timaeus + Critias*, one cannot but doubt that Plato ever intended to rewrite his *Republic*. Why should he have wished to rewrite it, when a recapitulation—as it appears in the beginning of the *Timaeus*—made any further revisions unnecessary?

4. This was the thesis of Krohn, Pfleiderer, and Rohde. Opposed to it are Hirzel, I, 257; Ritter, *Untersuchungen*, p. 177; A. Rivaud, *Timée* (*Platon Budé*, X, 1925), pp. 19ff.; F. M. Cornford, *Plato's Cosmology* [XXII[13]], pp. 4ff.

5. No conversation took place on the previous day between Socrates and the four others about the state. Instead, according to the fiction of the dialogue, Socrates reported to them yesterday a conversation conducted previous to that, as is indicated by the wording of *Timaeus* 17C: τῶν ὑπ' ἐμοῦ ῥηθέντων λόγων περὶ πολιτείας, and 20B: ὑμῶν δεομένων τὰ περὶ τῆς πολιτείας διελθεῖν. This resolves the contradiction between the dates. To Wilamowitz (II, 255), the purpose of the different dates is not evident. I disagree. By means of the different dates, Plato expressly calls attention to the fact that he is dealing with different conversations (or at the utmost, with different reports of the same conversation). Hirzel (I, 257) saw this even before. The note in Diogenes Laërtius III 37 (Εὐφορίων δὲ καὶ Παναίτιος εἰρήκασι πολλάκις ἐστραμμένην εὑρῆσθαι τὴν ἀρχὴν τῆς Πολιτείας) agrees with what the rhetoricians say (see Wilamowitz, II, 257f.). Whatever may be true in Diogenes' statement, however, an extensive revision is not at all attested by it. The beginning of the *Theaetetus* now offers us a parallel as to what may be learned from the antique commentaries. / It should be recognized that dating the Panathenaia after the festival of Bendis—see Proklos, *In Tim. Comm.* [XXIV[40]], I, p. 85, l. 26—is only an attempt to combine the incompatible. Cf. August Mommsen, *Feste der Stadt Athen im Altertum* (Leipzig, 1898), pp. 52f. / A suggestion akin to what I say here in the text appears in Salin, *Utopie*, p. 270. Also see Rivaud, *Timée*, pp. 19ff.; Cornford, *Cosmology*, pp. 4f.

6. A misunderstanding of Plato is behind Ritter's attempt (*Untersuchungen*, p. 178) to explain as follows: "What is left out no longer lies close to the heart of the philosopher, or perhaps he no longer considers it correct."

7. Starting with the Neoplatonists, there has been much discussion about the τέταρτος in 17A 1. See Proklos, *In Tim. Comm.*, I, p. 9, 11. 13ff. Ritter's opinion (*Untersuchungen*, p. 181) that Plato by means of a fourth person kept the way open for expanding the trilogy into a tetralogy is unsatisfactory. Just as unacceptable is the view of A. E. Taylor, *A Commentary on Plato's "Timaeus"* (Oxford, 1928), p. 45, that since Timaios embodied an impure Pythagorism, he appears as the substitute for a real Pythagorean. Rivaud (p. 18) and Cornford (*Cosmology*, p. 3) follow Ritter.

8. For the opposite view, see Wilamowitz, I, 586 (I^2, 592); II, 256. The sentence "Although the *Timaeus* implies that Plato will forego completing the *Critias*, he nevertheless wrote as an addition several pages which were later published from his legacy" should rather be turned around. Since the *Critias* presupposes the *Timaeus* as we have it, and since the *Timaeus* prepares the way for the *Critias* as we have it, the *Timaeus* must have been written with regard to the *Critias* which would follow. Thus, the trilogy has been developed up to the point where the *Critias* breaks off.

9. See *Plato* 1, pp. 198ff.

10. Ingeborg Hammer-Jensen, "Demokrit und Platon," *AfGP*, XXIII (1910) pp. 92ff., 211ff., sets up the theory that Plato supposedly met Demokritos when he was writing what is now *pag.* 45 of his *Timaeus*, and that this meeting changed Plato's concept. Such a thesis is altogether untenable (even if we completely disregard Demokritos). For this opposition, it is sufficient to refer to Wilamowitz, II, 258ff. Yet, strong opposition notwithstanding, the effect of Hammer-Jensen's view is still evident, as in Apelt's n. 124 to his translation of the *Timaeus* (2d edn., Leipzig, 1922). There Apelt also states that Plato "was not yet completely certain about his physics, nor about its place in the over-all structure." A prerequisite for any correct evaluation is, of course, that one not be misled by Plato's irony (49A: τότε μὲν οὐ διειλόμεθα νομίσαντες τὰ δύο ἕξειν ἱκανῶς · νῦν δὲ ὁ λόγος ἔοικεν εἰσαναγκάζειν). / In our first edition (1930), the *Timaeus* chapter was more strongly tinged with polemic against the Demokritos-thesis than is necessary today. But see Ahlvers, *Zahl und Klang* [XXI^{20}], ch. 4, "Die Pythagoreer oder Demokrit?" Clearly, one bias must not be substituted for another.

11. If we recall Aristophanes' myth of the creation in the *Symposium* (189c *et seq.*), we cannot disregard the grotesque element here in the construction of the human body. / On what follows about the mirror image, see Cornford, *Cosmology*, pp. 154f.

12. Cf. Wilamowitz, I, 581 = I^2, 587. In all fairness, it should be said that in Archer-Hind's commentary to the *Timaeus* [XXIV^5], Demokritos' importance for Plato is not unduly exaggerated. Natorp's *Ideenlehre*,

p. 442, might more fittingly be called the forerunner of the thesis expounded by Hammer-Jensen (see above, n. 10). By avoiding major misunderstandings like the comparison of Plato with the student of Leukippos, however, we do not in any way diminish the admirable polyhistory of Demokritos. Moreover, without agreeing completely with all that Burnet—*Greek Philosophy* [XXIII²⁸], I, ch. 2—reports about Demokritos, I do concur in what he states about the secondhand nature of the reports, the vagueness of our knowledge, and the limited originality of this thinker. In his *Commentary* [XXIX⁷], Taylor also protests against the Demokritos-thesis, but he replaces it with yet another bias (p. 18): "We might say that the formula for the physics and the physiology of the dialogue is that it is an attempt to graft Empedoclean biology on the stock of Pythagorean mathematics." Taylor's view—(*1*) that the dialogue mirrors the scientific theories of its dramatic date, the third decade of the fifth century B.C.; (*2*) that it cannot be determined whether Plato completely advocated any one of the theories presented; and (*3*) that Socrates here, too, is the historical Socrates, who, according to Aristophanes, occupied himself also with science—is incompatible not only with our conception of Plato, Socrates, dialogue, and myth, but also with the dating established by the history of science (see Frank, *Pythagoreer*, pp. 21, 233ff., and *passim*). Even so, we need hardly state how greatly indebted we all are to Taylor's *Commentary* on the *Timaeus*. / Among those who oppose Taylor's fundamental thesis are Cornford (*Cosmology*, pp. vii ff.) and Festugière (*Révélation*, p. 94).

13. See *Plato* 1, p. 199. / In the sketch for his projected extensive commentary on the *Timaeus*, Boeckh (*Kleine Schriften* [XXI²⁰], III, 183) states: "*Nam ut Platonis philosophia summa est veteris totius, sic etiam dialogus hic quidquid fere priores de natura philosophati sunt, docet nova et propria via.*" In what follows, references are suggested but not completely listed. The indexes to Diels' *Doxographi Graeci* and *Die Fragmente der Vorsokratiker* are useful in tracing the material.

14. For Leukippos, see *Vorsokr.* 67 [54] B 2. For Empedokles, see *Vorsokr.* 31 [21] B 17, 18, 19, 21, 115. In B 115 *Neikos* is shown as belonging to the realm of *Ananke*. One should also remember that in the *Iliad* (XVIII 382), Hephaistos has for his wife a certain Charis, while it is Aphrodite in the *Odyssey* (VIII 267ff.).

15. For this supposition, T. H. Martin, *Études sur le "Timée" de Platon* (2 vols., Paris, 1841), II, 248, was the initiator whom Archer-Hind, and then many others (among them apparently Cornford; see p. 220) followed. On the material itself, see Kranz's *Wortindex* [XXI²³], *s.v.* κόσμος.

16. Natorp (*Ideenlehre*, p. 343 = 2d edn., p. 360) comments that "in particular, the singularity of this world is based on the necessary

conceptual unity of life." The mathematical-musical unifying principle seems to be lacking, however, in Natorp's overconceptualized interpretation.

17. Whether the number five is at all related to the five regular polyhedra is more than questionable, and the "how" of this relationship would still remain unexplained. Cornford correctly calls this section "extremely puzzling," and his treatment of it (in *Cosmology*) apparently remains unsatisfactory even to himself. But see Ahlvers, *Zahl und Klang* [XXI²⁰], p. 33, concerning the pentacle and its "mystical" significance. One should also bear in mind that this pentacle permits a three-dimensional development which would be still more suitable to ordering the five worlds in space than the surface pentacle would be. Plutarch, in *De defectu oraculorum* 22, refers to "not innumerable worlds, not one world, not five [!], but one hundred and eighty-three."

18. On the world-soul, see further Cornford, *Cosmology*, pp. 59ff.; Raven, pp. 237ff.

19. Wilhelm Windelband, *Lehrbuch der Geschichte der Philosophie* (5th edn., Tübingen, 1910), p. 401.

20. Cornford (*Cosmology*, p. 58) translates ἔξωθεν as "on the outside" and then struggles to prevent the potential misunderstanding. ἔξωθεν clearly has this sense: beginning from the surface of the sphere.

21. *Aristotelis . . . fragmenta*, Rose edn. [XXVII¹⁶], frag. 44; Plutarch, *De musica* ch. 22, and *De animae procreatione in Timaeo* ch. 10 *et seq.*; Theon of Smyrna, *Expositio rerum mathematicarum*, ed. E. Hiller (Leipzig, 1878), pp. 94ff. / On what follows, see Frank, *Pythagoreer*, pp. 163f., 263ff.; Cornford, *Cosmology*, pp. 66ff.; Ahlvers, *Zahl und Klang*, pp. 21ff.; B. Kytzler, "Die Weltseele und der musikalische Raum," *Hermes*, LXXXVII (1959), 393ff.

22. See *Plato* 1, ch. XIV, "Plato as Physicist." / On the first point below, and esp. Plato's mathematical reformulation, see Eva Sachs, *Die fünf platonischen Körper* (Berlin, 1917), pp. 188ff. Basically she saw the matter clearly, and commented (on 48ʙ *et seq.*) that "this censure is directed against all pre-Platonic doctrines of elements presented." Nevertheless, she then violently builds up everything as evidence for Demokritos. (As to this, one should analyze her discussion on p. 193.) / It is the simile of the letters, in 48ʙ *et seq.*, that is called on to serve as evidence for the Atomists, since they—according to Diels—discovered this simile. (Against Diels: Taylor, *Commentary*, p. 307; G. S. Claghorn, *Aristotle's Criticism of Plato's "Timaeus,"* The Hague, 1954, p. 20.) One need only read the *Cratylus*, the *Theaetetus*, and the *Philebus* to recognize how important letters and syllables are as symbols to Plato. Methodically wrong, first of all, is the thesis that only the reference to an external factor (i.e., Demokritos) can explain "why here [51 ʙ *et seq.*] with such passion and conviction the basis

of the doctrine of *Ideas* is stressed." Actually, what had previously been presented more as a simile concerning the relations of primary image, appearance, and ἐκμαγεῖον is now confirmed by being related to the forms of cognition. In short, the acceptance of a polemic—here as so often—merely serves as a substitute for comprehending the immanent structure. See further Stenzel, "Platon und Demokritos," *Kleine Schriften*, pp. 60ff. Rivaud (*Timée*, pp. 24ff.) is more cautious regarding the Demokritos-thesis, but his assumption that a kind of mathematical atomism might have existed before Plato is hardly justified by any evidence.

23. Parmenides, *Vorsokr*. 28 [18] B 8, ll. 55ff. Also see 28 [18] A 35, and compare A 33.

24. Archer-Hind's commentary [XXIV⁵] on this passage is excellent: "[Plato] excels Empedokles in the matter of φιλία: he is not content with the vague assertion that φιλία keeps the universe together; he must show how φιλία comes about." Archer-Hind also refers to Empedokles (see *Vorsokr*. 31 [21] B 38, l. 4) for the very exceptional σφίγγει in *Timaeus* 58A.

25. Eva Sachs, op. cit., pp. 228ff., with reference to Simplicius has made it clear, in my opinion, that Plato was restricted here by his stereometric system, and that according to his primary conception he would have liked to include in it the earth. Cherniss, *Aristotle's Criticism of Plato*, p. 150, opposes this view. See Ahlvers, *Zahl und Klang*, pp. 54ff., for "a relatively simple method of dividing the square [of the hexahedron] into harmonic triangles . . . which could not have been above the knowledge of a Theaetetus."

26. 49BC: ὕδωρ πηγνύμενον ὡς δοκοῦμεν λίθους καὶ γῆν γιγνόμενον ὁρῶμεν, τηκόμενον δὲ καὶ διακρινόμενον αὖ ταὐτὸν τοῦτο πνεῦμα καὶ ἀέρα. Also see Herakleitos, *Vorsokr*. 22 [12] A 1, par. 9: πηγνύμενον δὲ τὸ ὕδωρ εἰς γῆν τρέπεσθαι . . . ἐκ δὲ τούτου (τοῦ ὕδατος) τὰ λοιπά. . .

27. *Vorsokr*. 22 [12] B 60, 103. Cf. the Herakleitean "De victu," *Vorsokr*. 22 [12] C 1, par. 19. On what follows, see *Doxogr*., pp. 370f.

28. Eva Sachs, *Platon. Körper*, pp. 190f., is mistaken in her interpretation of 49E in opposition to Martin and Archer-Hind. Cf. Wilamowitz, I, 616, and also Apelt's translation [XXIX¹⁰], n. 141 (where, however, we may disregard his criticism of Plato "from the logical point of view"). πῦρ τὸ διὰ παντός is not the *Idea* or Form of fire. This appears only in 51B as an example and therefore has no thematic importance for the over-all structure. Richard Reitzenstein, *Studien zum antiken Synkretismus* (Bibliothek Warburg, Leipzig, 1926), p. 147, failed to interpret *Timaeus* 51B correctly and has therefore arrived at dangerous conclusions. According to Reitzenstein, the world of *Ideas* has receded here, and only one *Idea*, or rather fire-itself, i.e., the highest god of the Persian prophet, finds recognition. But what,

then, is πάντα περὶ ὧν ἀεὶ λέγομεν οὕτως αὐτὰ καθ' αὐτὰ ὄντα (cf. *Phaedo* 75D: περὶ ἁπάντων οἷς ἐπισφραγιζόμεθα τὸ αὐτὸ ὅ ἔστι)? And does not the whole connection make it clear that fire is used here only as an example although water or earth could have been used just as easily? See Taylor's *Commentary*, pp. 333ff. / Reitzenstein adds, "Whether or not Plato still holds the 'dialectical view' of the *Ideas* I do not dare to determine"—but such an ἐποχή is inconceivable. Without the *Eidos*, the *Timaeus* is reduced to a heap of absurdities, an account of creation in the manner of Hermes Trismegistos.

29. Cf. W. Schadewaldt, "Das Welt-Modell der Griechen," in *Hellas und Hesperien* (Zurich and Stuttgart, 1960), pp. 426ff. / Ever since Eva Sachs' proof, it has been established as a fact that in identifying his particles of space with regular spatial forms, Plato followed no one, not even the Pythagoreans. It is evident, nevertheless, that the mathematization of the matter is in a deeper sense "Pythagorean," as Frank (*Pythagoreer*, pp. 54ff.) also assumes.

30. See W. Kranz, "Empedokles und die Atomistik," *Hermes*, XLVII (1912), 24ff.

31. In his commentary on the *Timaeus* [XXIV⁵], Archer-Hind demonstrated that this is consistent with 58B (τὰ γὰρ ἐκ μεγίστων μερῶν γεγονότα μεγίστην κενότητα ἐν τῇ συστάσει παραλέλοιπεν, τὰ δὲ σμικρότατα ἐλαχίστην). It seems obvious that Plato had previously considered what Aristotle (*De caelo* III 8 306ᵇ 3 *et seq.*) censures as an ἄλογον in the Platonic thesis. T. H. Martin, *Études* [XXIX¹⁵], II, 255f., believes he can show the lack of consistency also in the fact that the triangles which make up the polyhedra are thin, small leaves containing empty space. In my opinion, however, there is an error in Martin's thinking. The areas of the polyhedra do not include "empty space"; rather, they shape that variously named x, which Plato calls—among other names—χώρα, into something that we name either after fire or after earth. The thin leaves are mythical playthings for mathematical planes. / As to that x, see further *Plato* 1, pp. 249f., and the literature cited on p. 382, n. 10. The fact that the modern writers single out the term χώρα from the many names that Plato gives to that x has at least two explanations: (1) Plato himself places the word χώρα at the end of this discussion—even if in doing so, he certainly does not intend to suppress the manifold other metaphors. (2) Only χώρα corresponds—or seems to correspond—to a modern scientific term. It should be mentioned that, in contrast to modern one-sidedness, Aristotle, in *Physics* IV 2 209ᵇ 11, does indeed identify his ὕλη with Plato's χώρα, but nevertheless goes on in an entirely similar discussion, in *De generatione et corruptione* II 1 329ᵃ 13 *et seq.*, to choose the Platonic metaphors πανδεχές and τιθήνη rather than χώρα. Also see Plutarch, *De animae procreatione in Timaeo* ch. 27: χώραν γὰρ καλεῖ τὴν ὕλην, ἔστιν ὅτε καὶ ὑποδοχήν. / It is worth notic-

ing how Chalcidius, in ch. 308 of his commentary on the *Timaeus* (ed. J. Wrobel, Leipzig, 1876), attempts to render Plato's diverse expressions for what previously, following Aristotle, the commentator had called *silva* (=ὕλη) and *materia* as "*rerum receptaculum*, *matrem, nutricem totius generationis*—yet only for χώρα he seems to have no translation. / The manifold expressions of Plato and of the ancient commentators on his writings may stand in contrast to some examples of today's one-sidedness: Rey, pp. 246ff., "La chôra et l'idée de l'espace"; Rivaud, *Timée*, pp. 63ff., "La théorie du Lieu"; Cornford, *Cosmology*, pp. 191ff., "Form, Copy, and Space"; Festugière, *Révélation*, pp. 117ff., "La Χώρα puissance du désordre" (although on p. 129, Festugière more precisely uses the expression "*la* Χώρα-*matière*").

32. Plato's ordering of the sense perceptions "from below to above" is the opposite of Demokritos' and of Aristotle's. See Aristotle's *Über die Seele*, tr. Willi Theiler (Berlin, 1959), pp. 119f.

33. Concerning the eye, Empedokles, *Vorsokr.* 31 [21] B 84, ll. 10f.: ὕδατος μὲν βένθος ἀπέστεγον . . . πῦρ δ' ἔξω διίεσκον, ὅσον ταναώτερον ἦεν. On the same subject, Demokritos, *Vorsokr.* 68 [55] A 135, par. 50: τὸ μὲν πυκνὸν οὐ δέχεσθαι, τὸ δ' ὑγρὸν διιέναι. And Plato, *Timaeus* 45B: τὸ γὰρ ἐντὸς ἡμῶν . . . πῦρ εἰλικρινὲς ἐποίησαν διὰ τῶν ὀμμάτων ῥεῖν λεῖον . . . τὸ μὲν ἄλλο ὅσον παχύτερον στέγειν πᾶν, τὸ τοιοῦτον δὲ μόνον αὐτὸ καθαρὸν διηθεῖν. Evidently Plato is more closely related to Empedokles than to Demokritos.

34. For Alkmaion, see *Vorsokr.* 24 [14] A 5 (= Theophrastus, *De sensu* 26). For Pythagoras and Parmenides, see *Doxogr.*, p. 404. Cf. Martin, *Études* [XXIX¹⁵], II, 159. It is worth mentioning that in the *Timaeus*, as well as in the *Placita*, the theory of the mirror follows the theory of the act of seeing.

35. Concerning the opposition of Goethe to Newton, see W. Heisenberg, "Die Goethische und die Newtonsche Farbenlehre im Lichte der modernen Physik," in *Wandlungen in den Grundlagen der Naturwissenschaft* (9th edn., Stuttgart, 1950), pp. 85ff.; P. Bamm, "Humanität und Naturwissenschaft," in *Robert Boehringer: Eine Freundesgabe* (Tübingen, 1957), pp. 3ff.; C. F. von Weizsäcker, "Über einige Begriffe aus der Naturwissenschaft Goethes," *ibid.*, pp. 697ff.; H. Henel, "Type and Proto-phenomenon in Goethe's Science," *PMLA*, LXXI (1956), 651ff.; and the discussion between Henel and R. King, *PMLA*, LXXIII (1958), 433ff.

36. Cf. Max Wellmann, *Die Fragmente der sikelischen Ärzte* (Berlin, 1901), I, 49f. Wellmann understands the testimony of Diokles (as quoted by Vindicianus) as a polemic against Diogenes. In the wording of Vindicianus, however, there is no basis for such an assumption. The brain is *sine sono* just because the *apprehensio audiendi* resides in it. Being soundless itself, it receives sounds. The agreement of Diokles

with Diogenes is extensive. And Plato agrees with the two about as much as he departs from them.

37. Compare *Timaeus* 66D with Empedokles, *Vorsokr.* 31 [21] A 86, par. 7, and *Timaeus* 65c with Diogenes, *Vorsokr.* 64 [51] A 22. For the sake of her thesis, Hammer-Jensen, "Demokrit und Platon" [XXIX¹⁰], p. 225, attempts to make it seem plausible that Empedokles had derived his theory of the ἀπορροαί and the πόροι from Leukippos because he has made use of the hypothesis everywhere— including where neither we nor Theophrastus agree with it. This attempt is arbitrary. Cf. Kranz, "Empedokles . . ." [XXIX³⁰], pp. 18ff.

38. More sharply perhaps than necessary, but nevertheless pertinently, the contrast between Plato and Demokritos was formulated by Theophrastus in *De sensu* 61: ὁ μὲν γὰρ (Demokritos) πάθη ποιῶν τῆς αἰσθήσεως καθ' αὑτὰ διορίζει τὴν φύσιν. ὁ δὲ (Plato) καθ' αὑτὰ ποιῶν ταῖς οὐσίαις πρὸς τὰ πάθη τῆς αἰσθήσεως ἀποδίδωσι.

39. Diogenes, *Vorsokr.* 64 [51] A 19, par. 43 (Theophrastus). According to Wellmann, *Fragmente*, I, 89, the contrast between κατὰ φύσιν and παρὰ φύσιν refers to Diokles.

40. The whole subject of Plato's view of medicine needs a complete revision after Franz Poschenrieder's *Die platonischen Dialoge in ihrem Verhältnisse zu den hippokratischen Schriften* (1882). Ernst Hoffmann (in Zeller, 5th edn., pp. 1070ff.) refers to the fundamental significance of medicine for Plato. In the recent literature see W. Jaeger, *Diokles von Karystos* (Berlin, 1938), and *Paideia*, III, 3ff.; Cornford, *Cosmology*, pp. 332ff.; J. Bidez and G. Leboucq, "Une anatomie antique du coeur humain: Philistion de Locres et le *Timée* de Platon," *RevÉtGr*, LVII (1944), 7ff.; H. W. Miller, "The Aetiology of Disease in Plato's *Timaeus*," *TAPA*, XCIII (1962), 175ff.

41. See *Anonymus Londinensis* XX, 25ff. (in *Supplementum Aristotelicum*, III/1, Berlin, 1893); Wellmann, *Fragmente*, I, 110, frag. 4; Carl Fredrich, *Hippokratische Untersuchungen* (Berlin, 1899), p. 47. Wilamowitz (II, 258) even dates the *Timaeus* after the third journey because the dialogue presupposes a knowledge of Sicilian medicine. But why should Plato have become acquainted with this precisely during the third journey, and indeed why on a journey at all? We know that Philistion was in Athens.

42. *Anonymus Londinensis* XIX, 18ff. Menekrates, like Philistion and Plato too, precedes his etiology of diseases with a brief doctrine of the elements. For Diokles, see Wellmann, *Fragmente*, p. 74. Wellmann's rationale (see his p. 69) is that "Diokles' notorious dependency upon the doctrines of Philistion forces us to assume that wherever Plato and Diokles agree, Philistion is the source." This hypothesis cannot be proved by means of any evidence. On the basis of his dating

Diokles' work at about the year 300, however, Jaeger (*Diokles*, p. 212) agrees with Wellmann in this matter of sources.

43. The author of *De natura hominis* does not argue against an Empedoklean, however, as Diels, *Elementum* [XXIII⁶⁷], pp. 16f., might lead us to believe, but argues rather against those physicians who (in the sense of the monistic physicists) trace man's essence back to one primary substance, either air, fire, water, or earth, but not to all four.

44. Alkmaion, *Vorsokr.* 24 [14] B 4. Cf. *Timaeus* 82A, and also *Laws* X 906c. The subject matter had appeared earlier, in *Symposium* 188AB. Taylor's *Commentary* [XXIX⁷] on *Timaeus* 82A traces the word πλεονεξίη back to Hippokrates' treatise, Περὶ ἀδένων.

45. Fredrich, op. cit., p. 47; Wellmann, *Fragmente*, p. 9. See also W. Jaeger, "Das Pneuma im Lykeion," *Hermes*, XLVIII (1913), 50ff., and Cornford, *Cosmology*, pp. 340f.

46. See Fredrich, pp. 35ff., who recognizes in Plato's writing "an approximation to the doctrine of the island of Cos" (p. 48).

47. Albrecht Goetze, "Persische Weisheit im griechischen Gewande?" in *Zeitschrift für Indologie und Iranistik* (Leipzig), II (1923), 86. Also see Kranz, *Philosophie*, pp. 20, 210.

48. Reitzenstein, *Synkretismus* [XXIX²⁸], pp. 147f., as a conjecture traces the physiology of the *Timaeus* to Iranian doctrines. I refrain from making a judgment and will mention only that Reitzenstein does not consider this to be "borrowings and imitations in the usual sense," but rather "competitive creation based on entirely different presuppositions and with entirely different tools."

49. See Archer-Hind's "*Timaeus*" [XXIV⁵], p. 319; U. von Wilamowitz, *Griechisches Lesebuch* (Berlin, 1902), II/1, 269; H. Gossen, in *R-E*, V, col. 426; M. Pohlenz, *Gestalten aus Hellas* (Munich, 1950), pp. 335ff.

50. Wilamowitz (*Platon*, I, 619f.) believes that Plato, fatigued, abruptly terminated this dialogue. My presentation, on the contrary, has attempted to show that the composition of the *Timaeus* is strictly planned and executed throughout.

XXX: *Critias*

RECENT EDITIONS AND TRANSLATIONS: O. Apelt, PhB 179 (1922); A. Rivaud, *Platon Budé*, X (1925).

RECENT INTERPRETATIONS: H. Herter, "Altes und Neues zu Platons *Kritias*," *RhM*, n.s., XCII (1944), 236ff.; P. Friedländer, *Plato 1*, ch. XVII, "Plato as City Planner"; Reinhardt, *Vermächtnis*, pp. 280ff.; Lesky, pp. 534ff.

ADDITIONAL BIBLIOGRAPHY: Shorey, p. 620; Geffcken, Notes, p. 126; Leisegang, cols. 2512f.; Rosenmeyer, p. 178; Cherniss, *Lustrum*, pp. 79ff.

1. T. G. Rosenmeyer, "Plato's Atlantis Myth: *Timaeus* or *Critias?*" in *The Phoenix* (Toronto), X (1956), 163ff., clearly sets forth the unevennesses here, little as one need follow some of his judgments and suppositions. Rosenmeyer is right (p. 172): "There must be simpler explanations of the difficulties which we have noted."

2. Hans Meyerhoff, *The Philosophy of History in Our Time* (New York, 1959), p. 1, sees in Plato's *Critias* "possibly an attempt to construct a mythology, or philosophy, of history analogous to his philosophy of nature in the *Timaeus*. . . ."

3. See *Plato* 1, pp. 202ff.

4. *Plato* 1, chs. XV (esp. pp. 273ff.) and XVII. The circular naval harbor of Carthage should have been mentioned (in ch. XVII) among Plato's models for the city of the Atlantides. Cf. Theodor Mommsen, *Römische Geschichte* (7th edn., Berlin, 1881), II, 31; R. Oehler, *R-E*, X, col. 2183; Karl Lehmann-Hartleben, *Die antiken Hafenanlagen des Mittelmeeres* (Klio, n.s., I, Leipzig, 1923), pp. 72, 85 (n. 2), Plan XXII; C. Corbato, "Platone e Cartagine," *Archeologia Classica*, V (1953), pp. 232ff. Plato certainly had heard more exact information about Carthage in Syracuse. And he could see for himself in Syracuse examples of the bridges under which ships could pass, and the double ship-sheds; cf. Lehmann-Hartleben, pp. 85 (n. 2), 112. It is significant that Rudberg (pp. 51ff.) criticizes an earlier article of his own— in Swedish, "Atlantis och Syrakusai," *Eranos*, XVII (1919), 1ff.— as follows: "In this article of mine I emphasized, certainly too strongly, the similarities and associations which I thought I found between Plato's picture in *Timaeus-Critias* and ancient Syracuse." But even in his revision, Rudberg still exaggerates the importance of the immediate models that Plato may have found in Syracuse. See also Wilamowitz, I, 590.

XXXI: *Laws*

RECENT EDITIONS AND TRANSLATIONS: C. Ritter (Leipzig, 1896); O. Apelt, PhB 159, 160 (1916); E. B. England (London, 1921); A. Diès, L. Gernet, and É. des Places, *Platon Budé*, XI/1–2 (1951), XII/1–2 (1956); F. Adorno (Turin, 1958); J. M. Pabón and M. F. Galiano (Madrid, 1960).

RECENT INTERPRETATIONS: Salin, *Utopie*, pp. 63ff.; J. Bisinger, *Der Agrarstaat in Platons "Gesetzen"* (Klio, n.s., IV, Leipzig, 1925); W. G.

Becker, *Platons "Gesetze" und das griechische Familienrecht* (Munich, 1932); A. H. Chase, "The Influence of Athenian Institutions upon the *Laws* of Plato," *Harvard Studies in Classical Philology*, XLIV (1933), 131ff.; Shorey, pp. 355ff.; F. Guglielmino, *Preconcetti teorici e realismo in Platone* (Catania, 1936), pp. 33ff., "Il codice penale di Platone e l'involontarietà del male"; R. G. Bury, in *RevÉtGr*, L (1937), 304ff.; K. von Fritz, "Philippos von Opus," *R-E*, XIX (1938), cols. 2358ff.; F. Pfister, "Die Prooimia der platonischen *Gesetze*," *Mélanges Émile Boisacq*, II (Brussels, 1938), 173ff.; A. Meremetis, *Verbrecher und Verbrechung* (Leipzig, 1940); G. R. Morrow, "Plato and the Rule of Law," *PR*, L (1941), 105ff.; Solmsen, chs. 8, 9; O. Reverdin, *La religion de la cité platonicienne* (Paris, 1945); Jaeger, *Paideia*, III, pp. 213ff.; Barker, ch. 13; H. Cairns, *Legal Philosophy from Plato to Hegel* (Baltimore, 1949), pp. 29ff. (also in P. Friedländer, *Plato* 1, ch. XVI, "Plato as Jurist"); Festugière, *Révélation*, II, ch. 5; III, ch. 3; P. Haliste, "Zwei Fragen zum Katasterwesen in Platons *Gesetzen*," *Eranos*, XLVIII (1950), 93ff.; Dodds, pp. 207ff.; V. Martin, "Sur la condamnation des athées par Platon au Xe Livre des *Lois*," *Studia Philosophica* (Lvov), XI (1951), 103ff.; T. A. Sinclair, "Myth and Politics in the *Laws* of Plato," *Actes Congrès Internat. Études Class.* (Paris, 1951), pp. 273ff., and also *A History of Greek Political Thought*, pp. 186ff.; Stanka, pp. 164ff.; W. Theiler, in *Schweizer Archiv für Volkskunde*, XLVII (1951), pp. 192ff.; G. Müller, *Studien zu den platonischen "Nomoi"* (Munich, 1951), and the review by H. Cherniss in *Gnomon*, XXV (1953), 367ff.; E. Michelakis, *Platons Lehre von der Anwendung des Gesetzes und der Begriff der Billigkeit bei Aristoteles* (Munich, 1953); R. Schaerer, "L'itinéraire dialectique des *Lois* . . ." in *Revue Philosophique*, CXLIII (1953), 379ff.; G. R. Morrow, "The Demiurge in Politics," *Proc. Amer. Philos. Assoc.*, XXVII (1954), 5ff.; M. Vanhoutte, *La philosophie politique de Platon dans les "Lois"* (Louvain, 1954), and the review by H. Kuhn in *Gnomon*, XXVII (1955), 49f.; Wolff, pp. 291ff.; Luccioni, *passim*; H. Görgemanns, *Beiträge zur Interpretation von Platons "Nomoi"* (Munich, 1960); W. Knoch, *Die Strafbestimmungen in Platons "Nomoi"* (Wiesbaden, 1960); G. R. Morrow, *Plato's Cretan City* (Princeton, 1960); Lesky, pp. 536ff.

ADDITIONAL BIBLIOGRAPHY: Shorey, p. 622; Geffcken, Notes, pp. 127ff.; Leisegang, cols. 2513ff.; Rosenmeyer, pp. 180ff.; Cherniss, *Lustrum*, pp. 103ff.

1. See *Plato* 1, p. 115.
2. *Letter III* 316A. Joseph Souilhé (*Lettres, Platon Budé*, XIII/1, 1926, p. lxxxv) calls this passage suspect—without justification—by referring to *Letter VII* 341B. The two passages bear no relation to each

other. Concerning the authenticity of Plato's letters, see *Plato* 1, ch. XIII.

3. The contrary view (i.e., that Plato's *Laws* has nothing to do with the legislation for Syracuse) is just as unthinkable, in the vital unity of the Platonic life, as the other thesis (like that of F. Blass) is incredible: that in the *Laws* we actually possess the legislation of Syracuse. Wilamowitz (in *Hermes*, XLV, 1910, p. 405) is probably overcautious in stating that the *Laws* represents "in my opinion, the work of [Plato's] last decade in which many older notes could have been employed." Singer, p. 245, calls the dialogue "a monument testifying to the spirit in which [Plato and Dion] wanted to transform the state of Syracuse."

4. According to Wilamowitz (*Aristoteles und Athen*, Berlin, 1893, I, 194; *Platon*, I, 694 = I², 701), "Plato's *Laws* has created the *Ephebia*."

5. See Olof Gigon, "Das Einleitungsgespräch der *Gesetze* Platons," *MusHelv*, XI (1954), 207ff.

6. Salin, *Utopie*, p. 69. Gigon misunderstands this symbolism when he states that in the original conception the goal must have been the essential point, and the ascent to the cave of Zeus the factor determining the legislation. How is one to imagine this?

7. This is one of the passages that George Sarton should have considered before writing his invective against Plato: *A History of Science* (Cambridge, Mass., 1952), I, 408ff.

8. See *Plato* 1, pp. 133ff.

9. The scholiast and many other commentators—beginning with Cicero, *De legibus* I 15—simplify the relation as ἔστι δὲ Πλάτων. Susemihl (II, 668) views the Athenian stranger as "the idealized common Attic spirit." This is not quite wrong, apart from its formulation, but neither is it sufficient.

10. Eduard Zeller, *Studien* [XXIV²³], pp. 45f., and Ivo Bruns, *Platons "Gesetze"* (Weimar, 1880), p. 108, considered this "superstition" un-Platonic. This is correct in a way, but certainly not in the sense intended by Zeller and Bruns.

11. The discussion about the τρίτη πολιτεία in 739A 7 and E 5 seems to be endless. διαπερανούμεθα means to complete not λόγῳ but rather ἔργῳ. The misinterpretation that Plato is speaking here of a third state or body of legislation ἐν λόγοις—see, for example, the commentary on this passage in E. B. England, *The "Laws" of Plato* (2 vols., London, 1921); Theodor Gomperz, "Platonische Aufsätze, III," *SBWien*, CXLV (1902), 2; G. Müller, *Studien zu . . . "Nomoi"* [XX³⁶], p. 173—has led to fantastic conclusions. Susemihl (II, 644) argued against this misinterpretation as even more strongly did C. Ritter, *Platons "Gesetze": Kommentar zum griech. Text* (2 vols., Leipzig, 1896), I, 143. Ritter goes astray, however, in concluding that the διαπεραίνειν of the τρίτη πολιτεία lies in its legislating matters of

minor importance. Rather, the essential fact is that the τρίτη πολιτεία is not ἐν λόγοις, as the second one still is. The state to be erected on the soil of Crete (or perhaps somewhere else) is, as it were, τρίτη ἀπὸ ἀληθείας. Cf. É. des Places, *Les lois* (*Platon Budé*, XI/2, 1951), p. 96, n. 1.

12. The text of 626D 8 contains errors. The preceding discussion in the dialogue has shown that all are hostile toward all others, δημοσίᾳ καὶ ἰδίᾳ. In addition, as a third member, the inner enmity within oneself appears. Therefore ⟨καὶ⟩ ἑκάστους must be written. This is confirmed by the disappearance of the very strong hiatus between ἰδίᾳ and ἑκάστους. Obviously, καὶ ἰδίᾳ and καὶ ἑκάστους are not real hiatuses.

13. Gigon, discussing 631A in "Einleitungsgespräch" [XXXI⁵], refers to "a hastiness and superficiality . . . which could almost be termed atrocious."

14. The κατ' εἴδη ζητεῖν in 630E designates the meaningful order, while the words that follow—οἱ τῶν νῦν (namely, νομοθέται) εἴδη προτιθέμενοι ζητοῦσιν—describe the opposite, the unsystematical arrangement. This characterization would be fitting, for example, for the ancient Gortyn; cf. J. Kohler and E. Ziebarth, *Das Stadtrecht von Gortyn* (Göttingen, 1912), p. 43. / τοὺς πόρρω ⟨νοῦ⟩ νομοθέτας in 630D 3 seems to me more appropriate than τοὺς πόρρω νομοθεσίας.

15. Solon I 37 *et seq.*, and scholium 7 (8). See further *Hermes*, LXIV (1929), 381f. To this statement one should add that while ἡβᾶν μετὰ τῶν φίλων in the scholium does not correspond to the Solonic ἄλλος δειλὸς ἐὼν ἀγαθὸς δοκεῖ ἔμμεναι ἀνήρ, nevertheless for Plato ἰσχὺς εἴς τε δρόμον καὶ εἰς ἄλλας πάσας κινήσεις τῷ σώματι (*Laws* I 631C 3) stands between the two.

16. Bruns's "*Gesetze*" [XXXI¹⁰], pp. 11ff., has the merit of having forcefully brought out the significance of the "disposition" in 631B *et seq.* Bruns's view (p. 155), however, that it represents the remainder of the original plan "intended to demonstrate the Spartan-Cretan constitution as the model state" rests in the end on a misunderstanding of the irony in 632D. Zeller, *Studien* [XXIV²³], p. 76, also missed the ironic element, but not so Susemihl, who argued against Zeller on this passage. It was always Plato's intention for ἐχρῆν in 631B 3 and ἤθελον in 632D 1 to remain in the sphere of irreality, and for ἔτι νῦν βούλομαι in 632D 2 and τοῖς δ' ἄλλοις ἡμῖν οὐδαμῶς ἐστι καταφανής in 632D 6 to be understood as ironical. (In his *Kommentar*, pp. 4f., Ritter correctly rejects Bruns's hypothesis, but then Ritter himself fails to do justice to the significance of the passage.) The arrangement in 631B *et seq.* is essentially that of the legislation which follows in the dialogue. (Cf. A. Boeckh, *In Platonis . . . Minoem*, Halle, 1806, p. 98.) Yet, in the so-called disposition, the basic reality of the legislation is hidden under principles so general that one is unable either to assert or to deny agreement between details. The parallel

between the more general topics may be clarified, however, by the following table (which should be compared to that of des Places in *Platon Budé*, XI/1, 1951, p. 12, n. 1).

Laws 631B et seq.	ARRANGEMENT OF THE LAWS
Table of goods, including the ἀρεταί up to the νοῦς ἡγεμών.	Discussion of the ἀρεταί: Books I, II, and IV (715E et seq.).
Laws on marriage and children.	Marriage: Book IV (720E et seq.) and Book VI (771E). Education: Book VII.
Laws about deeds of passion.	Criminal offenses: Book IX. (Those deriving from emotions—854A 6, 867C 6, 869E 7, 870A and C.)
Laws on economic relations.	Civil laws: Books XI and XII.
Laws concerning tombs and honors to the dead.	Funerals: Book XII.
The guardians of this legislation.	Guardians: Book XII (964B et seq.).

17. Was it an insight of Plato's own, or perhaps that of some "sophist" whom we cannot name? Herakleitos' view of Πόλεμος, and Empedokles' conception of Νεῖκος "of which infinite time will never be emptied" (*Vorsokr.* 31 [21] B 16), appear here in a political context. Intrinsically, however, the sentence about eternal war is fully implied in the νόμος expressed by the Athenians in Thucydides V 105 2: οὗ ἂν κρατῇ, ἄρχειν—for since this law is always valid, it presupposes the continuous state of war.

18. H. Fuchs, *Augustin und der antike Friedensgedanke* (Berlin, 1926), pp. 117ff., 135ff., has traced these relationships.

19. Bruns ("*Gesetze*," p. 24), for example, does not see this—and he is hardly alone among the interpreters, who generally fail to recognize the dramatic movement.

20. Zeller, *Studien*, p. 59; Bruns, p. 18; Müller, *Studien zu . . . "Nomoi*," p. 18. The objections of Susemihl (II, 613) and Ritter (*Kommentar*, p. 9) still need to be sharpened. / See further England's commentary [XXXI[11]] on this passage.

21. Bruns (p. 21) calls this probably "one of the most curious creations ever to spring from the head of a philosopher speculating about the state." Yet, in speaking of "drinking societies" rather than "symposia," Bruns misunderstands the facts and thereby disturbs the clarity of the whole picture (syssitia are not dining societies either). Nevertheless, the fact that Bruns could be so mistaken reveals how vaguely

Plato expressed himself on this matter: ἡ ἐν οἴνοις διατριβή (645c 3), ἡ ἐν οἴνῳ συνουσία (652a 4), περὶ μέθης (637d 6). In order not to exaggerate the "curiosity," one should at least disregard the temporal distance and think of groups like student fraternities and officers clubs, where the goal striven for, even if in terms only of μέρος ἀρετῆς, is still intended as a παιδεία διὰ μέθης.

22. Bruns (pp. 53f.) objects to a certain vacillation in the discussion between πεῖραν λαμβάνειν and μελετᾶν, which are placed together in 649d 8 with a πρῶτον μέν and εἶτα. The objection is unjustified, however, because the two belong close together. The fact that sometimes one and then sometimes the other is more strongly expressed is due in general to the vitality of informal speech. And we can state, in particular, why at the end of the first book our attention is focused on the πεῖρα: in order that in the beginning of Book II μελέτη and thus "education" may emerge as the subject still to be completed.

23. ὅπως ἂν ἐν ἡμῖν τὸ χρυσοῦν γένος νικᾷ τἆλλα γένη (645a 7). Here we are also reminded somewhat of the tale about the men of metal in *Republic* III 414d *et seq.* (see further pp. 134ff., above). And τῇ καλλίστῃ ἀγωγῇ reminds us of the guidance by the string and also of education. Cf. Krämer, p. 147; Aichroth, pp. 101ff.

24. Apelt (*Aufsätze*, p. 165) does not view this passage seriously enough. On the other hand, Bruns's desire (pp. 95f.) to ascribe this utterance to Philippos of Opus, rather than to Plato, is a matter on which one had better remain silent. But see further England's commentary on 804b 8. (παθών most probably means "under this impression," "on the basis of this experience"—"this impression" or "experience" being the one expressed in ἀπιδών.)

25. According to Bruns, "*Gesetze,*" ch. 1 (esp. pp. 37ff.), the "drinking societies" of the first book and the Dionysian chorus of the second exclude each other. Against this it should be stated (1) that in Book I the subject is not drinking societies, but rather social drinking in general (see n. 21, above), and (2) that the symposia and the Dionysian chorus do not exclude each other but instead from the beginning have nothing in common. The general legislation about wine-consuming begins with II 666a. Moderate consumption is permitted to those between the ages of eighteen and thirty, but μέθη καὶ πολυοινία are prohibited. In Book I, these prohibitions are not mentioned. But the examination of the σωφροσύνη, which is emphasized there, can actually take place only within the framework of such a law. In 671a *et seq.*, the effect of wine on the chorus of elders is described. Plato inserts this as a connecting link between the institution of drinking and the educational choruses. Taylor (*Plato*, p. 468) correctly states that "Plato has ingeniously made the problem of the right use of wine lead up to that of the use of music and poetry as a vehicle of early moral education." Bruns (p. 30) calls special attention to the words

ἄνευ παιδείας τῆς πάσης in 642A 5, as a plan that is carried out not in Book II, but only in Book VII. To this one should reply: the words are not intended to mean that the entire field of education is actually to be surveyed in Books I and II. They only point to the whole field. Still, Bruns has set up the very important problem of the connection between Book II and Book VII. To this we shall return later. / On the passage in general, see Ritter, *Kommentar*, pp. 54ff.; Müller, *Studien zu . . . "Nomoi,"* pp. 6f.

26. Although it is not my intention to write a detailed analysis, several remarks should be made on the technique that links Book I and Book II. The wine motif of Book I is suggested in 653D 4 and 665A, is expressed more clearly in 666A *et seq.* and 671A, and is brought to a conclusion in 673D *et seq.*, where the motif of the wine and that of the institution of the chorus are merged. Bruns ascribes this fusion to his assumed "reviser." I see here Plato's own technique of fusion—and whether or not the technique can be considered completely successful does not matter. Plato, in any case, had other concerns. The much-discussed πρῶτον μέν (666C 3) which is not followed by a corresponding ἔπειτα δέ, does not justify such far-reaching conclusions as Bruns's (p. 44).

27. Regarding this concept here in Book II and the educational regulations of Book VII, see R. G. Bury, "The Theory of Education in Plato's *Laws*," *RevÉtGr*, L (1937), 304ff.

28. This formulation probably is too simple. We must realize what we would be expecting of the aged Plato if we were to imagine that he himself wrote or dictated the *Laws* from beginning to end. This is almost as unthinkable as it is that every inch of Michelangelo's or Raphael's Roman frescoes is by the master's own hand. And yet it is hard to imagine that *no* part of the *Epinomis* was written or dictated by Plato—even if Raeder (p. 414) certainly oversimplifies in the opposite direction in believing the *Epinomis* to be a genuine Platonic work. A thoroughgoing analysis could perhaps make it possible to distinguish what Plato himself wrote from what belongs to Philippos of Opus.

29. The contrast between the two treatments may lead us astray, according to G. A. Finsler, *Platon und die aristotelische Poetik* (Leipzig, 1900), pp. 230f. But how is it possible to overlook the fact that the *Republic*, like the *Laws*, intends not the exclusion but rather the purging of poetry? It is sufficient to compare *Republic* X 607A: ὅτι ὅσον μόνον ὕμνους θεοῖς καὶ ἐγκώμια τοῖς ἀγαθοῖς ποιήσεως παραδεκτέον εἰς πόλιν with *Laws* VII 801E: μετά γε μὴν ταῦτα ὕμνοι θεῶν καὶ ἐγκώμια κεκοινωνημένα εὐχαῖς ᾄδοιτ' ἂν ὀρθότατα.

30. *Laws* II 656B 4: ὁμοιοῦσθαι δή που ἀνάγκη τὸν χαίροντα ὁποτέροις ἂν χαίρῃ. *Republic* VI 500C: ἢ οἴει τινὰ μηχανὴν εἶναι, ὅτῳ τις ὁμιλεῖ ἀγάμενος μὴ μιμεῖσθαι ἐκεῖνο;

31. See *Plato* 1, pp. 119ff.

32. 668B: ἐκείνην τὴν ἔχουσαν τὴν ὁμοιότητα τῷ τοῦ καλοῦ μιμήματι. In addition, *Laws* VII 814E and 816A should be considered.

33. Bruns (*"Gesetze,"* pp. 73f.) states correctly that ἐφεξῆς does not mean "later on," but "successively," "in turn" (*"à son tour,"* in des Places' *Budé* translation). In Bruns's view, the real connection between Book II and Book VII is originally a spatial correlation. Later on we shall have to clarify in what sense this could be correct. In any case, however, it is not correct according to the interpretation of Bruns himself, who believes that a "reviser" established the present state of the text. Gomperz, "Aufsätze" [XXXI[11]], p. 20, deduces from ἐφεξῆς that what now appears in Book VII should originally have occurred sooner; that after changing his plan, Plato ought to have replaced this word by εἰσαῦθις; and that, therefore, the "final wording" has not been reached. This solution is unsatisfactory. It disregards the fact that the connection made by ἑξῆς is reciprocal. This very same objection may be made also to the reasoning of Ritter (in his *Kommentar*, pp. 86f.), since he regards ἐφεξῆς as evidence for a gap. And England's commentary [XXXI[11]], I, 342f., is not satisfactory either, for he does not even discuss this passage of Book VII. In my view, ἐφεξῆς refers to the spatial connection or that of the subject matter (namely, the "continuation"). If the connection of the subject matter is meant, then, in my opinion, a direct spatial connection is not required (although ἐφεξῆς naturally may designate such a connection). It is particularly clear that the connection concerns only the subject matter because in Book II ἐφεξῆς means the sequence *music, gymnastics*, while ἑξῆς in Book VII means the reverse. Cf. *Republic* IV 420C, αὐτίκα σκεψόμεθα—which does not take place until Books VIII and IX. Also see Epicurus, Περὶ φύσεως, end of Lib. II (*Hercul. vol. coll. pr.*, Oxford, 1809, II, 25): τὰ δ' ἁρμόττοντα ἐφεξῆς τούτοις ῥηθῆναι ἐν τοῖς μετὰ ταῦτα διέξιμεν.

34. Steinhart, VII/1, 168: "The theory of the origin of the states in Book II of the *Republic*, contrary to historical data, is replaced here by another theory, better supported by history and quite correct in its basic assumptions." But right and wrong in the sense of modern sociology or prehistory are mixed in both constructions. The major aim should be to grasp the fundamentally different character of each construction. / On *Laws* III and IV, see further G. Rohr, *Platons Stellung zur Geschichte* (Berlin, 1932), pp. 9ff.

35. If Plato himself did not refer to a system of four stages (683A 7), one rather would be inclined to regard the βασιλεία δικαιοτάτη (680E 3) as the second level and the level introduced by μετὰ δὲ ταῦτα (680E 6) as the third. It is curious that no one, so far, seems to have claimed that this slight unevenness might be due to an ancient revision.

36. The expanding addition τετάρτη πόλις, εἰ δὲ βούλεσθε ἔθνος in 683A 7 obviously cannot imply a true difference.

37. Bruns ("*Gesetze*," pp. 66f.) expresses the most radical view, claiming that the words must refer to a theoretical discussion deleted by an "editor." England (I, 360) rightly remarks how improbable such behavior would have been for this imagined editor. England himself believes that these words refer to a fictitious discussion—which he places before Book I—among the same participants. This is impossible, however, if only because of the word ὑμνδή. Ritter (*Kommentar*, pp. 97ff.) believes that Books I and II contain several passages that might be interpreted in the sense of the words in question (for which Steinhart, not very appropriately, refers to *Laws* I 629 *et seq.*, and des Places—in *Platon Budé*, XI/2, pp. 20f.—refers to 626E), but Ritter leaves open the possibility that the reference is to the first part of Book III. Gomperz, "Aufsätze" [XXXI[11]], p. 19, believes that this general sentence results from the described transformation of the constitutions; yet, according to him, the reference points back to another general sentence which has been omitted. F. Döring (*De legum Platonicarum compositione*, Leipzig diss., 1907, p. 47) even believes that the reference is to *Republic* VIII 545D. A similar view is that of Diès (see *Platon Budé*, XI/1, p. xx).

38. 687A 8, B 1, B 7, C 1, C 9.

39. For example, compare *Laws* 687A 8 *et seq.*: καὶ ὅλως ἐν ἀνθρώποις πᾶσι καὶ "Ελλησι καὶ βαρβάροις πράττειν ὅτι ἐπιθυμοῖεν with *Alcibiades* 105BC: μέγιστον δυνήσεσθαι . . . ἐν "Ελλησι . . . ἐν βαρβάροις . . . εἰ μὴ ἐμπλήσεις . . . πάντας . . . ἀνθρώπους. And compare *Laws* 687D with *Lysis* 207D *et seq.*

40. See esp. 693B 1, 2, 5, 7. Also see Wilamowitz, I, 659 = I², 666; Rand, *The Building of Eternal Rome* [XXVII[32]], p. 10.

41. τρέφειν, παιδεύειν, and the substantives occur in 694C 6, D 2, D 8, E 4; 695A 2, A 6, A 7, B 2, B 6, C 7, E 2, etc. / The words about Cyrus in 694C 6–7 have been connected with Xenophon's Κύρου Παιδεία; see Gellius, *Noctes Atticae* XIII 3 3.

42. τιμή, τιμᾶν, τίμιον, ἄτιμον: 696A 7, B 2, D 5, D 11, E 4, E 6; 697B 2, B 3, B 7, etc.

43. Pohlenz (*Werdezeit*, pp. 253ff.) has shown this parallel. Compare also *Republic* IX 573B 9: μεθυσθείς and 573C 3: μαινόμενος with *Laws* III 695B 5: μαινόμενος ὑπὸ μέθης. For reminiscences of the Orient in Plato's portrayal of the tyrannical nature, see *Republic* IX 572E 4: οἱ δεινοὶ μάγοι τε καὶ τυραννοποιοί, and 573A 8, E 7: δορυφορεῖται, δορυφόροι.

44. Bruns ("*Gesetze*," pp. 146f.) has made this observation, but at the same time has drawn from it false and exaggerated conclusions. The passages 682E and 702A are connecting links between the independently moving discussions of Book III and Books I–II. It is curious that the tables of goods described in *Laws* I 631B *et seq.* and in III 697BC bear no relation to each other; this, however, is only one particularly strong expression of the fact just established.

45. See Zeller, *Studien* [XXIV²³], pp. 57f.; cf. the view of Susemihl, II, 649.

46. Thus, in brief, the objections of Bruns—pp. 65ff.—are accepted and used constructively: one merely needs to take Plato himself as the "editor" whom Bruns assumes (and, all in all, disregard Bruns's petty criticism). Taken in this way, the observations of Bruns become valuable even though they have not been fully pursued as yet. We should not say, however, that the reader is altogether unable to understand the words of *Laws* II 659A 1 (ἕνα τὸν ἀρετῇ καὶ παιδείᾳ διαφέροντα) before VI 765D *et seq.* when the supervisor of education is introduced. Anyone acquainted with Book VI certainly can understand the εἷς of Book II in the same manner. Plato probably intended this reference. Yet, is not εἷς, put in a general way, meaningful and effective even without any such reference?

47. See, for example, 705D–E, 707D 1, 708D 8.

48. Otto Kern, *Die Inschriften von Magnesia am Maeander* (Berlin, 1900), pp. 14f. (Nr. 17). Cf. Wilamowitz, in *Hermes*, XXX (1895), 185ff. (reprinted in his *Kleine Schriften*, Berlin, 1935–37, V/1, 86ff.). The Magnesians are mentioned first in *Laws* VIII 848D, and then again in IX 860E, XI 919D, and XII 946B. Boeckh, *In Platonis . . . Minoem* [XXXI¹⁶], p. 68, cites these passages.

49. The word φύσις occurs in 704D 7, 705C 7.

50. On this see further A. Lesky, *Thalatta: Der Weg der Griechen zum Meer* (Vienna, 1947), pp. 214ff.; A. E. Raubitschek, "Meeresnähe und Volksherrschaft," *WienStud*, LXXI (1958), pp. 112ff. (Incidentally, *"Die grässliche Flotte"* was a political slogan in Germany around 1900.)

51. Therefore, what Plato stands for is exactly the opposite of that which Meyer (V, § 524) describes as "the indestructible faith in the omnipotence of the laws and the conscious rejection of the powers decisive in human life."

52. The "separatists" seem not to have noticed that, strictly taken, the question in 709D 10 disagrees with the foundation as determined in 702C.

53. μεταβολή, μεταβάλλειν: *Laws* IV 711A 3, B 5, C 6; *Republic* V 473B 6, C 2, C 3.

54. See *Plato* 1, pp. 86f.

55. *Laws* 711C 8 *et seq.*: οὐκ ἀδύνατον . . . ἀλλὰ χαλεπόν. 712A 6: τῇ μὲν χαλεπόν, τῇ δὲ τάχιστον καὶ ῥᾷστον. *Republic* 473C 3: οὐ μέντοι σμικροῦ γ᾽ οὐδὲ ῥᾳδίου, δυνατοῦ δέ. 502B 8: οὐ δήπου ἀδύνατον. 502C 5: χαλεπὰ δὲ γενέσθαι, οὐ μέντοι ἀδύνατά γε.

56. *Laws* 711D 3: ὅταν δὲ συμβῇ, μυρία καὶ πάντ᾽ ἐν πόλει ἀγαθὰ ἀπεργάζεται. *Republic* 502C 2: βέλτιστα, εἴπερ δυνατά. *Republic* 502C 6: ἄριστα μὲν εἶναι ἃ λέγομεν, εἰ γένοιτο.

57. Zeller, *Studien* [XXIV²³], pp. 42f., turned this into an argument for its unauthenticity.

58. This becomes evident in 712c.

59. The strange use of the expression τῇ τυραννουμένῃ ψυχῇ has caused concern to the interpreters (among them England, des Places, Ritter), and has led some to change the text: τῇ τοῦ τυράννου ψυχῇ (Cornarius); τῇ τυραννούσῃ ψυχῇ (des Places). Yet the expression in the *Laws* may be read *sensu medio*, as in Ast's interpretation, once the relation to the identical expression in *Republic* 577DE is recognized.

60. For τὴν τοῦ νοῦ διανομὴν ἐπονομάζοντας νόμον (714A), translators either have to get along with a version similar to ours (see also Müller and Apelt), or else, like des Places, must give up all attempts at an even approximate translation.

61. To regard this passage (ψυχὴν ἡδονῶν καὶ ἐπιθυμιῶν ὀρεγομένην, 714A 3) with England as a hendiadys ("coveted delights") does not do justice to the beautiful expression. Goethe's *Faust* is of more help: "Thus in desire I hasten to enjoyment, / and in enjoyment pine to feel desire."

62. *Republic* I 338c; see *Plato* 2, pp. 60f. *Gorgias* 493B *et seq.* and *Republic* IX 586B are also germane. Cf. *Plato* 2, pp. 263ff., and above, p. 119.

63. On the paradox εὐθείᾳ . . . περιπορευόμενος in 716A, see the comments of the scholiast and also of England.

64. In 716A 2, τῷ δ' ἀεὶ συνέπεται Δίκη is better than . . . δίκη, as also in 716B 4. τιμωρός and the whole sentence remind us of Herakleitos, *Vorsokr.* 22 [12] B 94.

65. Compare *Laws* 716AB with the beginning and end of the *Alcibiades Major* and with *Republic* 494B *et seq.*, and also see above, pp. 110f. Cf. É. des Places, *Platon Budé*, XI/2, p. 66, n. 1. Gerhard Müller, *Studien zu . . . "Nomoi,"* p. 171, considers the allusion to Alkibiades improbable since the point is lacking (i.e., the relation: Socrates, Alkibiades, the people). But is not this reference clearly present, the one to Socrates in *Laws* 716A 7–8, and the other to the people in 716B 3 and 5?

66. Robert Boehringer, "Alkibiades," in *Sang der Jahre* (Godesberg, 1944), p. 63.

67. Wilamowitz (II, 311) misunderstands this relationship because he is too intent on accusing Plato of "killing all progress as well as all individualism." (Have we not advanced tremendously through progress and individuality!) Far more valuable is the view of England (I, 459): "It is a rich piece of Platonic humour which gives the much decried and dangerous poet the task of teaching the νομοθέτης his duty."

68. Fritz Wehrli, "Der Arztevergleich bei Platon," *MusHelv*, VIII (1951), 178ff., offers parallel passages from the Hippokratic literature.

69. 721B 1 should read μέχρι [ἐ]τῶν πέντε. Cf. IV 721B 6 and VI 785B 4.

70. γενέσει τῆς ἀθανασίας μετειληφέναι (721c 6) is expressed as a provoca-

tive paradox, which has not been understood by the commentators or the translators. γένεσις, used usually in sharp contrast to ἀθανασία, is used here as the means to obtain it. γένεσις expresses both the general concept of becoming and the particular concept of birth. See also *Symposium* 206C: ἀθάνατον ἐν θνητῷ, and 206E: ἀθάνατον ὡς θνητῷ ἡ γέννησις. *Philebus* 26D: γένεσις εἰς οὐσίαν. *Statesman* 283D: γενέσεως οὐσία.

71. See C. F. von Nägelsbach, *Nachhomerische Theologie* (2d edn., Nürnberg, 1861), pp. 252ff., 275; R. Hirzel, *Agraphos Nomos* (*AbhLeipz*, 1903), XXIII, 32; Diels, in Dittenberger, *Sylloge* [XXVIII²⁴], inscr. 1268; K. Latte, *Archiv für Religionswissenschaft*, XX (1920), 264f. γονέας τιμᾶν is more or less an established term and almost always occurs in the second place. At the first place θεοὺς σέβειν or σέβεσθαι is usually found. The earliest evidence for this is the poem Χίρωνος Ὑποθῆκαι, according to Pindar, *Pythian* VI 23 *et seq.* (although this quotation is missing in Rzach's edition of the fragments). Anaximenes, *Rhetorica* ch. 1 counts as ἔθος ἄγραφον: γονέας τιμᾶν καὶ φίλους εὖ ποιεῖν καὶ τοῖς εὐεργέταις χάριν ἀποδιδόναι. Aeschylus, *Eumenides* 545 connects τοκέων σέβας εὖ προτίων and ξενοτίμους ἐπιστροφὰς δωμάτων αἰδόμενος. The longest series appears in Plutarch, *De lib. educ.* X 7E: ὅτι δεῖ θεοὺς μὲν σέβεσθαι, γονέας δὲ τιμᾶν, πρεσβυτέρους αἰδεῖσθαι, νόμοις πειθαρχεῖν, ἄρχουσιν ὑπείκειν, φίλους ἀγαπᾶν, πρὸς γυναῖκας σωφρονεῖν, τέκνων στερκτικοὺς εἶναι, δούλους μὴ περιυβρίζειν.

72. ἀκούοι δὴ πᾶς at the beginning is probably a ritual form similar to ἀκούετε λεῴ.

73. ἑαυτὸν καὶ τὰ ἑαυτοῦ is the expression that refers to the soul and the body (730B). This order occurs for the first time in the *Alcibiades* (127E *et seq.*).

74. τιμᾶν, ἀτιμάζειν, βλάπτειν are the key words which are repeated again and again, like a refrain.

75. 727A 3: θεῖον γὰρ ἀγαθόν που τιμή, τῶν δὲ κακῶν οὐδὲν τίμιον. The commentators have criticized this sentence in various ways. Replacing τιμή with ψυχή (Schanz) would only repeat what had been stated in 726A 3 and would not do justice to the fact that the concept τιμή has been transformed. Deleting ἀγαθόν (Susemihl) makes the sentence τῶν δὲ κακῶν unintelligible. Stallbaum's θείων ἀγαθῶν would mean "since the divine good can be honored only in one way." As England remarks, however, "We are not to wait till this imperfection is removed to honour the soul." Ritter's θετέον ἀγαθόν is bad Greek and expresses only what everyone would recognize. θεῖον ἀγαθόν τι οὗ τιμή (Apelt) sounds awkward in wording as well as in thought. And England is not altogether correct either. τιμή is an ἀγαθόν, and did not occur just accidentally on both tables of goods. Thus, it is not "benefit" but "good" in its strict sense. Neither is it "priceless"—but

rather it designates the highest level (cf. 631B). In the sentence τῶν δὲ κακῶν οὐδὲν τίμιον, the word τίμιον means that nothing bad merits honor (or can truly be honored), and this is then explained in detail. As to τίμιον, cf. 728D 7. / The text of des Places (*Platon Budé*, XI/2, p. 78) is correct.

76. Cf. Susemihl, II, 636.

77. Stenzel treats envy and the lack of it several times in his *Platon der Erzieher* (see, for example, pp. 243ff.), apparently without including any reference to the *Laws*. Yet φθόνος is a key word in 730E 5 and 731A 3 and 5.

78. 731E 5: τυφλοῦται γὰρ περὶ τὸ φιλούμενον ὁ φιλῶν. Max Scheler, "Liebe und Erkenntnis," in *Krieg und Aufbau* (Leipzig, 1916), p. 393, mentions the customary and "specifically modern bourgeois" opinion that love blinds rather than gives sight. Yet, as the quotation shows, this opinion is certainly not modern. For 731E Apelt refers to *Republic* V 474DE. See also Lucretius IV 1153 *et seq*.

79. See *Plato 2*, pp. 28ff., 240f., 256ff.; also see above, in the text, pp. 117ff. The fact that a part of the argument is anticipated in the doctrine of education in *Laws* II 663A *et seq*. conforms fully with the intertwining tendency of the dialogue, and cannot be used—as in Bruns's "*Gesetze*," p. 120—to attack the unity of the work.

80. The passage at 734E 3 – 735A 6 is difficult in its details. The changes proposed by Wilamowitz (*Platon*, II, 397; as also earlier in *Hermes*, XLV, 1910, p. 398) are impossible for the first sentence. The musical metaphor justifies νόμον, but with μᾶλλον the intended reality replaces this metaphor. Is not the lack of an article before πολιτείας to be explained similarly to the lack of an article preceding νόμον? / Concerning the structure of the long anacoluthic sentence, see Reinhard, *Anakoluthe* [XXI²⁷], p. 45. Whether one should extend the metaphor of spinning further into στροφαῖς is more than questionable ("a general word as τρόπος is quite in place," comments England). It is improbable that in what follows, the μεγάλαι ἀρχαί are to be interwoven with the μικραί (according to Buecheler's conjecture of σμικράς). Instead, in the second part of the sentence one expects the governed people to be mentioned—as Aristotle, *Politics* 1265ᵇ 18 *et seq*., also understood the sentence.

81. Concerning the intimate relationship between the administrative bodies and the law in Greece, see E. Weiss, *Griechisches Privatrecht* (Leipzig, 1923), I, 30.

82. Diès (see *Platon Budé*, XI/1, p. vi) in his schematic plan of the dialogue divides the *Laws* into three major parts: (*1*) Books I–III, (*2*) Books IV–VIII, and (*3*) Books IX–XII. No one doubts that the first three books form the "general introduction," but a division between Book VIII and Book IX separates closely related matter. Far

more important, however, this division destroys the fundamental insight that Plato's body of laws is based on the coherence of human life.

83. Bruns ("*Gesetze*," p. 111) has stressed the contradiction between 796B 6 *et seq.*, where the treatment of gymnastics is explicitly concluded, and 796B 1 where reference is made to a later treatment that actually appears in 813A 7. But this only appears to be a contradiction, as must necessarily be so. (Indeed, to invent a "reviser" so irrational as to be inconsistent within the space of a few lines—796B— is a poor hypothesis.) In 813 the concern is with something altogether different—namely, with τὸ διδασκαλικόν—although the ordering principle there, too, is grounded in human life. What is concluded in 796B is the physical education of the youth rather than gymnastics as a whole.

84. Bruns, pp. 129ff., correctly mentions (*1*) that the passage about the Egyptians in Book VII does not at all describe the Egyptian custom, but rather legislates the laws for Magnesia; and (*2*) that the passage about the Egyptians in Book VII does not refer to that in Book II. If we "replace" Bruns's supposed editor with Plato himself and imagine the procedure as being less mechanical, we may arrive at this view: that in connection with the doctrine of education in Book VII, Plato described the Egyptian model, reassessed it as law, and transferred the description into the context of Book II, while the *re-evaluation* in Book VII remained, unrelated to the earlier passage. / For a contrary view, see Müller, *Studien zu . . . "Nomoi"* [XX³⁶], pp. 84f.

85. This insight is based on the research of Bruns, "*Gesetze*," pp. 76ff. But rather than troubling to invent a reviser, I believe that Plato himself transformed his original work.

86. Richard Maschke, *Die Willenslehre im griechischen Recht* (Berlin, 1926), pp. 116ff.

87. The subjection of the Lokroi (I 638B) dates the first book of the *Laws* but not the entire work. This event occurred in the year 356 or 352; cf. Boeckh, *In Platonis . . . Minoem* [XXXI¹⁶], p. 73, and also Meyer, V, § 1000. Hackforth and England have used *Laws* IV 711E 5 for dating purposes, but this is very questionable. Most of the legislation (i.e., Books V–XII) definitely could be older than the frame dialogue of the first four books. Nevertheless, within the group of Books V–XII, it is highly probable that Books VII, X, and the conclusion of XII are of relatively recent origin. In general, there is still much room for stylistic analysis—even if L. Billig ("Clausulae and Platonic Chronology," *JPhilol*, XXXV, 1920, p. 236) concludes quite implausibly that "of the chronology of the *Laws* there is little to say. The rhythms show it to be a homogeneous whole, written probably in the order in which we have it." All we can conclude is that rhythmical analysis has not or at least has not as yet contributed anything

toward establishing different levels of composition. And we can readily identify one of Billig's basic mistakes. From Aristotle's statement that the fourth paeon is a preferred concluding rhythm and the first paeon a favored introductory rhythm, it may be understood that the one long syllable is the cause for differentiating. Therefore, it is a mistake to regard the concluding rhythms ∪ ∪ ∪ ∪ and ∪ ∪ ∪— as identical. Walther Kaluschka, in *WienStud*, XXVI (1904), 197, makes this same mistake.

88. See Döring, *De legum compositione* [XXXI[37]], pp. 79ff.; also Wilamowitz, II, 314.

89. On Book X see Solmsen, pp. 131ff.; Greene, *Moira*, pp. 295f.; J. Kerschensteiner, *Platon und der Orient* (Stuttgart, 1945), pp. 66ff.; Festugière, *Révélation*, ch. 5; W. J. Verdenius, "Platons Gottesbegriff," in *La notion du divin depuis Homère jusqu' à Platon* (Fondation Hardt, Entretiens sur l'Antiquité Classique, I, Vandoeuvres / Geneva, 1954), pp. 241ff., and the bibliography on p. 293.

90. See above, pp. 71ff. Cf. Diès, *Platon*, pp. 523ff.

91. τῷ παλαιῷ νόμῳ ἐπίκουρον γίγνεσθαι λόγῳ (890D). Despite Apelt's argument (see his PhB edition, 2 vols., Leipzig, 1916), the two different datives are not in the least objectionable from a grammatical point of view.

92. For Anaxagoras, see *Vorsokr.* 59 [46] B 1. Protagoras, *Vorsokr.* 80 [74] B 1. Herakleitos, *Vorsokr.* 22 [12] B 1. Parmenides, *Vorsokr.* 28 [18] B 8, 20. Melissos, *Vorsokr.* 30 [20] B 1, 2. / As to what follows, Diels (see *Vorsokr.* 31 [21] A 48) has claimed for Empedokles this passage of the *Laws* (889B 1 − c 6). It is improbable, however, that Plato is aiming here at specific doctrines of particular physicists. See Apelt's edition, II, p. 536, n. 19.

93. Should not καὶ ⟨καθ'⟩ ἕνα λόγον be written in 898A 9? νοῦν τήν τ' ἐν ἑνὶ φερομένην κίνησιν in 898B 1 certainly alludes in an etymological pun to the φρόνησις. Cf. *Cratylus* 411D: φορᾶς καὶ νοῦ νόησις. / Since H. Scholz, *Eros und Caritas* (Leipzig, 1929), p. 19, acknowledges that he has exactly understood only the determining elements ὡσαύτως and περὶ τὰ αὐτά, the following should be added: In speaking of the true being in contrast to γένεσις and μεταβολή, Plato usually places κατὰ ταὐτά and ὡσαύτως, here connected by καὶ, beside each other *without* connecting them (see *Phaedo* 78D, *Sophist* 284A), so that they reinforce each other and so that there can be no real difference between them. ἐν τῷ αὐτῷ means the movement of the sphere around its own center (*Laws* 898A 3). But what does πρὸς ταὐτά mean? Does it express the οὗ ἕνεκα, the eternal and constant goal of the movement? Cf. Parmenides, *Vorsokr.* 28 [18] B 8, l. 29; and for *Laws* 898B 2, cf. *Vorsokr.* 28 [18] B 8, l. 43.

94. Jaeger, *Aristotle*, p. 131: "At that time the Academy was the centre of a very strong interest in the Orient." R. Reitzenstein, J. Bidez,

and J. Kerschensteiner favor Oriental models. See *Plato* 1, p. 373, n. 39. W. J. W. Koster, *Le mythe de Platon, de Zarathoustra et des Chaldéens* (Leiden, 1951), argues against Oriental influence here, and cites E. R. Dodds, A.-J. Festugière, and O. G. von Wesendonk as fellow opponents. Some skepticism may be detected in the position of Simone Pétrement (*Le dualisme chez Platon, les Gnostiques et les Manichéens*, Paris, 1947), who remarks (p. 23) that the question of Oriental influence "perhaps does not have a definite solution." / Incidentally, Mlle. Pétrement quotes Bréhier's remark (in a seminar at the Sorbonne in 1919) that "in Plato's world there would be good soul and bad soul, just as there is pure water and impure water." This agrees with the formulation attempted above in the present work. And thus it is not the good soul, or the bad soul. Perhaps we should not say soul at all—but instead the spiritual power or the force of life. (See also Frank, *WWG*, p. 34: "The Greek word *psyche* has little in common with what we mean by 'soul.'")

95. See Schuhl, *Études*, ch. 9, "Un cauchemar de Platon?"

96. This word with its related terms predominates as the key word in 904c—e.

97. One fails to understand why for 905e 3 Burnet and England prefer the ἐντελεχῶς of the manuscripts to Stobaeus' ἐνδελεχῶς. (*1*) ἐντελέχεια can be understood only as an artificial word coined by Aristotle. (*2*) It is hardly an accident that neither an adjective nor an adverb derived from this word can be found anywhere. (*3*) The concern here in the *Laws* is not τέλος but rather continuity. Support for ἐνδελεχῶς is stated by Festugière, *Révélation*, III, p. 188, n. 6, and by Diès, *Les lois* (*Platon Budé*, XII/1, 1956), p. 176, n. 2.

98. See E. A. Wyller, "Platos Gesetz gegen die Gottesleugner," *Hermes*, LXXXV (1957), pp. 292ff.

99. Walther Judeich, *Topographie von Athen* (Munich, 1905), p. 318.

100. See the index in Apelt's edition [XXXI[91]], II, 557. / It is not quite so easy to be specific about the relation of these νομοφύλακες to the εὔθυνοι (according to *Laws* XII 945b *et seq.*, the highest body politic of the new state). W. Theiler, "Die bewahrenden Kräfte im Gesetzesstaat Platos," *Schweizer Archiv für Volkskunde*, XLVII (1951), 199, believes that the εὔθυνοι are placed even above the "custodians." Against this, it may be pointed out that the εὔθυνοι are incorporated by Plato into the book of laws only, while the "custodians of the law" are instituted in Book I (632c) and appear actively many times within the conversation surrounding the book of laws. To this the following is related: In contrast to the εὔθυνοι, the "custodians" are officials not of the new state alone. Of these thirty-seven officeholders, eighteen are citizens of Cnossus, and nineteen are colonists (VI 752e *et seq.*). Within the body of "custodians," therefore, the colonists have a majority of one vote, but the founding city

participates almost up to the half. See G. R. Morrow, "The Nocturnal Council in Plato's *Laws*," in *AfGP*, XLII/3 (1960), 229ff., and also in his book, *Plato's Cretan City* (Princeton, 1960).

101. See *Plato* 1, pp. 111ff.
102. Cf. Susemihl, II, 633ff.; Zeller, p. 966.
103. In the words of A. E. Taylor (*Plato*, p. 497), "Though the name 'dialectic' is not used, the demand for the thing remains unabated." This, in any case, is a more accurate view than that found in Zeller, p. 953, or in Gomperz, III, 247. John Burnet (*Platonism*, Berkeley, 1928, p. 119) discovers in the *Laws* "no trace of the theory of ideas," while Müller, *Studien* [XX³⁶], p. 97, thinks that here "the doctrine of ideas . . . has completely disappeared." For the opposed view, see Cherniss, *Riddle*, pp. 60, 82f., and in *Gnomon*, XXV (1953), 375; H. Görgemanns, *Beiträge zur Interpretation von Platons "Nomoi"* (Munich, 1960), pp. 218ff.; Lesky, pp. 536f.
104. Compare *Laws* 967c 8 – D 1: τοὺς φιλοσοφοῦντας κυσὶ ματαίαις ἀπεικάζοντας χρωμέναισιν ὑλακαῖς with Sophron, frag. 6 (in G. Kaibel, *Comicorum Graecorum fragmenta*, Berlin, 1899, I, 1): κύων πρὸ μεγαρέων μέγα ὑλακτέων.

AFTERWORD: *On the Order of the Dialogues*

1. Lewis Campbell, *The "Sophistes" and "Politicus" of Plato* [XXIII²⁸]; F. Blass, *Attische Beredsamkeit* (2d edn., Leipzig, 1892), II, 458f.; G. Janell, "Quaestiones Platonicae," *Jahrbücher für klassische Philologie*, Suppl. Vol. XXVI (1901), pp. 263ff.
2. See von Arnim, *Sprachliche Forschungen*. Those opposed to von Arnim's method describe it variously as "an erring into spiritless mechanism" (Ritter); "micrology and mechanical statistics" (Jaeger); "a mechanical procedure" (Cherniss). For arguments against those who dispute this method, see *DGrA*, II, 57; cf. Rudberg, pp. 26f. M. Warburg, *Zwei Fragen* [XXIII⁶⁰], has made an inadequate attempt to devaluate the statistical method—but then in the conclusion of his book arrives at a statistic of his own. Against all of this, see von Arnim, *Die sprachliche Forschung als Grundlage der Chronologie der platonischen Dialoge und der "Kratylos"* (*SBWien*, 1929). Cf. P. Kretschmer, in *Glotta*, XX (1932), 231f., who, however, is too brief in his remarks. / Concerning the fruitless efforts made so far to use the concluding rhythm of the sentence for dating purposes, see above, ch. XXXI, n. 87.
3. Regarding the less recent attempts (up until 1910) to establish an order of the dialogues, see Ritter, *Platon*, I, 230, and also Ernst Hoffmann, in *Jahresbericht des philologischen Vereins* (Berlin, 1910),

p. 344. The treatises of von Arnim are cited in Geffcken, Notes, pp. 137ff. See also Ross, ch. 1; Lesky, pp. 515ff.

4. See von Arnim, *Sprachliche Forschungen*, pp. 216, 228.

5. Taylor places it even after the *Gorgias*. For the opposed view, see *Plato* 2, p. 356, n. 30. Jaeger (*Paideia*, II, 107, 385) places the *Protagoras* between the first dialogues and the *Gorgias* as the work in which "Plato for the first time lifts the veil that has hung over his early dialogues."

6. Diogenes Laërtius III 35. Also Προλεγόμενα τῆς Πλάτωνος φιλοσοφίας ch. 3 (*Appendix Platonica*, ed. K. F. Hermann, Leipzig, 1920, p. 199).

7. Meyer, IV, § 438, remarks that "the assumption (that during the life of Socrates, Socratic dialogues were already composed—and even by Plato) belongs to the monstrosities of modern research." This is an appeal to emotion, however, instead of an argument. Geffcken (Notes, p. 29) admits, "I cannot imagine Platonic dialogues being written during the life of Socrates." Jaeger (*Paideia*, II, 17) concludes, partly from internal evidence, that "it is impossible to say definitely whether some of these [dialogues] were published during Socrates' lifetime, but it is highly probable that they were not." Cf. Olof Gigon, "Platons *Euthyphron*," in *Westöstliche Abhandlungen* (Wiesbaden, 1954), pp. 6ff.: ". . . Plato, when he started writing (perhaps a decade or more after the death of Socrates) . . ." Also see G. Müller, in *Gnomon*, XXXVI (1964), 124.

8. Wilamowitz, I, 136 = I², 138.

9. In this E. Dupréel (*La légende socratique et les sources de Platon*, Brussels, 1922, p. 260) sees "*quelque chose de déconcertant.*"

INDEX